International Investments
Third Edition

Bruno Solnik

H.E.C. School of Management
Groupe H.E.C.

Addison-Wesley Publishing Company

Reading, Massachusetts ▪ Menlo Park, California ▪ New York
Don Mills, Ontario ▪ Wokingham, England ▪ Amsterdam ▪ Bonn
Sydney ▪ Singapore ▪ Tokyo ▪ Madrid ▪ San Juan ▪ Milan ▪ Paris

The foreign currency image on the front cover is reproduced courtesy of Telegraph Colour Library/FPG International Corp.

Sponsoring Editor: Denise Clinton
Associate Editor: Lena Buonanno
Production Supervisor: Juliet Silveri
Production Services: Barbara Pendergast
Art Coordinator: Susan London-Payne
Cover Design Supervisor: Barbara Atkinson
Manufacturing Manager: Hugh Crawford

Library of Congress Cataloging-in-Publication Data

Solnik, Bruno H., 1944-
    International investments / Bruno Solnik. — 3rd ed.
        p.   cm.
    Includes bibliographical references and index.
    ISBN 0-201-56707-5
    1. Investments, Foreign.   I. Title.
  HG4538.S52   1996
  332.6'73—dc20   95-9342
                                     CIP

ISBN   0-201-89501-3   (paperback CFA edition)
ISBN   0-201-56707-5   (hardcover edition)

3 4 5 6 7 8 9 10 11-MA-97 9695

About the Author

*B*runo Solnik is a Professor of Finance at HEC-School of Management in France, where he chairs the Finance and Economics Department. He holds an Engineer degree from Polytechnique in Paris and a Ph.D. from Massachusetts Institute of Technology. Before joining HEC he was on the faculty of the Stanford Business School.

Professor Solnik has been a visiting professor at the University of California at Berkeley, U.C.L.A., Strathclyde University, and the Université de Genève. He was the founding President of the European Finance Association. He has written seven books, five in France and two in the United States, including *International Investments*. He has published some fifty articles in leading finance journals such as the *Journal of Finance,* the *Financial Analysts Journal, Journal of Financial and Quantitative Analysis,* and the *Journal of Portfolio Management.* He has received many prizes, including a 1994 Graham & Dodd award by the *Financial Analysts Journal.* He also serves on the board of editors of several major finance journals in America, Europe, and Asia.

Professor Solnik's work focuses on international financial markets, from exchange risk to international portfolio diversification. His expertise has been called upon by many pension funds and banks in Europe, the United States, and Asia. He serves on the Council for Education and Research of the AIMR (Association for Investment Management Research).

Preface

*I*n 1974 I published an article entitled "Why not diversify internationally rather than domestically?" in the *Financial Analysts Journal.* At the time, U.S. pension funds had never invested outside of the United States. The situation was not very different in most other countries in which international investment by pension funds and other institutional investors was legally prohibited or regarded as exotic. Although European banks and private investors have long been international investors by cultural heritage as well as necessity (given the small size of each country), pension funds guidelines often limited or prohibited international investments. Because pension plans are large and sophisticated investors, their absence on the international scene was significant.

Back in 1974 the world stock market capitalization stood below $1 trillion, and the U.S. market share was close to 60%. Since the publication of the first edition of this book, the world stock market capitalization has passed the $12 trillion mark, and the U.S. stock market share has dropped to 30%. It is now common to see U.S. pension funds with 10% or 15% of their assets invested internationally. The value of foreign assets held by U.S. pension funds has been multiplied by a factor of 100 in the past 10 years, reaching more than $300 billion by 1994. A similar trend toward international investing can be seen in all countries and, notably, Japan and Europe. For example, ABP, the pension fund of Dutch civil servants and one of the largest in the world with total assets close to $100 billion, decided in 1989 to move from a purely domestic strategy to invest a growing percentage of its assets abroad.

The rapid pace of international investing is due to a change in mentality based on many factors. First, the benefits of international diversification in terms of risk and return have progressively been recognized; they are detailed in this book. This has led to a push toward guidelines and legislation more favorable to foreign investments. For example, many U.S. public pension funds have obtained, or try to obtain, a modification of their investment constraints. A second factor is the deregulation and internationalization of financial markets throughout the world. This integration of financial markets leads to reduced costs, easier access to information, and the development of a worldwide expertise by major financial institutions. In 1986 foreign organizations and banks were allowed to become members of the Tokyo and London stock exchanges. A similar step was taken in France in 1988 and in Spain in 1989. Computerized quotation and trading systems have been developed that allow global round-the-world and round-the-clock trading. At the start of 1990 restrictions to capital flows were removed within the countries of the European Union (EU); European-based investment management firms can freely market their products to residents of any EU member state. This internationalization of investment management has led to increased competition among money managers of all nationalities, as well as to a wave of alliances, mergers, and acquisition among financial institutions in order to extend their international management expertise and the geographic coverage of their client base. The trend is most visible in Europe, where banks and insurance companies have acquired brokers (at home or abroad) and engaged in alliances and takeovers to access the global European market. It is also visible in the United States and Japan. For example, Sumitomo Bank took a participation in Goldman Sachs. Wells Fargo and Nikko Securities, two leading money managers in the United States and Japan, merged their pension fund management activities in a joint company that manages more than $130 billion of assets.

Target Audience

This book is designed for MBA students and professionals working in the investment area. In some cases it has been used for senior-level undergraduates majoring in finance. The book is to a large extent self-contained and does not take a specific national viewpoint (e.g., American); hence it has been successfully used in courses and professionals' seminars throughout the world. As of 1995, this book is a recommended reading for the CFA examination.

Structure of This Book

The greatest challenge faced by an international money manager is dealing with the sheer complexity of the international capital markets. It requires a familiarity with foreign cultures, financial instruments, and markets. Financial traditions vary across the world and strongly influence the organization and functioning of markets. A global investor must obtain information from different sources and be able to interpret it. Regulations, dealing practices, taxes, and costs complicate the investment process. The diversity and complexity of instruments available worldwide are an intellectual challenge. Different techniques and concepts must be applied to satisfy the range of objectives sought by the investors the manager serves. But the most difficult achievement is probably to operate in a complex *multicurrency* environment. This explains why this book starts with a detailed analysis of foreign exchange.

This third edition is divided into six parts. *Part One* deals with the international monetary environment. Its three chapters are designed to provide a sufficient understanding of the relation across national monetary variables and of the determinants of foreign exchange rates. *Part Two* introduces the case for international investing and its theoretical framework. Readers already familiar with foreign exchange could enter this book by going directly to the second part, which motivates international investing. The next three parts discuss the institutional features, concepts, and techniques of the major investment and risk-management vehicles. *Part Three* focuses on stock market investments, from the institutional aspects to the concepts and techniques used in global equity investing. A specific chapter is devoted to emerging stock markets. *Part Four* deals with fixed-income investment, from the institutional aspects to the concepts and techniques used in global fixed-income investing. The last chapter in this part is devoted to swaps; this introduction to derivatives is a transition to *Part Five*, which focuses on futures, options, and alternative investments. *Part Six* deals with some strategic and organizational issues.

A basic investment course is a useful prerequisite to this text. Some knowledge of international economics may also be of help in the early chapters. Some familiarity with discounting techniques and basic statistics (e.g., standard deviation, correlation) will make some of the chapters easier to read. However, this book is intended to be accessible to students and portfolio managers without recent training in portfolio theory. Concepts and theories are presented with a focus on their practical relevance rather than on their mathematical formulation. The more advanced sections are put in chapter appendixes. Each chapter ends with a large number of questions and problems. Brief solutions to selected problems marked with an asterisk (*) are provided at the end of the book.

New to the Third Edition

As with the previous editions, this new edition provide students and practitioners with comprehensive yet accessible coverage of international investments.

The third edition is a major revision in terms of both content and presentation. Each chapter has been updated and rewritten to reflect the most current developments in the investment field. In response to both investment trends and reviewers' recommendations, I have added five chapters to this edition:

- Chapter 2, Foreign Exchange Parity Relations

- Chapter 3, Foreign Exchange Determination and Forecasting

- Chapter 8, Emerging Stock Markets

- Chapter 11, Swaps

- Chapter 16, International Performance Analysis

The chapters on foreign exchange were needed to provide a better description and understanding of the complexities of the multicurrency environment. Emerging markets have grown rapidly in the past 10 years and had to be included. Swaps are derivatives extensively used in international finance; they allow one to design sophisticated investment strategies cutting across currencies and borders. Performance analysis is an important issue for institutional investors, and the difficulties of performance measurement in a global environment justify a separate chapter.

Solving problems is probably the more efficient learning device in the field of international investments. End-of-chapter problems have therefore been tripled to give students more opportunities to apply and practice the concepts learned. The answers to selected problems are located in the back of the text so that students can check their own work at their own pace. A glossary of terms is also new to this edition. The glossary allows students a quick reference to the key terms presented in the book.

Teaching Aids

An *Instructor's Manual* is available to adopters. The manual includes summaries, detailed answers to all questions and problems, and transparency masters of key texts and figures. Each problem and solution in the *Instructor's Manual* has been prepared by me and checked for accuracy by Laurence Bousquet, Olivier Lendrevie, and Jahangir Sultan. A *data disk* is also available to adopters. This disk contains monthly stock indexes, bond indexes, interest rates, exchange rates, and inflation rates for major countries and a sample of emerging countries. This allows the student to conduct tests of various theories presented in the text.

Acknowledgments

This book is the result of 20 years of teaching international investment to students and executives on four continents. My interest in this topic started with my doctoral dissertation at the Massachusetts Institute of Technology, and I am grateful to my former teachers R. Merton, F. Modigliani, S. Myers, G. Pogue, and M. Scholes. I also owe a special debt to many colleagues at universities where I taught international investment: Stanford, Berkeley, École Polytechnique, Université de Genève, and HEC (formerly named CESA). In times when international diversification was often regarded as an exotic idea, several organizations supported me in spreading the *bonne parole*. Special thanks are due to N. de Rothschild (Banque Rothschild), D. Nichol (Ivory Sime), J. Twardowski (Frank Russell and Q. Group), G. Stevenin (Rondeleux Oudart), K. Mathysen-Gerst and P. Keller (Lombard Odier), H. P. Baljet (Lombard Odier Nederland), F. Grauer (Wells Fargo), C. Nowakowski (Intersec), J. D. Nelson, L. R. Golz and D. Umstead (State Street Bank), F. s'Jacob and R. Van Maasdyck (LOIPM), Y. Sakaguchi (NIMCO), S. Fukabori (Kokusai), R. and S. Toigo (IFE), M. Leibowitz (Salomon Brothers), J. Gillies (Frank Russell Co.), J. Frijns and J. Overmeer (Inquire Europe), B. Goodsall (Inquire U.K.), and J. Vertin, D. Tuttle, and K. Sherrerd (AIMR).

From my 15-year association with Lombard Odier, I discovered not only that no theory could ever reflect the complexity of international finance but also that many ideas and techniques presented in this book could provide valuable assistance to investment management. Thierry Lombard provided constant stimulation for this book, and Patrick Odier contributed so much that he came close to becoming a co-author.

Numerous people have assisted me in the preparation of this third edition. Special thanks are due to Nathalie Seillé, and Vincent Solnik. Laurence Bousquet offered remarkable assistance in the preparation of this edition. Several colleagues provided suggestions for revisions and chapter organization. I am especially grateful to James Ang, Alexandros Benos, James Lothian, John Olienyk, Hervé Stolowy, Jahangir Sultan, Chris Telmer, and Linda Tesar.

My final words are for my wife, Catherine, who suffered through my sixth book (four in French and two in English). She has now enjoyed all the exciting aspects of the leading financial cities of the world and the top 10 hotels of *Institutional Investor's* list, with the exception of those located in Paris. She also shared numerous sleepless, interminable airplane hauls and middle-of-the night phone calls from Hong Kong, Tokyo, or San Francisco. Let this book add to the long list of pleasures and suffering we happily share.

Paris   Bruno Solnik

Contents

17   Structuring the International Investment Process   575

P A R T   O N E

The International Monetary Environment

1

Foreign Exchange

*T*he international investor is faced with a complex task. The financial markets throughout the world are quite different from one another, and information on them is sometimes difficult to obtain. Trading in different time zones and languages further complicates the task. But the most important aspect of international investment is the use of multiple currencies. An American investing in France must do so in French francs; therefore the performance (and risk) of the investment will depend partly on changes in the French franc/U.S. dollar exchange rate. Because of the importance of exchange rates in international investment, we start this book with a chapter describing the foreign exchange market.

A Few Historical Comments

Each country uses a different currency. This means that an exchange rate (i.e., a spot exchange rate) must be set in order for trade in goods and assets to occur between countries. The traditional method has been to use a common standard for assessing the value of each currency. Over the centuries various physical commodities have served as the international standard, including small sea shells, salt, and metals, such as bronze, silver, and gold (the best known and most recent). Silver played an important role until the middle of the nineteenth century, when gold was found in Transvaal and California. During the era of the gold standard, gold was the international means of payment, and each currency was assessed according to its gold value. At the time, one could exchange French francs for British pounds in exact proportion to their gold value. For example, if one ounce of gold bullion was worth ten francs in France and two pounds in the United Kingdom, the exchange rate was five French francs per British pound, or 0.2 British pounds per French franc. The domestic purchasing power of a currency, i.e., its *gold content*, was set by the domestic monetary authorities, who thereby controlled the exchange rate.

Adjustments in exchange rates occurred only rarely, when a government was forced to reduce the gold content of its currency. To maintain equilibrium in the system, gold bullion was used to settle international transactions. The balance of all monetary flows in and out of a country was usually referred to as the *balance of payments* and accounted for all monetary flows over a given time period. These flows were linked to either trade (payments of imports and exports) or capital flows (borrowing and lending abroad). A deficit in the balance of payments resulted in a gold outflow and a reduction in the domestic reserves; this was equivalent to a reduction in the domestic money supply, since the gold stock of a country was its real money supply. Gold made up all the international reserves of a country.

In order to soften the impact of balance of payments deficits or surpluses on the domestic economy, hard currencies were introduced to increase international reserves. These currencies—the U.S. dollar, followed by the British pound and Deutsche mark—were freely convertible into gold. This Bretton Woods system, or gold exchange standard, also allowed exchange rates to fluctuate in a wide band around fixed parities. It further allowed for infrequent devaluation or revaluation of the fixed parities. The gold exchange rates lasted for about 20 years after World War II.

But in the early 1970s international trade and financial transactions grew to the point where this direct link of currencies to a gold standard with fixed parities exploded. The international monetary system progressively evolved toward a system of floating exchange rates. Under the current system, the price of each currency is freely determined by market forces. Exchange rate parities are not fixed by governments but fluctuate according to supply and demand. The important dates in the evolution of the international monetary system since World War II are given in Exh. 1.1.

In this world of flexible exchange rates, some governments have linked their currency to others. Sometimes the link is rigid. For example, 14 African countries that are former French colonies tie their currencies to the French franc. The franc used by these countries is exactly equal to one French centime. Many currencies are linked tightly or loosely to the U.S. dollar. Others are linked to a basket of currencies, such as the Special Drawing Right (SDR).[1] However, the most important linkage affecting major investment currencies is the original system put into place by the European Union: the European Monetary System (EMS), often called the Snake. As of 1995 the European Union comprised the following countries:

- Austria

- Belgium

- Denmark

- Finland

- France

- Germany

- Greece

- Ireland

- Italy

- Luxembourg

- Netherlands

- Portugal

- Spain

- Sweden

- United Kingdom

The European Union (EU) is the new name given to the European Economic Community. Fifteen countries belonged the EU in 1995, but only nine were part of the EMS. Although the United Kingdom has been part of the EU for a while, its currency joined the EMS only at the end of 1990 and left it again in 1992. Italy had to leave the EMS in 1992, and the Greek Drachma had not yet been included in the EMS, partly because of the high Greek inflation. The European integration called for by the Maastricht treaty should lead to closer monetary and economic policies, reducing the tensions within the EMS. This should be further strengthened by the creation of the European central bank in Frankfurt (European Monetary Institute).

The European system may be characterized as a joint float. The currencies float freely relative to the U.S. dollar and other currencies but maintain a narrow range of exchange rate flexibility among themselves. In other words, a central exchange rate is set for the currencies, and the individual rates are allowed to fluctuate only within a band around this central rate. Changes are occasionally made in the central rates by the European monetary authorities when there is too much tension in the system. A byproduct of this system is the European Currency Unit (ECU), which is used in the accounting of the European Monetary System. The ECU is a composite currency, i.e., the weighted average of the European Union currencies. Each currency's share in the basket of currencies is weighted broadly, in line with the respective country's gross national product and foreign trade. The weights are periodically adjusted. Recently the ECU has been used in private transactions, and several bonds denominated in the ECU have been issued. The exchange rate arrangements as of 1994 are given in Exh. 1.2.

The current international monetary system may be characterized as a system of floating exchange rates with constraints. The forces of supply and demand continually move the prices of major currencies, but the exchange rates are also constrained by certain institutional agreements, such as the EMS, which are adjusted only infrequently.

EXHIBIT 1.1

Important Dates in the International Monetary System Since 1940

1944   Creation at Bretton Woods of a fixed exchange rate system based on gold and the dollar (gold exchange standard). The International Monetary Fund (IMF) and the World Bank are also created.

1950   U.S. balance of payments is in deficit and remains so for many years.

1958   The Common Market, or European Economic Community, is created. European countries restore the convertibility of their currencies into dollars and gold for nonresidents.

1960   A rush on gold causes the creation of the London gold pool by major central banks to hold the price of gold down.

1963   The United States levies the interest equalization tax on foreign borrowing by U.S. residents.

1967   A world monetary crisis follows the devaluation of the British pound.

1968   A new run on gold forces governments to adopt a two-tier gold market. Central banks trade at the official price, but a market is established for other investors where the price fluctuates freely. The United States imposes mandatory control on direct foreign investment.

1969   The Deutsche mark floats for a few weeks and then is revalued.

1970   Special Drawing Rights are created at the IMF to supplement gold and the dollar as international reserves.

1971   The United States runs an international trade deficit for the first time this century and a massive balance of payments deficit. Because of the conversion of dollars by other nations, the gold stock of the United States falls below $10 billion. On August 15 the convertibility of the U.S. dollar into gold is suspended and the dollar floats. On December 17 a new international monetary system is prepared at the Smithsonian Institution. The dollar is devalued, and new central rates are set with a wide fluctuation margin (2.25%) on either side. Dollar convertibility into gold is not reinstated.

1972   The Common Market countries, the United Kingdom, and Denmark join a European Monetary Union. The two latter countries quickly leave the system.

1973   International monetary pressures are high and remain so until 1975. Many currencies float while the dollar drops. The European Monetary Union (less Italy) floats against the dollar.

1976   A new international monetary system is agreed on in Jamaica. Currencies are allowed to float, and reference to the price of gold is abandoned.

1979   A new European Monetary System is created where parities between European currencies are maintained with narrow margins. The European Snake is allowed to float against all other currencies, particularly the U.S. dollar.

1985   The U.S. dollar hits a high of 3.45 Deutsche marks while the United States runs a current account deficit of $30 billion per quarter.

1985   The Group of Five (France, West Germany, Japan, the United Kingdom, and the United States) announces the coordination of national policies to push the dollar down. Following this announcement in September, the dollar drops and hits a low of 1.65 Deutsche marks in November 1987.

1990   East Germany merges with West Germany, and its currency is replaced by the Deutsche mark. The Soviet Union takes the first step toward full convertibility of the ruble by opening a foreign currency market. A wave of liberalization and reforms in Eastern Europe leads to the opening of the economies and financial markets of many countries of this region.

1992   The Portuguese escudo joins the European Monetary System, which comes under attack. The British pound and Italian lira leave the system, and numerous devaluations of other member currencies take place. On September 2 the U.S. dollar hits a low of 1.3885 Deutsche marks.

1993   On August 2 the finance ministers from the 12 European Union countries decide to widen the fluctuation margins in the exchange rate mechanism of the European Monetary System to 15% on either side of the EMS bilateral central rates, from 2.25% and 6% previously. After this meeting, virtue is rewarded with the gradual return of the French franc and other core currencies to levels that were either within, or close to, the old central rate against the Deutsche mark.

Foreign Exchange Quotations

Basic Principles

All currencies are quoted against the U.S. dollar. For example, the value of the French franc is quoted as 8.00 French francs per U.S. dollar. In other words, one dollar can be exchanged in the foreign exchange market for 8.00 francs. Conversely, the value of one French franc in terms of U.S. dollars is given by the reciprocal of 8.00, which is 0.125 dollars. We will define FF/$ as the number of French francs per dollar and $/FF as the number of dollars per French franc:

FF/$ = 8.00 and

$/FF = 0.125.

Similarly, the Deutsche mark (DM) may be quoted as 2.5 Deutsche marks per dollar, so that one Deutsche mark is worth $0.40. From the quotation of two currencies against the U.S. dollar, one can derive the cross exchange rate between the two currencies:

FF/$ = 8.00 and

DM/$ = 2.50 implies that

FF/DM = 3.20.

In this example one Deutsche mark is worth 3.20 French francs, or one French franc is worth 0.3125 Deutsche mark.

Foreign exchange quotations are difficult to follow for someone who does not trade in currency frequently. This is because a single number is usually quoted without any indication of the role played by each currency. Foreign exchange quotations are therefore confusing if one is not familiar with the usual direction of quotation. For example, the French franc/U.S. dollar may be quoted in terms of either francs per dollars or dollars per francs.

EXHIBIT 1.2

Exchange Rate Arrangements

Currency Pegged to

US dollar	French franc	Other currency	SDR	Other composite[1]
Angola	Benin	Azerbaijan (Russian ruble)	Libya	Algeria
Antigua & Barbuda	Burkina Faso	Bhutan (Indian rupee)	Myanmar	Austria
Argentina	Cameroon		Rwanda	Bangladesh
Bahamas, The	C. African Rep.	Estonia (deutsche mark)	Seychelles	Botswana
Barbados	Chad	Kiribati (Australian dollar)		Burundi
Belize	Comoros			Cape Verde
Djibouti	Congo			Cyprus
Dominica	Côte d'Ivoire	Lesotho (South African rand)		Czech Republic
Grenada	Equatorial Guinea			Fiji
Iraq	Gabon	Namibia (South African rand)		Hungary
Liberia	Mali			Iceland
Marshall Islands	Niger	San Marino (Italian lira)		Jordan
Micronesia, Fed. States of	Senegal			Kuwait
Oman	Togo	Swaziland (South African rand)		Malawi
Panama				Malta
St. Kitts & Nevis				Mauritania
St. Lucia				Mauritius
St. Vincent and the Grenadines				Morocco
Suriname				Nepal
Syrian Arab Rep.				Papua New Guinea
Yemen, Republic of				Solomon Islands
				Thailand
				Tonga
				Vanuatu
				Western Samoa
				Zimbabwe

[1]Comprises currencies which are pegged to various "baskets" of currencies of the members' own choice, as distinct from the SDR basket.

Flexibility Limited in Terms of a Single Currency or Group of Currencies			More Flexible		
Single currency[2]	**Cooperative arrangements[3]**	**Adjusted according to a set of indicators[4]**	**Other managed floating**	**Independently floating**	
Bahrain	Belgium	Chile	Belarus	Afghanistan, Islamic State of	Latvia
Qatar	Denmark	Colombia	Cambodia	Albania	Lebanon
Saudi Arabia	France	Madagascar	China, P.R.	Armenia	Lithuania
United Arab Emirates	Germany	Nicaragua	Ecuador	Australia	Macedonia, FYR
	Ireland		Egypt	Bolivia	Moldova
	Luxembourg		Greece	Brazil	Mongolia
	Netherlands		Guinea	Bulgaria	Mozambique
	Portugal		Guinea-Bissau	Canada	New Zealand
	Spain		Indonesia	Costa Rica	Nigeria
			Israel	Croatia	Norway
			Korea	Dominican Rep.	Paraguay
			Lao P.D. Rep.	El Salvador	Peru
			Malaysia	Ethiopia	Philippines
			Maldives	Finland	Romania
			Mexico	Gambia, The	Russia
			Pakistan	Georgia	Sierra Leone
			Poland	Ghana	South Africa
			Sao Tome & Principe	Guatemala	Sweden
			Singapore	Guyana	Switzerland
			Slovenia	Haiti	Tanzania
			Somalia	Honduras	Trinidad and Tobago
			Sri Lanka	India	Uganda
			Sudan	Iran, I.R. of	Ukraine
			Tunisia	Italy	United Kingdom
			Turkey	Jamaica	United States
			Turkmenistan	Japan	Zaire
			Uruguay	Kazakhstan	Zambia
			Venezuela	Kenya	
			Viet Nam	Kyrgyz Rep.	

[2]Exchange rates of all currencies have shown limited flexibility in terms of the U.S. dollar.

[3]Refers to the cooperative arrangement maintained under the European Monetary System.

[4]Includes exchange arrangements under which the exchange rate is adjusted at relatively frequent intervals, on the basis of indicators determined by the respective member countries.

Source: International Monetary Fund, *International Financial Statistics,* May 1994. Reprinted by permission.

Quotations are generally made in terms of the amount of local currency required to purchase one unit of foreign currency. For example, the French quote the Deutsche mark exchange rate as 3.20 FF/DM; the Germans quote 0.3125 DM/FF. Because of the leading role played by the British pound up to the twentieth century, London quotations are the reverse of Continental quotations. In other words, London bankers quote the amount of foreign currency required to purchase one pound. The Americans decided to adopt the British convention in the early 1980s. In New York the pound exchange rate is still quoted as the number of dollars required to purchase one pound, given the historical dominance of the pound sterling. As a result, the dollar/French franc exchange is quoted in exactly the same way in Paris and in New York (i.e., the French franc value of one dollar).

Depending on the direction of quotation, an increase in the exchange rate may mean an appreciation or a depreciation of the currency. If the French franc rate moves from 8.00 to 9.10, the French franc depreciated; equivalently, the U.S. dollar appreciated relative to the franc.

Organization of the Market

The foreign exchange market is a worldwide interbank market. Only the major banks and specialized brokers who act as middlemen for some local markets are admitted to this club, which is linked by telephone and telex. The market is organized like an international over-the-counter market. A customer wanting to buy a specified amount of a currency will call several banks to get the best price. The foreign exchange dealer does not quote a single price but rather two. The *bid* price is the exchange rate at which the dealer is willing to buy a currency; the *ask* (or offer) price is the exchange rate at which the dealer is willing to sell a currency. An example may help to show how a transaction is initiated and completed.

Example of a Transaction　A U.S. portfolio manager wants to buy $1 million worth of French bonds. The manager calls several banks to get their French franc quotation, without indicating whether a sale or a purchase of francs is desired. Bank A gives the following quotation:

FF/$ = 8.0000–8.0025.

In other words, Bank A is willing to buy a dollar for 8.0000 French francs or to sell a dollar for 8.0025 French francs. To make the quotation faster, only the last digits, called the *points*, are quoted. The preceding quotation would usually be given as follows:

FF/$ = 8.0000–25

or even

FF/$ = 000–25.

Traders who follow the market immediately understand the missing figures. Because these are <u>net prices,</u> there is no commission, so the spread between the bid and ask prices is a form of remuneration for the dealer who makes a firm quotation without knowing whether the customer wants to buy or sell.

Returning to the example, let's assume that the portfolio manager gets the following quotations from three different banks:

	Bank A	*Bank B*	*Bank C*
FF/$ =	8.0000–25	7.9985–20	7.9995–30

The manager will immediately choose Bank A and indicate that he or she will buy 8 million French francs for $1 million. Both parties indicate where each sum should be transferred. The portfolio manager indicates that the French francs should be transferred to an account with the Société Générale, the manager's business bank in Paris, whereas Bank A indicates that it will receive the dollars at its account with Bankers Trust in New York. Telexes are exchanged to confirm the oral agreement. The settlement of the transaction takes place simultaneously in Paris and in New York two days later.

Most currencies are quoted against the U.S. dollar, so that cross rates must be calculated from dollar quotations. For example, the FF/DM rate is calculated using the DM/$ and FF/$ rates. This usually implies a larger bid-ask spread on cross exchange rates.

Below are the quotations given by Bank A:

FF/$ = 8.0000–25

DM/$ = 2.5000–20

The FF/DM quotation is obtained as follows:

- The FF/DM bid price is the price at which Bank A is willing to buy Deutsche marks against French francs, i.e., the number of francs it is willing to pay for one Deutsche mark. This transaction (buy Deutsche marks–sell French francs) is equivalent to selling French francs to buy dollars (at a bid rate of 8.0000) and then reselling those dollars to buy Deutsche marks (at an ask rate of 2.5020). Mathematically, the transaction is as follows:

bid FF/DM = 8.0000/2.5020 = 3.1974.

- The FF/DM ask price is the price at which Bank A is willing to sell Deutsche marks for French francs, i.e., the number of francs it wants to get for selling one Deutsche mark. This transaction (sell Deutsche marks–buy French francs) is equivalent to buying French francs with dollars (at an ask rate of 8.0025) and simultaneously purchasing these dollars against Deutsche marks (at a bid rate of 2.5000). This may be expressed as follows:

ask FF/DM = 8.0025/2.5000 = 3.2010.

The resulting quotation by the bank is

FF/DM = 3.1974–3.2010.

Arbitrage aligns exchange rate quotations throughout the world. The quotation for the DM/$ rate must be the same, at a given instant, in Frankfurt and in New York. If quotations deviated by more than the spread, a simple phone call would allow one to make enormous profits. There are enough professionals in the world watching continuous quote fluctuations to rule out such riskless profit opportunities.

Quotations are directly available on-line from many financial institutions that have their own computer services. International database services, such as Reuters and Telerate, provide continuously revised quotations for several banks. Portfolio managers armed with this information on market prices can rapidly arbitrage or hedge their portfolios of foreign assets.

Market Structure   Only major players of the world are allowed as market participants of this worldwide telecommunication market. This means that a club of around 200 financial institutions act as market makers and trade around-the-clock in the major currencies. All the other banks act only as clients to these market makers. Some foreign exchange brokers take part in this market. They are used by some of the big banks to preserve anonymity when they want to unload or take a large position. These brokers seldom take a position as principal. They find matching deals for two banks, without revealing their identity.

The daily turnover averages $1 trillion, according to the Bank for International Settlement (BIS). The minimum size of a transaction depends on the foreign currency involved but is usually several million U.S. dollars. Although some transactions go through a computerized trading system developed by Reuters, the bulk of the big transactions take place by telephone, with telex or fax confirmation. Because banks in all these various countries do not use similar accounting and settlement systems, there can be only limited computerization of the market. In such a small club, an oral commitment is binding; failure to honor such an oral commitment means immediate exclusion from the club. The international litigation process would be too costly and uncertain to allow any risk of a failed transaction.

Statistics on the foreign exchange markets are not easy to get, and the best source is the BIS. Their survey suggests that a majority of the trades are not motivated by commercial transactions but are interbank trades. Traders take positions for the bank. These positions are often undone within a few minutes or hours. Taking positions is quite necessary for a dealer to assume its market-making role. But it is clear that foreign exchange traders go well beyond their market-making role. A major motivation is to make a speculative profit. This speculative behavior helps to maintain an active and, hopefully, efficient market. It also leads to large trading gains or losses for the bank and bonuses for the trader.

One should not confuse this international foreign exchange market with the organization of fund transfers that is associated with any foreign exchange transaction. Suppose that a Société Générale trader agrees by telephone to sell $10 million to J.P. Morgan for FF 80 million. By telephone, the Société Générale trader will indicate the account where the francs should be transferred, and the J.P. Morgan trader will indicate the account where the dollars should be transferred. As far as the banks are concerned, these are two separate cash transfers in two different national settlement systems. The Société Générale uses one of its New York accounts to transfer the dollars to J.P. Morgan, and J.P. Morgan uses one of its franc accounts in Paris to transfer the francs to Société Générale. This will be settled by the back offices of the two banks with a two-day value date. To avoid any risk of default on one side of the foreign exchange deal, the time of settlement is set to be exactly identical on the two transfers. The banks could also use international communication networks to arrange the bank transfers. SWIFT (Society for Worldwide Interbank Financial Telecommunication) is the major international network routing transfer orders through a network of computers in Europe and the United States. U.S. banks also use CHIPS (Clearing House Interbank Payments System) to settle their foreign exchange and Eurodollar transactions. Again, one must understand that the traders do not worry about these back-office transfers and that a deal is struck a soon as the oral commitment is made by the two traders.

One sometimes wonders why all currencies are traded only against the U.S. dollar. This comes from the fact that with n currencies, $n–1$ exchange rates are sufficient to deduce the exchange rates of any currency pair. We have seen that a cross exchange rate can easily be deduced by observing two exchange rates with the dollar. Someone wishing to sell Spanish pesetas to buy Italian liras has to go through two transactions involving the U.S. dollar (sell pesetas against dollars and buy liras with dollars). In terms of bid-ask quotations, the peseta/lira quote will basically include the sum of two bid-ask spreads: peseta/dollar and lira/dollar bid-ask spreads. One wonders if the creation of a direct market of the lira against the peseta would not reduce the bid-ask spread. The answer is no, because of a liquidity problem. Within a short time period, there is little demand for peseta/lira transactions. So the bid-ask spread on this exchange rate would have to be large to cover the risk of a market maker making firm quotations and having to carry a position for a long time before finding an offsetting transaction. However, there might be demand for peseta/DM, peseta/FF, peseta/yen, and so on. It is better to group all transactions involving the peseta into a transaction against the U.S. dollar. A direct market excluding the dollar exists only for currency pairs of active trading partners, as is the case for a Deutsche mark/French franc rate.

The market for the smaller currencies is less active, with just a few banks specializing in each lesser-traded currency. These banks are usually the major domestic banks of this currency, plus a few international banks. The domestic central bank tends to intervene frequently, and various regulations and restrictions sometimes constrain the foreign exchange market of some smaller currencies.

Dual foreign exchange markets existed for many developing or Communist countries. Even major European countries, such as Britain and France, used dual exchange rates for financial and commercial transactions. In a dual exchange rate system some types of transactions are settled using one exchange rate, whereas other transactions must use another exchange rate. Until the mid-1980s French residents wishing to invest in foreign securities had to buy foreign currencies at a higher rate known as *devise titre*. British investors had to use a *dollar premium*. The internationalization of financial markets led to a removal of all or most of these arrangements. A good example is China, which maintained two currencies. The RMB yuan was used by Chinese in their daily lives, whereas FEC (Foreign Exchange Certificates) yuans had to be used by foreigners in all their transactions with China. The FEC quoted at a large premium to the RMB in terms of dollars. The FEC was dismantled in 1993, and China moved progressively toward full convertibility of the yuan. In several Latin American and Communist countries, the existence of severe foreign exchange restrictions led to the development of an unofficial black market. Political developments and the general trend toward deregulation have led to the disappearance of most of these unofficial markets.

So far we have discussed only the interbank market, which is a large wholesale market for currencies. A normal transaction amounts to $1 million or more. A U.S. customer wanting to buy French bonds for $10,000 will not be charged these interbank rates. The bank used by the money manager adds a commission to the exchange rate. The commission is usually a function of the size of the transaction. For small transactions (a few thousand dollars) the commission is often very large (sometimes up to 0.5%), but the commission is nominal for large transactions (above $1 million). In other words, a customer must pay a larger spread than the interbank quotation. When the quote is

$$FF/\$ = 8.0000-25,$$

the small-transaction customer may receive only 7.9800 francs for each dollar purchased. This means that a commission of two French centimes per U.S. dollar is charged for the transaction, or 0.25%.

It should be stressed that the interbank spread and commissions are very small for the major investment and trade currencies (U.S. dollar, Deutsche mark, British pound, Swiss franc, French franc, and Japanese yen). Transaction costs increase for less-traded currencies, such as the Swedish krona or Thai bath.

Satellite Markets

Forward Markets

Spot exchange rates are quoted for immediate currency transactions, although in practice the settlement takes place 48 hours later. Spot transactions are extensively used to settle commercial purchases of goods, as well as for investments.

Foreign exchange dealers also quote forward exchange rates in the interbank market. These are rates contracted today but with delivery and settlement in the future, usually 30 or 90 days hence. For example, a bank may quote the one-month FF/$ exchange rate as 8.0200–50. This means that the bank is willing to commit itself today to buy dollars in one month for 8.0200 French francs or to sell them for 8.0250 French francs. In a forward, or futures, contract (described in detail in Chapter 12) a commitment is irrevocably made on the transaction date, but delivery, i.e., the exchange of currency, takes place later, on a date set in the contract. The origins of the forward currency market may be traced back to the Middle Ages, when merchants from all over Europe met at major trade fairs, where they made forward contracts for the next fair.

Forward exchange rates are often quoted as a *premium*, or *discount*, of the exchange rate. There is a premium when the forward exchange rate is higher than the spot rate and a discount otherwise. If the one-month forward exchange rate is FF/$ = 8.0200 and that spot rate is FF/$ = 8.0000, the dollar quotes with a premium of 0.02 franc, or two centimes. Consequently, when a trader announces that a currency quotes at a premium, the premium should be added to the spot exchange rate to obtain the value of the forward exchange rate. If a currency quotes at a discount, the discount should be subtracted from the spot exchange rate to obtain the value of the forward rate.

The forward discount, or premium, is often calculated as an annualized percentage deviation from the spot rate as given by the following formula:

$$\text{Annualized forward premium (discount)} = \left(\frac{\text{Forward rate} - \text{Spot rate}}{\text{Spot rate}} \right) \times \left(\frac{12}{\text{No. months forward}} \right) 100\%.$$

The percentage premium (discount) is annualized by multiplying by 12 and dividing by the length of the forward contract in months.

$$\text{Annualized forward premium} = \left(\frac{8.02 - 8.00}{8.00} \right) \left(\frac{12}{1} \right) 100\% = 3.0\%.$$

The interbank quotations are often done in the form of an annualized premium (discount) for reasons that will become obvious in the next section. However, forward rates quoted to customers are usually outright (e.g., FF/$ = 8.0200–50).

Exhibit 1.3 gives the spot and forward dollar exchange rates as found in the *Financial Times*. For example, the spot DM/$ exchange rate on July 14, 1986, was DM/$ = 2.1790–2.1800. At the same time, the Deutsche mark for delivery three months later quoted at a premium of 1.18–1.13 pfennig (one pfennig is one hundredth of one Deutsche mark). In other words, the dollar quoted at a discount, since a Deutsche mark premium as indicated in the exhibit is a dollar discount. The forward DM/$ is therefore quoted outright as DM/$ = 2.1672–2.1687, where the forward bid is obtained by subtracting the bid premium/discount of 0.0118 Deutsche marks from the spot bid of 2.1790. The annualized percentage premium is equal to 2.11% per annum; this is obtained by taking the middle premium of 1.15 pfennig and dividing it by the middle spot rate of 2.1795.

<u>**EXHIBIT 1.3**</u>

Foreign Exchange Quotations

July 14		Closing	Three months Rate	% PA
UK[†]	(£)	1.4810 – 1.4820	1.30 – 1.25c pm	3.44
Ireland[†]	(I£)	1.3745 – 1.3755	1.25 – 0.80 pm	2.99
Canada	(C$)	1.3760 – 1.3770	0.58 – 0.63 dis	−1.76
Netherlands	(Fl)	2.4565 – 2.4575	0.61 – 0.56 pm	0.95
Belgium	(BFr)	44.85 – 44.95	3 – 5 dis	−0.40
Denmark	(DKr)	8.14½ – 8.15	4.00 – 4.60 dis	−2.10
W. Germany	(DM)	2.1790 – 2.1800	1.18 – 1.13 pm	2.11
Portugal	(Es)	150 – 150¼	250 – 550 dis	−10.65
Spain	(Pta)	138.85 – 138.95	250 – 350 dis	−8.60
Italy	(L)	1495¾ – 1496¼	17 – 20½ dis	−4.99
Norway	(NKr)	7.63¾ – 7.64¼	14.25 – 14.75 ds	−7.57
France	(FFr)	7.0075 – 7.0125	1.05 – 1.20 dis	−0.64
Sweden	(SKr)	7.14¼ – 7.14¾	5.60 – 6.00 dis	−3.24
Japan	(Y)	160 – 160½	0.85 – 0.80 pm	2.04
Austria	(Sch)	15.34 – 15.34½	7 – 5 pm	1.56
Switzerland	(SFr)	1.7785 – 1.7796	0.84 – 0.79 pm	1.82

[†]UK and Ireland are quoted in U.S. currency. Forward premiums and discounts apply to the U.S. dollar and not to the individual currency.

Belgian rate is for convertible francs. Financial franc 45.15–45.25.

Source: *Financial Times*, July 15, 1986. Reprinted by permission.

$$\text{Annualized three - month forward premium} = \left(\frac{0.0115}{2.1795}\right)\left(\frac{12}{3}\right)100 = 2.11\%.$$

Eurocurrency Market

The interbank forward exchange market is closely linked to the *Eurocurrency* market, often called the *Eurodollar* market, although several other currencies are traded. This interbank market for short-term borrowing and lending is an offshore market and therefore beyond the purview of domestic regulations. This market started during the cold war between the Soviet Union and the United States, when the Soviets feared that the U.S. dollars they owned as reserve currencies might be frozen by U.S. authorities. Typically these U.S. dollar reserves were invested with the Federal Reserve Bank. To avoid any problems, the Banque Commerciale de l'Europe du Nord and the Narodny Bank, which are the Soviet banks in Paris and London, were asked to remove these dollars and lend them to a European bank. This started a market between European-based banks in short-term dollar deposits. Soon the European branches of U.S. banks joined the active market. Other currencies started being traded on the Eurocurrency market, such as the British pound, Deutsche mark, Swiss franc, French franc, Japanese yen, Dutch guilder, and Canadian dollar, and now the Eurocurrency market is enormous.

One should be careful to distinguish between the Eurocurrency market and the *Eurobond* market. The Eurobond market, which is described in Chapter 9, is a traditional bond market whereby a syndicate of underwriters is assembled and in a few weeks floats a bond for a specific company. By contrast, the Eurocurrency market is an interbank market closely linked to the foreign exchange market. Bank credits are extended to corporations on the basis of these Eurocurrency interest rates plus a spread reflecting the credit risk borne by the bank in its lending to a "risky" corporation. On the same telecommunication network, banks quote spot currencies as well as term currencies, i.e., interest rates with maturities from one day to one year. If a foreign exchange trading room is asked for its quotation on the three-month Deutsche mark, it will give the interest rate quotation on a three-month Euro-Deutsche mark in the form of a bid-ask spread. For example, a quotation of 4½–4⅝ indicates that the bank stands ready to borrow Deutsche marks for 90 days at 4½% or to lend Deutsche marks at 4⅝%. As with foreign exchange, Eurocurrency quotations can change at any instant to reflect changes in the market. When a trader gives a quotation, it means that the bank is ready to borrow from or lend to any institution of good standing at these rates. The minimum amount is usually $1 million. Maximums are set by the borrowing bank to limit the risks. A corporation or investor wanting to invest in this market will receive the bid rate minus a commission. For example, a customer might be able to lend at 4⁷⁄₁₆% if the bank charges a commission of ¹⁄₁₆%. Similarly, a customer wanting to borrow will be charged the ask rate plus a commission. This commission may be large because it includes a risk premium. A good-quality corporate customer might borrow at 5⅛%, i.e., 4⅝% plus a commission of ½% over the interbank market rate.

It should be stressed that the worldwide convention in quoting short-term interest rates is to quote "simple" or "linear" annualized rates. The rate to be paid over the period is simply equal to the annual rate multiplied by the length of the period, as a proportion of a year. For example, a three-month interest rate of 4% means that the interest rate paid after three months will be:

$$4\%\left(\frac{3}{12}\right) = 1\%.$$

Years are assumed to be made of 360 days, in all major currencies except the British pound, for which the convention is 365 days. Someone quoted a rate r for a maturity of T days will have to pay

$$r\left(\frac{T}{360}\right).$$

This is simply a convention of quotation. If the convention had been to quote rates using a year of 365 days, the interest rate quoted would have been slightly higher. Long-term interest rates are usually quoted differently, as can be seen in Chapter 10.

EXHIBIT 1.4

Eurocurrency Quotations

EUROCURRENCY INTEREST RATES

July 14	Short term	7 days notice	One month	Three months	Six months	One year
Sterling	9 5/8 – 9 7/8	9 13/16 – 9 15/16	10 – 10 1/15	10 – 10 1/8	10 – 10 1/8	9 15/16 – 10 1/16
US Dollar	6 1/2 – 6 5/8	6 9/16 – 6 11/16	6 9/16 – 6 11/16	6 9/16 – 6 11/16	6 9/16 – 6 11/16	6 5/8 – 6 3/4
Can. Dollar	8 1/4 – 8 1/8	8 1/4 – 8 1/2	8 1/8 – 8 3/8	8 1/8 – 8 3/8	8 3/8 – 8 5/8	8 1/2 – 8 3/4
Dutch Guilder	5 5/8 – 5 7/8	5 5/8 – 5 7/8	5 3/4 – 5 7/8	5 9/16 – 5 11/16	5 7/16 – 5 9/16	5 3/8 – 5 1/2
Swiss Franc	2 3/4 – 3	2 3/8 – 2 5/8	4 15/16 – 5 1/16	4 16/16 – 5 1/15	4 15/16 – 5 1/16	4 7/8 – 5
D-Mark	4 7/16 – 4 9/16	4 1/2 – 4 5/8	4 7/16 – 4 9/16	4 1/8 – 4 5/8	4 9/16 – 4 11/16	4 5/8 – 4 3/4
French Franc	7 1/8 – 7 1/4	7 1/8 – 7 1/4	7 1/8 – 7 1/4	7 3/4 – 7 4/10	7 1/4 – 7 3/8	7 1/4 – 7 3/8
Italian Lira	9 – 10 1/8	10 1/4 – 11 1/4	10 3/4 – 11 1/2	11 – 11 1/2	11 1/8 – 11 1/2	10 7/8 – 11 3/8
Belgian Franc	7 1/8 – 7 3/8	7 1/8 – 7 3/8	7 1/8 – 7 3/8	7 1/8 – 7 3/8	7 – 7 1/4	7 – 7 1/4
B.Fr.(Con)	7 – 7 1/8	7 – 7 1/2	7 – 7 1/2	6 7/8 – 7 3/8	6 7/8 – 7 3/8	6 7/8 – 7 3/8
Yen	4 3/8 – 4 1/2	4 5/8 – 4 11/16	4 11/16 – 4 3/4	4 5/8 – 4 11/16	4 9/16 – 4 5/8	4 5/8 – 4 11/16
Danish Krone	8 3/4 – 9 1/4	9 – 9 1/2	8 3/4 – 9 1/4	8 3/4 – 9 1/4	9 1/4 – 9 3/4	9 1/2 – 10
Asian $Sing	6 3/8 – 6 3/4	6 5/8 – 6 3/4	6 9/16 – 6 11/16	6 9/16 – 6 11/16	6 9/16 – 6 11/16	6 5/8 – 6 3/4

Long-term Eurodollars: Two years 7–7 1/4 per cent; three years 7 1/8–7 1/4 per cent; four years 7 1/4–8 per cent; five years 8–8 1/4 per cent nominal. Short-term rates are call for US Dollars and Japanese Yen; other, two days' notice.

Source: Financial Times, July 15, 1986. Reprinted by permission.

Exhibit 1.4 gives some Eurocurrency interest rate quotations. These short-term investments are sometimes called *fiduciary deposits* because of the legal form they take. They are not tradable.

As we can see, the Eurocurrency market functions like the foreign exchange market, into which it is thoroughly integrated. The default risk are larger, so banks exert better control over term transactions (Eurocurrency) than spot transactions (foreign exchange). On the other hand, access to the club of this huge and extremely rapid market is reserved to institutions of top quality. This is necessary to ensure that vast amounts of money are reliably transacted over the telephone between institutions located throughout the world and functioning under different regulations.

The forward exchange market and the Eurocurrency market are so closely tied to each other that only one of the two markets needs to exist.

Exchange Rate and Interest Rate Markets

Spot exchange rates, forward exchange rates, and interest rates are technically linked for all currencies that are part of the free international market. The relation known as *interest rate parity* states that the forward discount, or premium, is equal to the interest rate differential between two currencies. In other words, the forward exchange rate is equal to the spot exchange rate adjusted by the interest rate differential. The interest rate parity relation derives from the fact that arbitrage exists. If it did not, riskless arbitrage would occur. The following example illustrates how the arbitrage is done.

Assume that the following data exist for French francs and U.S. dollars:

Spot exchange rate   FF/$ = 8.00

One-year interest rates

   French franc   14%

   U.S. dollar   10%

To take advantage of the interest rate differential, a speculator could borrow dollars (at 10%), convert them immediately into French francs (at a rate of FF/$ = 8.00), and invest the francs (at 14%). This action is summarized in Exh. 1.5. The speculator makes a profit of 4% on the borrowing/lending position but runs the risk of a large depreciation of the French franc.

In Exh. 1.5 borrowing dollars means bringing money from the future to the present; lending mean the reverse. At time 1, the speculator must convert French francs into U.S. dollars at an unknown rate to honor the claim in dollars.

This position may be transformed into a covered (riskless) interest rate arbitrage by buying simultaneously a forward exchange rate contract to repatriate in one year the French francs into U.S. dollars at a known forward exchange rate of FF/$ = 8.08. In the process described in Exh. 1.6, the investor still benefits on the interest rate differential (a gain of 4%) but loses on the repatriation of French francs into dollars on the forward contract. In one year the exchange rate loss will be equal to

$$\frac{8.00 - 8.08}{8.00} = -1\%.$$

Per dollar borrowed, the net gain on the position is 3%. This gain is certain at time 0, since all interest rates and exchange rates are fixed at that time.

<u>**EXHIBIT 1.5**</u>

Currency Speculation

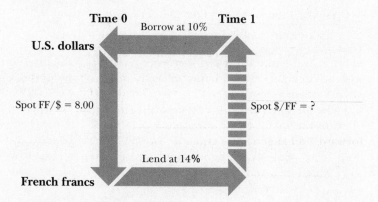

EXHIBIT 1.6
Covered Interest Rate Arbitrage

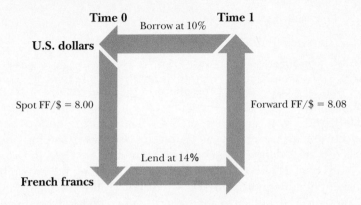

No capital is invested in the position, which is a pure swap with simultaneous borrowing and lending. If such rates were quoted in reality, banks would arbitrage to exploit this riskless profit opportunity. Enormous swaps could occur, since no capital needs to be invested. To prevent this obviously riskless arbitrage, the forward discount must exactly equal the interest rate differential. More exactly, the various rates must adjust so that interest rate parity holds. Note that if the forward discount were larger than the interest rate differential, the arbitrage would simply go the other way. Arbitrageurs would borrow French francs and swap them for U.S. dollars.

The exact mathematical relationship is slightly more complicated, because one must buy a forward contract covering both the principal and the accrued interest in order to achieve a perfect arbitrage. In the previous example, for every dollar borrowed, the forward hedge should cover eight francs plus the interest rate of 14%, i.e., 8.00 (1.14) = 9.12. The exact mathematical formula is given by

$$\frac{\text{Forward rate}}{\text{Spot rate}} = \frac{1 + \text{currency B interest rate}}{1 + \text{currency A interest rate}} = \frac{1 + r_B}{1 + r_A}, \tag{1.1}$$

where r_A is the interest rate of currency A, and r_B is the interest rate of currency B, and the exchange rates are quoted as the price of one unit of currency A in terms of units of currency B.

The forward premium (discount) is equal to

$$\frac{\text{Forward rate} - \text{Spot rate}}{\text{Spot rate}} = \frac{r_B - r_A}{1 + r_A}.$$

If one returns to the previous example, where exchange rates are quoted as the price of one U.S. dollar (currency A) in terms of French francs (currency B), arbitrage ensures that

$$F(1 + r_\$) = S(1 + r_{FF}),$$

$S = FF/\$$

where S and F are the spot and forward exchange rates (French franc price of one U.S. dollar) and r_{FF} and $r_\$$ are the interest rates in French francs and U.S. dollars. This relation implies that

$$\frac{F - S}{S} = \frac{r_{FF} - r_\$}{1 + r_\$}.$$

If the spot exchange rate is FF/$ = 8.00 and the dollar and franc interest rates are 10% and 14%, the forward exchange rate must equal

$$F = S \frac{1 + r_{FF}}{1 + r_\$} = 8.00 \frac{1.14}{1.10} = 8.2909.$$

The calculation of forward exchange rates is often confusing if one does not frequently trade in the currencies involved. In Eq. (1.1) it is easy to confuse the role played by the two currencies, depending on the direction of quotation. Here one should remember that a currency with a high interest rate is considered weak and that a currency with a low interest rate is considered strong. A currency with a high interest rate should trade with a forward discount, reflecting the expectation that it will depreciate. A currency with a low interest rate should trade with a forward premium, reflecting the expectation that it will appreciate. To cite the example, the French franc trades with a forward discount relative to the U.S. dollar, whereas the U.S. dollar trades with a forward premium relative to the French franc.

A similar arbitrage relation holds for maturities of less than a year, provided that the right interest rates are used. Annual interest must be converted into rates over the investment period. For a contract with n months maturity, the quoted interest rate must be divided by 12 and multiplied by n. As an illustration, assume that the following data hold:

Spot exchange rate   FF/$ = 8.00

Three-month interest rates

    French franc   13%

    U.S. dollar   10%

The three-month forward exchange rate is equal to

$$\text{Forward exchange rate} = \text{Spot exchange rate} \frac{1 + r_{FF}}{1 + r_{\$}}$$

$$= 8.00 \frac{1 + \left(13\dfrac{3}{12}\%\right)}{1 + \left(10\dfrac{3}{12}\%\right)} = 8.00 \frac{1 + 3.25\%}{1 + 2.50\%} = 8.0585.$$

The forward exchange rates and interest rates on July 14, 1986, given in Exhs. 1.3 and 1.4, broadly verify the relationship. For example, the three-month interest rate on dollars is 6%₁₆–6¹¹⁄₁₆, whereas the interest rate on Deutsche marks is 4½–4%. The forward premium of 2.11% is indeed consistent with the interest rate differential. Of course, the bid-ask spreads define a band for the value of the premium, and it is easy to verify that the premium (discount) lies within that band. The interest rate parity relation holds only at a given point in time; one has to compare interest rates and exchange rates quoted at the same point in time.

An example of the calculation of the implied forward exchange rate using bid-ask spreads can be performed using the following data:

Spot exchange rate   FF/$ = 8.000–8.0025

One-year interest rates   in FF   14–14¼%

                           in U.S. $10–10¼%

The bid forward exchange rate can be calculated as

$$\text{Bid forward FF/\$} = 8.0000 \frac{1 + 0.1400}{1 + 0.1025} = 8.2721.$$

$$\text{Ask forward FF/\$} = 8.0025 \frac{1 + 0.1425}{1 + 0.1000} = 8.3117.$$

The equation for the bid forward exchange rate can be obtained by noting that the bank that quotes the forward rate to buy a dollar forward at 8.2721 FF can cover itself in the marketplace by doing the following combined operations:

- borrow one dollar in the market at 10¼%

- exchange this dollar for 8.0000 FF in the spot exchange rate market

- lend these 8.0000 FF at 14%

The reverse hedging operation applies to the ask forward exchange rate.

The reader might find the following tips useful:

- If we look at the FF/$ forward rate, the FF interest rate should be on top, and the $ interest rate should be at the bottom of the fraction.

- The bid forward exchange rate obtains by taking the combination of bid and ask quotes (for the spot exchange rate and the interest rates) that leads to the smallest quote for the forward exchange rate.

- The ask forward exchange rate obtains by taking the combination of bid and ask quotes (for the spot exchange rate and the interest rates) that leads to the largest quote for the forward exchange rate.

It is clear that forward exchange rates and interest rates are direct substitutes, and one need trade in only one of the two investments. Because the market for interest rates is very large for purposes other than forward exchange transactions, it must exist anyway. This means that forward exchange contracts are not traded on the interbank market. Forward exchange rates are simply calculated by applying interest rate differentials to spot exchange rates. If a bank needs to hedge a forward contract written to a customer, it will engage in a swap, as described in Exh. 1.6. The bid and ask forward exchange rates are calculated using the bid-ask quotations on spot exchange rates and interest rates. For currencies that are not available on the Eurocurrency market, the bank calculates an implicit forward exchange rate by engaging in a swap on the domestic interest rate markets.

Long-term forward exchange rates are based on swaps between bonds denominated in two different currencies. The pricing formula is somewhat more complex, as shown in Chapters 10 and 11.

Euronote Market

A market for international short-term notes became quite active in the 1980s. This market is a complement to the traditional international system of interbank time deposits and bank credits. Euronotes take several forms, such as bankers' acceptance, Eurocommercial papers, and certificates of deposit. They are often issued with numerous option clauses, and the techniques used by banks placing these notes are somewhat complex and will not be detailed here. Bankers usually call the techniques Note Issuance Facilities (NIF). Altogether, the volume for the various forms of Euronotes, commercial papers, and banker's acceptance reached more than $100 billion (U.S.) in 1989. Euronotes replaced the traditional short-term credits granted by pools of international banks. They witnessed the evolution toward a greater "securitization" of credit markets. This means that traditional bank credits are progressively replaced by negotiable securities, which provide greater liquidity to the lending party and give direct access to other, nonbank investors. The secondary market is not yet very liquid, but it offers a welcome extension to the Eurocurrency market. The interest rates on these facilities are closely linked to the interest rates quoted on the Eurocurrency market.

Summary

1. The international monetary system has evolved toward a system of floating exchange rates constrained by some institutional agreements, such as the European Monetary System.

2. The foreign exchange market is an international interbank market. Transactions take place by telephone throughout the world.

3. The markets for forward exchange and Eurocurrency interest rates are directly linked to the foreign exchange market.

4. Forward exchange rates are rates quoted for future delivery. These rates are often quoted as a premium or discount from the spot exchange rate. This premium or discount is equal to the interest rate differential for the two currencies.

Questions and Problems

1. Briefly describe the current international monetary system.

2. In 1993 the European Monetary System came under severe speculative pressures. Several currencies, including the French franc, were pushed down to the limit of their allowed fluctuation margin against the DM, e.g., the franc could not stay within 2.25% of its central parity with the DM. One solution would have been to devalue the parity of the franc against the DM by 5 to 10%. Instead, the EU decided to keep the same bilateral parities but to widen the allowed fluctuation band to 15% on each side of the parity. What, do you think, are the advantages and disadvantages of both solutions? Which one is more likely to prevent currency speculation?

3*. You heard on the radio that the dollar appreciated by 20% against the French franc: The FF/$ rate moved from five francs per dollar to six. By what percentage did the franc depreciate against the dollar?

4*. Here are some quotes of the Italian lira/U.S. dollar spot exchange rate given simultaneously on the phone by three banks:

Bank A   1560–1562

Bank B   1563–1565

Bank C   1561–1565

Are these quotes reasonable? Do you have an arbitrage opportunity?

5. You visit the foreign exchange trading room of a major bank. A trader asks for quotations of the French franc to various corespondents and hears the following quote:

From Bank A   7.9610–50

From Bank B   6.20–55

What do they mean?

*6**. The French franc is quoted as FF/$ = 7.9610–50, and the Deutsche mark is quoted as DM/$ = 2.4100–40. What is the implicit FF/DM quotation?

7. The French franc is quoted as FF/$ = 7.9610–50, and the Dutch guilder is quoted as DG/$ = 2.0510–60. What is the implicit DG/FF quotation?

*8**. The spot FF/$ is equal to 7.9630. The one-year interest rates on the Eurocurrency market are 13% in French francs and 9% in U.S. dollars. What is the one-year forward exchange rate? The one-month interest rates are 12% in French francs and 8% in U.S. dollars. What is the one-month forward exchange rate?

9. The bid-ask rates are as follows:

DM/$	2.4100–40
1-year Euro-DM	4½–⅝
1-year Euro-$	9⅛–¼

What is the quotation for the one-year DM/$ forward exchange rate?

*10**. The bid-ask rates are as follows:

DM/$:	2.4100–40
1-month Euro-DM	5½–⅝
1-year Euro-DM	6¼– ½
1-month Euro-$	6⅛–¼
1-year Euro-$	6½–¾

What are the quotations for the one-month and one-year DM/$ forward exchange rate?

11. Here are some quotes for spot exchange rates and three-month interest rates:

FF/$	5.8650–80
DM/$	1.8100–30
3-month Euro-$	3–3¼
3-month Euro-FF	7¼–7½
3-month Euro-DM	6¼–6½

What should the quotes be for:

1. The FF/DM spot exchange rate
2. The FF/$ 3-month forward exchange rate
3. The FF/DM 3-month forward exchange rate

12. A French company knows that it will have to pay 10 million Swiss francs in three months. The current spot exchange rate is 4.00 FF/SF. The three-month forward rate is 4.02 FF/SF. The treasurer is worried that the French franc will depreciate in the next few weeks. What action can be taken? Three months later, the spot exchange rate turns out to be 4.15 FF/SF; was it a wise decision?

13. Paf is a small country that wishes to control international capital flows. Its currency, the pif, is worth about one dollar. Paf put in place an exchange control whereby all current account transactions can be transferred using the normal exchange rate, but capital account transactions must be transferred at a financial Pif rate. In other words, foreigners wishing to invest in assets of Paf must buy them at the financial Pif rate, whereas dividends are repatriated at the normal pif rate. The current financial pif rate is 0.8 pif per dollar or 1.25 dollar per financial pif. The financial rate quotes at a premium of 25% over the normal rate.

- Assume that the premium of the financial rate stays constant over time. Will an American make the same return on investment as a resident of Paf, once the asset is resold?
- You hear rumors that the exchange controls may be lifted and that the financial rate will disappear. Would this be good news to a foreign investor?

14. *Project:* Collect monthly exchange rates of the French franc, British pound, and U.S. dollar against the DM over the past 10 years. Write all the exchange rates as the number of non-German currency units per DM (i.e., $/DM, FF/DM, £/DM).

  The franc and DM have been linked by the EMS with a few devaluations of the franc and periodic adjustments of the allowed fluctuation band. The British pound has been part of the EMS for only a few years. Of course, the dollar has remained outside the EMS. Hence we would expect to find that the FF/DM rate has been more stable than the £/DM and $/DM rates. Is this the case?

  Plot the three exchange rates and try to comment on their historical evolution.

Notes

1. The SDR is a basket of currencies. The composition of the basket of currencies has changed over time, but the dollar value of the SDR is calculated daily, based on the country weights and the market exchange rate for each currency. Beginning January 1, 1991, the SDR valuation basket consists of the currencies of the five members having the largest exports of goods and services during the period 1985 to 1989, i.e., the U.S. dollar, Deutsche mark, French franc, Japanese yen, and British pound. The weights for the five currencies (U.S. dollar, 40%; Deutsche mark, 21%; Japanese yen, 17%; French franc and British pound, 11% each) broadly reflect the relative importance of these currencies in international trade and finance. The weights are revised every five years.

Bibliography

Antl, B., and Ensor, R. *The Management of Foreign Exchange Risk*, London: Euromoney Publications, 1982.

Bank for International Settlements. *Annual Report*, various issues.

Coninx, R. *Foreign Exchange Dealer's Handbook*, Homewood, IL: Dow Jones–Irwin, 1986.

Dornbusch, R. *Open Economy Macroeconomics*, New York: Basic Books, 1988.

Evans, J.S. *International Finance: A Markets Approach*, Fort Worth, TX: Dryden Press, 1992.

International Monetary Fund. *International Financial Statistics*, various issues.

———. *Annual Report of Exchange Arrangements and Exchange Restrictions*, various issues.

Riehl, H., and Rodriguez, F. *Foreign Exchange and Money Markets*, New York: McGraw-Hill, 1983.

2

Foreign Exchange Parity Relations

 *F*luctuations in exchange rates seem to be generated by a large variety of economic and political events. Exchange rate uncertainty adds an important dimension to the economics of capital markets. Before presenting some of the basic models of exchange rate determination in Chapter 3, it may be useful to recall well-known international parity conditions linking domestic and foreign monetary variables: inflation rates, interest rates, and foreign exchange rates. These relations are the basis for a simple model of the international monetary environment. Given the complexity brought by a multicurrency environment, it is most useful to start by building a simplified model linking the various domestic and foreign monetary variables. The second part of this chapter will then discuss the empirical validity of the various building blocks and their practical implications.

International Parity Relations: Inflation, Interest, and Exchange Rates

Traditionally, different nations use different currencies. This allows each nation some independence in setting its national interest rate and monetary policy. Thus inflation rates and interest rates can differ markedly across countries. This also implies that the currencies' exchange rates will not stay fixed over time. We will now study how these variables should be linked in a simple and perfect world.

Some Definitions

We need to recall some notations introduced in Chapter 1:

- *The spot exchange rate, S.* The rate of exchange of two currencies tells us the amount of foreign currency that one unit of domestic currency can buy. *Spot* means that we refer to the exchange rate for immediate delivery. For example, the French franc/U.S. dollar spot exchange rate might be $S = 8.00$, indicating that one U.S. dollar is worth eight French francs.

- *The forward exchange rate, F.* The rate of exchange of two currencies set on one date for delivery at a future specified date, the *forward* rate is quoted today for a delivery taking place at a future date. For example, the French franc/U.S. dollar forward exchange rate for delivery in one year is 8.2909 French francs per U.S. dollar.

- *The interest rate, r.* The rate of interest for a given time period is a function of the length of the time period and the denomination of the currency. Interest rates are usually quoted in the marketplace as an annualized rate. For example, the one-year rate on U.S. Treasury bills might be $r_\$ = 10\%$, and the one-year rate on French franc bills might be $r_{FF} = 14\%$. In this case the *interest rate differential* is equal to 4% ($r_{FF} - r_\$ = 4\%$).

- *The inflation rate, I.* This is equal to the rate of consumer price increase over the period specified. The *inflation differential* is equal to the difference of inflation rates between two countries. For example, if the inflation in France is $I_{FF} = 12.87\%$ and $I_\$ = 8.91\%$ in the United States, the inflation differential over the period is approximately 4%.

The theoretical parity relations of international finance[1] are:

1. the *purchasing power parity* relation, linking spot exchange rates and inflation

2. the *international Fisher* relation, linking interest rates and inflation

3. the *foreign exchange expectation* relation, linking forward exchange rates and expected spot exchange rates

4. the *interest rate parity* relation, linking spot exchange rates, forward exchange rates, and interest rates

Purchasing Power Parity

Purchasing power parity[2] (PPP) is a well-known relation in international finance. It states that the spot exchange rate adjusts perfectly to inflation differentials between two countries. PPP comes in two versions: absolute PPP and relative PPP.

Absolute PPP   This version of PPP is inspired by a basic idea known as the <u>law of one price</u>, which states that the real price of a good must be the same in all countries. If goods prices rise in one country relative to another, the country's exchange rate must depreciate to maintain a similar real price for the goods in the two countries. This argument is obvious for traded goods with no trade restrictions. Let's consider the following scenario: The French price of wheat is 32 francs per bushel, and the U.S. price is 4 dollars per bushel; the exchange rate is 8 francs per dollar. In the next year, the French franc price of wheat rises by 12.87%, the

French inflation rate, whereas the U.S. dollar price of wheat rises by only 8.91%, the U.S. inflation rate. If the French franc depreciation does not offset this 4% inflation differential, it will make French wheat less competitive in the international market and induce trade flows from the United States to France to take advantage of this price differential. If trade could take place instantaneously, at no cost and with no impediments, one would expect the law of one price to hold exactly for all traded goods.

If we take a weighted average of the prices of all goods in the economy, absolute PPP claims that the exchange rate should be equal to the ratio of the average price levels in the two economies. So absolute PPP is some "average" version of the law of one price. If the weights differ across countries, absolute PPP could be violated even if the law of one price held for each individual good. In practice, determining an average national price level is a daunting task never undertaken. Rather than calculating average price *levels*, expressed in francs in France and dollars in the United States, countries calculate movements in price indexes. A price index can be based on a representative sample of produced goods (GNP deflator) or a representative basket of consumed goods (consumer price index). A price index is a pure number, without meaning in itself. Its purpose is to calculate price increases, *inflation rates*, from one period to the next.

Relative PPP   Most economists care about relative PPP when they talk about purchasing power parity. Because of domestic inflation, a currency loses some of its purchasing power. For example, a 10% monthly inflation rate in Brazil implies that one Brazilian real (the new currency unit in Brazil) loses 10% of its purchasing power: At the end of the month, a carioca can buy 10% less goods with one real. Relative PPP focuses on the general, across-the-board inflation rates in two countries and claims that the exchange rate movements should exactly offset any inflation differential between the two countries.

The purchasing parity relation might be written as follows:

$$\frac{S^1}{S^0} = \frac{1+I_F}{1+I_D},$$

(2.1)

where

S^0 is the spot exchange rate at the start of the period (the foreign price of one unit of the domestic currency),

S^1 is the spot exchange rate at the end of the period,

I_F is the inflation rate, over the period, in the foreign country, e.g., France, and

I_D is the inflation rate, over the period, in the domestic country, e.g., the United States.

Using the figures given previously for our French/American illustration, the end-of-period spot exchange rate should be equal to S^1, such that:

$$\frac{S^1}{8.00} = \frac{1.1287}{1.0891} \text{ and}$$

$$S^1 = 8.00 \frac{1.1287}{1.0891} = 8.2909.$$

Let's define s, the exchange rate movement:

$$s = \frac{S^1 - S^0}{S^0} = \frac{S^1}{S^0} - 1.$$

The purchasing power parity relation is often presented as the linear approximation stating that the exchange rate variation is equal to the inflation rate differential:

$$s = \frac{S^1}{S^0} - 1 \cong I_F - I_D.$$

This is only a first-order approximation of the exact relation (Eq. 2.1). This purchasing power parity relation is of major importance in international portfolio management. If it holds, purchasing power parity implies that the real return on an asset is identical for investors from any country. For example, consider an Italian asset with an annual rate of return equal to 20% in lira. Assume that the inflation rate is 10% in Italy and 2% in the United States and that purchasing power parity is verified so that the lira depreciated against the U.S. dollar by about 8%. With the linear approximation, the dollar rate of return on this Italian asset is roughly 12% (20% – 8% of lira depreciation). The real rate of return is approximately 10% for an Italian investor (20% – 10% of Italian inflation) and an American investor (12% – 2% of U.S. inflation). Since investors should care about real returns, they all agree, whatever their nationality, on the return and risk of a specific asset. Exchange rate movements have no influence, since they only mirror inflation differentials and equalize real return across countries.

International Fisher Relation

The *international Fisher* relation states that the interest rate differential between two countries should be equal to the expected inflation rate differential over the term of the interest rate. This relation is inspired by the *domestic* relation postulated by Irving Fisher (1930). Let's first define the real interest rate: The nominal interest rate, r, is the sum (or rather the compounding) of the real interest rate, p, and of expected inflation over the term of the interest rate, $E(I)$:

$$(1 + r) = (1 + p)(1 + E(I)).$$

The nominal interest rate is observed in the marketplace and is usually referred to as *the interest rate*, while the real interest rate is calculated from the observed interest rate and the forecasted inflation. For example, let's suppose a nominal U.S. interest rate of 10% and an expected inflation rate of 8.91%. The real interest rate is equal to 1%, since:

$$1 + 0.10 = (1 + 0.01)(1 + 0.0891).$$

This relation is often presented with the linear approximation[3] stating that the interest rate is equal to a real interest rate *plus* expected inflation:

$$r \cong p + E(I).$$

The economic theory proposed by Fisher (1930) is that real interest rates are very stable over time. Hence fluctuations in interest rates are caused by revisions in inflationary expectations, not by movements in real interest rates.[4]

The international counterpart of this domestic relation is that the interest rate differential between two countries is linked to the difference in expected inflation:

$$\frac{1 + r_F}{1 + r_D} = \frac{1 + p_F}{1 + p_D} \times \frac{1 + E(I_F)}{1 + E(I_D)}.$$

The international Fisher relation claims that real interest rates are equal across the world; hence differences in nominal interest rates are caused only by differences in national inflationary expectations. The international Fisher relation can be written as:

$$\frac{1 + r_F}{1 + r_D} = \frac{1 + E(I_F)}{1 + E(I_D)} \tag{2.2}$$

or, with the linear approximation:

$$r_F - r_D = E(I_F) - E(I_D).$$

Note that our French/American illustration verifies the international Fisher relation if we expect a continuation of inflation at the same levels. The real rates are identical in the two countries and equal to 1%:

$$(1 + r) = (1 + p)(1 + E(I)).$$

In France

$$1 + 0.14 = (1 + 0.01)(1 + 0.1287)$$

and in the United States

$$1 + 0.10 = (1 + 0.01)(1 + 0.0891)$$

and

$$\frac{1 + r_F}{1 + r_D} = \frac{1 + 0.14}{1 + 0.10} = \frac{1 + E(I_F)}{1 + E(I_D)} = \frac{1 + 0.1287}{1 + 0.0891}.$$

Purchasing power parity combined with the international Fisher relation implies that the interest differential between two countries is expected to be offset by the currency depreciation over the term of the interest rate. This can easily be seen by taking the expected values of the future exchange rate and of inflation in the PPP Eq. (2.1). PPP applied to expected values implies:

$$\frac{E(S^1)}{S^0} = \frac{1+E(I_F)}{1+E(I_D)}.$$

Replacing in Eq. (2.2), we get:

$$\frac{1+r_F}{1+r_D} = \frac{E(S^1)}{S^0} \tag{2.3}$$

or, with the linear approximation:

$$r_F - r_D = E(s).$$

In other words, the movement in exchange rate should offset, on the average, the interest rate differential. The basic idea behind the international Fisher relation is that differences in real interest rates across countries would motivate capital flows between countries to take advantage of these real interest rate differentials. These capital flows would lead to an equalization of real interest rates across the world.

Let's for a moment consider a simple world in which goods and financial markets are perfect, i.e., *costless* arbitrage can take place instantaneously, throughout the world, for physical goods and financial assets. Let's further assume that all nationals consume the same good and that there is *no uncertainty*. Hence we know *exactly* what the inflation and the exchange rates will be in the future. In this simple world the previous parity relations can be shown, by arbitrage, to hold exactly. If the exchange rate does not adjust to the inflation differential as claimed by PPP, one would simply have to buy the goods in the country with the low real price and ship it for sale in the country with the high real price to make a certain profit. In a perfect world with costless and instantaneous shipping, such attractive situations cannot exist for long; the proposed arbitrage will make the exchange rate movement adjust exactly to inflation in both countries. In the same spirit if the interest rate differential does not reflect exactly the anticipated and certain exchange rate movement, an arbitrageur would simply borrow in one currency, transfer the amount in the other currency, and lend it at that currency interest rate. By so doing, the arbitrageur will make a certain profit with no capital investment. This riskless profit opportunity will attract huge arbitrage capital, and market rates will have to adjust to "prevent" such an arbitrage.

In reality, the future exchange rate is uncertain, and arbitrage in the goods market cannot be instantaneous and costless. So the parity relations developed here are only *theories* that claim that real prices and rates should be equalized across the world. The empirical evidence on the validity of these relations is presented in the second part of this chapter.

The next two parity relations involve the forward exchange rate.

Foreign Exchange Expectations

The *foreign exchange expectation* relation states that the forward exchange rate, quoted at time 0 for delivery at time 1, is equal to the expected value of the spot exchange rate at time 1. This can be written as:

$$F = E(S^1). \tag{2.4}$$

This relation would certainly hold if the future values of exchange rates were known with certainty. If one were sure at time 0 that the exchange rate would be worth S^1 at time 1, the current forward rate for delivery at time 1 would have to be S^1; otherwise, a riskless arbitrage opportunity would exist.

Let's assume, for example, that we know for sure that the spot exchange rate will be 8.2909 FF/\$ in a year and that the one-year forward rate is only 8 FF/\$. One could then do the following arbitrage:

- Buy dollars forward at eight francs per dollar and hold the contract until maturity.

- At maturity simultaneously deliver the forward contract and take an offsetting position in the spot exchange rate market.

On the forward contract the arbitrageur pays eight francs per dollar but receives 8.2909 francs on the spot market, leading to a profit of 0.2909 francs per dollar. If the expected spot exchange rate is certain, this is a riskless arbitrage that requires no invested capital on the forward commitment. Banks would keep doing this arbitrage until the buying pressure pushed the forward exchange rate to 8.2909 FF/\$.

Of course this parity relation depends strongly on the certainty assumption. However, it is sometimes claimed that the forward exchange rate should be an unbiased predictor of the future spot exchange rate in the presence of uncertainty, thereby leading to Eq. (2.4). Other researchers claim the existence of a risk premium appended to this relation.[5]

The foreign exchange expectation relation is often stated relative to the current spot exchange rate. If we subtract S^0 on both sides of Eq. (2.4) (remember that the current spot exchange rate is known with certainty) and divide by S^0, we get:

$$\frac{F - S^0}{S^0} = E\left(\frac{S^1 - S^0}{S^0}\right) = E(s).$$

The left-hand side is usually referred to as the forward discount, or premium, denoted *f*. It is the percentage deviation of the forward rate from the current spot rate. This relation states that the forward discount (or premium) is equal to the expected exchange rate movement and can be written as:

$$f = E(s).$$

The practical relevance of this foreign exchange expectation relation is obvious. If verified, it means that there is, on the average, no reward for bearing foreign exchange uncertainty. If a risk premium were to be added to the relation, the symmetry of the exchange rate means that it will be paid by some investors (e.g., those selling forward liras for dollars) and received by other investors (e.g., those buying forward liras for dollars). A zero-risk premium means that a forward hedge, i.e., the use of forward currency contracts to hedge the exchange risk of a portfolio of foreign assets, will be "costless" in terms of expected returns (except for commissions on the forward contracts).

Interest Rate Parity

The *interest rate parity* relation states that the interest rate differential must equal the forward discount (or premium). The exact mathematical relation, mentioned in Chapter 1, can be written as:

$$\frac{F}{S^0} = \frac{1 + r_F}{1 + r_D} \tag{2.5}$$

or, with the first-order linear approximation

$$s = \frac{F - S^0}{S^0} = \frac{r_F - r_D}{1 + r_D} \cong r_F - r_D.$$

Again, the linear approximation might be quite wrong when interest rates are high. Interest rate parity is not an economic theory but rather a technical *arbitrage* condition that is demonstrated in Chapter 1. It must hold; otherwise, riskless arbitrage would take place to exploit this situation.

Note that this interest rate parity relation is verified in our simple example, where

$$\frac{F}{8.00} = \frac{1 + 0.14}{1 + 0.10},$$

and *F* is 8.2909 francs per dollar.

Combining the Parity Relations

The four parity relations might be combined in several ways to link the four variables:

- the interest rate differential
- the inflation differential

- the forward discount or premium

- the exchange rate movement

For example, the interest rate parity relation combined with the foreign exchange expectation relation implies that the difference in interest rates is equal to the expected exchange rate movement.

The various parity relations are illustrated in Exh. 2.1. They provide a very useful base to the relationship among exchange rates, inflation, and interest rates. Using this simple framework as a starting point, an international investor can draw several practical implications:

- Interest rate differentials reflect expectations about currency movements. In other words, the expected return on default-free bills should be equal across countries. This is true whether we measure return in a common currency or in real terms.

- Exchange risk reduces to inflation uncertainty. An investor caring about real returns would not be affected by exchange rate uncertainty.

EXHIBIT 2.1

International Parity Relations
Linear approximation

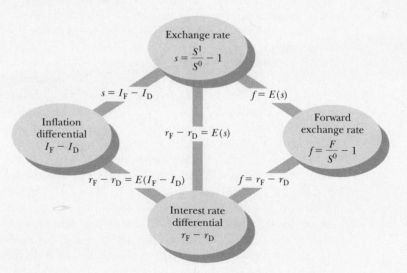

The Empirical Evidence

The economic theory presented so far is a useful framework in which to analyze the international interplay of monetary variables. As a theory, it relies on restrictive assumptions about the perfection of trade and money markets. In the real world future inflation and exchange rates are uncertain: Goods cannot be transferred instantaneously from one country to another, shipping costs are high, and import restrictions of various forms restrict international trade. Although the stylized system of equilibrium as presented is a useful starting point for understanding the international financial environment, its empirical validity must be studied. The next step is to evaluate the extent to which each link holds true and to examine the causes of deviation.

Purchasing Power Parity

Purchasing power parity is a poor explanation for short-term exchange rate movements. Regression of monthly or quarterly exchange rate movements on inflation differentials yields a low explanatory power (R^2) for the recent period of floating exchange rates. Little exchange rate volatility is explained by inflation. For example, Adler and Dumas (1983) found that inflation differentials explained less than 5% of monthly exchange rate movements in the 1970s. In other words, 95% of currency movements were not caused by current inflation. Nonetheless many believe that although purchasing power parity may not hold for short periods (from one month to a year), it does hold over the long run.

PPP is probably the economic subject that has attracted the largest number of empirical articles. The empirical findings can be summarized as disappointing.[6] The "optimistic" researchers conclude that it seems to take many years before a deviation from purchasing power parity is corrected in the foreign exchange market. The "pessimistic" researchers suggest that short-term movements in the real exchange rate, i.e., the exchange rate adjusted for the inflation differential, tend to follow a random pattern; in other words, deviations from PPP are never corrected.[7]

The econometric methodology has moved from the traditional regression techniques to a cointegration approach. This later approach states that the exchange rate and the price level series should be cointegrated if the PPP holds as a long-term equilibrium relation.[8] All tests performed on the recent period of floating exchange rates (since the early 1970s) for major currencies tend to reject or provide only weak support for PPP. Tests performed on longer time periods or involving high-inflation countries provide stronger support for PPP.[9]

There are several explanations for this phenomenon. First, the mere definition of an inflation rate is questionable. Investors throughout the world have different consumption preferences, and a common basket of consumption goods does not exist. In the short run, relative prices of different consumption goods vary extensively with specific influences on specific consumption baskets. As an illustration, the price of sake might double in Japan (thereby affecting the local price index), but the price rise should have little influence on the yen exchange rate, since few foreigners consume sake, and it has little international trade. In the long run, consumption substitution will take place in Japan to reflect the higher price of sake, and Japanese people may consume more beer or wine.

Second, transfer costs, import taxes and restrictions, as well as export subsidies may prevent arbitrage in the goods markets to restore purchasing power parity. In the long run, however, industries from countries with overvalued currencies will make direct investments in undervalued countries. For example, the U.S. dollar was vastly overvalued in terms of purchasing power parity in the early 1980s. This meant that the real price of U.S. goods was high compared to that of foreign countries. Because the U.S. dollar was strong, wages were lower in France than in the United States when converted into dollars. U.S. exports were not competitive, because of their high prices, which were a result of the exchange rate; similarly, foreign imports to the United States were cheap. Because the situation persisted, many U.S. companies built plants abroad to take advantage of this deviation from purchasing power parity. Such behavior leads in time to a restoration of purchasing power parity.

Many factors other than inflation influence exchange rates. Because physical goods arbitrage is constrained, purchasing power parity plays only a small role in the short run; other variables have a major impact on the short-run behavior of exchange rates. The practical implications of these deviations from purchasing power parity are very important. The real returns of one asset as measured by investors from different countries are different. For example, assume that the lira keeps a constant exchange rate with the dollar, despite the 8% inflation differential mentioned in the preceding illustration. Then the real return for an Italian investor is 10%, whereas that of a U.S. investor in 18% (20% asset return in dollars minus 2% U.S. inflation rate). Furthermore uncertainty about the real exchange rate adds uncertainty to the dollar return of a foreign investment.

International Fisher Relation

The international Fisher relation is somewhat supported empirically when applied to the major currencies. Kane and Rosenthal[10] studied the Eurocurrency market for six major currencies during the period 1974 to 1979 and found support for this model. Studies on a more recent period (post-1979) seem to indicate that real interest rates are variable over time and differ across countries. This is illustrated in Exh. 2.2, which reproduces the real interest rate for three-month bills for the three major international currencies over the past 20 years. The calculation of the real interest rate is somewhat difficult, since it requires a measure of expected inflation. In Exh. 2.2 expected inflation is simply replaced by the realized inflation over the life of the three-month bill; real rates observed each quarter have been averaged over the year. Real rates differed markedly during the first oil shock of 1973–74. Real rates were very high in the 1980s and became much lower on the U.S. dollar than on other currencies in the early 1990s.

EXHIBIT 2.2

Real Interest Rates

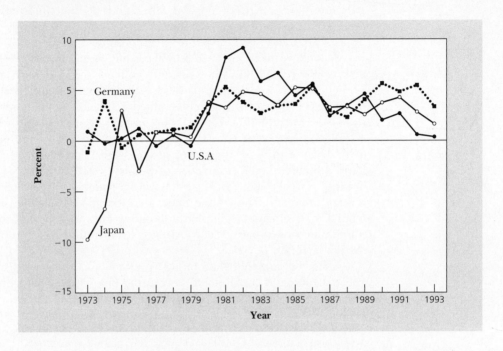

Foreign Exchange Expectations

The foreign exchange expectations relation links the expected exchange rate movement to the forward discount/premium. Exchange rate expectations are not directly observable, so the ex-post movements are used instead, assuming that the realized exchange rate movement is equal to its expectation plus a random unpredictable element. This relation is usually tested by running a regression of the ex-post exchange rate movement s_{t+1} over the period $t+1$, on the forward discount/premium f_t observed at the start of the period:

$$s_t = \alpha + \beta f_t + \varepsilon_t,$$

where α should be equal to 0 and β to 1, according to the theory.

The explanatory power (R^2) of the regression is usually quite low, and the slope coefficient β is generally negative rather than equal to 1. At least two explanations can be advanced for this finding. First, exchange rates are so unpredictable that the statistical power of this test, using ex-post data for projections, is very poor. Second, Eq. (2.4) should include a risk premium term because of the uncertainty in exchange rates, and risk premiums change over time. Fama (1984) and other researchers[11] have found some evidence of the existence of such a time-varying risk premium. Fama further suggests that the variation in risk premium is too large to be reasonable and able to explain the deviations from the foreign exchange expectations relation. Numerous theories and models of exchange rate behavior have been developed, including that of speculative bubbles, but it is fair to say that none provides a satisfactory description of observed behavior of foreign exchange rates.

Other researchers[12] have tested this relation by drawing exchange rate expectations from survey data. In these surveys foreign exchange specialists are periodically asked to provide their short-term forecasts for the major currencies. Again, these studies tend to conclude that the participants are irrational or that the market is inefficient.

The current variability of exchange rates is very large compared to that of interest rates and inflation rates. So risk must be an important factor in the foreign exchange relation and all relations involving the expected exchange rate. Any arbitrage strategy built to take advantage of real interest rate differentials or of expected exchange rate movements has a very uncertain outcome.

Interest Rate Parity

As demonstrated in Chapter 1, the interest rate parity relation is derived from arbitrage among the various money markets. If these markets are free and deregulated, interest rate parity *must* hold, within transaction costs; we showed in Chapter 1 how the bid-ask spreads on exchange and interest rates affect this relation. The Eurocurrency market, in which major currencies can be borrowed and lent freely, fits this description. As the bid-ask spreads are very tiny on the Eurocurrency market, interest parity is always verified within a few basis points. This is confirmed by the casual observation of trading screens and by studies.[13] However, many countries, especially developing ones, still impose various forms of capital controls and taxes that impede arbitrage. Furthermore many smaller currencies can be borrowed and lent only domestically; the domestic money markets are often subject to political risk and various types of costly regulations and controls. Frankel and MacArthur (1988) have confirmed that deviations from interest rate parity can be quite large for what they call "closed less-developed countries." The continuing deregulation and international integration of financial markets throughout the world is certain to reduce these deviations in the future, even for emerging markets.

The Past Two Decades

It might be useful to go beyond a summary of research results and to provide a quick look at the international monetary environment of the past 20 years, from the mid-1970s to the mid-1990s. Without getting into sophisticated statistical methodologies, Exh. 2.3 indicates the relationships among inflation rates, interest rates, and exchange rates. Two pairs of countries and their exchange rates are analyzed: U.S. dollar/Japanese yen and Deutsche mark/British pound. For each year, the figure indicates in percentages the inflation differential, the exchange rate movement, and the interest rate differential. Differentials are calculated as the value for the first country minus that of the second one. For example, Exh. 2.3

EXHIBIT 2.3

Annual Comparison of Interest Rate Differentials, Exchange Rate Movements, and Interest Rate Differentials, 1976 to 1993

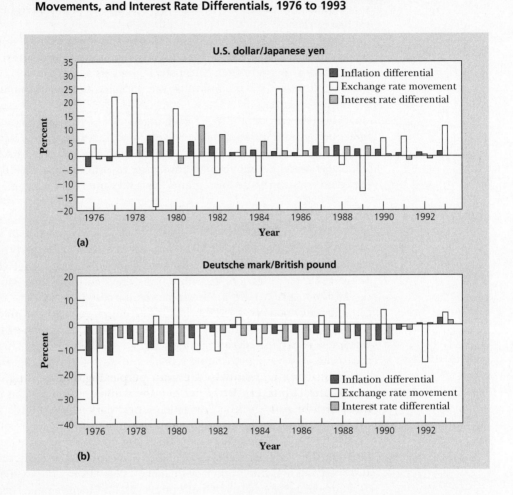

(a)

(b)

shows that in 1983 the United States had about two percent more inflation than Japan and a higher short-term interest rate (a differential of approximately four percent). The currency is calculated as the value of the second country's currency. For example, in Exh. 2.3 we can track the dollar value of the Japanese yen. In 1983 the yen appreciated by approximately two percent relative to the U.S. dollar. In theory we would expect all three values to be of the same sign and magnitude: For each year the three bars should be at the same level, but they typically are not.

Although the interest rate and inflation differentials tend to be of the same sign and magnitude, this is not the case for exchange rate movements. For many years the exchange rate has moved in the opposite direction from interest differentials (hence from the forward exchange rate discount, or premium). Note that this effect is not dollar-specific, since it also applies the Deutsche mark/pound exchange rate. For example, Exh. 2.3 shows that in 1985 the dollar depreciated by more than 20% relative to the yen, although their inflation and interest rates were fairly close.

The various building blocks of the theory are more tenable over the long run, as can be seen in Exh. 2.4. The means for inflation rate differentials, interest rate differentials, and exchange rate movements are calculated for the period from 1973 to 1993 and for a larger sample of currencies. Note that there was more inflation in the United States than in Switzerland, Germany, and to some extent Japan but less than in France or the United Kingdom. In keeping with the theory, the dollar appreciated against the British pound and depreciated against the Deutsche mark, Swiss franc, and Japanese yen. Yet although the signs of the three variables are the same for each country pair, their magnitude is sometimes quite different. It appears clearly that the dollar has been systematically weak compared to the inflation and interest rate fundamentals. Although the inflation rate differential of foreign countries relative to the United States is on the average reflected in the interest rate differential (within about one percent), the U.S. dollar has experienced a much higher average rate of depreciation than these two differentials would suggest. For an American investor, investing in foreign interest rate assets provided a much higher return than did investing in dollar interest rate assets. The story is somewhat different for other exchange rates that do not involve the U.S. dollar, especially among European currencies. Over 20 years the parity relations have been fairly well verified for the British pound/Deutsche mark exchange rate, as can be seen in Exh. 2.4.

These empirical findings are both perplexing and exciting. Exchange rates are a matter of concern for all international investors because the evidence shows that they do not simply neutralize inflation differentials in real terms.

EXHIBIT 2.4

Exchange Rate Movements, Inflation Rate Differentials, and Interest Rate Differentials
Average annual rate, 1973 to 1993

Countries	Exchange Rate Movement %	Inflation Rate Differential %	Interest Rate Differential %
U.S./Japan	5.40	1.13	2.21
U.S./Germany	3.70	2.34	2.24
U.S./U.K.	−1.52	−2.95	−3.05
U.S./Switzerland	5.49	2.11	3.69
U.S./France	0.02	−1.10	−2.63
Germany/U.K.	−4.63	−5.30	−5.29

Furthermore movements do not generally correct interest rate differences between two currencies. Basically, one cannot rely on money markets to correctly assess and neutralize future exchange rate movements. This gives economists a chance to improve significantly the performance of a portfolio by forecasting exchange rates correctly, a topic addressed in Chapter 3. Exchange rates add a dimension to international investments not encountered in the domestic situation, which makes it all the more important to gain an understanding of the influence of international monetary variables on equity and bond prices and to develop international asset pricing models that explicitly incorporate exchange risk.

Summary

1. A simple understanding of the interaction of international monetary variables can be obtained by looking at various parity relations linking exchange, interest, and inflation rates.

2. *Purchasing power parity* states that exchange rates adjust to inflation differentials between two countries. Although this relation is reasonably verified in the very long run, it does not explain short-term variations in exchange rates.

3. The *international Fisher* relation states that the difference is interest rates between two countries is explained by their inflation differential. There is some empirical support in the short run and the long run for this proposition. However, real interest rates can be quite different across countries.

4. The *foreign exchange expectations* relation states that the expected spot exchange rate is equal to the current forward exchange rate. No empirical support is found for this relation.

5. *Interest rate parity* states that the forward discount (or premium) is equal to the interest rate differential. This is a relation that must hold by financial arbitrage and is therefore verified on free money markets.

6. The parity relations provide a useful framework for understanding the international links among monetary variables, but they leave many questions unanswered.

Questions and Problems

1*. The current Swiss franc/U.S. dollar spot exchange rate is 2 Swiss francs per dollar, or SF/$ = 2. The expected inflation over the coming year is 2% in Switzerland and 5% in the United States. What is the expected value for the spot exchange rate a year from now, according to purchasing power parity?

2. The spot exchange rate is SF/$ = 2.00. The one-year interest rate is equal to 4% in Switzerland and 8% in the United States. What should the current value of the forward exchange rate be?

3. The yen/DM spot exchange rate is 60 yen per DM. Inflation rates in Japan and Germany are similar. Over the past year the yen/DM rate moved from 55 to 60. Is it good news or bad news for Japanese firms competing with German firms in the automobile market?

4*. Let's consider a utopian world in which there are only three goods:

- Japanese consume only a locally produced food, called sake, and an industrially produced and traded good, called TV sets.
- Americans consume only a locally produced food, called beer, and an industrially produced and traded good, called TV sets.

TV sets are produced in both countries and actively traded; their local prices follow the law of one price. Foods are produced only locally and are not traded.

The consumption basket of a Japanese consists of two thirds sake and one third TV sets. The consumption basket of an American consists of one half beer and one half TV sets. Prices of beer and TV sets in the United States are constant over time, in U.S. dollars. Japanese are very competitive and export a lot of TV sets. Japanese farmers want to share in the increased national wealth, and the price of sake is rising at a rate of 10% per year, in yen. Assume that the yen/dollar exchange rate stays constant. What is the consumer price index inflation in Japan? Is PPP verified? Should it be verified?

5. Foreign companies are complaining that they are prevented from exporting to Japan by all kinds of official or unwritten impediments. Try to list some of these impediments. What are the implications in terms of PPP?

6*. Should nominal interest rates be equal across countries? Why?

7. Should real interest rates be equal across countries? Can a financial arbitrage take place in case of significant and persistent real interest rate differences? To answer this question, first assume that exchange rates are fully predictable and follow purchasing power parity (PPP). Then assume that they are uncertain but that PPP holds. Finally, assume that exchange rates are uncertain and that PPP does not hold.

8*. Here are some statistics:

	FF	US$
Inflation (annual rate)	6%	?
One-year interest rate	8%	7%
Spot exchange rate (FF per US$)		?
Expected exchange rate (in one year)		6
One-year forward exchange rate (FF/$)		?

Replace the question marks by appropriate answers, assuming the perfect world described in Exh. 2.1.

9. Here are some statistics:

	UK£	DM
Inflation (annual rate)	10%	4%
One-year interest rate	12%	?
Spot exchange rate (DM per £)		3
Expected exchange rate (in one year)		?
One-year forward exchange rate (DM/£)		?

Replace the question marks by appropriate answers, assuming the perfect world described in Exh. 2.1.

10*. You believe that the DM will strongly appreciate against the French franc in the next few weeks. What action can you take?

11. Assume that foreign exchange rates are totally unpredictable, as claimed by some theories and empirical studies, so that the best prediction of the future spot rate is the current spot rate. Back in 1982, would you have suggested investing in U.S. dollar bills or in DM bills? What about in 1992? (Look at Exh. 2.2, knowing that inflation rates were similar in the two countries.)

12*. In the early 1990s France and Germany had similar current and forecasted inflation rates. However, political/economic uncertainties were higher in France, which in the 1980s had had several political changes leading to several devaluations of the French franc. Do you expect to observe equal interest rates in the two countries? Why?

13. *Project:* One would expect that purchasing power parity (PPP) would be better verified for countries with high inflation. Look at the validity of PPP for Latin American countries relative to the United States.

   ▪ Take end-of-quarter consumer price index data for a sample of high-inflation emerging countries and the United States; take a period of ten years. For each country, divide its price index by that of the United States to obtain its relative price index.
   ▪ Take end-of-quarter exchange rates against the U.S. dollar.
   ▪ For each country, perform various statistical tests to compare the two series. For example, you can first plot them, using a common base. You can also calculate their quarterly percent variation and compare the means of the two series (average inflation differential and average depreciation of the currency). You could do a regression of the quarterly exchange rate variations on the quarterly inflation differential and look at the regression coefficients, as well as at the *R*-square.
   ▪ Do a similar calculation for some developed countries (e.g., Japan, Germany, and the United Kingdom) relative to the United States. Are the conclusions similar?

Notes

1. A derivation of these relations may be found in Giddy (1976); Roll and Solnik (1979); and B. Solnik, "International Parity Condition and Exchange Risk: A Review," *Journal of Banking and Finance*, 2, 1978, pp. 281–293.

2. This theory was originally presented by Cassel (1916). A review of purchasing power parity may be found in Shapiro (1983).

3. The linear approximation ignores the cross-product term $p.E(I)$ in the exact relation. This cross-product may be significant, especially in countries with high inflation rates. The same applies to all the parity relations.

4. Keynesians disagree with this theory and provide a different explanation for fluctuations in nominal short-term interest rates. They claim that monetary shocks leave short-term inflation unaffected because of sticky good prices, whereas real interest rates react immediately to liquidity conditions. For example, a sudden contraction in the money supply growth rate leads to an immediate increase in the nominal interest rate: The real interest rate goes up because money becomes rare and expensive, whereas short-term inflationary expectations are unchanged. Those expectations adjust only gradually to the slowdown in money supply. See Dornbusch (1988).

5. See Solnik (1974); Roll and Solnik (1979); Stulz (1981); and Adler and Dumas (1983).

6. For surveys of the empirical literatures, see L.H. Officer, "The Purchasing Power Theory of Exchange Rates: A Review Article," *IMF Staff Papers*, March 1976; R. Dornbusch, "Purchasing Power Parity," in J. Eatwell, M. Milgate, and P. Newman, eds., *The New Palgrave: A Dictionary of Economics*, New York: Stockton, 1987; and M.D.D. Evans and J.R. Lothian, "Response of Exchange Rates to Permanent and Transitory Shocks," *Journal of International Money and Finance*, 12, December 1993.

7. See R. Roll, "Violations of Purchasing Power Parity and Their Implications for Efficient International Commodity Markets," in M. Sarnat and G. Szego, eds, *International Finance and Trade*, Cambridge, MA: Ballinger, 1979. This is usually referred to as the "efficient market" version of PPP. This theory claims that the foreign exchange market immediately discounts the influence of expected inflation and that any future exchange rate movement is affected by future inflation, not by past inflation rates. See also on this topic R. Meese and K. Rogoff, "What is Real? The Exchange Rate–Interest Rate Differential Relation over the Modern Floating-Rate Period," *Journal of Finance*, September 1988; and M. Adler and B. Lehman, "Deviations from Purchasing Power Parity in the Long Run," *Journal of Finance*, December 1983.

8. See, among others, W. Enders, "ARIMA and Cointegration Tests of PPP under Fixed and Flexible Exchange Rate Regimes," *Review of Economics and Statistics*, 70, August 1988; N. Mark, "Real and Nominal Exchange Rates in the Long Run: An Empirical Investigation," *Journal of International Economics*, 28, February 1990; N. Abouaf and P. Jorion, "Purchasing Power Parity in the Long Run," *Journal of Finance*, 45, March 1990; and M.K. Pippenger, "Cointegration Tests of Purchasing Power Parity: The Swiss Case," *Journal of International Money and Finance*, 12, February 1993.

9. See N. Abouaf and P. Jorion, "Purchasing Power Parity in the Long Run," *Journal of Finance*, 45, March 1990, for long-term time-series investigation. See also R. McNown and M. Wallace, "National Price Levels, Purchasing Power Parity and Cointegration: A Test of Four High Inflation Countries," *Journal of International Money and Finance*, 8, December 1989; or K. Phylaktis, "Purchasing Power Parity and Cointegration: The Greek Evidence from the 1920s," *Journal of International Money and Finance*, 11, October 1992.

10. See E. Kane and L. Rosenthal, "International Interest Rates and Inflationary Expectations," *Journal of International Money and Finance*, April 1982; F.S. Mishkin, "Are Real Interest Rates Equal Across Countries: An Empirical Investigation of International Parity Relations?" *Journal of Finance*, December 1984; N. Mark, "Some Evidence on the International Equality of Real Interest Rates," *Journal of International Money and Finance*, 4, June 1985; and M.M. Dutton, "Real Interest Rate Parity: New Measures and Tests," *Journal of International Money and Finance*, 12, February 1993.

11. See R. Roll and B. Solnik, "A Pure Foreign Exchange Asset Pricing Model," *Journal of International Economics*, May 1977; E. Fama, "Forward and Spot Exchange Rates," *Journal of Monetary Economics*, November 1984; R.J. Hodrick and S. Srivastava, "An Investigation of Risk and Return in Forward Foreign Exchange," *Journal of International Money and Finance*, April 1984; R.E. Cumby and M. Obstfeld, "A Note on Exchange Rate Expectations and Nominal Interest Rate Differentials," June 1981; A. Giovanini and P. Jorion, "Interest Rates and Risk Premia in the Stock Market and the Foreign Exchange Market," *Journal of International Money and Finance*, 6, April 1987; R.J. Hodrick, *The Empirical Evidence on the Efficiency of Forward and Futures Foreign Exchange Markets,* Chur, Switzerland: Harwood Academic Publishers, 1987; G. Kaminsky and R. Peruga, "Can a Time-Varying Risk Premium Explain Excess Returns in the Forward Market for Foreign Exchange," *Journal of International Economics*, 28, February 1990; and G. Bekaert and R.J. Hodrick, "On Biases in the Measurement of Foreign Exchange Risk Premiums," *Journal of International Money and Finance*, 12(2), April 1993.

12. See J.A. Frankel and K. Froot, "Using Survey data to Test Standard Propositions Regarding Exchange Rate Expectations," *American Economic Review*, 77, March 1987; S. Takagi, "Exchange Rate Expectations: A Survey of Survey Studies," *IMF Staff Papers*, June 1991; P.C. Liu and G.S. Maddala, "Rationality of Survey Data and Tests of Market Efficiency in the Foreign Exchange Market," *Journal of International Money and Finance*, 11, August 1992; and S. Cavaglia, W.F.C. Verschoor, and C.P. Wolff, "Further Evidence on Exchange Rate Expectations," *Journal of International Money and Finance*, 12, February 1993.

13. See K. Clinton, "Transaction Costs and Covered Arbitrage: Theory and Evidence," *Journal of Political Economy*, 88, April 1988; M. Taylor, "Covered Interest Parity: A High-Frequency, High-Quality Data Study," *Econometrica*, 54, May 1987; and J. Frankel and M.A. MacArthur, "Political vs Currency Premia in International Real Interest Differentials: A Study of Forward Rates for 24 Countries," *European Economic Review*, 32, June 1988. A study supporting interest rate parity for long-term rates can be found in H. Popper, "Long-Term Covered Interest Parity: Evidence from Currency Swaps," *Journal of International Money and Finance*, 12, August 1993.

Bibliography

Adler, M., and Dumas, B. "International Portfolio Choice *and* Corporation Finance: A Synthesis," *Journal of Finance*, 38, June 1983.

Branson, W.H. "Exchange Rate Policy after a Decade of Floating," in J. Bilson, and R. Marston, eds., *Exchange Rate Theory and Practice*, Chicago: University of Chicago Press, 1984.

Cassel G. "The Present Situation on the Foreign Exchanges," *Economic Journal*, 1916, pp. 62–65.

Cumby, R.E., and Obstfeld, M. "A Note on Exchange Rates Expectations and Nominal Interest Rates Differentials," *Journal of Finance*, June 1981.

Dornbusch, R. *Open Economy Macroeconomics*, New York: Basic Books, 1988.

Fama, E. "Forward and Spot Exchange Rates," *Journal of Monetary Economics*, November 1984.

Fisher, I. *The Theory of Interest*, New York: Macmillan, 1930.

Giddy, I. "An Integrated Theory of Exchange Rate Equilibrium," *Journal of Financial and Quantitative Analysis*, December 1976.

Hodrick, R.J., and Srivastava, S. "An Investigation of Risk and Return in Forward Foreign Exchange," *Journal of International Money and Finance*, April 1984.

Kravis, I.B., Heston, A., and Summers, L. *World Production and Income: International Comparisons of Real GDP*, Baltimore, MD: Johns Hopkins University Press, 1982.

Meese, R., and Rogoff, K. "What is Real? The Exchange Rate–Interest Rate Differential Relation over the Modern Floating-Rate Period," *Journal of Finance*, September 1988.

Mishkin, F.S. "Are Real Interest Rates Equal Across Countries? An Empirical Investigation of International Parity Relations," *Journal of Finance*, December 1984.

Officer, L.H. "The Purchasing Power Theory of Exchange Rates: A Review Article," *IMF Staff Papers*, March 1976.

Roll, R. "Violations of Purchasing Power Parity and Their Implications for Efficient International Commodity Markets," in M. Sarnat and G. Szego, eds., *International Finance and Trade*, Cambridge, MA: Ballinger, 1979.

Roll, R., and Solnik, B. "A Pure Foreign Exchange Asset Pricing Model," *Journal of International Economics*, 7, May 1977.

———. "On Some International Parity Conditions," *Journal of Macroeconomics*, Summer 1979.

Shapiro, A. "What Does Purchasing Power Parity Mean?" *Journal of International Money and Finance*, December 1983.

Solnik, B. "An Equilibrium Model of the International Capital Market," *Journal of Economic Theory*, 8, July/August 1974.

Stulz, R. "A Model of International Asset Pricing," *Journal of Financial Economics*, 9, December 1981.

3

Foreign Exchange Determination and Forecasting

M ajor currencies are traded on an international monetary market, and their exchange rates fluctuate extensively. In a system of *fixed* exchange rates,[1] the rate fluctuates within a small band around the fixed central parity. Tensions in the system can lead to infrequent realignments of the central parity. In such a monetary system one must try to understand what drives the fluctuations of the exchange rate within the band and, eventually, the time and magnitude of a change in parity. Monetary authorities decide on parity changes, but they are often compelled to act by market forces. These market forces are often called "speculation" by the media and governments. In a system of *floating* exchange rates there is no central parity, and the exchange rate can fluctuate freely. However, governments often have target policies for the exchange rate of their currencies and tend to intervene to keep their currencies from deviating too much from those targets. In both cases it is useful to understand the long- and short-term determinants of the exchange rate fluctuations. Experience shows that this is a difficult task. Chapter 2 introduced a simple framework to analyze the links among exchange rates, inflation, and interest rates. It was shown that exchange rates exhibit a volatility that cannot be directly explained by these parity conditions. We now go one step further and give a brief review of the simple economic models of the exchange rate.[2] We then examine various models used in foreign exchange forecasting.

 ## Exchange Rate Determination

The traditional view, introduced in Chapter 2, is that exchange rates should adjust the purchasing power of the two currencies. It is worth looking again at this relation.

Purchasing Power Parity Revisited

Chapter 2 showed that the *short-run* behavior of the exchange rates does not conform to purchasing power parity (PPP). Exhibit 2.3 demonstrated that yearly exchange rates can deviate significantly from the inflation differentials between countries. The *real* exchange rate is the observed exchange rate adjusted for inflation. Hence, movements in the real exchange rate are equal to movements in the exchange rate minus the actual inflation differential between the two countries.

The definition of a proper inflation index is open to question. The estimation of the inflation rate depends on the basket of goods chosen for the index. Different baskets of goods will exhibit different price increases, as the relative prices of the goods change over time. For example, the price of a haircut or of bread in Uruguay does not closely track that of an imported computer. An inflation rate measured from an index of consumed goods will be different from an inflation rate measured from an index of produced goods, because of differences in imported and exported goods. Monetarists view inflation as a depreciation of the real value of a currency. One would expect PPP to be better verified for countries with hyperinflation, as was the case with some South American countries in the 1980s, since relative price movements are small compared to general monetary inflation. Even for these countries, the short-term volatility of the real exchange rate can be quite high. These movements in the real exchange rate create arbitrage opportunities on the physical goods market. Clearly a physical arbitrage cannot take place for many of the home goods consumed, e.g., haircuts and bread. Even for internationally traded goods the law of one (real) price does not hold in the short run. Market segmentation, tariffs, quota, as well as the costs and risks involved in such an arbitrage, can explain large price differentials for traded goods.

Even over the *long run*, say a 20-year period, annual violations of PPP can cumulate to offer very significant deviations from the theory. For example, the average deviation from PPP between Japan and the United States is 4% per year for a 20-year period starting in 1973, as reported in Exh. 2.4. Back in 1970, the final days of the fixed exchange rate system, one dollar was worth 360 yen. The exchange rate went below 100 in 1994. Over the same period, the cumulated inflation differential for consumer prices between the two countries was less than 20%.

A major question is what can explain such movements in the real exchange rate over the long run. The explanation must come from more fundamental economic reasons than the difficulty of goods arbitrage. Economic activity is the major determinant of the long-run behavior of the real exchange rate. Assume that a country exhibits a significant rise in productivity with a rapid growth in manufacturing. This gain in productivity will make the manufactured goods competitive in the international marketplace and will increase exports. The increased economic activity will raise demand for labor and will lead to an increase in wages and to a rise in consumer prices. If the exchange rate is *fixed*, this growth in productivity and activity would simply lead to higher domestic inflation. The *real* exchange rate of the home currency appreciates. If the exchange rate is *flexible*, the necessary adjustment can also take place through an appreciation of the domestic currency. Nationals will start to consume more of the foreign goods imported at a cheaper home-currency price because of the appreciation of the domestic currency. Inflation will be less than in the case of fixed exchange rates (because of the drop in the price of imported goods), but the net result will also be an appreciation in the real exchange rate of the home currency.

Differential in productivity growth influences the real exchange rate in the long run. This explanation applies well to the Japanese yen/U.S. dollar rate in the past 30 years. Similarly, the Hong Kong dollar had been pegged to the U.S. dollar for many years before 1997. Inflation was much higher in Hong Kong than in the United States, but the Hong Kong dollar remained pegged to the U.S. dollar, thanks to the growth in Chinese productivity and economic activity.

Although growth in economic activity and differences in productivity can be a good determinant of the very long-term real exchange rate, it appears clearly that shorter-term variations can be explained only by more elaborate models. The general impression is that exchange rates can become grossly misaligned and stay so for several years without a correction. This correction will take place, but it may take several years, and its timing is unclear.

The Balance of Payments Approach

Historically, an analysis of the balance of payments provided the first approach to the economic modeling of the exchange rate.

Definition   The balance of payments tracks all financial flows crossing the borders of a country during a given period (a quarter or a year). For example, an export creates a positive financial inflow for the country, whereas an import creates a financial outflow (a negative financial inflow). A resident's purchase of a foreign security creates a negative financial inflow, whereas a loan made by a foreign bank to a resident bank induces a positive financial inflow. The balance of payments compiles all financial flows, not the transaction that induced them. The convention is to treat all financial inflows as a credit to the balance of payments.

A balance of payments is not an income statement or a balance sheet but rather a cash balance of the country relative to the rest of the world. As long as a country is not bankrupt, the balance of all financial flows must be equilibrated, like any cash balance. In other words, the final balance *must* be zero.

This concept is not always easy to understand and can be best confirmed by a simple example. Let's consider a small country whose only international transactions consist of exports and imports of goods. Its central bank has a large reserve of foreign currencies accumulated over the years. Assume that in the year 2000, this country runs a trade deficit of $1 million (imports greater than exports). Then the central bank will need to use $1 million of reserve to offset this deficit. The net balance will then be zero. Of course, the importers could instead borrow $1 million abroad to finance the payment of the trade balance; this will create a capital inflow that will be recorded in the balance of payments as a positive inflow offsetting the trade deficit. Again the balance of payments will be equilibrated.

A parallel can be drawn with the cash balance of an individual. If expenses exceed receipts at the end of the month, an individual must use his or her reserves to cover the deficit, borrow money from the outside world, or sell some assets to the outside world. The net balance must be zero. Hence what is interesting is to analyze and interpret the various components of the balance of payments, as we know that the final balance must be zero.

The tradition is to separate the balance according to the type of transaction involved. There are indeed many types of international transactions, including the following:

- international trade leads to the payment of goods imported and exported

- payments of services, such as tourism and consulting contracts

- income received (and paid) on loans and existing investments

- direct investments made by domestic corporations abroad and by foreign corporations at home

- portfolio investments, such as purchase of foreign securities by domestic investors and purchase of domestic securities by foreign investors

- all types of short-term and long-term capital flows

- sale of foreign currency reserves by the central bank

Several chapters could be devoted to the accounting details of the balance of payments and to the controversy surrounding the various accounting conventions. The establishment of a balance of payments requires the collection of statistics from many different sources, e.g., customs data, central bank statistics, and bank reports of transactions. Some countries, such as the United States, construct their balance of payments from a sampling of transactions. Most other countries engage in an attempt to trace every single international transaction. It is common to see the balance of payments figures revised periodically after a few months or years to reflect corrected data or a change in accounting conventions.

To simplify the presentation of a balance of payments, it is useful to consider three component groups of lines:

- current account

- capital account

- official reserve account

The *current account* includes the balance of goods and services, income received or paid on existing investments, and unrequited transfers. Exports, or income received from abroad, appear as credits to the balance. It must be stressed that the current account does not include the amounts paid for investments abroad but only the income received on current holding of foreign assets, usually in the form of dividends or interest payments. Actual investments are reflected in the capital account section. Unrequited (or unilateral) transfers correspond to flows entailing no compensation (in the form of goods, services, or assets). This covers, for example, aid programs in favor of poor countries and expropriation losses.

An important component of the current account, often mentioned by the news media, is the *trade balance*, which is simply the balance of merchandise exports minus merchandise imports. Many consider that the merchandise trade balance is given too much importance and that services should be added to the trade balance. Altogether, the current account gives a more global view of all current (i.e., noninvestment) transactions. Introducing straightforward notations, the current account CA is the sum of the following:

Trade balance	TB
Balance of services	BS
Net income received	NI
Unrequited transfers	UT
Current account	CA

The *capital account* includes all short-term and long-term capital transactions. In our definition we exclude transactions made by the central bank, which will be assigned to the official reserve account. The capital account includes direct investment, portfolio investment, other capital flows (especially short-term capital), and net errors and omissions. Direct investment is the net amount of direct purchases of companies or real estate made by a resident abroad and by foreigners at home. "Direct" means that the purchase did not go through the capital market and involves some form of control in the foreign company, as opposed to portfolio investment. The purchase (sale) of a foreign company by a resident is treated as a debit (credit), as it corresponds to a financial outflow (inflow). The purchase (sale) of a domestic company by a foreign resident is treated as a credit (debit), as it corresponds to a financial inflow (outflow). Portfolio investments correspond to the balance of investments made on financial markets by domestic and foreign investors. "Other capital flows" includes many types of private and official capital flows, including short-term deposits made by foreigners at domestic banks and vice versa. "Net errors and omissions" is very shameful for balance of payments accountants. At the end of the day, when all statistics are collected from many different sources, the balance of payments must balance, like any cash balance. "Net errors and omissions" includes a few unaffected transactions but consists mostly of whatever is needed to equilibrate the final balance to zero. Apparently disliking this terminology, the United States in 1976 preferred to change it to "statistical discrepancy." This line is assigned to the capital account because transactions in the current account are more reliably tracked than capital transactions.

Introducing straightforward notations, the capital account (KA) is the sum of:

Direct investment   DI

Portfolio investment   PI

Other capital flows   OK

Net errors and omissions   NE

Capital account   KA

The sum of the current account and the capital account is generally called the *overall balance* (IMF terminology). Denoting *OB* the overall balance, we have:

$$OB = CA + KA.$$

The *official reserve account* reflects net changes in the government's international reserves.[3] These reserves can take the form of foreign currency holdings and loans to foreign governments. Conversely, liabilities that constitute foreign governments' reserves come in deduction of the domestic reserves. When the Federal Reserve Bank sells foreign currencies to equilibrate a deficit in the current and capital accounts, it will receive dollars in exchange. This inflow of dollars is treated as a credit to the balance of payments. This means that a *reduction* in the official reserves has a *positive* sign in the balance of payments accounting. This is very often a source of confusion, as most of us tend to regard a drop in reserves as "bad" or "negative." However, this convention is quite logical. If a country sells goods or services, it receives a financial flow in exchange for these goods or services. If its government sells foreign currencies, it receives a financial flow in exchange for this special type of note. Similarly, if a government is forced to borrow abroad to finance a deficit, the loan will induce a financial inflow and hence a credit to the balance of payments. This credit is treated as an increase in official liabilities and hence as a reduction in official reserves.

By definition of a balance of payments, the sum of the current account (*CA*), the capital account (*KA*), and the change in official reserves (*OR*) must be equal to zero:

$$CA + KA + OR = 0.$$

In other words, the change in official reserves simply mirrors the overall balance:

$$OR = - OB.$$

To illustrate this discussion, we present in Exh. 3.1 the 1993 balance of payments statistics for France, Germany, Japan, the United Kingdom, and the United States. The United States has been running a very large current account deficit for many years, and the 1993 deficit reached $109 billion. A positive balance for services and net income received from abroad are far from compensating a huge deficit in the U.S. merchandise trade balance ($132.5 billion). The U.S. capital account is in surplus ($41 billion), despite the fact that Americans have been net direct and portfolio investors abroad (–$18.7 and –$23.9 billion, respectively).

EXHIBIT 3.1

1993 Balance of Payments of Five Major Countries *Billions of U.S. dollars*	France	Germany	Japan	U.K.	U.S.A.
Current account	**11.9**	**−21.4**	**131.5**	**−16.1**	**−109.3**
Exports	196.3	349.5	351.3	181.3	456.8
Imports	−187.9	−306.3	−209.7	−201.5	−589.3
Trade balance	*8.4*	*43.1*	*141.6*	*−20.2*	*−132.5*
Balance of services	19.8	−37.4	−41.3	6.9	41.1
Net income	−9.6	4.1	37.3	4.8	14.6
Unrequited transfers	−6.7	−31.2	−6.1	−7.6	−32.5
Capital account	**−4.5**	**8.1**	**−103.8**	**6.5**	**41.4**
Direct investment	0.4	−14.0	−13.6	−10.8	−18.7
Portfolio investment	3.3	132.0	−65.7	−85.8	−23.9
Other capital flows	−12.3	−95.8	−24.3	100.4	57.1
Net errors & omissions	4.1	−14.1	−0.2	2.7	26.9
Official reserve account	**−7.4**	**13.3**	**−27.7**	**9.6**	**67.9**

Source: International Monetary Fund, *International Financial Statistics,* August 1994.

This is in contrast with the 1980s, when extensive direct and portfolio investments by foreigners led to huge surpluses of these two lines and of the capital account. The 1993 surplus in the U.S. capital account is explained by the fact that foreigners are happy to lend (invest) money to the United States (other capital flows of $57.1 billion). However, the surplus in the capital account is insufficient to cover the huge current account deficit, and the United States must use its official reserves to finance the overall balance deficit ($67.9 billion). This use of reserves has mostly taken the form of an increase in liabilities to foreign monetary authorities.

Japan has a very different balance of payments structure. Japan runs a huge trade surplus, with a current account surplus of $131 billion. This allows Japan to invest heavily abroad while retaining a balanced reserve account.

Germany has a surplus in its trade balance but a deficit in its balance of services, plus large unrequited transfers abroad (indemnizations). The capital account surplus ($8.1 billion) is insufficient to cover the current account deficit (−$21.4 billion), and the German central bank has to use its reserve assets to cover the deficit of the overall balance ($13.3 billion).

The Exchange Rate and the Balance of Payments   The traditional approach to foreign exchange rate determination is to focus on the influence of balance of payments flows. Let's consider a country in which capital flows are restricted, as is often the case with developing nations. A trade deficit would lead to a reduction in the country's reserves and ultimately to a depreciation of the home currency. In turn this depreciation would improve the terms of trade. National exports will become cheaper abroad and more competitive: Exports should grow. Imported goods will become more expensive: Imports should drop. This should lead to an improvement in the trade balance, and the currency should stabilize.

For example, the drop in oil prices in 1985 and 1986 led to a Mexican trade balance deficit; the value of the oil that Mexico exported suddenly dropped, without a corresponding reduction in imports. This deficit forced the Mexican government to borrow abroad to offset the imbalance; it also led to a depreciation of the peso. This devaluation helped restore the terms of trade.

The analysis requires us to estimate the trade flow elasticities in response to a movement in exchange rate: How will imports and exports react to an exchange rate adjustment and vice versa? The answers have to be built on often complex models of the economy. Furthermore the model must be dynamic, as the improvement in the trade balance will be only progressive. The immediate technical effect is not a quantity adjustment (more exports and less imports) but a price adjustment. Because imports are more expensive after the devaluation, the trade deficit will immediately increase, given the new exchange rate. Furthermore the rise in import prices can feed higher inflation at home, leading to a further depreciation of the currency. The monetary authorities will have to adjust their monetary/fiscal policy to control this "imported" inflation.

The analysis becomes even more complex when one considers capital flows. It is necessary to analyze the various components of the balance of payments. One must draw the line between flows that are autonomous—caused by current economic or political conditions—and those that are created to compensate for a potential imbalance.

The United States has run systematic, large trade deficits from the 1970s without a structural depreciation of its currency, because of a capital account surplus. Foreign investors were happy to hold an increasing amount of dollar assets. Similarly, fast-growing countries, such as Thailand, have been able to entertain a systematic deficit in their trade balance and current account, offset by a surge in foreign capital investment attracted by high expected returns. The net result has been a buildup of official reserves. The story for the United States is shown in Exh. 3.2, which gives the three major components of the U.S. balance of payments, as well as the real effective exchange rate index, as calculated by the IMF. The real effective exchange rate index is the weighted average of the currencies of selected trading partners of the United States, adjusted for relative inflation differentials. It is more representative of the value of the U.S. dollar than any single exchange rate. A real appreciation of the dollar would lead to an increase in the effective exchange rate index. To analyze Exh. 3.2, remember that a positive official reserve account means a drop in reserves. In 1978 and 1979 the combined deficits of the current and capital accounts led to a drop in official reserves, as well as to a depreciation of the dollar. The improvement in the balance of payments

EXHIBIT 3.2

Balance of Payments and the Dollar Exchange Rate

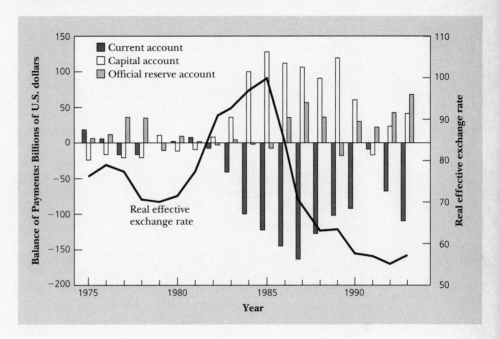

(stable reserves, no trade deficit) from 1979 to 1982 led to an appreciation of the dollar. From 1983 to 1985 the United States started to run a huge trade and current account deficit. However, this current deficit was offset by fast-growing foreign investments, and the reserves did not deteriorate: The dollar kept rising. By 1986 the capital flows became insufficient to cover the current account deficit, the official reserve position deteriorated, and the dollar started to slide. After 1990 the capital account began to deteriorate. The big surge in capital investment in the 1980s came partly from Japanese investors who engaged in real estate and business acquisitions in the United States. The Japanese were running huge surpluses in their trade and current account balances, which allowed them to invest extensively in the United States and other countries (a Japanese deficit of the capital account).

Although this story sounds reasonable, it is difficult to understand the huge swings in the value of the dollar. The timing of these swings is also difficult to forecast. Small changes in current account flows cannot justify such dramatic turning points and volatility in the exchange rate. In particular, one wonders what drives the behavior of foreign investors and their willingness (or unwillingness) to hold U.S. dollars.

The Asset Market Approach

Many economists reject the view that the short-term behavior of exchange rates is determined in flow markets. Exchange rates are asset prices traded in an efficient financial market. Indeed, an exchange rate is the relative price of two currencies and therefore is determined by the willingness to hold each currency. Like other asset prices, the exchange rate is determined by expectations about the future, not current trade flows.

A parallel with other asset prices may illustrate the approach. Let's consider the stock price of a winery traded on the Bordeaux stock exchange. A frost in late spring results in a poor harvest, in terms of both quantity and quality. After the harvest, the wine is finally sold, and the income is much less than in the previous year. On the day of the final sale, there is no reason for the stock price to be influenced by this flow. First, the unusually low level of income has already been discounted for several months in the winery stock price. Second, the stock price is affected by future, in addition to current, prospects. The stock price is based on expectations of future earnings, and the major cause for a change in stock price is a revision of these expectations.

A similar reasoning applies to exchange rates: Contemporaneous international flows should have little effect on exchange rates to the extent that they have already been expected. Only news about future economic prospects will affect exchange rates. Since economic expectations are potentially volatile and influenced by many variables, especially those of a political nature, the short-run behavior of exchange rates is volatile.

The opposition of the traditional balance of payments approach and of the asset market approach may be illustrated as follows. In a simple balance of payments approach domestic real growth tends to be bad for the domestic currency in the short run: Higher domestic growth leads to a boost in imports necessary for the higher production; exports do not increase, since foreign activity is unchanged. The net result is a trade balance deficit that leads to a depreciation of the domestic currency. By contrast, proponents of the asset market approach contend that prospects for higher domestic growth lead to capital inflows caused by foreign investments attracted by the higher returns. This results in increased demand for the home currency and a stronger currency, not a weaker one. This scenario took place in the United States in the period 1983 to 1984, accompanied by rapid economic growth, a widening trade balance deficit, and an appreciating dollar.

The challenge of this approach is to specify the news that should affect the exchange rate and quantify its *à priori* influence. One of the important components of such an approach is the modeling of the behavior of monetary authorities, as investors will try to guess their reactions. This issue will be further discussed in the next section.

Exchange Rate Forecasting

Exchange rate forecasting is novel to traditional portfolio investors. Rather than examining companies or industrial sectors, financial analysts must study the relative social, political, and economic situations of several countries. Two methods are actively used to forecast exchange rates: Economic analysis is the usual approach for assessing the fair value, present and future, of foreign exchange rates. However, it is often argued that technical analysis may better explain short-run exchange rate fluctuations. This brings us back to the traditional segmentation of financial analysts into fundamentalists and technicians. Both methods use quantitative models that make extensive use of computers, as well as qualitative (or judgmental) analysis.

Before proceeding any further, it is important to determine what our naive forecast would be in the absence of any specific model or information. In other words, assuming efficient foreign exchange markets, what is the exchange rate prediction implicit in market quotations? As discussed previously, the forward exchange rate (or spot exchange rate plus the interest rate differential) is the rational, expected value of the future spot exchange rate in a *risk-neutral* world. Therefore if the spot French franc is quoted at 8.00 francs per dollar on January 1 and if the one-year interest rates are 14% for the French franc and 10% for the U.S. dollar, the implied market prediction for the FF/$ rate on December 31 would be

$$8.00\,\frac{1.14}{1.10} = 8.2909.$$

If this forward exchange rate did not reflect all information available to the market, arbitrageurs would buy (or sell) currency forward and arbitrage away profit opportunities. Note that the international money market does in fact meet most of the technical criteria of an efficient market, at least for the major currencies. A huge volume of quick and almost costless transactions is performed by numerous informed and competent traders. The only restriction on the market might be central bank intervention. On the other hand, central banks may simply be regarded as transactors like any others, though having somewhat different motives. The main upshot of this scenario is that investors should average the same returns on their deposit in every currency, the reason being that short-term interest rate differentials are expected to offset exchange rate movements.

In a *risk-averse* world forward exchange rates deviate from the pure expectation value by a risk premium. If the direction and magnitude of this bias are unpredictable and volatile over time, the best market estimate of the future spot exchange rate is still the forward rate.

As mentioned in the previous chapters, several studies have shown that forward exchange rates are poor indicators of future spot rates. This does not necessarily mean that a better forecasting model can be found. It may be the case that unanticipated news has a frequent and strong influence on spot rates, making them inherently volatile and unpredictable. Before reviewing the various approaches to foreign exchange forecasting, it is useful to ask whether the foreign exchange market treats information efficiently or whether market participants are rational. This seems a reasonable question in view of the negative comments often made by the press and government officials.

Is the Market Efficient/Rational?

In an efficient market all information should be immediately reflected in the exchange rates. Rational market traders should base their forecasts on all available information. Consider an information set Φ_t known at time t; the spot exchange rate for time $t+1$ forecasted, or expected, at time t and based on this information set is usually denoted

$$E(S_{t+1}|\Phi_t). \tag{3.1}$$

Finance tends to focus on rates of returns and percentage variations. Using the notations introduced in Chapter 1, we have

$$s_{t+1} = (S_{t+1}-S_t)/S_t$$

$$E(s_{t+1}|\Phi_t) = [E(S_{t+1}|\Phi_t) - S_t]/S_t$$

The forecast error is defined as the deviation of the realized rate at time $t+1$ from the expected rate:

$$e_{t+1} = s_{t+1} - E(s_{t+1}|\Phi_t). \tag{3.2}$$

If market participants are rational, the forecast error should be uncorrelated with the information previously available at time t. Deviations from the expected value should be caused only by unpredictable news. Any information already available at time t should be reflected in the forecast and could not explain subsequent deviations from the forecast.

In a *risk-neutral* world, the forward exchange rate should be the best predictor of the future spot rate. It should already incorporate all relevant information available at the time of quotation. Let's denote F_t the forward rate quoted at time t for maturity $t+1$ and f_t its percentage deviation from the spot exchange rate:

$$f_t = (F_t - S_t)/S_t.$$

Remember that f_t is also called the forward premium (discount) and is equal, by arbitrage, to the interest differential. We should get

$$F_t = E(S_{t+1}|\Phi_t)$$

$$f_t = (F_t - S_t)/S_t = E(s_{t+1}|\Phi_t).$$

The forecast error of the exchange rate movement is given by

$$e_{t+1} = s_{t+1} - f_t. \tag{3.3}$$

One simple way to test that the foreign exchange market is efficient in processing information, and therefore that the forecast error is uncorrelated with f_t, is to run a regression between the realized exchange rate movement and the forward premium/discount:

$$s_{t+1} = \alpha + \beta f_t + \varepsilon_{t+1}. \tag{3.4}$$

We should find that α is equal to 0 and that β is equal to 1.

Numerous studies have tested this relation on many currencies and for various time periods.[4] They all find that the slope coefficient β is significantly smaller than 1 and even negative. This negative sign is surprising. It means that a successful strategy would be to bet against the forward exchange rate. When a currency quotes with a forward premium, it should depreciate rather than appreciate. Since the forward premium (discount) is equal to the interest rate differential, the currency with the highest interest rate tends to appreciate. This is illustrated over the period 1973–1993 in Exh. 3.3, which gives the result of the regression for monthly rates of seven major currencies relative to the U.S. dollar. Slope coefficients range from −0.4 to −2.1 instead of +1. Of course, the R-squares of the regressions are very low, but the results are statistically significant. They imply that expected exchange rate movements vary over time in a somewhat predictable fashion as a function of the interest rate differential.

Another common finding is that the forecast errors appear to be positively correlated over successive periods. In other words, exchange rates appear to trend.

EXHIBIT 3.3

Regression of Monthly Ex-post Exchange Rate Movement on Forward Premium (Discount) Relative to the U.S. Dollar, 1973–1993
Standard deviations of estimates appear in parentheses
$$s_{t+1} = \alpha + \beta f_t + \varepsilon_{t+1}$$

Currency	α	β	R-square (%)
Canada	−2.4	−1.1	1.6
	(1.1)	(0.5)	
France	−2.6	−1.0	0.7
	(3.3)	(0.8)	
Germany	4.6	−0.4	0.1
	(3.4)	(0.8)	
Japan	8.7	−1.5	1.5
	(3.0)	(0.8)	
Netherlands	4.6	−1.0	0.6
	(2.9)	(0.8)	
Switzerland	10.0	−1.2	0.9
	(4.4)	(0.8)	
U.K.	−7.8	−2.1	2.5
	(3.5)	(0.8)	

Again, this is not consistent with market rationality. It seems that exchange rate movements (or forecast errors) are positively correlated over time for short horizons (one or two years) and start to exhibit negative autocorrelation for long horizons (several years). A possible justification for this finding is that exchange rates tend to exhibit *jumps*. They tend to trend slowly until a sudden turning point. If one looks at short periods that exclude the jump, exchange rates appear to trend, and forecast errors exhibit positive autocorrelation. This phenomenon disappears when the jump takes place and is included in the data. Market traders expect this jump but do not know when it will take place. The exchange rate drifts away from its fundamental, or equilibrium, value, and the correction can take several years to materialize but in a brutal fashion. This is sometimes referred to as the "peso problem." The Mexican peso used to see its real exchange rate against the U.S. dollar appreciate progressively until the Mexican government finally devalued the peso (generally after an election). Such bubbles are more likely to appear on foreign exchange markets, where participants try to forecast the policy and timing of monetary authorities, than on other capital markets, such as stock markets. Surveys of foreign exchange expectations formulated by various market participants conducted in New York, London, and Tokyo suggest that expectations extrapolate the recent trend for short time horizons and predict a reversal for long horizons.[5]

Another possible explanation for the autocorrelation of forecast errors is the existence of a time-varying risk premium. The forward exchange rate could deviate from the future expected value of the spot exchange rate by a risk premium rp_t which can change over time:

$$f_t = E(s_{t+1} \mid \Phi_t) + rp_t.$$

The forecast error becomes:

$$e_{t+1} = s_{t+1} - f_t + rp_t,$$

and autocorrelation in forecast errors could come from the time-series properties of the required risk premium. However, the magnitude and volatility of this risk premium would have to be very large to justify the observed phenomenon. Several studies reject this type of explanation.[6]

Any test of market efficiency/rationality is confronted with serious econometric problems. Clearly exchange rates are not stationary in the sense that exchange rate movements are not identically independently distributed, as a statistician would say. Expected returns vary over time in a somewhat predictable fashion, but more work is needed to attempt to model these time-varying expectations (see the Appendix and Chapter 17). The volatility of an exchange rate is not constant, and researchers have found evidence of GARCH effects (see the appendix to this chapter).[7] The modeling of variance is quite difficult, given the existence of infrequent jumps whose timing and magnitude are unknown.

It seems fair to say that current empirical research has not solved the exchange rate puzzle. More work is needed to establish rationality and to understand the behavior of exchange rates over time.

The Economic Approach

Advisory services and institutional investors that have developed foreign exchange forecasting tools may use a *subjective* approach, an *econometric* model, or both. An econometric approach implies that a quantitative model of the exchange rate is estimated on past data and is used to make predictions. A subjective approach implies that a large number of parameters are taken into account in a subjective, not quantitative, way. One set of models attempts to deduce theoretical values for current exchange rates. If the values deviate from going market rates, the models assume that the deviation will be quickly corrected by the market. Another set of models assumes that current exchange rates are correctly priced, or in equilibrium, and attempts to forecast rates in the future based on the present and predicted values of other variables.

Econometric models, which are statistical estimations of the economic theories, make it feasible to take complex correlations between variables into account explicitly. Parameters for the models are drawn from historical data. Then current and expected values for causative variables are entered into the model, producing forecasts for exchange rates. Econometric models clearly suffer from two drawbacks. First, most of them rely on predictions for certain key variables (money supply, interest rates) that are not easy to forecast. Second, the structural correlation estimated by the parameters of the equation can change over time, so that even if all causative variables are correctly forecast, the model can still yield poor exchange rate predictions. In periods when structural changes are rapid compared with the amount of time-series data required to estimate parameters, econometric models are of little help.[8] In these instances subjective analysis is generally more reliable.

Many econometric forecasts rely on a single equation founded on PPP and equated to an expression containing variables for interest rates, trade balances, and money supply. Other models rely on sets of 10 to 900 simultaneous equations, which no doubt provide a more satisfactory description of international correlations than simplistic single-equation models. But at the same time, complex models cannot be revised frequently. Moreover, it is time consuming to simulate each scenario, as the amount of inputs required is very large.

The recent models developed for exchange rate forecasting take the view that an exchange rate is the price of an asset (the currency). This asset market approach implies that the short-term behavior of exchange rates is influenced mostly by news. News appears when economic data or a political statement is different from its predicted value. The time-series properties of the exchange rate are specifically modeled with a focus on time variations in expected returns and volatility. These models seem to fare better than the traditional economic approach.

Several banks and advisory services make their models available worldwide on time-sharing systems. Using terminals with simple telephone modems, subscribers may input their own forecasts for the causative variables and even change parameters in the model equations. In fact, it is not uncommon to see portfolio managers use home or hotel telephones to connect portable terminals to any one of several wire services that provide information ranging from up-to-date economic forecasts, to quoted prices, and to investment management packages. In periodic reports econometric forecasts are generally combined with more subjective discussions of the international scene.

Technical Analysis

Technical analysis of exchange rates bases predictions solely on price information. The analysis is technical in the sense that it does not rely on fundamental analysis of the underlying economic determinants of exchange rates but only on extrapolations of past price trends.[9] Technical analysis looks for the repetition of specific price patterns. Once the start of such patterns has been detected, it automatically suggests what the short-run behavior of an exchange rate will be.

Technical analysis has long been applied to commodity and stock markets. Its application to the foreign exchange market is a recent phenomenon but has attracted a wide and rapidly growing audience. One difference that sets the currency market apart from other markets is that data for trading volume are not available for currencies, so price history is the only source of information. As for economic analysis, technical analysts often use quantitative computer models or subjective analysis based on the study of charts (*chartism*).

Computer models attempt to detect both major trends and critical, or turning, points. These models are usually very simple and rely on *moving averages, filters,* or *momentum.* With all computer models the objective is to detect when a sustainable trend has begun.

- In moving-average models, buy and sell signals are usually triggered when a short-run moving average (SRMA) of past rates crosses a long-run moving average (LRMA). The aim of a moving average is to smooth erratic daily swings of exchange rates in order to signal major trends. An LRMA will always lag an SRMA because the LRMA gives a smaller weight to recent movements of exchange rates than an SRMA does. If a currency is moving downward, its SRMA will be below its LRMA. When it starts rising again, as in Exh. 3.4a, it soon crosses its LRMA, generating a buy signal. The converse holds true for sell signals.

- Filter methods generate buy signals when an exchange rate rises *X* percent (the filter) above its most recent trough and sell signals when it falls *X* percent below the previous peak. Again, the idea is to smooth (filter) daily fluctuations in order to detect lasting trends (see Exh. 3.4b).

- Momentum models determine the strength of a currency by examining the change in velocity of currency movements. If an exchange rate climbs at increasing speed, a buy signal is issued (see Exh. 3.4c).

In a sense these models monitor the derivative (slope) of a time-series graph. Signals are generated when the slope varies significantly.

Note that there is a good deal of discretionary judgment inherent in these models. Signals are sensitive to alterations in the filters used, the period lengths

EXHIBIT 3.4

Computer Methods in Technical Analysis

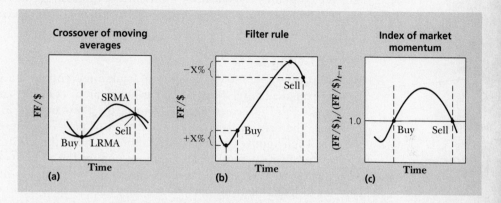

used to compute moving averages, and the methods used to compute rates of change in momentum models. Recently more sophisticated statistical models have evolved, some of which are direct applications of statistical models developed for other disciplines, such as physics and seismology. Among them are wave-and-cycle models, chaos theory, or ARIMA estimations à la Box-Jenkins. Some powerful quantitative methods have recently been applied to forecast the short-term behavior of foreign exchange rates, such as the multivariate vector autoregressive methods, the multivariate spectral methods, ARCH models, and the nonlinear autoregressive methods. Some of these methods are described in the appendix to the chapter.

Chartism technical analysis relies on the interpretation of exchange rate charts. Analysts usually attempt to detect recurrent price formations on bar charts that plot daily price ranges as vertical bars. They also use line charts connecting daily closing prices, or point-and-figure charts, which take into account a series of price movements in the same direction.

Numerous price patterns are considered significant by chartists. Each pattern is representative of a typical market situation, the outcome of which is usually predictable, thereby giving clear sell or buy signals. The various patterns are interpreted as logical sequences, in various market phases (accumulation, resistance, breakaway, reaction). Colorful terminology is generally used to describe the various patterns, including *flag*, *pennant*, *head and shoulder*, and *camel*.

Obviously chartism is more an art than a science. Its main tenet is that market participants tend to behave in the same way over time when confronted with a similar market environment. This repetition of response is ascribed partly to emotional factors and partly to the regulatory and other constraints imposed on major market participants, such as multinational companies' treasurers, bankers, and central bankers. In other words, guidelines, regulations, and central bank intervention help cause repeated and predictable currency market patterns.

Charts are sometimes used to time purchases and sales of currencies when large actors, such as central banks, intervene in the market. With the development of graphics software on microcomputers, many more people now engage in technical analysis. One should be aware that technical models, such as moving averages, are constantly calculated by thousands of investors. As a result, those who use this method rarely beat the market, because so many others use similar models.

Central Bank Intervention

It might seem strange to discuss central bank intervention in a section devoted to foreign exchange forecasting. But the behavior of central bankers is somewhat predictable, and forecasters attempt to factor their market intervention in the forecasts. The central banks are major types of players in the foreign exchange markets. Their motives are somewhat different from those of most other market participants. Some central banks are renowned for the active management of their foreign currency reserves, but most of them do not attempt to profit from trading. They try to implement the monetary policy and exchange rate targets defined by their monetary authorities. In the early 1970s the Bretton Woods system of semifixed exchange rates exploded because of the magnitude of speculative flows and the unreasonable attitude of some governments attempting to defend unrealistic exchange rates. In a semifixed exchange rate system, exchange rates must stay within a narrow band of a fixed central parity. When a currency is under too much pressure, the monetary authorities must de(re)value its central parity. Let's assume that because of political and economic fundamentals, the British pound is "weak," as was the case in 1967. Speculators can speculate against the pound with little risk. They sell pound forward against dollar. If the Bank of England is successful in defending the parity of the pound, the exchange rate will stay constant, and the speculators will lose nothing or very little. If the Bank of England exhausts its foreign currency reserves in defending the pound and is forced to devalue, the speculators will pocket the amount of devaluation by buying back the pound at a cheaper price. It is a game in which there can be only one loser: the central bank. Of course, monetary authorities and market forces will lift the interest rates of the weak currencies, but this is a small cost to speculation, given the speed at which it can succeed in forcing a de(re)valuation.

In the late 1960s, the amount of capital available for currency speculation became large compared to the amount of official reserves of central banks, and the number of currencies forced to de(re)value became large, leading to large losses for central banks. Within two months, one saw the Dutch guilder forced to devalue by almost 10% and then forced to revalue by a similar amount. Indeed, Taylor reports that the central banks of Canada, the United States, and six European nations experienced collective losses of more than $10 billion from 1973 to 1979.[10] The move to floating exchange rates made this type of speculation against the central banks much more problematic. Unfortunately monetary authorities tend to forget fairly quickly lessons from the past. The attempt to maintain fixed central parities within the EMS has been fairly costly to European central banks, especially France. The European Monetary System relies on a collective defense of the central parities by all its members, thereby increasing the amount of reserves usable to defend the parities. Unfortunately for the central banks, the amount of private speculative capital also increased. In 1992 and 1993 several European central banks lost many billions of dollars unsuccessfully defending their currencies against a devaluation relative to the Deutsche mark. Conversely, hedge funds and George Soros became notorious for their profit in currency speculation.

One should not believe that speculation against central banks is an easy game. Big losses made by these same currency hedge funds in early 1994 illustrate this point. But it is clear that a lucid analysis of the policy and objectives of a country's monetary authorities can help, in some cases, forecast the short-term behavior of speculation and of the exchange rate. In the face of an uncertain social, political, and even electoral environment, monetary authorities are inclined to defend a currency beyond dangerous levels. More generally the various aspects of the policy of central banks should be incorporated in a forecasting model for the exchange rate. Although the French are famous for their desire to keep a "strong" franc, the English have often resorted to "competitive" devaluation to improve the international competitiveness of British firms and to stimulate domestic activity.

An illustration of the importance of news about official intervention is given in Exh. 3.5, which tracks the DM/$ exchange rate around October 20, 1994. On October 20, U.S. Treasury Secretary Lloyd Bentsen made a surprise, and imprudent, announcement that the U.S. had no plans to intervene in the foreign exchange market to defend the dollar, sending the market into a frenzy when the statement appeared on the traders' Reuters screens. The next morning Treasury

---

EXHIBIT 3.5

An Example of the Impact of News about Central Bank Intervention

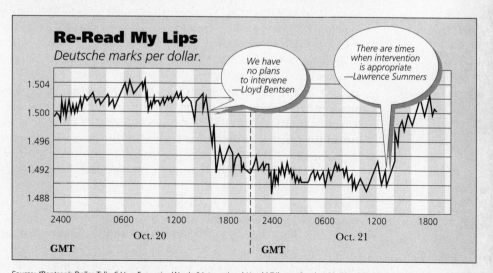

Source: "Bentsen's Dollar Talk: 6 Very Expensive Words," *International Herald Tribune,* October 22–23, 1994. © International Herald Tribune. Reprinted by permission.

Undersecretary Lawrence Summers corrected the statement and suggested that there were times when an intervention was appropriate. The dollar immediately rebounded.

The Use and Performance of Forecasts

Technical analysts closely follow the market and forecast the very near future. Detecting a pattern is beneficial if the market continues to follow that pattern faithfully. But no pattern can be expected to last for more than a few days, possibly weeks; market inefficiencies are corrected just too quickly. Indeed, if a technical analyst persuades enough clients to act on his or her recommendations, prices will move rapidly to a level that rules out additional profits. The more publicity a successful analyst gets, the more quickly the market corrects the inefficiencies he or she reports. As a result, all systematic black-box models must be continually modified to counter this self-correcting process. A client must react very quickly to a technical recommendation. Unfortunately there are often time lags between the moment a technical service issues a recommendation, the time it takes to reach the money manager, and the moment it is finally implemented. For this reason immediate transmission via telephone, fax, or computer terminal of buy and sell signals is essential in order to make a profit.

The corporate treasurer who manages a complex international position with daily cash flows and adjustments in his or her foreign exchange exposure can respond readily to technical analysis recommendations. This is not the case for portfolio managers; they cannot continually adjust their long-term asset allocation on the basis of technical signals on currencies. In practice, therefore, technical foreign exchange models are used mainly by money managers for timing their investment sales and purchases or for currency-hedging decisions using derivatives. Transaction costs on equity are just too high to make an active trading strategy based on short-term currency forecasts worthwhile. Part of an institutional portfolio is sometimes entrusted to a currency-overlay money manager. The objective of a currency-overlay strategy is to benefit from currency forecasts. Such managers often resort to short-term currency trading strategies that make use of technical analysis and interpret interventions by central banks. Currency hedge funds have also developed. These are leveraged funds that take bets on currencies and engage in active trading. Banks also trade extensively in currencies for their proprietary accounts. All these traders make use of all the available short-term forecasting techniques described here.

By contrast, long-term economic forecasts for currencies and interest rates are a basic component of the international asset allocation decision. In fact, currency analysis is one of several economic analyses of the international environment that a manager must undertake. Briefly, economic models of exchange rates are commonly used for long-term asset allocation, whereas technical models are more helpful for timing transactions. When the Bank of England conducted a survey among chief foreign exchange dealers based in London, it found that 90% of the respondents place some weight on technical analysis when forming views at one or more time horizons.[11] Although technical analysis is extensively used for very short-term forecasts, fundamental economic analysis becomes dominant for longer-term forecasts.

One question that remains for the user of foreign exchange forecasts is: How does one measure the performance of these forecasts, and what is their track record? All methods compare a particular forecast to the forward exchange rate, which is both the implied market forecast and the price at which an investor may contract to try and make a profit based on his or her specific forecast. In order to study the performance of a given forecasting model over a specific time period, one must collect the values for the following series:

- forecasts formulated in t for time $t + n$, $E(S_{t+n}|\Phi_t)$
- forward rates quoted in t for time $t + n$, F_t
- spot rates realized in t (S_t) and $t + n$, (S_{t+n})

With this set of data in hand, several methods may be used to evaluate the performance of a forecast relative to the forward rate.

A common statistical approach is to compare the forecast errors of the two models (the forecasting model versus the forward rate). The percentage forecast errors (ε and e) for each forecast are computed as

$$\varepsilon_{t+n} = [S_{t+n} - E(S_{t+n}|\Phi_t)]/S_t$$

$$e_{t+n} = [S_{t+n} - F_t]/S_t.$$

Average forecasting accuracy is usually measured by the mean squared error (MSE). The error is squared because a positive error is no better than a negative one; the MSE averages the squared errors over all forecasts. A forecasting model is more accurate than the forward rate if it has a smaller MSE.

This commonly used statistical measure of forecasting accuracy does not satisfy those managers for whom the important contribution of a forecast is the generation of correct buy and sell signals, even if the magnitude of the expected move is inaccurate. In other words, those managers want to know the number of times the forecast turns out to be on the correct side of the forward exchange rate. The fraction P = correct forecast/total forecasts estimates the probability of making correct forecasts during a given period. If the model has no forecasting ability, P is close to 0.5. If it is unusually accurate, P should be larger than 0.5, and its statistical significance may be measured.

A final method for evaluating forecasting performance is to assume that the money manager systematically buys forward contracts if the forecast is above the forward rate and sells them if the forecast is below the forward rate. The ex-post financial return on this strategy is then computed, and the forecasting ability is judged on the basis of the manager's return on the capital invested.

In the 1980s *Euromoney* provided an annual performance review of major foreign exchange advisory services, using the three methods mentioned previously.

Although results vary every year, there is no doubt that exchange rate forecasting is very difficult. In some years advisory services have consistently underperformed the forward exchange rate. As one might expect, the reward for active exchange rate forecasting strategies is potentially large, but so are the risks. Technical models seem to have a slightly better track record, at least in the short run. But those models are quite difficult for the international portfolio manager to use systematically, because the transaction costs are so high.

An illustration of the rather poor performance of forecasters is given in the summary of the 1984 *Euromoney* survey. The average return is very poor (4.5%), and no single service was able to beat the Treasury bill rate over 1983.

> *Euromoney's* sixth annual survey of foreign exchange forecasters finds that technical services were once again profitable. But their performance declined in terms of return on capital at risk, from 10.8% in 1982 to 4.5% in 1983. In addition their percentage of correct signals was only 44.9%, worse than the toss of a coin.[12]

As a group, forecasters tend to look at the same variables, using methodologies that are often close, and come up with forecasts that are often mostly in the same direction. Given the high volatility of exchange rates, it is not surprising to find that they do quite badly as a group in a given year. However, the long-term record is not that bad. For example, several studies indicate that technical analysis has been able to take advantage of exchange rate trending behavior to generate large returns.[13] It also seems possible to model the time variation of expected exchange rate movements in a fashion that can lead, in the long run, to profitable returns on an active asset allocation strategy (see also Chapter 17).[14] Because central banks seem to be consistent losers in the foreign exchange market, with a somewhat predictable trading strategy, one should not be surprised to find that active currency strategies could lead to profits, despite the high risks involved.

Summary

1. In the long run, purchasing power parity should guide the exchange rate. Differences in national productivity can explain the long-run behavior of the real exchange rate.

2. The balance of payments, which tracks all financial flows crossing the borders of a country, is the cash balance of a country relative to the rest of the world. By nature the balance of payments must be equilibrated; otherwise, a country is in default.

3. The balance of payments can be separated into three major blocks:

The *current account* tracks all current transactions: trade and services, income paid and received, and unrequited transfers (gifts).

The *capital account* tracks all short-term and long-term investment transactions (excluding transactions by the central bank).

The *official reserve account* tracks net changes in the government's international reserves.

The sum of the three accounts must be 0.

4. A deficit in the current account must be offset by a capital account surplus or by central bank intervention. The balance of payments approach to the exchange rate focuses on the relation between the current account and the exchange rate.

5. The asset market approach treats the foreign exchange rate as a financial price determined by *expectations* about the future. It focuses on the relation between the capital account and the exchange rate. Many types of news will affect the investment demand for a currency.

6. Foreign exchange forecasting is a difficult exercise, and no theory of exchange rate determination can claim to be consistently successful.

7. Forecasters resort to *economic* analysis or *technical* analysis methods. Technical analysis focuses on the short-run behavior of exchange rates, whereas the economic approach is by nature better designed for long-run forecasts. A modeling of central bank intervention sometimes helps to understand the short-term behavior of foreign exchange rates.

8. Different measures of forecasting ability can be used. The track record of forecasters shows the difficulty of the task.

Questions and Problems

1. The Thai bath is pegged to a basket of currencies. In practice, assume that the bath exchange rate is set at 25 baths per U.S. dollar. Thailand is experiencing rapid economic growth, with extensive ongoing foreign investment. CPI inflation is somewhat higher than in the United States, but Thailand has no problem in maintaining its fixed exchange rate with the dollar. Explain why the Thai bath does not depreciate as suggested by PPP.

2*. Paf is a small country. Its currency is the pif, and the exchange rate with the U.S. dollar is 0.9 Pif per dollar. Here are some transactions affecting Paf's balance of payments during the quarter:

   1. Paf exports for 10 million pifs of local products.
   2. Paf investors buy foreign companies for a total cost of $3 million.
   3. Paf investors receive $0.1 million of dividends on their foreign shares.
   4. Many tourists visit Paf and spend $0.5 million.
   5. Paf pays 1 million pifs as interest on Paf bonds currently held by foreigners.

     6. Paf imports for $7 million of foreign goods.

     7. Paf receives $0.3 million as foreign aid.

    What is Paf's balance of payments for the quarter? How are official reserves affected?

3*. In late 1994 it was announced that the monthly current account of Japan was shrinking and that this effect could be permanent. Is this news good or bad for the Japanese yen? Why?

4. Because of the relative rise in local production costs brought about by the appreciation of the yen, many Japanese corporations decide to delocalize their production abroad. What should be the immediate and future impact on the Japanese balance of payments?

5*. Look at Exh. 3.1. Provide an analysis of the French balance of payments.

6. Look at Exh. 3.1. Provide an analysis of the U.K. balance of payments.

7. The Japanese balance of payments from 1987 to 1993 follows. All numbers are reported in billions of U.S. dollars. The last line gives the real effective exchange rate index of the yen relative to other currencies. An increase in the index means a real appreciation of the yen.

	1987	1988	1989	1990	1991	1992	1993
Merchandise: Exports	224	260	270	280	307	331	351
Merchandise: Imports	–128	–165	–193	–217	–203	–198	–210
Services: Credit	29	35	40	41	45	48	52
Services: Debit	–48	–64	–75	–82	–85	–90	–93
Income: Credit	51	77	104	125	144	146	152
Income: Debit	–37	–60	–85	–106	–121	–114	–115
Unrequited transfers	–4	–4	–4	–6	–12	–5	–6
Direct investment	–18	–35	–45	–45	–29	–15	–14
Portfolio investment	–91	–53	–33	–14	35	–28	–66
Other capital flows	64	21	30	39	–78	–64	–24
Net errors and omissions	–4	3	–22	–21	–8	–10	0
Reserve account							
Real effective yen rate	128	135	128	114	122	127	160

1. Calculate the trade balance, current account, capital account, and official reserve account for each year.

2. Use these numbers to describe what has happened in terms of Japanese financial transactions with the rest of the world.

8*. The domestic economy seems to be overheating, with rapid economic growth and low unemployment. News has just been released that the monthly activity level is even higher than expected (as measured by new orders to factories and unemployment figures). This news leads to renewed fears of inflationary pressures and likely action by the monetary authorities to raise interest rates to cool the economy down. State reasons why this news should be good or bad for the exchange rate.

9. In the 1970s France had in place a dual exchange rate system for its residents. All business trade transactions took place at the official, or "commercial," exchange rate (say, 5 francs per U.S. dollar). All foreign investments by French industrial corporations were subject to prior government authorization. The regulation was even stricter for French financial institutions or private residents. They were not allowed to transfer currency abroad. French tourists could not take abroad more than FF 5,000 (or its equivalent in foreign currency) per year. French residents could buy foreign securities but had to use a special "financial" rate to purchase these foreign currencies. Basically, the supply of foreign currency assigned to "financial" francs was fixed. To buy foreign securities, residents had to use the proceeds of the sales of foreign securities by other French residents. This led to a separate market for the "financial" franc with a different exchange rate. Foreign income and dividends paid were repatriated at the "commercial" franc rate and did not increase the supply of "financial" currency available. By contrast, foreigners were free to buy and sell French securities at the "commercial" rate, but they were not allowed to borrow francs.

   Explain why this type of control imposed on French residents helps defend the French franc, which was periodically under devaluation pressure. Would you expect the "financial" exchange rate to be higher or lower than the "commercial" rate?

10*. The current Swiss franc/Deutsche mark rate is 1.2 francs per DM. Inflation rates are 2% in Switzerland and 3% in Germany. One-year interest rates are 4% in Switzerland and 5% in Germany. What would be a natural forecast for the Swiss franc/DM exchange rate next year?

11*. You have a simple forecasting model for the one-year exchange rate, adapted from Exh. 3.3. A currency should appreciate over the year by the amount of the interest rate differential quoted today. For example, if the DM exchange rate is DM/$ = 2 and the one-year interest rates in DM and $ are 4% and 7%, respectively, the dollar should move up by 3% relative to the DM, and your forecast for the exchange rate at the end of the year is DM/$ = 2.06.

   - What is the current forward exchange rate?
   - What type of forward transaction would you conduct to capitalize on your forecast?
   - If everyone were using your model and following your strategy, what would happen to the exchange and interest rates?

12. Is foreign exchange forecasting consistent with market efficiency? What would be the expected exchange rate movements in an efficient market, assuming that you know the interest rates for all maturities and that you have reliable forecasts for inflation rates?

13. What is the danger of using forecasting methods based on trends?

14*. Paf is a country with a fixed exchange rate with the U.S. dollar, set at 0.9 pif per dollar. The Paf government intends to defend this central parity but has no exchange controls; it can use only an interest rate policy to defend its national currency, the pif. The pif comes under severe speculative devaluation pressures because of a drop in the official reserves of Paf. The current (annualized) one-month interest rates are 18% for the pif and 6% for the dollar.

   - What type of borrowing/lending action could you take to try to take advantage of a devaluation of the pif?

- How much would you stand to lose if Paf is successful in defending its currency?
- How much would you stand to gain if the pif is devalued to 1 pif per dollar within the next month?

15. *Project*: Take a time series of monthly exchange rates of a major currency relative to the U.S. dollar. Try to derive a technical analysis that would yield a profitable trading strategy over the period studied. For example, you could simulate various moving average strategies discussed in the text or simulate various filter strategies. Apply the strategy that seems most profitable for the previous exchange rate to other currencies. Perform the same exercise for nondollar exchange rates (for example, for the DM/£ rate or the FF/DM rate). What do you conclude?

Notes

1. Exhibit 1.2 summarizes the current international monetary arrangements.

2. These models are detailed in standard international economics textbooks. See, for example, Dornbusch (1988).

3. The official reserve account is sometimes included as a subcategory of the capital account. Here, we follow the current IMF presentation, which allows an easier interpretation of the balance of payments.

4. For tests of foreign exchange market efficiency, see Hodrick (1987); Meese and Rogoff (1988); Froot and Thaler (1990); Bekaert and Hodrick (1992); and Evans and Lewis (1993).

5. See Frankel and Froot (1987); Dominguez (1986); and Liu and Maddala (1992).

6. See Fama (1984); Giovanini and Jorion (1989); and Bekaert and Hodrick (1992).

7. See Wasserfallen (1989); Baillie and Bollerslev (1991); Goodhart and Figliuoli (1991); Bollerslev and Domowitz (1993); and Dacorogna, Müller, Nagler, Olsen, and Pictet (1993).

8. The failure of econometric models to satisfactorily depict the behavior of the exchange rates is illustrated in Meese and Rogoff (1983); and Huizinga (1987).

9. For a general description of technical analysis, see Levine (1975); Murphy (1986); Edwards and Magee (1992); Pring (1985). See also Rosenberg (1981); and Kritzman (1989).

10. See Taylor (1982); and Goodhart (1993).

11. See Taylor and Allen (1992).

12. *Euromoney*, August 1984.

13. See several articles in Antl and Ensor (1982); and Levich and Thomas III (1993). Levich and Thomas III studied the exchange rate of five major currencies relative to the U.S. dollar, from January 1976 to December 1990.

14. See Solnik (1993); and Glen and Jorion (1993).

Bibliography

Adler, M., and Dumas, B. "International Portfolio Choice and Corporation Finance: A Survey," *Journal of Finance*, June 1983.

Antl, B., and Ensor, R. *The Management of Foreign Exchange Risk*, London: Euromoney Publications, 1982.

Baillie, R.T., and Bollerslev, T. "Intra-Day and Inter-Market Volatility in Foreign Exchange Rates," *Review of Economic Studies*, May 1991.

Bekaert, G., and Hodrick, R.J. "Characterizing Predictable Components in Excess Returns on Equity and Foreign Exchange," *Journal of Finance*, June 1992.

Bollerslev, T., and Domowitz, I. "Trading Patterns and Prices in the Interbank Foreign Exchange Market," *Journal of Finance*, September 1993.

Coninx, R. *Foreign Exchange Dealer's Handbook*, Homewood, IL: Dow Jones-Irwin, 1986.

Dacorogna, M.M., Müller, U.A., Nagler, R.J., Olsen, R.B., and Pictet, O.V. "A Geographical Model for the Daily and Weekly Seasonal Volatility in the Foreign Exchange Market," *Journal of International Money and Finance*, August 1993.

Dominguez, K.M. "Are Foreign Exchange Forecasts Rational?: New Evidence from Survey Data," *Economic Letters*, 21, 1986, pp. 277–281.

Dornbusch, R., *Open Economy Macroeconomics*, New York: Basic Books, 1988.

Edwards, R.D., and Magee, J. *Technical Analysis of Stock Trends*, Boston: New York Institute of Finance, 1992.

Evans, M.D., and Lewis, K.K. "Trends in Expected Returns in Currency and Bond Markets," University of Pennsylvania, Wharton School, working paper 93–4, 1993.

Fama, E. "Forward and Spot Exchange Rates," *Journal of Monetary Economics*, April 1984.

Frankel, J.A., and Froot, K.A. "Using Survey Data to Test Standard Propositions Regarding Exchange Rate Expectations," *American Economic Review*, March 1987.

Froot, K.A., and Thaler, R.H. "Anomalies: Foreign Exchange," *Journal of Economic Perspectives*, 4, 3, 1990.

Giovanini, A., and Jorion, P. "Time-Variation of Risk and Return in the Foreign Exchange and Stock Markets," *Journal of Finance*, June 1989.

Glen J., and Jorion, P. "Currency Hedging for International Portfolios," *Journal of Finance*, December 1993.

Goodhart, C.A.E. "Central Bank Forex Intervention Assessed in Continuous Time, "*Journal of International Money and Finance*, August 1993.

Goodhart, C.A.E., and Figliuoli, L. " Every Minute Counts in Financial Markets," *Journal of International Money and Finance*, March 1991.

Grossman, G., and Rogoff, K., eds. *Handbook of International Economics*, Amsterdam: North Holland, 1995.

Hodrick, R.J. *The Empirical Evidence on the Efficiency of Forward Futures Foreign Exchange Market*, Chur, Switzerland: Harwood Academic, 1987.

Huizinga, J. "An Empirical Investigation of the Long Run Behavior of Real Exchange Rates," in K. Brunner and A. Meltzer, eds., Carnegie-Rochester Series on Public Policy, 27, Amsterdam: North Holland, 1987.

Kritzman, M. "Serial Dependence in Currency Returns: Investment Implications," *Journal of Portfolio Management*, Fall 1989.

Levich, R. "Evaluating the Performance of the Forecasters," in B. Antl and R. Ensor, eds., *The Management of Foreign Exchange Risk*, London: Euromoney Publications, 1982.

Levich, R.M., and Thomas, L.R. III, "The Significance of Technical-Trading Rule Profits in the Foreign Exchange Market: A Bootstrap Approach," *Journal of International Money and Finance*, October 1993.

Levine S., ed., *Financial Analyst's Handbook*, Homewood, IL: Dow Jones–Irwin, 1975.

Liu, P.C., and Maddala, G.S. "Rationality of Survey Data and Tests for Market Efficiency in the Foreign Exchange Markets," *Journal of International Money and Finance*, August 1992.

Meese, R., and Rogoff, K. "Empirical Exchange Rate Models of the Seventies: Do They Fit Out-of-Sample?" *Journal of International Economics*, February 1983.

———. "What Is Real? The Exchange Rate–Interest Rate Differential Relation over the Modern Floating-Rate Period," *Journal of Finance*, September 1988.

Murphy, J.J. *Technical Analysis of the Futures Markets: A Comprehensive Guide to Trading Methods and Applications*, New York: Prentice Hall, 1986.

Pring, M.J. *Technical Analysis Explained: The Successful Investor's Guide to Spotting Investment Trends and Turning Points*, New York: McGraw-Hill, 1985.

Rosenberg, M. "Is Technical Analysis Right for Currency Forecasting?" *Euromoney*, June 1981.

Solnik, B. *Predictable Time-Varying Components of International Asset Returns*, Charlottesville, VA: The Research Foundation of Chartered Financial Analysts, 1993.

Soros, G. *The Alchemy of Finance*, New York: Simon and Schuster, 1987.

Taylor, D. "Official Intervention in the Foreign Exchange Market, or Bet against the Central Bank," *Journal of Political Economy*, April 1982.

Taylor, M.P., and Allen, H. "The Use of Technical Analysis in the Foreign Exchange Market," *Journal of International Money and Finance*, June 1992.

Wasserfallen, W. "Flexible Exchange Rates: A Closer Look," *Journal of Monetary Economics*, June 1989.

Chapter 3: Appendix
Statistical Supplements on Forecasting Asset Returns

The reader is assumed to have some familiarity with standard statistics. This appendix is intended as a brief but somewhat technical introduction to less conventional statistical models used in forecasting. The basic question is: How can we describe the time behavior of a random variable in a tractable way, i.e., in a model whose statistical properties are such that it can be easily estimated from past data and used to forecast the future value of the variable?

Some Notations

Prices move over time in a somewhat random fashion. It is common in finance to focus on the stochastic process followed by the rate of return of an asset, i.e., its percentage price movement. Let's introduce some mathematical notations:

r_{t+1}	the rate of return observed at time $t+1$
$E_t(r_{t+1})$	the rate of return *expected* in period t for period $t+1$
e_{t+1}	the deviation of the rate realized in period $t+1$ from its expected value in period t: $e_{t+1} = r_{t+1} - E_t(r_{t+1})$; sometimes called *forecast error* or *shock* or *innovation*
σ^2_{t+1}	the *variance* of the rate of return r_{t+1}; also the variance of e_{t+1}; its square root, σ_{t+1}, is the standard deviation of returns

In this appendix we will denote in bold italic type any variable that is uncertain at time t.

The process for the rate of return can be written as:

$$r_{t+1} = E_t(r_{t+1}) + e_{t+1}, \tag{3.5}$$

where the forecast error e_{t+1} has a zero expected return and a variance σ^2_{t+1}. The variance is equal to

$$\sigma^2_{t+1} = E_t(e^2_{t+1}).$$

The variance and expected returns are called *moments* of the probability distribution of the rates of returns. The variance is a measure of the *volatility* of the asset.

The notations may seem a little bit complicated but are necessary. They stress that the expectation and variance estimates are taken at time *t*, for a return to be realized at time *t+*1. At this point we do not assume that expected returns and variances are constant over time. They are assumed to be *conditional* on some set of information available at time *t*. A more descriptive notation would be

$$E_t(r_{t+1}) = E_t(r_{t+1} \,|\, \Phi_t)$$
$$\sigma^2_{t+1} = E_t(e^2_{t+1} \,|\, \Phi_t),$$

where the notation $|\,\Phi_t$ means that the expectation is conditional on an information set Φ_t known at time *t*.

Traditional Statistical Models with Constant Moments

The traditional approach to statistical modeling are models with constant expected returns and variances.

Normal Distribution   The most simple and common statistical model describing the process followed by an asset rate of return is the *normal* distribution, with constant expected return and variance. A normal, or Gaussian, distribution is completely summarized by its mean and variance. The distribution takes the famous bell shape. At each time period *t+*1, rates of return are assumed to be drawn independently from the same distribution; they are identically independently distributed (i.i.d.). In other words, the rate of return for each time period *t+*1 is independent from what happened in the past and always has the same expected return and variance. We have

$$E_t(r_{t+1}) = E(r) = \text{constant}$$
$$\sigma^2_{t+1} = \sigma^2 = \text{constant}$$

and

$$r_{t+1} = E(r) + e_{t+1} \tag{3.6}$$

This distribution is *unconditional*, in the sense that its expected return and variance are constant through time and not conditional on time or current information.

Let's now see how one would empirically estimate the parameters of such a model and use it to forecast. One would look at past data; the expected return is simply estimated as the mean return over the sample. Hence the best empirical estimate of the future return is the mean return estimated over past data. In the foreign exchange market the best forecast for a future movement in the exchange rate is its past trend.

Jumps   Some asset prices are likely to exhibit infrequent big *jumps*. For example, exchange rates are periodically devalued or revalued under speculative pressures. The date of the jump is uncertain.

The statistical distribution of daily exchange rate movements could be thought of as a combination of daily normal movements and infrequent jumps.[1] The simplest jump process is a binomial approach, whereby a jump of size J has a probability p to take place at time $t+1$ and a probability $1-p$ not to take place. Hence the return on date $t+1$ is a random variable λ_{t+1} such that

$$\lambda_{t+1} = \begin{vmatrix} J \text{ with probability } p \\ 0 \text{ with probability } 1-p \end{vmatrix} \tag{3.7}$$

This can lead to so-called *Poisson* distributions.

Note that both types of distributions—normal and Poisson—are i.i.d. and unconditional. In the simple jump process described, the probability of occurrence of a jump is independent of what happened in the previous periods or independent of current information. Hence the expected return and the variance are the same for each period. Such a simple statistical jump process is not satisfactory for describing the behavior of exchange rate movements. The probability of a jump in exchange rate is clearly a function of past jumps. If a big jump (e.g., a devaluation) has just taken place, it is unlikely to take place again in the very near future. Also the magnitude of the jump is uncertain. Unfortunately, complex time-dependent jump processes are untractable from a practical viewpoint.

Traditional Statistical Models with Time-Varying Moments

No theory claims that the expected return on an asset should always stay the same. The assumption that the expected return is constant through time can be relaxed in a number of ways. A first one is to assume that past returns influence future returns in a specified manner. A second one is to model the influence of a change in the economic environment by stating a linear relation between current observed economic variables and future returns. A third one is to assume that a change in market volatility affects the expected return.

Time-Varying Expected Return: ARIMA   A first approach is to assume that future returns are a function of past returns. A powerful model of time dependence in returns is the ARIMA (AutoRegressive Integrated Moving Average) process. Its theory was developed by Box and Jenkins.[2] The basic idea is that the return at time $t+1$ will be affected by past returns in a specified and predictable way. A general ARIMA process can be written as

$$r_{t+1} = a_0 + b_0 r_t + b_1 r_{t-1} + b_2 r_{t-2} + \ldots + c_0 e_t + c_1 e_{t-1} + c_2 e_{t-2} + \ldots + e_{t+1}. \tag{3.8}$$

The variance of the innovations e_{t+1} is assumed to be constant.

The terms with the b's coefficients are the moving-average terms. The terms with the c's coefficients are the autoregressive terms. The *order* of the ARIMA process is the number of lags included on the right-hand side. The number of lags for the moving-average terms and for the autoregressive terms can be different. We stopped detailing the terms at order 3 for both.

One must clearly understand what is known at time t. All past returns, including r_t have been observed at time t. All innovation terms, including e_t have also been observed at time t. Hence, and assuming an ARIMA process of order 3, the expectation formulated at time t for the return for time $t+1$ is equal to

$$E_t(r_{t+1}) = a_0 + b_0 r_t + b_1 r_{t-1} + b_2 r_{t-2} + c_0 e_t + c_1 e_{t-1} + c_2 e_{t-2}. \tag{3.9}$$

To use this model in forecasting, one would first estimate the coefficients c's and b's over past data, using standard ARIMA econometric software. The forecast for $t+1$ would then be derived using Eq. (3.9).

Expected returns can depend on past returns in ways other than specified by ARIMA processes. Technical analysis uses a variety of methods, such as filter rules or charts, described in this chapter.

Time-Varying Expected Return: Information Variables　The economic environment changes over time. Clearly the level of interest rates or the business cycle could affect expectations on future asset returns. A wide body of literature[3] has modeled a linear relation between time-varying expected returns and a set of n observed economic variables Z_t. This can be written as

$$E_t(r_{t+1}) = d_0 + d_1 Z_{1t} + d_2 Z_{2t} + ... + d_n Z_{nt}. \tag{3.10}$$

The process followed by r_{t+1} can then be written as

$$r_{t+1} = d_0 + d_1 Z_{1t} + d_2 Z_{2t} + ... + d_n Z_{nt} + e_{t+1}. \tag{3.11}$$

where the variance of innovation e_{t+1} is assumed constant.

It must be stressed that the information variables are known at time t when the forecast of the return for $t+1$ is formulated. The information variables commonly used are the level of interest rates, the spread between short- and long-term interest rates, the interest rate differential between two currencies, and so on.

To use this model in forecasting, one would first estimate the coefficients d's over past data, using a regression technique. The forecast for $t+1$ is obtained by observing the current value Z_t of the information variables and inputting them in Eq. (3.10).

Time-Varying Variances: GARCH　Financial market volatility changes over time in a somewhat predictable fashion. This implies that the variance of the returns changes over time in a predictable fashion, conditional on a set of information. To be more precise, the *conditional* variance for period $t+1$ estimated in t, σ^2_{t+1}, depends on the information set available at time t.

The simplest specification of the conditional variance is the ARCH(p) model, in which the conditional variance is simply a weighted average of p past squared forecast errors:

$$\sigma^2_{t+1} = \alpha + \beta_1 e^2_t + \beta_2 e^2_{t-1} + \ldots + \beta_p e^2_{t-p-1}. \tag{3.12}$$

The order of the ARCH process is the number p of lags included in the equation. A natural generalization is to allow past conditional variance to enter the equation. This is known as Generalized ARCH, or GARCH.[4] The GARCH(p,q) model is written as

$$\sigma^2_{t+1} = \alpha + \beta_1 e^2_t + \ldots + \beta_p e^2_{t-p-1} + \gamma_1 \sigma^2_t + \ldots + \gamma_q \sigma^2_{t-q-1}. \tag{3.13}$$

The orders of the GARCH process are the number of lags for the squared error terms (p) and for the past variances (q). Most researchers have found that a GARCH(1,1) is generally an excellent model for modeling and forecasting the volatility of asset returns. The GARCH(1,1) is written as

$$\sigma^2_{t+1} = \alpha + \beta_1 e^2_t + \gamma_1 \sigma^2_t. \tag{3.14}$$

This model means that the current volatility estimate can be deducted from the volatility estimated in the previous period, σ^2_t, modified by the innovation, or shock, e^2_t, just observed. The observation of large shocks leads to an increase in forecasted volatility.

The estimation of the GARCH coefficients requires some specialized econometric software using a so-called maximum-likelihood algorithm. One is sometimes faced with convergence problems in such an algorithm. Once the parameters ß's and γ's have been estimated, Eq. (3.14) can be used to forecast the next-period volatility, using the past-period volatility and observed shocks.

It is possible to model simultaneously the time variation in expected return and in volatility. For example, the variance of the forecast error in Eq. (3.11) could be modeled as a GARCH process, and the conditional variance could be added as an explanatory variable in the conditional expected return. This known as a GARCH-M process. Numerous variants of GARCH models have been developed.

Nontraditional Models

Numerous models developed in other fields, such as physics and artificial intelligence, have been applied to forecasting financial returns. These are various classes of nonlinear models, and only the most widely quoted of them are briefly described here.

Chaos Theory   Scientists have observed that some mathematical and physical systems that exhibited an enormously complicated behavior that appears random were actually generated by some simple nonlinear deterministic models. A *deterministic* model is governed by some mathematical rules that involve no random elements, so that its outcome can be fully described and explained, once the rules are known. However, the future behavior is extremely difficult to predict, because of the high dependence of these systems on the initial conditions. Such nonlinear deterministic systems, which are highly sensitive to initial conditions, are called *chaotic* systems.[5]

A classic example of chaos is the weather system. The famous "butterfly problem" in weather forecasting is that the wing flapping of a butterfly in a specific spot at a specific time may cause a hurricane several months later in another place. Although weather systems appear to be random, they follow very precise models but are very sensitive to small changes in initial conditions. A reasonable weather forecast for tomorrow can be the same weather as today, but precise forecasts for the weather in 30 days are not possible. Another example of a chaotic system is a random-number generator used on computers. These random numbers are indeed generated by a deterministic system, but they look random for all practical purposes.

Chaos is caused by exact nonlinear mathematical functions but appears to be virtually random, and the next state of the system appears virtually unpredictable. Chaotic systems periodically settle into regular cycles, which leads the observer to believe that the system is predictable, but they suddenly explode in wild movements. A simple definition of a chaotic system could be a system generated by nonlinear dynamics whereby small differences in starting values can have a very large influence on the time-series dynamics of the variable.

Similarly, financial markets could be chaotic in the sense that financial prices appear to follow random movements, although they follow a set of exact rules. Forecasting returns is extremely difficult, because a minor change in initial conditions can lead to major changes in forecasts. At best, chaos theory could help detect "pockets" of stability that could help the astute forecaster. The estimation of a chaotic system is a difficult empirical exercise that will not be discussed here. It is very difficult, if not impossible, to differentiate between a stochastic process, whereby random shocks affect the financial variable studied, and a deterministic chaotic process whose underlying model is unknown.

Chaotic systems are one class of *nonlinear dynamic* systems. They are related to *fractal* models and other nonlinear dynamic models that will not be discussed here.[6]

Artificial Intelligence, Expert Systems, and Neural Networks

Artificial intelligence attempts to computerize human reasoning. An *expert system* is a simple class of artificial model that attempts to learn from the behavior of market participants and that translates this learning into a set of program rules. In the 1980s expert systems became quite fashionable in financial markets. They are used in risk management, trading, and forecasting. The computer program attempts to replicate the *sequential* decision process of interviewed "experts" in the field. An expert system is a computer program that uses a set of rules, procedures, and facts to make inferences to simulate the problem-solving ability of human experts. Although these systems are well adapted to replicate the classic behavior of a portfolio manager or a trader, they have not been very successful in being applied to forecasting financial prices. One of the problems with expert systems is that they are sequential processes based on fixed decision rules that need to be adapted continuously. In other words, the market learns more quickly than the expert system designed to mimic the behavior of market participants.

Another approach to artificial intelligence, favored in the 1990s, is constructing programs that mimic the architecture and processing capabilities of the brain. These are known as *artificial neural networks (ANN)*, or more simply *neural networks.*[7] Conventional computer programs (like earlier expert systems) process information *sequentially*; the innovation in neural networks is the massively *parallel* processing of information, in the sense that, as in a brain, all information is processed simultaneously. A human brain is composed of interconnected neurons. An artificial neural network consists of a set of layers of neurons. Each neuron receives inputs, processes them, and delivers a single output. This output can be an input to another neuron or a final output. The network structures can have different shapes. A typical neural network used in finance would have three layers of 10 to 1,000 neurons.

The development of a neural network needs a vast amount of data, because little *a priori* theoretical structure is assumed. The data are separated into a *training* set and a *test* set. The training set is used to determine the parameters of the neural network system, and the test set is used to validate, or test, the network. Once the neural network has been validated, it can be used in forecasting. The observed values of the relevant variables are entered as inputs, and the neural network generates a forecast.

Data Mining, Data Snooping, and Model Mining

A word of caution is required after this review of models used in forecasting. All these models used for forecasting are estimated over some past data. Although the models may look very attractive over the data sample on which they are estimated, their out-of-sample forecasting performance can be very bad. The problems come from the fact that researchers report and use only the models that best fit the past data, although they search ("*mine*") a very huge number of possible models.

Data Mining   *Data mining* refers to the fact that when a given database is studied by researchers long enough, they are likely to find some strong, but spurious, association between some sets of variables. This relation just happened by chance over the specific period covered by the data set and is not likely to repeat over the future. A statistician would say that the relation is not stable. There is an obvious selection bias in trying a large number of models and reporting only the one that yields the bet explanatory power in-sample.

For example, let's assume that a regression is performed, over the past 10 years, between the French stock index return and a large number of economic and financial variables from many countries. The researcher attempts to find a combination of any five variables observed at time t that have a good explanatory power for French stock return in the next month (time $t+1$). By chance, a good explanatory power will be found if we mine across a large number of variables. For example, it could be that the French stock market went up, by chance, on the very months when it rained in Australia or when there was a full moon in South China. Such a relation found over a past data set would be of little practical help for the future, because it is only a statistical artifact of the studied data sample, not a reasonable economic model.

Data Snooping *Data snooping* can be defined as using the data mining of other researchers on a similar database. For example, a bank could estimate only one forecasting model, which is quite close to the one published by another researcher after extensive data mining. To use a parallel, data mining is like cheating at an exam by bringing unauthorized notes, whereas data snooping is like looking over the shoulder of your neighbor to read his unauthorized notes.

In data snooping you can genuinely claim that you did not engage personally in any data mining and that hence your model cannot be guilty of the statistical biases just reported. However, it should be clear that your model is no more likely to work well out-of-sample.

Model Mining In traditional statistical models, as described earlier, a theoretical model is postulated, and its parameters are estimated over a set of data. The problem of data mining is already present for these traditional econometric models, which clearly expose their underlying theoretical logic. It is more acute for complex systems whose underlying structure is primarily empirical and that need a long data history to be estimated and revised. In artificial intelligence systems the estimation procedure searches through a huge number of possible model classes. This means that the researcher can also be guilty of *model mining*. It is even less likely that a model that fits well over some past data will do so in the future.

Appendix Notes

1. See, for example, P. Jorion, "On Jump Processes in the Foreign Exchange and Stock Markets," *Review of Financial Studies*, 1, 3, 1989.

2. See G.E. Box and G.M. Jenkins, *Time Series Analysis, Forecasting and Control*, San Francisco: Holden Day, 1976.

3. A review of the literature can be found in B. Solnik, *Predictable Time-Varying Components of International Asset Returns*, Charlottesville, VA: The Research Foundation of Chartered Financial Analysts, 1993.

4. A review of GARCH models can be found in R. Engle, "Statistical Models for Financial Volatility," *Financial Analysts Journal*, January/February 1993; and T. Bollerslev, R.Y. Chou, and K.F. Kroner, "ARCH Modelling in Finance: A Review of the Theory and Empirical Evidence," *Journal of Econometrics*, 52, 1992.

5. Most references on chaos theory are very technical. A good introduction to chaos theory and its implications for portfolio management can be found in J.J. Angel,

"Implications of Chaos for Portfolio Management," *Journal of Investing*, Summer 1994. See also E. Peters, *Fractal Market Analysis*, New York: Wiley, 1994.

6. *Ibid.*

7. A good nontechnical description of neural networks can be found in L. Medsker, E. Turban, and R. Trippi, "Neural Network Fundamentals for Financial Analysts," *Journal of Investing*, Spring 1993. See also L. Kryzanowski, M. Galler, and D.W. Wright, "Using Artificial Neural Network to Pick Stocks," *Financial Analysts Journal*, July/August 1993.

P A R T   T W O

International Investing and Market Equilibrium

4

The Case for International Diversification

*I*nternational portfolio investment has long been a tradition in many European countries, but it is a more recent practice in North America.[1] However, there is now a strong trend toward international diversification in all countries, especially among U.S. institutional investors, such as corporate and public pension funds. Total assets of U.S. pension funds have grown very rapidly over the past 20 years and surpassed $4 trillion[2] U.S. ($4,000 billion) at the start of 1994. In 1973 these institutional investors basically held no foreign assets; the percentage of foreign assets got close to 10% of total assets by 1995. British institutional investors hold more than 25% of their assets in non-British securities. Some Dutch pension funds have more than half of their assets invested abroad. Recently private investors have joined the trend toward global investment, and international mutual funds were the fastest-growing segment of the U.S. mutual fund industry in the early 1990s.

Indeed, the mere size of foreign markets justifies international diversification even for U.S. investors. At the end of 1994, the world stock market capitalization was over $10 trillion U.S. The U.S. stock market accounted for roughly 35% of the world market size. The growth of the world stock market since 1974 has been remarkable. In 1974 the New York Stock Exchange was the only significant market in the world, representing 60% of a world market capitalization of less than a trillion dollars. As can be seen in Exh. 4.1, the size of the world market multiplied by a factor of 12 in the next 20 years, and the share of U.S. equity moved from 60% to roughly a large third of the world market. The Asian region now makes up a big third of the world stock market and Europe a small third.[3] The world market capitalization of publicly issued bonds was estimated by Salomon Brothers to be around $16 trillion at the start of 1994. U.S. dollar bonds accounted for roughly 45% of the world bond market, yen bonds accounted for approximately 18%, and bonds denominated in European currencies for over 30%.

EXHIBIT 4.1

Stock Market Capitalization
Developed markets

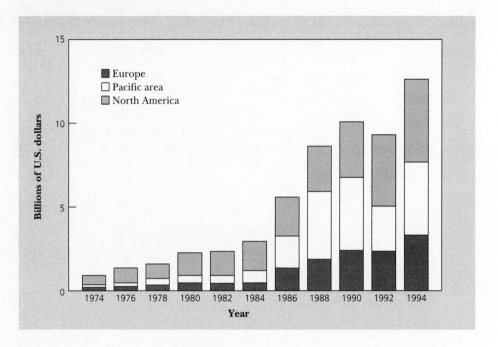

In a fully efficient, integrated, international capital market, buying the world market portfolio would be the natural strategy. However, the case for an integrated international capital market has not yet been fully built (see Chapter 5); furthermore numerous constraints may give a competitive advantage to domestic investors. If buying the market is not the obvious strategy for all investors, the case for international diversification has to be established empirically. Since foreign exchange risk hedging may not be available, we assume in this chapter that exchange risk is fully borne by international investors; this tends to penalize foreign investments in terms of risk.

Even then the basic arguments in favor of international diversification are that foreign investments offer additional profit potentials while reducing the total risk of the portfolio. In other words, international diversification helps to improve the risk-adjusted performance of a domestic portfolio.

Domestic securities tend to move up and down together because they are similarly affected by domestic conditions, such as money supply announcement, movements in interest rates, budget deficit, and national growth. This creates a strong positive correlation among all national securities traded in the same market. The correlation applies equally to stocks and bonds; bond prices on a national market are very strongly correlated. Investors have searched for methods to spread their risks and diversify away the national market risk. Foreign capital markets, in their variety, provide good potential for diversification beyond domestic instruments and markets.

This chapter presents the major arguments in favor of international investment. Our case has been supported by extensive empirical evidence provided by academicians as well as practitioners. The strong advantages have to be weighed against some of the impediments to foreign investment, which are discussed in the last section.

Before discussing the increased profit opportunities offered by international investment, we will present the well-established case of international risk reduction.

Risk Diversification

The argument often heard in favor of international investment is that it lowers risk without sacrificing expected return. A prerequisite for this argument is that the various capital markets of the world have somewhat independent price behavior. If the Paris Bourse and the London Stock Exchange moved in parallel with the U.S. market, diversification opportunities would not exist.

Market Correlation

An impression of the relative independence of the world stock markets may be obtained by looking at the performance of major stock markets as plotted in Exh. 4.2. Each reader, however, may have his or her own interpretation of this graph; thus Exh. 4.3 is more reliable in evaluating market independence.[4] The correlations between various stock and bond markets are systematically monitored by major international money managers, and they arrive at the same conclusions regardless of the period of time analyzed. Although the correlation coefficients between markets vary over time,[5] they are always far from unity. For the portfolio manager this means that there is ample room for successful risk diversification.

Equity Exhibit 4.3 gives the correlations across national stock markets with returns measured in two different numeraires. The bottom-left part of the matrix gives the correlation when all returns are measured in U.S. dollars. The top-right part of the matrix gives the correlation when the foreign investments are fully hedged against currency risk; in other words, the foreign currency is assumed to be sold forward for an amount equal to that of the foreign stock investment. Let's first examine the correlations when no currency hedging is undertaken.

For example, Exh. 4.3 indicates that the correlation between the German and U.S. stock markets is 0.36. The square of this correlation coefficient, usually called R^2, indicates the percentage of common variance between the two markets. Here only 13% ($R^2 = 0.36^2$) of stock price movements is common to the German and U.S. markets.[6] Note that on the average the common variance between the U.S.

EXHIBIT 4.2

Performance of Major Stock Markets in U.S. Dollars, Logarithmic Scale, 1975–1994

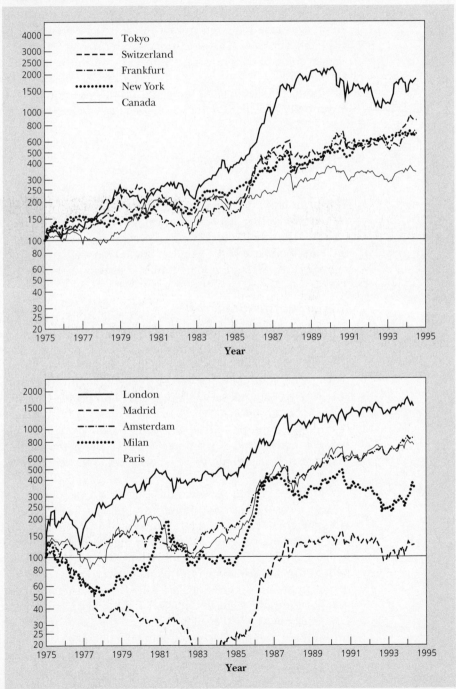

Source: Lombard Odier and Cie, *International Financial Markets,* June 1994. Reprinted by permission.

and other markets is less than 25% (average R of less than 0.5). The correlation with Canada is, of course, quite strong (0.68), because the two economies are closely linked. Other groups of countries are also highly correlated, indicating strong regional links. The Deutsche mark block, for instance, is readily apparent. Germany, Switzerland, the Netherlands, and France tend to have high correlations because their currencies and economies are interrelated. Conversely, Hong Kong and Singapore show little correlation with European markets.

The last two rows and columns in Exh. 4.3 give the correlation of each national market with two international indexes. The world index is a market capitalization–weighted index of all the major stock markets of the world. The Europe, Australia, and Far East (EAFE) index is the non-American world index and is made up of stock markets from those parts of the world. Both indexes are computed in U.S. dollar terms by Morgan Stanley Capital International. The correlation of the U.S. market with the EAFE index is only 0.47. Therefore the overall common variance between U.S. and non-U.S. stock indexes is 22% $R^2 = 0.47^2 = 22\%$. This implies that any well-diversified portfolio of non-U.S. stocks provides an attractive risk-diversification vehicle for a domestic U.S. portfolio. The same holds true for any other domestic portfolio.

The correlation of the U.S. stock market with the world index is much larger ($R^2 = 0.82^2 = 67\%$) than it is for the EAFE index. But this should not be surprising, since the U.S. market accounts for a significant share of the world market.

After the United States, the most "international" market, in terms of correlation with the world index, is the Dutch stock market; much of the Dutch market capitalization is accounted for by truly multinational firms with international ownership, including Royal Dutch–Shell, Unilever, Philips, and AKZO.

In general, we find that all stocks within a given market tend to move up and down together, whereas stocks in different national markets as a rule do not. This provides opportunities for the expert international investor to time the markets by buying those markets that he or she expects to go up and neglecting the bearish ones. It also allows naive investors to spread risk, since some foreign markets are likely to go up when others go down. Actually, this reasoning is simply a variation on the traditional domestic diversification argument, except that it is extended to a larger universe of fairly independent markets.

The degree of independence of a stock market is directly linked to the independence of a nation's economy and government policies. To some extent, common world factors affect expected cash flows of all firms and therefore their stock prices. However, purely national or regional factors seem to play an important role in asset prices, leading to sizable differences in the degrees of independence between markets. It is clear that constraints and regulations imposed by national governments, technological specialization, independent fiscal and monetary policies, and cultural and sociological differences all contribute to the degree of a capital market's independence. On the other hand, when there are closer economic and government policies, as among the Benelux countries or the members of the European Union, one observes more commonality in capital market behavior. In

EXHIBIT 4.3

Correlation Matrix Stock Markets, 1971–1994
Monthly returns in U.S. dollars (bottom left) and currency-hedged (top right)

	France	Germany	Italy	Nether.	Spain	Sweden	Switz.	U.K.	Austr.
France	**1.00**	0.53	0.41	0.53	0.34	0.30	0.54	0.50	0.38
Germany	0.60	**1.00**	0.33	0.60	0.36	0.37	0.64	0.38	0.33
Italy	0.43	0.39	**1.00**	0.36	0.39	0.32	0.35	0.32	0.27
Netherlands	0.60	0.68	0.37	**1.00**	0.36	0.40	0.65	0.62	0.43
Spain	0.40	0.40	0.38	0.39	**1.00**	0.41	0.33	0.30	0.30
Sweden	0.36	0.44	0.35	0.46	0.39	**1.00**	0.44	0.36	0.34
Switzerland	0.60	0.69	0.35	0.70	0.35	0.48	**1.00**	0.56	0.42
U.K.	0.53	0.43	0.36	0.64	0.33	0.42	0.55	**1.00**	0.45
Australia	0.36	0.29	0.25	0.40	0.30	0.36	0.37	0.45	**1.00**
Hong Kong	0.26	0.26	0.22	0.40	0.24	0.27	0.32	0.35	0.34
Japan	0.39	0.39	0.38	0.42	0.38	0.36	0.40	0.35	0.24
Singapore	0.28	0.28	0.22	0.42	0.19	0.35	0.38	0.50	0.41
Canada	0.42	0.31	0.29	0.55	0.25	0.35	0.45	0.51	0.57
U.S.A.	0.44	0.36	0.23	0.58	0.27	0.38	0.47	0.51	0.47
Gold mines	0.20	0.12	0.16	0.19	0.02	0.10	0.23	0.11	0.21
EAFE	0.62	0.61	0.53	0.68	0.50	0.51	0.62	0.68	0.44
World	0.62	0.56	0.46	0.73	0.46	0.53	0.64	0.68	0.54

any case, the covariation between markets is still far from unity, leaving ample opportunities for risk diversification.

One asset class considered in Exh. 4.3 is gold mining shares. Its correlation with all of the stock markets in the world is very weak and sometimes negative. The risk protection property of gold assets is discussed in Chapter 15.

Let's now examine the correlation across stock markets when full currency hedging is undertaken. The correlation coefficients are very similar to the U.S. dollar correlations. The correlation between the U.S. and German markets increases slightly to 0.39, but many other correlations are slightly smaller. There is little difference between stock market correlations when we look at hedged and unhedged returns.

Exhibit 4.3 does not report correlation coefficients measured from a non-U.S. viewpoint. Odier and Solnik (1993) look at the benefits of international diversification from the point of view of investors from different nationalities. For example, Exh. 4.4 reports in a synthetic manner the correlations estimated for a Japanese, a British, and a German investor, respectively, over the period 1980–1990. Again, the correlations across stock markets tend to be all positive but quite low.

	Hong Kong	Japan	Sing.	Canada	U.S.A.	Gold Mines	EAFE	World
France	0.22	0.30	0.26	0.45	0.47	0.14	0.49	0.55
Germany	0.26	0.30	0.27	0.33	0.39	0.02	0.44	0.47
Italy	0.21	0.31	0.23	0.27	0.24	0.09	0.40	0.38
Netherlands	0.36	0.34	0.40	0.55	0.58	0.09	0.46	0.58
Spain	0.22	0.32	0.21	0.27	0.30	−0.03	0.39	0.41
Sweden	0.19	0.27	0.32	0.31	0.38	0.02	0.32	0.41
Switzerland	0.30	0.34	0.43	0.51	0.59	0.12	0.47	0.59
U.K.	0.35	0.29	0.52	0.52	0.56	0.03	0.55	0.61
Australia	0.30	0.23	0.41	0.56	0.52	0.21	0.43	0.56
Hong Kong	**1.00**	0.21	0.48	0.30	0.31	−0.02	0.32	0.37
Japan	0.24	**1.00**	0.33	0.29	0.33	0.09	0.70	0.63
Singapore	0.48	0.33	**1.00**	0.41	0.46	0.05	0.42	0.50
Canada	0.29	0.27	0.40	**1.00**	0.71	0.26	0.47	0.69
U.S.A.	0.29	0.27	0.45	0.68	**1.00**	0.08	0.47	0.82
Gold mines	−0.01	0.12	0.08	0.26	0.08	**1.00**	0.18	0.19
EAFE	0.31	0.82	0.47	0.47	0.47	0.18	**1.00**	0.87
World	0.35	0.67	0.53	0.68	0.82	0.19	0.87	**1.00**

Bonds Similar conclusions can be reached for bonds, as can be seen in Exh. 4.5, which is presented in a fashion similar to Exh. 4.3. Let's first look at the correlation of the various bond markets when returns are all expressed in U.S. dollars (the bottom-left part of the exhibit). For example, the correlation of U.S. dollar returns of U.S. and German bonds is only 0.31, or an average percentage of common variance less than 10% (the square of 0.31). The correlations of U.S. bonds with all foreign bonds are around 0.3, except for the Canadian dollar bonds, whose returns are strongly correlated with the return on U.S. dollar bonds. These surprisingly low coefficients reflect two factors. First, contrary to comments often made by politicians, long-term yield variations are not strongly correlated across countries. Second, returns on a bond investment in a foreign country are strongly influenced by the performance of the country's currency, and currency movements are correlated only weakly with long-term yield movements.

The general observation is that national monetary/budget policies are not fully synchronized. For example, the growing U.S. budget deficit in the mid-1980s, associated with high U.S. interest rates and a rapid weakening of the dollar, was not matched in other countries. The relative independence of national monetary/budget policies, influencing both currency and interest rate movements, leads to a surprisingly low correlation of the U.S. dollar returns on the U.S. and

EXHIBIT 4.4

Correlation for Non-U.S. Stock Markets
In local currency, monthly returns

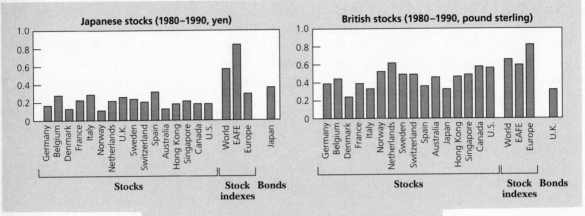

foreign bond markets. Hence foreign bonds allow one to diversify the risks associated with the domestic monetary/budget policies; this conclusion would be even stronger if we measured risk and return in real terms rather than in nominal terms.

Let's now examine the correlations found for bond investments fully hedged against currency risk (top-right part of the matrix). The correlations of foreign bond markets with the U.S. bond market are quite similar to those found for unhedged returns; this can be seen by comparing the U.S.A. row and column of the matrix. However, from the viewpoint of a U.S. investor, the returns on various foreign bond markets appear to be much more correlated between themselves when the returns are measured in U.S. dollars than when they are hedged against

EXHIBIT 4.5

	France	Germany	Italy	Nether.	Switzer.	U.K.	Japan	Canada	U.S.A.	U.S.A. Stocks

Correlation Matrix Bond Markets, 1971–1994
Monthly returns in U.S. dollars (bottom left) and currency-hedged (top right)

	France	Germany	Italy	Nether.	Switzer.	U.K.	Japan	Canada	U.S.A.	U.S.A. Stocks
France	**1.00**	0.33	0.26	0.39	0.32	0.25	0.25	0.25	0.24	0.16
Germany	0.77	**1.00**	0.07	0.59	0.42	0.24	0.39	0.38	0.37	0.17
Italy	0.60	0.58	**1.00**	0.11	0.10	0.17	0.09	0.21	0.14	0.12
Netherlands	0.79	0.92	0.59	**1.00**	0.49	0.16	0.33	0.31	0.33	0.14
Switzerland	0.66	0.78	0.49	0.77	**1.00**	0.33	0.31	0.28	0.33	0.17
U.K.	0.45	0.46	0.40	0.16	0.44	**1.00**	0.24	0.30	0.24	0.14
Japan	0.58	0.60	0.45	0.60	0.57	0.46	**1.00**	0.27	0.28	0.09
Canada	0.22	0.32	0.26	0.31	0.26	0.35	0.28	**1.00**	0.73	0.28
U.S.A.	0.26	0.31	0.22	0.32	0.24	0.25	0.25	0.65	**1.00**	0.31
U.S. stocks	0.12	0.10	0.08	0.09	−0.01	0.09	0.04	0.29	0.31	**1.00**

currency risk. This is explained by the fact that currency risk is a large component of the total risk of a foreign bond investment (although it is only a small part of a foreign stock investment). When the U.S. dollar depreciates, all foreign bonds tend to have a positive return when measured in U.S. dollars, because of the currency component of the total return. This is not the case when we look at currency-hedged returns; hence the unhedged correlation across foreign bond markets tends to be higher than the hedged correlation.

Finally, the last asset class in Exh. 4.5 is U.S. equity. The correlation of foreign bonds with the U.S. stock market is also weak. This is not surprising, given the independence between U.S. and foreign national economic and monetary policies. The correlation of the U.S. bond and stock markets indicates the well-known reaction of stock prices to movements in domestic interest rates (see Chapter 5). However, the correlation is generally very weak in the case of foreign bond markets. Clearly foreign monetary and budgetary policies have little impact on U.S. economic growth and U.S. share prices. Foreign bonds offer excellent diversification benefits to a U.S. stock portfolio manager.

Exhibit 4.6 reports in a synthetic manner the correlations estimated for a Japanese, a British, and a German investor, respectively, in the local currencies and over the period 1980–1990. Again, the correlations across bond markets tend to be quite low and sometimes even negative. The explanation for the negative correlation in national bond returns can be found in Chapter 5. Many countries have periodically adopted a "leaning-against-the-wind" monetary policy. In periods of weakness of the domestic currency, monetary authorities have often resorted to a policy of increasing domestic interest rates, which affected bond yields. This leads simultaneously to a drop in domestic bond prices and a rise in the local-currency value of foreign assets because of the appreciation of foreign currencies.

EXHIBIT 4.6

Correlation for Non-U.S. Bond Markets
In local currency, monthly returns

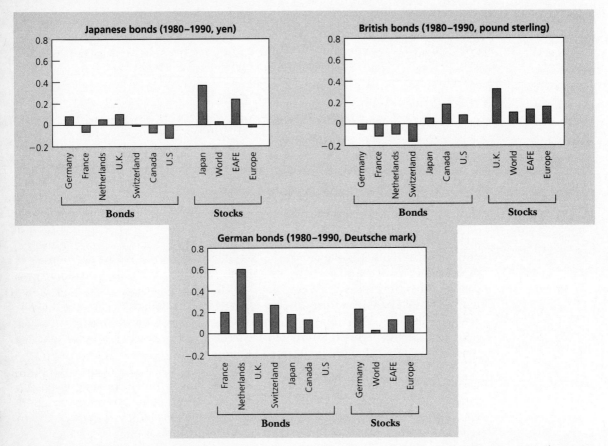

More on Correlation   So far we have talked about the contemporaneous correlation across markets taking place when an event or factor affects two or more markets simultaneously. Some investigators have attempted to find leads or lags between markets. For example, they studied whether a bear market in February on Wall Street would lead to a drop in prices on other national markets in March. No evidence of a systematic delayed reaction of one national market to another has ever been found, except for daily returns as outlined later. The existence of such simple market inefficiencies is, indeed, unlikely, since it would be easy to exploit them to make an abnormal profit. However, one must take into account the time differences around the world before assessing whether some national market leads or lags other markets.

The stock exchanges in New York and Tokyo are not open at the same time. If important news hits New York prices on a Tuesday, it will impact Tokyo prices only on Wednesday. If important news hits London prices on a Tuesday, it will impact New York prices the same day, as New York generally lags London by five hours. Indeed, when it is Tuesday noon in New York, it is already Tuesday 17:00 (or 5 P.M.) local time in London and Wednesday 02:00 (or 2 A.M.) in Tokyo.[7] The opening and closing times of the three major stock markets are depicted in Exh. 4.7, where the trading hours are indicated using both the universal GMT (Greenwich Mean Time) and the American EST (Eastern Standard Time). It can be seen that New York and Tokyo official trading hours never overlap. London and New York trading hours generally overlap for three hours. If the markets are efficient, international news should affect all markets around the globe simultaneously, with markets closed at that hour reflecting the news immediately upon opening. For example, if important news is revealed after noon EST, it can be impounded in Japanese and British stock prices only the next day; because of the time overlap involved, we should not be surprised to find a lagging correlation of Tokyo and London with New York when returns are measured from closing price to closing price. This lagged correlation can be explained by the difference in time zones, not by some international market inefficiency that could be exploited to make a profit. The price adjustment to news revealed at noon EST should take place as soon as the Tokyo and London markets open the next day. Once this opening-price adjustment has taken place, the open-to-close return in London and Tokyo should not be affected by prior news and therefore should not be correlated with the previous-day return on the NYSE. Susmel and Engle (1994) look at hourly

---

EXHIBIT 4.7

Stock Exchange Trading Hours in GMT and EST clocks

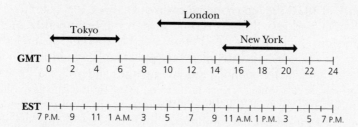

quotations on the London and New York stock markets. They conclude that the markets are efficient and that the correlations are consistent with the absence of arbitrage opportunities. Other studies looking at the correlation of London, Tokyo, and New York are broadly consistent with this conclusion.[8]

Another important issue is whether the correlation across markets remains constant over time. It is often stated that the progressive removal of impediments to international investment, as well as the growing political, economic, and financial integration, affects international market linkages. This could lead to a progressive increase in the intentional correlation of financial markets. Several studies have looked at the stability of international correlation over long time periods.[9] Kaplanis studied the stability of the correlation matrix of monthly returns of 10 markets over a 15-year period (1967–1982). The null hypothesis that the correlation matrix is constant over two adjacent subperiods of four years could not be rejected at the 15% confidence level. Longin and Solnik (1995) studied a longer period (1960–1990), using a GARCH methodology. They found a modest but significant increase in international correlation over this 30-year period. However, one must point out that the correlations dropped back to a lower level in the early 1990s after the conclusion of their study; this can be seen in Exh. 4.8. Exhibit 4.8 reports the average correlation of the U.S. market with the seven other major stock markets; the estimation is performed over successive subperiods of two years. The observation that the international correlation across stock markets has not trended more rapidly over the past 30 years is somewhat puzzling. This may be explained by the growing competition among national economies and the recent importance of monetary factors on the behavior of security prices. Increased international competition has led to national specialization. For example, the French industry has become famous for its luxury goods, its food and beverage companies, and its aircraft and train production. National monetary/budget/fiscal factors do not appear to be well coordinated across the world or even within a region like Europe. Even if the stock markets of developed countries were to become more correlated, thereby reducing the potential benefits of global diversification, new stock markets are emerging. As discussed in Chapter 8, these developing economies, located in Asia, Latin America, and Central Europe, could become in the future the Japan of the 1970s and 1980s.

To be sure, correlation coefficients are not constant. In some periods all stock markets are affected by the same worldwide factors. This was the case with the oil shock of 1974, the international crash of October 1987, and the Gulf crisis of 1990. In other periods all markets tend to move independently and even in opposite directions. Indeed, a question often raised is whether the international correlation increases in periods of high turbulence. The international correlation increases when global factors dominate domestic ones and affect all financial markets. The dominance of global factors tends to be associated with very volatile markets (e.g., the oil crisis or Gulf war). Using high-frequency data surrounding the crash of 1987, several studies have found that international correlation tends to increase in periods of high turbulence.[10] Longin and Solnik (1995) looked at monthly data

EXHIBIT 4.8

Mean Correlation of U.S. Stocks with Other Markets and U.S. Stock Market Volatility

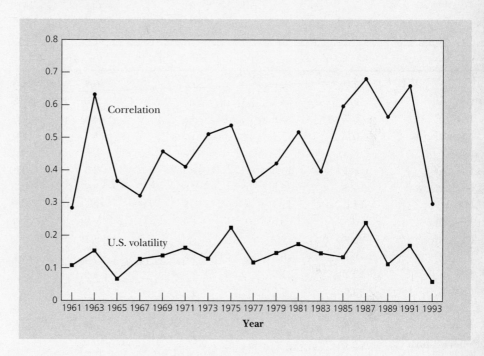

for the period 1960–1990, which covers several business cycles and crises, and confirm that international correlation tends to increase in periods of high stock market volatility. Exhibit 4.8 also reports the volatility of the U.S. stock market alongside its average correlation with the other major stock markets. The volatility is estimated as the standard deviation over a two-year subperiod. The link between volatility and correlation appears clearly. Although this link between correlation and volatility is unfortunate, it does not negate the benefits of international diversification.

To summarize, all capital markets move together to some extent, but their relatively high degree of independence leaves ample room for risk diversification on both foreign stock and foreign bond markets.

Portfolio Volatility

One argument against foreign investment by U.S. investors is that foreign markets are more volatile than the U.S. domestic market, especially if currency risk is taken into consideration. Supporting evidence of this volatility is found in Exh. 4.9,

EXHIBIT 4.9

Risk and Return for U.S. Dollar Investors, 1971–1994
Percent per year

	(1) Annual Return %	(2) Capital Gain %	(3) Dividend Interest Income %	(4) Currency Gain %	(5) Total Risk %	(6) Domestic Risk %
Stocks						
France	14.0	9.0	5.4	−0.4	24.6	21.7
Germany	14.2	6.1	4.5	3.6	21.2	18.0
Italy	6.7	8.5	3.1	−4.8	27.0	25.6
Netherlands	16.7	7.4	6.2	3.1	18.4	17.1
Spain	8.5	4.7	7.3	−3.5	23.2	20.8
Sweden	16.4	14.6	4.3	−2.5	22.3	22.0
Switzerland	14.3	6.3	2.8	5.2	20.1	16.9
U.K.	14.6	11.3	5.8	−2.5	26.3	23.5
Australia	10.5	8.0	4.9	−2.5	26.9	23.1
Hong Kong	22.2	19.3	5.0	−2.1	42.3	39.7
Japan	18.1	10.4	1.8	5.8	23.3	18.8
Singapore	17.7	11.9	2.6	3.3	31.1	30.4
Canada	9.6	7.0	4.0	−1.3	19.2	17.5
U.S.A.	11.0	6.5	4.5	0.0	15.5	15.5
Gold mines	16.8	8.3	8.5	0.0	45.5	45.5
International stock indexes						
EAFE	14.6	11.0	3.6	0.0	18.2	15.3
World	12.2	8.2	4.0	0.0	14.6	13.3
Bonds						
France	11.0	0.1	11.3	−0.3	13.8	6.8
Germany	12.0	0.4	8.1	3.5	14.5	5.8
Italy	8.2	−0.5	13.6	−4.9	13.9	8.2
Netherlands	12.0	0.5	8.6	3.0	13.7	5.8
Switzerland	10.3	0.1	5.2	5.0	14.4	3.5
U.K.	9.3	0.0	11.7	−2.4	17.0	10.9
Japan	14.4	1.1	7.6	5.6	14.9	6.2
Canada	8.2	−0.9	10.4	−1.3	11.1	8.9
U.S.A.	8.8	−0.4	9.2	0.0	8.6	8.6

	(1) Annual Return %	(2) Capital Gain %	(3) Dividend Interest Income %	(4) Currency Gain %	(5) Total Risk %	(6) Domestic Risk %
Cash (3-month)						
France	11.1	0.0	11.4	−0.3	11.5	
Germany	10.0	0.0	6.5	3.5	12.2	
Italy	8.6	0.0	13.5	−4.9	10.8	
Netherlands	10.1	0.0	7.2	2.9	11.8	
Switzerland	9.9	0.0	5.0	5.0	14.0	
U.K.	9.6	0.0	12.0	−2.4	11.5	
Japan	12.2	0.0	6.6	5.5	11.3	
Canada	8.4	0.0	9.8	−1.3	4.6	
U.S.A.	8.8	0.0	8.8	0.0		

These calculations are based on monthly index values and coupons obtained from Morgan Stanley Capital International (stocks) and Lombard Odier (bonds, cash).

which shows the recent performance of various market indexes. The average annual total return for a U.S. investor investing in each market is given in column 1. Columns 2, 3, and 4 segment this return into capital gains, yield, and the influence of exchange rate movements. The total risk of the market, measured by the annualized standard deviation[11] of U.S. dollar monthly rates of return, is given in column 5, and the risk measured in local currency is given in column 6.

The objective of risk diversification is to reduce the total risk of a portfolio. Of course, one hopes simultaneously to achieve high expected returns, as discussed in the next section. The total risk of most stock markets is larger than that of the U.S. market when the dollar is used as the base currency, even though the domestic risk of many markets is less than that of the U.S. market. Because of the exchange risk component, the same conclusion holds true for a Swiss, German, or Japanese investor if returns are computed in Swiss francs, Deutsche marks, or yen, respectively. Nevertheless, the addition of more risky foreign assets to a purely domestic portfolio still reduces its total risk as long as the foreign assets correlation with the domestic market is not large. The following example demonstrates this mathematically.

Assume that the domestic and foreign assets have standard deviations (σ) of $\sigma_d = 10\%$ and $\sigma_f = 12\%$, respectively, with a correlation of $R = 0.3$. The variance (σ^2) of the total portfolio equally invested in both assets σ_p^2, is given by

$$\sigma_p^2 = 0.5^2[\sigma_d^2 + \sigma_f^2 + (2R\sigma_d\sigma_f)]$$

$$\sigma_p^2 = 0.5^2[100 + 144 + (2 \times 0.3 \times 120)] = 79.$$

Hence the standard deviation σ_p is given by $\sqrt{79}$, or 8.88%, which is significantly less than that of the domestic asset. Since one can diversify in several foreign markets, the total risk of the portfolio could be further reduced.

Column 6 in Exh. 4.9 shows that the volatility of stock markets measured in their domestic currency is higher or comparable to that of U.S. markets. Hong Kong's, however, is much more volatile, as are some of the smaller markets (Singapore and Italy).

A significant part of the market capitalization–weighted world stock index is U.S. securities, yet the index also includes some highly volatile markets, such as Hong Kong. Nevertheless, the total risk of this internationally diversified index ($\sigma = 14.6\%$) is considerably less than that of a well-diversified U.S. portfolio (15.5%).

A similar conclusion holds for bond markets. For several years Salomon Brothers, J.P. Morgan, Lombard Odier, and others have computed monthly or daily bond indexes for the major domestic and European markets. They generally find that the world-weighted bond index, in U.S. dollars, is less volatile than the U.S. government bond index. For example, Salomon Brothers found a monthly standard deviation of dollar returns (interest plus price movement) equal to 3.48% for the U.S. government bond index and 3.18% for the world bond index over a six-year period from January 1978 to December 1983.

Solnik (1994) studied the benefits of international diversification for European pension funds. He showed that a broad passive international diversification offers a significant reduction in volatility compared to the local stock market for all nationalities. This is shown in Exh. 4.10 for British, French, and Dutch investors and applies equally to stocks and bonds.

Although the evidence is compelling at the market index level, it is not clear that the same diversification payoffs can be obtained by a practicing portfolio manager who selects only a few issues in a few markets. For example, is it true that a portfolio diversified across 50 foreign and domestic securities is less risky than a portfolio made up of 50 domestic securities? The answer to this question again is affirmative.

Exhibit 4.11 shows the total risk of domestic and internationally diversified portfolios as a function of the number of securities held. Let us first consider the top curve (U.S. stocks); 100% represents the typical risk of a single U.S. security. When more U.S. stocks are added to the portfolio (all securities are randomly selected), its total risk (standard deviation or variance) is quickly reduced. Beyond 40 or 50 stocks, the addition of more domestic securities provides little reduction in risk. That is why the top curve reaches an asymptote corresponding to the U.S. market risk, which represents roughly 30% of the typical risk of a single security. Adding foreign stocks to a purely domestic portfolio reduces risk much more quickly, as can be seen on the bottom curve (international stocks). Indeed, with as few as 40 securities equally spread among the major U.S. and European stock markets, the risk for a U.S. investor is less than half that of a purely domestic portfolio of comparable size. The same finding has been attained for real or simulated portfolios over various time periods, including the recent era of volatile exchange

EXHIBIT 4.10

Stock and Bond Market Volatility: Selected Markets, 1971–1992
(Domestic currencies)

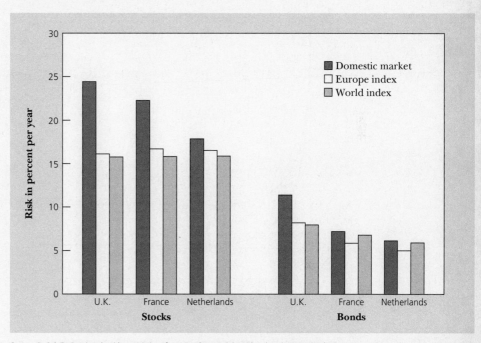

rates. In all cases international diversification provided a better and quicker reduction in risk, even for a portfolio with a limited number of securities.

Currency Risk

Another argument against international diversification is that currency risks (i.e., exchange risks) more than offset the reduction in security risks achieved by international diversification. Indeed, currency fluctuations affect both the total return and volatility of any foreign currency–denominated investment. From time to time, in fact, its impact on the investment return may exceed that of capital gain or income, especially over short periods of time. But currency fluctuation has never been the major component of total return on a diversified portfolio over a long period of time. This stems from the fact that the depreciation of one currency is often offset by the appreciation of another. Since exchange rates are so difficult to forecast, we will focus on the contribution of exchange rate uncertainties to the total risk of the portfolio rather than to expected returns. Empirical studies

EXHIBIT 4.11

International Diversification

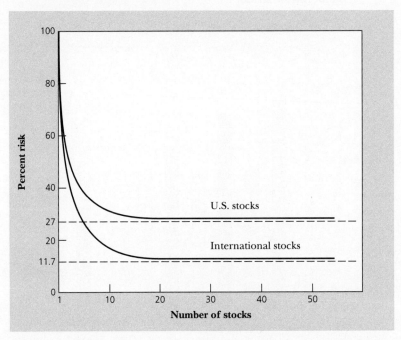

indicate that currency risk, as measured by the standard deviation of the exchange rate movement,[12] is smaller than the risk of the corresponding stock market. This is shown by a comparison of the last two columns of Exh. 4.9. On the other hand, currency risk is often larger than the risk (in local currency) of the corresponding bond market. It would seem, then, that foreign investors stand to lose more, at least in the short run, on currency than on bond price movements. Does this mean that currency risk is so large that investors should avoid foreign investment? Not at all, and for several reasons.

First, market risks and currency risks are not additive. This would be true only if the two were perfectly correlated. In fact, there is only a weak, and sometimes negative, correlation between currency and market movements. If σ_D is the market risk in the domestic currency, σ_F the exchange rate volatility, σ the total risk in U.S. dollars, and R the correlation coefficient between the two risks, we have

$$\sigma^2 = \sigma_D^2 + \sigma_F^2 + 2R\sigma_D\sigma_F,$$

implying that

$$\sigma \leq \sigma_D + \sigma_F,$$

since $R < 1$.

To illustrate this point, Exh. 4.9 shows the risk of each market measured in both U.S. dollars and domestic currency. The difference between the two is the contribution of currency risk to the total risk. Worldwide, exchange risk broadly amounts to 15% of the total stock market risk. For example, the French stock market has a risk of 21.7% when measured in local currency and a risk of 24.6% when measured in U.S. dollars. The contribution of currency risk is equal to the difference, 2.9%; this is far below the standard deviation of the French franc/U.S. dollar exchange rate, which is equal to 11.5%. Equity investment risk is actually very small for some markets, such as Singapore. By contrast, exchange risk amounts to roughly 50% of the risk involved in foreign bonds and, of course, is the major source of risk for short-term investments.

Chapter 5 features a discussion of the theoretical relationship between asset prices and exchange rates. A question often raised in this regard is: What is the appropriate numeraire to measure returns? Should a pension fund be concerned about real returns, adjusted for inflation, rather than nominal dollar returns? If so, the appropriate measure of currency risk should be in terms of purchasing power and its effect on the real returns for a domestic investor.

Second, the exchange risk of an investment may be hedged for major currencies by selling futures or forward currency contracts, buying put currency options, or even borrowing foreign currency to finance the investment. Naturally the cost of hedging should be weighed against the risk it eliminates.

Third, the contribution of currency risk should be measured for the total portfolio rather than for individual markets or securities. The reason is that part of that risk gets diversified away by the cocktail of currencies represented in the portfolio.

As can be seen in Exh. 4.9, the currency component accounts for less than 20% of the total risk of the EAFE stock index. With no currency movements, the risk of this index would have been 15.3%, compared to 18.2% with the exchange rate movements. Given the large share of the U.S. market in the world portfolio, the currency contribution to the total risk of the world stock market portfolio is rather weak.

As stressed by Jorion (1989), the contribution of currency risk to the total risk of a portfolio that includes only a small proportion of foreign assets (say, 5%) is insignificant. The contribution of currency risk is larger if one holds the world market portfolio and hence a large share of foreign assets. Then the question of the optimal currency-hedging policy becomes more relevant. This issue is discussed in Chapters 5 and 17.

Risk-Adjusted Return

We have devoted so much attention to the risk-reduction benefits of international investment because risk diversification is the most established and frequently invoked argument in favor of foreign investment and justifies foreign investment even to the naive investor. However, it is not the sole motive for international investment. Indeed, mere risk reduction could more easily be achieved by simply investing part of one's assets in domestic risk-free bills. For that matter, the risk level of a domestic portfolio can be carefully modulated by changing its bill-bond-equity mix. Unfortunately, although the inclusion of risk-free bills lowers the portfolio risk, it also lowers expected return. In the traditional framework of the capital Asset Pricing Model (CAPM), the expected return on a security is equal to the risk-free rate plus a risk premium. In an efficient market reducing the risk level of a portfolio by adding less-risky investments implies reducing its expected return. International diversification, however, implies no reduction in return. It lowers risk by eliminating nonsystematic volatility without sacrificing expected return. Before presenting some empirical evidence on the risk-return characteristics of international investment, let us examine why this apparent free lunch exists.

To some extent the strictly domestic (noninternational) investor is like a U.S. investor who ignores all industrial sectors except chemicals on the New York Stock Exchange. By restricting oneself to the equity of chemical firms, the investor incurs unnecessary risk. If stocks in other industries have the same expected return, the investor would be better off diversifying into those U.S. sectors, whether they be energy, high technology, banking, or something else. By so doing, the risks are considerably reduced without sacrificing return. The same argument holds for a domestic investor investing in foreign capital markets even when he or she does not expect a better performance in the foreign markets. One buys stocks abroad because the low correlation between national markets implies that it is likely that other markets will go up when the domestic stock market falls. Of course, during any given period the foreign portfolio segment may underperform the domestic segment, but on average the risk of loss is reduced.

The second argument in favor of international investment is that more profitable investments are possible in an enlarged universe. Higher returns may arise from faster-growing economies and firms located around the world or simply from currency gains.

Long-Term Performance

American money managers can rightfully call attention to the excellent track records of international portfolios since the 1960s or the 1970s. This is illustrated in Exh. 4.9, which shows that the Morgan Stanley Capital International EAFE stock index markedly outperformed the U.S. stock index (14.6% per year versus 11.0%) between 1971 and 1994. The average annual total performance of the world stock

EXHIBIT 4.12

**Risk/Return Trade-off of an Internationally Diversified Portfolio:
1971 to 1994**

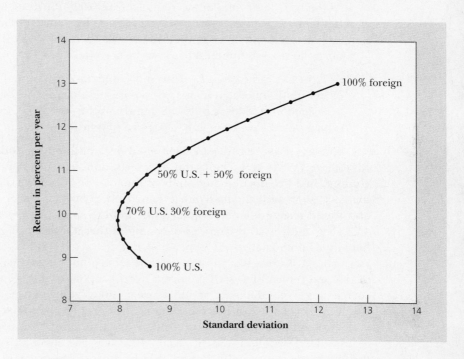

index[13] in U.S. dollars was 12.2% compared to 11% for the U.S. index, and the volatility was much smaller (14.6% versus 15.5%). Although these differences in mean annualized rates of return could look small, they compound into dramatically different wealth over 20 years. One hundred dollars invested in the U.S. stock index at the start of 1971 would be worth $1,084 dollars at the end of 1994. The same $100 would be worth $1,409 if it had been invested in the world index; $2,227 if it had been invested in the EAFE index.

A similar conclusion is reached for bonds, or for a combination of bonds and stocks, as seen in the next section. The case for the international diversification of a purely U.S. bond portfolio is illustrated in Exh. 4.12. We ran a simulation of the risk and return of a portfolio including various percentages of U.S. and foreign bonds. The foreign bonds are represented by a passive market–capitalization-weighted index of non-U.S. bonds. Currency risk is fully borne. The period is 1971 to 1994, as used before in various exhibits. We start from a portfolio fully invested in U.S. bonds (return of 8.8% and volatility of 8.6%). Introducing 5% of foreign bonds allows for a significant reduction of volatility and an increase in return. We increase the proportion of foreign bonds by increments of 5% and come up with the following conclusions:

- As the U.S. bond content was reduced, portfolio return rose. This reflects the fact that foreign bonds outperformed U.S. bonds over the period.

- As the U.S. bond content was reduced from 100% to 70%, the volatility portfolio for a U.S. investor was reduced. This reflects the fact that returns on U.S. and foreign bonds were not highly correlated. At a 70% U.S. bond content, portfolio risk was minimized, as can be seen in Exh. 4.12.

- As Exh. 4.12 indicates, a U.S. investor could have committed up to 50% of his or her funds to foreign bonds without raising the level of risk above the level associated with holding only U.S. bonds. At the same time, the total annual return would have been enhanced by a significant amount.

Similar studies have been conducted over different periods by Barnett and Rosenberg (1983) and Chollerton, Pieraerts, and Solnik (1986) with similar conclusions. In a well-documented study of the total performance of the world capital markets, using annual data from 1960 to 1984, Ibbotson, Siegel, and Love (1985) also found a superior performance for non-U.S. investments, as shown in Exh. 4.13. This study is all the more interesting in that it covers a period for which we have little bond data.

One must stress that the expected benefits of international investing in terms of risk and return of a portfolio are different. Because of the low (less than one) correlation across different national assets, the volatility of a portfolio is *less* than the average volatility of its components. Risks get diversified away. This international risk reduction appears from any currency viewpoint. However, the return on a diversified portfolio is exactly *equal* to the average return of its components. By definition, the return on the world index is the average return of all national markets. In other words, some countries will outperform the world index, whereas others will underperform the world index. Although international diversification has looked attractive over the past 20 or 30 years from both a risk and a return viewpoint for an American investor, this is not the case for a Japanese investor, whose national stock market outperformed the world index. A Japanese investor benefited only from the risk reduction provided by a passive global portfolio, such as the world index.

The fact that national stock markets have different long-term performances is not surprising and could justify an active asset allocation strategy. In the long run the performance of stock markets can be explained by national economic factors. The difference in performance between the American and Asian equity markets reported in Exh. 4.13 is largely the result of higher real growth rates in most Asian economies. From 1960 to 1984 the real gross domestic product grew at an average annual rate of 3.4% in the United States compared to over 4% in the other industrial countries. Over the same period, the annual real growth rate was 7.5% in Japan and 8.7% in Korea. Such differences in growth rates are likely to persist, as evidenced in forecasts by the World Bank or the Organization for Economic Cooperation and Development (OECD). Some emerging economies offer attractive investment opportunities. The local risks (volatility, liquidity, political) are

EXHIBIT 4.13

World Capital Market Total Annual Returns, 1960 to 1984

	Compound Return	Standard Deviation
Equities		
United States	8.81	16.89
Foreign		
Europe	7.83	15.58
Asia	15.14	30.74
Other	8.14	20.88
Foreign total	9.84	16.07
Equities total	9.08	15.28
Bonds		
United States		
Corporate	5.35	9.63
Government	5.91	6.43
United States total	5.70	7.16
Foreign		
Corporate domestic	8.35	7.26
Government domestic	5.79	7.41
Crossborder	7.51	5.76
Foreign total	6.80	6.88
Bonds total	6.36	5.50
Cash Equivalents		
United States	6.49	3.22
Foreign	6.50	7.10
Cash total	6.38	2.92

Source: Data from R. Ibbotson, L. Siegel, and K. Love, "World Wealth: Market Values and Returns," *Journal of Portfolio Management,* Fall 1985.

higher, but the expected profit is large. Among the fast-growing economies with emerging stock markets, portfolio investors should seriously consider Thailand, Korea, Philippines, Sri Lanka, China, India, Chile, Peru, Turkey, Hungary, and many other countries in Asia, Latin America, and Central Europe. These emerging markets and their contribution to a global investment strategy are examined in Chapter 8.

Economic flexibility is also an important factor in investment performance, which may explain differences between past and future performances among these countries. Wage and employment rigidity is bad for the national economy. In countries such as France, Canada, and Sweden, companies have a difficult time adjusting to slowing activity; on the other hand, they do not take full advantage of growth opportunities, since they are reluctant to hire new employees whom they cannot fire if the activity slows. The degree of socialization of the economy is also an important issue. Some international money managers like to correlate the prospects of an economy and its stock market with the so-called lawyer intensity. They claim that stock market growth is negatively related to the time and costs lost in legal procedures; they recall that in 1983 there were 2.67 lawyers per 1000 persons in the United States, 1.0 lawyer per 1000 persons in the United Kingdom, 0.57 lawyer per 1000 persons in West Germany, and only 0.1 lawyer per 1000 persons in Japan.[14]

It should be stressed that there is no guarantee that the past will necessarily repeat itself. Indeed, over any given period one national market is bound to outperform the other, and if one had perfect foresight, the best strategy would be to invest solely in the top-performing market or even in the top-performing security in that market. But because of the great uncertainty of forecasts, it is always better to spread risk in the fund by diversifying internationally across markets with comparable expected return. This ensures a favorable risk-return trade-off, or in the jargon of theory, higher risk-adjusted expected returns. If managers believe that they have some relative forecasting ability, they will engage in active investment strategies that reap the benefits of international risk diversification while focusing on preferred markets. For example, an American investor may concentrate on U.S. and Japanese stocks if he or she is bullish on those markets and may avoid France for political or currency reasons.

Optimal International Asset Allocation

So far we have focused on the risk-diversification advantage of passive international diversification. But global asset allocation can also provide better profit opportunities and hence improve a portfolio's risk/return trade-off. Odier and Solnik studied optimal asset allocations over the 10-year period 1980–1990.[15]

Exhibit 4.14 shows optimal international stock allocations for different risk levels and for a U.S. investor. The mean annual return is given on the *Y*-axis, and the asset volatility (standard deviation) is given on the *X*-axis. Each asset or portfolio is represented by one point on the graph. The U.S. stock market has a risk of 16.2% and a total return of 13.3%. Other stock markets are more volatile, partly because of currency risk. By combining the various national stock markets, we get diversified portfolios whose returns and risks can be calculated, because we know the returns and covariances of all the assets. The well-known idea popularized by the 1990 Nobel prize winner Markowitz is that investors building a portfolio will try to obtain the best return while attempting to minimize the risk of loss. They will thus select asset allocations that lie in the top-left part of the figure.

The best achievable risk/return trade-offs—the optimal asset allocations—lie on the efficient frontier.[16] As Exh. 4.14 shows, international diversification of a pure U.S. stock portfolio would greatly enhance return without a large increase in

EXHIBIT 4.14

Efficient Frontier for Stocks (U.S. dollar, 1980–1990)

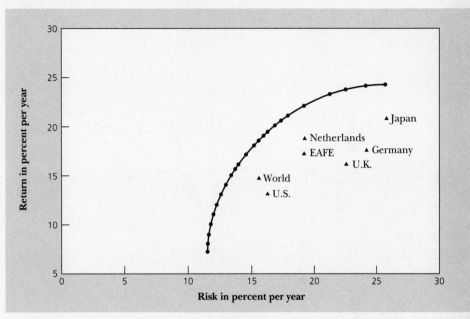

risk. An international stock portfolio with the same risk level as the purely U.S. stock portfolio (16.2% per year) would achieve an annualized total return above 19%, compared with 13.3% for the U.S. portfolio.

Can bonds help improve the risk-adjusted performance of globally diversified portfolios? The question addressed here is not whether one should prefer portfolios made up solely of bonds or solely of stocks but whether bonds should be added to a stock portfolio in a global investment strategy. Exhibit 4.15 gives the efficient frontier for a global asset allocation allowing for bonds and stocks, foreign and domestic. No investment constraints other than no short-selling are applied; no currency hedging is included. To keep the figure readable, we did not plot individual bond and stock markets but only the U.S. bond and stock indexes, as well as the world stock index. Their relative positions are consistent with theory. U.S. bonds have a lower risk and a lower return. Over the long run, riskier stock investments are compensated for by a risk premium. The U.S. equity risk premium has been around 0.5% per annum over the past 10 years. This is low compared with the risk premium observed over the past 20 years (around 2% per annum) or over longer time periods. As noted, world stocks have had less risk and a better return than U.S. stocks. The global asset allocations on the efficient frontier

Efficient Frontier for Stocks and Bonds (U.S. dollar, 1980–1990)

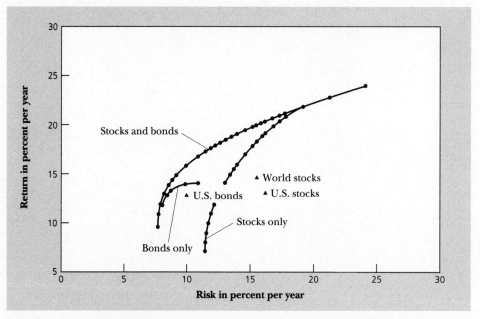

strongly dominate U.S. investments. The global efficient asset allocation with a return equal to that of the U.S. stock market (13.3% annualized) has a risk equal to only one third that of the U.S. stock market. Conversely a global efficient allocation with the same risk as the U.S. stock market outperforms the U.S. stock market by 8% per annum. Similarly, any domestic U.S. stock/bond strategy is strongly dominated by a global stock/bond strategy. A domestic portfolio of U.S. stocks and bonds tends to have half the return of that on an international efficient allocation with the same risk level.

Exhibit 4.15 also shows the efficient international frontier for stocks only (same as Exh. 4.14), as well as the efficient international frontier for bonds only. Clearly, stocks offer a strong contribution to a bond portfolio in terms of risk/return trade-off; the bond-only efficient frontier is also dominated by a global strategy. A theoretician might regard Exh. 4.15 as a simple test of the efficiency of the world market portfolio. Without resorting to sophisticated econometric procedures, this figure indicates, at least visually, that the world stock index is far from efficient when the universe of all national stock markets is included.

Exhibit 4.16 shows the efficient frontiers for Japanese, German, and British investors. All calculations are performed in the respective national currency. The

EXHIBIT 4.16

Efficient Frontiers for Non-U.S. Investors

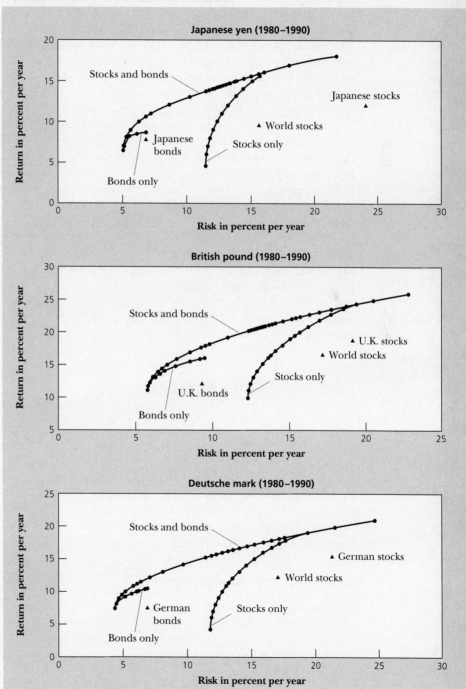

return on the world stock index is simply the average, market capitalization–weighted return on all stock markets. Hence the world index underperforms some national markets and overperforms others. However, risks get diversified away in the world index, and its volatility is always less than that of any national stock market. The conclusions about optimal international asset allocations derived earlier for an American investor also apply to the other nationalities. Global asset allocation seems to offer large potential in terms of risk-adjusted performance for investors of all major countries. This conclusion emerges from a study of the past 10 years, but a similar result would hold for a longer time period. The asset allocation strategy was kept constant over the whole period; performance could be further improved by allowing periodic revisions of the allocation over time. Also, Odier and Solnik ruled out any form of currency hedging; systematic or selective currency hedging could have further improved the risk profile.[17]

The potential profits are large but require some forecasting skills. A major question is how much of the potential can be achieved through superior management skills. Even if only 20% of the profits could be reaped, international asset allocation would seem to be very valuable in risk/return terms. It is, of course, quite difficult to know in advance what these optimal asset allocations will be. Therefore all we can conclude is that the opportunities for increased risk-adjusted returns are sizable and that the performance gap between optimal international asset allocations and a simple index fund is potentially quite wide. Whether any money manager has sufficient expertise to realize most, or even part, of this performance differential is yet another question.

Constraints and Misconceptions

The relative size of foreign capital markets would justify extensive foreign investment by investors of any nationality. Empirical studies build a strong case for international diversification. However, international investment, although rapidly growing, is still not widespread in several countries and certainly is far from what it should be according to the world market portfolio weights. This conservative behavior may be explained by the prevalence of misconceptions and constraints. Although some barriers to foreign investment exist, they are usually exaggerated. We will now address the often-mentioned barriers to foreign investment.

Familiarity with Foreign Markets

A major impediment to foreign investment is cultural differences. Investors are often unfamiliar with foreign cultures and markets. They feel uneasy about the way business is done in other countries: the trading procedures, the way reports are presented, different languages, different time zones, and so on. Because of these familiarity and communication problems, institutional investors often prefer to do their foreign trades through domestic brokers. Many investors, especially Americans, feel more comfortable staying at home with local markets, even though this is a myopic and nonprofitable attitude. Foreign markets are perceived as more risky simply because they are unfamiliar.

It is clearly worth the effort to break this psychological barrier and invest some time in understanding foreign markets and business cultures. Corporations have understood the benefits of direct foreign investment for a long time and possess truly multinational operations. It is interesting to find numerous private corporations that are very international on their corporation side but very parochial on their pension plan. Again, the argument is not that one should go international because overseas is better than home but rather that international investment is part of a global strategy of improving the risk-return trade-off.

Regulations

In some countries regulations constrain the amount of foreign investment that can be undertaken by local investors. At some times and in some countries investors are prohibited from investing abroad for capital or currency control purposes. Investors in some European countries have had to use a special "financial" exchange rate to invest abroad, called the *dollar premium* in the United Kingdom, the *devise titre* in France, and the *financial franc* in Belgium. These regulations applied to domestic investors wishing to buy foreign shares; they do not apply to foreigners investing on the domestic market. Institutional investors in most countries are often constrained on the proportion of foreign assets they can hold in their portfolios. However, there has been a slow but general worldwide relaxation of these constraints. The "prudent man" rule for U.S. pension plans allows for more extensive international diversification, and the proportion of foreign assets in U.S. pension plans is rapidly increasing, although it has not yet reached the level of U.K. or Dutch pension funds. Private pension funds have led the way toward international investment (several U.S. funds have more than 15% of their assets in foreign investments), and public funds follow the lead when their legislatures pass a "prudent man" management rule.

Other countries limit the amount of foreign ownership in their national companies. This is typically the case for emerging countries, which tend to limit foreign ownership to a maximum percentage of the capital of each firm This is also the case for some developed countries. For example, Swiss corporations tend to issue special shares to foreign owners, and these shares trade at a premium over those available solely to Swiss nationals. Again, the trend is toward a progressive removal of these constraints. For example, the European Union prohibits any ownership discrimination among its members. Such constraints are rarely found for bond investments. All governments are happy to have foreign investors subscribe to their bond issues financing their budget deficit.

Market Efficiency

A first question in market efficiency is that of liquidity. Some markets are very small; others have a large volume for many issues traded. As mentioned previously, non-American markets are similar, in terms of size and trading volume, to the U.S. stock and bond markets. U.S. institutions can easily find a few hundred foreign issues with good liquidity.

Of course, some issues on the major markets, as well as some of the smaller national markets, trade on little volume. Large institutional investors may wish to be careful and invest only a small part of their portfolios in these small-capitalization, less-liquid shares. Indeed, it may be difficult to get out of some national markets on a large scale. An excellent performance on a local index may not be transformed into a realized performance on a specific portfolio, because of the share price drop when liquidating the portfolio. This was the experience in Spain and Italy in the 1980s and suggests that one may improve liquidity by investing in a passive index portfolio of the local stock market, which by definition has the same performance as the market, whatever the liquidity problems, rather than by picking a few attractive stocks.

Another liquidity risk is the imposition of capital controls on foreign portfolio investments. Such capital control prevents the sale of a portfolio of foreign assets and the repatriation of proceeds. This has never happened on any of the major capital markets of the world; the cost of such a political decision would be very high for any government, as it would reduce its borrowing capacity on the international capital market. However, it is a definite risk for investments in some emerging countries. Such capital controls may be imposed in an extreme financial or political crisis, and international money managers carefully monitor a few high-risk countries.

Another issue in market efficiency is price manipulation. If foreign markets were too inefficient, a manager would probably not run the risk of investing in these markets to benefit the domestic speculators. As mentioned in Chapter 5, a number of studies have established that all major stock markets are nearly efficient in the usual sense. Stock prices seem close to following a random walk, and systematic inefficiencies are difficult to detect and never exist for long.

Risk Perception

Any unknown is perceived as risky; foreign capital markets are perceived as very risky by investors who are not familiar with them. But this is not a rational financial approach.

The true measure of the market risk borne by a portfolio is international market risk, and international diversification allows the elimination of all unnecessary national risks. Foreign assets might look more volatile than domestic assets, but their inclusion in a domestic portfolio will reduce, not increase, the total risk of the portfolio because of the low correlation between the various national markets. Remember that a good diversification asset is one with high volatility and low correlation with the portfolio. This phenomenon, amply demonstrated previously, runs against the intuition of some investors. But again, the net result of international diversification is the reduction of the magnitude of potential losses in any given time period. It should be stressed that a diversification of risk is not a complete insurance; diversification reduces risk but does not eliminate it. A good diversification eliminates all unnecessary risks while keeping profit opportunities intact, which is not the case with a fully hedged or insured program. The purpose is not to eliminate risk but to get rid of unnecessary risks while trying to maximize the performance. Some international investors focus solely on performance and build undiversified international portfolios; this might lead to a more risky portfolio with large potential losses. In all cases, risk should be closely monitored.

A major cause for the higher volatility of foreign assets is currency risk. As mentioned previously, currency risk should not be overstated:

- Currency risk gets partly diversified away in a well-diversified portfolio.

- Currency options and futures contracts may be used to fully or partly hedge currency risk if so desired.

- Currency risk may be desired by investors. Foreign currencies sometimes provide attractive profit opportunities to domestic investors. They also allow diversification of domestic monetary risks. All private investors and pension sponsors should worry about the real purchasing power of their assets, not their nominal performance. Since foreign goods represent a sizable part of any consumption basket, foreign currency assets allow one to hedge the local price variation of these foreign consumption goods. Equally important is the fact that one major factor of domestic risk is monetary policy uncertainty. This domestic monetary risk cannot be diversified away locally, since domestic stock and bond prices react in the same direction to news on monetary policy. On the other hand, a loose monetary policy will generally lead to a depreciation of the domestic currency and a good performance of foreign assets because of the currency component.

Costs

Costs of international investments tend to be higher than those of domestic investments. This effect is more pronounced for investors in countries where all costs tend to be very low (e.g., the United States and France). This cost has several components, which are detailed in the appendix to this chapter.

Conclusions

Altogether, foreign investment may not seem more costly for a resident from a high-cost country, such as Switzerland or the Netherlands, but it is clearly more expensive for a U.S. resident. For a U.S. investor, a ballpark estimate of the increase in total costs (management fee, commissions, custody) is on the order of

0.2 to 0.75% for stocks and 0.2% for bonds. The difference would be less for a passively managed fund. These figures are still small compared to the return-risk advantage of foreign investment, as presented in the first part of this chapter. However, they could explain why one would desire to overweigh the domestic component of the portfolio compared to the world market portfolio weights. Information and transaction costs, differential taxes, and sometimes political or transfer risk give a comparative advantage to the domestic investor on the home market. This does not imply that foreign investment should be avoided altogether.

We have seen that international diversification reduces domestic market risk and therefore improves risk-adjusted performance, even for a passive international portfolio. An active international market, currency, or security selection strategy can further improve performance.

Although European investors, and even U.S. corporations, find foreign investment routine, psychological and cultural barriers still inhibit many U.S. investors from following suit. The issue is not whether or not foreign markets systematically outperform the U.S. market but whether or not so effective a means of diversification should remain untapped. Since the benefits of foreign diversification can be achieved with only a few securities, there is no need to invest in politically risky markets or illiquid issues. The advantages of international diversification seem to exceed the costs and difficulties associated with investment in foreign markets.

Summary

1. Non-American capital markets account for more than half of the world market capitalization. The mere size of foreign markets justifies extensive international investment for the U.S. investor. This argument is even stronger for nationals of other countries.

2. Markets across the world display only limited correlation. When one national market goes down, another is likely to go up simultaneously. Their relative independence leaves ample room for risk diversification on foreign stock and bond markets.

3. Although foreign securities may sometimes look more volatile, especially because of exchange risk, their addition to a purely domestic portfolio reduces the total risk of the portfolio. This is caused by the less than perfect correlation between foreign securities and the domestic market. The same risk reduction appears both for market indexes and for small portfolios made up of only a few securities.

4. Currency risk can be hedged to reduce the total risk of a foreign portfolio. Anyway, currency risk gets partly diversified away in portfolios including assets from several countries. Currency risk is the major source of risk for cash investments; it is a significant part of the total risk of a foreign bond portfolio but only a small part of the total risk of a stock portfolio.

5. In the past U.S. investors would have improved the portfolio risk-adjusted performance by diversifying a portfolio internationally. In other words, international (U.S. plus foreign) portfolios yielded both a higher return and a lower volatility than purely domestic U.S. portfolios. Foreign bonds allow diversification of U.S. monetary policy risk without sacrificing returns.

6. Higher growth rates in foreign economies explain part of their superior performance. Differences in real growth rates are likely to persist over time.

7. Several misconceptions and constraints may explain why foreign portfolio investment is still not widespread in some countries, such as the United States. Some of these constraints are probably overstated; they should be carefully investigated and possibly relaxed so that the risk and return benefits of international diversification can be realized.

Questions and Problems

1*. The estimated volatility of a domestic asset is 15% (annualized standard deviation of returns). A foreign asset has a volatility of 18% and a correlation of 0.5 with the domestic asset. What is the volatility of a portfolio invested for 80% in the domestic asset and 20% in the foreign asset?

2*. Here are the expected returns and risks of two assets:

$$E(r_1) = 10\% \qquad \sigma_1 = 10\%$$

$$E(r_2) = 14\% \qquad \sigma_2 = 16\%$$

$$\text{Correlation} = 0.2$$

Calculate the expected return and risk of portfolios invested in the following proportions:

Asset 1	Asset 2
100%	
80%	20%
60%	40%
50%	50%
40%	60%
20%	80%
	100%

Draw all the portfolios made up of the two assets in an Expected return/Risk graph (same as in Exh. 4.12).

3. Here are the expected returns and risks of two assets:

$$E(r_1) = 10\% \qquad \sigma_1 = 16\%$$

$$E(r_2) = 14\% \qquad \sigma_2 = 16\%$$

- Assume a correlation of 0.5 and draw all the portfolios made up of the two assets in an Expected return/Risk graph (same as in Exh. 4.12).
- Same question assuming successively a correlation of –1, 0, and +1.
- Looking at the four graphs, what do you conclude about the importance of correlation in risk reduction?

4*. The annualized performance of the U.S. and EAFE stock indexes are;

$Return_{us} = 11\%$ $\sigma_{us} = 15.5\%$

$Return_{eafe} = 14.6\%$ $\sigma_{eafe} = 18.2\%$

   Correlation = 0.47

What would be the return and risk of a portfolio invested half in the U.S. market and half in the EAFE index? What if the correlation increases to 0.6?

5. The best diversification vehicle is an asset with high volatility and low correlation with the portfolio. What do you think of this statement?

6. Let's look at some numbers in Exh. 4.3. Which are the markets most (least) correlated with Germany? Can you provide some explanations?

7*. Same question as above for the United States.

8*. Let's look at Exh. 4.13. Explain the motivations for diversifying a U.S. dollar bond portfolio into foreign currency bonds.

9. In 1994 the United States was experiencing a fairly strong economic recovery, ahead of other nations. Fears of an overheating economy led to sudden inflationary fears for the next few years. Would you expect U.S. interest rates to rise or drop? Would you expect the dollar to depreciate or appreciate? Would you expect a foreign bond portfolio to be a good investment compared to a U.S. dollar portfolio under that scenario?

10. Try to find some reasons why
- stock and bond markets should be strongly correlated across the world and
- stock and bond markets should be weakly correlated.

11. It is often claimed that financial markets are getting increasingly integrated worldwide. Advance some reasons for this trend. Also try to explain the rapid growth in equity markets.

12. Let's look at Exh. 4.9. Take the difference between the figures reported in columns 5 and 6 (total risk and domestic risk) for stock or bond investments. Why is this difference not equal to the figure reported in column 5 for cash investments?

13*. Let's look at Exh. 4.9. The domestic volatility of the German stock market (in DM) is 18%. The volatility of the Deutsche mark against the U.S. dollar is 12%. What would be the dollar volatility of the German market for a U.S. investor if the correlation between the stock market returns and exchange rate movements were zero? Compare to the figure reported in Exh. 4.9 and conclude about the correlation between the two types of risk.

14. Let's look at Exh. 4.9. The domestic volatility of the German bond market (in DM) is 5.8%. The volatility of the Deutsche mark against the U.S. dollar is 12%. What would be the dollar volatility of the German market for a U.S. investor if the correlation between the bond market returns and exchange rate movements were zero? Compare to the figure reported in Exh. 4.9 and conclude about the correlation between the two types of risk. What can explain this correlation?

15. Here are some statements heard recently at a conference for institutional investors:

    (A German national): "My money manager knows the German firms very well; why should I bother to invest in French and American shares? I am not familiar with their names or their operations, and I will have to pay much higher costs to buy them."

    (A French national): "Why should I buy German and American shares? The foreign brokers will give preferential treatments to their domestic clients, and I am going to get a lousy deal in terms of prices and costs. Furthermore, I cannot read the financial statements of these companies, as they are written in German or English, and with different accounting methods."

    (An American national): "I cannot even pronounce the names of these foreign companies; how could I defend investing abroad in front of my board of trustees? By the way, what is the capital of Switzerland: Geneva or Zurich?"

    How would you try to convince these people if you were the marketing representative of a big international money manager?

16. *Project*: Take monthly values of the stock indexes of a selected group of developed and emerging stock markets over a period of 10 years.

    - Calculate the correlation of returns, in local currency, among them.

    - Break the period into two five-year subperiods and compare the calculated correlations over the two subperiods.

    - Multiply the stock prices by the exchange rate and calculate the correlation of U.S. dollar returns. Do the figures change dramatically for developed markets? Do the figures change dramatically for emerging markets?

    - Focus on emerging markets experiencing high inflation. Why is it important to perform the calculations using a single base currency when one looks at countries with high inflation from a foreign viewpoint?

Notes

1. The terminology varies across countries. Americans use the word "international" to refer to non-American investments and "global" to refer to American plus non-American investments. Other English-speaking nationals tend to use the word "foreign" to refer to nondomestic investments and "international" to refer to domestic plus foreign investments.

2. Another $2 trillion of pension assets are found in the rest of the world. However, this can be a conservative estimate, depending on the definition of what constitutes a pension fund, especially in countries like Japan.

3. Details on the geographical breakdown of the world market capitalization are provided in Chapter 6. Emerging markets are detailed in Chapter 8.

4. A correlation coefficient between two random variables lies between −1.0 and + 1.0. A coefficient of +1.0 means that the two markets go up and down in exact phase, whereas a coefficient of −1.0 means that they are exactly countercyclical. By way of illustration, two industry indexes on the same national market typically have a correlation of approximately 0.8.

5. Tests of stability of international correlation coefficients and their implications may be found in Jorion (1985); Kaplanis (1988); and Longin and Solnik (1995).

6. An R^2 of 13% may be interpreted as follows: Thirteen percent of the German stock price movements are the result of influences common to the U.S. stock market. In other words, 87% of the price movements are independent.

7. Europe and America, but not Asia, change time during the summer (daylight savings time in the United States), but not on the same date. Hence the time difference between Europe and the United States generally increases by one hour during a few weeks in the year.

8. See Lau and Diltz (1994); Hamao, Masulis, and Ng (1990); and Lin, Engle, and Ito (1994). Another issue is whether an increase in volatility of one national market spills over to another. The studies above find some weak evidence of volatility spillover between stock markets.

9. See Kaplanis (1988); Erb, Harvey, and Viskanta (1994); and Longin and Solnik (1995).

10. See Bertero and Mayer (1987); King and Wadhwani (1990); King, Sentana, and Wadhwani (1994); and Longin and Solnik (1995).

11. Remember that the standard deviation of returns is the simplest statistical measure of volatility of a market or an asset. It is traditionally used to indicate the risk of a market or an asset. The square of the standard deviation is the variance.

12. The bottom part of Exh. 4.9 gives the return and risk of investments in short-term (three-month) deposits denominated in the major currencies. The annual volatility of returns on such investments is caused mostly by exchange rate volatility. Hence the standard deviation of exchange rates, against the U.S. dollar, can be approximated by the figures given in column 5 for cash investments.

13. The total performance includes capital gains, dividends, and currency gains. All returns are measured before taxes. Many countries impose a withholding tax, generally 15%, on dividends paid by local firms to foreign investors. Part of the withholding taxes on dividends might be lost by a nontaxable investor. In the extreme case in which no withholding taxes could be recovered by an American investor, the annual return on the world stock index would be lowered by less than 0.30% per year. As explained in Chapter 6, international tax treaties generally allow a foreign investor to claim the tax withheld as a tax credit at home or the tax can be reclaimed abroad after submitting a tax reclaim. Withholding taxes have been removed on most bond markets.

14. See *Forbes*, January 1984.

15. This section draws heavily on P. Odier and B. Solnik, "Lessons for International Asset Allocation," *Financial Analysts Journal*, March/April 1993. Adapted, with permission, from *Financial Analysts Journal*, March/April 1993. Copyright 1993, Association for Investment Management and Research, Charlottesville, VA. All rights reserved.

16. The calculation of the efficient frontier is based on mean returns and covariances over the 10 years 1980–90. No short-selling or currency hedging was used. Exhibit 4.14 restricts the investment universe to the 15 largest stock markets; no bond investments were made, but no maximum constraint on foreign investments was set.

17. See Jorion (1989); Solnik (1993); and Glen and Jorion (1993).

Bibliography

Adler, M., and Dumas, B. "International Portfolio Choice and Corporation Finance: A Synthesis," *Journal of Finance*, June 1983.

Barnett, G., and Rosenberg, M. "International Diversification in Bonds," *Prudential International Fixed Income Investment Strategy*, Second Quarter 1983.

Berryessa, N., and Kirzner, E. *Global Investing: The Templeton Way*, Homewood, IL: Dow Jones–Irwin, 1988.

Bertero, E., and Mayer, C. "Structure and Performance: Global Interdependence of Stock Markets around the Crash of October 1987," *European Economic Review*, December 1990.

Chollerton, K., Pieraerts, P., and Solnik, B. "Why Invest into Foreign Currency Bonds?" *Journal of Portfolio Management*, Summer 1986.

Erb, C.B., Harvey, C.R., and Viskanta, T.E. "Forecasting International Correlations," *Financial Analysts Journal*, November/December 1994.

Eun, C., and Resnick, B. "Estimating the Correlation Structure of International Share Prices," *Journal of Finance*, December 1984.

Glen, J., and Jorion, P. "Currency Hedging for International Portfolios," *Journal of Finance*, December 1993.

Hamao, Y., Masulis, R.W., and Ng, V. "Correlations in Price Changes and Volatility across International Stock Markets," *Review of Financial Studies*, May 1990.

Hanna, J. "Why Americans Should Have Diversified," *Euromoney*, March 1980.

Ibbotson, R., and Brinson, G. *Global Investing*, New York: McGraw-Hill, 1993.

Ibbotson, R., Siegel, L., and Love, K. "World Wealth: Market Values and Returns," *Journal of Portfolio Management*, Fall 1985.

Jorion, P. "Asset Allocation with Hedged and Unhedged Foreign Stocks and Bonds," *The Journal of Portfolio Management*, Summer 1989.

———. "International Portfolio Diversification with Estimation Risk," *Journal of Business*, July 1985.

Kaplanis, E. "Stability and Forecasting of the Comovement Measures of International Stock Market Returns," *Journal of International Money and Finance*, March 1988.

King, M., and Wadhwani, S. "Transmission of Volatility between Stock Markets," *Review of Financial Studies*, 3 May 1990.

King, M., Sentana, E., and Wadhwani, S. "Volatility and Links between National Stock Markets," *Econometrics*, July 1994.

Lau, S.T., and Diltz, J.D. "Stock Returns and the Transfer of Information between the New York and Tokyo Stock Exchanges," *Journal of International Money and Finance*, April 1994.

Lessard, D.R. "International Portfolio Diversification: A Multivariate Analysis for a Group of Latin-American Countries," *Journal of Finance*, June 1973.

Levy, H., and Lerman, Z. "The benefits of International Diversification of Bonds," *Financial Analysts Journal*, September/October 1988.

Levy, H., and Sarnat, M. "International Diversification of Investment Portfolios," *American Economic Review*, September 1970.

Lin, W.L., Engle, R.F., and Ito, T. "Do Bulls and Bears Move across Borders? International Transmission of Stock Returns and Volatility," *Review of Financial Studies*, Fall 1994.

Longin, F., and Solnik, B. "Is the International Correlation of Equity Returns Constant: 1960–1990?" *Journal of International Money and Finance*, February 1995.

Maldonado, R., and Saunders, A. "International Portfolio Diversification and the Intertemporal Stability of International Stock Market Relationships," *Financial Management*, Autumn 1981.

Odier, P., and Solnik, B. "Lessons for International Asset Allocation," *Financial Analysts Journal*, March/April 1993.

Rhee, S.G., and Chang, R.P., eds. *Pacific-Basin Capital Market Research*, Amsterdam: North-Holland, 1990.

Roll, R. "The International Crash of October 1987," *Financial Analysts Journal*, September/October 1988.

Solnik, B. "Why Not Diversify Internationally Rather than Domestically?" *Financial Analysts Journal*, July/August 1974.

———. *Predictable Time-Varying Components of International Asset Returns*, Charlottesville, VA: The Research Foundation of the Institute of Chartered Financial Analysts, August 1993.

———. *Fundamental Considerations in Cross-Border Investments: The European View*, Charlottesville, VA: The Research Foundation of the Institute of Chartered Financial Analysts, 1994.

Solnik, B., and Noetzlin, B. "Optimal International Asset Allocation," *Journal of Portfolio Management*, Fall 1982.

Susmel, R., and Engle, R.F. "Hourly Volatility Spillovers between International Equity Markets," *Journal of International Money and Finance*, February 1994.

Tapley, M., ed. *International Portfolio Management*, London: Euromoney Publications, 1986.

Vertin, J., ed. *International Equity Investing*, Homewood, IL: Dow Jones–Irwin, 1984.

Chapter 4: Appendix
Costs in International Investment

Transaction Costs

It is difficult to calculate the average transaction cost on a typical trade, given the many ways a commission is charged (bid-ask spread, variable schedule, negotiable commissions). However, brokerage commissions on stocks tend to be low in the United States (typically 0.10% for large transactions) and higher in foreign countries (ranging from 0.10% to above 1.0%). In some countries commissions are fixed, and a stamp tax applies. However, the deregulation of capital markets is lowering these commissions. For example, they became negotiable for large trades in France in 1985, and "the big bang" in London drastically reduced the commissions charged in 1986. Commissions are detailed in Chapter 6.

It is even more difficult to quote a so-called average commission for bonds. On most of the major bond markets (including the Eurobond market), prices are quoted net, so that the commissions have to be inferred from the bid-ask spread, which depends on the volume of transactions on a specific bond. In general, commissions on bonds tend to be very low on all markets.

Because of poor liquidity, a given transaction may have an impact on the market price. Several U.S. studies have estimated the market price impact of a typical stock trade as a function of its size. Studies for other markets come up with conflicting estimates of the market impact of a transaction (see Chapter 6). The lower the average liquidity (turnover) in the market for shares, the higher the market impact.

Custody Costs

International custody costs tend to be higher for international investment because here one engages in a two-level custodial arrangement; a money manager generally acquires a master custodian with a network of subcustodians in every country. Higher costs are also incurred because of the necessity of a multicurrency system of accounting, reporting, and cash flow collection.

Some countries have a very inexpensive and efficient centralized custodial system with a single clearinghouse, and local costs tend to be less than in the United States. However, the need for the international network may raise the annual cost to more than 0.10% of assets.

Withholding Taxes

Withholding taxes have been progressively eliminated on bonds. Coupon hopping is a technique to avoid the taxes where they exist. In many markets regulated institutional investors (e.g., insurance companies, which in Japan, France, and Switzerland cannot treat unrealized capital gains as profit) have a demand for income, so they may want to buy bonds before the coupon date and sell them shortly after the coupon is paid. A foreign investor wanting to avoid withholding tax on the coupon can sell the bond before the coupon date and repurchase it a day later at little or no cost.[1] This is more difficult on stock markets where the institutional demand for coupon hopping is weaker, transaction costs are higher, and the gain is less, since the yield is lower on equity than on bonds.

Withholding taxes exist on most stock markets (see Chapters 6 and 9). This tax can usually be reclaimed after several months; this time lag creates an opportunity cost. In a very few cases part of the tax is completely lost, according to the tax treaty between the two countries. Alternatively, a taxable investor may claim this amount as a tax credit in his or her home country, but this is not possible for a nontaxable investor, such as a pension plan. However, the withholding tax (generally 15%) applies only to the dividend yield. For a yield of 4%, a total loss of withholding tax on common stocks would imply a 0.60% reduction in performance.

Management Fee

Fees charged by international money managers tend to be higher than those charged by domestic management. This is justified by the higher costs borne by the money managers in terms of

- international database subscription,
- data collection,
- research,
- international accounting system, and
- communication costs (international telephone, computer links, and travel).

Management fees for foreign portfolios typically run 0.10% to 0.30% higher than fees on similar domestic portfolios. Some investors believe that they can limit costs by simply buying foreign firms listed on their domestic markets (called American Depository Receipts, or ADRs, in the United States; see Chapter 6). Although this may be a practical alternative for the private investor, it is a questionable strategy for larger investors. A growing number of companies have multiple listings, but they tend to be large multinational firms that provide fewer foreign diversification benefits than a typical foreign firm. Also, the foreign share price of a company (e.g., the U.S. dollar ADR price of a French firm) is often determined by its domestic market price adjusted by the exchange rate. When a large order to buy an ADR is received, brokers will generally arbitrage between the prices in New York and the local market. This means that on most ADRs, the execution will be made at a high price compared to the domestic price (adjusted for the exchange rate). The commission seems low, but the market impact on the price tends to be very high. It is often in the best interest of a large customer to deal on the primary market, where there is the largest transaction volume for the shares. However, there are significant exceptions. Several Dutch and British companies have a very large transaction volume on U.S. markets. London is an important trading center for south African gold mining shares and for many European shares.

Appendix Notes

1. In many countries only the payment of the interest coupon is treated as income for tax purposes, so only the bondholder of record on the date of coupon payment is liable for income tax. Accrued interest is added to the bond price and treated as capital gain.

5

International Asset Pricing: Theory and Tests

*T*he case for global investment is quite convincing. A major question remains: What would happen if all investors diversified their portfolios internationally? What would be the asset prices resulting from such a market equilibrium? What type of risks should be priced in the marketplace? Should taking currency risk be rewarded, and what should be the optimal currency-hedging policy?

Answers to these questions require some theoretical market equilibrium framework. In this chapter we review the theory of international asset pricing and its empirical validation. All asset pricing theories start from the assumption that markets are efficient, and the first section is devoted to this concept. The second section reviews international asset pricing models. The last section presents some discussion of the relation between exchange rates and asset prices, a central issue in international asset pricing. This is the most theoretical chapter of this book, but attempts have been made to stress the concepts rather than the mathematical formulation.

Efficient Markets

The Concept of Market Efficiency

The notion of an efficient market is central to finance theory. In an *efficient market any new information would be immediately and fully reflected in prices.* Since all current information is already impounded in the asset price, only news, i.e., unanticipated information, could cause a change in price in the future.

Let's see why a financial market *quickly*, if not instantaneously, discounts all available information. Any new information will be immediately used by some privileged investors, who will take positions to capitalize on this news, thereby making the asset price adjust (almost) instantaneously to this piece of information. For example, a new balance of payments statistic would immediately be used by foreign exchange traders to buy or sell a currency until the foreign exchange rate reached a level considered consistent with the new information. Similarly, surprise information about a company, such as a new contract or changes in forecasted income, might be used by insiders to reap a profit until the stock price reached a level consistent with the news. The adjustment in price would be so rapid that it would not pay to buy information that has already been available to other investors. Hundreds of thousands of expert financial analysts and professional investors throughout the world search for information and make the world markets *close* to fully efficient.

In an efficient market the typical investor could consider an asset price to reflect its true *fundamental value* at all times. The notion of fundamental value is somewhat philosophical; it means that at each point in time, each asset has an intrinsic value that all investors try to discover. Since the true fundamental value is unknown, the only way to test for market efficiency is to detect whether some specific news is not yet impounded in the asset price and could therefore be used to make some abnormal profit in the future.

Testing for Market Efficiency of Individual Markets

In this section we start by a review of efficiency tests for individual national markets. Most of the tests have been performed on stock markets because there is a huge amount of information on individual firms that could be exploited to make profit in an inefficient market. Our review will therefore focus on stock markets.

Rational market traders should base their forecasts on all available information. Consider an information set Φ_t known at time t. The asset rate of return for time $t+1$ forecasted, or expected, at time t and based on this information set is usually denoted

$$E(r_{t+1}|\Phi_t). \tag{5.1}$$

Using the notations introduced in Chapter 3, the forecast error is defined as the deviation of the realized rate at time $t+1$ from the expected rate:

$$e_{t+1} = r_{t+1} - E(r_{t+1}|\Phi_t). \tag{5.2}$$

If the market is efficient, the forecast error should be uncorrelated with the information previously available at time t. Deviations from the expected value should be caused only by unpredictable news. Any information already available at time t should be reflected in the forecast and could not explain subsequent deviations from the forecast.

The various efficiency tests differ by the information set that is used in the test. To test for market efficiency, one must first specify a form of possible violation of efficiency and test for its existence. Traditionally, tests have been grouped under three categories:

- *Weak form*: Do past returns predict future returns?

- *Semistrong form*: How quickly do asset prices reflect all public information?

- *Strong form*: Do some investors have information or methods that enable them to "beat" the market, i.e., to outperform simple passive investment strategies, such as "buying the market"?

Recently Fama (1991), who suggested in 1970 the previous classification, proposed a slightly different classification of market efficiency test:

- *Return predictability*: Are returns predictable in a way that is inconsistent with market efficiency?

- *Event studies*: How quickly do asset prices reflect all public information?

- *Private information*: Do some investors have information or methods that enable them to "beat" the market?

The major difference, besides terminology, comes in the first category of tests.

Return Predictability   Traditional research in the 1960s tested whether past returns could be of some use to forecast future stock price movements, under the restrictive assumption that expected stock returns were constant over time. More recent research is more general, as the tests relax the assumption that expected returns stay constant over time. On the other hand, it becomes difficult to conclude whether a perceived predictability of return is explainable by a rational change in market expectations or by some form of market inefficiency.

Weak form tests assume that the available information is only the past realized returns: r_t, r_{t-1}, r_{t-2}, r_{t-3},.... These old tests made the additional assumption that the *expected return was constant*. They also assumed a constant variance. This amounted to a test that rates of returns were uncorrelated through time. Most tests in the 1960s and 1970s concluded that equity returns were very close to follow a *random walk*, i.e., that asset returns exhibited a very low autocorrelation for short time horizons (see Fama (1970) and an international review by Hawawini (1984). Past returns give little or no indication on the next-period return.

More recent research has focused on the autocorrelation of returns over long time horizons (a few years). Shiller (1989) and Summers (1986) suggest that asset prices are driven by *fads* or irrational *bubbles*. The prices slowly decay away from the fundamental value, so there is little autocorrelation at a short time horizon. At some point in the future they revert toward their fundamental values, and long-horizon returns exhibit strong negative autocorrelation. Some evidence of this autocorrelation structure for all major stock markets has been reported by Cutler, Poterba, and Summers (1991) and Solnik (1993). However, the conclusion that this phenomenon is driven by irrational fads or bubbles is controversial. Fama (1991) argues that this phenomenon could also be created by time variation in expected returns. Indeed, the efficient-market hypothesis never claims that expected returns on assets should be constant over time. As soon as the hypothesis of a constant mean return is relaxed, it becomes very difficult to differentiate between a phenomenon caused by time variation in expected returns and one caused by some market inefficiency.

Many authors have found that the time variation in expected returns could be predicted by a set of economic variables.[1] The most commonly cited variables are:

- the level of the interest rate

- the level of the dividend yield on equity

- the term spread (the difference between the yields on long-term bonds and one-month bills)

- the default spread (the difference between the yields on lower-grade and Aaa long-term corporate bonds)

This return predictability is usually not interpreted as evidence of market irrationality or inefficiency, for a couple of reasons. First, the time variation in expected returns is related to the various stages of the business cycle, so they can be logically explained. Second, the phenomenon seems to be common to both stocks and bonds and similar in most foreign markets. So it can hardly be interpreted as a bubble affecting some specific securities or markets.

Other deviations from the hypothesis of a constant expected return have been found. They are referred to a *seasonality in returns*, or *anomalies*, because little logical explanations have been found. For example, it has been found that stock returns tend to be different on different days of the week or different months of the year. Among the most robust return anomalies[2] found across the world are the following:

- *Day-of-the-week* effect: Lowest and negative returns tend to occur on Mondays in many national stock markets and on Tuesdays in other countries. Highest returns tend to occur on Fridays.

- *Turn-of-the-month* effect: Returns tend to be larger on the last trading day of the month. This is more pronounced in December.

- *Holiday* effect: Returns tend to be higher the day before a holiday.

- *January* effect: Monthly returns tend to be higher in January than in the other months of the year. The effect is more pronounced for shares of small firms.

- *Intraday* effect: Most of the average daily return comes at the beginning and end of the day.

These seasonal patterns in returns are anomalies in the sense that we do not have asset pricing theories to predict them. However, they do not lead to a rejection of market efficiency. The anomalies cannot be exploited to make a profit, because the bid-ask spreads are higher than the potential profit opportunities they create—see Lakonishok and Smidt (1988). Furthermore, so many possible anomalies (e.g., Friday 13th, lunar month, Super Bowl week, election month, and so on) have been tested by so many academics and practitioners that the existence of data mining is obvious. There is a serious risk that most of these anomalies are spurious and will not be robust in the future.

We have come to realize that expected returns and risks vary over time as a function of the economic and political environment. The observation that expected returns and risks are not constant is, of course, not inconsistent with market efficiency. It simply means that the task of financial analysts and portfolio managers is somewhat more complex than in an unchanging world.

Other tests of efficiency are joint tests of a theoretical asset pricing model. Some authors suggest that stock markets are too volatile to be efficient, or rather that investors are irrational.[3] Other researchers have claimed that stock markets are inefficient because they did not properly compensate for risk.[4] The econometric approach of all these studies has been extensively criticized. A test of efficient asset pricing requires a cross-sectional comparison of returns across securities; it also requires use of a presupposed asset pricing model to indicate what should drive differential returns across securities. Hence we get joint tests of two hypotheses: market efficiency and a specific asset pricing model. A brief discussion of tests of international asset pricing is provided later in this chapter.

Event Studies Events studies permit a direct look at market efficiency. One should focus on news that has a large impact on stock prices and whose exact announcement date is known. Such news can be earnings announcements or news about a merger or acquisition, for example. In an efficient market the stock price reaction should be immediate. In his 1991 review Fama concludes:

> There is a large event-study literature on issues in corporate finance. The results indicate that on average stock prices adjust quickly to information about investment decisions, dividend changes, changes in capital structure, and corporate control transactions. This evidence tilts me toward the conclusion that prices adjust efficiently to firm-specific information. (p. 1607)

Studies for non-American markets also show that stock prices quickly adjust to public information.

Private Information Another direct test of market efficiency is to study the performance of those investors and traders who are most likely to be in a position to benefit from private information not available immediately to the general investor. Researchers have looked at the performance of financial analysts' recommendations on individual stocks.[5] For example, the *Value Line Investment Survey* publishes weekly rankings of 1700 U.S. common stocks in five groups, from best investment prospect (group 1) to worst (group 5). The announcement by Value Line that a stock is changing group is associated with a market price adjustment in the day following the announcement. Hence Value Line seems to possess private information that is not yet impounded in current market prices. However, the price adjustments are generally small (around 1% on the average). Liu, Smith, and Syed (1990) have surveyed the market impact of the widely read *Wall Street Journal* column "Heard on the Street," which provides recommendations for stock investments. The market price change of the studied stocks on the publication day is around 1.7%. These studies suggest that some analysts have private information that is not yet reflected in stock prices. However, the impact on stock prices is relatively small. Except for the London market, few exhaustive studies of analysts' recommendations exist on non-American markets.

Portfolio managers could have access to private information and models that should allow them to "beat" the market. The analysis of the performance of professional portfolio managers has been the subject of a large number of studies. The general conclusion is that this performance is disappointing on all developed markets. For example, Brinson, Hood, and Beebower (1986) examined 91 large U.S. corporate pension funds and found that their performance was 1.1% per year below that of passive benchmarks. This underperformance could be explained by the management and transaction costs incurred by the pension funds. Numerous studies have shown that the performance of mutual funds was, on the average, below that of their investment objective as measured by a passive benchmark (e.g., the S&P 500 index for a U.S. common stock mutual fund). However, some studies have suggested that the performance of professional managers could be better than passive strategies.[6]

At the very least, studies of the performance of professional managers show that useful private information is not widely available among money managers, contrary to the folklore and myth that often surround them. Several firms specialize in evaluating the performance of money managers (see Chapter 16), and their conclusions are widely reported. In a very competitive world in which a large number of professional money managers compete among themselves and incur costs to do so, it is not surprising to find that the profession in the aggregate tends to underperform passive benchmarks.

Conclusions   The final word will never be said on the issue of market efficiency, leaving plenty of hope for the astute money manager or academic researcher. But all in all the general conclusion is that individual markets across the world are quite efficient, probably due to the intense competition among professional security analysts and managers in each national market. In addition, the number of foreign investors and securities firms bringing their own techniques of financial analysis has increased, helping to make the national market more efficient. Of course, the degree of efficiency is likely to vary across countries, depending on the maturity, liquidity, and degree of regulation of the markets. However, one must be aware that it is not easy to "beat" the market in any developed stock market. This observation also suggests that theoretical asset pricing models, based on the premise that markets are efficient, are useful guides to investment policy.

International Market Efficiency

Each national market is quite efficient, making it difficult to consistently outperform the local index, but the question of international market efficiency remains unanswered. Could active asset allocation among countries consistently outperform the world market index? There is less competition among countries than within a single market. So far, there is little empirical evidence on the international efficiency of national markets. The fundamental issue of international market efficiency is often viewed in terms of international market *integration* or *segmentation*. An integrated world financial market would achieve international efficiency, in the sense that arbitrage across markets would instantaneously take advantage of any new information throughout the world. For example, an international investor would not hesitate to move money from Germany to France if the investor forecasted an election result in France that would improve the competitiveness of French firms against German firms. Similarly, a portfolio manager would arbitrage an Italian chemical stock against a U.S. chemical stock, based on new information on their prospective earnings and market shares. In an efficient, integrated international market prices of all assets would be in line with their relative investment values.

It is sometimes claimed, however, that international markets are not integrated but segmented. Although each national market might be efficient, numerous factors might prevent international capital flows from taking advantage of relative mispricing among countries:

- *Psychological barriers.* Unfamiliarity with foreign markets, language, sources of information, etc., might curtail foreign investment.

- *Legal restrictions.* Institutional investors are often constrained in their foreign investments. Also, some national markets regulate foreign investment flowing into or out of the market. Foreign ownership is sometimes constrained to avoid loss of national control.

- *Transaction costs.* The costs of foreign investment are high. Access to sources of information throughout the world is costly, as are international transaction costs, management fees, and custodial services.

- *Discriminatory taxation.* Foreign investment might be more heavily taxed than domestic investment. Withholding taxes might lead to double taxation.

- *Political risks.* The political risks of foreign investment might dampen the enthusiasm for international diversification. This political transfer risk might take the form of a prohibition on repatriation of profits or capital investment from a foreign country. Although the risk is extremely small in the major markets, the associated potential loss is large.

- *Exchange risks.* Foreign investments bear the risk of the local market and the foreign exchange rate.

All these factors tend to reduce international capital flows and lead to somewhat segmented national markets. However, international integration requires only a sufficient flow of capital to make the world market efficient and to eliminate relative mispricing among countries. In many countries private and institutional investors are extensively invested abroad. All major corporations have truly multinational operations; their shares are often listed on several stock exchanges. Large corporations, as well as governments, borrow internationally and quickly take advantage of relative mispricing, thereby making the markets more efficient. The flow of foreign investment has been rapidly growing through the years; thus it does not seem that the international markets are fully segmented. The exact degree of international market efficiency is an empirical question that has not yet been answered.

Asset Pricing Theory

The Domestic Capital Asset Pricing Model

The value of an asset depends on its discounted anticipated cash flows adjusted for risk. For example, the value of a risk-free bill is equal to the repayment value of the bill discounted at the risk-free interest rate. There is a direct relationship between the price of an asset and its expected return and risk. Modern portfolio theory has proposed models of asset pricing in fully *efficient markets*. All of them attempt to determine what should be the expected return on an asset in an efficient market given the risk borne by the owner. Market equilibrium requires that the expected return be equal to the risk-free rate plus risk premia to reward the various sources of risk borne by the investor. The major challenge is to determine the relevant measures of risk, as well as the size of the associated premia.[7] The Capital Asset Pricing Model (CAPM) is the first well-known model of market equilibrium. Since the reality of the international market is extremely complex, entailing a huge number of securities and sources of uncertainties, the objective of the model is to provide a simplified view of the world so as to capture the major aspects of reality. This simplification is required to allow the formation of operational concepts.

The domestic Asset Pricing Model is built on fairly restrictive assumptions regarding investors' preferences. Many of these original assumptions can be somewhat relaxed, leading to more complex (and less operational) versions. The assumptions of the original CAPM may be recalled:

- Investors care about risk and return. They are risk-averse and prefer less risk and more expected return.

- A consensus opinion among all investors holds, and everyone agrees about the expected return and risk of all assets.

- Investors care about nominal returns, e.g., U.S. investors care about U.S. dollar returns.

- There exists a risk-free interest rate with unlimited borrowing or lending capacity at this rate.

- There are no transaction costs or taxes.

In the CAPM all investors determine their demands for each asset by a mean-variance optimization (expected-utility maximization). The demands from each investor are aggregated and set equal to the supply of assets, their market capitalization. The net supply of borrowing and lending (the risk-free asset) is assumed to be zero.

Two conclusions emerge from the domestic CAPM.

Separation Theorem   The *normative* conclusion of the domestic CAPM is that everyone should hold the same portfolio of risky assets. This portfolio of risky assets must therefore be the *market portfolio*, made up of all assets traded in proportion to their market capitalization. All investors should hold a combination of:

- the risk-free asset
- the market portfolio

Investors adjust their risk preference by putting some of their money in the risk-free asset (more risk-oriented investors will borrow, instead of lend, at the risk-free interest rate). In other words, investors need only two portfolios to design their investment strategies: a market index fund and the risk-free asset.

Risk-Pricing Relation   The *descriptive* conclusion of the CAPM is that the equilibrium expected return of an asset should be equal to the risk-free rate plus a risk premium proportional to the covariance of the asset return with the return on the market portfolio. The notation beta, β, is used to represent the ratio of the covariance between the asset and the market return to the variance of the market return; it is the measure of the sensitivity of the asset return to market movements. The risk-pricing relation of the CAPM for asset i can be written as

$$E(R_i) = R_0 + \beta_i \times RP_m, \qquad (5.3)$$

where

$E(R_i)$ is the expected return on asset i

R_0 is the risk-free interest rate

β_i is the sensitivity of asset i to market movements

RP_m is the market risk premium equal to $E(R_m)-R_0$.

Equation (5.3) describes the risk-pricing relation for all assets i. So RP_m and R_0 are constant, whereas $E(R_i)$ and β_i vary, depending on the asset i considered. The operational application of this theory is summarized in Chapter 7.

The simplifying assumptions of any theory, including the CAPM, are never verified exactly in the real world. The empirical question is whether the results are robust. A major problem mentioned by Roll (1977) is that the CAPM requires an exact identification of the market portfolio, including all investable assets. Hence a proper CAPM should include all world assets in the market portfolio, but this would require a model that accounts for a multicurrency environment.

The International Capital Asset Pricing Model

Attempts have been made to justify the use of the domestic CAPM in an international context, whereby investors in different countries use different currencies and have different consumption preferences.[8] This can be done only with the addition of two unreasonable assumptions:

- Investors throughout the world have identical consumption baskets.

- Real prices of consumption goods are identical in every country. In other words, purchasing power parity holds exactly at any point in time.

In this type of perfect world, exchange rates would simply mirror inflation differentials between two countries. Exchange rate uncertainty would simply be money illusion; it would not matter whether one used French francs or ten-dollar bills or five-dollar bills. The exchange rate would be a pure translation-accounting devise, and real exchange risk would not exist. Then the CAPM would hold, with the market portfolio being the market capitalization–weighted portfolio of all assets in the world.

However, it has been shown repeatedly that deviations from purchasing power parity are the major source of exchange rate variation (see Chapter 2). Similarly, consumption preferences differ among countries. It follows that investors will want to hedge against foreign exchange risk, which is sometimes called real currency risk or purchasing power risk.

An international CAPM (or ICAPM) can be developed under the assumption that nationals of a country care about returns and risks measured in their *home currency* (e.g., the U.S. dollar for American investors and the French franc for French investors).[9] All the assumptions of the CAPM still hold. In particular, investors can freely borrow or lend in any currency. By interest rate parity (discussed in Chapters 1 and 2), investors can therefore freely replicate forward currency contracts to hedge currency risk. It must be stressed that a dollar short-term bill that is risk-free for a U.S. investor becomes risky for a foreign investor, caring about returns in his/her currency, because of exchange risk.

As in the domestic CAPM, all investors determine their demands for each asset by a mean-variance optimization (expected-utility maximization), *using their home currency as base currency*. The demands from each investor are aggregated and set equal to the supply of assets, their market capitalization. The net supply of borrowing and lending (the risk-free asset), *in each currency*, is assumed to be zero.

Two conclusions emerge from this international CAPM.

Separation Theorem   The *normative* conclusion is that the optimal investment strategy for any investor is a combination of two portfolios: a risky portfolio common to all investors and a personalized hedge portfolio used to reduce the purchasing power risks. If there is no uncertainty about future inflation rates in any country, the personalized hedge portfolio reduces to the national risk-free asset, and a simpler separation theorem can be demonstrated.[10] All investors should hold a combination of:

- the risk-free asset in their own currency

- the world market portfolio partly hedged against currency risk

This world market portfolio, partly hedged against currency risk, is the same and only portfolio of risky assets that should be held by any investor. However, it must be stressed that the optimal currency hedge ratio need not be unitary and will generally be different for different assets and currencies.[11]

Risk-Pricing Relation The international equilibrium risk-pricing relation is more complex than in the domestic CAPM, where the expected return on any asset is simply a function of its covariance with the world market portfolio. In the presence of exchange risk, additional risk premia must be added to the risk-pricing relation to reflect the covariance of the asset with the various exchange rates (the currencies' betas). If there are $k+1$ countries, there will be k additional currency risk premia. Hence the expected return[12] on an asset is the sum of the market risk premium plus various currency risk premia:

$$E(R_i) = R_0 + \beta_{iw} \times RP_w + \gamma_{i1} \times RP_1 + \gamma_{i2}\, RP_2 + \ldots + \gamma_{ik}\, RP_k \tag{5.4}$$

where

R_0 is the risk-free interest rate

β_{iw} is the sensitivity of asset i to market movements

RP_w is the world market risk premium equal to $E(R_w) - R_0$

γ_{i1} to γ_{i1} are the sensitivities of asset i to the currencies 1 to k

RP_1 to RP_k are the risk premia on currencies 1 to k.

For an asset that is uncorrelated with the various exchange rates or that is optimally hedged against currency risk, the traditional CAPM with a single-market risk premium function of the covariance of the asset with the world market portfolio still applies. So the traditional CAPM applies only to securities or portfolios perfectly hedged against currency risk.

Equation (5.4) also applies to exchange rates. The expected return on a foreign risk-free bill is equal to the interest rate in that currency plus the expected exchange rate movement. Hence Eq. (5.4) indicates that the expected exchange rate movement should be equal to the interest differential plus a summation of risk premia. For example, the expected French franc/U.S. dollar exchange rate movement would be equal to the FF/$ interest rate differential plus risk premia linked to the covariance of the FF/$ exchange rate movements with the price movements on the market portfolio and on the various currencies.

Currency Risk Hedging

In a perfect world, with no inflation and following the assumptions described, everyone should hold a combination of domestic (risk-free) bills and of the same world market portfolio of equity hedged against currency risk. In the theoretical derivations, we assume the existence of two types of assets: equity, with a net supply equal to their market capitalization, and national bills (often called bonds by various authors), with a zero net supply for each of them. As can be seen in Chapter 1, a forward currency contract is equivalent to being short in the foreign bill (borrowing in the foreign currency) and long in the domestic bill (lending in the domestic currency). To make things simple, let's consider a risk-averse investor who holds a combination of domestic (risk-free) bills and of the common risky portfolio made up of the world market portfolio of equity and of positions in all national bills. Although the weights of each national bill in this portfolio are complex functions, it is not unreasonable to assume, for illustrative purposes, that they are negative. These negative weights in the foreign bills correspond to selling forward currency contracts, except, of course, for the domestic bill position.

Black (1989, 1990) uses this result, derived by Solnik (1974), Sercu (1980), and Adler and Dumas (1983), to suggest that there exists a "universal hedging formula" that every investor should use, independently of nationality and fairly easily estimated.[13] Indeed everyone hedges the world market portfolio with national bills, or forward currency contracts, in the same way, since everyone holds the same risky portfolio. The aggregate hedge ratio need not be unity, and Black provides a historical estimate around 0.7. Unfortunately, this "universal hedging formula" gives only the aggregate dollar amount of foreign and domestic bills used to hedge as a proportion of the total dollar value of the world market portfolio of equity. We have no indications on how to achieve such an aggregate hedge using individual forward currency contracts. We also know that these individual currency hedge ratios are complex, since they depend on such parameters as the covariance structure of assets and currency, the risk aversion of investors from various countries, and their relative wealth. As individual preferences and relative wealth are not observable, the optimal currency hedging policy cannot be deduced from market-observable data.

There are many ways to achieve a given *aggregate* hedge ratio, but only one is optimal. Another problem is that the proportion of the foreign portfolio optimally hedged with foreign currency contracts is nationality dependent. Using Black's definition, the aggregate hedge ratio is universal (the same for everyone) because it includes both *domestic* and foreign currencies. So we add to foreign currency hedges some artificial domestic currency hedge that corresponds to no physical action or forward contract. Whereas the total demand for domestic bills can always be split in two components, it does not change the fact that the proportion of foreign forward currency contracts to be used to hedge depends on nationalities.

Equally important, this nice result of a unique aggregate hedge ratio breaks down if, for theoretical or practical purposes, investors do not hold the world market portfolio. The simple fact that inflation differs across countries and varies randomly destroys the result that the hedged world market portfolio is efficient. This is not a trivial observation, since interest and currency rates are clearly linked to inflation. For all kinds of additional reasons, investors tend to underweight foreign assets relative to the world market weights. For example, in 1994 U.S. pension funds held only 10% of their holdings in foreign assets, although they represent around 70% of the world market portfolio. Even if a U.S. pension fund puts its 10% of foreign assets in a rest-of-the-world index fund, there is no theoretical ground to suggest using the same hedge ratio that should be used if the fund were invested 70% in rest-of-the-world assets. Intuitively the risk diversification benefits brought to the U.S. portfolio by the foreign assets are different in the two cases. The currency risk component may actually lower the total risk of a portfolio with only a small investment in foreign assets (say, 5%) because it provides some diversification of the U.S. monetary policy risk. For example, Jorion (1989) conducted an empirical study of optimal asset allocations for a U.S. investor. He concluded that the importance of currency hedging depends on the proportion of foreign assets held in the portfolio and states that "this question of hedging may not matter so much if the amounts invested in the foreign assets are small, in which case overall portfolio volatility is not appreciably influenced by hedging. Hedging therefore brings no particular benefits in terms of risk reduction...." (p. 54) The difference should be even more pronounced if the portfolio of foreign assets is actively managed with country weights that differ markedly from the rest-of-the-world market index.

In the very simple theoretical world described, simple aggregation results could be obtained from the fact that at equilibrium, every investor held the same market portfolio, with bills in zero net supply. International asset pricing theory cannot help us much to decide on an optimal hedging policy when investors strongly deviate from holding the world market portfolio. Hence currency hedging becomes an individual empirical decision, function of the portfolio to be hedged, and risk preferences matter.

Market Imperfections and Segmentation

The international asset pricing relation described applies to all securities only in an integrated world capital market. Financial markets are segmented if securities with the same risk characteristics but listed in two different markets have a different value.

In many countries various types of institutional investors face severe legal constraints on their international investments. This is often the case with public pension funds or insurance companies that have liabilities denominated in their national currencies and are required to invest their assets in assets denominated in the same currency. The psychological aspects are also important. Investors are much more familiar with their local financial market than with foreign markets. Hence they feel somewhat uneasy about investing their money in a remote country or an exotic currency.

If currency hedging is not available either physically or legally, the simple pricing relation breaks down. Furthermore official restrictions, fear of expropriation, discriminatory taxes, and higher investment costs will push domestic investors to underinvest in foreign assets compared to the world market portfolio. An investment is viewed as more risky and less profitable by a foreign investor than by a resident of the country in which the asset is traded. For example, a German investor might perceive French stocks as more risky and more costly than does a French investor and therefore underinvest in French shares relative to German shares. French investors might have a comparative advantage in buying French shares;

they might have better and quicker access to company information, as well as lower taxes. For example, French investors benefit from an *avoir fiscal*, a tax credit for French taxes paid by the corporation. This tax advantage is not easily transferred to foreign residents. However, French shares are still a unique diversification vehicle with good potential return for German investors. Germans will invest in French shares, but their French counterparts will invest more.

The argument might sometimes go the other way. Before a French election whose results might negatively affect all French assets, French investors might want to diversify away the most liquid part of their wealth by investing in foreign capital markets. German investors might be willing to gamble for the higher French expected return, since only a small part of their total wealth is exposed to the French election–associated risk.

The argument for international comparative advantage in imperfect markets might be firm-specific; investors might prefer foreign companies that aren't found in other places of the world, e.g., Club Méditérranée, and avoid companies that are deemed sensitive to national interests or in countries in which foreign interests might get expropriated on short notice, e.g., armament companies.

If all these impediments to international investments are of significant magnitude, buying the market is not a reasonable first-cut strategy. While it certainly does not mean that one should not have any foreign investments, the additional costs and risks of foreign investment may cause market segmentation and affect asset pricing.

International asset pricing under various forms of market segmentation, including differential taxes, has been studied, and more complex asset pricing relations have been found.[14] The risk premium has a more complex form than in the traditional Capital Asset Pricing Model. It generally depends on the form of market imperfection, the relative wealth of investors, and parameters of their utility. However, most forms of market imperfections and constraints to foreign investments cannot be incorporated easily in an equilibrium asset pricing framework. Hence their precise influence on the resulting optimal portfolio holdings cannot be easily modeled.

Tests of the International Asset Pricing Model

A brief look at investors' portfolio holdings would suggest that a major conclusion of the international asset pricing model is violated. Portfolios are strongly biased toward domestic investments. U.S. investors devote almost all of their equity portfolio to U.S. securities, although the theory would have them hold the world market portfolio. French and Poterba (1991), Cooper and Kaplanis (1994), and Tesar and Werner (1995) present evidence of a home preference in portfolio investment and fail to find satisfactory explanations for such a large bias. This does not mean that financial markets are necessarily segmented and that the theory does not provide useful and robust implications regarding the pricing of securities. The international capital market would be integrated if all securities followed the same international risk pricing relation outlined here.

Few tests of international market integration and asset pricing models have been performed so far. One problem has been the limited amount of long-term historical data available on international capital markets. Other problems are methodological and affect the testing of any CAPM, whether domestic or international. They have to do with the difficulty of exactly identifying the market portfolio and with the time-varying nature of the expected return and risk measures. The ongoing controversy regarding empirical validation of the domestic CAPM extends to the international version. Tests of the international risk pricing relation have followed various routes,[15] summarized in Dumas (1994). Additional assumptions have to be formulated, which lead to different econometric methodology. A major difference is whether the tests are *conditional* or *unconditional.* In unconditional tests one assumes that expected returns and risk measures are constant over time. This approach will not be detailed here. In conditional tests expected returns and risk measures are allowed to vary in some specified way. Chan, Karolyi, and Stulz (1992) used a GARCH representation (see Chapter 3 Appendix) of the variance/covariance matrix of the U.S. and Japanese stock markets. They do not include currency risk factors. They find no evidence that the pricing of risk differs between Japanese and U.S. equity or of market segmentation. Harvey (1991) designed a methodology that allows the risk measures to vary freely over time, while expected asset returns are assumed to vary over time as a linear function of a set of information variables; currency risk factors are not included. Dumas and Solnik (1994) extended this approach to allow for currency risk factors. Looking at the major capital markets, they find support for international asset pricing and market integration. They also find that currency risk factors are significant and reject a domestic CAPM in which the world market portfolio risk is priced.

The current empirical evidence is still fragmentary, and the results are likely to evolve as the world financial markets are increasingly liberalized and transaction costs are driven down. A summary of current research tends to support the conclusion that assets are priced in an integrated international financial market. The evidence can be somewhat different for emerging and smaller markets, in which constraints are still serious (see Chapter 8).

Security Prices and Monetary Variables

The relation between asset returns and exchange rate movements is central to international asset pricing. Chapter 3 focused on models of the exchange rate; it now seems appropriate to investigate the link between security prices and exchange rates, in theory and in practice. Because of the close relationships among inflation, interest, and exchange rates, it is useful to include in this review the influence on security prices of both *domestic* and *international* monetary variables.[16]

Domestic Monetary Variables

Equity Prices, Inflation, and Interest Rates: The Theory   Stocks are claims on cash flows generated by real assets. Traditional wisdom maintains that stocks provide a hedge against expected and unexpected inflation, but empirical studies consistently disprove this.[17]

The negative correlation between returns on equity investments and inflation has been justified by numerous ad hoc explanations, which will not be detailed here, because they are unsatisfactory. However, two well-documented theories that rely on the monetary links between inflation and real economic activity have recently been proposed. Both theories hinge on the observation that equity prices are good indicators of future changes in real economic activity. It appears that returns on stock markets satisfactorily forecast the real GNP growth rate, industrial production, corporate earnings, and employment.[18]

Fama (1981) proposes a money-demand explanation for the negative correlation between returns on equity investments and inflation. Using a traditional version of the quantity theory of money demand, he claims that lower anticipated growth rates of real activity (hence lower real returns on equities) are associated with higher inflation. Lower activity implies a decrease in demand for real balances. With a fixed money supply, this results in a relative increase in goods prices and therefore inflation.

Geske and Roll (1983) favor a money supply explanation. Their basic model holds that economic slowdowns lead to a reduction in tax revenues. With fixed expenditures, this results in an increase in a country's budget deficit, which inflationary measures are expected to finance. In other words, a drop in stock prices signals a drop in economic activity, which leads to a revision of expected inflation. They further argue that because a government will borrow to finance a deficit, the real interest rate may increase (assuming partial debt monetization). Therefore a fall in equity prices should go hand in hand with an increase in Treasury bill rates, because both expected inflation and real interest rates are seen as rising. This real-interest-rate effect is what people usually have in mind when they argue that high interest rates are bad for the economy. When interest rates rise well above inflation, corporate sales and profit margins do not keep pace with the increase in financing costs. (The scenario is somewhat different when a rise in interest rates is simply a response to an increase in inflation and therefore in sale prices and profit margins.) Conversely, a drop in the real interest rate paid by corporations should improve their operating earnings, as borrowing costs will go down in real terms. From 1991 to 1993 real U.S. short-term interest rates dropped dramatically, as can be seen in Exh. 2.2. Salomon Brothers estimated that "about 28% in the increase in S & P industrial operating earnings over the 1991–93 period was generated by falling interest expenses" (Equity Research publication, July 1994, p.2).

Equity Prices, Inflation, and Interest Rates: The Empirical Evidence

Although empirical studies on the U.S. capital market abound, fewer studies have been performed on other countries. (These studies are referenced in notes 17 and 18.) The disruption of the international monetary system in 1971 and the subsequent unpegging of foreign exchange rates gave rise to autonomous monetary policies and diverse domestic inflation rates. This means that different inflationary processes may be observed in different countries, which was theoretically not possible under the previous system of fixed exchange rates. Indeed a single theoretical model need not apply to every country if it relies, as Geske and Roll's does, on the behavior of fiscal and monetary authorities.

In a test conducted from January 1973 to December 1993, monthly real equity returns have regressed against the level and changes in nominal interest rates for each country's stock market. The results presented in Exh. 5.1 show the consistently strong negative correlation between equity returns and changes in interest rates for every country studied. The correlations between interest rate changes and a country's stock market returns are large and significant for every country. In fact, this seems to be the dominant monetary influence on all stock markets.

Separating inflationary expectations and real-rate effects is a difficult task, since there is no direct measure of real rates and expected inflation. A sophisticated

---

EXHIBIT 5.1

The Relationships Among Monthly Real Stock Returns, Interest Rates, and Changes in Interest Rates, 1973 to 1993[a]: Regression Results

Country	Interest Rate Coefficient[b]	Change in Interest Rate Coefficient[b]	$R^2(\%)$
Canada	−1.9	−21.6	9.0
	(1.1)	(4.7)	
France	−1.2	−8.2	5.6
	(1.1)	(2.4)	
Germany	−1.4	−18.0	4.4
	(1.5)	(5.5)	
Japan	−3.5	−23.5	4.4
	(1.6)	(9.5)	
Netherlands	−3.6	−6.7	4.0
	(1.4)	(4.0)	
Switzerland	−2.7	−16.4	7.6
	(1.3)	(4.2)	
U.K.	−2.3	−23.0	13.9
	(1.4)	(3.8)	
U.S.	−2.0	−14.0	9.1
	(0.9)	(3.2)	

[a]All returns have been annualized (i.e., monthly rates of returns are multiplied by 1200) to be consistent with annualized interest rate quotations. They are total returns on MSCI indexes adjusted for inflation.
[b]Standard deviations of coefficient estimates appear in parentheses.

econometric method proposed by Geske and Roll can be used.[19] The major finding is that the real-rate effect is significant, although often small, in most countries. It is greatest in countries that tend to demonetize their budget deficits, such as Japan, Germany, and Switzerland. Demonetization means that governments finance unplanned deficits by borrowing on future taxes (or later surpluses), ultimately off-setting the increases in borrowing. The real-rate effect was weak in the 1970s for the United States and the United Kingdom, which increased their money supplies mostly to finance unplanned deficits. The change in U.S. monetary policy in the 1980s shows up in the data, with a stronger real-rate effect.

Some companies might be more sensitive than others to interest rates. A rise in expected inflation and interest rates affects a company's future cash flows. It will also increase its cost of financing and its required rate of return on equity. Banks might be more sensitive to interest rate movements. For example, their portfolios of existing fixed-interest loans drop in value if interest rates rise. This could lead to a severe drop in banks' stock prices. Banks might try to manage their interest rate exposure by adjusting their liabilities or by using interest rate futures to hedge interest rate risk.

Bonds   Bond prices react negatively to a rise in interest rates; this is a technical (actuarial) relationship (shown in Chapter 10). An increase in inflationary expectations or in the real interest rate leads to an increase in interest rates and a drop in bond prices. There is a whole-term structure of interest rates, depending on the maturity of the bonds considered. A temporary rise in the short-term real interest rate might leave long-term interest rates and, therefore, bond prices unaffected. However, there is generally a negative relationship between bond prices and interest rates or inflation.

International Monetary Variables: Exchange Rates

Let us now turn to the question of whether exchange rates affect domestic asset prices, and if so, in what way and to what extent. From a practical standpoint, any investor should be concerned about the reaction of the domestic capital market to international monetary disturbances, such as exchange rate movements. The international investor who uses domestic currency to value a portfolio measures total return as the sum of returns on the assets, in local currencies, plus any currency movements; the investor bears both market and exchange risk. Setting aside considerations of portfolio diversification, the reaction of asset prices to fluctuations in asset currencies is a matter of prime concern for international investors. A major question is whether stocks and bonds provide a hedge against exchange rate movements.

Let's consider a U.S. investor holding shares of the French company Michelin and study various scenarios of the correlation of the price of Michelin stock with the French franc/U.S. dollar exchange rate. At time 0 a share of Michelin is worth 3000 francs, and one dollar is worth eight French francs (FF/$ =8.00); this means that one franc is worth one-eighth, or 0.125, dollar ($/FF = 0.125). The dollar price of Michelin is $375 (3000/8.00). Let's now assume a sudden depreciation of the French franc to 0.120 U.S. dollar ($/FF = 0.120 and FF/$ = 8.333). This means a 4% loss on the French currency for the U.S. investor. However, the price of Michelin shares may react in different fashions to this exchange rate movement:

- A zero correlation between stock returns and exchange rate movements would mean no systematic reaction to exchange rate adjustments. The immediate rate of return on Michelin shares would tend to be zero for French investors (the French franc price of Michelin does not move) and –4% for U.S. investors because of the currency translation into U.S. dollars: One share of Michelin was worth $375 (3000 × 0.125); it would now be worth $360 (3000 × 0.12).

- A positive correlation would mean that the local stock price benefits from a depreciation of the local currency. In other words, the loss on the French currency would be partly offset by a French franc capital gain on the stock price. A perfect currency hedge would be attained if the French franc price of Michelin moved up to 3125 francs. Then the return to a U.S. investor would be exactly zero, since the final dollar price of Michelin would be unchanged at $375 (3125 × 0.12).

- A negative correlation would mean that the local stock price would be negatively affected by a depreciation of the local currency. For example, Michelin might drop to $2950 with news of the franc depreciation (or go up, following a franc appreciation). The dollar return to a U.S. investor would be –5.6%, since the dollar price of Michelin moved from $375 to $354 (2950 × 0.12). In this case, foreign asset prices would compound the currency effect and might be considered a negative hedge against currency movement.

Equity Prices: The Theory   To the extent that purchasing power parity holds, i.e., if exchange rates exactly adjust to inflation differentials, exchange rate movements simply mirror relative inflation and do not add another dimension to the analysis. They have no specific influence on the economy or equity prices beyond that of domestic inflation. But virtually all studies indicate that purchasing power parity does not hold, especially since the advent of floating exchange rates. This means that real exchange rate movements (deviations from purchasing power parity) are the relevant variable to study, and the actual effect of real exchange rate movements is large compared to inflation-induced variations. As such, real currency movements may have a significant influence on domestic economies and hence on stock markets.

It might be useful to look at an individual firm to examine the influence of a real exchange appreciation. Let's consider a strong real appreciation of the U.S. dollar relative to all currencies, including the French franc, as was the case from 1984 to 1985. Typically, a U.S. tourist had great incentive to spend a vacation in France, since the dollar purchased much more in terms of accommodations and food. Conversely, Michelin tires manufactured in France were highly price competitive when exported to the United States. The 50% real appreciation of the U.S. dollar in the early 1980s meant that Michelin could lower its U.S. selling price without reducing its French franc profit margin.[20] The effect of this real dollar appreciation is the opposite for the Goodyear Tire Company; it gives them incentives for establishing plants in countries such as France, where they can benefit from lower costs. Note, however, that the importance of the exchange rate for an individual firm depends on the currency structure of its exports, imports, and financing. For example, a French firm importing U.S. typewriters and financed in U.S. dollars is badly hurt by the real dollar appreciation. An interesting analysis of the influence of a currency movement on the value of the firm is provided in Heckman (1985, 1986). She looks at the economic currency exposure of a corporation rather than its accounting exposure.

In the macroeconomic approach it is widely recognized that economic activity is a major determinant of stock market returns, so the influence of exchange rate movements on domestic economic activity may explain the relation between exchange rate movements and stock returns. Various economic theories have been proposed to explain the influence of real exchange rate movements on domestic economies.

The traditional approach can be sketched as follows: A decline in a currency's real exchange rate tends to improve competitiveness, whereas the concomitant deterioration in the terms of trade increases the cost of imports, which creates additional domestic inflation and reduces real income and, hence, domestic demand and production. The initial reduction in real GNP caused by a deterioration in the terms of trade should eventually be offset by improved international competitiveness and export demand until purchasing power parity is restored.

A simple example may help to illustrate this phenomenon. Let's assume a sudden 10% depreciation of the French franc. Let's also assume that the French trade balance (French exports minus imports) is in deficit, which it was in the early 1980s. The immediate effect of a 10% depreciation of the franc is to make current imports more expensive in terms of francs; if all imports were denominated in foreign currency, the cost of imports would immediately increase by 10%. This increase in cost has two major effects. First, the French trade balance deficit measured in francs widens. Although the franc value of exports increases somewhat because part of the export sales are contracted in foreign currency, the percentage of export denominated in foreign currency is usually smaller than that of import. Second, the rise in imported goods prices leads to an increase in the domestic price index and imports inflation. Both of these effects are bad for the French economy, and in a sense the real wealth is reduced. However, this currency depreciation makes French firms more competitive; they can lower the price of their products by 10% in terms of foreign currency without lowering the French franc income. In the long run this should help increase foreign sales and stimulate the French economy. However, if the economy is slow to improve, this cycle of events threatens to become a vicious circle: The immediate economic and trade balance worsens, leading to a further currency depreciation, which in turn may worsen domestic economic conditions, and so on.

The stock market, which immediately discounts the overall influence on the economy of an exchange rate movement, may be positively or negatively affected, depending on whether the short-term or long-term effect dominates. In late 1985 the U.S. dollar was at its highest point, well above its purchasing power parity value. The Group of Five leading industrialized nations (United States, Japan, United Kingdom, West Germany, and France) met at the Plaza Hotel and made the surprise announcement that they would coordinate their intervention policies to lower the value of the dollar on the foreign exchange market. The reaction to this news was immediate; the dollar fell by 5%, and the U.S. stock market rose by more than 1%, anticipating that the dollar depreciation would have an overall positive effect on the U.S. economy. However, in many cases a currency depreciation is not followed by this type of stock market reaction.

A money demand model has also been proposed.[21] In this model real growth in the domestic economy leads to increased demand for the domestic currency through a traditional money demand equation. This increase in currency demand induces a rise in the relative value of the domestic currency. Because domestic stock prices are strongly influenced by real growth, this model justifies a positive association between real stock returns and domestic currency appreciation.

This book does not intend to get into the controversies surrounding various international economic theories. Although the traditional trade approach suggests that a real exchange rate appreciation tends to reduce the competitiveness of the domestic economy and therefore reduce domestic activity, the money demand approach leads to the opposite effect, whereby an increase in domestic economic growth leads to a real currency appreciation.

Equity Prices: The Empirical Evidence   The empirical evidence for these theories is somewhat puzzling. All studies[22] point toward a very low correlation between stock returns and exchange rate movements. At the aggregate stock market level, little correlation exists between stock market indexes and currency movements. Exhibit 5.2 reports the sample correlation between monthly returns on equities and individual exchange rate fluctuations; each row gives the correlation coefficients between domestic stock market returns and the exchange rates of all currencies versus the domestic one. For example, 0.04 is the correlation coefficient between the U.S. market and the French franc/U.S. dollar rate; a positive coefficient means that the U.S. stock market tends to go up when the French franc appreciates (the U.S. dollar depreciates). Similarly, the U.S. stock market tends to go up when the Deutsche mark appreciates. But in both cases the correlation is very weak. On the other hand, the German stock market tends to go down when the French franc appreciates (relative to the Deutsche mark), as is indicated by a correlation coefficient of –0.02, and tends to go up when the British pound appreciates (indicated by a positive correlation coefficient of 0.06). Different national monetary policies may explain differences among countries.

EXHIBIT 5.2

Correlation Coefficient Between Stock Returns[a] and Exchange Rates, 1973–1993

Stock Market	Currency							
	Canadian dollar	French franc	Deutsche mark	Japanese yen	Dutch guilder	Swiss franc	British pound	U.S. dollar
Canada		–0.06	–0.05	–0.07	–0.05	–0.04	–0.02	–0.29
France	0.04		–0.04	0.06	–0.04	–0.05	0.01	0.00
Germany	0.07	–0.02		0.04	0.06	–0.03	0.06	0.06
Japan	–0.11	–0.15	–0.11		–0.11	–0.11	–0.07	–0.15
Netherlands	0.27	–0.02	–0.01	0.15		–0.03	0.13	0.23
Switzerland	0.19	0.15	0.10	0.11	0.17		0.17	0.16
U.K.	0.04	–0.02	–0.06	0.00	–0.05	–0.09		0.01
U.S.	0.16	0.04	0.04	–0.01	0.04	–0.04	0.00	

[a]Stock returns are total returns on MSCI indexes, measured in local currency.

It must be stressed that most correlation coefficients are very small. One usually takes the square of the correlation (the R^2) to measure the percentage of common variance. A correlation of 0.10 translates into an R^2 of 0.01, or only 1% of common variation. Exchange rate movements seem to have only a small systematic influence on stock prices, and the influence is weaker than expected. Similar conclusions have been reached in all studies. As Adler and Simon (1986) stress, foreign stock investments are poor hedges against currency movements. In other words, the dollar return on a French stock portfolio tends to follow movements in the dollar/franc exchange rate, since franc prices of French stock are affected little by exchange rate movements.

A couple of exceptions are worth mentioning. The Canadian stock market tends to go down in periods when the U.S. dollar appreciates relative to the Canadian dollar (correlation of –0.29). The observation that the U.S. dollar is the only exchange rate with a significant influence on the Canadian equity market is not surprising, given the dominant role of the United States for the Canadian economy. A common explanation is that periods of higher inflation in Canada tend to be bad for both the Canadian dollar and the Canadian stock market. On the other side, the Dutch stock market reacts favorably to an appreciation of the U.S. dollar relative to the Dutch guilder. More than 50% of the Dutch stock market capitalization is made up of three multinational firms (Royal Dutch/Shell, Unilever, and Philips). The ownership of these firms is truly international, and their shares are traded mostly in New York and London. If the dollar value of these shares remains constant, their guilder value will go up when the guilder depreciates relative to the dollar. A similar, but weaker, phenomenon can be found for the Swiss multinational firms. Although the overall relation between stock markets and exchange rate movements is very weak, these last results would suggest that the relation could be firm-specific, depending on the geographical distribution of the firm's activities, its export/import structure, and so on. This issue will be raised in Chapter 7. Although there has not been much research on this topic, most studies suggests that a firm-specific exchange rate influence on equity prices is quite weak.[23] An extract from an article in *Fortune* after the G5 meeting referred to earlier illustrates this point:

> Though they welcomed the general prospect of a weaker dollar with a brief cheer— the Dow Jones industrial average rose more than 18 points the day after the Plaza Hotel announcement—investors couldn't find much cause for excitement among individual U.S. stocks.[24]

Bonds   Since bond prices are directly linked to long-term interest rates, the story for bonds is told by the relation between changes in long-term interest rates and exchange rates. There is a mathematical relation, outlined in Chapter 10, between changes in long-term interest rates and bond returns. Bond returns are negative when interest rates rise.

In an early study Chollerton, Pieraerts, and Solnik (1986) showed that all non-U.S. bond markets tend to react negatively to a depreciation of their national currency relative to the U.S. dollar. This is confirmed in Exh. 5.3, which presents the correlation of monthly national bond returns with the exchange rate movements of various foreign currencies (relative to the home currency).

It is often stated that a rise in the national real interest rate leads to the appreciation of the home currency, because of international investment flows attracted by the higher real interest rate. Indeed the values of the U.S. dollar and U.S. interest rates tend to be positively related, so that a drop in U.S. bond prices (rise in U.S. long-term interest rates) tends to be associated with a depreciation of all

EXHIBIT 5.3

Correlation Coefficient Between Bond Returns[a] and Exchange Rates, 1973–1993

Bond Market				Currency				
	Canadian dollar	French franc	Deutsche mark	Japanese yen	Dutch guilder	Swiss franc	British pound	U.S. dollar
Canada		0.02	0.08	0.11	0.09	0.11	0.09	−0.31
France	−0.06		−0.06	0.08	−0.07	−0.18	−0.12	−0.08
Germany	−0.14	−0.10		−0.04	0.05	−0.03	−0.10	−0.19
Japan	−0.35	−0.15	−0.09		−0.11	−0.14	−0.16	−0.40
Netherlands	−0.10	−0.03	0.05	0.01		−0.08	−0.20	−0.12
Switzerland	−0.02	0.00	0.02	0.11	0.05		−0.07	−0.02
U.K.	−0.13	−0.21	−0.23	−0.05	−0.21	−0.22		−0.16
U.S.	0.16	0.18	0.21	0.18	0.22	0.17	0.15	

[a]Bond returns are total returns on Lombard Odier indexes, measured in local currency.

foreign currencies (a rise in the U.S. dollar). In Exh. 5.3 the correlation of U.S. bond returns with the dollar value of foreign currencies is positive and ranges from 0.15 to 0.22. This is consistent with the theory that a rise in the domestic interest rate supports the home currency. However, one should be careful in differentiating between an interest rate movement caused by a rise in the real rate of interest and an interest rate movement caused by changes in inflationary expectations (Fisher effect). Early in 1994 a strong U.S. economic recovery led to renewed inflationary fears. This induced simultaneously a dramatic rise in the U.S. long-term interest rate (Fisher effect) and a severe drop of the dollar against all currencies.

On the other hand, nondollar interest rates tend to be negatively related to the value of their national currencies against the U.S. dollar. As can be seen in the last column of Exh. 5.3, non-U.S. bond returns tend to be negative when the U.S. dollar rises. For example, the Japanese bond market has a correlation of –0.40 with the dollar, implying that Japanese bond prices tend to go down when the dollar appreciates against the yen (the yen drops). This phenomenon is usually explained by the exchange rate policy followed by most countries. A fall in the domestic currency induces the monetary authorities to raise real interest rates to defend the currency, and a strong domestic currency induces the authorities to ease the interest rate policy. Branson (1984) calls this exchange rate polity reaction a "leaning-against-the-wind" policy, whereby foreign monetary authorities use interest rates to stabilize the exchange rate of their home currency. For example, European governments adopted a monetary policy of high interest rates in the 1980s to slow the decline of their currencies relative to the U.S. dollar; rising interest rates led to a decline of bond prices correlated to the decline of the local currency. These correlations depend on the monetary policy adopted by a government and show the key role played by the U.S. dollar on the international monetary scene.

Concluding Remarks

To summarize, the specific influence of international variables, such as exchange rates, is weak compared to that of domestic variables, such as changes in inflationary expectations and interest rates. This may be comforting to domestic government policies in times of highly volatile exchange rates. It implies that either the effects of international monetary disturbances on domestic economic activity are weak and delayed or that markets expect governments to adopt economic and monetary countermeasures. Most of the apparent association between equity prices and currency movements seems to result from changes in domestic interest rates, which influence both variables, so that the specific influence of foreign variables is small when isolated from domestic monetary variables.The effect of foreign variables on major markets seems too small to justify extensive research by financial analysts, especially since exchange rate movements are so difficult to predict.

It should be stressed that the negative correlation between returns on equity investments and interest rates, which has been consistently observed in the United States, also applies strongly to other major stock markets. Surprisingly the same structural model seems to be at work in all countries; different coefficients depend on the country's fiscal-monetary policy mix. A more detailed study of domestic links between government policy and stock market behavior would be fruitful and rewarding for international investors.

It appears that stocks are a short-term negative hedge against inflation and climbing interest rates in all countries. Furthermore they do not correct real exchange rate movements and are therefore a bad monetary hedge. Because real currency movements are somewhat unpredictable, foreign portfolios are subject to foreign exchange, as well as domestic monetary, risks.

Summary

1. Market efficiency is an important issue in investment management. In efficient markets investors would move to passive investment strategies focusing on risk management. In inefficient markets investors would attempt to "beat" the market.

2. All major national capital markets are regarded as quite efficient. However, we have as yet less evidence on the interefficiency of these markets, i.e., on whether international mispricing is arbitraged between markets. Transaction costs, political risks, legal restrictions on foreign investment, differential taxes, and exchange risk may limit international investment. International portfolio investment is, however, extensive and rapidly growing, which should lead to greater international market integration.

3. International asset pricing models have been developed assuming efficient markets. When exchange risk can be fully hedged, i.e., if there exist forward exchange contracts in all currencies, it is shown that all investors should hold a combination of their national risk-free asset and the world market portfolio (partly) hedged against currency risk. A risk pricing relation in the CAPM spirit applies, which states that the expected return on an asset should be a linear function of risk premia on the market portfolio and on all currencies.

4. Many forms of market imperfections or the absence of exchange risk hedging possibilities can alter the previous conclusion.

5. The relation between asset returns and exchange rate movements is central to international asset pricing. In all countries equity prices react fairly strongly to domestic variables, such as interest rates. The reaction to international monetary variables, such as exchange rates, is much weaker.

6. Bond prices tend to be more strongly correlated to exchange rate movements because of the relationships between interest rates and exchange rates.

Questions and Problems

1*. Traditional weak-form tests of market efficiency look for autocorrelation of successive daily or weekly stock returns. Assume that you look at stock returns of a specific company and find that returns over two successive weeks have a correlation of 0.2. What would you do to attempt to benefit from this finding?

2. A broad-based stock market index is made up of a large numbers of issues, with many of them trading infrequently. Assume a national stock market with little trading activity. Each company is traded only every other day (half the stocks trade on even days, and the other half trade on odd days). Explain why an index calculated on the basis of last available prices would exhibit positive autocorrelation of daily returns.

3*. Do you expect that the autocorrelation in stock indexes induced by infrequent trading (see above) to be larger for narrow-based or broad-based indexes? If you were to design a futures contract on the national stock index, would you choose a narrow-based or a broad-based index as the underlying asset?

4. In several stock markets, e.g., U.S., U.K., and Switzerland, Monday returns (from Friday close to Monday close) are negative (say, –0.1% per day on the average). In other countries, e.g., France and Japan, the negative returns are of the same magnitude but show on a Tuesday (from Monday close to Tuesday close). In all countries there is an unusual positive mean return on Friday (say, +0.1% per day). The mean daily return across all days is around 0.05% per day, or 10% per year. What trading strategies would you use to take advantage of this seasonality in daily returns?

   Some potential explanations for this day-of-the-week effect are provided below; what is your opinion for each of them?

   - Corporations delay announcement of bad news until the weekend, when the market is closed.

   - Trades are settled with a five-day delay in New York, three days in Zurich, and four days in Tokyo.

   - Markets across the world are strongly correlated, but they are open at different times because of time zones (see Exh. 4.7).

   - Investors do not like to go back to work on Mondays after a nice weekend.

5*. France and Italy settle all their trades only once a month. These markets are like forward markets, with all transactions taking place during the month settled (cash payment and share delivery) on the last day of the month. What kind of seasonality in daily returns should be induced by this settlement procedure (assume that the one-month interest rate is equal to 1% per month, or 12% per year)?

6. Ireland and the U.K. settle all their trades only once every two weeks. These markets are like forward markets, with all transactions taking place during the fortnight settled (cash payment and share delivery) on the Mondays following the two-week period. What kind of seasonality in daily returns should be induced by this settlement procedure (assume that the one-month interest rate is equal to 1% per month, or 12% per year)?

7*. Paf is a small country that used to be closed to foreign stock investment. Paf nationals are prohibited from investing abroad. The one major corporation is Pafpaf Inc., whose returns are highly volatile. This volatility cannot be diversified away; hence Paf investors require a high risk premium to buy the shares. This means that the expected return is high and that the stock price is low in comparison with the expected earnings of the firm. Suddenly the government decides to allow foreigners to buy shares of Pafpaf Inc. to attract capital flows, but foreign investment remains prohibited for Paf nationals. What should happen to the share price of Pafpaf Inc.?

8. Thailand limits foreign ownership of Thai companies to a maximum percentage of all the shares issued (see, for example the article by Bailey and Jagtiani, 1994). The limit is generally 50% but can be lower for some industries or firms. Once a company has reached this limit, it starts to be traded on two different boards. Foreigners must trade on the Alien Board, but Thai investors still trade in the same share on the Main Board. Main and Alien Board shares are identical in all other respects.

   - Why does this segmentation ensure that the limit on foreign ownership is respected?

   - Shares listed on the Alien Board trade at a fairly large premium over their Main Board counterparts. Give some likely explanations.

9. Swiss corporations like to control their ownership and issue different categories of shares traded separately. All types of shares enable the owner to receive the same dividend. Registered shares are available only to Swiss investors, whereas others, bearer shares, are also available to foreigners (see, for example, the article by Stulz and Wasserfallen, 1994). Which type of shares should have the higher price? Recently Nestlé decided to remove all restrictions on foreign ownership. What do you think happened to the prices of the two types of Nestlé shares when this restriction was lifted?

10. List reasons why an international extension of the capital asset pricing model is problematic. Why would the optimal portfolio differ from the world market portfolio, as suggested by the traditional CAPM, even if the markets are fully efficient?

11. Give some intuitive explanations for the negative relation between stock returns and changes in interest rates.

12. Consider two French firms listed on the Paris stock market:

   - *Meca* manufactures engine parts in France for export, and the prices are set and paid in dollars. Production costs are mostly domestic (the labor force) and considered to follow the French inflation rate.

   - *Club* imports computers from the United States and sells them in France to compete with French products.

   What will happen to the earnings of the two companies if there is a sudden depreciation of the French franc (say, 20%)? What is the difference between the short-run effect and long-run adjustments? Would your findings be the same if the French depreciation were only a progressive adjustment to the U.S.-France inflation differential that reflected the higher French inflation rate?

13*. Consider two Australian firms listed on the Sydney stock exchange:

   - *Australia I.* Its stock return shows a consistent positive correlation with the value of the U.S. dollar. The stock price of Australia I (in Australian dollars) tends to go up when the U.S dollar appreciates relative to the Australian dollar.

- *Australia II.* Its stock return shows a consistent negative correlation with the value of the U.S. dollar. The stock price of Australia II (in Australian dollars) tends to go down when the U.S. dollar appreciates relative to the Australian dollar.

A U.S. investor wishes to buy Australian stocks but hesitates between Australia I and Australia II. She is afraid of a depreciation of the Australian dollar. Which of the two investments would offer some protection against a weak Australian dollar?

14. The two Australian firms discussed above have the same β relative to the market portfolio. Assuming that there are risk premia associated to currencies, should the equilibrium expected returns be the same on the two shares? Why?

15*. The currencies of several emerging countries depreciate at a rapid pace. Does it imply that you should not invest in their stock markets? For example, the Polish zloty went from 15,767 to 21,444 zlotys per U.S. dollar in 1993. The Polish stock market went from 1,040 to 12,439 during the same period. Guess why the zloty depreciated.

16*. Refer to the statistics given in Exh. 5.3. In 1985 a strong depreciation of the U.S. dollar was expected over the next two years. Were nondollar bonds a good investment for U.S. investors? Why?

17. As a U.S. money manager, you are asked to advise a client about investing in foreign bonds to diversify domestic inflation risk. In 1993 you fear that the strong economic recovery observed in the United States but not yet in Europe would feed inflationary anticipations in the United States. Try to build a "marketing" case for international bond diversification. You can use data from Exh. 5.3.

Notes

1. See, for example, C. Harvey, "The World Price of Covariance Risk," *Journal of Finance*, March 1991; B. Solnik, *Predictable Time-Varying Components of International Asset Returns*, Charlottesville, VA: The Research Foundation of Chartered Financial Analysts, 1993; and G. Hawawini and D. Keim, "On the Predictability of Common Stock Returns: World-wide Evidence," in R.A. Jarrow, V. Maksimovic, and W.T. Ziemba, eds., *Handbook in Operations Research and Management Science: Finance Volume*, Amsterdam: North-Holland, 1994.

2. See, for example, A. Agrawal and K. Tandon, "Anomalies or Illusions? Evidence from Stock Markets in Eighteen Countries," *Journal of International Money and Finance*, February 1994.

3. For tests of excessive volatility, see R. Shiller, *Market Volatility*, Cambridge, MA: MIT Press, 1989. For criticisms of this approach, see A. Kleidon, "Variance Bounds Tests and Stock Price Valuation Models," *Journal of Political Economy*, December 1986; and S.P. Kothari and J. Shanken, "Stock Returns and Variation in Expected Dividends: A Time-Series and Cross-Sectional Analysis," *Journal of Financial Economics*, April 1992.

4. See E. Fama and K. French, "The Cross-Section of Expected Stock Returns," *Journal of Finance*, June 1992; and a criticism in R. Jagannathan and Z. Wang, "The CAPM is Alive and Well, NBER working paper, 1994.

5. For a study of Value Line recommendations, see S.E. Stickel, "The Effect of Value Line Investment Survey Rank Changes on Common Stock Prices," *Journal of Financial Economics*, March 1985. For a study of the *Wall Street Journal's* recommendations, see P. Liu, S.D. Smith, and A.A. Syed, "Security Price Reactions to the *Wall Street Journal's* Securities Recommendations," *Journal of Financial and Quantitative Analysis*, June 1990.

6. See R.A. Ippolito, "Efficiency with Costly Information: A Study of Mutual Fund Performance, 1965–1984," *Quarterly Journal of Economics*, 1990. A detailed critique of this study is found in E.J. Elton, M.J. Gruber, S. Das, and M. Hlavka, "Efficiency with Costly Information: A Reinterpretation of Evidence on Managed Portfolios," *Review of Financial Studies*, Spring 1993.

7. See H. Levy and M. Sarnat, *Portfolio and Investment Selection: Theory and Practice*, Englewood Cliffs, NJ: Prentice Hall, 1988; E. Elton and M. Gruber, *Modern Portfolio Theory and Investment Analysis*: New York: Wiley, 1991; and W.F. Sharpe, *Investments*, Englewood Cliffs, NJ: Prentice Hall, 1991.

8. See F. Grauer, R. Litzenberger, and R. Stehle, "Sharing Rules and Equilibrium in an International Capital Market Under Uncertainty," *Journal of Financial Economics*, June 1976.

9. See B. Solnik, "An Equilibrium Model of the International Capital Market," *Journal of Economic Theory*, July/August 1974; P. Sercu, "A Generalization of the International Asset Pricing Model," *Revue de l'Association Française de Finance,* June 1980; and M. Adler and B. Dumas, "International Portfolio Choice and Corporation Finance: A Synthesis," *Journal of Finance*, June 1983.

10. It has been repeatedly observed that the variability of inflation rates is very small compared to that of exchange rates or asset returns. Therefore the assumption of using nominal returns to measure returns is quite reasonable from a practical viewpoint.

11. The hedge ratio is the proportion of the value of the portfolio (or component of a portfolio) that is currency hedged.

12. As stressed by Adler and Dumas (1983), Eq. (5.4) applies to returns measured in any base currency. For example, one could choose arbitrarily to measure all returns in U.S. dollars; then Eq. (5.4) would apply for dollar returns, and R_0 would be the U.S. risk-free rate.

13. For a critique of Black's conclusions, see M. Adler and B. Solnik, Letter to the Editor, "The Individuality of 'Universal' Hedging," *Financial Analysts Journal*, May/June 1990; M. Adler and B. Prasad, "On Universal Currency Hedges," *Journal of Financial and Quantitative Analysis*, February 1992; and B. Solnik, "Currency Hedging and Siegel's Paradox: On Black's Universal Hedging Rule," *Review of International Economics*, June 1993.

14. See Black (1974), Subrahmanyam (1975), Stappleton and Subrahmanyam (1977), Stulz (1981), Errunza and Losq (1985 and 1989), Eun and Janakiramanan (1986), and Hietla (1989).

15. See C. Cho, C. Eun, and L.W. Senbet, "International Arbitrage Pricing: An Empirical Investigation," *Journal of Finance*, June 1986; P. Jorion and E. Schwartz, "Integration

versus Segmentation in the Canadian Stock Market," *Journal of Finance*, July 1986; S. Wheatley, "Some Tests of International Equity Integration," *Journal of Financial Economics*, September 1988; M. Gultekin, B. Gultekin, and A. Penati, "Capital Controls and International Capital Market Segmentation: The Evidence from the Japanese and American Stock Markets," *Journal of Finance*, September 1989; C. Harvey, "The World Price of Covariance Risk," *Journal of Finance*, March 1991; R. Korajczyck and C. Viallet, "Equity Risk Premia and the Pricing of Foreign Exchange Risk," *Journal of International Economics*, February 1992; K.C. Chan, G.A. Karolyi, and R. Stulz, "Global Financial Markets and the Risk Premium on U.S. Equity," *Journal of Financial Economics*, October 1992; R. Bansal, D. Hsieh, and R. Viswanathan, "A New Approach to International Arbitrage Pricing," *Journal of Finance*, December 1993; and B. Dumas and B. Solnik, "The World Price of Foreign Exchange Risk," *Journal of Finance*, June 1995.

16. This section draws on B. Solnik, "Capital Markets and International Monetary Variables," *Financial Analysts Journal*, March/April 1984. Reprinted by permission.

17. See, for example, P. Cagan, "Common Stock Values and Inflation: The Historical Record of Many Countries," *Annual Report Supplement*, NBER, Cambridge, MA, 1974; E. Fama and W. Schwert, "Asset Returns and Inflation," *Journal of Financial Economics*, November 1977; B. Solnik, "The Relation Between Stock Prices and Inflationary Expectations," *Journal of Finance*, March 1983; N.B. Gultekin, "Stock Market Returns and Inflation: Evidence from Other Countries," *Journal of Finance*, March 1983. J. Boudoukh and M. Richardson, "Stocks Returns and Inflation: A Long Horizon Perspective," *American Economic Review*, December 1993, use data from 1802 to present some evidence that U.S. and U.K. stocks are a partial hedge against inflation in the very long run.

18. See also E. Fama, "Asset Returns, Expected Returns and Real Activity," *Journal of Finance*, September 1990; W. Schwert, "Stock Returns and Real Activity: A Century of Evidence," *Journal of Finance*, September 1990; G. Mandelker and K. Tandon, "Common Stock Returns, Real Activity, Money and Inflation: Some International Evidence," *Journal of Finance*, March 1983; M. Asprem, "Stock Prices, Asset Portfolios and Macroeconomic Variables in Ten European Countries," *Journal of Banking and Finance*, August 1989.

19. See R. Geske and R. Roll (1983) and B. Solnik (1983).

20. The story is only partially true, since the real dollar appreciation raises the cost of some imported goods required to manufacture tires. Eighty percent of Michelin turnover is realized outside of France, and 30% of the turnover comes from the United States.

21. See, for example, Lucas (1982).

22. See M. Adler and D. Simon, "Exchange Rate Surprises in International Portfolios," *Journal of Portfolio Management*, Winter 1986; B. Solnik, "Capital Markets and International Monetary Variables," *Financial Analysts Journal*, March/April 1984; R. Roll, "Industrial Structure and the Comparative Behavior of International Stock Market Indices," *Journal of Finance*, March 1992; M. Drummen and H. Zimmerman, "The Structure of European Stock Returns," *Financial Analysts Journal*, July-August 1992.

23. See B. Solnik and A. de Freitas, "International Factors of Security Returns," in S. Khoury and A. Ghosh, eds., *Recent Developments in International Finance and Banking*, Lexington, MA: Lexington Books, 1988; P. Jorion, "The Exchange Rate Exposure of U.S. Multinationals," *Journal of Business*, July 1980; G. Bodnar and W.M. Gentry, "Exchange Rate Exposure and Industry Characteristics: Evidence from Canada, Japan and the USA," *Journal of International Money and Finance*, February 1993; and A. Khoo, "Estimation of Foreign Exchange Exposure: An Application to Mining Companies in Australia," *Journal of International Money and Finance*, June 1994.

24. "Toppling the Dollar Could Cost a Lot," *Fortune*, October 28, 1985.

Bibliography

Adler, M., and Dumas, B. "International Portfolio Choice and Corporation Finance: A Synthesis," *Journal of Finance*, June 1983.

Adler M., and Prasad, B. "On Universal Currency Hedges," *Journal of Financial and Quantitative Analysis*, February 1992.

Adler, M., and Simon, D. "Exchange Rate Surprises in International Portfolios," *Journal of Portfolio Management*, Winter 1986.

Adler, M., and Solnik, B. Letter to the Editor, "The Individuality of 'Universal' Hedging," *Financial Analysts Journal*, May/June 1990.

Bailey, W., and Jagtiani, J. "Foreign Ownership Restrictions and Stock Prices in the Thai Capital Market," *Journal of Financial Economics*, August 1994.

Bansal, R., Hsieh D., and Visvanathan, R. "A New Approach to International Arbitrage Pricing," *Journal of Finance*, December 1993.

Berglund, T., and Liljebom, E. "Market Serial Correlation on a Small Security Market: A Note," *Journal of Finance*, December 1988.

Black, F. "International Capital Market Equilibrium with Investment Barriers," *Journal of Financial Economics*, December 1974.

———. "Universal Hedging: Optimizing Currency Risk and Reward in International Equity Portfolios," *Financial Analysts Journal*, July/August 1989.

———. "Equilibrium Exchange Rate Hedging," *Journal of Finance*, July 1990.

Branson, W.H. "Exchange Rate Policy after a Decade of Floating," in J. Bilson, and R. Marston, eds., *Exchange Rate Theory and Practice*, Chicago: University of Chicago Press, 1984.

Brinson, G.P., Hood, L.R., and Beebower, G.L. "Determinants of Portfolio Performance," *Financial Analysts Journal*, July–August 1986.

Chan, K.C., Karolyi, G.A., and Stulz, R. "Global Financial Markets and the Risk Premium on U.S. Equity," *Journal of Financial Economics*, October 1992.

Chollerton, K., Pieraerts, P., and Solnik, B. "Why Invest in Foreign Currency Bonds," *Journal of Portfolio Management*, Summer 1986.

Cooper, I., and Kaplanis, E. "Home Bias in Equity Portfolios, Inflation Hedging and International Capital Market Equilibrium," *Review of Financial Studies*, Spring 1994.

Cutler, D.M., Poterba, J., and Summers, L.H. "Speculative Dynamics," *Review of Economic Studies*, May 1991.

Dornbusch, R. *Open Economy Macroeconomics*, New York: Basic, 1980.

Dumas, B. "Partial Equilibrium versus General Equilibrium Models of the International Capital Market," in F. Van Der Ploeg, ed. *The Handbook of International Macroeconomics*, Cambridge, MA: Blackwell, 1994.

Dumas, B., and Solnik, B. "The World Price of Foreign Exchange Risk," *Journal of Finance*, June 1995.

Elton, E., and Gruber, M. *Modern Portfolio Theory and Investment Analysis*, New York: Wiley, 1991.

Errunza, V., and Losq, E. "International Asset Pricing Under Mild Segmentation: Theory and Test," *Journal of Finance*, 40, March 1985.

———. "Capital Flow Controls, International Asset Pricing and Investor's Welfare: A Multi-Country Framework," *Journal of Finance*, September 1989.

Eun, C., and Janakiramanan, S. "A Model of International Asset Pricing with a Constraint on the Foreign Equity Ownership," *Journal of Finance*, September 1986.

Fama, E. "Stock Returns, Real Activity, Inflation and Money," *American Economic Review*, September 1981.

———. "Efficient Capital Markets: A Review of Theory and Empirical Work," *Journal of Finance*, May 1970.

———. "Efficient Capital Markets II," *Journal of Finance*, December 1991.

Fama, E., and French, K. "The Cross-Section of Expected Stock Returns," *Journal of Finance*, June 1992.

French, K., and Poterba, J. "Investor Diversification and International Equity Markets," *American Economic Review*, March 1991.

Geske, R., and Roll, R. "The Fiscal and Monetary Linkage Between Stock Returns and Inflation," *Journal of Finance*, March 1983.

Harvey, C. "The World Price of Covariance Risk," *Journal of Finance*, March 1991.

Hawawini, G. *European Equity Markets: Price Behavior and Efficiency*, Monograph 1984–4, Solomon Brothers Center, New York University, 1984.

Heckman, C.R. "A Financial Model of Foreign Exchange Exposure," *Journal of International Business Studies*, Summer 1985.

Heckman, C.R. "Don't Blame Currency Values for Strategic Errors: Protecting Competitive Position by Correctly Assessing Foreign Exchange Exposure," *Midland Corporate Finance Journal*, Fall 1986.

Hietla, P.T. "Asset Pricing in Partially Segmented Markets: Evidence from the Finnish Market," *Journal of Finance*, July 1989.

Jagannathan R., and Wang, Z. "The CAPM is Alive and Well," NBER working paper, 1994.

Jorion, P. "Asset Allocation with Hedged and Unhedged Foreign Stocks and Bonds," *Journal of Portfolio Management*, Summer 1989.

Jorion, P., and Schwartz, E. "Integration Versus Segmentation in the Canadian Stock Market," *Journal of Finance*, July 1986.

Korajczyk R., and Viallet, C. "Equity Risk Premia and the Pricing of Foreign Exchange Risk," *Journal of International Economics*, February 1992.

Lakonishok, J., and Smidt, S. "Are Seasonal Anomalies Real?: A Ninety Year Perspective," *Review of Financial Studies*, 1, 1988.

Levy, H., and Sarnat, M. *Portfolio and Investment Selection*, Englewood Cliffs, NJ: Prentice Hall, 1988.

Liu P., Smith, S.D., and Syed, A.A.. "Security Price Reactions to the *Wall Street Journal* Securities Recommendations," *Journal of Financial and Quantitative Analysis*, June 1990.

Lucas, R. "Interest Rates and Currency Prices in a Two-Country World," *Journal of Monetary Economics*, November 1982.

Roll, R. "A Critique of the Asset Pricing Theory's Test: On Past and Potential Testability of the Theory," *Journal of Financial Economics*, 4, March 1977.

————. "Violations of Purchasing Power Parity and Their Implications for Efficient International Commodity Markets," in M. Sarnat, and G. Szego, eds. *International Finance and Trade*, Cambridge, MA: Ballinger, 1979.

Sercu, P. "A Generalization of the International Asset Pricing Model," *Revue de l'Association Française de Finance*, June 1980.

Sharpe, W.F. *Investments*, Englewood Cliffs, NJ: Prentice Hall, 1991.

Shiller, R. *Market Volatility*, Cambridge, MA: MIT Press, 1989.

Solnik, B. "An Equilibrium Model of the International Capital Market," *Journal of Economic Theory*, July/August 1974.

————. "Capital Markets and International Monetary Variables," *Financial Analysts Journal*, March/April 1984.

————. "Currency Hedging and Siegel's Paradox: On Black's Universal Hedging Rule," *Review of International Economics*, June 1993.

————. "The Relationship Between Stock Prices and Inflationary Expectations," *Journal of Finance*, March 1983.

————. "The Validity of the Random Walk for European Stock Prices," *Journal of Finance*, December 1973.

————. *Predictable Time-Varying Components of International Asset Returns*, Charlottesville, VA: The Research Foundation of Chartered Financial Analysts, 1993.

Solnik, B., and de Freitas, A. "International Factors of Security Returns," in S. Khoury and A. Ghosh, eds., *Recent Developments in International Finance and Banking*, Lexington, MA: Lexington Books, 1988.

Stapleton, R.C., and Subrahmanyam, M.G. "Market Imperfections, Capital Asset Equilibrium and Corporation Finance," *Journal of Finance*, 32, May 1977.

Stulz, R. "A Model of International Asset Pricing," *Journal of Financial Economics*, 9, December 1981.

————. "On the Effect of International Barriers to International Investment," *Journal of Finance*, September 1981.

————. "The Pricing of Capital Assets in an International Setting: An Introduction," *Journal of International Business Studies*, Summer 1984.

————. "International Portfolio Choice and Asset Pricing: An Integrative Survey," Unpublished working paper, Ohio State University, 1994.

Stulz, R., and Wasserfallen, W. "Foreign Equity Investment Restrictions and Shareholder Wealth Maximization: Theory and Evidence," Unpublished working paper, NBER, 1994.

Subrahmanyam, M.G. "On the Optimality of International Capital Market Integration," *Journal of Financial Economics*, August 1975.

Summers, L.H. "Does the Stock Market Rationally Reflect Fundamental Values?" *Journal of Finance*, July 1986.

Tesar, L., and Werner, I. "Home Bias and High Turnover," *Journal of International Money and Finance*, August 1995.

Wheatley, S. "Some Tests of International Equity Integration," *Journal of Financial Economics*, September 1988.

PART THREE

Stock Market Investment

6

Equity: Markets and Instruments

The financial specialist is often struck by the differences among stock market organizations across the world. Traditionally national stock markets have not only different legal and physical organizations but also different transaction and accounting methods. The international investor must have a minimum familiarity with these technical differences because they influence the price, commission, speed, and accounting of every transaction.

This chapter begins with a statistical overview of the activity of the major stock exchanges of the world. It then highlights some important differences among the markets. The move toward automation in trading raises several microstructure issues, which are addressed next. Finally, several practical aspects are discussed, including listing of foreign stocks, transaction costs, taxation, and the availability of stock indexes. Emerging markets are often treated as a different asset class; their presentation is detailed in Chapter 8.

Some Statistics

Market Size

The U.S. stock exchanges are the largest exchanges in the world. Since 1970, U.S. stocks have represented between 35% and 60% of world market capitalization. The market values of the major stock exchanges are given in Exh. 6.1. Japan has the largest market outside of the United States, with a capitalization larger than that of all the European markets combined.

It is worth noting that the U.S. capital market is very large compared to the U.S. economy. The U.S. stock market capitalization represents roughly 60% of the U.S. gross national product; the corresponding figure for France is only 30%. This difference between the United States and France has several explanations. Most U.S. firms prefer to go public,

EXHIBIT 6.1

Comparative Market Sizes of Developed Markets
Billions of U.S. dollars

Area or Country	1994	1992	1990	1988	1986	1984	1982	1980	1978	1976	1974
Europe	**3275**	**2353**	**2322**	**1860**	**1338**	**489**	**408**	**457**	**362**	**239**	**198**
United Kingdom	1145	915	882	718	440	219	182	190	118	65	38
Germany	477	326	342	241	246	78	69	71	83	54	45
France	444	333	296	224	150	40	29	53	45	28	26
Switzerland	284	195	163	148	132	43	41	46	41	22	13
Netherlands	224	130	114	86	73	31	22	25	22	17	11
Italy	177	124	148	135	141	23	20	25	10	9	12
Spain	151	95	105	87	42	12	10	16	15	18	31
Sweden	118	87	93	89	49	19	17	12	10	10	8
Belgium	84	63	65	58	36	12	8	10	12	9	8
Other countries	171	84	90	74	29	12	9	9	6	6	5
Europe as percent of world	**26%**	**25%**	**28%**	**24%**	**24%**	**17%**	**18%**	**20%**	**22%**	**17%**	**22%**
Pacific area	**4435**	**2717**	**3070**	**4104**	**1910**	**722**	**496**	**479**	**378**	**217**	**141**
Japan	3624	2331	2805	3840	1746	617	410	357	327	179	116
Australia	212	133	106	134	78	52	41	60	27	20	18
Singapore	139	75	68	43	33	27	24	24	11	6	3
Hong Kong	241	162	83	74	53	26	21	38	13	12	4
Pacific as percent of world	**35%**	**29%**	**36%**	**47%**	**34%**	**25%**	**21%**	**21%**	**23%**	**16%**	**16%**
North America	**4914**	**4243**	**3035**	**2702**	**2369**	**1709**	**1413**	**1353**	**884**	**908**	**554**
United States	4626	4023	2813	2481	2203	1593	1308	1240	817	856	510
Canada	288	220	222	221	166	116	105	113	67	52	44
U.S.A. as percent of world	**36%**	**43%**	**33%**	**29%**	**39%**	**54%**	**56%**	**54%**	**50%**	**62%**	**57%**
World	**12,640**	**9320**	**8444**	**8680**	**5642**	**2945**	**2317**	**2289**	**1625**	**1371**	**892**

Source: Morgan Stanley Capital International

whereas in France, as well as in the rest of Europe, tradition calls for maintaining private ownership as much as possible. In many European countries corporations are undercapitalized and rely heavily on bank financing. Germany, where banks assist corporations extensively, thereby reducing the need for outside equity capital, is a typical example. In Europe banks tend to provide corporations with all financial services, assisting them in both their commercial needs and their long-term debt and equity financing.

It is common for European banks to own shares of their clients. By contrast, U.S. commercial banks are prohibited by law (Glass-Stegall Act) from participating in their clients' equity. This forces U.S. companies, especially small- and medium-size ones, to go public and raise capital in the marketplace, thereby increasing the public stock market capitalization. In other countries many large firms are nationalized and therefore not listed on the capital markets. In France, for example, large portions of steel, arms manufacturing, oil, chemical, electronic, automobile, banking, insurance, and transportation industries are owned by the government.

The size of the world stock market grew steadily in the 1970s and 1980s and passed the $12 trillion mark in 1993. It has multiplied by 14 since the end of 1974. Currency movements induce changes in the total size and geographical breakdown of the world market. A drop in the value of the dollar reduces the market share of U.S. stocks; the dollar value of non-U.S. stocks increases by the amount of the dollar depreciation, assuming that the stocks' values in domestic currency do not change and that the dollar value of U.S. stocks stays constant. For example, the share of the U.S. market dropped from 55% in mid-1985 to 45% in mid-1986 because of a dramatic drop in the dollar value. The structure of the world financial market has undergone a dramatic change in the past decades. As we can see in Exh. 6.1, the share of U.S. markets has decreased from two thirds of the world market capitalization in 1972 to only one third by the early 1990s. Although the share of European markets remained constant, at around 20% to 25%, the importance of Asia grew dramatically, and its share of the world market tripled. Japan accounts for roughly 30% of the world market capitalization. This figure is somewhat inflated by the practice of cross-holding of stocks among publicly traded Japanese companies and financial institutions. McDonald (1989) conducted a detailed study of this effect (called "Mochiai") and reported that the weight of Japan in the world market portfolio at the end of 1988 should be revised from 44% to 39%.

The 1980s saw the emergence and rapid growth of stock markets in many developing countries. In Africa stock markets opened in Egypt, Morocco, and the Ivory Coast but with limited growth. The growth has been somewhat faster in Latin America, especially in Brazil or Mexico. However, the most spectacular change has been witnessed in Asia. Stock markets have rapidly grown in India, Indonesia, Malaysia, Thailand, Korea, and Taiwan. Many of these markets were closed to foreign investors but are progressively opening up. At the start of 1994, the market capitalization of Taiwan, Korea, and Thailand was, respectively, 195, 139, and 130 billions of U.S. dollars, compared to 456, 136, and 78 billions for France, Italy, and Belgium. The total capitalization of emerging markets represents around 12% of the world stock market capitalization. In addition, the transaction volume on some of these markets is very large in regard to their size. For example, Taiwan's transaction volume in 1993 was larger than that of France or Germany. A wave of liberalization and reforms took place in Eastern Europe in the early 1990s. Stock markets have opened in Hungary and Poland—countries that are moving away from communism. All these emerging countries are liberalizing their economies and quickly opening up their financial markets to foreign investment.

Transaction Volume

Another measure of the bourse activity is transaction volume. Once again New York and Tokyo have the largest share turnover, as revealed in Ex. 6.2.

Depending on market activity, these figures can vary widely from one year to the next. In fact, annual turnover as a percentage of market capitalization varies significantly over time. For example, the U.S. annual turnover as a percentage of market capitalization varied from 30% to 75% between 1974 and 1994; the same statistic ranged from 20% to 80% for France. The turnover in Japan soared in the late 1980s to surpass that of the NYSE but dropped dramatically in 1992 and 1993. Therefore comparison of national market liquidity based on this variable could lead to different conclusions if different years were observed. During any given year, Japan, Hong Kong, France, Germany, the United States, or some other country may turn out to be the most active market in proportion to its size.

EXHIBIT 6.2

Turnover on Major Developed Stock Exchanges
Billions of U.S. dollars

Stock Exchange	1993	1992	1990	1988	1986	1984	1982	1980	1978	1976	1974
United States (NYSE)	2283	1765	1071	1356	1374	756	751	381	200	164	99
Japan (First Section)	764	466	1204	2181	954	267	213	157	148	76	42
United Kingdom	418	327	151	166	133	48	43	36	20	13	15
Germany	562	429	498	174	136	30	33	15	17	10	5
Canada	137	78	68	68	57	25	29	29	11	7	6
France	168	124	115	69	56	10	12	14	11	6	5
Netherlands	66	44	40	30	30	12	10	5	5	3	2
Sweden	36	21	16	19	20	9	10	2	0.4	0.5	0.5
Australia	67	45	38	38	27	11	9	10	1	0.8	0.8
Hong Kong	133	75	35	26	15	6	5	19	6	3	2
Singapore	72	17	19	6	5	7	9	4	1	0.5	0.5
Italy	64	26	43	31	45	4	4	8	2	2	3
Belgium	11	6	9	11	7	3	3	2	1	1	1
Spain	44	42	40	28	16	3	1	2	1	3	4
Denmark	21	19	12	5	0.2	0.2	0.2	0.1	0.1	0.1	0.1
Austria	7	5	10	1	0.5	0.1	0.1	0.1	0.1	0.1	0.1
World	**4884**	**3508**	**3387**	**4211**	**2877**	**1190**	**1134**	**683**	**425**	**290**	**186**

Figures for Switzerland are not available.

Source: Morgan Stanley Capital International.

Another informative statistic is the degree of concentration of the market capitalization found in the major markets. It is important for the investor to know whether a national market is made up of a myriad of small firms or concentrated in a few large firms. Institutional investors are reluctant to invest in small firms for fear that they offer poor liquidity. Also, it is easier for the investor to track the performance of an index fund (i.e., national market capitalization weighted) if it is dominated by a few large issues. On the other hand, a market dominated by a few large firms provides fewer opportunities for risk diversification and active portfolio strategies.

As shown in Exh. 6.3., the U.S. stock exchange is a diverse market in which the top 10 firms represent less than 12% of the total market capitalization. In the United States the largest firm represents less than 2% of the capitalization for the New York Stock Exchange. At the other end of the spectrum, the top 10 Dutch multinational firms account for more than 70% of the Amsterdam Stock Exchange. Only four Dutch companies make up more than 50% of the Dutch market capitalization. It should be stressed that a large number of Japanese and European firms are on the list of the 50 largest international companies, using market capitalization as a ranking criterion.

As indicated in Chapter 7, non-U.S. companies make up the majority of the top 50 industrial or banking corporations when sales (or assets) are used as a ranking criterion. These observations suggest that there exists a large number of U.S., Japanese, and European companies offering sufficient market capitalization and liquidity even to the largest institutional investors. Similar statistics for emerging markets are discussed in Chapter 8.

Major Differences among Markets

Financial paper has long been traded in Europe, whereas trading in company shares is relatively recent. The Amsterdam Bourse is usually considered the oldest stock market. The first common stock to be publicly traded in the Netherlands was the famous East Indies Trading Company (Verenigde Oost-Indische Compagnie) in the seventeenth century.[1] In Paris a stock market was started on a bridge (Pont au Change). In London the stock market originated in a tavern; churches and open-air markets were also used as stock markets on the Continent. For example, the Amsterdam Bourse spent some time in the Oude-Kerk (Old Church) and later in the Nieuwe-Kerk (New Church). Most of these European exchanges became recognized as separate markets and were regulated around 1800. Stock exchanges in the United States and Japan are more recent creations.

Historical and cultural differences explain most of the significant differences in stock-trading practices around the world. Rather than engage in a detailed analysis of each national market, we will try to bring out the major oppositions in terms of market structures and trading procedures.

EXHIBIT 6.3

The Ten Largest Market Capitalizations and Their Share of the National Stock Market

	USD million	% of total		USD million	% of total		USD million	% of total
U.S.A.			**Switzerland**			**Singapore**		
General Electric Co.	81950	1.8	Roche Holding	46888	17.1	Singapore Telecommuni- cations	34503	26.8
Exxon Corp.	78091	1.7	Nestle	32660	11.9			
American Telephone & Telegraph Co.	70663	1.5	Schweiz Bankgesellschaft UBS	22014	8.0	OCBC Bank	6515	5.1
						Singapore Airlines	6100	4.7
			Sandoz	19195	7.0	Development Bank of Singapore	4759	3.7
Wal-Mart Stores	58320	1.3	Ciba-Geigy	18047	6.6			
Coca-Cola Co.	52569	1.1	CS Holding	12593	4.6	United Overseas Bank	4646	3.6
Philip Morris Cos.	47577	1.0	Schweiz Bankverein SBS	10405	3.8			
General Motors Corp.	40113	0.9				Keppel Corporation	3416	2.7
Merck & Co.	40035	0.9	Zurich Versicherung	8245	3.0	City Developments	3096	2.4
E.I. Du Pont de Nemours & Co.	39215	0.9	BBC Brown Boveri	7748	2.8	Fraser & Neave	2644	2.1
Procter & Gamble Co.	38604	0.8	Schweiz Ruckversicherung	5671	2.1	Singapore Press Holdings	2511	2.0
						Overseas Union Bank	2131	1.7
Total top ten	**547137**	**11.9**	**Total top ten**	**183466**	**67.0**	**Total top ten**	**70321**	**54.6**
Total stock market USD	**4608 billion**		**Total stock market USD**	**274 billion**		**Total stock market USD**	**129 billion**	
Germany			**Italy**			**Japan**		
Allianz Holding	30952	6.5	Assicurazioni Generali	20877	10.4	NTT	134496	3.9
Daimler-Benz	25028	5.3	Sip	18067	9.0	Mitsubishi Bank	75745	2.2
Siemens	24981	5.3	Stet	16852	8.4	Industrial Bank of Japan	73075	2.1
Deutsche Bank	22060	4.7	Fiat	15023	7.5			
Bayer	16089	3.4	Alleanza Assicurazioni	7294	3.6	Toyota Motor Corp.	71804	2.1
Munchener Ruckversicherung	14650	3.1	Montedison	5656	2.8	Sumitomo Bank	65483	1.9
VEBA	14238	3.0	Mediobanca	5638	2.8	Fuji Bank	64343	1.9
RWE	13798	2.9	San Paolo di Torino	5162	2.6	Sanwa Bank	61882	1.8
Hoechst	12373	2.6	Imi Istituto Mobiliare Italiano	5016	2.5	Dai-Ichi Kangyo Bank	57155	1.7
BASF	11609	2.5				Sakura Bank	44888	1.3
			Banca di Roma	4563	2.3	Nomura Securities Co.	42632	1.2
Total top ten	**185778**	**39.2**	**Total top ten**	**104148**	**51.7**	**Total top ten**	**691503**	**20.2**
Total stock market USD	**473 billion**		**Total stock market USD**	**202 billion**		**Total stock market USD**	**3431 billion**	

Source: Morgan Stanley Capital International. Reprinted with permission.

The Ten Largest Market Capitalizations and Their Share of the National Stock Market

	USD million	% of total		USD million	% of total		USD million	% of total
France			**Netherlands**			**United Kingdom**		
ELF Aquitaine	18488	4.0	Royal Dutch Petroleum Co.	59754	31.7	Shell Transport & Trading	36752	3.3
Alcatel Alsthom	17007	3.7	Unilever NV	18052	9.6	British Tele-communications	35827	3.2
Total	13035	2.8	Int'le Nederlanden Groep	11023	5.8	British Petroleum	32777	2.9
LVMH	12530	2.7	ABN-AMRO Holding	9729	5.2	HSBC Holdings	28099	2.5
Generale des Eaux	12429	2.7	Philips Electronics	9565	5.1	Glaxo Holdings	25790	2.3
L'Oreal	12307	2.7	Akzo Nobel	8434	4.5	Hanson	20880	1.9
BSN	10130	2.2	Polygram	7460	4.0	BTR	20725	1.9
Saint-Gobain	9636	2.1	Elsevier	5842	3.1	BAT Industries	20486	1.8
Carrefour	9206	2.0	Aegon	5210	2.8	British Gas	19482	1.7
Société Générale	8786	1.9	Heineken NV	5128	2.7	Marks & Spencer	18296	1.6
Total top ten	**123554**	**26.7**	**Total top ten**	**140197**	**74.3**	**Total top ten**	**259114**	**23.2**
Total stock market USD		**463 billion**	**Total stock market USD**		**189 billion**	**Total stock market USD**		**1117 billion**
Hong Kong			**Spain**			**Canada**		
Hong Kong Telecommuni-cations	21365	7.9	Endesa	12688	10.5	Seagram Co.	11167	3.9
Hutchison Whampoa	15082	5.6	Telefonica de Espana	12685	10.5	BCE Inc.	11034	3.9
Sun Hung Kai Properties	13308	4.9	Repsol	9888	8.2	Northern Telecom	7653	2.7
Hang Seng Bank	12875	4.8	Iberdrola	6522	5.4	Thomson Corp.	7393	2.6
Swire Pacific	11815	4.4	Banco de Bilbao Vizcaya	5518	4.6	American Barrick Resources	6382	2.2
China Light and Power	10564	3.9	Argentaria (Corp Bancaria)	5454	4.5	Royal Bank of Canada	6310	2.2
Cheung Kong	10524	3.9	Banco de Santander	4774	3.9	Imperial Oil	6236	2.2
Wharf Holdings	8613	3.2	Banco Central Hispano-americano	3942	3.3	Canadian Pacific Ltd.	5677	2.0
Henderson Land & Development	8057	3.0	Banco Popular Espanol	3320	2.7	Placer Dome	4847	1.7
Hongkong Land Holdings	7720	2.9	Banco Exterior de Espana	3253	2.7	Alcan Aluminum	4826	1.7
Total top ten	**119923**	**44.4**	**Total top ten**	**68044**	**56.2**	**Total top ten**	**71525**	**25.2**
Total stock market USD		**270 billion**	**Total stock market USD**		**121 billion**	**Total stock market USD**		**284 billion**

(continued on next page)

EXHIBIT 6.3 (CONTINUED)

The Ten Largest Market Capitalizations and Their Share of the National Stock Market

	USD million	% of total		USD million	% of total		USD million	% of total
Australia			**Malaysia**			**Sweden**		
Broken Hill Proprietary	20222	10.0	Tenaga Nasional	16756	9.5	Astra	12159	10.7
			Telekom Malaysia	14385	8.1	LM Ericsson	9311	8.2
News Corp.	12722	6.3	Malayan Banking	6358	3.6	ASEA	7374	6.5
National Australia Bank	11309	5.6	Resorts World	6046	3.4	Volvo	7026	6.2
			Genting	5198	2.9	Sandvik	4172	3.7
CRA	7158	3.5	Sime Darby	4045	2.3	Electrolux	3749	3.3
Westpac Banking	6077	3.0	Technology Resources Industries	3026	1.7	Pharmacia	3688	3.2
BTR NYLEX	5748	2.8				Skandinaviska Enskilda Banken	3583	3.1
Commonwealth Bank	5241	2.6	Malaysian Int'l Shipping	2701	1.5	Svenska Handelsbanken	3515	3.1
Western Mining	4747	2.4	United Engineers (Malaysia)	2375	1.3	Investor	3295	2.9
ANZ Banking Group	4582	2.3				**Total top ten**	**57872**	**51.1**
AMCOR	4198	2.1	Magnum Corp	2347	1.3	**Total stock market USD**	**114 billion**	
Total top ten	**82004**	**40.6**	**Total top ten**	**63237**	**35.8**			
Total stock market USD	**202 billion**		**Total stock market USD**	**177 billion**				

Historical Differences in Market Organization

Each stock exchange has its own unique characteristics and legal organization, but broadly speaking all exchanges are one of three market organization types:

- Public bourse
- Private bourse
- Bankers' bourse

We will briefly describe the major characteristics of these three structures and highlight specific aspects of the major representative markets where it is appropriate. To be sure, some national markets display characteristics of more than one of these structures.

Public Bourses   The public bourse market structure has its origin in the legislative work of Napoleon I, the French emperor. He designed the bourse to be a public institution, with brokers appointed by the government and enjoying a monopoly over all transactions. Brokerage firms are private, and new brokers are proposed to the state for nomination by the brokers' association. Stock exchanges organized under the authority of the state are found in the historical sphere under the influence of Napoleon I: Belgium, France, Spain, Italy, Greece, and some Latin American countries.

Before its deregulation, the Paris Bourse was a good example of a capitalistic market under the authority of the government. Until 1989 commissions were set by the Ministry of Finance, but a certain amount of regulatory authority was delegated to the association of brokers. The advantage to the brokers of this highly regulated market was that they had a monopoly. Their number was fixed, and all transactions had to legally go through them. So even for a private deal arranged by two banks, the transaction had to be registered by a broker, and a minimum commission paid. On the other hand, the commission for small trades was low compared to those of other stock markets. As in most countries, stock brokers may engage in portfolio management activities. Both bonds and stocks are traded on the bourse. Deregulation is progressively affecting all public bourses. The French brokers have progressively lost their monopoly, and their capital is now fully open to domestic and foreign financial institutions. Fixed commissions have been abolished. A similar "big bang" has taken place in Spain, Italy, and Belgium, meaning that banks are becoming brokers.

Private Bourses   Private stock exchange corporations are founded by independent members for the purpose of securities trading. Several private stock exchanges may compete within the same country, as in the United States, Japan, and Canada. In other countries, such as the United Kingdom, one leading exchange has emerged through either attrition or absorption of its competitors. Although these bourses are private, they are not free of public regulation. But the mix of self-regulation and government supervision is oriented more toward self-regulation than in the public bourses.

Private exchanges often require members to perform all of their transactions on the floor of the exchange. Commissions are usually set by the exchange and sometimes require the agreement of the public authority. They are fully or partly negotiable in most countries. Canada, Australia, South Africa, Japan, and the Far East operate private bourses that are organized according to the Anglo-American model.

Bankers' Bourses   In some countries banks are the major, or even the only, securities traders. In Germany the Banking Act grants a brokerage monopoly to banks. Bankers' bourses are found in the German sphere of influence: Austria, Switzerland, Scandinavia, and the Netherlands. (Amsterdam is to some extent a hybrid private and bankers bourse, where nonbank members are active participants. All members must deal through the exchange.)

Bankers' bourses may be either private or semipublic organizations, but their chief function is to provide a convenient place for banks to meet. Many regional bankers' bourses, in fact, have been founded by local chambers of commerce and are not even incorporated. Sometimes trading takes place directly between banks without involving the official bourse at all. Government regulation is imposed both on the bourse itself and directly on the banks.

Differences in Trading Procedures

Apart from legal structure, numerous other differences ar found in the operation of national stock markets. The most important differences are in the trading procedures.

Cash versus Forward Markets   In most markets stocks are traded on a cash basis, and transactions must be settled within a couple of days. To allow more leveraged investment, margin trading is available on many cash markets, such as those of the United States, Canada, Japan (for domestic investors), and Switzerland. In margin trading the investor borrows money (or shares) from a broker to finance a transaction. The following example illustrates how a margin purchase works.

An investor buys 100 shares of XYZ at $100 per share but not having much cash, borrows $10,000 from a broker to make the purchase. The broker holds the shares as collateral. But this collateral, or guarantee, can drop in value if there is a decline in stock prices. If XYZ's price drops to $80, the stock loses $20 per share in value, or $2000. Margin deposits of 30% (of stock value) are therefore required to guarantee that an investor will cover potential losses. The margin deposit must be increased immediately to match any decline in stock value and reconstitute the guarantee. Moreover, interest charges must be paid on the money that has been borrowed.

Margin trading is very costly compared to trading on an organized futures market, because private contracts must be arranged for each deal. This is still a cash market transaction, and delivery of the shares takes place immediately; however, a third party steps in to lend money (shares) to the buyer (seller) to honor a cash transaction commitment.

In contrast, forward stock markets provide an organized exchange for levered stock investment. Some of these forward stock markets, such as those in Rio de Janeiro and the Far East, have sprung up quite recently as competitors to old cash stock markets. But the major forward stock markets—for example, those in London and Paris—are old, established markets.

The Paris bourse illustrates how forward markets function. All major stocks are traded on a forward market (*marché à terme* or *règlement mensuel*). To simplify the clearing operations all transactions are settled at the end of the month on the settlement day. This is a periodic settlement system. Of course, a deposit is required to guarantee a position, as on most forward markets. Moreover, the transaction price is fixed at the time of the transaction and remains at this value even if the market price has changed substantially by the settlement time. Settling all accounts once a month greatly simplifies the security clearing system. But it also opens the door to short-term speculation and to frequent misconceptions on the part of foreign investors who are unfamiliar with the technique. For example, U.S. institutions sometimes credit their newly purchased French shares immediately in their portfolio accounting, even though the cash outflow occurs at the end of the month. This leads to an overvaluation of the account. If an investor insists on being paid cash for a sale, the broker will advance the transaction proceeds minus a fee corresponding to an interest charge up to the settlement date. On the Paris bourse both infrequently traded smaller issues and bonds are negotiated on a cash basis.

The British system is quite similar to the French system except that the account period is shorter. All deals are settled fortnightly, although accounts can run as long as three weeks because of public holidays. Gilts (government bonds) are traded on a cash basis. Other stock markets in both the Far East (Singapore) and Europe (Switzerland) offer the option of a more remote settlement day.

These settlement procedures allow some form of forward transaction, but they differ from the newly introduced futures contracts on financial instruments. Futures contracts on stock indexes are reviewed in Chapter 12.

Call versus Continuous Quotation   U.S. investors are accustomed to a *continuous* market, whereby transactions take place all day and *market makers* (also called *dealers*) ensure market liquidity at virtually any point in time. On the NYSE the market maker, called *specialist*, has a monopoly for a given security. In other markets the market makers compete with one another. The market maker quotes both a *bid* price (the price offered for buying the security) and an *ask* price (the price offered for selling the security). The ask price is sometimes called the *offer* price. These quotes are firm commitments by the market maker to transact at those prices for a normal transaction size. The client will turn to the market maker who provides the best quote. Of course, market makers adjust their quotes continuously to reflect supply and demand for the security as well as their own inventory. This type of market is often referred to as a *dealer market*. It is also known as a *price-driven* market (or *quote-driven* markets), because market makers publicly post their bid-ask prices that will induce orders.

In other markets and countries, however, active market makers do not exist, and the supply and demand for securities is directly confronted in an *auction market*. Because the quantities demanded and supplied are a function of the transaction price, there will exist a price that equilibrates demand and supply. In a traditional auction market liquidity requires that an asset be traded only once or a few times per day. This is known as a *call* or *fixing* market, whereby orders are batched together until the auction and are executed at a single price that equilibrates demand and supply. This auction price maximizes trade volume. Before studying the detailed mechanics used by each market to arrive at a transaction, it is useful to understand how a call auction works. This is illustrated by looking at the system used on the Paris bourse until 1990. The *criée* (call) is a good example of a tatonement process used to determine the equilibrium price on a call market.

Until the late 1980s Parisian floor brokers used to assemble when the name of a firm (e.g., Club Méditérannée) was called out at its trading post. The bourse clerk's job is to determine the equilibrium price that allows demand to equal supply. This is done through an open auction system. The clerk calls out an initial price for Club Méditérannée and writes it on a blackboard. Then brokers begin shouting how many shares they are willing to buy or sell at this price. The transactions are conducted among the floor brokers themselves. If there is still a net demand of shares at the price on the board, the clerk will write a higher price; all previous transactions are canceled, and the shouting starts again. Two major types of orders are submitted in an auction market. A *market order* implies that the customer will accept the price set in the auction, whatever the price. A *limit order* states the maximum price at which a customer is willing to buy the shares (for a purchase), or the minimum price at which the customer is willing to sell the shares (for a sale). When the clerk writes a higher price, some limit buy orders will be removed from the supply of shares, and some limit sell orders will be added to the demand for shares. The process converges more or less rapidly to an equilibrium price bringing silence. This price becomes the official opening price and applies to all transactions negotiated during that auction. Although the largest volume of transactions took place at this opening criée, other trades could periodically take place in the following hours, again on a competitive call auction basis. Stocks with smaller trading volume have their price determined once a day in an auction system but without a criée. Orders are batched by the bourse clerk and entered in a book throughout the day. At the end of the day, the clerk determines the price at which the maximum volume of transactions occur. Again, the result is a single price for all transactions. An automated trading system replaced this criée in the early 1990s.

In Frankfurt all stocks trade according to a call auction system that begins at noon. Orders are accumulated before the opening of the market and crossed at a price that maximizes the volume of trading. Stocks with a large trading volume are also traded in a continuous market with market makers, but the opening and closing prices are determined by a call auction.

In Tokyo, a call auction system, called *itayose*, is used to establish prices at the start of the morning and afternoon sessions. During the sessions, a continuous auction is used to treat new orders. This auction system, called *zaraba*, is still an order-matching method and does not require the intervention of a market maker.

On the New York Stock Exchange, the opening price is determined through a call auction.

A call auction market is also known as an *order-driven* market because all traders publicly post their orders, and the transaction price is the result of the equilibrium of supply and demand.

Automation on the Major Stock Exchanges

Trading on a floor where participants noisily meet is increasingly being replaced by computerized trading. Automation allows a more efficient handling of orders, especially when there is a large number of small orders. The increase in the volume of trading pushed the need for computerized systems. This includes price quotation, order routing, and automatic order matching. Trading hours have to be extended to accommodate investors from different time zones. Although a single call auction provides an excellent liquidity at one point in time, it makes trading at other times difficult. Hence the market-making function is being developed on all call auction markets, such as Paris, Tokyo, or Frankfurt, to allow the possibility of trading throughout the day. The design of the automated systems reflects the historical and cultural heritage of the national market. The trading algorithm programmed in the computers simply automates the trading rules adopted by the stock exchange. For example, auction markets have moved to computerized continuous trading. But in the absence of market makers, they still resort to a direct confrontation of order demand and supply, with a transaction price determined by electronic auction.

Before discussing some major issues in market microstructure, we will start by a quick review of the automated systems developed by the five largest stock exchanges.[2] Technology is evolving very quickly, leading to continuous adaptations in the systems described below.

New York Stock Exchange (NYSE)   Still organized around a trading floor, the NYSE is a mixture of an auction and a dealer market. Seventeen trading posts are located on the trading floor, and all stocks are assigned to a trading post (an average of 160 different issues are traded per post). The trading post is where the specialist and clerks are posted and where floor brokers congregate, forming the *trading crowd*. Each stock is assigned to a single specialist, who acts as an auctioneer and a market maker. Orders arrive on the floor either electronically through the SuperDOT system[3] or by telephone and brokers' proprietary automated systems to the floor brokers. A member can send an order from anywhere via a SuperDOT terminal and receive report of execution of the order via the same system. Around 75% of all orders arrive via the SuperDOT system, but they tend to be small orders and represent only about 30% of all orders in terms of share volume. Using floor brokers to transmit orders is justified only for large orders that must be *worked* (exposed to the market progressively). At the post, orders appear on the specialist's Display Book screen, an electronic system that keeps track of all limit orders and incoming market orders. The Display Book sorts the limit orders and displays them in price/time priority. The specialist is the only member of the NYSE to have access to this limit-order book. New limit orders simply enter the limit-order book. The specialist may execute a market order against another market order in the book, against his or her inventory, or against an order presented by a floor broker in the trading crowd. If the specialist does not intervene for proprietary trading, the transaction price is determined in a simple auction process involving the limit-order book and the trading crowd. The specialist can also use an electronic system called ITS (Intermarket Trading System) to get the order executed on another market that displays a better quote.[4] Clearly, orders are almost never executed automatically on the NYSE.

One important measure of automation efficiency is the turnaround time, the time interval between a specialist's receiving the order through SuperDOT and sending out the execution report. In 1993 the NYSE set a standard turnaround time for a SuperDOT order at 60 seconds. If the turnaround time exceeds 60 seconds, the NYSE will take action to improve the specialist's performance. An average turnaround time is now around 20 seconds. Once the order is executed, a report is sent electronically via the same route it arrived. The execution report is private information. However, the U.S. exchanges and the NASD implemented a system to publicly disseminate transaction data within 90 seconds of execution. This system, approved by the SEC, is known as CTS (Consolidated Tape System). Since 1993 all exchange members must also report all transactions conducted outside business hours, as well as in foreign markets. Recent bid-ask quotes are reported on a Consolidated Quote System (CQS).

The specialist, charged with maintaining a fair and orderly market, acts as an auctioneer, dealer, and broker. As an auctioneer, the specialist must maintain a fair market for all participants; in particular, the specialist sets a market opening price based on an auction. As a dealer, the specialist buys and sells for his or her own account. As a broker, the specialist supervises the execution of orders contained in the limit-order book and collects a commission on these trades. The specialist's own account trading cannot take precedence over the limit-order book or any market order. Because of its important role and its monopoly position, the performance of a specialist is closely monitored via automated control systems.

To summarize, the NYSE is highly automated to bring the transactions to the point of sale on the floor of the exchange and to report executions. However, the transaction itself is not automated. The NYSE claims that customers will benefit from the human judgment of an agent on either side of the transaction, one who is acting solely in the customer's best interest. This agent is supposed to be able to get price improvement for the customer.

Several trading systems have developed in competition with the NYSE and with different levels of functions and regulation. NASDAQ (National Association of Securities Dealers Automated Quotation) is a price-driven screen system used for over-the-counter transactions. This is a dealer market, in which market makers post their bid-ask quote on a screen available to all traders. This system has inspired the London Stock Exchange. Other systems developed for large transactions of institutional investors include the Arizona Stock Exchange, Instinet (a subsidiary of Reuters), and Posit.

London Stock Exchange   The most important feature of this dealer market, or price-driven market, is an automated dealer quotation system known as SEAQ (Stock Exchange Automated Quotation). Any member of the exchange is free to register as a market maker (or dealer) in any shares. In practice only a few brokers act as market makers, and most market makers tend to specialize in some groups of shares. Stocks are categorized as alpha, beta, and gamma as a function of their market capitalization and liquidity, alpha shares being the most actively traded ones. Registered market makers in alpha and beta shares are obliged to quote firm bid-ask prices at which they stand ready to trade. This information is carried on SEAQ screens available to all members of the stock exchange. The screen carries the name of the market maker, the quotes, and the maximum size of the transactions for which these quotes are firm. For gamma stocks, the quotes are indicative, not firm. Small orders can be entered in an automated execution system known as SAEF (SEAQ Automated Execution Facility), but most other transactions are concluded by calling the market maker. A member of the exchange will contact the market maker by phone and negotiate the transaction price, which may be better than the price quoted on the screen. It can never be a worse price than quoted on the screen, within the maximum transaction size indicated, as SEAQ quotes are firm. Executed transactions must be reported on SEAQ screens within a couple of minutes.[5] Members are allowed to deal directly between themselves, without going through a market maker, but these trades must also be reported on SEAQ. Floor trading has disappeared from the London Stock Exchange, after the Big Bang of 1986 and the introduction of SEAQ.

Market makers can deal between themselves through an IDB system (Inter Dealer Broker) for posting quotes and expressing interest in trading blocks in some shares. Only market makers can deal through IDB. Trading is anonymous.

As opposed to the NYSE or to order-driven markets, the routing of orders is not automated through a central system. Brokers use their proprietary routing systems to centralize orders from their clients and execute limit orders themselves when the market permits. They do not make their order book information available to the market.

The London Stock Exchange has put in place various automated systems to control the trading activity of its members.

London has become a major market for international stock trading. A significant share of transactions in French, German, Swiss, Dutch, and even Italian shares is taking place on SEAQ, especially for large transactions. This can be explained by the presence of highly professional market makers providing market liquidity and low-cost execution, as well as the absence of any British taxation on trading in foreign shares.

Tokyo Stock Exchange This is the largest Japanese stock exchange, with more than 80% of all transactions; Osaka is the second largest exchange (about 15% of all transactions). By tradition, the Tokyo Stock Exchange is an auction, or order-driven, market without market makers. Trades are concluded by *saitoris* (or *order clerks*) who match buyers and sellers without taking positions for their own accounts. The saitori maintains a limit-order book, which is open to all exchange members. The saitori must execute the transactions according to the rules of the exchange and earn a commission on each trade. Orders are matched according to the following precedence rules, standard on order-driven markets:

- *Price priority*: The highest bid and the lowest ask have priority over all other orders.

- *Time priority*: Orders at the same price are treated on a "first-come, first-served" basis.

- *Order priority*: Market orders have priority over limit orders.

Orders are now routed to the saitori book electronically through computer systems known as CORES (Computer-assisted Order Routing and Execution System), for the majority of shares, and FORES (Floor Order Routing and Execution System) for the 150 most active stocks. CORES can be described as automated order-routing, execution, and trade-reporting systems. The automated execution system replicates the trading rules of the Tokyo Stock Exchange. Floor trading is still dominant for the 150 major stocks. A large proportion of transactions take place at the opening of the market sessions with a special auction called *itayose.* All orders that have rached the saitori book before opening are executed at a single price that equilibrates demand and supply. If the orders on each side of the market do not match exactly in size, a limit order is split to make up the balance. The philosophy of this *itayose* is similar to the call system of the Paris bourse. After this opening auction, all orders are executed as they arrive on the floor under continuous auction. When a new order arrives, it will be matched against the saitori book of limit orders or other market orders arriving simultaneously. In the absence of market makers trading for their accounts, sometimes a wide gap appears between the highest bid or lowest ask in the book, and the last executed price. Hence the execution of a newly arrived market order could lead to a huge price movement. The exchange requires the saitori not to execute the trade but to indicate for a few minutes a special quote close to the previous transaction price. This special quote is designed to attract further interest in the share and is progressively adjusted as time passes by.

All these order-matching functions can be automated fairly easily, except maybe for this last feature. However, the move toward a fully automated transaction system has been fairly slow.

Paris Bourse   This auction, or price-driven, market adopted a computerized trading system named CAC (Cotation Assistée en Continu) initially patterned after the Toronto CATS. Orders are automatically routed and executed. All members have trading screens in their offices, and floor trading has disappeared. Trading takes place against the computerized limit-order book, which is basically public. When a new order arrives in the system, it is immediately executed against the limit-order book if possible, or entered in the book. Orders are executed following price/time/size priority rules. Brokers can enter orders for their clients or for their own accounts. However, market-making activity is still very limited. Investors are very reluctant to expose their large orders in a public limit-order book, and the Paris Stock Exchange has allowed blocks (large orders) to be negotiated off CAC. Blocks, negotiated by telephone, are then reported into CAC, and all limit orders in the book that would have been executed under the new block's trade price must be cleared at their limit price.[6] Small orders can be directly traded by brokers acting as principals and need not be routed to CAC for execution (but the trade must be reported in CAC). In the morning an automatic auction system determines the opening price that equilibrates supply and demand of accumulated orders, by maximizing trade volume.

Frankfurt Stock Exchange   The largest of eight German bourses, with about 70% of the volume in German equities, the Frankfurt Stock Exchange is also the last of the major stock exchanges to become automated. Banks act as brokers on the exchange, and some specialists, called *makler*, traditionally have responsibility for setting the price at the periodic auctions and, to some extent, act as dealers. The trading system in Frankfurt was a call auction that evolved to accommodate continuous trading. Small orders accumulate, and an auction around noon determines a single equilibrium price that maximizes trade volume. Trading can take place continuously during the day, especially for large orders. An automated trading system known as IBIS II (Integriertes Börsenhandels- und Informations-System) was introduced in 1990 and functions as a trading and settlement system. Members can enter limit orders for their clients, as well as bid-ask quotes, when they trade for their own accounts. IBIS II is therefore a mixture of a price-driven system in which market makers disseminate their best quotes, and an order-driven auction system in which orders are entered, and the book is public. Banks are becoming both market makers and brokers.

Other Stock Exchanges   These, including most emerging markets, have become automated. They generally follow a computerized, order-driven system close to the Paris CAC.

Issues in Market Microstructure

Trading in securities has become increasingly globalized, and the microstructure of all markets has evolved rapidly due to automation. This raises the issue of determining the "best" market organization for securities trading. The criteria used to determine what constitutes the "best" market structure are controversial. The basic function of any trading market mechanism is to facilitate the process of *price discovery*. All stock exchanges in the world are now resorting to computer technology to automate the trading process. However, the philosophy of the automation can differ fundamentally across markets. An automated market structure consists of a communication technology for exchanging messages among traders. The market structure is governed by a set of rules stating the type of message that each participant can send and receive and governing the way these messages are transformed into transactions through a programmed computerized algorithm. This system should allow the trader to discover the best price available. By "best" traders often have in mind such issues as:

- getting a fair price, without some counterparty getting an overly favorable deal

- getting a low transaction cost

- having a liquid market

- having a transparent but anonymous market

Many of these issues cannot be stated in simple terms acceptable to everyone. For example, there is a lot of disagreement on how to measure transaction costs. A frequent definition of *transaction cost* is the difference between the price, including commissions, at which you trade and the price that existed prior to the market's knowing about your trade. In other words, it is the sum of commissions, taxes, and the market impact of a trade. The difficulty in measuring transactions costs is assessing what would have been the "true" market price of the security if your trade had not taken place. In an attempt to design the best market structure, stock exchanges are confronted with various issues and major choices to be made. Furthermore, one should not forget that the historical heritage cannot be simply discarded when a market becomes automated. The automation of each national market builds on its historical structure.

The study of the various market microstructures raise numerous questions and issues.

Price-Driven versus Order-Driven Systems

Automated trading systems have followed two different paths, depending on whether the traditional market organization was dominated by dealers making the market or by brokers acting as agents in an auction system. The London SEAQ and the U.S. NASDAQ are typical *price-driven* systems (also called quote-driven systems). The automated system posts firm quotes by market makers. There is no automatic trading mechanism for orders and no centralized book of limit orders. When posting a quote, the market maker does not know what trades it will generate. In a price-driven system a market maker is basically placing the equivalent of limit orders: a buy limit order at the bid and a sell limit order at the ask.

At the other extreme auction markets, such as Paris and Tokyo (and most other European and Asian markets), have put in place *order-driven* systems. The computer stores all orders that become public knowledge. The limit-order book is the hub of these automated systems. Viewing all standing orders, a trader knows exactly what trades will be executed if he or she enters a new quote or limit order.

The NYSE is a mixture of these two types of systems. There is a limit-order book, but it is the private knowledge of the specialist. Brokers are likely to hide some of their limit orders and keep them with their floor brokers to trade in the most appropriate manner. Given the importance of floor trading, the NYSE is the less automated market in its trading function.

Automation brings many improvements in the speed and costs of trading. However, it forces one side of the transaction to expose itself first and therefore to run the risk of being "picked off."

In all cases a limit order gives a free trading option to other market participants. In an order-driven market it is the trader who has submitted the order who implicitly gives the free option to the rest of the market. In a price-driven market it is the dealer who posts a firm quote who gives this free option. To understand this concept, assume that an investor entered on the CAC a limit order to sell Club Méditérannée shares at 300 francs while the market price was 290. If favorable information arrives suddenly that justifies a higher price for Club Méditérannée— say, 350—other market participants have an option worth 50 francs per share, and the investor gets "picked off." Now assume that on SEAQ a market maker posts a bid-ask quote for Club Méditérannée of 300–310. Under the same scenario market participants suddenly get a free option worth 40 (they can buy at 310 from the market maker a share worth 350). In a price-driven market dealers run the risk of being "picked off." The danger of automation is to reduce market liquidity by affecting the willingness of dealers (in a price-driven system) or public investors (in an order-driven system) to place limit orders.

SEAQ and NASDAQ have introduced rules to protect market makers ("time delays" banning of "professional" traders). Such rules are more difficult to implement for an order-driven system with many small orders. London dealers make firm quotes for large sizes, compared to all the other markets, and their cost of being "picked off" by not updating quickly their posted quotes is potentially large. There seems to be a tendency to post fairly wide bid-ask spreads on SEAQ and to provide better terms by telephone.

Another drawback of a continuous order-driven system, in the absence of developed market making, is the danger in placing market orders. As mentioned, the Tokyo Stock Exchange has a special procedure to limit this risk. Other markets are trying to implement rules protecting market orders.

In the absence of active market makers, trading a block (a large transaction) on an automated order-driven system is also difficult. Because of the lack of depth in the market, it may take a long time to trade the block. This will leave the trader who discloses the block on the system fully exposed to all the risks. Blocks are generally traded off the automated system.

Informed Traders and Transparency

Transparency is a desired property of a financial market. It means that information on recent trades and outstanding orders is made public to all market participants. Automation increases transparency because a great amount of information on orders, or quotes, and completed transactions is disseminated in real time. Transparency is achieved on an order-driven system by making the limit-order book public. Clearly the NYSE is less transparent, as the limit-order book is private information of the specialist, and brokers are inclined not to reveal their large orders and keep them with their floor brokers. However, transparency has also a cost due to informational trading.

Some investors are *liquidity traders*: They trade because they need to trade, not because they possess some private information on the shares they are selling or buying. For example, a pension fund has to invest its monthly contributions or to reinvest dividends received. Other investors, called *informed traders*, trade on the basis of private information. The presence of these informed traders complicates the design of automated trading systems. Liquidity traders and market makers fear to systematically lose to informed traders. An informed trader can "pick off" an uninformed trader the moment the order (or the market-maker quote) appears on the screen. To some extent automation allows for one side to remain anonymous while observing posted orders (in an order-driven system) or posted quotes (in a price-driven system). Informed traders can wait behind their screens for the incoming orders of uninformed traders. On the London market, where competing dealers post quotes for substantial transaction sizes, the informed trader can conduct trades with multiple dealers before any of them becomes aware of the large transaction. Conversely informed traders do not wish to reveal their information. Entering publicly a large order reveals information to the rest of the market, which will immediately discount it in their valuation of the share. The problem is once more the forceful exposition of one side of the transaction by the automated system. The problem becomes acute for large transactions, usually called *blocks.* The problem of informational trading also exists in a floor or telephone trading, but experience seems to indicate that block traders tend to prefer face-to-face or telephone contact with an *identified* party, to get a better feel for the motivation of a trade. Indeed the general automated trading systems have never been very successful for block trading. In all countries specific systems have been developed to handle blocks, and other specific systems have been developed to handle small orders. Blocks are often traded *upstairs*, meaning in the offices upstairs from the floor and via telephone, because these transactions require negotiation, which is difficult in a fully transparent environment. These transactions are then reported in the main trading systems, and the exchange edicts rules to clear limit orders that would have been hit if the block had come to the main automated system. London has taken steps to ensure that SEAQ keeps the large transactions. The London Stock Exchange allows the publication of the large transaction (price and volume) to be delayed for 90 minutes to allow time for market makers to unwind the position they have taken.

Index traders are a special type of liquidity traders. An index fund holding a portfolio that tracks a stock market index does not trade to benefit from information on specific firms. An index trader is not an informed trader and is therefore less risky for a counterparty. This means that index traders wish to get better prices than a typical investor by making the transaction fully transparent. A market maker should stand ready to quote tighter bid-ask spreads to this type of investor, as the risk of being picked off is nonexistent. Index funds now represent major traders on most markets and deserve special treatment. They need to trade simultaneously a whole portfolio of securities, not a couple of specific stocks. Their goal is to match exactly the performance of some index. Because performance is compared to the value of the index calculated at the market close, they often wish to trade *market-on-close*, i.e., trade at the closing price for all stocks in the index. Computerized basket trading arrangements have been made on many stock markets (e.g., Crossing Sessions on the NYSE).

Anonymity and Reputation

Many investors desire anonymity, e.g., informed traders and those who wish to hide their action and believe that they can get a better price by remaining anonymous. On the other hand, market makers and brokers often wish to build a reputation for their skills in handling a client. They wish to give publicity to their activity to attract more business. In an automated execution system, such as CAC or even the London SAEF for small orders, anonymity can be preserved at the expense of reputation. In some systems, such as the London SAEF or the NASDAQ Small Order

Execution System, brokers can indicate a preference for some market maker. However, this is a dangerous procedure, as it weakens the dealers' incentive to quote the best prices.

Market Fragmentation

Deregulation and technological advances have led to the development of new markets and have increased competition among markets domestically and across borders. For example, the London Stock Exchange is believed to account for 20% to 50% of the volume of transaction in French, Dutch, and German shares. Stocks listed on the NYSE are extensively traded on competing automated markets, designed mostly for institutional investors. Buying a futures contract on some index is sometimes an alternative to buying a diversified portfolio of shares. This leads to a fragmentation of the market. Established national stock markets are defending their vested interests by fighting against this fragmentation and by calling for increased regulation of these off-exchange trades.

The very presence of fragmentation and competition implies that the market has become more efficient. It is clearly the pressure of competition that leads to an improved efficiency of the long-established stock markets. Modern technology provides instant information on all markets and allows the investor to search for the best price of a security worldwide.

Internationalization

The development of global investment calls for an increase in international trading. This need can be fulfilled in several ways.

To service international investors, U.S., British, Japanese, and other securities firms have developed an international network of offices. The required staff and investment make this strategy very expensive. International financial centers have removed constraints to foreign securities firms; they have opened their doors to remain competitive with New York or London.

Some stock markets believe that they can safeguard their share of global trading by establishing links with other markets. This trend was most apparent among futures and options markets but also affected stock markets. For example, in 1985 the American Stock Exchange and the Toronto Stock Exchange inaugurated an automated trading link for a few of the major companies listed on their markets. The results were disappointing, and the agreement was dropped in 1988. The volume on most of these linkages was small, due partly to legal and technical problems and to the advantage of the largest, more liquid market. The European stock markets are studying various linkage alternatives.

These linkages could be superseded by around-the-clock electronic trading. The NASDAQ system is being made available to investors in the U.K. and Singapore. The International Stock Exchange in London and the NASD have agreed not to compete, by avoiding electronic quotes and trading for the same stocks. Some markets believe that they need not join a cooperative agreement with other national markets but that they should simply make their own automated trading system available worldwide on a 24-hour basis. With modern telecommunications, it is relatively easy to connect a screen on a computer system anywhere in the world. To be attractive, such a system requires more than the computer software; it also requires round-the-clock market makers and sufficient liquidity to attract active participation by international investors. Efficient clearing and settlement procedures are also needed. Global electronic trading may also be offered by vendors of trading information, such as Reuters or others.

As of the mid-1990s, some stock exchanges have been successful in attracting a significant proportion of the trading volume in some major foreign shares. SEAQ international is now a natural location for large trades in French, German, Dutch, or Italian shares. The volume of trading in some ADRs listed in New York is quite large compared to their domestic counterparts. At this time it is too early to tell which type of global trading system or linkages will emerge, but it is certainly a major challenge to the profession and its future.

Some Practical Aspects

Multiple Listing and ADR

Some companies are listed on several stock markets around the world.[7] Multinational firms, such as Royal Dutch–Shell or Ciba-Geigy, are traded on more than a dozen markets. The procedure for admitting foreign stocks to a local market varies; in some markets the regulations are quite lax. For example, in 1986 the Quebec Securities Act allowed a foreign company to list in Montreal simply by meeting the same regulatory requirements as those in its own jurisdiction. In other markets foreign companies must abide by the rules of the local exchange. For instance, foreign companies wanting to be listed on U.S. stock exchanges must satisfy the requirements of both the exchange and the U.S. Securities and Exchange Commission. Although this SEC regulation offers some protection to the U.S. public, it imposes substantial dual-listing costs on foreign companies, which have to produce frequent reports in English.

In the United States and France trading takes place in special shares of the foreign company. U.S. investors deal in American depository receipts (ADRs). Under this arrangement foreign shares are deposited with a U.S. bank, which in turn issues ADRs in the name of the foreign company. To avoid unusual share prices ADRs may represent a combination of several foreign shares. For example, Japanese shares are often priced at only a few yen per share. They are therefore combined into lots of 100 or more so that their value is more like that of a typical U.S. share price.

The shares of foreign companies can be traded in several different ways in the United States. An ADR program created without the company's involvement is usually called an *unsponsored* ADR. These over-the-counter shares are traded through *pink sheets*, electronic bulletin boards, or an electronic trading system called Portal. An ADR program created with the assistance of the foreign company is called *sponsored* ADR. These sponsored ADRs are often classified at three levels:

- *Level I:* The company does not comply with SEC registration and reporting requirements, and the shares can be traded only on the over-the-counter market (but not NASDAQ).

- *Level II:* The company registers with the SEC and complies with its reporting requirements. The shares can be listed on an official U.S. stock exchange (NYSE, ASE) or NASDAQ.

- *Level III:* The company is listed on a U.S. stock exchange or NASDAQ and raises capital in the United States through a public offering.

A nonregistered company can also raise capital in the United States, but it has to be done through a private placement under rule 144A. A drawback of this private placement is that only some private investors and qualified institutional buyers (QIBs) can participate. The retail sector is excluded. Furthermore, liquidity of ADRs on the OTC market is not good. The cost of being registered with the SEC is the public reporting that has to be performed. The foreign company must file a Form 20-F annually. If domestic statements using national accounting standards are presented as primary statements on Form 20-F, the company must provide a reconciliation of earnings and shareholder equity under domestic and U.S. GAAP (Generally Accepted Accounting Principles). This implies that the company must supply all information necessary to comply with U.S. GAAP. Furthermore the stock exchanges require timely disclosure of various information, including quarterly accounting interim statements.

In Chapter 7 we discuss the relation between various national accounting principles and market valuation, especially whether the use of U.S. GAAP allows investors to get a better information on the value of the foreign firm and therefore affects stock prices. Some national accounting practices can very easily be reconciled with U.S. practices. For example, the SEC considers that Canadian accounting practices are similar to U.S. practices and accepts Canadian statements: Canadian firms do not have to go through an ADR program and simply list their shares on a U.S. stock exchange. Many companies from Bermuda, Cayman Islands, the Netherlands Antilles, Hong Kong, or Israel simply use the U.S. GAAP statements as their primary financial statements, so they do not even need to provide reconciliation data. At the other extreme, German and Swiss firms have been very reluctant to list shares in the United States because of the difficulty of reconciling U.S. and German or Swiss accounting practices and the detailed information that these firms are not accustomed to disclosing. German and Swiss firms tend to smooth reported earnings by using various hidden reserves. In 1993 Daimler-Benz became the first German company to be listed on the NYSE, but the general reluctance of German companies to do so can be illustrated by the published statement that follows.

BMW AG's chief financial officer, Volker Doppelfeld, said a New York Stock Exchange listing of the company's shares "would cost money and achieve nothing," claiming that quarterly accounting requirements of the exchange would undermine long-term corporate planning by emphasizing short-term profits.[8]

At the start of 1994, there were about 1200 ADR programs in the United States, with 193 foreign companies listed on the NYSE. Three of these firms (Telefonos de Mexico, Glaxo, and Royal Dutch) are among the top 21 most active stocks of the NYSE. The total turnover of stocks of foreign firms represents almost 10% of the NYSE transaction volume.

Some firms have issued Global Depositary Receipts (GDR) that are simultaneous listed on several national markets. These GDRs give the firms access to a larger base to raise new capital. Several Japanese and Chinese firms have seized this opportunity.

London is another market with very active trading of foreign stocks. SEAQ has captured a significant share of trading in French, German, Dutch, Swiss, and Italian stocks. Other non-U.K. shares are also actively traded on SEAQ. Trade takes place in the regular shares of the company. The motivation for trading on SEAQ is to reduce transaction costs by avoiding some taxes or high commissions charged on the home market and to benefit from the liquidity provided by highly professional market makers based in London. The companies whose shares are traded do not get involved in this market and derive little direct benefits from being traded in London.

Multiple listing implies that the share values of a company are linked on several exchanges.[9] One company should sell at the same share price all over the world, once adjustments for exchange rate and transactions costs have been made. Arbitrage among markets ensures that this is so. An important question is: What is the dominant force affecting the stock price of a multiple-listed company? In a dominant/satellite market relationship the home market is the dominant force, and the price in the foreign market (the satellite) simply adjusts to the home market price. This is clearly the case for many dual-listed stocks where only a very small proportion of capitalization is traded abroad. However, the answer is less obvious for a few British, Dutch, and Swiss companies that have a very active market in other countries (especially the United States). The influence of time zones should also be noted. Since stock trading takes place at different times around the world, U.S. stocks listed on the Paris bourse are traded before the opening of the U.S. markets. Their French prices reflect the previous close in New York and the current exchange rate but also anticipation about today's new price, based on new information that surfaced during the night.

A domestic investor wanting to buy foreign shares has several alternatives. First, the investor can check whether the foreign firm is listed on the domestic market. If it is, these shares can most conveniently be bought domestically. The advantage of ADRs for a U.S. investor is simply their convenience; they are traded just like domestic securities. Another alternative is to check on whether certain local institutions make a market in the foreign stock. For example, U.S. and British brokers maintain an active over-the-counter market for numerous foreign issues. The third alternative is to buy the shares abroad, directly on the company's primary market. Whereas the small investor may find it more convenient to trade in foreign shares listed on the home market, the large investor may often find the primary market of overseas companies to be more liquid and cheaper. In all cases price levels, transaction costs, taxes, and administrative costs should be major determinants of which market the investor chooses.

Foreign companies have a variety of reasons for being listed on several national stock markets, despite the costs involved. Multiple listing gives them more access to foreign ownership, allowing a better diversification of their capital and access to a larger amount of funds than is available from smaller domestic equity markets. Diversified ownership in turn reduces the risk of a domestic takeover. Also, foreign listing raises the profile of a firm in foreign markets, which enables it to raise financing more easily on both the national level and abroad, and is good advertising for its product brands. The only danger from foreign listing may be the increased volatility of the firm's stock in responses to domestic economic news. Bad political and economic news in the Scandinavian countries, for example, has frequently been followed by an immediate reflux of shares from foreign markets. Scandinavian shareholders display less volatile behavior than foreign investors for two reasons: They are not as shaken by bad domestic news, and controls and regulations give them few attractive investment alternatives.

Tax Aspects

Foreign investments may be taxed in two locations: the investor's county and the investment's country. Taxes are applied in any of three areas: transactions, capital gains, and income (dividends, etc.).

Some countries impose a tax on transactions. This tax is sometimes proportional to the amount transacted, as in Switzerland, with a federal stamp tax of 0.075%. The United Kingdom has a tax of 0.5% on purchases of domestic securities (but not on sales), whereas Japan has a tax of 0.3% on sales (but not on purchases). In countries where brokers charge a commission rather than trade on net prices, a tax proportional to the commission is sometimes charged. For example, France levies an 18.6% VAT (Value Added Tax) on commissions (not on the transaction value), like on any service. Market makers are usually exempted from these taxes when they trade for their own accounts. Although transaction taxes are usually small, institutional investors tend to trade on markets where these taxes can be avoided. This has led to the development of foreign stock trading in London where trading in foreign securities is exempt from taxation. In reaction most countries have now eliminated or drastically reduced their transaction taxes, with the few remaining taxes among major markets as mentioned.

Capital gains are normally taxed where the investor resides, no matter what the national origin of the investment is. In other words, domestic and international investments are taxed the same way.

Income on foreign stocks is paid from the legal entity of one country to a resident of another country. This often poses a conflict of jurisdiction, since both countries may want to impose a tax on that income. The international convention on taxing income is to make certain that taxes are paid by the investor in at least one country. That is why withholding taxes are levied on dividend payments. Since many investors are also taxed on income received in their country of residence, double taxation can result from this practice but is avoided through a network of international tax treaties. An investor receives a dividend net of withholding tax plus a tax credit from the foreign tax government. The investor's country of residence imposes its tax on the gross foreign dividends, but the amount of this tax is reduced by the withholding tax credit. In other words, the foreign tax credit is applied against the home taxes.

To a tax-free investor, such as a pension fund, this tax credit is worthless, since the investor does not pay taxes at home. In this case the investor can reclaim the tax withheld in the foreign country. Reclaiming a withholding tax is often a lengthy process requiring at least a few months and even up to a couple of years to recover the money. In a few countries part of the withholding tax is kept by the country of origin. Tax rules change frequently; Exh. 6.4 indicates the major withholding tax rates that were in effect in 1994. Note that some investors, such as public funds, can obtain complete exemption from withholding taxes. Also, withholding-tax treatment is quite different for bonds. No withholding tax is applied to Eurobonds, and many countries have removed withholding taxes on domestic bonds purchased by nonresidents (see Chapter 9).

To illustrate these fiscal aspects, let's consider a U.S. investor who buys 100 shares of Heineken listed in Amsterdam for 170 guilders. She goes through a U.S. broker, and the current exchange rate is one Dutch guilder = 0.3 U.S. dollars. Her total cost is $5100, or $51 per share of Heineken (170 times 0.3 $/DG). Three months later, a gross dividend of 6 guilders is paid (15% withholding tax), and our American decides to sell the Heineken shares. Each share is now worth 160 guilders, and the current exchange rate is $/DG = 0.4, since the guilder has sharply risen against the dollar. The same exchange rate applied on the dividend payment date. Here is the cash flow she received in U.S. dollars:

Dividend payment minus withholding tax ($/DG = 0.4)

	Net Dividend	Tax Credit
In guilders per share	5.1	0.9
In dollars per share	2.04	0.36
Net in dollars	204	36

Sale of Heineken shares ($/DG = 0.4)

In guilders per share	160
In dollars per share	64
Net in dollars	6400

Our investor has made a capital gain of $1300 ($6400 − $5100), which will be taxed in the United States at the U.S. capital-gain tax rate. She will also declare a total gross dividend of $240 as income, which will be taxed at her income tax rate. However, she can deduct from her income tax a tax credit of $36, thanks to the United States–Netherlands tax treaty.

Commissions and Price Impact

Commissions vary across markets. The deregulation and increased globalization of all stock markets has led to a global trend toward negotiated commissions. The dealers bid-ask spread should also be taken into account. The total cost could be estimated as the difference between the price paid (or received) and the value of the share if the transaction had not taken place. Of course, the total transaction cost is a function of the size of the transaction and the market depth. Various studies come up with different estimates. Exhibit 6.5 reports some cost estimates for trading in the shares of the national stock index of developed markets. Trading in non-U.S. securities tends to be somewhat more expensive than trading in U.S. stocks.

Stock Market Indexes

Stock market indexes allow one to measure the average performance of a national market. One or several market indexes may track a national market at any given time.

International Stock Indexes Morgan Stanley Capital International (MSCI) publishes national market value–weighted indexes on 22 countries based on approximately 1500 stocks. MSCI also publishes several regional indexes. The major ones are:

- World (approximately 1500 stocks)

- Europe (approximately 600 stocks)

- Europe, Australia, and the Far East (EAFE, approximately 1000 stocks)

These indexes are widely used by international money managers for asset allocation decisions and performance measurements. They cover about 60% of each market capitalization, which means that 40% of the market is not represented. Hence more broadly based indexes can have significant differences in performance. These indexes have been available since 1970. Morgan Stanley Capital International also publishes related information on their sample of stocks, including financial ratios, such as price earnings, price-to-book value ratios, and yield. Worldwide industry indexes are available.

EXHIBIT 6.4

Dividend Taxation, 1994

Company's Domicile

Shareholder's Domicile[a]	Australia	Austria	Belgium	Canada	Denmark	Finland	France	Germany	Hong Kong	Ireland	Italy	Japan
Australia		15	15	15	15	15	15	15	0	15	15	15
		C	C	C	C	C	C	C	—	C	C	C
Austria	15		15	15	10	10	15	25	0	15	15	20
	—		C	C	C	C	C	C	—	C	C	C
Belgium	15	15		15	15	15	15	15	0	0	15	15
	D	D		D	D	D	D	D	—	—	D	D
Canada	15	15	15		15	15	15	15	0	0	15	15
	C	C	C		C	C	C	C	—	—	C	C
Denmark	15	10	15	15		15	0	15	0	15	15	15
	C	C	C	C		C	—	C	—	C	C	C
Finland	15	10	15	15	15		15	15	0	15	15	15
	C	C	C	C	C		C	C	—	C	C	C
France	15	15	15	15	0	0		15	0	0	15	15
	C	C	C	C	—	—		C	—	—	C	C
Germany	15	22	15	15	15	15	0		0	0	15	15
	C	C	C	C	C	C	—		—	C	C	C
Hong Kong	30	22	25.8	25	30	25	25	25		0	32.4	20
	—	—	—	—	—	—	—	—		—	—	—
Ireland	15	10	15	15	15	15	15	15	0		15	15
	C	C	C	C	C	C	C	C	—		C	C
Italy	15	15	15	15	15	15	15	15	0	0		15
	C	C	C	C	C	C	C	C	—	—		C
Japan	15	20	15	15	15	15	15	15	0	0	15	
	C	C	C	C	C	C	C	C	—	—	C	
Luxembourg Holding	30	22	25.8	25	30	25	25	25	0	0	32.4	20
	—	—	—	—	—	—	—	—	—	—	—	—
Malaysia	15	10	15	15	0	15	15	15	0	0	10	15
	C	C	C	C	C	C	C	C	—	—	C	C
Netherlands	15	15	15	15	15	15	15	15	0	0	15	15
	C	C	C	C	C	C	C	D	—	—	C	C

[a]Top number indicates the effective rate of dividend withholding tax. Bottom letter describes the treatment of the foreign withholding tax in the shareholder's country of residence: D = deduction for foreign tax paid; i.e. the shareholder's country of residence imposes its tax on net foreign dividends. C = credit for foreign tax paid; i.e. the shareholder's country of residence imposes its tax on gross foreign dividends, but the amount of this tax is reduced by the amount of the foreign dividend withholding tax.

Dividend Taxation, 1994

Shareholder's Domicile[a]	Luxembourg	Malaysia	Netherlands	New Zealand	Norway	Singapore	Spain	Sweden	Switzerland	U.K.	U.S.A.
Australia	25	0	15	15	15	0	15	15	15	15	15
	C	—	C	C	C	—	C	C	C	C	C
Austria	15	0	15	30	15	0	15	10	5	15	15
	C	—	C	D	C	—	C	C	C	C	C
Belgium	15	0	15	15	15	0	15	15	15	20	15
	D	—	D	D	D	—	D	D	D	D	D
Canada	15	0	15	15	15	0	15	15	15	15	15
	C	—	C	C	C	—	C	C	C	C	C
Denmark	15	0	15	15	15	0	15	15	0	15	15
	C	—	C	C	C	—	C	C	—	C	C
Finland	15	0	15	15	15	0	15	15	10	15	15
	C	—	C	C	C	—	C	C	—	C	C
France	15	0	15	15	15	0	15	0	5	15	15
	C	—	C	C	C	—	C	—	C	C	C
Germany	15	0	15	15	15	0	15	15	15	0	15
	C	C	C	C	C	—	C	C	C	—	C
Hong Kong	25	0	25	30	25	0	25	30	35	0	30
	—	—	—	—	—	—	—	—	—	—	—
Ireland	15	0	15	15	10	0	25	15	15	15	15
	C	—	C	C	C	—	D	C	C	C	C
Italy	15	0	15	15	15	0	15	15	15	15	15
	C	—	C	C	C	—	C	C	C	C	C
Japan	15	0	15	15	15	0	15	15	15	15	15
	C	—	C	C	C	—	C	C	C	C	C
Luxembourg Holding		0	25	30	25	0	25	30	35	0	30
	—	—	—	—	—	—	—	—	—	—	—
Malaysia	25		15	15	0	0	25	0	15	15	30
	C		C	C	C	C	C	C	C	C	C
Netherlands	15	0		15	15	0	15	15	15	15	15
	C	—		C	C	—	C	C	C	C	C

EXHIBIT 6.4 (CONTINUED)

Dividend Taxation, 1994

Shareholder's Domicile[a]	Company's Domicile											
	Australia	Austria	Belgium	Canada	Denmark	Finland	France	Germany	Hong Kong	Ireland	Italy	Japan
New Zealand	15	22	15	15	15	15	15	15	0	15	15	15
	C	C	C	C	C	C	C	C	—	C	C	C
Norway	15	15	15	15	15	15	15	15	0	0	15	15
	C	C	C	C	C	C	C	C	—	—	C	C
Singapore	15	22	15	15	15	15	15	15	0	0	10	15
	C	D	C	C	C	C	C	C	—	—	C	C
Spain	15	15	15	15	15	15	15	15	0	0	15	15
	C	C	C	C	C	C	C	C	—	—	C	C
Sweden	15	10	15	15	15	15	15	15	0	15	15	15
	C	C	C	C	C	C	C	C	—	C	C	C
Switzerland	15	5	15	15	0	5	15	10	0	15	15	15
	C	C	C	C	—	C	C	C	—	C	C	C
U.K.	15	15	10	15	15	15	15	15	0	15	15	15
	C	C	C	C	C	C	C	C	—	C	C	C
U.S.A.	15	11	15	15	15	15	15	10	0	0	15	15
	C	C	C	C	C	C	C	C	—	—	C	C

Since 1987 the *Financial Times* has published the FT-Actuaries world indexes in association with Goldman Sachs and WM Company. Twenty-four national indexes are provided, as well as numerous industrial and regional indexes. The most important regional indexes are the world index, the Europe index, the Pacific Basin index, and the Europe and Pacific index. The FT-Actuaries indexes have a wider coverage than the MSCI indexes, since they are based on a sample of around 2400 stocks and cover more than 70% of each market capitalization. Worldwide industry indexes are available.

MSCI and FT-Actuaries indexes reported daily do not include dividends. Cum-dividend indexes are available monthly, but the treatment of dividends is somewhat rudimentary (one twelfth of the annual dividend yield is added to the monthly rate of return).

In 1987 Salomon Brothers and Frank Russell also launched the Salomon/Russell Global Equity indexes. They are widely available.

Other international indexes are available. Union de Banques Suisses (UBS) calculates regional and world indexes based on the major national indexes most

EXHIBIT 6.4

Dividend Taxation, 1994

Shareholder's Domicile[a]	Company's Domicile										
	Luxembourg	Malaysia	Netherlands	New Zealand	Norway	Singapore	Spain	Sweden	Switzerland	U.K.	U.S.A.
New Zealand	25	0	15		15	0	25	15	15	15	15
	C	—	C		C	—	C	C	C	C	C
Norway	15	0	15	15		0	15	15	15	15	15
	C	—	C	C		—	C	C	C	C	C
Singapore	25	0	15	15	0		25	15	15	15	30
	D	C	C	C	—		D	C	C	C	D
Spain	15	0	15	30	15	0		15	15	15	15
	C	—	C	C	C	—		C	C	C	C
Sweden	15	0	15	15	15	0	15		15	15	15
	C	C	C	C	C	—	C		C	C	C
Switzerland	15	0	15	15	15	0	15	15		15	15
	C	C	C	C	D	—	C	C		C	D
U.K.	15	0	15	15	15	0	15	5	15		15
	C	—	C	C	C	—	C	C	C		C
U.S.A.	12.5	0	15	15	15	0	15	15	15	15	
	C	—	C	C	C	—	C	C	C	C	

Source: Morgan Stanley Capital International. Reprinted by permission.

commonly used in each market. These daily indexes are market value–weighted averages of the national indexes presented in Exh. 6.6. Recently Dow Jones has started to compile international indexes. The *International Herald Tribune* and Bloomberg are publishing market indexes based on a small sample (10 or 20) of the major stocks in each country.

Indexes for emerging markets also exist and are reviewed in Chapter 8.

Domestic Stock Indexes Domestic investors usually prefer indexes that are calculated and published locally. Exhibit 6.6 lists the most commonly used stock indexes for the major stock markets. Most of these are broadly based, market value–weighted indexes. In other words, each company is assigned an index weight proportional to its market capitalization. Market value–weighted indexes are true market portfolio indexes in the sense that when the index portfolio is held by an investor, it truly represents movements in the market. This is not true of equal-weighted indexes, such as the U.S. Dow Jones or the Japanese Nikkei/Dow Jones.

EXHIBIT 6.5

Cost Estimates for One-way Trades

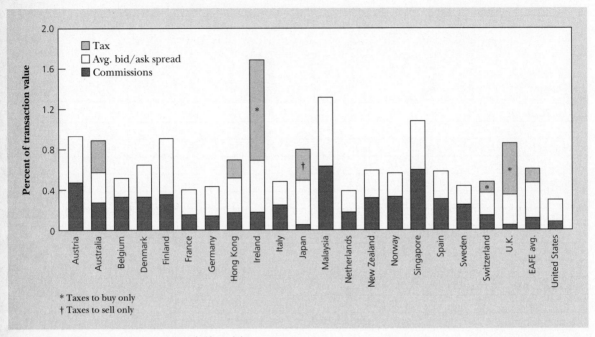

* Taxes to buy only
† Taxes to sell only

Source: Wells Fargo Nikko Investment Advisors. Reprinted with permission.

The Dow Jones Industrial Average (DJIA) simply adds up the stock price of 30 corporations. In other words, each company is assigned an index weight proportional to its market price. Not only is the DJIA narrowly based but also its weighting method is artificial; for example, IBM was removed from the index in the 1970s because its price was too high compared to the other 29 corporations. Most stock indexes published do not include dividends, although some countries also report dividend-adjusted indexes. A notable exception is the German DAX index, which is only a total return index (price plus net dividend based on a specific tax rate assumption).

Local indexes are widely used by domestic investors. Private investors often prefer these indexes over such international indexes as MSCI or FT-Actuaries, for several reasons:

- In most cases the local indexes have been used for several decades.

- Local indexes represent a broader coverage of securities.

- Local indexes are calculated immediately and are available at the same time as stock market quotations on all electronic price services.

EXHIBIT 6.6

Major National Stock Indexes
The approximate number of securities in the index is given in parentheses for leading markets. All indexes are market capitalization–weighted indexes except as noted.

Locality	Exchange	Index
United States	New York Stock Exchange (NYSE)	Dow Jones industrial (30)[a]
	NYSE	Standard and Poor's (500)
	NYSE	NYSE Composite (about 1500)
	American Stock Exchange	AMEX index
	Over the counter	NASDAQ index (3000)
Canada	Toronto	TSE (100) (200)
Japan	Tokyo	Nikkei Average (225)[a]
	Tokyo	Topix (about 12,300)
Hong Kong	Hong Kong	Hang Seng (33)[a]
Singapore	Singapore	Straits Times (30)[a]
Australia	Sydney	All Ordinaries
South Africa	Johannesburg	Composite, JSE Actuaries
Austria	Vienna	ATX index
Belgium	Brussels	Brussels Return
	Brussels	BEL (20)
Denmark	Copenhagen	KFX index
Finland	Helsinki	HEX index, FOX (25)
France	Paris	CAC (40)
	Paris	SBF (120, 250)
Germany	Frankfurt	Commerzbank (60)
	Frankfurt	FAX Aktien (100)
	Frankfurt	DAX (30)
Italy	Milan	Mibtel index (152)
	Milan	BCI All Share (300)
	Milan	BCI (30)
	Milan	MIB (80)
Netherlands	Amsterdam	CBS General
	Amsterdam	EOE Index (25)[b]
Norway	Oslo	OBX
Spain	Madrid	General SE/Madrid SE
	Madrid	IBEX (35)
Sweden	Stockholm	Affaersvaerlden
Switzerland	Zurich	Swiss Market Index (21)
	Zurich	SBC Index
	Zurich	Crédit Suisse
United Kingdom	London	Financial Times (30)
	London	Financial Times–Stock Exchange (100)/FT–SE 100
	London	FT-All Shares (750)

[a]Price-weighted index
[b]Weights are based on liquidity and size, with target percentage weights of 5% or 3.33%

- Local indexes are available every morning in all the newspapers throughout the world.

- The risk of error in prices and capital adjustment is minimized in local indexes by the fact that all calculations are done locally, with excellent information available on the spot.

Institutional investors, on the other hand, prefer to use the MSCI, FT-Actuaries, or other international indexes for the following reasons:

- The pension funds do not need up-to-the-minute indexes.

- The indexes on all stock markets are available in a central location, whereas local indexes must be drawn from several locations.

- All MSCI or FT-Actuaries indexes are calculated in a single consistent manner, allowing for direct comparisons between markets.

- They provide global indexes (world, EAFE), which are what international money managers need to measure overall performance.

- They also provide indexes cum-dividends.

The choice of index is important. In any given year the difference in performance between two indexes for the same stock market can be significant by as much as several points. This is illustrated in Exh. 6.7, which plots two widely used Japanese stock indexes from 1980 to 1995. The solid line is the Morgan Stanley Capital International index and the dotted line is the Nikkei 225 index. To allow for comparisons, both indexes are set at 100 on December 31, 1979.

Marked divergences appear over the years. The MSCI index strongly outperformed the Nikkei index from 1985 to 1990, when both indexes converge again. From 1990 to 1995 the MSCI index outperformed the Nikkei index by some 15%.

Summary

1. The world market size is over $10 trillion. The world market capitalization is spread somewhat evenly among North America, Asia, and Europe. Tokyo and New York are the largest national markets. European countries tend to be underrepresented compared to the relative size of their economies. European companies tend to rely more on banks for debt and equity financing and have less need for external equity financing. Other companies are not listed on the stock exchanges, because they are owned by the state. Emerging countries, especially in Asia, contributed to the rapid growth in world stock market capitalization in the 1980s; Eastern Europe and Latin America could provide further growth in the 1990s.

2. The degree of stock market concentration varies greatly among countries. However, an extensive number of companies with large market capitalization and good liquidity are available in Europe, Japan, and North America.

EXHIBIT 6.7

Comparative Performance of Two Japanese Stock Indexes

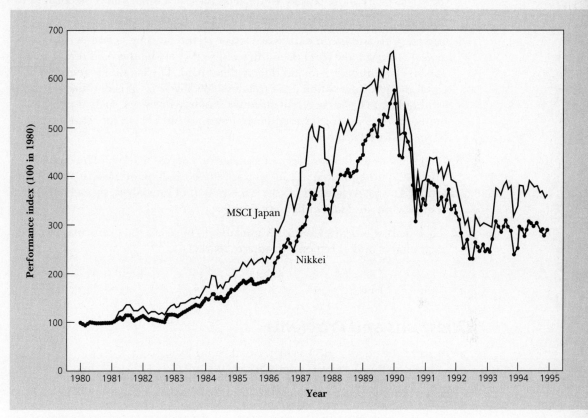

Source: Lombard Odier and Cie. Reprinted with permission.

3. Stock market structures differ considerably among countries. The different organizations and trading procedures are inherited from tradition and culture. The various stock exchanges, or bourses, may be classified into three historical categories: public bourses, private bourses, and bankers' bourses.

4. Among the many differences in trading procedures, the major one is the difference between a call auction and a dealer market. In a call auction market, purchase and sell orders are confronted at any given point in time, and the equilibrium price is determined. In a continuous dealer market, market makers continuously quote bid and ask prices at which they stand ready to buy or sell shares.

5. Stock exchanges have become extensively automated. Order-driven systems and price-drive systems proceed from two different philosophies. Both raise several microstructure issues.

6. Numerous companies are now listed on foreign stock markets. The shares of foreign companies dual-listed in the United States are called ADRs. Although these shares are more readily available to local investors, it may be cheaper to buy shares directly on their home markets.

7. Capital gains and income taxes are levied by the investor's country of residence. However, the foreign country where the dividend is paid often imposes a withholding tax on the dividend paid. The tax rate is generally equal to 15%. International tax treaties allow investors to claim this foreign withholding tax as a tax credit at home. Tax-free investors, such as pension funds, have no use for tax credits, so they must file a claim for refund of the tax in the foreign country.

8. Commissions and various securities taxes vary across markets. The commission is either negotiable or follows a schedule function of the size of the transaction. The total transaction cost is a function of the bid-ask spread quoted, commissions, and taxes when applicable.

9. Stock market indexes are readily available to measure the performance of each market and of regional groups of markets.

Questions and Problems

1. Describe the trends in stock market growth, using Exh. 6.1

2. Compare national turnover ratios (ratio of annual turnover to market capitalization). Do you have any explanation for the difference across markets and over time?

3. Collect data on the gross national product (or gross domestic product) for various countries. These statistics can be found in the monthly edition of the IMF *Financial Statistics* or OCDE publications. Make a scatter plot of the various countries, with the stock market capitalization on the *Y*-axis and the GNP on the *X*-axis. What comments can you make?

4*. The value of the U.S. dollar went down after 1985. How did it affect the geographical breakdown of the world market capitalization?

5. Let's consider the French stock market. Collect data on France's gross national product (or its gross domestic product) for the years covered in Exh. 6.1. These statistics can be found in yearbook editions of the IMF *Financial Statistics* or in OCDE publications. Look at the ratio of the French market capitalization to GNP and provide some interpretation for its evolution.

6*. You are a French institutional investor and wish to buy 1000 shares of General Motors. Your U.S. broker quotes 45–45$^{1/4}$, with a commission of 0.20% of the transaction value. Your bank quotes the FF/$ rate at 5.3000–5.3100 net. What would be your total costs in French francs?

7*. A French investor bought 100 shares of IBM on January 1 on the New York Stock Exchange at $120. The exchange rate was FF/$=7.00. Over the year, the investor has received a gross dividend of $4 per share; the net dividend received is $3.4 because of a 15% withholding tax levied by the United States. The exchange rate at the time of dividend payment was FF/$=7.1. By December 31 the investor resells the IBM shares at $140, but the exchange rate has dropped suddenly to FF/$=6.8. Ignoring commissions, what is the rate of return on the investment, in dollars and francs, gross and net of taxes? Our French investor is taxed at 50% on income and 15% on capital gains; the U.S. withholding tax can be used as a tax credit in France.

8. You are the manager of an American pension fund and decide, on January 5, to buy 10,000 shares of British Airways listed in London. You sell them on February 5. Here are the quotes that you can use:

	January 5	February 5
British Airways	3.50–3.52 £	3.81–3.83 £
$/£	1.5000–1.5040	1.4500–1.4540

You must pay the U.K. broker a commission of 0.2% of the transaction value (on the purchase and on the sale). There is a 0.5% U.K. securities transaction tax on purchase (but not on sale); this tax cannot be recovered. Foreign exchange rates are net of commissions and taxes. What is your dollar rate of return on the operation? Would the rate of return be the same for a British investor using the British pound as reference currency?

9. You hold some shares of BMW listed in Frankfurt. The share price is DM750, and a gross dividend of DM30 is paid. The current exchange rate is 1.55 DM/$. The German government imposes a 15% withholding tax on dividends paid to U.S. investors. Your marginal tax rate is 30%.

   ■ What dividend per share will you receive in U.S. dollars?

   ■ What tax will you have to pay to the U.S. government on the dividend received?

10. Your pension fund decides to invest in many national stock markets in a passive way. The objective is to try to match the performance of the local market capitalization–weighted index in each country. You do not buy national index funds but invest directly in companies listed on each market. Because of the limited size of your portfolios, you can buy only 10 issues in each market. In which national markets are you likely to track the index well or badly?

11*. You are a U.S. investor and wish to buy 10,000 shares of Club Méditérannée (Club Med). You can buy them on the Paris bourse or on SEAQ in London. You ask the brokers to quote you net prices (no commissions paid). There are no taxes on foreign shares listed in London. Here are the quotes:

Club Med

London (in £)	$56^{3/4}$–$57^{1/4}$
Paris (in FF)	450–460
$/£	1.5000–1.5040
FF/$	5.3000–5.3100

What is your total dollar cost if you buy the Club Med shares at the cheaper place? Are there arbitrage opportunities between London and Paris?

12. Royal Dutch is listed as an ADR on the New York Stock Exchange. It is also listed in Amsterdam. Here are some quotes:

Royal Dutch

NYSE (in $)	$107^{1/2}$–$108^{3/8}$
Amsterdam (in DG)	187–188
Dutch guilder/$	1.7360–1.7380

In addition, you have to pay a commission of 0.3% in New York or 0.5% in Amsterdam.

   - Where should you buy (sell) Royal Dutch shares if you were a U.S. investor?
   - If all commissions were waived for a large transaction, would your answer be the same?
   - Answer the same questions for a Dutch investor.

13. Some Dutch, Swiss, and British companies with multiple listing are famous for having a very large transaction volume on foreign stock markets. Why? Some newly privatized firms, such as British Telecom, have a very large trading volume in New York. Advance some reasons.

14. It is often argued that automated trading systems (order-driven) must provide special arrangements for small trades, as well as for block trading. Advance some explanations.

15. Why is the NYSE trading procedure considered a mixture of a dealer market (price-driven) and an auction market (order-driven)?

16*. The following statement was heard in Paris:

   In the traditional criée system of the Paris bourse, investors were sure to obtain a fair price, but transactions could take place only once a day. The computerized CAC system with continuous trading is more risky for investors.

   - What do you think of this statement?
   - Why do trading halts (the Japanese system) make sense?

17*. Is an automated price-driven system likely to induce financial firms to become market makers in the less liquid issues? How is it different on an order-driven system?

Notes

1. A good historical review of the development of stock exchanges can be found in M. Tapley, ed., "Historical Introduction," in *International Portfolio Management*, London: Euromoney Publications, 1982; see also R.C. Michie, *The London and New York Stock Exchanges, 1850–1914*, London: Allen and Unwin, 1987.

2. See also R.D. Huang and H.R. Stoll, "The Design of Trading Systems: Lessons from Abroad," *Financial Analysts Journal*, September-October 1992. Description of various national microstructures can be found in H. Stoll, ed., *Micro-structure of World Trading Markets*, Norwell, MA: Kluwer Academic Publishers, 1993; R.A. Schwartz, *Equity Markets: Structure, Trading and Performance*, New York: Harper & Row, 1988; R.R. Lindsey and U. Schaede, "Specialist vs. Saitori: Market Making in New York and

Tokyo," *Financial Analysts Journal*, July-August 1992; B.N. Lehmann and D.M. Modest, "Trading and Liquidity on the Tokyo Stock Exchange: A Bird's Eye View," *Journal of Finance*, July 1994.

3. SuperDOT (Designated Order Turnaround) is part of a global order routing and communication network that embraces many subsystems: CMS (Central Message Switch), PPS (Post Support System), and so on. The OARS (Opening Automated Report System) is used to set the opening price of all stocks, using an auction system.

4. ITS is an electronic network linking most U.S. stock exchanges and the OTC (over-the-counter) market to facilitate execution of orders in eligible securities at the best available quote.

5. Some restrictions have ben introduced for large trades. See the following discussion.

6. This is somewhat different from the NYSE procedure, whereby limit orders are cleared at the block's transaction price, not at their limit price.

7. *Euromoney* periodically provides a list of companies with multiple listing in its annual equity market review.

8. *International Herald Tribune*, June 25, 1994.

9. Some discussion of dual-listed securities can be found in K.D. Garbade and W.L. Silber, "Dominant and Satellite Markets: A Study of Dually Traded Securities," *Review of Economics and Statistics*, August 1979; N. Jayaramanan, K. Shastri, and K. Tandon, "The Impact of International Cross-Listings on Risk and Return: The Evidence from American Depository Receipts," *Journal of Banking and Finance*, March 1993; F.R. Edwards, "Listing of Foreign Securities on U.S. Exchanges," *Journal of Applied Corporate Finance*, Winter 1993; and C.S. Eun and H. Jang, "Price Interactions in a Sequential Global Market: Evidence from the Cross-Listed Stocks," Working paper, College of Business and Management, University of Maryland, March 1994. An interesting study of the stock price of Royal Dutch/Shell and Unilever is provided in L. Rosenthal and C. Young, "The Seemingly Anomalous Price Behavior of Royal Dutch/Shell and Unilever NV/Plc," *Journal of Financial Economics*, July 1990.

Bibliography

"Annual Equity Market Review," *Euromoney*, various issues.

Edwards, F.R. "Listing of Foreign Securities on U.S. Exchanges," *Journal of Applied Corporate Finance*, Winter 1993.

Eun, C.S., and Jang, H. "Price Interactions in a Sequential Global Market: Evidence from the Cross-Listed Stocks," Working paper, College of Business and Management, University of Maryland, March 1994.

Garbade, K.D., and Silber, W.L. "Dominant and Satellite Markets: A Study of Dually Traded Securities," *Review of Economics and Statistics*, August 1979.

Huang, R.D., and Stoll, H.R. "The Design of Trading Systems: Lessons from Abroad," *Financial Analysts Journal*, September-October 1992.

Jayaramanan, N., Shastri, K., and Tandon, K. "The Impact of International Cross-Listings on Risk and Return: the Evidence from American Depository Receipts," *Journal of Banking and Finance*, March 1993.

Kemp, L.J. *A Guide to World Money and Capital Markets*, New York: McGraw-Hill, 1992.

Lehmann, B.N., and Modest, D.M. "Trading and Liquidity on the Tokyo Stock Exchange: A Bird's Eye View," *Journal of Finance*, July 1994.

Levine, S.M., ed., *Global Investing: A Handbook for Sophisticated Investors*, New York: HarperBusiness, 1992.

Lindsey, R.R., and Schaede, U. "Specialist vs. Saitori: Market Making in New York and Tokyo," *Financial Analysts Journal*, July-August 1992.

McDonald, J. "The Mochiai Effect Japanese Corporate Cross-holdings," *Journal of Portfolio Management*, Fall 1989.

Rhee, S.G., and Chang, R.P., eds. *Pacific-Basin Capital Market Research*, Amsterdam: North-Holland, 1990.

Roll, R. "The International Crash of October 1987," *Financial Analysts Journal*, September/October 1988.

Schwartz, R.A. *Equity Markets: Structure, Trading and Performance*, New York: Harper & Row, 1988.

Stoll, H., ed. *Micro-structure of World Trading Markets*, Norwell, MA: Kluwer Academic Publishers, 1993.

Takagi, S. "The Japanese Equity Market: Past and Present," *Journal of Banking and Finance*, September 1989.

Tapley, M., ed. *International Portfolio Management*, Euromoney Publications, 1986.

7

Equity: Concepts and Techniques

*I*nvesting in foreign stocks poses at least two types of problems:

- First, the portfolio manager must gain sufficient familiarity with the operations, trading mechanisms, costs, and constraints of foreign markets. This issue was addressed in Chapter 6.

- Second, the portfolio manager's investment approach must be global; that is, his or her method for analyzing and selecting stocks should be part of an optimal worldwide investment strategy. The technical aspects of this analysis are discussed in this chapter. Chapter 16 is devoted to designing a global international asset allocation strategy.

The greatest challenge faced by an international money manager is dealing with the sheer complexity of the international capital markets. Among the many factors the manager must take into account are the following:

- the large variety of instruments that currently exist, including stocks, bonds, short-term bills, and derivatives

- the large number of national markets and currencies that are found worldwide

- the many sectors from which to choose, ranging from industrial to geographic sectors

- the range of objectives sought by the investors the manager serves

In order for our approach to international investment to be effective, these aspects must be incorporated into both the operational design and the performance controls of our investment strategy. In this chapter we deal with investing in common stocks.

Analyzing a particular investment is a technical undertaking that will lead to some *forecasts* about its future value, but it is only a first step. The next step is to analyze each investment in terms of a *tractable number of parameters*, so we need to identify the major *factors* influencing international security price behavior and determine the *sensitivity* of each security to these factors. Only then can we directly compare the alternatives and thereby reach our overall investment objectives.

Hence the purpose of this chapter is to present some methods used to reduce the complexity of a detailed analysis of a company stock to a limited number of parameters. These parameters are then used to structure a global portfolio consistent with a desired strategy, as outlined in Chapter 17. We will review the common problems of international financial analysis and then identify the major factors influencing stock price behavior. From this foundation we will discuss the applicable theoretical framework.

Approaching International Analysis

There is nothing unique to financial analysis in an international context. U.S. analysts must already take foreign variables into account in evaluating domestic U.S. firms. After all, product markets in which many domestic industrial companies compete are international.

Large domestic firms tend to export extensively and head a network of foreign subsidiaries. These companies must be analyzed as international firms, not purely domestic ones. In many sectors the competition is fully international. Exhibit 7.1 indicates the 50 largest industrial corporations, ranked by sales. Most of the world's major car manufacturers appear on this list (they all belong on the top-100 list); the same holds true for other industrial sectors, such as petroleum, chemicals, and electronics. Nineteen European and 13 Japanese corporations appear on this list but only 15 U.S. corporations. A similar ranking of banks according to different criteria is published yearly by *Fortune* and *Euromoney*. The 1994 ranking of banks by *Fortune*, based on total assets, is given in Exh. 7.2. Only 5 U.S. banks are among the top 50 institutions. Twenty-three Europe and 21 Japanese banks are represented in the top 50.

The methods and data required to analyze U.S.-, French-, or Italian-type manufacturers are quite similar and for this reason are not covered in detail here. In brief, research on a company should produce two pieces of information:

- *Expected return.* The expected return on an investment can be measured by a rate of return over some time period, by a potential price appreciation, or by some other quantified form of buy or sell recommendation.

- *Risk sensitivity.* Risk sensitivity measures how much a company's value responds to certain key factors, such as economic activity, energy costs, interest rates, currency volatility, and general market conditions. Risk analysis enables a manager or investment policy committee to simulate the performance of an investment in different scenarios. It also helps them to design more diversified portfolios.

EXHIBIT 7.1

The World's Largest Industrial Corporations

Corporation	Nationality	Sales $ billions	Assets $ billions
1. General Motors	U.S.	133.6	188.2
2. Ford Motor	U.S.	108.5	198.9
3. Exxon	U.S.	97.8	84.1
4. Royal Dutch–Shell	Britain/Netherlands	95.1	99.7
5. Toyota Motor	Japan	85.3	88.2
6. Hitachi	Japan	68.6	87.2
7. I.B.M.	U.S.	62.7	81.1
8. Matsushita Electric Inc.	Japan	61.4	80.0
9. General Electric	U.S.	60.8	251.5
10. Daimler-Benz	Germany	59.1	52.3
11. Mobil	U.S.	56.6	40.6
12. Nissan Motor	Japan	53.8	71.6
13. British Petroleum	Britain	52.5	45.8
14. Samsung	South Korea	51.3	50.5
15. Philip Morris	U.S.	50.6	51.2
16. IRI	Italy	50.5	N.A.
17. Siemens	Germany	50.4	46.2
18. Volkswagen	Germany	46.3	45.6
19. Chrysler	U.S.	43.6	43.8
20. Toshiba	Japan	42.9	52.3
21. Unilever	Britain/Netherlands	41.8	24.7
22. Nestlé	Switzerland	38.9	30.2
23. Elf Aquitaine	France	37.0	45.5
24. Honda Motor	Japan	35.8	28.5
25. ENI	Italy	34.8	51.9
26. Fiat	Italy	34.7	48.9
27. Sony	Japan	34.6	41.7
28. Texaco	U.S.	34.4	26.6
29. NEC	Japan	33.2	39.5
30. E.I. DuPont de Nemours	U.S.	32.6	37.0
31. Chevron	U.S.	32.1	34.7
32. Philips Electronics	Netherlands	31.7	23.8
33. Daewoo	South Korea	30.9	44.4
34. Procter & Gamble	U.S.	30.4	24.9
35. Renault	France	30.0	35.9
36. Fujitsu	Japan	29.1	35.0
37. Mitsubishi Electric	Japan	28.8	32.8

EXHIBIT 7.1 (CONTINUED)

The World's Largest Industrial Corporations

Corporation	Nationality	Sales $ billions	Assets $ billions
38. ASEA Brown Boveri	Switzerland	28.3	25.0
39. Hoechst	Germany	27.8	22.5
40. Alcatel Alsthom	France	27.6	43.9
41. Mitsubishi Motors	Japan	27.3	23.6
42. PEMEX	Mexico	26.6	49.3
43. Mitsubishi Heavy Ind.	Japan	25.8	39.2
44. Peugeot	France	25.7	21.4
45. Nippon Steel	Japan	25.5	42.4
46. Amoco	U.S.	25.3	28.5
47. Boeing	U.S.	25.3	20.5
48. Pepsico	U.S.	25.0	23.7
49. Bayer	Germany	24.8	23.1
50. BASF	Germany	24.5	23.2

Source: Fortune International, July 25, 1994.

The overall purpose of our analysis is to find securities with superior expected returns, given current (or foreseeable) domestic and international risks.

Quantifying the analysis facilitates a consistent global approach to international investment. This is all the more desirable when the parameters that must be considered are numerous and their interrelationships are complex. Although qualitative analysis is easier to conduct in some institutions than in others, it must be very carefully structured so that it is consistent for every security. For a qualitative method to be effective, it must offer the same investment guidance as mathematically derived factor sensitivity coefficients.

The Information Problem

Information on foreign firms is often difficult to obtain; once obtained, it is often difficult to interpret and analyze, using domestic methods. It is no wonder, then, that comparisons of similar figures for foreign firms are often misleading.

In the United States companies publish their quarterly earnings, which are publicly available within just a couple of weeks. The 10-K reports are particularly useful for trend analysis and intercompany comparisons. Moreover, these reports are available on computerized databases. In contrast certain European or Far Eastern firms publish their earnings only once a year. French companies follow this pattern and don't actually publish their earnings until six months after the end of their fiscal years.[1] As a result, French earnings estimates are outdated

EXHIBIT 7.2

The World's Largest Banks

Bank	Nationality	Assets $ billions	Deposits $ billions
1. Fuji Bank	Japan	538.2	381.7
2. Dai-Ichi Kangyo Bank	Japan	535.4	435.5
3. Sumitomo Bank	Japan	531.8	435.4
4. Sanwa Bank	Japan	525.1	435.3
5. Sakura Bank	Japan	523.7	436.6
6. Mitsubishi Bank	Japan	487.5	399.4
7. Norinchukin Bank	Japan	435.6	311.1
8. Industrial Bank of Japan	Japan	414.9	331.0
9. Crédit Lyonnais	France	337.5	143.2
10. Bank of China	China	334.7	147.0
11. Mitsubishi Trust & Banking	Japan	330.5	297.6
12. Tokai Bank	Japan	328.7	253.9
13. Deutsche Bank	Germany	320.0	283.1
14. Long-Term Credit Bank of Japan	Japan	315.0	259.8
15. Sumitomo Trust & Banking	Japan	305.3	277.5
16. HSBC Holdings	Britain	304.5	231.2
17. Mitsui Trust & Banking	Japan	296.9	269.6
18. Crédit Agricole	France	281.8	208.5
19. Asahi Bank	Japan	277.7	235.6
20. Bank of Tokyo	Japan	273.8	205.5
21. Daiwa Bank	Japan	262.6	227.3
22. Société Générale	France	259.1	212.8
23. ABN AMRO Holding	Netherlands	252.2	133.2
24. Banque Nationale de Paris	France	249.1	198.6
25. Barclays Bank	Britain	245.3	206.3
26. Yasuda Trust & Banking	Japan	235.5	215.4
27. Cie Financière de Paribas	France	229.0	126.7
28. National Westminster Bank	Britain	225.9	186.8
29. Dresdner Bank	Germany	218.9	198.2
30. Citicorp	U.S.	216.6	145.1
31. Union Bank of Switzerland	Switzerland	209.2	120.3
32. Toyo Trust & Banking	Japan	204.0	181.6
33. Westdeutsche Landesbank	Germany	191.2	170.8
34. Bankamerica Corp.	U.S.	186.9	141.6
35. Nippon Credit Bank	Japan	168.1	146.7
36. Bayerische Vereinsbank	Germany	166.3	158.1

(*continued on next page*)

EXHIBIT 7.2 (CONTINUED)

The World's Largest Banks

Bank	Nationality	Assets $ billions	Deposits $ billions
37. Commerzbank	Germany	164.1	113.9
38. Shoko Chukin Bank	Japan	160.9	147.0
39. Nationsbank Corp.	U.S.	157.7	91.1
40. Crédit Suisse	Switzerland	156.0	136.8
41. Groupe des Caisses d'Epargne	France	156.0	17.6
42. Bayerische Hyp. & Wechsel	Germany	152.7	141.6
43. Chemical Banking Corp.	U.S.	149.9	98.3
44. Bayerische Landesbank	Germany	149.6	132.5
45. Ist. Banc. San Paolo di Torino	Italy	145.9	126.2
46. Banca di Roma	Italy	141.8	79.3
47. Swiss Bank Corp.	Switzerland	139.1	97.7
48. Zenshinren Bank	Japan	137.4	101.5
49. J.P. Morgan & Co.	U.S.	133.9	40.4
50. Rabobank	Netherlands	130.0	73.6

Source: Fortune International, August 22, 1994.

before they become public. To remedy this lack of information, international corporations with large foreign ownership have begun announcing quarterly or semi-annual earnings estimates. The format and reliability of these announcements vary from firm to firm, but overall they help investors to get better-quality financial information more quickly. Like U.S. firms, British firms publish detailed financial information frequently. Similarly Japanese firms have begun publishing U.S.-style financial statements, though not as frequently as U.S. firms.

Other problems arise from the language and presentation of the financial reports. Many reports are available only in a company's local language. Whereas multinational firms tend to publish both in their local language and in English, many smaller but nevertheless attractive foreign firms do not. In general, financial reports vary widely from country to country in format, degree of detail, and reliability of the information disclosed. Therefore additional information must sometimes be obtained directly from the company. Differences in national accounting standards are discussed later in this chapter.

As international investment has grown, brokers, banks, and information services have, fortunately, started to provide more financial data to meet investors' needs. In fact, today many large international brokerage houses and banks provide analysts' guides covering companies from a large number of countries. The guides include information ranging from summary balance sheet and income statement information to growth forecasts, expected returns on equity investments, and risk measures, such as betas, which are discussed later. The reports are usually available in both the domestic language and English. Similarly several data services, such as Extel, DAFSA, Reuters, and Moody's, are extending their international coverage on companies and currently feature summary financial information on an increasing number of foreign corporations. Some financial firms, such as I/B/E/S, Euro-Equity, or Associés en Finance, have specialized in collecting earnings forecasts from financial analysts worldwide. They provide a service giving the individual analyst's forecast for most large companies listed on the major stock exchanges of the world. They also calculate a consensus forecast, as well as various other global statistics.

Despite these developments, to get the most timely information possible, financial analysts may have to visit foreign corporations. This, of course, is a time-consuming and expensive process. Moreover, the information obtained is often not homogenous across companies and countries. The next section reviews differences in international accounting standards.

A Vision of the World

A major challenge faced by all investment organizations is structuring their international research efforts. Their choice of method depends on what they believe are the major factors influencing stock returns. The objective of security analysis is to detect relative misvaluation, i.e., investments that are preferable to other *comparable* investments. That is why sectoral analysis is so important. A financial analyst should be assigned the study of securities that belong to the same sector, i.e., that are influenced by the *same* common factors and that can therefore be directly compared. The question is to determine these sectors, or common factors. For example, one can reasonably claim that all dollar Eurobonds with fixed coupons belong to the same sector. Another sector would be French common stocks, which are all influenced by national factors. An alternative would be all high-technology companies across the world, which are supposed to be influenced by similar worldwide industrial factors. In a homogeneous sector, research should detect securities that are underpriced or overpriced relative to the others.

A first step for an organization to structure its global equity investment requires that it adhere to some vision of the world regarding the dominant factors affecting stock returns. Traditionally investment organizations use one of two major approaches to international research, depending on their vision of the world:

- If a portfolio manager believes that all securities in a national stock market are influenced primarily by domestic factors, his or her research effort should be structured on a country-by-country basis. The most important investment decision in this approach is how to allocate assets among countries. Thereafter, securities are given a relative valuation within each national market.

- If a portfolio manager believes that the value of companies worldwide is affected primarily by international industrial factors, his or her research effort should be structured according to industrial sectors. This means that companies are valued relative to others within the same industrial sector, e.g., the chemical industry. Naturally financial analysts who use this approach are specialists in particular industrial sectors. Unfortunately this approach has major drawbacks. As shown later in this chapter, the stock return on most companies is influenced primarily by domestic factors, not industrial factors. Also, there are a number of practical impediments to conducting a comparative analysis of companies located in different countries, as we shall soon discover.

In general, an organization must structure its investment process based on some vision of the major common factors influencing stock returns worldwide. These are discussed later on.

Differences in National Accounting Standards

We will now detail the difficulties encountered when analyzing and comparing the financial information and statements published by companies based in different parts of the world.

Are Financial Statements Comparable Internationally?

Trying to compare financial statements from different countries is a difficult task. Different countries employ different accounting principles, and even where the same accounting methods are used, cultural, institutional, political, and tax differences can make between-country comparisons of accounting numbers hazardous and misleading.

For example, the treatment of depreciation and extraordinary items varies greatly among countries, so much so, in fact, that an analyst would probably have to double the net income of many Swedish, German, or Japanese firms in order to make a meaningful comparison with the corresponding figures for British or U.S. firms. This disparity is partly the result of different national tax incentives and the creation of "secret" reserves in certain countries. German and Swiss firms, for example, are known to stretch the definition of a liability; that is, they tend to overestimate contingent liabilities and future uncertainties when compared to U.S. firms.

German firms create hidden reserves—sometimes equal to 100% of fixed assets—to economize on taxes and to smooth reported earnings. Their inventories tend to be understated for tax purposes and are not revalued when goods prices go up. Mergers and takeovers are reported in the balance sheet based on book value, not on actual transaction prices, so underestimating the value of equity. German reports to stockholders have to be those produced for tax purposes. Since corporations use accounting techniques to reduce taxable earnings, the reported earnings understate the true economic earnings compared to a similar U.S. or English company. Similarly, Sweden has a very favorable tax system for corporations. Tax incentives, such as accelerated depreciation, inventory write-off, and various other provisions, cause Swedish firms to report what are considered distorted net income figures by the standards of the U.S. generally accepted accounting principles (GAAP).

Comparing Japanese and U.S. earnings figures or accounting ratios is virtually meaningless.[2] As a result, many large Japanese companies now publish secondary financial statements in English that conform to the U.S. GAAP and are audited by major U.S. accounting firms. But even when we examine these statements, we find that financial ratios differ markedly between the two countries. For example, financial leverage is high in Japan compared to the United States, and coverage ratios are poor. But this does not mean that Japanese firms are more risky than their U.S. counterparts, only that the relationship between banks and their client corporations is different from that in the United States.

Major Differences in Accounting Practices

Each country follows a set of accounting principles that are usually prepared by the accounting profession and the national authorities. These sets of accounting principles are called national GAAP (generally accepted accounting practices). Two different models apply to the preparation of these national accounting principles:

- In the Anglo-American model accounting rules are set in *standards* prepared by a well-established, influential accounting profession.[3]

- In Continental Europe and Japan accounting rules are set in a codified *law* system; governmental bodies write the law, and the accounting profession is less influential than in the Anglo-American model.

Anglo-American countries typically report financial statements intended to give a *true and fair view* of the firm's financial position. Hence there can be big differences between *accounting statements*, whose intent is to give a fair representation of the firm's financial position, and *tax statements*, whose intent is to reflect the various tax provisions used to calculate the amount of income tax owed. Many other countries (France, Germany, Italy, and Japan, for example) have a tradition that the reported financial statements and earnings conform to the method used to determine taxable income. This implies that financial statements are geared to satisfy tax provisions and may not give the true and fair view of the firm. This confusion between tax and book accounting is slowly disappearing under the pressure of international harmonization, as stressed later.

An overview of national accounting principles can be found in international accounting textbooks.[4] It appears that the most important differences arise in numerous areas shown in Exh. 7.3. Some of these differences are detailed in the following discussion.

EXHIBIT 7.3

Major Differences in Accounting Practices among Countries

Publication of consolidated statements

Publication of accounts corrected for fiscal distortion

Treatment of goodwill and intangibles

Inflation and revaluation accounting

Depreciation methods

Existence of "hidden" reserves

Treatment of pension liabilities

Research and development

Currency adjustments and treatment of currency hedging

Treatment of extraordinary expenses

Inventory valuation

Stability of accounting principles used

Consolidation   In most countries corporations publish financial statements that consolidate, to some extent, the accounts of their subsidiaries and affiliates. A full range of consolidation practices is observable.[5] In all countries majority interests in domestic subsidiaries are typically consolidated. This is not always the case when dealing with foreign subsidiaries or with minority interests. In Germany or Japan, for example, minority interests are typically valued at historical cost on the balance sheet, with no impact on the earnings statement, except for the dividend paid by the subsidiary. In France there is considerable leeway in the method used for consolidation. Japanese companies, like many German firms, tend to prefer to publish separately the (nonconsolidated) financial statements of the various companies belonging to the same group. This can be partly explained by the extent of cross-holdings in these countries. The perimeter of consolidation is often difficult to establish in Japan because of the extent of cross-holding. The practice of publishing (partly) nonconsolidated statements renders the valuation of a company a difficult exercise.

Goodwill   Goodwill can appear in various ways. Most commonly, goodwill is created when a company engages in an acquisition or merger at a market value different from the book value. In the United Kingdom goodwill is written off against reserves immediately and does not affect the income statement. In the United States goodwill is capitalized as an asset and is amortized progressively over an appropriate period, up to 40 years. In order words, this depreciation affects the income statement until full amortization. Everything else being equal, this convention tends to inflate British earnings compared to U.S. earnings. On the other hand, the British practice tends to increase book leverage (gearing) because equity is immediately reduced by the amount of goodwill. Practices in other countries tend to lie between those two extremes. New rules are being enacted in the United Kingdom that would narrow the difference with U.S. GAAP.

Asset Revaluation   Revaluation of assets is not permitted in the United States and Germany but is normally practiced in the United Kingdom. Revaluation of assets, especially real estate, is practiced to reflect inflation. The effect of asset revaluation is to increase simultaneously the value of assets and equity (revaluation reserves). It also leads to higher depreciation charges in subsequent years. In countries where financial statements are tax-driven, asset revaluation is unusual. Special laws have permitted periodic revaluation in France, Italy, and Spain in order to compensate for inflation, but the tax implications of these revaluations has sometimes been bad, making revaluation unpopular. Countries with higher inflation, such as Brazil, tend to have systems for automatic inflation indexation.

Depreciation   In most countries fixed assets are depreciated according to the straight-line formula. In the Anglo-American model assets are depreciated over their useful lives, whereas in other countries depreciation follows tax schedules. Furthermore, some countries (Japan, Korea, Germany, and the Scandinavian countries) make use of accelerated depreciation (a faster way to depreciate an asset). The use of accelerated depreciation allows tax reductions but tends to understate earnings.

Provisions   A provision is an estimate of a likely future loss or expense. It appears as a liability on the balance sheet and is deducted from current reported earnings when initially taken. In many countries, such as the United States, United Kingdom, Italy, and Spain, provisions can be taken only for *specific* and *likely* future events. In Germany and Switzerland generous provisions can be taken for all types of general risks. In good times German firms will build provisions to reduce earnings growth; in bad times German firms will draw on these provisions to boost reported earnings. These provisions are called *hidden reserves* because they do not appear as equity reserves on the balance sheet but rather as general liability (debt). However, they can be used to boost profits in bad times. This important difference between U.S. GAAP and German rules can lead to marked differences in reported total equity and earnings. In 1993 Daimler-Benz became the first German company to be listed on the NYSE. This forced Daimler-Benz to file a reconciliation statement with U.S. GAAP (form 20-F). Because Daimler-Benz drew on hidden reserves during the recession of 1993, its German reported profit was a small, but positive, DM615 million. It translated into a DM3.6 billion loss according to U.S. GAAP. Daimler's 1993 net worth translates from DM18.15 billion under German rules to DM23.92 billion under U.S. GAAP.

Pensions   The accounting for pensions and retirement liabilities differs widely across countries, in part because of the national differences in pension systems. A first difference is whether pension liabilities are *accrued*, i.e., whether there is an actuarial evaluation of future pension expenses (and on what basis). A second difference is whether the pensions are *funded* off balance sheets or whether pension assets and liabilities remain on the balance sheet of the company. Some countries, e.g., France and Italy, have primarily a national pay-as-you-go pension system, whereby current workers pay for the pensions of retired workers; companies contribute to pensions, but future pension liabilities are neither accrued nor funded, and current pension costs are expensed as incurred. In the United States, the Netherlands, Switzerland, the United Kingdom, and to some extent Japan, pensions are accrued and funded off balance sheets; a separate entity, called *pension fund*, manages the pension assets and liabilities. In Germany or Spain, pensions are accrued but not funded, so pension assets remain on the company's balance sheet. The assumptions used to estimate accrued pension liabilities also vary across countries and firms.

Research and Development Expenditures   The conservative approach used in the United States is to require such expenditures to be expensed as incurred. In other countries, such as the United Kingdom, such research and development costs may be capitalized and progressively amortized over the life of the research investment. In countries where financial statements are tax-driven, these expenses must often be capitalized and then progressively amortized like any fixed asset, because they are not immediately tax-deductible as expenses.

Currency Hedging   The accounting treatment of currency translation is a very complex area, and many national differences in accounting practices can be found.[6] The treatment of currency risk hedging can introduce major differences in reported earnings. Currency hedging takes place when a specific foreign currency asset is funded by a loan in the same foreign currency or when the currency risk on a specific foreign currency asset or liability is hedged using derivative contracts (forward exchange contracts, currency options, swaps, and so on). To illustrate the differences in accounting treatment, let's assume that a corporation has funded a foreign asset with a loan in the same foreign currency and that the foreign currency appreciates. This would lead to a (currency) gain on the asset and a (currency) loss on the loan. U.K. rules allow an offset of the currency losses and gains on the foreign currency asset and on the foreign currency loan. In the United States and most other countries, the loss on the loan must be taken through the income statement but not the appreciation in asset value. The impact on current earnings can be significant. For example, British Airways hedges its purchase of new planes, paid in dollars. In the fiscal year 1993 British Airways had a profit of U.K.£178 million, using British accounting standards. Because British Airways is traded as an ADR on the NYSE, it reported that its profits according to U.S. GAAP would have been reduced to U.K.£45 million because of the differential treatment in foreign currency hedging.

International Harmonization in Accounting Practices

Investors exert pressure to harmonize national accounting principles. The International Accounting Standard Committee (IASC) was set up in 1973 by leading professional accounting organizations in 9 countries and now represents a large number of organizations in more than 70 countries. The major objective of the IASC is to develop international accounting standards (IAS) that meet the needs of the capital markets in terms of accounting standards and disclosure. The IASC also wants the standards to meet the needs of developing and newly industrialized countries. In the past the IASC has met with limited success because of its lack of enforcement power. However, several emerging countries, as well as Hong Kong, have recently adopted the IAS as a basis for their accounting standards. The FASB has announced that it will consider the IAS when setting its own international standards. The International Organization of Securities Commissions (IOSCO) has also endorsed some of the standards set forth by the IASC.

The harmonization of European accounting principles has come mostly through directives published by the European Union. These EU Directives are drafted by the EU Commission and are adopted by member states' parliaments. The national legislations must then be rewritten to conform with these EU Directives. As of 1995, the EU has issued 12 directives dealing with accounting principles. The *Fourth Directive*, issued in 1978, deals with accounting rules. It sets forward the principle that financial statements must give a *true and fair view* of the company's financial situation. The *Seventh Directive*, issued in 1983, deals with the consolidation of financial statements. To be acceptable by all member states, these directives have to be drafted in fairly general terms, and their translation in national accounting standards is quite slow. There is considerable leeway in the implementation of these directives at the national level.

The Impact of Accounting Principles on Earnings and Stock Prices

Accounting Standards and Reported Earnings   The same company using different national accounting standards could report different earnings as was illustrated. Some accounting standards are more conservative than others, in the sense that they lead to smaller reported earnings. Several comparative studies have attempted to measure the relative conservativeness of national standards.[7] For example, Radebaugh and Gray (1993) conclude that U.S. accounting principles are significantly more conservative than U.K. principles but significantly less conservative than Japanese and Continental European accounting principles. If the United States is rated at 100, Japanese earnings would rate at 66, German earnings at 87, French earnings at 97, and British earnings at 125. Various studies come up with somewhat different adjustments, so these figures should be interpreted with some caution.

These national accounting principles also affect the reported book value of equity. Speidell and Bavishi (1992) report the adjustment that should be made to the book value of foreign shareholders' equity if U.S. GAAP were used. They find that the book value of equity would be increased by 41% in Germany and 14% in Japan and would be reduced by 14% in the United Kingdom and 28% in France.

Price-earnings (PE) ratios are of great interest to international investors, who tend to compare the PE ratios of companies in the same industrial sector across the world. The PE ratio divides the market price of a share by its current or estimated annual earnings. Japanese companies have traditionally traded at very high PE ratios in comparison with those of U.S. companies. For comparison purposes, these PE ratios should be adjusted because of the differences in accounting earnings. They should also be adjusted to reflect the fact that Japanese firms tend to report nonconsolidated statements despite the extent of cross-holding. For example, if Company A owns 20% of the shares of Company B, it will include in its own earnings only the dividend paid by Company B, not a proportion of Company B's earnings. In the PE ratio of Company A, the stock price reflects the value of the holding of shares of Company B, but the earnings do not reflect the earnings of Company B. For all these reasons, French and Poterba (1991) claim that the average Japanese PE ratio in 1989 should be adjusted from 53.7 to 32.6. Other authors come up with an even bigger reduction in Japanese PE ratios.

The Information Content of International Differences in GAAP   Investors request companies to disclose accurate information on a timely basis. The national GAAP dictate the format in which the information is disclosed. Investors would like companies to use accounting principles that provide the most informative presentation of the accounting numbers. It is difficult to tell if there exists an optimal accounting standard that would apply equally to all nations. The SEC requests that all foreign firms listed on a public stock exchange in the United States, including NASDAQ, provide financial reports along the U.S. GAAP (form 10-K) or provide all necessary reconciliation information (form 20-F). This is a controversial policy, as many foreign firms, especially medium-size ones, do not wish to carry the burden and costs of presenting all their financial statements under two different accounting standards. For example, this has deterred most Continental European companies from a dual listing on the NYSE. U.S. investors wishing to buy the shares of these European companies have to do it in London, which does not impose such a requirement for foreign firms, or on the respective national stock exchanges. This reduces the international role of U.S. stock exchanges. Hence a major question is whether the presentation of earnings using U.S. GAAP provides useful information above their presentation using domestic GAAP. If the difference between the two numbers has some information content, it should affect the stock price. The difference in earnings under U.S. and other national accounting principles has been illustrated for Daimler-Benz and British Airways.

A major question for investors is determining which GAAP provide the best information. It is difficult to find the answer to such a question. Some insights can be gained by looking at the reaction of stock prices to earnings reported according to different national standards. Studies have focused on foreign firms dually listed in the United States, which must also provide earnings calculated according to U.S. GAAP.[8] If U.S. GAAP provide incremental information relative to foreign GAAP, stock prices should show some reaction to the difference between the two reported earnings. Preliminary evidence seems to suggest that "the GAAP earnings adjustments add marginally to the ability of earnings to explain returns" (Pope and Rees, 1992, p. 190).

Another approach has been to survey international money managers to see if they find added value in obtaining financial statements under different national GAAP.[9] Choi and Levich (1991) surveyed a variety of capital market participants (institutional investment managers, corporate issuers, and regulators) and found that roughly half of them feel that their capital market decisions are affected by accounting diversity. However, most of them find ways to cope with this diversity. Some restate all financial statements to a common, more familiar accounting framework; others have become familiarized with foreign accounting practices and adopt a local perspective when analyzing foreign statements; others simply do not use accounting numbers in their investment decisions. Bhushan and Lessard (1992) surveyed 49 U.S.-based international money managers. All of them regard accounting harmonization as a good thing but do not find that providing reconciled accounting information is crucial; they tend to focus on valuing firms within their own markets and stress the importance of the quality and timeliness of the information disclosed.

Indeed the quality and speed of information disclosure is of paramount importance to investors. Restating the same information in a different accounting standard does not address the issue of the quality of the information disclosed or the firm's future prospects. Investment managers deciding to include a specific stock in a portfolio need to do more than simply look at past accounting data.

Stock Market Valuation

The valuation of a common stock is usually conducted in two steps. First, the company must be valued within its market. Second, the national stock market must also be valued relative to the other markets.

Individual Stock Valuation

To evaluate a company, its financial statements are studied along with its overall market and growth potential. On the basis of this analysis, a forecast is made of the company's future earnings. Next, an assessment is made of how the stock market will value these forecasts. In other words, the first level of analysis is specific to the company and its product market; the second level is general, focusing on the relative valuation of the company within the stock market. The traditional measures for these two forms of analyses are, respectively, expected earnings per share (EPS) and the price earnings (PE) ratio. This simple approach to stock market valuation is sometimes replaced by a more quantitative approach based on projecting dividend streams (rather than earnings) and requiring the use of a dividend discount model as described later. But no matter how the financial analysis is done, problems arise at both levels of valuation.

Stock markets in different countries value different attributes. Thus the same earnings forecast can lead to a different stock price valuation, depending on the nationality of the corporation. For example, the average price-earnings ratio varies greatly among countries, as shown in Exh. 7.4. Indeed we find that comparable firms in the same industry but in different countries can have markedly different PE ratios. For example, U.S. and U.K. corporations tend to have much lower PE ratios than do German or Japanese firms. Therefore the cheapest companies are not necessarily the most attractive. This result obtains even if we adjust the earnings estimates for differences in national accounting principles. All this indicates is that there are national differences in earnings accounting and stock market perception rather than mispricing of comparable firms.

In Europe Swedish and German companies tend to sell well above their accounting book values if their ratios of stock price to book value are compared to those of Dutch, French, or Italian firms But this does not mean that German equity should be arbitraged against Dutch equity. Rather, it means that the two markets react differently.

Investors often rely on a dividend discount model (DDM) for estimating the expected return on a stock investment. The value of an asset is determined by the stream of cash flows it generates for the investor. In a DDM the stock market price is set equal to the stream of forecasted dividends.

$$P = \frac{D_1}{1+r} + \frac{D_2}{(1+r)^2} + \frac{D_3}{(1+r)^3} + \dots \qquad (7.1)$$

Financial analysts take great care in forecasting future earnings and hence dividends. A typical DDM approach is to decompose the future in three phases. In the near future (e.g., the next two years), earnings are forecasted individually. In the second phase (e.g., years two to five), a general growth rate of the company's earnings is estimated. In the final stage the growth rate in earnings is supposed to revert to the average rate of all firms in the market. Application of Eq. (7.1) where the expected dividends (D_t) and the current stock market price (P) are known allows the derivation of the expected return (r) on an investment in the company's stock.

These models readily permit the direct comparison of corporations traded on the same stock market (after adjusting for risk, as described later). But to make an international comparison of expected returns requires an accurate forecast of currency movements as well. The presence of so many differences among countries explains why most international money managers value corporations relative to their domestic markets, before even attempting to value them globally in relation to their direct product market competitors. The logic behind this country-specific approach is amply supported by study of the major factors influencing stock returns.

EXHIBIT 7.4

Stock Market Valuation				
P/BV	P/CE	P/E	Yield	Index
				International indexes
2.26	9.9	26.7	2.2	World
2.51	10.0	20.1	2.8	North America
2.13	9.9	33.8	1.9	EAFE
1.94	8.3	22.6	3.1	Europe
2.30	12.2	53.1	1.0	Pacific
				National indexes
1.72	10.6	17.2	3.4	Australia
1.67	7.5	loss	1.1	Austria
1.59	6.9	20.1	4.2	Belgium
1.77	11.4	44.7	2.5	Canada
2.40	8.7	19.2	1.7	Denmark
1.50	10.2	loss	0.9	Finland
1.55	7.7	27.2	3.1	France
2.10	6.2	60.3	2.4	Germany
2.16	14.2	16.6	2.9	Hong Kong
1.97	11.6	15.3	2.4	Ireland
1.77	7.9	n.s.	1.4	Italy
2.33	11.9	88.0	0.7	Japan
3.61	19.5	28.4	1.0	Malaysia
1.71	7.8	17.6	3.5	Netherlands
1.89	10.1	13.7	4.3	New Zealand
1.95	6.6	16.3	1.7	Norway
1.96	12.6	20.4	1.3	Singapore
1.50	6.7	n.s.	3.4	Spain
2.31	12.0	30.1	1.3	Sweden
2.10	9.6	17.5	1.8	Switzerland
2.22	9.7	15.5	4.2	United Kingdom
2.58	9.9	19.5	2.8	U.S.A.

Valuation: P/BV: price to book-value ratio;
P/CE: price to cash earnings (earnings + depreciation) ratio;
P/E: price earnings ratio;
Yield: gross dividend yield;
n.s.: not significant.
Source: Morgan Stanley Capital International, May 31, 1994.

Country Analysis

Asset allocation is a major decision in international portfolio management. The choice of instruments, markets, and currencies often has more impact on portfolio performance than the selection of specific securities within each market. So the relative valuation of national stock markets is of paramount importance in the construction of a portfolio of individual securities. An active allocation strategy requires the study and forecast of changes in at least three types of financial variables: currencies, interest rates, and stock markets.

The latter two variables affect the performance of bond and stock portfolios. Currency not only is one of the many variables indirectly affecting asset prices but directly affects the domestic performance of all foreign assets through the translation of foreign currency into the domestic one. The issue of currency forecasting was addressed in Chapter 3, where we stressed that it is difficult. It is not easier to forecast the relative performance of national stock markets. In each country economists try to monitor a large number of economic, social, and political variables, such as

- anticipated real growth

- monetary policy

- wage and employment rigidities

- competitiveness

- social and political situations

- fiscal policy (including fiscal incentives for investments)

- economic sensitivity to energy costs

Real economic growth is probably the major influence on a national stock market. Of course, stock markets react to anticipated growth. If the past gives any indication of the future, Exh. 7.5 indicates marked differences in real growth among countries. This figure shows the cumulative growth rate of the gross domestic product (GDP) of the United States, the major industrial countries,[10] and selected Asian countries. Although the United States had a cumulative real growth rate close to 150% from 1962 to 1993, this is below the average of industrial countries and well below that of most Asian countries. The economic growth of Japan, Hong Kong, and Singapore explains their excellent long-term stock market performance. The volatility of economic growth in developing countries explains in part the greater volatility of their stock markets.

Many researchers have found that expected returns on national stock markets vary over time in a somewhat predictable fashion.[11] As discussed in Chapter 5, there is no reason for risk premia to stay constant over time. For example, Harvey (1991) found that variations in expected stock returns could be explained by U.S. and national variables, such as the term spread (the difference between long- and short-term interest rates), the default-risk spread (the difference between yields on Aaa and junk bonds), and the interest rate differential between two countries, a foreign exchange variable. This line of research uses only market-observable financial variables. There is no need to estimate future macroeconomic variables for the

EXHIBIT 7.5

Cumulative Percentage Change in Real GDP

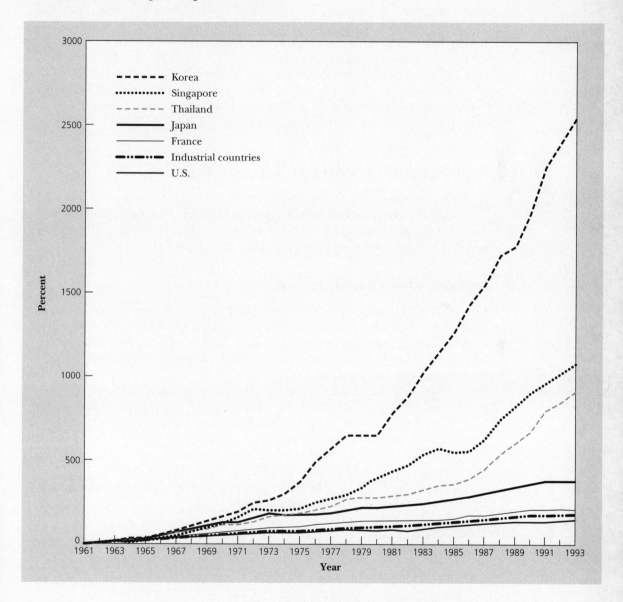

next few years, and there are no problems of measurement. These models are usually estimated in the form of regressions of the next-period realized stock market return on the observed financial variables. Although the explanatory power of the regressions is often small, the parameters are statistically significant. So these forecasts, conditional on the financial environment, tend to have some predictive ability. Harvey (1994) found good predictive ability for emerging stock markets. Solnik

(1993a, 1993b) used forecasts derived from these models to build optimal international asset allocation strategies that are optimal in a risk/return framework. He found that these conditional strategies dominate passive investment strategies. Although the difference in return can be very large, it takes many years to be reasonably assured that the conditional strategies will dominate passive strategies. Furthermore, one cannot be sure that the results are not caused by data mining or data snooping, as discussed in the Chapter 3 appendix. These models have led to the development of *Tactical Asset Allocation (TAA)* strategies, which use quantitative models that automatically rebalance the international asset allocation, based on a change in the financial environment (see Chapter 17).

International Factors in Security Returns

To structure a portfolio properly, a manager must have a clear understanding of the main factors influencing the return on a security. We now present empirical evidence on the relative importance of international factors.

Domestic versus International Factors

Lessard (1976) and Solnik (1976) researched the relative importance of industry, domestic, and international factors. They concluded that there existed an international influence on stock returns but that domestic effects were much stronger. International industry effects appeared weak compared to national effects. These studies used old data (prior to 1973) from a time when most exchange rates were fixed. Since 1973 and the advent of flexible exchange rates, currency movements make a significant contribution to the total return of a foreign portfolio, and their influence on stock return must be further studied. Solnik (1984) and Adler and Simon (1986) suggest a weak correlation between stock market indexes and currency movements, but this does not rule out the existence of a selective exchange rate influence on specific firms, depending on the activity of the firm.

A simple approach to determining the relative importance of each factor is to separately correlate each individual stock with:

- the world stock index

- the appropriate (international) industrial sector index

- the currency movement

- the appropriate national market index

The first three factors may be regarded as international; the last one as domestic.

This approach was taken in a study by Solnik and de Freitas.[12] The R^2 is a measure of correlation that tells us which of the four factors is most important in explaining the return of a particular stock. The average R^2 for all companies from a given country are reported in the first four columns of Exh. 7.6. The behavior of the domestic market is by far the most important factor affecting individual stock

EXHIBIT 7.6

Relative importance of world, industrial, currency, and domestic factors in explaining return of a stock

Average R^2 of Regression on Factors

Locality	Single-factor tests				Joint test all four factors
	World	Industrial	Currency	Domestic	
Switzerland	0.18	0.17	0.00	0.38	0.39
Germany	0.08	0.10	0.00	0.41	0.42
Australia	0.24	0.26	0.01	0.72	0.72
Belgium	0.07	0.08	0.00	0.42	0.43
Canada	0.27	0.24	0.07	0.45	0.48
Spain	0.22	0.03	0.00	0.45	0.45
United States	0.26	0.47	0.01	0.35	0.55
France	0.13	0.08	0.01	0.45	0.60
United Kingdom	0.20	0.17	0.01	0.53	0.55
Hong Kong	0.06	0.25	0.17	0.79	0.81
Italy	0.05	0.03	0.00	0.35	0.35
Japan	0.09	0.16	0.01	0.26	0.33
Norway	0.17	0.28	0.00	0.84	0.85
Netherlands	0.12	0.07	0.01	0.34	0.31
Singapore	0.16	0.15	0.02	0.32	0.33
Sweden	0.19	0.06	0.01	0.42	0.43
All countries	0.18	0.23	0.01	0.42	0.46

returns; on the average, this factor explains 42% of the return on individual securities. The world and industrial factors explain 18% and 23% of the return, whereas the influence of currency movements on the local stock prices is almost insignificant. Note that the various correlations do not add up; the four factors are correlated with one another. In fact, most of the influence of the world factor is common to that of the domestic factor. This is revealed by running a multiple regression including all four factors. The average R^2 of this joint regression is given in the last column of Exh. 7.6. The simple regression of stock returns on the domestic market index return has an average R^2 of 0.42; the value rises to 0.46 when the three international factors are added in the regression. This is a rather small improvement in R^2. However, the story differs among countries; the increase in R^2 is fairly large for companies in the United States (from 0.35 to 0.55) and in France (from 0.45 to 0.60). A detailed analysis of the results indicates that the marginal contribution of the international industrial factor is generally positive and significant. The contribution of the currency movement is generally very weak but positive and appears to be country specific but not company specific. A local currency appreciation tends to be good for the local stock market.

Factor analysis was also used in this study to extract common factors from the sample of companies and to correlate them with the four sets of indexes. The previous conclusions were confirmed; the influence of the domestic market is dominant, although weaker industrial factors are significant. The influence of exchange rates is very weak and usually positive. There is little evidence of firm-specific currency influence.

Note that this last result indicates that stocks tend to be poor hedges against currency movements. When translated into the investor's home currency, all stock prices of a given foreign market tend to go up and down with the exchange rate.

Grinold, Rudd, and Stefek (1989) used a slightly different methodology to study the relative importance of country and industry factors in stock returns over the period 1983 to 1988. They also conclude that country factors are more important than industry factors. However, some industry factors are more "global" than others. For example, they found that the oil industry factor is highly significant, which is not the case for the factor of consumer goods. Drummen and Zimmerman (1992) analyzed daily returns on 105 European stocks in the late 1980s. They found that national factors clearly dominate industrial factors; the contribution of currency factors is relatively minor. This result is all the more important in that it concerns a set of companies that belong to a closely integrated European market. Heston and Rouwenhorst (1994) studied monthly returns on 829 European firms from 1978 to 1992 and confirm that the industrial structure explains very little of the cross-sectional difference in European country returns and volatility. The country effect strongly dominates the industry effect. Wadhwani (1991) confirms this conclusion. He finds that the average correlation of stocks within the same European industrial sector is a mere 0.040 when country effects have been taken into account. This extremely low correlation means that European stocks have very little common price movement within the same industrial sector. A major exception is oil stocks and, to a small extent, the sectors of financial institutions, transport, auto components, and beverages/tobacco.

To summarize, there is strong, although somewhat surprising, evidence that the stock price of a company is affected primarily by domestic factors.

The Valuation of Multinational Firms: Domestic or International?

Some companies conduct a large percentage of their activities abroad. The largest companies in Switzerland (Nestlé and Ciba-Geigy) and in the Netherlands (Royal Dutch–Shell, Philips, and Unilever), for example, derive most of their profits from foreign sales and operations. Many of the largest corporations in the world, including quite a few U.S. ones, derive more than 50% of their earnings and sales from abroad.[13]

The extent of foreign operations for many multinational firms (MNFs) raises the following question: Can a portfolio of MNF stocks achieve true international diversification? In order words, do MNF stock prices behave like diversified international stocks, thereby offering a good substitute to direct foreign portfolio investment?

This issue is most relevant to a U.S. money manager who may invest in the large universe of United States–based MNFs. Ideally the manager would want to monitor his or her exposure in specific countries by buying or selling the shares of U.S. companies with important activities in these countries. This would avoid the difficulties and costs involved in investing directly in foreign capital markets. Furthermore, better information is available on U.S. companies than on many of the exotic firms quoted in distant stock markets.

Few studies have focused on MNF stock price behavior, but the conclusions reached by Senschack and Beedles (1980) are a good summary of the current evidence. They state that "the evidence seems to support strongly the behavior guide to investors that positioning in U.S. multinational firms does not provide all the benefits available from direct investment in foreign securities" (page 56). Specifically, they found that the total risk of a portfolio of U.S. MNFs is no smaller than that of a portfolio of U.S. stocks with predominantly domestic activities. Indeed MNFs do not even provide additional diversification benefits to a portfolio of purely domestic firms.

Similarly, Jacquillat and Solnik (1978) examined firms from nine countries and found that MNF stock prices behave very much like those of purely domestic firms (Exh. 7.7). Their approach was to formulate a multifactor model whereby each factor represented a national market index. Their results show that MNF stock prices are more strongly affected by the domestic market index than by foreign factors in most cases. This is especially true for U.S. and British firms, where the addition of foreign factors to the (domestic) market model does not significantly improve its explanatory power (R^2). This is less true for French, Swiss, Belgian, and Dutch companies. But even in these countries, the impact of foreign factors is much less than that of the domestic factor, despite the fact that many of their firms are more active abroad than domestically. Dada and Williams (1993) confirm that holding the shares of domestic MNFs is not a good alternative to international portfolio diversification.

The impact of national control and management policy, as well as government constraints on a firm's performance, may explain why multinationals are not a good substitute for international portfolio diversification. National influence on the prices of the major stock market on which the firm is traded may also be a factor.

The dominance of the national factor is compounded by the currency translation common to all securities of a local market. From a domestic viewpoint, all stocks of a foreign market tend to have a fairly similar price behavior because of both the local market factor and the exchange rate movement when translated into the domestic currency. Note that a similar conclusion holds for bonds. The return on all bonds issued in a given currency are mostly affected by movements in that currency's interest rate and the exchange rate. Differences in bond price behavior between securities issued in the same currency are, however, minor compared to the national factor. These conclusions do not rule out international asset pricing; they suggest that investment analysis ought to be structured on a geographic top-down approach.

EXHIBIT 7.7

Average Betas of Portfolios of Domestic MNF's with Selected National Indexes

| | National Index | | | | | | |
Nationalities of MNF	United States	Netherlands	Belgium	West Germany	Italy	Sweden	France
American MNF	*0.94*	1.12	–0.05	–0.01	–0.04	0.04	0.02
Dutch MNF	0.31	*0.76*	0.09	0.16	–0.02	–0.28	0.25
Belgian MNF	–0.27	0.07	*1.04*	0.06	0.03	0.19	0.06
German MNF	0.24	0.03	–0.21	*1.18*	–0.02	–0.01	0.10
Italian MNF	–0.10	0.06	0.10	0.01	*0.83*	0.11	–0.19
Swedish MNF	0.06	–0.15	–0.02	0.08	–0.10	*0.96*	0.01
French MNF	–0.10	0.14	0.33	0.18	0.02	–0.16	*0.95*
Swiss MNF	–0.12	–0.23	–0.04	–0.09	–0.02	0.16	–0.11
British MNF	–0.10	–0.11	0.30	0.09	–0.04	–0.13	–0.09

Risk and Return: An International CAPM

The International CAPM Theory

Forecasting the expected return on a security is not sufficient. Returns on very risky assets should be higher than returns on less risky security: A risk premium should compensate the risk-averse investor for the extra risk borne. For example, an investment in Daimler-Benz shares should be considered only if the expected return is at least higher than the interest rate on a short-term Euro-Deutsche mark deposit. Risk-averse investors would take into account the possibility of incurring a sizable loss on their shares of Daimler-Benz if their forecast is proved wrong.

To determine if a security is under- (or over-) valued in the market, we must decide if the expected return is too large (or small) given the risks incurred. This means that we need a theory to tell us what the normal (or required) expected return should be on a security given its risks and what that relevant measure of risk is.

The international Capital Asset Pricing Model (CAPM), discussed in Chapter 5, proposes a simple and operational theory of asset pricing. This model relies, as does any theory, on simplifying assumptions. The major conclusion of the model for asset pricing is given in Eq. (5.4), repeated here without detailing again the notations:

$$E(R_i) = R_0 + \beta_{iw} \times RP_w + \gamma_{i1} \times RP_1 + \gamma_{i2} \times RP_2 + \ldots + \gamma_{ik} \times RP_k. \tag{5.4}$$

This relation can be summarized as follows:

- The relevant measures of risk are the sensitivity, or beta, of the asset return to the return on the world market portfolio and the sensitivities of the asset return to exchange rate movements.

	National Index				
Nationalities of MNF	**Switzerland**	**United Kingdom**	R^2 **adjusted**	**Single-index beta**	**Single-index** R^2 **adjusted**
American MNF	−0.01	−0.07	0.31	1.02	0.29
Dutch MNF	−0.21	−0.06	0.63	0.98	0.50
Belgian MNF	0.08	0.07	0.58	1.03	0.45
German MNF	−0.15	−0.11	0.74	1.18	0.65
Italian MNF	−0.16	0.20	0.51	0.91	0.47
Swedish MNF	0.15	0.02	0.50	0.92	0.42
French MNF	−0.22	0.03	0.62	1.08	0.45
Swiss MNF	*1.74*	0.16	0.75	1.39	0.52
British MNF	0.07	*0.84*	0.49	1.06	0.44

Source: B. Jacquillat and B. Solnik, "Multinationals Are Poor Tools for International Diversification," *Journal of Portfolio Management,* Winter 1978.

- The asset risk premium, i.e., the difference between the expected return on the asset and the risk-free interest rate, is a linear function of this beta and of the currency risk measures.

We have seen repeatedly that the covariance of stock returns with exchange rate movements is quite small. To simplify the analysis, we will *temporarily* assume that these gammas are equal to zero.

The total risk of a security can be broken down into two parts: its market risk, which is proportional to the risk of the market portfolio, and its specific risk, which is uncorrelated with the market risk. In a diversified portfolio all specific risks of individual securities are diversified away, and only the market risk proportional to the beta of the portfolio remains. The CAPM makes the commonsensible claim that only the market risk (ß) should be compensated by a risk premium in an efficient market, not the specific risks, which can be easily eliminated by diversification. This model implies that the risk that is priced in the market is measured by the *international* beta of a security, that is, the beta relative to the world market portfolio.

The question is: How can this theory be reconciled with our empirical observation that the domestic market factor is the major source of influence on the return of a security? To answer this question, we now introduce a simple multicountry model, or top-down approach.

A Multicountry Model

The Model According to the simple, descriptive, multicountry model, each security is influenced by its domestic market factor, which in turn is influenced by

EXHIBIT 7.8

A Multicountry Model

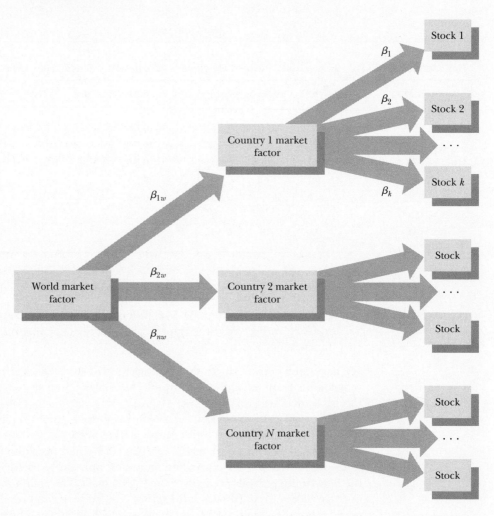

the single world market factor and, possibly, currency risk factors. In other words, a security is indirectly sensitive to the world market factor through its national market factor.[14] National market risk may be dissected into a risk caused by world factors and a risk specific to the country.

The sensitivity a country displays to this world market factor is the result of many influences, including its degree of international trade and investment, domestic monetary and economic policy, regulation and controls of international trade, and capital flows. Thus the world beta of a security (β_{iw}) is the product of its domestic beta (β_i) and the sensitivity of the domestic country factor to the world market factor (β_{cw}). This is illustrated in Exh. 7.8.

The theoretical implication of this international CAPM is that each security's expected return is proportional to *both* its world beta (β_{iw}) and its domestic beta (β_i). This implication is consistent with the domestic versions of the traditional CAPM.

The Model's Practical Use   Although this theoretical framework is useful for structuring the investment process, most money managers do not regard the world capital market as fully efficient. Therefore this model of international security returns leads to a multicountry, or top-down, approach to the international investment process of trying to exploit inefficiencies within a coherent framework. The first step in the top-down approach requires economists and analysts to attempt to forecast national market returns and currency movements. These forecasts lead to international asset allocation with an under- (or over-) weighting of some markets relative to the world index. In the second step individual companies are valued within the context of their national market. Superior performance can come from two sources: (1) country selection and (2) individual selection within a national market.

A good forecast of the domestic factor is very important because it affects the return of all stocks of the country through their domestic betas. The returns are compounded by currency movements, which affect all the local stocks from a foreign investor's viewpoint.

Beta coefficients have to be estimated, which is no simple task. The simplest method used by large investment institutions is to employ a simple regression model over past data. Many data services, brokers, and banks make these beta estimates available in frequent publications or on time-sharing systems across the world, but one must often refer to several institutions to get betas from different countries. Institutions with a large in-house historical database have an obvious advantage in being able to compute betas directly for all the stocks under their management. A second method of determining betas is to adjust the regression estimates to factor in certain statistical properties of the estimation, as well as other information on the company studied.

Both methods are based on the notion that risk estimates are stable over time, so that past data give indications on what the beta for the new period will be. Again, we use past data only to the extent that they help us to estimate the future betas, since money managers are interested only in the future stock sensitivity to domestic and international factors.

To summarize, a financial analyst should compute both the expected return and the risk of stocks relative to their domestic markets. This allows a list of stocks with abnormally high expected returns given their risk level to be drawn. From the list the manager can select securities to achieve the desired international asset allocation among markets, which is based on general forecasts of markets, interest rates, and currencies. A manager who is bullish on a particular national stock market should select stocks with high betas for that market. On the other hand, a manager who is bullish in the currency but quite uncertain about the market itself should select only low-beta stocks in that market.

The Problems with CAPM

The multicountry model approach has several drawbacks. Market and currency risk factors are unstable over time. That is unfortunate, because they are constructed mostly as statistical estimates from past data. It is not easy to construct good future estimates of these betas, as we have no *a priori* theory to explain what causes differences in these risk measures across stocks. An international Capital Asset Pricing Model is also difficult to defend on theoretical grounds in the presence of market imperfections (see Chapter 5). Furthermore all the criticisms of the practical use of the domestic CAPM apply to the international version. Roll (1987) showed that if the market portfolio were not identified exactly, the practical use of the CAPM was difficult. Yet internationally the mere definition of a world market portfolio is close to impossible. Ideally it includes the whole range of instruments, stocks, bonds, short-term deposits in foreign currencies, gold, and so on, yet the market size of many instruments is not known precisely. In addition, restrictions on investment, limited negotiability, differential taxes, and high transaction costs make the design of a complete world market equilibrium model a hopeless operational task.

Even if all equities were priced consistently with their international betas (a doubtful hypothesis), a portfolio manager who actively trades individual stocks still needs information on the reaction of each security price to *all* the important factors that can affect their prices.

A single world factor model plainly fails to accurately describe international stock price behavior. The multicountry model presented previously is better, since the national market factor picks both the real and monetary influences on all stocks traded in the same market and currency. Also, we have seen that this domestic factor was the dominant influence in stock price behavior. Although a security is influenced mostly by the domestic factor, it seems unlikely that all domestic influences, whether real or monetary, can be summarized in a single domestic factor identical for every firm. As we already discussed, each security reacts somewhat differently to currency movements or is influenced by factors specific to its industry.

In short, the simple multicountry model is a good practical step toward describing the true complexity of international stock price behavior, but it needs refinement. The next step requires the introduction of multifactor models.

Arbitrage Pricing Theory

More complete multifactor models have been developed, with a theoretical underpinning found in Arbitrage Pricing Theory (APT) initiated by Ross (1976). One advantage of APT is that it can be applied to a subset of investments, so that we do not need to consider every single world asset, as we did in the asset pricing model. It starts with a *descriptive model*, whereby the return on a security is determined by a number of common factors plus a term specific to the security and leads to an *asset pricing* theory of what expected returns should be in an efficient market.

The Descriptive Model   The multifactor model, where R is the rate of return on the security, may be written mathematically as

$$R = a + \beta_1 f_1 + \beta_2 f_2 + \ldots + \beta_k f_k + \varepsilon, \tag{7.2}$$

where a is a constant, $f_1 \ldots f_k$ are the k factors common to all securities, and ε (epsilon) is a random term specific to this security and therefore independent of all fs (factors) and other εs, the specific risks of all other securities. The ε is the source of idiosyncratic or diversifiable risk, and $\beta_1 \ldots \beta_k$ represent the sensitivity, or *risk exposure*, of this security to each factor. The betas vary among securities. Some stocks may be highly sensitive to certain factors and much less sensitive to others, and vice versa.

The Asset Pricing Theory   Arbitrage ensures that only the βs should be priced, so that $E(R)$, the expected return on a security, is a linear function of these betas:

$$E(R) = R_0 + \beta_1 RP_1 + \beta_2 RP_2 + \ldots + \beta_k RP_k, \tag{7.3}$$

where RP_i is the risk premium associated to factor i and R_0 is the risk-free rate. This relation states that the expected return on a stock should be a linear function of its risk exposures (or betas) to the various factors. Hence the risk of an asset is decomposed into several risk components linked to the various common factors.

According to the CAPM, we need to identify all securities in the world in order to construct the world market portfolio and derive the theoretical pricing relation. This is not necessary for APT, because it focuses on the relative pricing of the securities under study, the common factors being exogenous.

The next question is, What are the factors that determine the return on a security? The answer is that they must be either estimated from the data or postulated *à priori*; they are not specified by the theory.

Multifactor Models in Practice

Three types of factors are being used in practice. They have to be common factors in the sense that they have an influence on many stocks rather than being specific to a single stock.

Statistical Factors   From a historical database of stock returns, it is possible to "extract" factors. For example, one can use statistical methods, known as *factor analysis* or *principal component analysis*, to estimate the set of common factors that best explain the past variation in stock returns. These *statistical factors* suffer from two problems. First, they are very difficult to interpret, as they are simply a statistical estimate of some linear combination of stocks or underlying economic forces. Furthermore they change over time. Second, the statistical technique used tries to maximize the explanatory power of the factors in-sample; this is prone to discovering spurious correlations that will not be stable in the next periods.

Macroeconomic Factors   Factors can be postulated *a priori* as sources of risk that are common to all companies. This clearly leads us to some macroeconomic variables that affect the economics of all firms, as well as the behavior of stock market participants who price those firms.

Selecting a set of *macroeconomic factors* is as much an art as a science. These factors must be logical choices, easy to interpret, robust over time, and able to explain a significant percentage of variation in stock returns. Some macroeconomic variables are logical candidates as factors but suffer from serious measurement error or long publication lags. For example, the evolution in industrial production is a logical candidate, but it is difficult to get timely, good-quality, reliable data.

Burmeister, Roll, and Ross (1994) propose a set of five factors, based on their experience with macroeconomic factors at BIRR.[15] These five factors apply to domestic U.S. stocks. These factors are as follows:

- *Confidence factor* (f_1). This factor is measured by the difference in return on risky corporate bonds and on government bonds. The default-risk premium required by the market to compensate the risk of default on corporate bonds is measured as the spread between the yields on risky corporate bonds and government bonds. A decrease in the default-risk spread will give a higher return on corporate bonds and implies an improvement in the investors' confidence level. Hence confidence risk focuses on the willingness of investors to undertake risky investments. Most stocks have a positive exposure to the confidence factor ($ß_1 > 0$), so their prices tend to rise when the confidence factor is positive ($f_1 > 0$). The underlying idea is that in periods when investors are becoming more sensitive to risks (less confident with $f_1 < 0$), they require a higher premium on risky corporate bonds compared to government bonds. They also require a higher risk premium on stocks and will bid their prices down, inducing a negative stock price movement.

- *Time horizon factor* (f_2). This factor is measured as the difference between the return on a 20-year government bond and a one-month Treasury bill. A positive difference in return is caused by a decrease in the term spread (long minus short interest rates). This is a signal that investors require a lesser premium to hold long-term investments. Growth stocks are more exposed (higher $ß_2$) to time horizon risk than income stocks. The underlying idea is to view the stock price as the discounted stream of its future cash flows. The present value of growth stocks is determined by the long-term prospects about growing earnings while current earnings are relatively weak (high PE ratio). An increase in the market-required discount rate will penalize the price of growth stocks more than the price of value stocks.

- *Inflation factor* (f_3). This factor is measured as the difference between the actual inflation for a month and its expected value, computed the month before, using an econometric inflation model. An unexpected increase in inflation tends to be bad for most stocks ($ß_3 < 0$), so they have a negative exposure to this inflation surprise ($f_3 > 0$). Luxury-goods stocks tend to be most sensitive to inflation risk, whereas firms in the sectors of foods, cosmetics, or tires are less sensitive to inflation risk. Holdings of real estate benefit from increased inflation.

- *Business cycle factor* (f_4). This factor is measured by the monthly variation in a business activity index. Business cycle risk comes from unanticipated changes in the level of real activity. The business cycle factor is positive ($f_4 > 0$) when the expected real growth rate of the economy has increased. Most firms have a positive exposure to business cycle risk ($\beta_4 > 0$). Retail stores are more exposed to business cycle risk than are utility companies, because their business activity (sales) is much more sensitive to recession or expansion.

- *Market-timing risk* (f_5). This factor is measured by the part of the S&P 500 total return that is not explained by the first four factors. This factor captures the global movements in the market that are not explained by the four macroeconomic factors. The inclusion of this market-timing factor makes the CAPM a special case of the APT. If *all* relevant macroeconomic factors had been included, it would not be necessary to add this market-timing factor.

Macroeconomic multifactor models have also been proposed for non-U.S. markets and for global portfolios. Exchange rates are added as factors to make these models fully international and compatible with the international CAPM.

A common criticism to this approach is that the risk exposures (betas) have to be estimated statistically from past data and may not be stable over time.

Firm's Attribute Factors   *Attribute factors* relate to attributes of stocks. This approach claims that some companies' attributes are important in explaining cross-sectional differences in stock returns.[16] For example, a firm's *size* is an attribute: The stock prices of small firms and of large firms tend to behave differently, everything else being equal. Another example is the ratio of price-to-book value. Firms with a high stock market price relative to book value (growth stocks) tend to have a different market performance than firms with a low price-to-book ratio (value stocks). This does not mean that growth stocks will always outperform value stocks but rather that they will have a different performance (positive or negative) because of this difference in attribute value.

Attribute factors can be classified in two groups: fundamental and market. *Fundamental* attributes are some characteristics of the company's business activity or financial statements (size, earnings volatility, financial leverage). *Market* attributes are some characteristics of the company's stock market price behavior (volatility, share turnover).

Here again, selecting a set of attribute factors is as much an art as a science. These factors must be logical choices, easy to interpret, robust over time, and able to explain a significant percentage of cross-variation in stock returns. Some accounting attributes cannot be used, because of differences in accounting conventions and the delay in obtaining them. It is important to work with information that is timely and fully comparable across firms. The selection of relevant attributes is mostly an empirical question. Attributes are selected if they have explained cross-sectional return differences in the past. The rationale behind the empirical importance of an attribute factor is not always clear. An attribute factor can have a positive influence on returns in some periods and a negative influence in other periods.

Once the attributes have been identified, the approach is quite different from that used with macroeconomic factors. In the former approach the factors' returns were clearly identified (e.g., unexpected inflation), and the factor exposures had to be estimated with some statistical technique. In the attribute-factor approach it is the exposure to specific attribute factors that is clearly identified (e.g., the size of the firm), but the return on the factor itself must be estimated with some statistical technique. The factor exposure is simply the value of the attribute after some normalization. If we call X the value of the attribute for a given company (e.g., the size of the company), the risk exposure of that company to this attribute factor is typically measured as the deviation from the mean attribute value of all stocks (X mean), divided by the standard deviation of this attribute over all stocks ($SD(X)$):

$$\beta = \frac{X - X \text{ mean}}{SD(X)}. \tag{7.4}$$

Hence the mean factor exposure for each attribute is set equal to zero. A company with an attribute value smaller than the average value over all companies will have a negative exposure to that factor.

The factor returns are typically estimated ex-post by constructing portfolios of stocks that have a zero exposure to all factors except one. These portfolios are sometimes called *factor-mimicking portfolios*, because they mimic the behavior of one underlying factor. They can be long in some stocks and short in others.

Grinold and Kahn (1994) propose a set of factors based on their experience at BARRA. The major ones for U.S. stocks are as follows:

- *Industry* distinguishes companies by their business activity. Stocks are grouped into industries. There are as many factors as industries. Industry exposures are generally 0/1 variables. A company either belongs to a specific industry (exposure of 1) or it does not (exposure of 0). The exposure of large corporations with diversified activity is computed as the percentage of its activity in each industry.

- *Size* distinguishes large stocks from small stocks. Size is usually measured by the logarithm of the stock market capitalization of the company.

- *Value* distinguishes stocks by their fundamentals, including various ratios relating fundamental accounting data (earnings, dividend, cash flows, book value) to the market value of the company. This attribute measures whether the stock is expensive compared to current fundamentals.

- *Financial leverage* distinguishes stocks by their debt-to-equity ratios and their exposure to interest risk.

- *Earnings volatility* distinguishes stocks by their earnings stability.

- *Growth* distinguishes stocks by their past and anticipated earnings growth.

- *Volatility* distinguishes stocks by their degree of stability. This factor is clearly linked to the usual beta stated in the CAPM.

- *Liquidity* distinguishes stocks by how often they trade.

- *Momentum* or *Success* distinguishes stocks by their recent performance.

Other national models could use a larger or smaller set of attribute factors, depending on data availability and an identification of attributes that are useful in explaining differences in return across stocks. Grinold, Rudd, and Stefek (1989) present an international multifactor model applied to local currency returns of stocks from 24 countries. The six factors are:

- *Local stock market factor.* The risk exposure (beta) is measured relative to the local market index. This is a macroeconomic factor.

- *Industry.*

- *Size.*

- *Yield.*

- *Volatility.*

- *Success.*

Each of the last four attributes is normalized *within its own country.* So an Austrian firm that is large compared to other Austrian firms will have a large risk exposure to that factor, even if it is a small firm compared to the average Japanese firm. Clearly this model is quite national in its spirit. It attempts to enrich the multicountry approach detailed earlier.

A common critique to the attribute-factor models is that the theoretical rationale for many of the attribute factors is unclear. Hence it is difficult to make forecasts about these factor returns in the future.

Practical Use of Factor Models   Multifactor models are used in risk management and in selecting stocks. A major application is the analysis of the risk profile of portfolios. The exposure of the portfolio to the various factors is the weighted average of the exposures of the stocks making up the portfolio. A manager can estimate the risks taken and the exposure of the portfolio to the various sources of risk. If some specific stock index is assigned as a benchmark to measure performance, the manager can analyze the risks of deviations from the benchmark. This helps the manager identify and quantify the bets and risks that are taken in the portfolio.

Managers can also use multifactor models to tilt the portfolio along some factor bets. Assume, for example, that a manager believes that the economy is going to grow at a faster rate than generally forecasted, leading to some inflationary pressure. The manager will tend to increase the portfolio exposure to business risk but reduce its exposure to inflation risk. This could also lead the manager to take some industry bets and invest in small companies.

Summary

1. Faced with the complexities of international money management, an investor must analyze each particular investment in a systematic fashion. The end result should be reflected in a tractable number of parameters that can be used to structure the portfolio in a global approach. An investor needs indications of the expected return on the asset, as well as of the sensitivity of the asset price to the various sources of uncertainties, i.e., the major factors affecting an asset price behavior.

2. Financial analysis techniques are well known, but their application in comparing corporation values among countries poses numerous problems.

3. A majority of the largest industrial corporations and financial institutions are non-American. The analysis of any large company must be international to account for its worldwide market and competition. However, the available information on companies varies widely among countries. In many countries good-quality information is scarce and is subject to long delays before being published.

4. Differences in accounting principles make international comparisons of companies in the same industrial sector difficult, when based on accounting data. There are numerous areas in which national accounting principles differ. In some countries the objective of financial statements is to present a fair and true view of the firm's financial position, so they are geared to satisfy the needs of shareholders and creditors. In many other countries, however, financial statements are geared primarily to satisfy tax requirements. Different accounting principles can lead to different earnings figures, as is illustrated by non-U.S. firms listed on a U.S. stock exchange; these firms must provide estimates of their earnings computed using U.S. GAAP as well as their domestic accounting principles. On the average, it appears that U.S. accounting rules yield lower earnings than U.K. rules but markedly higher earnings than German or Japanese rules.

5. Different national stock markets value firms' attributes differently. For example, a leverage ratio may be regarded as too high by U.S. standards and reasonable by Japanese or German standards. A high price-earnings ratio in one country may be regarded as low in another country. Although relative valuation within a specific national market is useful, international value comparison is a very difficult exercise.

6. An empirical study of the major factors affecting stock price behavior indicates the dominance of domestic factors over foreign factors. Currency factors are very weak, and international industrial factors are significant, although dominated by the national market influence. The importance of national factors suggests that international investment analysis should be structured primarily along a top-down geographic approach.

7. Portfolio selection decisions should be structured around an analysis of risk and return. Managers should select both a risk level and securities with superior return for that risk level. A model of the world capital market is required to determine: (1) the appropriate measures of risk and (2) the normal return for a given risk level.

8. Several models of international asset pricing have been proposed in this chapter. Macroeconomic factors focus on proxies of the economic conditions that can affect the value of a stock. Attribute factors focus on differences in firms' characteristics that can lead to differences in returns across stocks. Multifactor models provide a fruitful approach to equity analysis and investment.

Questions and Problems

1. Explain why a corporation can have a stock market price well above its accounting book value.

2. The accounting and fiscal standards of many countries allow corporations to build general provisions (or "hidden" reserves) in anticipation of foreseen or unpredictable expenses. How would this practice affect the book value of a corporation and its ratio of market price to book value?

3*. List reasons why German earnings would tend to be understated compared to U.S. earnings.

4. List reasons why British earnings would tend to be overstated compared to U.S. earnings.

5. List reasons why the accounting net worth of German companies would tend to be understated compared to U.S. companies.

6*. In studying the impact of consolidation on PE ratios, there are four basic methods of consolidating the account of a subsidiary into the parent company:

- *Full consolidation.* Assets, liabilities, and earnings of the subsidiaries are fully incorporated, line by line, into the parent's accounts, with special care to avoid double counting.

- *Proportional consolidation.* Assets, liabilities, and earnings are consolidated line by line, proportionally to the percentage of ownership in the subsidiary.

- *Equity consolidation.* A share of the subsidiary profits are consolidated on a one-line basis, proportionally to the share of equity owned by the parent. The value of the investment in the subsidiary is adjusted to reflect the change in the subsidiary's equity.

- *No consolidation.* This is sometimes referred to as the cost method, whereby only dividends received from the subsidiary affect earnings of the parent. The value of the investment in the subsidiary is carried at cost in the book of the parent and is not revalued.

Here are the simplified 1997 accounts of Papa SA and Fille SA, two French firms. Papa SA owns 50% of Fille SA, a company created the previous year. Fille SA has not paid any dividend. The nonconsolidated accounts follow:

	Papa SA FF mios	**Fille SA** FF mios
Balance sheets, end-1977		
Fixed assets	400	80
Investment in subsidiary	50	
Current Assets	50	40
Total assets	500	120
Share capital	440	100
Net income 1997	60	20
Stockholders equity	500	120
Minority interests		
Total liabilities	500	120
Income statement 1997		
Revenues	300	80
Expenses	240	60
	60	20
Income from subsidiary		
Minority interests (−)		
Net income	60	20

The nonconsolidated accounts for Papa SA use the cost method, whereby the investment in the subsidiary is carried at historical cost in the balance sheet of the parent.

- Establish the consolidated accounts, using the three other methods outlined previously.
- Which method provides the highest reported net income for Papa SA?
- Which method provides the highest PE ratio, based on book value, for Papa SA?

7*. Japanese companies tend to belong to groups ("keiretsu") and to hold shares of one another. Because these cross-holdings are minority interest, they tend not to be consolidated in published financial statements. To study the impact of this tradition on published earnings, take the following simplified example.

Company A owns 10% of Company B; the initial investment was 10 million yen. Company B owns 20% of Company A; the initial investment was also 10 million yen. Both companies value their minority interests at historical cost. The year-end nonconsolidated balance sheets of the two companies follow.

	Company A Yen millions	**Company B** Yen millions
Balance sheet		
Current assets	70	120
Fixed assets	70	150
Minority investments	10	10
Total assets	150	280
Debt	50	80
Shareholders equity	100	200
Total liabilities	150	280

The annual net income of Company A was 10 million yen. The annual net income of Company B was 30 million yen. Assume that the two companies do not pay any dividends. The current stock market values are 200 million yen for Company A and 450 million yen for Company B.

- Restate the earnings of the two companies, using the equity method of consolidation. Remember that the share of the minority-interest profits are consolidated on a one-line basis, proportionally to the share of equity owned by the parent. The value of the investment in the subsidiary is adjusted to reflect the change in the subsidiary's equity.

- Calculate the PE ratios, based on nonconsolidated and consolidated earnings. Are they similar?

8. In 1989 Jaguar Plc, an English company, was listed on the London SEAQ and on NAS-DAQ. At the time one fourth of Jaguar common stock was held in the form of ADRs quoted on NASDAQ. Under U.K. accounting principles, Jaguar reported a 1988 net income (before extraordinary items) of £61 million, a *decrease* of 27% from 1987 net income. Under U.S. GAAP, Jaguar reported a 1988 net income (before extraordinary items) of £113 million, an *increase* of 89% over the comparable figure for 1987. What would your reaction be as an investor?

9*. In the past 20 years the best-performing stock markets have been found in countries with the highest economic growth rate. Should current growth rate guide you in picking stock markets if the world capital market is efficient?

10. Exhibits 7.6 and 7.7 indicate that the influence of the domestic market is dominant. Does this observation imply that international factors have no influence on individual stock prices?

11*. British Telecom is a British firm with extensive foreign ownership. It is traded in London and in New York in the form of ADR.

- Last week the London stock market went up by 2% and New York went down by 3%. The British pound appreciated by 1% against the U.S. dollar.

- What should have happened to the price of British Telecom? Are you sure of your answer?

12. You are a U.S. pension fund that cares about dollar return. The following are your forecasts for the coming year and the betas of stocks calculated relative to their domestic index.

Country	Expected Return (percent)	Beta
United States		
Current risk-free rate	8	
Stock market	10	1
Company A	13	1.2
Company B	9	0.9
Company C	11	1.5
France		
Current risk-free rate	10	
Stock market	11	1
Company D	12	0.8
Company E	12	2
Company F	11	1.1
Franc (against $)	−5	
Japan		
Current risk-free rate	6	
Stock market	14	1
Company G	16	1.25
Company H	18	1.1
Company I	12	0.9
Yen (against $)	+5	

You believe in the multicountry approach and feel that foreign exchange factors are totally unpredictable. How would you structure your portfolio? What risk considerations would you take into account?

13*. You use the five macroeconomic factors described in the text. The factor exposures of two stocks are as follows:

Factor	Stock A	Stock B
Confidence	0.2	0.6
Time horizon	0.6	0.8
Inflation	−0.1	−0.5
Business cycle	4.0	2.0
Market timing	1.0	0.7

What would be the factor exposures of a portfolio invested half in stock A and half in stock B?

Contrary to general forecasts, you expect strong economic growth with a slight increase in inflation. Which stock should you overweight in your portfolio?

14*. You invest in a country named Papaf, whose currency is the Pif. You observe the stock returns on a list of stocks during two periods.

Stock	Period 1	Period 2	Period 3
A	14.5%	–10.5%	14%
B	11%	–6.5%	10.5%
C	7.5%	–3%	8%
D	5.5%	–1%	5%
E	2%	2%	2.5%
F	–1.5%	5%	–1%

You consider explaining differences in returns by common factors, with a linear model as represented in Eq. (7.2). You have two candidates for factors: movements in interest rates and changes in the popularity of the president of Paf as measured by polls. The various values of these factors are given below.

Factor	Period 1	Period 2	Period 3
Change in interest rate	–3%	+3%	–3%
Change in popularity	–5%	–3%	+5%

Try to assess whether each factor has an influence on stock returns. Try to estimate the intercept and the factor exposures of each asset.

15*. Here is some return information on firms of various sizes and their price-to-book ratios. Can you tell us something about attribute factors?

Stock	Size	P/BV	Period return
A	Huge	2	4%
B	Huge	1	6%
C	Medium	2	9%
D	Medium	1	12%
E	Small	2	12%
F	Small	1	15%

16. You are an active British stock portfolio manager. Your performance is measured against the FTSE index, a broadly based British stock index.

It has been repeatedly observed that small-capitalization stocks outperform large-capitalization stocks over prolonged periods of time ("small-firm effect") but that there have been periods when the reverse was true. It has also been repeatedly observed that value stocks (firms with low price-to-book ratios) outperform growth stocks over prolonged periods of time ("value/growth effect") but that there have been periods when the reverse was true.

How would an attribute-factor model be useful in estimating the risks that your performance deviates from that of the assigned benchmark?

Notes

1. A study by the French Analysts Federation shows that corporations publish their annual reports with a lag after the end of the fiscal year that varies from country to country. The average lags are for the United States, 6 weeks; the Netherlands, 10 weeks; Japan, 12 weeks; the United Kingdom, 14 weeks; Germany, 16 weeks; and France, 24 weeks.

2. See, for example, Choi *et al.* (1983), Rutherford (1985), and Kester (1986).

3. Although Dutch accounting rules are codified in a law, the Netherlands is very much along the Anglo-American model. The Dutch accounting profession formed the influential NIvRA (Netherlands Institute of Registered Accountants). Recommended accounting standards are proposed by the CAR (Council for Annual Reporting), which is composed of representatives of the NIvRA, employers, employees, and various users of financial statements. There are several accounting bodies in the U.K., and the ASB (Accounting Standards Board) was set up in 1990 to issue accounting standards known as FRSs (Financial Reporting Standards). These FRSs were previously named SSAPs (Statements of Standard Accounting Practices). The American FASB (Financial Accounting Statement Board) was set up in 1973 to issue accounting standards, known as SFASs (Statements of Financial Accounting Standards); together these SFASs are the base of the U.S. GAAP. The SEC (Security and Exchange Commission) recognizes the GAAP embodied in the SFASs and requires all corporations to follow these accounting principles.

4. See, for example, Choi and Mueller (1992) and Radebaugh and Gray (1993).

5. A review of different consolidation methods is provided in Radebaugh and Gray (1993).

6. See Eiteman, Stonehill, and Moffett (1992), Shapiro (1992), Choi and Mueller (1992), and Radebaugh and Gray (1993).

7. See Weetman and Gray (1991), Speidell and Bavishi (1992), Choi *et al.* (1983), Radebaugh and Gray (1993), and French and Poterba (1991).

8. See Choi and Levich (1990), Pope and Rees (1992), McQueen (1993), and various issues of the *Journal of International Financial Management and Accounting* and of the *Journal of Accounting Research,* especially its *1993 Supplement.*

9. See Bhushan and Lessard (1992), Choi and Levich (1991), and Ennis, Knupp & Associates (1994).

10. This is the average over all major industrial countries as defined by the Organization for Economic Coordination and Development.

11. See Harvey (1991), Solnik (1993a, 1993b), Ferson and Harvey (1993), and Harvey (1994).

12. See B. Solnik and A. de Freitas, "International Factors of Stock Price Behaviour," in S. Khoury and A. Ghosh, eds., *Recent Developments in International Finance and Banking,* Lexington, MA: Lexington Books, 1988. They used monthly observations on a sample of 279 firms from 18 countries over the period December 1971 to December 1984. The country, industrial, and world indexes come from Morgan Stanley Capital

International. The currency movement is that of the local currency relative to the U.S. dollar (U.S. dollar price of one unit of local currency). The Deutsche mark replaced the U.S. dollar as the reference currency for tests on U.S. companies.

13. The ratio of foreign to total sales, earnings, and assets of major corporations is periodically reported by *Business International.* Although this information is publicly available for U.S. corporations, it is much more difficult to obtain for European and Asian corporations. Another interesting reference in J. Stopford and J.H. Dunning, *World Directory of Multinational Enterprises: Company Performance and Global Trends,* Woodbridge, IL: McMillan Pubns., 1983. Rugman (1976) reports that measures of foreign activities, such as sales assets, net income, and number of employees, are highly correlated (correlation of more than 0.8).

14. For a first approach to this multicountry model, see Solnik (1974) and Sharpe (1987). Remember that the famous beta, ß, is equal to the covariance of the return on the asset with the return on the market portfolio divided by (or normalized by) the variance of the market portfolio return. This is also equal to the slope of a regression of the asset return on the market portfolio return.

15. BIRR is an acronym for the firm Burmeister, Ibbotson, Roll and Ross. Earlier, Chen, Roll, and Ross had identified four factors for the U.S. equity market as growth rate in industrial production, unexpected inflation, twists in the yield curve (the difference between long- and short-term interest rates), and changes in the attitude toward risk as proxied by changes in the pricing of default risk implicit in the difference between yields on Aaa and Baa corporate bonds. See Chen, Roll, and Ross (1986).

16. A study of the cross-sectional difference in returns along various attributes can be found in Fama and French (1992). Capaul, Rowley, and Sharpe (1993) studied the "value-growth factor" on a large sample of stocks from France, Germany, Switzerland, the United Kingdom, Japan, and the United States. Chan, Hamao, and Lakonishok (1993) look at various attributes of Japanese stocks.

Bibliography

Adler, M., and Simon, D. "Exchange Risk Surprises in International Portfolios," *Journal of Portfolio Management,* Winter 1986.

Alexander, D., and Nobes, C. *A European Introduction to Financial Accounting,* Hemel Hempstead, UK: Prentice Hall, 1994.

Bhushan, R., and Lessard, D.R. "Coping with International Accounting Diversity: Fund Managers' Views on Disclosure, Reconciliation, and Harmonization," Cambridge, MA: M.I.T. Sloan School of Management Working Paper, October 1992.

Burmeister, E., Roll, R., and Ross, S. "A Practitioner's Guide to Arbitrage Pricing Theory," in *A Practitioner's Guide to Factor Models,* Charlottesville, VA: The Research Foundation of Chartered Financial Analysts, 1994.

Capaul, C., Rowley, I., and Sharpe, W.F. "International Value and Growth Stock Returns," *Financial Analysts Journal,* January-February 1993.

Chan, L.K.C., Hamao, Y., and Lakonishok, J. "Can Fundamentals Predict Japanese Stock Returns," *Financial Analysts Journal*, July-August 1993.

Chen, N., Roll, R., and Ross, S. "Economic Forces and the Stock Market," *Journal of Business* September 1986.

Choi, F.D.S., Hino, H., Min, S., Nam, S., Ujiie, H., and Stonehill, A. "Analyzing Foreign Financial Statements: The Use and Misuse of International Ratio Analysis," *Journal of International Business Studies*, Summer 1983.

Choi, F.D.S., and Levich, R.M. *Capital Market Effects of International Accounting*, Homewood, IL: Dow Jones–Irwin, 1990.

_____. "International Accounting Diversity: Does it Affect Market Participants?" *Financial Analysts Journal*, July-August, 1991.

Choi, F.D., and Mueller, G.G. *International Accounting*, 2d ed. Englewood Cliffs, NJ: Prentice Hall, 1992.

Dada, J., and Williams, T.J. "Is There a Shortcut to International Investing?" *Journal of Investing*, Winter 1993.

Drummen, M., and Zimmermann, H. "The Structure of European Stock Returns," *Financial Analysts Journal*, July-August 1992.

Eiteman, D.K., Stonehill, A.I., and Moffett, M.H. *Multinational Business Finance*, 6th ed. Reading, MA: Addison-Wesley, 1992.

Ennis, Knupp & Associates, *1993 Survey of non-U.S. Stock Market Suitability*, Chicago, 1994.

Fama, E.F., and French, K.R. "The Cross-Section of Expected Stock Returns," *Journal of Finance*, June 1992.

Ferson, W.E., and Harvey, C.R. "The Risk and Predictability of International Equity Returns," *Review of Financial Economics*, 1993.

_____. "Sources of Risk and Expected Returns in Global Equity Markets," *Journal of Banking and Finance*, 1994.

French, K.R., and Poterba, J.M. "Were Japanese Stock Prices Too High?" *Journal of Financial Economics*, October 1991.

Grinold, R., and Kahn, R.K. "Multiple-Factor Models for Portfolio Risk," in *A Practitioner's Guide to Factor Models*, Charlottesville, VA: The Research Foundation of Chartered Financial Analysts, 1994.

Grinold, R., Rudd, A., and Stefek, D. "Global Factors: Fact or Fiction," *Journal of Portfolio Management*, Fall 1989.

Hagigi, M. "Industry Versus Country Risk in International Investments of U.S. Pension Funds," *Financial Analysts Journal*, September/October 1988.

Harvey, C.R. "The World Price of Covariance Risk," *Journal of Finance*, March 1991.

_____. "Predictable Risk and Returns in Emerging Markets," working paper, Durham, NC: Duke University, 1994.

Heston, S.L., and Rouwenhorst, K.G. "Does Industrial Structure Explain the Benefits of International Diversification?" *Journal of Financial Economics*, August 1994.

_____. "Industry and Country Effects in International Stock Returns," *Journal of Portfolio Management*, Spring 1995.

Jacquillat, B., and Solnik, B. Multinationals Are Poor Tools for International Diversification," *Journal of Portfolio Management*, Winter 1978.

Kester, W.C. "Capital and Ownership Structure: A Comparison of U.S. and Japanese Manufacturing Corporations," *Financial Management*, Spring 1986.

Lessard, D. "World, Country and Industry Relationships in Equity Returns," *Financial Analysts Journal*, January/February 1976.

McQueen, P.D. "The Information Content of Foreign and US GAAP Earnings in SEC Form 10-F," CUNY-Baruch College working paper, September 1993.

Mueller, G.G., Gernon, H., and Meek, G.K. *Accounting: An International Perspective*, Burr Ridge, IL: Richard D. Irwin, 1994.

Pope, P.F., and Rees, W.P. "International Differences in GAAP and the Pricing of Earnings," *Journal of International Financial Management and Accounting*, 1992.

Radebaugh, L.H., and Gray, S.J. *International Accounting and Multinational Enterprises*, New York: Wiley, 1993.

The Research Foundation of Chartered Financial Analysts, *A Practitioner's Guide to Factor Models*, Charlottesville, VA, 1994.

Roll, R. "A Critique of the Asset Pricing Theory's Tests," *Journal of Financial Economics*, March 1987.

Ross, S. "The Arbitrage Pricing Theory of Capital Asset Pricing," *Journal of Economic Theory*, December 1976.

Rugman, A. letter to the editor, *Financial Analysts Journal*, March/April 1976.

Rutherford, J. "An International Perspective on the Capital Structure Puzzle," *Midland Corporate Finance Journal*, Fall 1985.

Senschack, A., and Beedles, W. "Is International Diversification Desirable?" *Journal of Portfolio Management*, Winter 1980.

Shapiro, A.C. *Multinational Financial Management*, 4th ed. Needham Heights, MA: Allyn and Bacon, 1992.

Sharpe, W. *Investments*. Englewood Cliffs, NJ: Prentice Hall, 1991.

Solnik, B. "L'Internationalisation des Places financières," *COB-Université*, 1976.

_____. "The International Pricing of Risk: An Empirical Investigation of the Work Capital Structure," *Journal of Finance*, May 1974.

_____. "Stock Prices and Monetary Variables: The International Evidence," *Financial Analysts Journal*, March/April 1984.

_____. "The Performance of International Asset Allocation Strategies Using Conditioning Information," *Journal of Empirical Finance*, March 1993a.

_____. *Predictable Time-Varying Components of International Asset Returns*, Charlottesville, VA: The Research Foundation of Chartered Financial Analysts, 1993b.

Solnik, B., and de Freitas, A. "International Factors of Stock Price Behaviour," in S. Khoury and A. Ghosh, eds., *Recent Developments in International Finance and Banking*, Lexington, MA: Lexington Books, 1988.

Speidell, L.S., and Bavishi, V.B. "GAAP Arbitrage: Valuation Opportunities in International Accounting Standards," *Financial Analysts Journal*, November-December 1992.

Stopford, J., and Dunning, J.H. *World Directory of Multinational Enterprises: Company Performance and Global Trends*, Woodbridge, IL: McMillan Pubns., 1983.

Wadhwani, S. "Are European Stock Markets Converging?" Goldman Sachs Portfolio Strategy Paper, 27 September 1991.

Weetman, P., and Gray, S.J. "A Comparative Analysis of the Impact of Accounting Principles in Profits: The U.S.A. versus the U.K., Sweden and the Netherlands," *Accounting and Business Research*, 21, 1991.

8

Emerging Stock Markets

A chapter on emerging stock markets is a well-deserved addition to this book. The international interest in emerging stock markets has come in several stages. In the 1980s the four Asian "tigers" (Hong Kong, Korea, Singapore, and Taiwan) attracted much attention because of their rapid economic growth rates. The expected entry of Greece and Portugal into the European Common Market provoked a financial boom in those countries in the mid-1980s. Latin American countries regained international honorability when Brady plans (see Chapter 9) brought a solution to the rescheduling of their nonperforming debts, and their stock markets offered attractive returns in the early 1990s. The disintegration of communism in Eastern Europe led to the development of market economies and the hope for attractive investment opportunities for foreigners. However, successful stock markets have so far developed only in the Czech Republic, Hungary, and Poland. China has started to industrialize and open up to foreign investment. Active stock markets have developed in Shanghai and Shenzen, and Chinese firms have issued shares in Hong Kong and New York. Some African markets, such as Zimbabwe or South Africa, are envisaged as part of a global diversification strategy.

Traditionally investors have considered only developed markets in their international diversification strategy. These are markets that have been in operation for a long time and whose economies are already in a developed stage. This selection was reinforced by the focus on performance measurement relative to international benchmarks (such as the MSCI or FT-A international indexes) including only developed markets. Stock markets from developing countries were not included in these indexes. However, investors came to realize the stock market development and economic growth potential of many emerging countries. The World Bank, which was very involved in assisting those developing countries, decided to promote their stock markets. The International Finance Corporation (IFC), a member of the World Bank Group, started to publish monthly Emerging Stock Market Indexes, which allowed money managers to measure the performance of their portfolios invested in developing countries. Since 1990, the amount of foreign investment in these

251

emerging markets has grown dramatically. The net foreign capital flow to emerging equity markets in 1993 was around $37 billion.

This chapter starts with a review of the economies and markets of emerging countries. Next, we detail the case for diversification into emerging markets. The remainder of this chapter is devoted to practical aspects of investing in those markets.

Some Statistics on Emerging Economies and Markets

It is never easy to classify economies and stock markets. We will use the segmentation adopted by IFC and followed by major investors.

The traditional criterion for ranking the state of development of a country is its level of income, measured by the gross national product (GNP) per capita. Developed countries have high income; developing countries have low income. Another criterion to deliver the label "emerging stock market" is whether the stock market has begun a process of change, growing in size, turnover, and sophistication. IFC has decided to follow these two criteria to include countries in its emerging market database. It uses the World Bank classification and defines as emerging a country with a low or middle income. It calculates market indexes only for those stock markets that have shown the promise of becoming mature.

In 1994 the cut-off between high-income countries and emerging countries was a 1992 GNP per capita of $8356. As of 1994, there were more than 200 countries of significant size, and only 38 of them were classified as developed. Many emerging economies have a stock market that is still in an embryonic stage. In 1994 IFC calculated stock indexes for 26 emerging markets.[1] Once a stock market is classified as emerging, it will remain as such for some time even if the economy later moves to the high-income group. For historical and practical reasons, the separation between emerging and developed stock markets is likely to persist for a while. The major emerging markets are represented in Exh. 8.1. Three emerging markets are in Africa, five in Europe, seven in Latin America, ten in Asia, and one in the Middle East. Some statistics on these markets and their underlying economies are provided in Exh. 8.2. Altogether, emerging countries have a share of 20% of world GNP; their populations represent 85% of world population.

The stock market capitalization of emerging countries has been growing rapidly, as can be seen in Exh. 8.3. The capitalization of all emerging stock markets stood at 12% of the total world market capitalization (developed plus emerging markets) at the end of 1993, as can be seen in Exh. 8.2.

Six emerging stock markets rank among the top 20 markets in the world in terms of capitalization. Malaysia, South Africa, Mexico, Taiwan, Korea, and Thailand have a larger market capitalization than does Spain or Sweden. Exhibit 8.4 shows that emerging markets are even more active in terms of transaction volume.

EXHIBIT 8.1

Major Emerging Stock Markets of the World

Asia

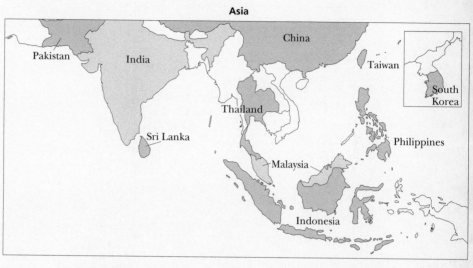

Latin America

Europe/Middle East

(continued)

EXHIBIT 8.1 (CONTINUED)

Africa

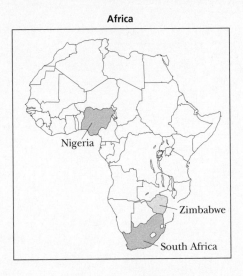

EXHIBIT 8.2

Summary Statistics on Major Emerging Markets

Economy	GNP (billions of US$) 1992	GNP per capita (US$) 1992	Inflation Rate (%) 1985–92	Real Growth Rate (%) 1985–92	Market Capitalization (billions of US$) end-1993
Developed					
Australia	299.3	17,070	5.2	0.7	204.0
Canada	565.8	20,320	3.7	0.3	326.5
France	1,278.7	22,300	3.1	2.2	456.1
Germany	1,846.1	23,030	2.9	2.2	463.5
Hong Kong	89.3	15,380	9.0	5.6	385.2
Italy	1,186.6	20,510	6.6	2.3	136.2
Japan	3,507.8	28,220	1.4	4.0	2,999.8
Netherlands	312.3	20,590	1.5	2.1	181.9
Singapore	44.3	15,750	2.7	5.9	132.7
Spain	548.0	14,020	6.9	3.8	119.3
Sweden	233.2	26,780	6.9	0.4	107.4
Switzerland	248.7	36,230	4.0	1.1	271.7
United Kingdom	1,024.8	17,760	6.0	1.5	1,151.6
United States	5,904.8	23,120	3.7	1.1	5,223.8

Economy	GNP (billions of US$) 1992	GNP per capita (US$) 1992	Inflation Rate (%) 1985–92	Real Growth Rate (%) 1985–92	Market Capitalization (billions of US$) end-1993
Emerging					
Argentina	200.3	6,050	495.7	0.5	44.0
Brazil	425.4	2,770	731.3	–0.7	99.4
Chile	37.1	2,730	19.7	6.1	44.6
China	442.3	380	7.5	6.0	40.6
Colombia	44.6	1,290	26.1	2.4	9.2
Greece	75.1	7,180	16.5	1.1	12.3
Hungary	30.7	3,010	18.5	–1.5	0.8
India	271.6	310	9.5	3.3	98.0
Indonesia	122.8	670	8.8	4.7	33.0
Jordan	4.4	1,120	7.2	–7.0	4.9
Korea	296.3	6,790	6.8	8.5	139.4
Malaysia	52.0	2,790	2.8	5.7	220.3
Mexico	294.8	3,470	52.7	1.1	200.7
Nigeria	32.9	320	28.0	3.4	1.0
Pakistan	49.5	410	8.6	1.7	11.6
Peru	21.3	950	736.8	–4.3	5.1
Philippines	49.5	770	10.1	1.9	40.3
Poland	75.3	1,960	124.2	–1.9	2.7
Portugal	73.3	7,450	13.6	5.5	12.4
South Africa	106.0	2,670	14.4	–1.3	217.1
Sri Lanka	9.5	540	11.3	2.2	2.5
Taiwan (est.)	208.8	10,120	2.6	6.3	195.2
Thailand	106.6	1,840	5.8	8.3	130.5
Turkey	114.2	1,950	54.7	2.7	37.5
Venezuela	58.9	2,900	35.8	1.1	8
Zimbabwe	5.9	570	17.6	–0.6	1.4
All developed	**18,297**	**22,100**			**12,464**
All emerging	**4,590**	**995**			**1,636**
World	**22,887**	**4,200**			**14,101**

EXHIBIT 8.3 GROWTH OF EMERGING MARKET CAPITALIZATION

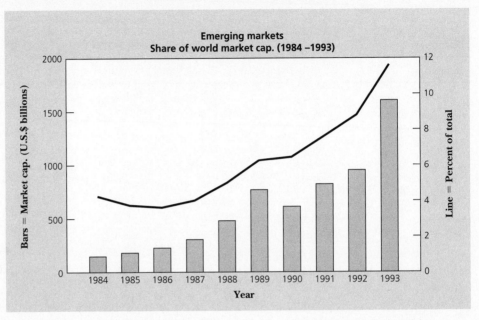

Source: *Emerging Stock Markets Factbook 1994*. International Finance Corporation, Washington, DC. Reprinted with permission.

Taiwan, Korea, and Malaysia were among the 10 more active markets during 1993. The nascent stock exchanges in China ranked twenty-first in terms of transaction volume. Trading in these emerging markets is not concentrated on a few companies. Many of these emerging markets trade a large number of domestic companies. For example, 6800 companies are listed in India, which ranks second to the United States in terms of the number of listed stocks. Korea has more companies listed than France or Germany. Still, some emerging markets are very concentrated, mostly because of the large size of some recently privatized companies. Exhibit 8.5 lists the 10 largest market capitalizations on each major emerging market. The top 10 Argentinean companies represent more than 60% of the total national market capitalization. The markets are much less concentrated in Korea, Thailand, Taiwan, or Turkey.

The Case for Investing in Emerging Markets

Each emerging market looks quite volatile and risky. However, the case for diversifying into emerging stock markets stems from the high growth potential of emerging markets, together with their low correlation with developed markets.

EXHIBIT 8.4

World Ranking of Market Capitalization, Value Traded, and Number of Listed Companies, 1993

Rank	Market	Total Market Cap (US$ millions)	Rank	Market	Total Value Traded (US$ millions)	Rank	Market	Number of Listed Domestic Companies
1	U.S.	5,223,768	1	U.S.	3,507,223	1	U.S.	7,607
2	Japan	2,999,756	2	Japan	954,341	2	India	6,800
3	U.K.	1,151,646	3	U.K.	423,526	3	Japan	2,155
4	Germany	463,476	4	Taiwan	346,487	4	U.K.	1,646
5	France	456,111	5	Germany	302,985	5	Canada	1,124
6	Hong Kong	385,247	6	Korea	211,710	6	Australia	1,070
7	Canada	326,524	7	France	174,283	7	Korea	693
8	Switzerland	271,713	8	Switzerland	167,880	8	Pakistan	653
9	Malaysia	220,328	9	Malaysia	153,661	9	South Africa	647
10	South Africa	217,110	10	Canada	142,222	10	Israel	558
11	Australia	203,964	11	Hong Kong	131,550	11	Brazil	550
12	Mexico	200,671	12	Thailand	86,934	12	France	472
13	Taiwan	195,198	13	Singapore	81,623	13	Hong Kong	450
14	Netherlands	181,876	14	Australia	67,711	14	Germany	426
15	Korea	139,420	15	Netherlands	67,185	15	Malaysia	410
16	Italy	136,153	16	Italy	65,770	16	Spain	376
17	Singapore	132,742	17	Mexico	62,454	17	Thailand	347
18	Thailand	130,510	18	Brazil	57,409	18	Taiwan, China	285
19	Spain	119,264	19	Spain	47,156	19	Chile	263
20	Sweden	107,376	20	Sweden	43,593	20	Denmark	257
21	Brazil	99,430	21	China	43,395	21	Netherlands	245
22	India	97,976	22	Israel	30,327	22	Peru	233
23	Belgium	78,067	23	Turkey	23,242	23	Switzerland	215
24	Israel	50,773	24	India	21,879	24	Italy	210
25	Chile	44,622	25	Denmark	20,989	25	Sri Lanka	200
26	Argentina	43,967	26	South Africa	13,049	26	Mexico	190
27	Denmark	41,785	27	Belgium	11,199	27	China	183
28	China	40,567	28	Argentina	10,339	28	Portugal	183
29	Philippines	40,327	29	Indonesia	9,158	29	Argentina	180
30	Turkey	37,496	30	Norway	8,751	30	Philippines	180
31	Indonesia	32,953	31	Finland	8,112	31	Singapore	178
32	Austria	28,437	32	New Zealand	6,785	32	Indonesia	174
33	Norway	27,380	33	Philippines	6,785	33	Nigeria	174
34	New Zealand	25,597	34	Austria	6,561	34	Belgium	165
35	Finland	23,562	35	Portugal	4,835	35	Bangladesh	153
36	Luxembourg	19,337	36	Chile	2,797	36	Turkey	152
37	Portugal	12,417	37	Greece	2,713	37	Greece	143
38	Greece	12,319	38	Kuwait	2,612	38	Ecuador	142
39	Pakistan	11,602	39	Poland	2,170	39	New Zealand	136
40	Kuwait	10,103	40	Venezuela	1,874	40	Iran	124

Source: Emerging Stock Markets Factbook 1994, International Finance Corporation, Washington, DC. Reprinted with permission.

EXHIBIT 8.5

Top Ten Securities in MSCI Emerging Market Indexes

	Mkt Cap US $ Mil	% of Total		Mkt Cap US $ Mil	% of Total		Mkt Cap US $ Mil	% of Total
Argentina			**Brazil**			**Chile**		
YPF	9,161	20.8%	Telebras PN	10,012	10.3%	Telefonos de Chile A	4,639	10.6%
Telefonica de Argentina	8,657	19.7%	Eletrobras ON	6,855	7.0%	Endesa	3,750	8.6%
Naviera Perez Companc	2,836	6.4%	Vale do Rio Doce PN	4,162	4.3%	Enersis	2,750	6.3%
			Petrobras PN	3,961	4.1%	Copec	2,669	6.1%
BCO Galicia Buenos Aires	1,595	3.6%	Cemig PN	2,337	2.4%	Cartones	1,721	3.9%
			Banco Itau PN	2,294	2.3%	Cervezas	1,487	3.4%
Banco Frances	1,437	3.3%	Souza Cruz ON	2,181	2.2%	Entel	1,055	2.4%
Interamericana de Auto	1,144	2.6%	Banco Bradesco PN	1,993	2.0%	Madeco	940	2.2%
Astra	696	1.6%	Banco Bradesco ON	1,968	2.0%	Chilgener	890	2.0%
Molinos Rio de la Plata	532	1.2%				Vapores	666	1.5%
Dalmine Siderca	523	1.2%	Usiminas PN	1,585	1.6%	**Top ten**	**20,568**	**47.2%**
Bagley	371	0.8%	**Top ten**	**37,350**	**38.2%**	**Total stock market**	**43,592**	
Top ten	**26,952**	**61.2%**	**Total stock market**	**97,672**				
Total stock market	**44,053**							
Colombia			**Greece**			**Indonesia**		
Bavaria	1,118	10.4%	Hellenic Bottling CB	1,203	9.7%	Indocement	4,368	9.5%
Cementos Argos	994	9.2%				Barito Pacific Timber	4,244	9.2%
Banco de Bogota	862	8.0%	Credit Bank	677	5.5%			
Nacional de Chocolates	633	5.9%	National Bank	675	5.4%	Gudang Garam	2,011	4.4%
			Ergo Bank	661	5.3%	Astra International	1,835	4.0%
Banco ind de Colombia	538	5.0%	Intracom CB	589	4.8%	Indah Kiat Pulp & Paper	1,404	3.1%
Cementos del Caribe	500	4.6%	Heracles-Cement	444	3.6%	Unilever Indonesia	1,326	2.9%
			Delta C	384	3.1%			
Banco Ganadero	462	4.3%	Titan-Cement C	334	2.7%	Bank Int'l Indonesia	1,292	2.8%
Cadenalco	337	3.1%	Michaniki C	267	2.2%	Jakarta Int'l Hotel	1,175	2.6%
CIA Colombiana de Tabaco	285	2.6%	Elais Co	247	2.0%			
Colombiana de Tejidos	110	1.0%	**Top ten**	**5,481**	**44.2%**	Kalbe Farma	844	1.8%
Top ten	**5,839**	**54.1%**	**Total stock market**	**12,395**		Polysindo	745	1.6%
Total stock market	**10,786**					**Top ten**	**19,244**	**41.8%**
						Total stock market	**46,000**	

India	Mkt Cap US $ Mil	% of Total
Reliance Industries	2,719	3.0%
Hindustan Lever	2,566	2.9%
ITC	2,493	2.8%
Tata Iron & Steel	2,183	2.4%
Larsen & Toubro	1,616	1.8%
Colgate-Palmolive (India)	1,604	1.8%
Tata Eng & Locomotive	1,313	1.5%
Tata Chemicals	1,263	1.4%
Icici	1,185	1.3%
Grasim Industries	1,041	1.2%
Top ten	**17,983**	**20.1%**
Total stock market	**89,623**	

Jordan	Mkt Cap US $ Mil	% of Total
Jordan Cement Factories	209	4.3%
Jordan Phosphate Mines	165	3.4%
Arab Pharma-ceutical Mfg	104	2.1%
Housing Bank	95	2.0%
Jordan Petrol Refinery	90	1.9%
Arab Aluminium Industry	85	1.8%
Jordan National Bank	80	1.7%
Jordan Invest. & Finance	61	1.3%
Cairo-Amman Bank	55	1.1%
Bank of Jordan	47	1.0%
Top ten	**991**	**20.4%**
Total stock market	**4,855**	

Korea	Mkt Cap US $ Mil	% of Total
Korea Electric Power	16,506	11.8%
Pohang Iron & Steel	6,198	4.4%
Samsung Electronics	4,181	3.0%
Hyundai Motors	2,502	1.8%
Gold Star	2,466	1.8%
Daewoo Securities	2,132	1.5%
Daewoo Corp	1,933	1.4%
Korea First Bank	1,932	1.4%
Kia Motors	1,907	1.4%
Yu Kong	1,819	1.3%
Top ten	**41,575**	**29.8%**
Total stock market	**139,584**	

Sri Lanka	Mkt Cap US $ Mil	% of Total
Development Finance Corp.	199	7.9%
John Keells Holdings	127	5.1%
Hatton National Bank	91	3.6%
Commercial Bank Ceylon	90	3.6%
Asian Hotels Corp.	76	3.0%
Ceylon Grain Elevators	74	3.0%
Aitken Spence	74	3.0%
Hayleys	71	2.8%
Sampath Bank	49	1.9%
Pelwatte Sugar	29	1.2%
Top ten	**880**	**35.1%**
Total stock market	**2,510**	

Mexico	Mkt Cap US $ Mil	% of Total
Telmex L	26,273	13.3%
Grupo Televisa CPO	10,764	5.4%
Telmex A	9,400	4.8%
Cemex A	8,981	4.5%
Grupo Fin Banacci B	8,474	4.3%
Cifra B	7,766	3.9%
Grupo Fin Bancomer B	5,199	2.6%
Kimberly Clark Mexico A	3,749	1.9%
Fomento Economico Mex.	3,564	1.8%
Grupo Fin Banacci C	3,081	1.6%
Top ten	**87,251**	**44.1%**
Total stock market	**197,818**	

Malaysia	Mkt Cap US $ Mil	% of Total
Tenaga Nasional	21,505	9.9%
Telekom Malaysia	16,323	7.5%
Malayan Banking	8,023	3.7%
Resorts World	6,970	3.2%
Sime Darby	4,391	2.0%
Technology Resources Ind	3,525	1.6%
Magnum Corp.	2,956	1.4%
United Engineers (Mal)	2,877	1.3%
Rothmans Pall Mall (Mal)	2,756	1.3%
Malaysian Int'l Shipping	2,659	1.2%
Top ten	**71,984**	**33.1%**
Total stock market	**217,713**	

(*continued on next page*)

EXHIBIT 8.5 (CONTINUED)

	Mkt Cap US $ Mil	% of Total
Peru		
Telefonos B	825	14.7%
Banco de Credito	487	8.7%
Cerveceria Backus C	451	8.0%
Cementos Lima T	291	5.2%
Cerveceria Backus T	231	4.1%
Telephonos A	216	3.8%
Buenaventura C	156	2.8%
Nacional de Cerveza C	119	2.1%
Southern T	115	2.0%
Nacional de Cerveza T	48	0.9%
Top ten	**2,938**	**52.3%**
Total stock market	**5,616**	

	Mkt Cap US $ Mil	% of Total
Philippines		
Phil Long Distance Tel	4,340	11.1%
San Miguel Corp A	2,722	7.0%
Philippine National Bank	2,064	5.3%
San Miguel Corp B	1,985	5.1%
Meralco A	1,985	5.1%
Meralco B	1,554	4.0%
Ayala Land Inc. B	1,217	3.1%
ABS-CBN Broadcasting	598	1.5%
Far East Bank & Trust	506	1.3%
ICTSI	485	1.2%
Top ten	**17,457**	**44.6%**
Total stock market	**39,099**	

	Mkt Cap US $ Mil	% of Total
Pakistan		
Fauji Fertilizer	959	8.3%
Dewan Salman Fibre	426	3.7%
Pakistan State Oil	408	3.5%
ICI (Pakistan)	374	3.2%
Engro Chemicals Pakistan	361	3.1%
Sui South Gas Pipelines	311	2.7%
Pakistan Int'l Airlines	304	2.6%
Lever Brothers (Pakistan)	286	2.5%
Muslim Commercial Bank	284	2.5%
Sui North Gas Pipelines	279	2.4%
Top ten	**3,992**	**34.5%**
Total stock market	**11,588**	

	Mkt Cap US $ Mil	% of Total
Portugal		
BCP Nom	1,6551	14.2%
Banco Totta & Acores	1,021	8.8%
BPI Nom	661	5.7%
Sonae	368	3.2%
Jeronimo Martins	359	3.1%
Uniao Cervejerira (Unicer)	293	2.5%
Seguros Tranquilidade	242	2.1%
Marconi Nom	236	2.0%
Marconi Port	219	1.9%
Soares Costa	155	1.3%
Top ten	**5,205**	**44.7%**
Total stock market	**11,643**	

	Mkt Cap US $ Mil	% of Total
Thailand		
Bangkok Bank	8,534	6.6%
Shinawatra Computer	4,775	3.7%
Siam Cement	4,322	3.3%
Bangkok Land	3,969	3.0%
Land and Houses	3,829	2.9%
Thai Farmers Bank	3,789	2.9%
Siam Commercial Bank	3,154	2.4%
Finance One	2,236	1.7%
Phatra Thanakit	1,863	1.4%
Dhana Siam Finance & Sec.	1,776	1.4%
Top ten	**38,246**	**29.4%**
Total stock market	**130,178**	

	Mkt Cap US $ Mil	% of Total
Turkey		
T.I.s Bankasi (C) 100%	1,728	4.7%
T. Garanti Bankasi	1,575	4.3%
Arcelik	1,115	3.0%
Eregli Demir Celik	1,096	3.0%
Otosan	811	2.2%
Yapi ve Kredi Bank	676	1.8%
Cukurova Elektrik	588	1.6%
Ege Biracilik	581	1.6%
Aksa Akrilik Kimya	465	1.3%
Bekoteknik Sanayi	328	0.9%
Top ten	**8,963**	**24.5%**
Total stock market	**36,613**	

	Mkt Cap US $ Mil	% of Total		Mkt Cap US $ Mil	% of Total
Taiwan			**Venezuela**		
Cathay Life Insurance	14,207	7.4%	Electricidad de Caracas	1,457	18.1%
Chang Hwa Bank	7,141	3.7%	Banco de Venezuela	777	9.6%
Nan Ya Plastic	4,977	2.6%	Banco Union	444	5.5%
I.C.B.C	4,410	2.3%	Banco Provincial	407	5.0%
Formosa Plastic	3,731	1.9%	Venezolana de Cementos	364	4.5%
Tatung	2,881	1.5%			
Taiwan Cement	2,794	1.5%	Corimon	344	4.3%
Asia Cement	2,636	1.4%	Mavesa	275	3.4%
Evergreen Marine	2,623	1.4%	Siderurgica Venezolana	243	3.0%
China Development	2,502	1.3%	Banco Mercantil	192	2.4%
			Ceramica Carabobo	139	1.7%
Top ten	**47,902**	**25.0%**	**Top ten**	**4,642**	**57.5%**
Total stock market	**191,500**		**Total stock market**	**8,070**	

Source: Morgan Stanley Capital International Perspective, May 1994. Reprinted with permission.

Where Do We Stand?

In Exh. 8.6, which is presented in a fashion similar to Exh. 4.9, the first column gives the total annual return measured in a common currency, the U.S. dollar. The next three columns decompose this annual return into capital gains, dividend yield, and currency gains. The next two columns give the risk (standard deviation) of the emerging markets measured in dollars (*total risk*) and in their local currently (*domestic risk*). The last column gives the correlation of returns with the world index of developed markets. The selected emerging markets are those for which IFC indexes are available since the end of 1984. The first two lines give statistics for the U.S. stock market and for the MSCI world index of developed markets. The third line is the IFC composite index of emerging markets. Emerging markets have some special risk and return characteristics:

- First, the high *volatility* of emerging markets appears clearly. In U.S. dollar terms most markets have a volatility ranging between 30% and 70%, compared to 15% for the U.S. market. The figure can be even worse when measured in the local currency. For example, the Argentinean market had a

EXHIBIT 8.6

Return and Risk of Emerging Stock Markets
January 1985–December 1993, in U.S. dollars

	Annual Return %	Capital Gain %	Dividend Yield %	Currency Gain %	Total Risk %	Domestic Risk %	Correlation with World
U.S.A.	15.8	11.9	3.9	0.0	15.6	15.6	0.71
World ($)	16.9	13.8	3.1	0.0	15.4	14.3	1.00
Composite ($)	20.9	17.8	3.1	0.0	23.6	n.a.	0.31
Argentina	40.5	358.1	15.4	−333.0	106.2	173.4	−0.06
Brazil	13.3	731.4	46.9	−765.0	69.7	94.9	0.12
Chile	52.3	62.1	12.3	−22.0	27.3	26.4	0.11
Colombia	40.8	62.6	12.5	−34.3	31.9	30.8	−0.01
Greece	23.3	23.3	9.4	−9.4	45.2	44.2	0.16
India	19.4	29.3	2.9	−12.8	34.8	36.9	−0.15
Indonesia[*]	−2.6	3.9	0.5	−7.0	23.9	21.5	0.11
Jordan	9.5	11.4	4.7	−6.6	17.7	17.4	0.11
Korea	22.6	19.5	2.8	0.3	29.9	29.4	0.30
Malaysia	18.5	17.2	2.7	−1.4	26.5	26.7	0.42
Mexico	52.8	96.4	8.1	−51.7	46.1	46.5	0.25
Nigeria	−6.1	33.5	11.4	−51.0	42.5	12.0	0.07
Pakistan	24.3	26.3	7.7	−9.6	24.2	24.4	0.01
Philippines	53.8	54.8	4.4	−5.4	38.2	39.7	0.31
Portugal	25.1	22.9	2.7	−0.6	44.2	43.9	0.38
Taiwan	28.4	21.2	1.6	5.6	53.5	52.4	0.22
Thailand	38.1	30.8	6.3	1.0	31.0	31.1	0.30
Turkey	25.3	65.2	8.7	−48.7	65.1	66.2	0.04
Venezuela	26.4	56.6	3.2	−33.4	51.4	39.7	−0.04
Zimbabwe	28.2	39.6	12.3	−23.8	32.5	30.9	0.07

*From January 1990

volatility[2] of 173.4% in pesos, compared to 106.2 in dollars. This difference is explained by hyperinflation. The Argentinean peso depreciated by more than 300% per annum relative to the U.S. dollar, with a large volatility.

- The high *return* offered by many emerging markets appears in Exh. 8.6. Some markets had a spectacular growth. For example, the Philippines and Chile had an average dollar return of more than 50% per annum, compared to 15.8% for the United States. The IFC composite index of emerging markets had an average dollar return of 20.9% per annum compared to only 16.9% for the MSCI world index of developed markets. This difference of 4% in average annual return translates into a large compounded difference. From the start of 1985 to the end of 1993, the world index had a total return of 307%, compared to a total return of 453% for the composite index.

- The low *correlation* of emerging markets with the world developed index appears in the last column of Exh. 8.6. This is a strong advantage of emerging markets. Their economies tend to be less linked to the business cycles of developed nations. Economies that are more open to the world (Malaysia, Mexico, Korea, Portugal) tend to have the highest correlation with developed markets. On the average, the correlation of the composite emerging index with the world developed index is only 0.31.

In general, emerging markets provide some good diversification benefits to a portfolio invested solely in developed markets. The contribution to the long-term return can be excellent, and the risk of the overall portfolio can be reduced. However, the correlation is still generally positive. One should not be surprised to find that in some periods when developed markets drop, emerging markets also drop and by a large amount, because of their high volatility. This happened in early 1994. In other periods an appreciation of emerging markets can offset a loss in developed markets.

The risk/return case for international diversification into emerging markets is illustrated in Exh. 8.7, which reproduces the risk and return of various portfolios combining the world index and the composite index in various proportions. The minimum-risk strategy is to be invested for 22% in emerging markets and 78% in developed markets, a proportion not too different from the relative GNPs. The contribution of emerging stock markets to a global asset allocation, including domestic and foreign stocks and bonds, is illustrated in Exh. 8.8 for a Swiss investor. This exhibit, taken from Odier, Solnik, and Zucchinetti (1995), gives the efficient frontiers for global asset allocations with and without emerging stock markets. Here individual national stock and bond markets are selected on the basis of their returns and risks. All returns and risks are measured in real Swiss francs, adjusted for wage inflation; real Swiss francs should be the relevant numeraire for a Swiss pension fund paying pensions indexed on wage inflation. The gains from including emerging stock markets in the investment universe are very significant. Let's consider portfolios with a volatility of 19%, *equal* to that of the Swiss stock market. An efficient international portfolio solely invested in developed markets had a real return of 19% per annum compared to 11.5% for the Swiss market. This return is further increased to 28%, when both developed and emerging markets are considered in the optimal portfolio.

The Prospects

The question is whether these emerging markets will continue to grow and whether some small, lesser-known stock markets will become more mature and sophisticated and gain the status of emerging market. The factors that will affect the future growth of emerging markets can be grouped into institutional, economic, and political categories.

EXHIBIT 8.7

Combination of World Developed Index and Emerging Index

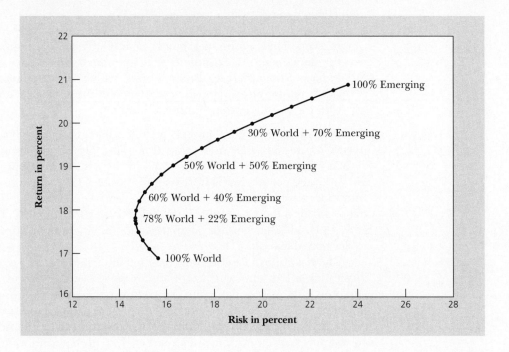

Institutional Factors   The role of multinational development banks in assisting emerging countries should not be underestimated. These banks include the World Bank, the Inter-American Development Bank, the African Development Bank, the Asian Development Bank, and the recently created European Bank for Reconstruction and Development. The International Bank for Reconstruction and Development (IBRD) was the first institution of the World Bank Group, which now also includes the International Development Association, the Multilateral Investment Guarantee Agency, and the International Finance Corporation (IFC), which focuses on private-sector development. Its purpose is "to further economic development by encouraging the growth of productive private enterprise in member countries." IFC is the largest source of multilateral loan and equity financing for private-sector projects in the developing world. IFC sponsors the development of stock markets as a means to further local economic development and also as a means of recovering quickly its investments after having accomplished its developmental role. It has developed a widely used database on emerging companies and stock markets and has launched numerous country and multinational emerging funds that have been subscribed by institutional investors across the world. It has also advised numerous emerging nations on the development of their financial markets. IFC has gained international credibility by being a profitable institution

EXHIBIT 8.8

Efficient Frontier with Emerging Markets

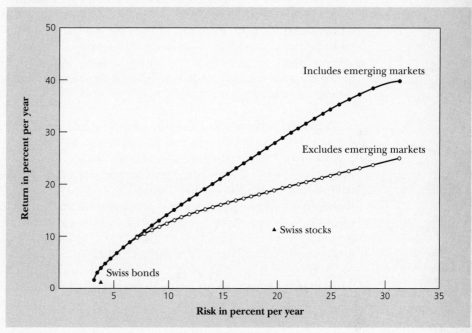

Source: P. Odier, B. Solnik, and S. Zucchinetti, "Global Optimization for Swiss Pension Funds," *Finanzmarkt und Portfolio Management,* June 1995.

while promoting efficient and competitive projects, without any government guarantee. Its recognized expertise allows IFC to mobilize additional capital from worldwide investors. This new role of the World Bank has therefore been instrumental in the growth of emerging stock markets and is likely to remain a positive factor for the development of emerging markets.

Economic Factors   Clearly a major argument for investing in emerging economies is their prospective economic growth. Exhibit 7.5 shows the high growth rate of such countries as Thailand or Korea compared to major industrialized nations. Portfolio managers want to find countries that will exhibit in the future the type of growth witnessed by Japan between the 1960s and the 1980s. Most analysts expect emerging economies to grow at a higher rate than developed nations, given the liberalization of international trade. Arguments frequently mentioned are lower labor costs, lower level of unionization and social rigidities, delocalization of production by high-cost developed countries, and rapid growth in domestic demand. The arrival of foreign capital helps those countries develop at a rapid pace and to compete on the world goods market. Some specific factors could also affect the local stock markets. For example, pension funds have recently been created in many Latin American countries and are likely to invest heavily in their local stock markets. Many countries are pursuing an active program of privatization, and more local firms are attracted by the financing potential of stock markets. Under pressure from international investors, emerging markets are becoming more efficient, providing more rigorous research on companies, and progressively applying stricter standards of market supervision. Most of these markets have automated their trading and settlement procedures, using computer software tested on developed markets.

Political Factors   The development of many emerging markets stems from the winds of political reform and liberalization. This is clearly the case in Central Europe with the fall of communism. This is also the case of China with its economic reforms. However, problems can easily materialize. Some emerging countries do not have a fully stable political and social situation. The explosive social transformation brought about by rapid, and sometimes anarchic, economic growth can lead to serious imbalances, causing social and political unrest. For example, some Chinese cities have industrialized very rapidly while rural regions became more aware of their poverty. Corruption is a rampant problem everywhere but may be more so in some emerging countries. The infrastructure can limit growth. Thailand and China, for example, have stretched the limit of their existing road infrastructures. Education structures are often insufficient to train a large number of workers and managers to modern international techniques. Multilateral development banks have made education a priority, but improvements are very slow, as local teachers must first be trained and are tempted to leave the education system after their training. The quality of goods produced may be below international standards because of a lack of training and different quality standards than those required in developed countries.

Despite all these problems, which create higher investment risks, emerging stock markets are an attractive investment opportunity. Again, the idea is that investors should be willing to buy emerging markets, which are inherently very volatile, because some of them are likely to produce very high returns. Altogether the contribution of emerging markets to the total risk of the global portfolio is not very large, because of their low correlation with developed markets.

Some Practical Issues and Problems

Stock Market Indexes

Local indexes are available on all emerging stock markets and are distributed by major information services. They are seldom used by global investors, because of their lack of comparability. These investors prefer to use emerging market benchmarks prepared by recognized international institutions. It is important to review these indexes, because they are extensively used as performance benchmarks. The performance of managed portfolios investing in emerging markets is measured relative to one or several of these emerging market indexes. The return on various emerging indexes can differ widely, so it is crucial to understand how they are constructed. We will review the major indexes, as of 1994, in their historical order of creation.

IFC Indexes   IFC proposes IFC Global (IFCG) and IFC Investable (IFCI) indexes on a weekly basis. As of 1994, the IFC global indexes covered all 26 countries mentioned in Exhs. 8.1 and 8.2. For each country the target aggregate market capitalization of IFCG indexes is from 60% to 75% of the total capitalization of all listed shares on the local bourse. Each stock enters the index in proportion to its market capitalization. IFC publishes an IFCG composite index of all emerging markets, as well as three regional indexes (Latin America, Asia, and Europe and the Middle East). IFC uses a "bottom-up" approach in constructing the composite index. Once a share is included in a national index, it will automatically enter the composite index with a weight proportional to its market capitalization. This implies that a country does not necessarily enter the composite index with a share proportional to its national market capitalization.[3] At the start of 1994, the IFCG composite index included some 1006 stocks. IFC investable indexes attempt to measure the market for shares available to foreign investors. For example, some Mexican shares cannot be purchased by foreign investors. These shares do not appear in the IFCI indexes. The weights of Korean and Taiwanese stocks are drastically reduced to reflect the degree to which foreigners can invest in those markets. A reduction also applies to other countries imposing restrictions on foreign ownership. IFCI composite and regional indexes are also published on a weekly basis. At the start of 1994, the IFCI composite index included some 644 stocks. All series are calculated on a price-only and a total-return basis, in local currency and in U.S. dollar terms. IFCG indexes have been available since December 1984, and IFCI indexes have been available since 1988. IFC also publishes IFCG and IFCI industry indexes across all emerging markets.

Morgan Stanley Capital International   Morgan Stanley Capital International (MSCI) proposes MSCI Global and MSCI Free indexes for 20 emerging markets on a daily basis. These are the 26 mentioned, minus Hungary, Jordan, Nigeria, Poland, South Africa, and Zimbabwe. For each country the target aggregate market capitalization is 60% of the total capitalization of all listed shares on the local bourse. Stocks are also selected on the basis of their liquidity and float. Efforts are made to obtain a sample of stocks with similar industry representation as the total market. Efforts are also made to have a representative sample of small, medium, and large capitalization companies in the sample selected. Once a stock is selected, it enters the index in proportion to its market capitalization.

MSCI also publishes an international index, simply called Emerging Markets Global (EMG), as well as regional indexes. At the start of 1994 the EMG index included 627 stocks. MSCI Free indexes excludes all stocks that cannot be purchased by foreign investors. MSCI publishes an international index called the Emerging Markets Free (EMF), which includes only investable stocks. To reflect foreign investment constraints, Taiwan is excluded from the EMF. For the same reason, MSCI retains only 20% of the Korean stocks capitalization. In other words, the Korean index enters the EMF index, but the market capitalization of all Korean stocks is divided by 5. These conventions would change if investment restrictions were eased. The EMF index included 560 stocks at the start of 1994. All series are calculated on a price-only basis and a total-return basis, in local currency and in U.S. dollar terms. MSCI publishes EMG industry indexes across all emerging markets. MSCI also calculates all-country indexes based on its market indexes for developed markets (world or EAFE) and for emerging markets (EMG or EMF). MSCI Emerging Markets indexes have been available since 1988.

Baring Indexes   Baring Emerging Markets Indexes (BEMI) cover 19 countries on a daily basis. These are the 26 countries mentioned, minus Hungary, Jordan, Nigeria, Poland, Sri Lanka, Venezuela, and Zimbabwe. Baring considers only major stocks that are available to foreign investors. Each national index consists of some 10 to 35 stocks weighted in proportion to their market capitalization. Baring also publishes a BEMI world index and regional indexes. Foreign investment restrictions are reflected in the world weightings. Some 403 stocks were included at the end of 1994. Some equally weighted indexes are also available. All series are calculated on a price-only and a total-return basis, in local currency and in U.S. dollar terms. BEMI indexes have been available since July 1992.

Goldman Sachs–Financial Times   Goldman Sachs collaborates with the *Financial Times* to produce the FT-Actuaries World indexes for developed markets. In 1994 indexes for several emerging markets (Brazil and Thailand) were added and others are likely to follow. Goldman Sachs publishes Extended Global Market Indexes (GS-EGMI), which cover developed and emerging markets. These indexes are a combination of the FT-Actuaries World indexes and of the IFC Investable indexes.

All the institutions named not only produce emerging markets indexes but also provide information on the companies included in the coverage of the indexes. Investors have developed a keen interest in emerging markets and need good-quality information. There is a continuous production of new emerging market indexes. Each year, new countries are included in the coverage provided by IFC, MSCI, Baring, or Financial Times–Goldman Sachs. South Africa was added by most services in 1994 or 1995. Israel became covered by MSCI in 1994. IFC launched *tradable* indexes in 1994. The IFC 100 is comprised of 100 very liquid, large-capitalization stocks in 13 emerging markets. The Asia50 is comprised of 50 very liquid Asian stocks, and the Latin50 is made up of 50 very liquid Latin American stocks. The objective of these new IFC indexes is to provide highly liquid indexes that would help traders create derivative investment strategies in emerging markets.

Emerging markets are very diverse and tend to have little correlation between themselves. Hence differences in the composition and geographical distribution of international indexes can lead to marked differences in performance. Meier (1994) provided a comparison of the international indexes calculated by the IFC, MSCI, and Baring from the start of 1989 to October 1993. He found that investable indexes (IFCI, MSCI Free, and BEMI) had very different return and risk characteristics from global indexes (IFCG, MSCI Global), as follows:

International Index	Return (% per year)	Risk (% per year)
IFC Global	11.3	20.9
IFC Investable	27.9	19.6
MSCI Global	14.7	21.6
MSCI Free	31.6	23.3
Baring	21.2	25.9

The major differences in performance come from the country weightings. Taiwan and Korea make up roughly a quarter of the global indexes but much less of the investable indexes. Taiwan is absent from the MSCI Free index but represents about 2% of the IFC Investable index.

Altogether, one should have a good knowledge of the construction of the emerging markets index that is being used to monitor portfolio performance, because these indexes will necessarily guide the investment strategy of the portfolio manager.

Information

Information on emerging-market activity is now readily available, as we have seen. For the sample of firms included in their indexes, the publishers provide some summary accounting information on the companies. In many markets accounting information is not reliable and even more difficult to get from newly listed companies. In some countries the earnings forecasts announced by companies that become publicly listed are totally unverifiable. An extreme case can be found with China. The rapid move from a centrally planned economy to a somewhat partly capitalistic system implies that the mere notion of accounting at the firm level is a new concept. State-owned companies have been listed on Chinese or foreign stock exchanges but have no tradition of having separate accounts and therefore have problems trying to identify earnings to shareholders during a given time period. It is equally difficult to assess who is the legal owner of some of the assets of a Chinese firm; the state, the province, and the municipality all lay some claim on existing firms' assets, and legal property titles do not exist historically. Shanghai Petrochemical Co., for example, was the largest company to be introduced on the NYSE in 1993. Its value is clearly a function of its properties and equipment. A letter from America Appraisal Hong Kong Ltd., included in the 1993 listing prospectus, illustrates that reliable information on companies from emerging markets is sometimes difficult to get.

> We have relied to a considerable extent on information provided by you . . . . As all the properties are situated in the People's Republic of China, we have not searched the original documents to verify ownership . . . . All dimensions, measurements and areas are approximate. We have inspected the exterior and, when possible, the interior of all the properties valued. However, no structural survey has been made and we are therefore unable to report as to whether the properties are or not free of rot, infestation or any other structural defects.

Given the uncertainty about a company's information, it is not surprising that its valuation is a matter of highly subjective judgment. This is all the more apparent when a firm is first floated on a stock exchange, so that no reference stock price can be used to determine its introduction price. In December 1994 China's state-owned Huaxin Cement Co. was introduced on the Shanghai bourse in the form of "B shares," available to foreign investors. The introduction price was determined by a major international bank underwriting the placement. Shares of Huaxin Cement Co. plunged 18.4% on their first day of trading. Such a dramatic drop in price would not take place on a developed market.

The uncertainty surrounding companies' information is damaging. Foreign investors tend to request a lower stock price when information is uncertain. Most emerging markets trade at low price-earnings ratios compared to developed markets with similar or lesser growth potential. Local authorities and the management of listed firms have come to realize that stricter standards must be applied to the timely release of reliable information. But progress can only be slow. IFC provides an evaluation of the quality of accounting standards and investor protection; these are summarized in Exh. 8.9.

Liquidity and Costs

Emerging stock markets tend to be very active, with large traded volume. As can be seen in Exh. 8.4, the turnover ratio (ratio of transaction volume to market capitalization) tends to be higher for emerging stock markets than for developed markets. However, there can be periods of liquidity problems because of the amount of "hot," or speculative, money invested in those markets. Late in 1994, many foreign investors wanted to sell their emerging market holdings, following the Mexican crisis. This led to a steep drop in most markets.

Transaction costs are not easy to assess with precision. Fixed commissions are often the rule on the smaller markets, but the price impact of a large trade can be significant. Hence estimates of the total transaction cost vary widely among international brokers. It is safe to say that transaction costs are higher than on large developed markets and can be from 50 to 100 basis points higher than what an international investor is accustomed to pay on a major developed market. The cost of transferring money, and converting it into the local currency, can also be high for some of the lesser traded currencies and for some countries with foreign exchange controls.

Taxes can also have a significant impact. Some of the countries impose a withholding tax on dividends paid. This tax can be used by a taxable investor as a credit

EXHIBIT 8.9

Information Disclosure Summary

Country	Accounting Standards	Investor Protection	Country	Accounting Standards	Investor Protection
Argentina	A	AS	Nigeria	A	AS
Brazil	G	GS	Pakistan	A	AS
Chile	G	GS	Peru	A	AS
China	P	PS	Philippines	G	AS
Colombia	A	AS	Poland	A	AS
Greece	A	AS	Portugal	A	AS
Hungary	A	AS	South Africa	n.a.	n.a.
India	G	GS	Sri Lanka	G	AS
Indonesia	P	AS	Taiwan	A	AS
Jordan	A	AS	Thailand	A	AS
Korea	G	GS	Turkey	A	AS
Malaysia	G	GS	Venezuela	A	AS
Mexico	G	GS	Zimbabwe	A	AS

KEY: G = Good, of internationally acceptable quality; A = Adequate; P = Poor; S = Functioning securities commission or similar government agency regulating market activity.

Source: Emerging Stock Market Factbook 1994, International Finance Corporation, Washington, DC. Reprinted with permission.

against home taxes, when an international tax convention allows it. It can often be fully or partly reclaimed by a foreign investor, but the process is lengthy. Some emerging countries impose taxes on capital gains made by foreign investors. These taxes are summarized in Exh. 8.10.

National Regulations and Controls

The growth of emerging stock markets has been remarkable. Their trading volume multiplied by a factor of 30 from the mid-1980s to the mid-1990s. The market capitalization multiplied by a factor of close to 20 over the same period. This extensive growth has been accompanied by progressive deregulation and liberalization, especially as far as foreign investors are concerned. Emerging countries need capital and have come to realize that equity investment is an attractive substitute for, or addition to, foreign commercial loans and aid from international organizations. They also realize that capital will flow more willingly to countries with the lowest barriers to entry and exit. Moreover, foreign investors look for an efficient regulatory environment that meets international standards.

Wide disparities still exist among emerging countries in the pace of financial deregulation and liberalization. Exhibit 8.11 summarizes investment regulations governing the entry and exit of foreign portfolio investment. The first group of countries is very liberal toward foreign capital. Others impose some form of

EXHIBIT 8.10

Withholding Taxes for Emerging Markets

Market	Interest (%)	Dividends (%)	Long-term Capital Gains on Listed Shares (%)	Market	Interest (%)	Dividends (%)	Long-term Capital Gains on Listed Shares (%)
Latin America and the Caribbean				**Europe/Mideast**			
Argentina	0	0	0	Cyprus	0	30	0
Barbados	15	15	0	Czech Republic	0	0	0
Brazil	15	15	0	Greece	15	0	0
Chile	15	23.5	15	Hungary	20	10	20
Colombia	12	12	30	Iran	10	0	0
Costa Rica	8	5	0	Jordan	0	0	0
Jamacia	15	15	0	Poland	0	20	0
Mexico	15	0	0	Portugal	25	15	0
Panama	0	10	0	Slovakia	15	15	15
Peru	0	10	0	Turkey	15	15	0
Trinidad and Tobago	30	25	0				
Venezuela	30	0	30				
Africa				**Asia**			
Botswana	15	15	0	China	10	20	0
Cote d'Ivoire	0	12	0	India	20	20	20
Ghana	30	10	0	Indonesia	12	15	0
Kenya	10	10	0	Korea	12	15	0
Mauritius	0	0	0	Malaysia	20	0	0
Morocco	0	15	38	Pakistan	12	10	0
Namibia	0	10	0	Philippines	20	25	0
Nigeria	5	5	20	Sri Lanka	0	15	0
South Africa	0	15	0	Taiwan	20	20	0
Swaziland	10	15	0	Thailand	15	10	15
Tunisia	15	0	0				
Zimbabwe	15	15	10				

Notes: Chile: Effective dividend withholding tax rate. Venezuela: Rate on capital gains in excess of Bs. 2 million. Zimbabwe: Rates as in effect from Jan. 1, 1994.

Source: *Emerging Stock Market Factbook 1994*, International Finance Corporation, Washington, DC. Reprinted with permission.

EXHIBIT 8.11

Investment Regulations Summary for Entering and Exiting Emerging Markets

Entry[a]	Exit[b]	
Are listed stocks freely available to foreign investors?	Repatriation of	
	Income	Capital
Free entry		
Argentina	Free	Free
Botswana	Free	Free
Brazil	Free	Free
Colombia	Free	Free
Czech Republic	Free	Free
Ghana	Free	Free
Greece	Free	Free
Hungary	Free	Free
Malaysia	Free	Free
Mexico	Free	Free
Pakistan	Free	Free
Peru	Free	Free
Poland	Free	Free
Portugal	Free	Free
South Africa	Free	Free
Turkey	Free	Free
Relatively free entry		
Bangladesh	Some restrictions	Some restrictions
Chile	Free	After 1 year
Costa Rica	Free	Free
Indonesia	Some restrictions	Some restrictions
Jamacia	Free	Free
Jordan	Free	Free
Kenya	Some restrictions	Some restrictions
Korea	Free	Free
Sri Lanka	Some restrictions	Some restrictions
Thailand	Free	Free
Trinidad and Tobago	Free	Free
Venezuela	Free	Free
Zimbabwe	Free	Free

(*continued on next page*)

EXHIBIT 8.11 (CONTINUED)

Entry[a]	Exit[b]	
Are listed stocks freely available to foreign investors?	Repatriation of Income	Capital
Special classes of shares		
China	Free	Free
Philippines	Free	Free
Authorized investors only		
India	Free	Free
Taiwan	Some restrictions	Some restrictions
Mauritius	Free	Free
Closed		
Nigeria	Some restrictions	Some restrictions

[a]*Key to Entry*: Free Entry: No significant restrictions to purchasing stocks. Relatively Free Entry: Some registration procedures required to ensure repatriation rights. Special Classes: Foreigners restricted to certain classes of stocks, designated for foreign investors. Authorized Investors Only: Only approved foreign investors may buy stocks. Closed: closed, or access severely restricted (e.g., for nonresident nationals only).

[b]*Key to Exit*: Repatriation of income: Dividends, interest, and realized capital gains. Repatriation of capital: Initial capital invested. Free: Repatriation done routinely. Some Restrictions: Typically, requires some registration with or permission of Central Bank, Ministry of Finance, or an Office of Exchange Controls that may restrict the timing of exchange release.

Notes: Some industries in some countries are considered strategic and are not available to foreign/nonresident investors, and that the level of foreign investment in other cases may be limited by national law or corporate policy to minority positions not to aggregate more than 49% of voting stock. The summaries above refer to "new money" investment by foreign institutions; other regulations may apply to capital invested through debt conversion schemes or other sources.

Source: *Emerging Stock Market Factbook 1994*, International Finance Corporation, Washington, DC. Reprinted with permission.

restrictions; Thailand is a typical example.[4] Foreign ownership of any Thai company is limited to 49%. This limit is lowered to 25% for banks and finance companies. As soon as the limit is reached, shares owned by foreigners start to be traded separately, on the *Alien Board*, where foreigners can buy and sell shares of that company. The price on the Alien Board is usually higher than on the *Main Board*, where Thai investors can trade the share. Any company that has not reached its limit on foreign ownership is traded only on the Main Board. A few countries require some registration procedures to ensure repatriation rights. In China and the Philippines foreign investors are restricted to certain classes of stocks. China has two types of shares, which are kept separate. "A shares" can be held only by Chinese; "B shares" can be held only by foreigners. A dual exchange rate system existed for the yuan until 1993; the RMB was used by domestic Chinese, and the FEC (foreign exchange certificates) was used by foreigners. This dual exchange rate system has been removed, but foreign investors still face some foreign currency restrictions. The situation in China is undergoing continuous and significant change and is a good example of how the need for foreign capital pushes toward rapid liberalization. India and Taiwan allow only approved investors to buy stocks;

these are typically foreign institutional investors, not private investors. Taiwan is one of the most restrictive markets. It imposes a foreign ownership limit on each Taiwanese company, as well as a global limit on the amount of foreign capital invested on the local stock market.

The pace of liberalization of emerging markets is rapid, and investors should be aware that the regulations outlined here are undergoing continual changes.

Foreign-Listed Shares

Investors wishing to get some participation in emerging markets have alternatives other than investing directly on the local emerging market. They can also buy foreign-listed shares and country funds.

Some companies from emerging countries have their shares listed on foreign stock markets. These are called ADRs (American Depositary Receipts) in the United States (see Chapter 6). Listing abroad allows access to a wider capital base and increases the business visibility of the firm. Chinese companies provide a good illustration of this opportunity. Shares of Chinese companies listed in Hong Kong are usually called "H shares," and those listed in New York are called "X shares." To list abroad, Chinese companies must gain government authorization. Foreign listing is the occasion to raise new capital abroad. The advantage for non-Chinese investors is that it is easier, and sometimes cheaper, to buy shares on a well-known, developed market. The currency of quotation for shares listed in the United States is the dollar, dividends are paid in dollars, and some information in English is provided. Emerging-country companies listed abroad tend to be some of the largest firms of their countries, and their number is still quite limited. Another alternative for participating in the growth of the Chinese economy is to buy Hong Kong firms that have extensive activities in China.

Country Funds

Closed-end country funds have been created for many countries, especially emerging countries.

Definition and Motivation   A closed-end fund is an investment vehicle that buys stocks in the market; in turn, shares of the closed-end fund are listed on some national market and are traded at a price determined by supply and demand for that fund. A closed-end fund is never liquidated, and the number of shares of the fund remains fixed. The fund's market price can differ from the value of the assets held in its portfolio, which is called the *net asset value* (NAV). The *premium* on the fund is the difference between the fund value (FV) and its NAV:

FV = NAV + Premium.

The premium is often expressed as a percentage of the NAV and is usually called a discount when negative. The situation is quite different for a portfolio directly entrusted to a portfolio manager or for an open-end fund, such as a mutual fund. There the value of the portfolio or fund is, by definition, equal to the market value of the invested assets (the NAV). The advantage of a closed-end fund for the investment manager is that he or she does not have to worry about redemptions; once a closed-end fund is initially subscribed, the investment manager keeps the money under management. This vehicle is well suited to investing in emerging markets, whereby the manager transfers the money to the emerging market and can invest it in the long term. The disadvantage for the closed-end shareholder is the uncertainty in the premium, as discussed later.

A *country fund* (e.g., the Korea Fund) is a closed-end fund whose assets consist primarily of stocks of the country for which the fund is named (e.g., stocks of Korean companies). A country fund is launched by a portfolio management firm with expertise in the local market (e.g., the Korea Fund was launched by Scudder Stevens & Clark/Daswoo Capital Management). Numerous country funds are listed in the United States, the United Kingdom, and major stock markets. To avoid confusion, we will call "local" the country where the fund is invested and "United States" the country where the fund shares are traded.

The motivation for investing in those country funds is twofold. First, they offer a simple way to access the local market and benefit from international diversification. For example, country funds invested in Italy, Spain, Australia, the United Kingdom, or Germany can be purchased in the United States. These funds invested in developed markets are of interest primarily to private investors, who find an easy way to hold a diversified portfolio of that country. Country funds are just managed portfolios specializing in stocks of a specific country. The case for country funds investing in emerging markets is more compelling, because the alternative of investing directly on emerging markets is a more difficult process. Furthermore, some countries, e.g., Brazil, India, Korea, and Taiwan, restrict foreign investment. Country funds, approved by the local government, are a way to overcome foreign investment restrictions. So foreign investment restriction is a second motivation for the creation and use of some of these country funds. Recently IFC has been instrumental in the launching of country funds on small emerging markets. In 1992 IFC established the Mauritius Fund, which invests exclusively in Mauritian companies. Mauritius's stock market opened to foreign investment only in 1994. IFC and Emerging Market Management (an investment manager) set up in 1994 the Africa Emerging Markets Fund. This is a regional fund placed with institutional investors and intended to invest in African stock markets being modernized. Here again, investors wishing to participate in the future growth of African stock markets have little realistic alternatives, because of foreign investment constraints.

The Pricing of Country Funds   The price of a country fund is seldom equal to its NAV. Some funds trade at a substantial premium or discount from their NAV.

This poses problems to investors. The change in market price of a country fund is equal to the change in NAV plus the change in the premium (discount). If the premium decreases or the discount widens, the return on the fund will be less than the return on underlying assets making up the portfolio.

Some country funds provide a unique way to invest in emerging countries with foreign investment restrictions. When these foreign investment restrictions are binding, one would expect the country fund to sell at a premium over its net asset value; see Bonser-Neal, Brauer, Neal, and Wheatley (1990) or Eun, Janakiramanan, and Senbet (1995). The premium should be equal to the amount that investors are willing to pay to circumvent the restriction. Indeed funds invested in India, Korea, Taiwan, or Brazil have generally sold at a steep but volatile premium. Emerging countries are progressively liberalizing foreign access to their financial markets. When the lifting of a foreign investment restriction is announced, the premium on a local-country fund should drop, as local shares will be more widely available to foreign investors. This drop in premium is a risk of these country funds. It can only be hoped that the local market will respond favorably to the prospect of attracting more foreign investors and that a rise in NAV will compensate for a drop in the fund's premium. The liberalization in Brazil and Korea has indeed led to large drops in the premium of closed-end funds invested in those countries.

The volatility in the value of the premium can add volatility to that of the underlying assets. Historically premiums on country funds have been very volatile. For example, the Italy Fund listed in New York had an average premium[5] over the period 1986–1990 of –12.5%, with variations between –39% and +43%. Johnson, Schneeweiss, and Dinning (1993) studied a sample of country funds listed in the United States and invested either in developed markets or in emerging markets. They measured the volatilities in U.S. dollars of the fund, its NAV, and the local underlying stock index (e.g., the Italian index for Italy Fund). For emerging-country funds, the volatility of the fund was about 30% more than that of its NAV and only 10% more than that of the local stock index. This additional volatility might be a necessary cost to bear when few other alternatives are open. Since these markets are becoming much more accessible, the attraction of country funds is reduced. For developed-country funds, they found that the volatility of the fund was almost twice as large as that of its NAV or of the local stock index. Given the high volatility of closed-end country funds invested in developed markets and the easy alternatives available, it is difficult to understand why investors would buy them. Instead, global portfolio management is now readily available in many different forms; for example, investors can buy open-ended funds or buy a portfolio directly on the local market. These portfolios will always be valued at their NAV, without premium or discount. It can be argued that the large discount observed on many developed-country funds simply reflects the large management fees charged by the fund's managers and the lack of liquidity of the market for the fund's shares.

Summary

1. Emerging stock markets can be found in countries with low GNP per capita and whose stock exchanges are being modernized. The International Finance Corporation (IFC) has been instrumental in prompting the development of emerging stock markets. Among the many stock markets across the world, roughly 26 qualify as active emerging markets, and many others are developing.

2. Emerging markets have been growing very rapidly, relative to developed markets, and represent well over 10% of the world market capitalization; this share is growing. Some of the emerging markets are among the top stock markets in the world in terms of transaction volume.

3. Emerging markets are quite volatile. They have offered attractive returns in the past, with a low correlation with developed stock markets. Because of this low correlation, the contribution to the total risk of a global portfolio is limited, and the profit potentials are large. Investors buying emerging stock markets intend to benefit from the future growth of their economies.

4. Several emerging markets indexes are available as benchmarks to measure performance. They can have markedly different return and volatility, so it is important to understand their differences.

5. Information on companies from emerging countries is sometimes difficult to get. Transaction costs can be quite high. Some restrictions on foreign investment apply in several emerging countries. However, the trend is toward rapid deregulation and liberalization of emerging stock markets, as most countries are trying to attract foreign capital.

6. Foreign-listed shares and closed-end country funds are an alternative to investing directly in the local markets. Country funds are sometimes set up to overcome foreign investment restrictions. One should be careful in assessing the price volatility of country funds in relation to that of their underlying assets.

Questions and Problems

1. Following is a list of countries and their stock market annual return, calculated in U.S. dollars, over the period 1985–1993:

Country	Mean return	Country	Mean return
France	25.4	Hong Kong	34.8
Germany	21.8	Chile	52.3
Japan	16.3	India	19.4
Spain	23.0	Portugal	25.1
U.K.	21.2	Taiwan	28.4
U.S.	15.8	Thailand	38.1
Canada	9.3	Turkey	25.3

Compare this stock market performance with the average growth rates in Exh. 8.2.

- What do you conclude?
- Can you advance some explanation for the surprising result of Japan?

2. Select a sample of countries and compute their ratio of market capitalization to GNP, using Exh. 8.2.

- Do developed and emerging countries have similar ratios?
- Advance some explanations for the difference.

3*. Use the figures reported in Exh. 8.6 to calculate the mean return and volatility in U.S. dollars of the following portfolios:

Portfolio

A	80% World	20% Composite
B	80% World	20% Thailand
C	90% World	10% Argentina
D	80% World	20% Argentina

4.* Here are some risk and return estimates for the future:

Market	Return	Risk
U.S.	10%	16%
EAFE	12%	17%
Composite	15%	25%

All return and risk measures are calculated in U.S. dollars and are expressed in % per year. The correlation matrix is given below:

	U.S.	EAFE	Composite
U.S.	1.0	0.5	0.2
EAFE	0.5	1.0	0.1
Composite	0.2	0.1	1.0

- Calculate the return and risk of a portfolio invested in the following proportions:

Portfolio	U.S.	EAFE	Composite
A	50%	50%	0%
B	45%	45%	10%
C	40%	40%	20%

- Try to derive some estimate of the efficient frontier obtained by using these three indexes (no short sales are allowed).

5. Thailand limits foreign ownership of Thai companies to a maximum percentage of all the shares issued; see, for example, Bailey and Jagtiani (1990). The limit is generally 49% but can be lower for some industries or firms. Once a company has reached this limit, it starts to be traded on two different boards. Foreigners trade on the Alien Board, but Thai investors must still trade in the same share on the Main Board. Main and Alien Board shares are identical in all other respects.

- Why does this segmentation ensure that the limit on foreign ownership is respected?
- Shares listed on the Alien Board trade at a fairly large premium over their Main Board counterparts. Give some likely explanations.

6*. The currencies of several emerging countries depreciate at a rapid pace. Does it imply that you should not invest in their stock markets? For example, the Polish zloty went from 15,767 to 21,444 zlotys per U.S. dollar in 1993. The Polish stock market went from 1,040 to 12,439 during the same period. Guess why the zloty depreciated.

7*. You consider investing in four very volatile emerging markets. These are small countries just opening up to foreign investment. You spread your money equally across them. After a year, the following observations are made on the performance of each market:

Country	Return in local currency	Currency depreciation	Comment
A	400%	20%	High inflation, high growth
B	60%	10%	
C	0	40%	High inflation, low growth
D	–100%	80%	Foreigners got expropriated

- Calculate the return, in dollars, on each market. The currency depreciation is equal to the drop in the dollar value of one unit of local currency. For example, if the peso moves from 1 dollar per peso to 0.8 dollar per peso, the depreciation of the peso is measured as 20%.
- What is the return on a portfolio equally invested in each market?

8*. Paf is an emerging country with severe foreign investment restrictions but with an active stock market open mostly to local investors. The exchange rate of the Pif, the local currency, with the U.S. dollar remains fixed at 1 Pif/$. A closed-end country fund, called *Paf Country Fund*, has been approved by Paf. Its net asset value is 100 dollars. It trades in New York with a premium of 30%.

- Give some intuitive explanations for this positive premium.
- Paf unexpectedly announces that it will lift all foreign investment restrictions. This has two effects. First, stock prices in Paf go up by 20% because of the expectation of massive foreign investment attracted by the growth opportunities in Paf. Second, the premium on the *Paf Country Fund* drops to zero. Is this scenario reasonable? What would be your total gain (loss) on the shares of *Paf Country Fund*?

9. *Project*: Select a sample of emerging countries. For each of them collect monthly stock market indexes, consumer price indexes, and exchange rates. Possible sources are the IMF and the IFC. Calculate the following:

- their mean return measured in local currency, in real terms (after local inflation adjustment), and in dollar terms
- their standard deviation of return measured in local currency, in real terms (after local inflation adjustment), and in dollar terms.
- the correlation across the various markets, using, successively, returns measured in local currency terms, in real terms (after local inflation adjustment), and in dollar terms.

Notes

1. The classification and coverage differ slightly across the major *emerging* index providers. For example, Malaysia and Mexico are classified as developed markets by some institutions. Indexes for South Africa have been offered only recently. Indexes for Israel are reported by MSCI. Some of the *developed* countries, primarily in the Middle East, have no stock markets, so only some 22 are usually considered as having a developed stock market.

2. Clearly the assumption of normality of returns is violated for hyperinflation countries. In nominal terms the rate of return on an investment can never be less than −100%, but it can be extremely large (several hundred percent) because of inflation. So the distribution of returns is not symmetric.

3. For instance, assume that Argentinean shares selected in the Argentine IFCG index cover 60% of the total market capitalization of Argentina, whereas Thai shares selected cover 75% of the total market capitalization of Thailand. Then Thailand will be over-represented in the composite index compared to its relative total market capitalization.

4. See an interesting study of the Thai stock market in Bailey and Jagtiani (1994).

5. See Chang, Eun, and Kolodny (1995).

Bibliography

Bailey, W., and Jagtiani, J. "Foreign Ownership Restrictions and Stock Prices in the Thai Capital Market," *Journal of Financial Economics*, August 1994.

Bailey, W., and Lim, J. "Evaluating the Diversification Benefits of the New Country Funds," *Journal of Portfolio Management*, Spring 1992.

Bonser-Neal, C., Brauer, G., Neal, R., and Wheatley, S. "International Investment Restrictions and Closed-End Country Fund Prices," *Journal of Finance*, June 1990.

Chang, E., Eun, C., and Kolodny, R. "International Diversification through Closed-End Country Funds," *Journal of Banking and Finance*, 1995.

Claessens, S., and Gooptu, S., eds. *Portfolio Investment in Developing Countries*, Washington, D.C.: International Finance Corporation, 1994.

Davis, L.H. "Portfolio Composition for Emerging Markets Equities," *Journal of Investing*, Winter 1994.

Divecha, A., Drach, J., and Stefek, D. "Emerging Markets: A Quantitative Perspective," *Journal of Portfolio Management*, Fall 1992.

Diwan, I., Errunza, V., and Senbet, L. "Country Funds for Emerging Economies," in Claessens and Gooptu, 1994.

Errunza, V. "Pricing of National Index Funds," *Review of Quantitative Finance and Accounting*, June 1990.

Eun, C., and Janakiramanan, S. "A Model of International Asset Pricing with a Constraint on the Foreign Equity Ownership," *Journal of Finance*, September 1986.

Eun, C., Janakiramanan, S., and Senbet, L.W. "The Design and Pricing of Country Funds under Market Segmentation," presented at the AFA annual meetings, January 1995.

IFC, *Emerging Stock Markets Factbook 1994*, Washington, D.C.: International Finance Corporation, 1994.

IFCA Continuing Education, *Managing Emerging Market Portfolios*, Charlottesville, VA: Association for Investment Management and Research, 1994.

Johnson, G., Schneeweiss, T., and Dinning, W. "Closed-End Country Funds: Exchange Rate and Investment Risk," *Financial Analysts Journal*, November-December 1993.

Meier, J., "A Comparison of Emerging Markets Benchmarks," *Journal of Investing*, Summer 1994.

Odier, P., Solnik, B., and Zucchinetti, S. "Global Optimization for Swiss Pension Funds," *Finazmarkt und Portfolio Management*, June 1995.

Park, K.K.H., and Van Agtmael, A.W., eds. *The World Emerging Stock Markets*, Chicago: Probus, 1993.

P A R T   F O U R

Fixed-Income Investment

9

Bonds: Markets and Instruments

*D*ebt certificates have been traded internationally for several centuries. Kings and emperors borrowed heavily to finance their wars. Bankers from neutral countries assisted in arranging the necessary financing and thereby created a market in the debentures. The Rothschilds, for example, became famous for supporting the British war effort against Napoleon I through their European family network. As a matter of fact, organized trading in domestic and foreign debentures took place well before the start of any domestic common stock market.

Although debt financing has always been international in nature, there is still no unified international bond market. Instead, the international bond market is divided into three broad market groups: *domestic bonds, foreign bonds,* and *Eurobonds.*

- Domestic bonds are issued locally by a domestic borrower and are usually denominated in the local currency.

- Foreign bonds are issued on a local market by a foreign borrower and are usually denominated in the local currency. Foreign bond issues and trading are under the supervision of local market authorities.

- Eurobonds are underwritten by a multinational syndicate of banks and are placed mainly in countries other than the one in whose currency the bond is denominated. These bonds are not traded on a specific national bond market.

Foreign bonds issued on national markets have existed for a long time. They often have colorful names, such as Yankee bonds (in the United States), Samuraï bonds (in Japan), Rembrandt (in the Netherlands), Matador (in Spain), Caravela (in Portugal), and Bulldog bonds (in the United Kingdom).

Because many non-American firms have financing needs in U.S. dollars, there has for some years been an incentive to issue bonds in New York. But to do so the bonds must satisfy the disclosure requirements of the U.S. Securities and Exchange Commission. This can be a costly process for non-English-speaking corporations that use different accounting standards. In 1963 the United States imposed an Interest Equalization Tax (IET) on foreign securities held by U.S. investors.[1] The tax forced non-U.S. corporations to pay a higher interest rate in order to attract U.S. investors. A few years later the Federal Reserve Board restricted both U.S. lending to foreigners and the financing of foreign direct investment by U.S. corporations. These measures simultaneously made the U.S. bond market less attractive to foreign borrowers and created a need for offshore financing of U.S. corporate foreign activities. This led to the development of the Eurobond market in the early 1960s. Because of the Glass-Steagall Act, U.S. commercial banks were prevented from issuing and dealing in bonds. Such restrictions do not apply to their offshore activities, and foreign subsidiaries of U.S. commercial banks became very active on the Eurobond market. The repeal of the IET in 1974, the partial relaxation of the Glass-Steagall Act, as well as various measures to attract foreign borrowers and issuers on the U.S. domestic market did not slow the growth of the Eurobond market.

In 1984 the United States rescinded the interest withholding tax on the earnings of foreign investors. Foreign investors could then directly purchase bonds on the U.S. market with the same fiscal treatment as on the Eurobond market. Some analysts expected that most of the U.S. dollar Eurobond market would move back to New York. This did not happen, and the Eurobond market continued to grow at a rapid pace; investors preferred the protection of anonymity offered by the Eurobond market and feared a change in U.S. regulations. More important, the Eurobond market came to be recognized by borrowers and investors alike as the most efficient, least costly, and most innovative market.

Bond investment is both technical and difficult. This stems from the vast diversity of markets, instruments, and currencies offered. Terminology and techniques vary from one market to the next, as do trading methods and costs. For example, U.S. yields are computed on an annual basis on the Eurobond market but on a semiannual basis on the U.S. market. Accrued interest is not included in the bond market price, except in the United Kingdom. And the Japanese use a simple-interest method to calculate yield-to-maturity rather than the usual compound-interest method. Moreover, instruments vary in these markets from straight bonds and floating-rate notes denominated in various currencies to bonds with numerous, and often exotic, option clauses.

This chapter first presents some statistics on the various bond markets. It then outlines the major differences among markets and describes the Eurobond market. The chapter ends with a review of investments in bonds from emerging countries.

Some Statistics

Bond Markets in the World

The rapidly growing world bond market is comprised of both the domestic bond markets and the international market, which includes foreign bonds and Eurobonds. The size of the world bond market was estimated at around $16 trillion at the start of 1994. The figure is even larger if we include private placements, in which bonds are placed directly among the clients of the underwriting bank and are not offered publicly. The world market capitalization of bonds is therefore somewhat bigger than that of equity. Bonds denominated in dollars currently represent roughly half the value of all outstanding bonds. Yen bonds represent roughly 20% of the world bond markets, and European currencies, 30%. A detailed analysis of the size of major bond markets is given in Exh. 9.1. Note that the relative share of each currency market depends not only on new issues and repaid bonds but also on exchange rate movements. For example, the U.S. dollar dropped by more than 40% against most currencies from 1985 to 1986, which substantially reduced the worldwide U.S. dollar bond market share.

As shown in Exh. 9.1, government bonds represent a large share, approximately two thirds, of all bonds issued in the world. The share is especially large for U.K. sterling, French franc, and Japanese yen bonds and is quite small for Swiss franc and Deutsche mark bonds.

The market value of international bonds (Eurobonds and foreign bonds) represents approximately 10% of all outstanding bonds publicly issued, although the percentage is probably larger if private placements are included. The share of international bonds in terms of new issues (rather than total market size) is much larger for two reasons: This market has grown rapidly only recently, and Eurobonds tend to be issued with short maturities. As a result, despite the smaller market capitalization, the pace of new issues is very rapid in the growing Eurobond market.

We now turn to a more detailed analysis of the international market.

The International Bond Market

Exhibits 9.2, 9.3, and 9.4 give some background statistics on new issues in the international bond market. The growth of the international bond market, especially Eurobonds, has been remarkable.

Currency Breakdown   As of 1994 the U.S. dollar was the major currency of denomination in the market, followed by the yen, the Deutsche mark, the French franc, and the Swiss franc. The importance of the Swiss franc as an investment

EXHIBIT 9.1

Size of Major Bond Markets at Year End, 1993
Nominal value outstanding, billions of U.S. dollars equivalent[a]

Bond Market	Total Publicly Issued	As a Pct. of Public Issues in All Markets	Central Govt.	Central Govt. Agency & Govt. Guaranty	State & Local Govt.
U.S. dollar	$7,547.2	46.3%	$2,274.8	$1,898.9	$988.4
Japanese yen	3,044.0	18.7	1,554.6	176.3	74.1
Deutsche mark	1,590.8	9.8	500.9	61.8	60.3
Italian lira	780.7	4.8	620.3	15.1	—
French franc	748.6	4.6	331.5	215.5	3.9
U.K. sterling	436.6	2.7	282.2	—	0.0
Canadian dollar	393.0	2.4	149.8	—	113.9
Belgian franc	301.3	1.8	159.2	12.8	—
Dutch guilder	227.5	1.4	142.0	—	2.6
Danish krone	227.4	1.4	72.9	—	—
Swiss franc	200.7	1.2	17.3	—	15.4
Swedish krona	186.4	1.1	61.8	—	0.6
European currency unit	144.6	0.9	49.3	—	—
Spanish peseta	144.4	0.9	100.9	5.3	—
Australian dollar	106.1	0.7	50.2	19.2	—
Austrian schilling	87.8	0.5	32.5	2.1	0.4
Norwegian krone	40.8	0.2	13.2	2.9	5.8
Finnish markka	33.7	0.2	12.7	—	1.2
Portuguese escudo	28.6	0.2	20.0	—	0.4
Irish pound	21.4	0.1	20.0	0.6	—
New Zealand dollar	15.0	0.1	10.2	1.6	—
Total	**$16,306.5**	**100.0%**	**$6,476.4**	**$2,412.0**	**$1,267.0**
Sector as a pct. of public issues in all markets	100.0%		39.7%	14.8%	7.8%

[a]Exchange rates prevailing as of December 31, 1993: ¥111.85/US$; DM1.7263/US$; Lit1,704/US$; Ffr5.8955/US$; £0.6751/US$; C$1.324/US$; Bfr36.11/US$; Dfl 1.9409/US$; Dkr6.773/US$; Sfr1.4795/US$; Skr8.3035/US$; Ecu0.8918/US$; Pta142.21/US$; A$1.4769/US$; ATS12.143/US$; Nkr7.518/US$; Fmk5.7845/US$; Esc176.81/US$; Irf0.7088/US$; and NZ$1.7895/US$.[b] Includes straight, convertible and floating-rate debt.[c] The German bond market does not distinguish between Euro and Foreign international issues.[d] Includes both Foreign and Eurobond Totals.[e] In additon, an unspecified amount of privately placed issues of the private sectors exists.

currency is surprising, given the small size of the country. Several factors explain this phenomenon. First, Switzerland has a history of stability and a strong currency. Second, Swiss banks have long specialized in international investment and are

| | Corp (Incl. Cvts.) | Other Domestic Publicly Issued | Int'l. Bonds[b] | | Private Place. Unclass. |
			Foreign Bonds	Euro-Bonds	
U.S. dollar	$1,455.3	$249.7	$126.0	$554.1	—
Japanese yen	314.9	700.7	66.3	157.2	$536.4
Deutsche mark	1.8	762.4	— $203.6[c]	—	367.7[e]
Italian lira	2.2	112.9	1.2	29.0	—
French franc	103.4	—	4.9	89.3	—
U.K. sterling	25.1	—	5.9	123.4	—
Canadian dollar	52.3	0.8	0.6	75.8	—
Belgian franc	7.4	101.9	19.5	0.4	—
Dutch guilder	49.6	—	6.1	27.2	—
Danish krone	—	151.5	—	3.0	—
Swiss franc	29.9	54.7	83.4	—	85.0[e]
Swedish krona	8.7	112.5	—	2.9	55.4
European currency unit	—	—	—	95.3	—
Spanish peseta	19.0	9.7	9.4	—	—
Australian dollar	19.4	—	—	17.3	—
Austrian schilling	2.8	47.5	2.5	—	7.0
Norwegian krone	2.7	15.8	0.3	0.0	—
Finnish markka	5.7	12.9	—	1.2	—
Portuguese escudo	2.5	3.9	1.8	—	—
Irish pound	0.4	—	0.1	0.3	—
New Zealand dollar	1.8	—	0.1	1.2	—
Total	**$2,105.1**	**$2,336.9**	**$1,709.1[d]**		**$1,051.6[e]**
Sector as a pct. of public issues in all markets	12.9%	14.3%	10.5%		

Source: "How Big Is the World Bond Market? 1994 Update," Salomon Brothers, August 1994. Reprinted by permission.

probably the largest investors in the international bond markets. Third, Switzerland is a large net exporter of capital. But note that their historical expertise in international financial intermediation has not prevented the Swiss Central Bank (Banque Nationale Suisse) from regulating the use of its currency on international capital markets. In fact, the Swiss Central Bank does not allow the Swiss

EXHIBIT 9.2

New Issues on the International Bond Market
Summary data by type of market and type of instrument (billions of U.S. dollars)

Market	1981	1982	1983	1984	1985	1986	1987	1988	1989	1990	1991	1992	1993
Eurobonds	31.3	50.3	50.1	83.7	136.7	187.0	140.5	177.2	212.8	180.1	258.1	276.1	394.6
Foreign bonds	25.8	25.2	27.0	27.8	31.0	39.4	40.2	47.7	42.9	49.8	50.6	57.6	86.4
Total	**52.8**	**75.5**	**77.1**	**111.5**	**167.7**	**226.4**	**180.7**	**224.9**	**255.7**	**229.9**	**308.7**	**333.7**	**481.0**
Instruments													
Fixed rate	n.a.	57.6	57.6	65.4	92.5	147.2	117.0	159.2	154.6	158.9	242.7	265.4	369.1
Floating rate and CDs	n.a.	15.3	13.8	38.2	58.4	50.7	13.0	23.1	17.8	37.1	18.3	43.6	69.8
Convertible and equity-warrant	n.a.	2.6	5.7	7.8	11.4	22.3	43.3	42.0	80.3	31.8	41.7	20.9	38.7
Other	—	—	—	—	5.4	6.2	7.4	0.6	3.0	2.1	6.0	3.8	3.4

n.a. – not available.

Source: Data adapted from *Financial Market Trends*, Organization for Economic Cooperation and Development, various issues, and *Quarterly Report of the Bank of England*.

franc to be used for Eurobond issues. Therefore foreign borrowers must issue bonds on the foreign Swiss market. But fortunately the regulations and administrative procedures for issuing foreign Swiss bonds are simple and straightforward, making access easy for foreign borrowers.

Until 1984 Japan prevented the use of the yen for Eurobond issues except by foreign governments and supranationals, such as the World Bank. As in Switzerland, the foreign yen (samuraï) bond market is relatively active. In 1984 the Japanese government relaxed its regulation of international financial activities, and the yen Eurobond market began opening up, under the supervision of Japanese authorities, to private borrowers. Since then, the share of the Japanese yen in the international bond market has increased rapidly.

It is perhaps surprising that a central bank can prevent its currency from being used in the Eurobond market, which is by definition an offshore market. This control is imposed through national financial institutions, which are the major sources of funds in a nation's domestic currency. In Japan domestic financial institutions must participate in a yen Eurobond syndicate for the issue to succeed, because they are the largest yen investors. The situation is similar elsewhere. If the government forbids the banks to participate, the issue must fail. As for Deutsche mark bonds, it is difficult to draw the line between foreign and Eurobonds; we have classified them as Eurobonds in these exhibits, following the OECD convention.

European Currency Unit   The European currency unit (ECU) has become an important currency of denomination. The ECU is a composite currency comprised

EXHIBIT 9.3

International Issues of Bonds
Breakdown by currency of issue (billions of U.S. dollars)

Issue	1982	1983	1984	1985	1986	1987	1988	1989	1990	1991	1992	1993
Eurobond issues by currency												
U.S. dollar	42.2	39.2	65.3	96.5	117.2	58.1	75.4	117.5	70.0	81.6	103.2	147.7
Deutsche mark	3.2	4.0	4.3	9.5	16.9	15.0	23.7	16.4	18.3	20.5	33.8	54.7
European currency unit	0.8	2.2	2.9	7.0	7.0	7.4	11.3	12.6	17.9	32.7	21.3	7.1
Yen	0.5	0.2	1.2	6.5	18.7	22.6	15.8	15.6	22.8	36.0	33.7	44.4
Sterling	0.8	2.2	4.0	5.8	10.5	15.1	21.7	18.5	20.9	25.8	23.3	42.7
Australian dollar	—	0.2	0.3	3.0	3.2	8.8	8.1	6.7	5.2	4.4	4.9	3.5
Canadian dollar	1.2	1.1	2.2	2.8	5.4	6.0	12.9	12.5	6.4	23.7	15.6	29.3
French franc	—	—	—	1.1	3.4	1.8	2.4	4.5	9.4	1.7	24.3	39.9
New Zealand dollar	0	0	0.1	1.0	0.4	1.5	0.8	0.7	0.5	0.3	0.1	0.1
Other	1.5	1.0	1.4	2.2	4.3	4.3	5.1	7.8	8.7	16.1	15.9	25.2
Total	**50.3**	**50.1**	**81.7**	**135.4**	**187.0**	**140.5**	**177.2**	**212.8**	**180.1**	**258.1**	**276.1**	**394.6**
Foreign issues by market												
Switzerland	11.3	13.5	13.1	15.0	23.4	24.3	26.6	18.6	23.2	20.2	18.1	27.0
Japan	3.3	3.9	4.9	6.4	4.8	4.1	6.4	8.2	7.9	5.2	7.4	15.2
United States	6.0	4.7	4.3	4.7	6.1	7.4	9.7	9.4	9.9	14.4	23.2	35.4
West Germany	2.1	2.6	2.4	1.7	—	—	—	—	—	—	—	—
Netherlands	0.9	0.9	0.9	1.0	1.8	1.0	1.0	—	0.6	0.1	0.2	0.9
United Kingdom	1.1	0.9	1.6	1.0	0.3	—	0.2	1.2	0.3	0.1	—	—
Other	0.5	0.6	0.6	1.2	2.1	3.5	3.8	5.5	7.9	10.6	8.7	7.9
Total	**25.2**	**27.1**	**27.8**	**31.0**	**38.44**	**40.3**	**47.7**	**42.9**	**49.8**	**50.6**	**57.6**	**86.4**

Source: Financial Market Trends, Organization for Economic Coordination and Development, various issues.

of a weighted basket of European currencies. The ECU exchange rate is an average exchange rate of all currencies in the basket. The ECU has attracted many borrowers from weak-currency countries, which cannot issue international bonds in their home currencies. For these borrowers the ECU reduces exchange risk relative to their home currency. At the same time, investors wanting to invest in nondollar bonds may directly diversify their portfolios of European currencies by investing in ECU-denominated bonds.

EXHIBIT 9.4

International Bond Issues
Breakdown by country of borrower (billions of U.S. dollars)

	1981	1982	1983	1984	1985	1986	1987	1988	1989	1990	1991	1992	1993
Industrial countries	**40.9**	**63.1**	**60.3**	**91.9**	**141.1**	**200.3**	**156.5**	**199.0**	**240.4**	**208.4**	**282.9**	**296.9**	**408.0**
United States	6.8	14.5	7.3	23.9	40.5	43.6	21.5	17.3	15.8	21.8	21.1	17.6	24.8
Japan	6.9	8.4	14.0	17.0	21.1	34.4	44.4	51.2	97.5	55.4	72.1	56.2	61.0
Developing areas	**4.9**	**5.0**	**2.5**	**3.6**	**7.9**	**4.2**	**3.1**	**4.2**	**2.6**	**4.5**	**9.4**	**14.0**	**45.6**
Latin America	3.7	2.5	—	0.2	0.2	0.4	—	0.8	—	1.0	5.0	8.0	23.7
Asia	1.1	2.1	2.2	3.0	6.9	3.7	3.1	2.9	1.9	3.1	4.1	5.8	13.0
Middle East	0.2	0.4	0.2	0.4	0.4	0.1	—	0.5	0.7	0.4	0.3	0.2	8.9
Centrally planned countries	—	—	**0.1**	**0.2**	**2.0**	**0.3**	**0.5**	**1.3**	**2.4**	**2.0**	**2.0**	**2.9**	**7.0**
International organizations	**7.2**	**9.9**	**13.4**	**11.7**	**17.7**	**19.5**	**20.4**	**21.7**	**10.3**	**15.0**	**14.4**	**19.9**	**20.4**
Total	**53.0**	**78.0**	**76.3**	**107.4**	**167.7**	**224.3**	**180.8**	**224.8**	**255.7**	**229.9**	**308.7**	**333.7**	**481.0**

Source: Data adapted from *Financial Statistics*, OECD, various issues.

Types of Instruments   Most issues on the international bond market are fixed interest bonds. However, floating-rate notes (FRNs) have become a sizable segment of the market, especially when interest rates are volatile. FRNs are usually issued in U.S. dollars. Japanese corporations rely heavily on convertible bonds, as do other borrowers. The many other types of instruments that have been issued on the international bond market are described in more detail here and in Chapter 10.

Borrowers   The major borrowers on the international bond markets are industrial countries and supranational organizations (see Exh. 9.4). U.S. and Japanese corporations are the heaviest borrowers. The governments of Canada and Scandinavia and Scandinavian corporations are also heavy borrowers. High-risk borrowers have no access to this market, so that Latin American countries virtually dropped out after 1982 but reappeared in the 1990s. Also note that supranationals, such as the World Bank, European Investment Bank, Asian and African Development Banks, International Development Bank, and the European Union, are heavy borrowers in the international bond market and that part of their funds are in turn loaned to higher-risk countries. Starting in 1990, the deterioration of the economic and political situation in Eastern Europe has led to drastic political changes in most countries of the region. The move to more liberal economic policies has been accompanied by large financing needs. An international bank was set up in 1990 by developed countries to assist the financing needs of Eastern

European economies. This international organization, known as the EBRD, is based in London and gives preferential treatment to private projects over public ones. At the end of 1989, the Brady plan was introduced to transform the market for emerging-countries debt. Bearing the name of the U.S. secretary of the Treasury, the Brady plan allows debtor nations to repackage large amounts of their debt into easily tradable bonds. This market for Brady bonds is described in the last section.

To summarize, the world bond market is becoming more integrated across currencies. The Eurobond market in particular is opening up to a variety of currencies, including the Spanish peseta, the Portuguese escudo, or the Danish krone. Many governments are encouraging foreign borrowers to tap their national markets. Governments are also encouraging foreign investors to buy domestic bonds, especially government bonds; withholding taxes have been removed for foreign investors on most national bond markets.

Large market makers perform an essential function in the world bond market because they deal simultaneously in both the Eurobond and national bond markets. Therefore an investor wanting to buy domestic bonds, foreign bonds, or Eurobonds can do so through one financial institution and receive equal tax treatment. In the future current differences in costs and trading procedures and other impediments are bound to disappear as the internationalization of the world bond market continues.

Major Differences among Bond Markets

A thorough technical knowledge of the various bond markets reduces an investor's trading costs and enhances his or her returns; it also helps one to understand better the risks involved. Because bond markets are still rapidly developing, new types of instruments and issuing techniques appear over the world all the time. For this reason, the following description of these markets is bound to become partially outdated over time; it is meant to serve chiefly as a broad guideline.

Types of Instruments

The variety of bonds offered to the international or even the domestic investor is amazing, due to the recent development of bonds with variable interest rates and complex optional clauses. This diversity is illustrated in the French bond market, where state or government agencies have issued the following types of bonds:

- Index-linked bonds, whose coupons or principal are indexed to the price of gold, energy costs, the stock market index, or another index.

- Straight bonds with simultaneous call and put options. These bonds can be redeemed early at a set price by either the bondholder or the issuer.

- Straight bonds renewable at maturity into new straight bonds with the same coupon and terms.

- Straight bonds exchangeable for FRNs at the option of the bondholder or the issuer.

- FRNs exchangeable for straight bonds at the option of the bondholder or the issuer.

- Zero-coupon bonds.

- FRNs with a coupon linked to the average market long-term interest rate.

- FRNs with a coupon indexed to a variety of short-term interest rates. The coupon may be either post- or predetermined. If it is postdetermined, the investor knows the value of the coupon only on the payment date (in reference to the average interest rate over the coupon period). If it is predetermined, the investor knows the value of the coupon for the coming coupon period (in reference to the interest rate during the previous coupon period). This reference interest rate may be an average over a period or a spot rate measured at a particular time.

- Straight bonds with warrants to purchase similar bonds.

- Straight bonds with warrants to purchase common stock or other types of assets.

- Convertible bonds.

Whereas the U.S. and French bond markets are among the more innovative markets, the Eurobond market is surely the most creative of all. Investment bankers from many countries bring their expertise to this unregulated market. Each month new instruments appear or disappear regularly. Some of the more complex bonds are analyzed in Chapter 10.

The Eurobond market's major difference from domestic markets lies in its multicurrency nature. Japanese firms, for example, have frequently issued Swiss franc–denominated bonds convertible into common shares of a Japanese company. A foreign investor can benefit from purchasing this bond in any one of three situations:

- a drop in the market interest rate on Swiss franc bonds (as on any straight Swiss franc bond)

- a rise in the price of the company's stock (because the bonds are convertible into stocks)

- a rise in the yen relative to the franc (because the bond is convertible into a Japanese yen asset)

An example of such a Eurobond issue is presented in Exh. 9.5. The tombstone in Exh. 9.5 advertises a bond issued in 1986 by NKK, a Japanese company. Several

EXHIBIT 9.5

Eurobond Tombstone

These securitites have been sold outside the United States of America and Japan. This announcement appears as a matter of record only.

22nd January, 1994

NKK

Nippon Kokan Kabushiki Kaisha

8 per cent. Dual Currency
Yen/U.S. Dollar Bonds Due 2004

Issue Price: 101 per cent. of the Issue Amount

Issue Amount:	**¥20,000,000,000**
Redemption Amount at Maturity:	**U.S.$110,480,000**

Nomura International Limited	**Mitsubishi Trust & Banking Corporation** (Europe) S.A.
Prudential-Bache Securtities International	**Yamaichi International (Europe) Limited**
Bankers Trust International Limited	**Crédit Lyonnais**
Credit Suisse First Boston Limited	**Dresdner Bank Aktiengesellschaft**
EBC Amro Bank Limited	**Fuji International Finance Limited**
Generale Bank	**Kleinwort, Benson Limited**
Lloyds Merchant Bank Limited	**Morgan Guaranty Ltd**
Morgan Stanley International	**Orion Royal Bank Limited**
Swiss Bank Corporation International Limited	**Union Bank of Switzerland (Securities)** Limited

S.G. Warburg & Co., Ltd.

Source: *Euromoney*, Euromoney Publications, July 1986. Reprinted by permission.

points are worth noting: First, the underwriting syndicate is made up of banks from numerous countries (Japan, France, the United States, Germany, the Netherlands, and Switzerland). The list of banks and countries is often much longer; it is not uncommon to see 50 or 100 banks from all over the world participating in a large issue. Also note that U.S. commercial banks (Morgan Guaranty, now J.P. Morgan) participate, as well as U.S. investment banks (Morgan Stanley, Prudential-Bache). Note, however, that the British subsidiaries of the U.S. banks are involved, not U.S. head companies. This is easily recognized by the word *Limited* at the end of the banks' names. Similarly, the Japanese and Swiss underwriters used a British-based company, with the exception of Yamaichi, which used a Benelux base. Another interesting feature of this bond is that it is a dual-currency bond: It is issued in yen (20 billion), with interest coupons fixed in yen (8%), but its principal repayment is fixed in U.S. dollars ($110,480,000). When this bond was issued, numerous other borrowers issued yen/dollar dual-currency bonds, including the Federal National Mortgage Association (Fannie Mae).

Issuing Techniques

Domestic bonds are usually underwritten by a syndicate of national banks. However, Dutch, British, Canadian, French, and Swiss government bonds are sold under a tender system, whereby banks place bids. In Great Britain once an issue has been listed, the Bank of England often sells part of a gilt (British government bond) issue directly on the market through its broker. It also issues new tranches of an old gilt with identical characteristics and sells those on the market. This technique, known as tapping the market, avoids a proliferation of different bonds. A similar technique is used for French government bonds, known as O.A.T. ("Obligations Assimilables du Trésor").

Eurobonds are issued through an international syndicate of financial institutions. However, institutional investors may buy new bonds directly a few days before they are officially issued. This is the so-called gray market, described later in this chapter.

Dealing and Quotations

On European bond markets, orders are generally sent to the exchange floors through brokers. In the United States trading usually takes place over the counter, although some bonds, especially foreign dollar bonds, are listed on the New York Stock Exchange. Trading of U.S. bonds is transacted between *market makers*, which are specialized financial institutions. Over-the-counter trading also takes place in some European markets (Switzerland, United Kingdom, Germany, the Netherlands) for nongovernment issues. In Japan bonds are traded both over the counter and on the securities exchanges.

In brokers' markets bond buyers and sellers pay the same price but must pay a commission to the broker. In the U.S. system prices are net of commissions, but there is a bid-ask spread on all quotations.

Although the Eurobond market has no physical location, most of the bonds are listed on the Luxembourg stock exchange to satisfy the requirement of obtaining a public quotation at least once a year or quarter. However, very few transactions go through the exchange. Instead, Eurobond dealers created an around-the-clock market among financial institutions across the world that formed the International Securities Market Association (ISMA), formerly AIBD. The geographical composition of the ISMA is shown in Exh. 9.6. The prominent role of London in the ISMA is unmistakable. Swiss banks are the largest investors in the market, but because of a local stamp tax on all Swiss transactions, they often consummate their deals offshore. Settlement procedures vary from one country to the next.

Bonds are usually quoted on a price-plus-accrued-interest basis. This means that the price is quoted separately (as a percentage of the bond's nominal value) from the percentage coupon accrued from the last coupon date to the trade date. The buyer pays (or the seller receives) both the market price of the bond and accrued interest. Thus the market price quoted is "clean" of coupon effect and allows meaningful comparisons between various bonds. This quoted price is often called a *clean* price. Unfortunately, this method of quotation is not universal. Convertible bonds, index-linked bonds, or FRNs where the coupon is determined ex-post (at the end of the coupon period) are quoted with coupons attached. Even some straight bonds follow this convention, as in the UK *gilt* market, the market for U.K. government bonds.[2] There, bonds with more than five years to maturity used to be traded without any separate allowance for accrued interest (i.e., with the coupon attached). This means that the price quoted falls on the *ex-dividend* date,

EXHIBIT 9.6

Geographical Breakdown of ISMA Members	
Locality	**Number of Members**
United States	31
Belgium	37
Denmark	20
France	43
Germany	74
Hong Kong	39
Italy	63
Luxembourg	67
Netherlands	48
Switzerland	136
United Kingdom	195

Source: International Securities Market Association, 1994.

or *ex date*, the date when the bond trades without the next coupon payment. To make matters worse, the ex date is normally 37 calendar days before each coupon date, plus or minus a couple of days to allow for weekends and vacations. An investor who buys the bond during this 37-day period does not receive the coupon. Instead, it goes to the previous bondholder. Furthermore, investors are allowed to trade *cum*, or *ex*-dividend, for a period of 21 days preceding the ex date. This is known as *special ex-dividend*. Exhibit 9.7 reproduces the unusual hypothetical market price behavior over time for a long-term U.K. bond, assuming that the market interest rate stays constant. Tax effects should also be taken into account. U.K. gilts, but not British corporate bonds or foreign bonds, are now traded on a clean price basis. However, the ex-dividend convention still applies, and the total value of the gilt (clean price plus accrued interest) still drops on the ex date as the security holder loses the right to the next coupon. Practitioners consider that there is a negative accrued interest between the ex date and the coupon date.

Bonds also differ in the way accrued interest is calculated. In the United States straight bonds usually pay a semiannual coupon. The day-count method used in accrued interest rate calculations for corporate and foreign bonds[3] assumes months of 30 days in a year of 360 days. In other words, the basic unit of time measurement is the month; it does not matter if a month is actually 28 or 31 days long. An investor holding a bond for one month receives 30/360, or ½, of the annual coupons (⅙ of the semiannual coupon). The same method is used in Germany, Scandinavia, Switzerland, and the Netherlands. By contrast, the United Kingdom, Canada, and Japan use a day count based on the actual number of days in a 365-day year, so that an investor receives accrued interest proportional to the number of days the bond has been held. Straight Eurobonds use the U.S. convention regardless of their currency of denomination, so that a yen or sterling Eurobond uses a 30-day month in a 360-day year. On the other hand, Euro-FRNs use actual days in a 360-day year, which is also the convention used for short-term deposits.[4]

EXHIBIT 9.7

Market Price Behavior of a U.K. Bond

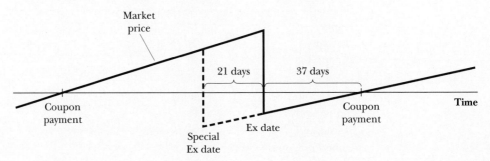

This follows naturally from the fact that FRN coupons are indexed to short-term interest rates. Straight Eurobonds pay annual coupons, whereas FRNs pay quarterly or semiannual coupons. The coupon characteristics of the major bond markets are summarized in Exh. 9.8.

The issue of yields also needs to be addressed. Most financial institutions around the world calculate and publish yields-to-maturity on bonds (see definition in Chapter 10). Unfortunately the methods used for this calculation vary among countries, so that yields are not directly comparable. Most Europeans, for instance, calculate an annual, and accurate, actuarial yield-to-maturity using the ISMA-recommended formula. U.S. (and often British) institutions publish a semiannual actuarial yield. For example, a U.S. bond issued at par with 12% coupons will pay $6 semiannually per $100 of face value and is reported as having a semiannual yield-to-maturity of 12%.

Europeans would quote this bond as having a 12.36% (annual) yield-to-maturity because of the compounding of the two semester coupons. Common sense dictates that yields for all maturities and currencies be compared in an iden-

EXHIBIT 9.8

Coupon Characteristics of Major Bond Markets (straight bonds)

Characteristic	United States	U.S. Treasuries	Canada
Usual frequency of coupon	Semiannual	Semiannual	Semiannual
Day count (month/year)	30/360	Actual/actual	Actual/365

Characteristic	Australia	United Kingdom	Switzerland
Usual frequency of coupon	Semiannual	Semiannual	Semiannual
Day count (month/year)	Actual/actual	Actual/365	30/360

Characteristic	Germany	Netherlands	France
Usual frequency of coupon	Annual	Annual	Annual
Day count (month/year)	30/360	30/360	Actual/365

Characteristic	Japan	Eurobonds	FRNs
Usual frequency of coupon	Semiannual	Annual	Quarter or semiannual
Day count (month/year)	Actual/365	30/360	Actual/360

tical fashion. The tradition of using semiannual yields is understandably confusing for international investors.[5] The situation is even worse in Japan, where financial institutions tend to report yield-to-maturity based on simple-interest calculation. The following simple formula shows how this is done:

$$\text{Yield} = \left(\text{Coupon rate} + \frac{100 - \text{Current price}}{\text{Years to maturtity}} \right) \frac{100}{\text{Current price}}.$$

This simple yield understates the true yield-to-maturity for bonds priced over par and overstates the yield for bonds priced below par. Again, the historical rationale for this incorrect formula is the ease of calculation.

Legal Aspects

Bonds are issued in either *bearer* or *registered* forms. On the Eurobond market, as well as in many European countries, the bearer of a bond is assumed to be its legal owner. In the United States and many other countries, owners must be registered in the books of the issuer. Share registration allows for easier transfer of interest payments and amortization. Coupons are usually paid annually on markets where bonds are issued in bearer form. This reduces the cost associated with coupon payments. Eurobond coupons in all currencies are paid this way. Bearer bonds provide confidentiality of ownership, which is very important to some investors.

In some countries investor purchase of foreign bonds is restricted. The motivation for these restrictions stems from exchange controls or attempts by governments to ensure domestic investor protection. In 1981 France imposed a special exchange rate (*devise titre*) for security transactions. This forced French investors to pay a currency premium to purchase and sell foreign bonds, although their coupons could be cashed in at the normal exchange rate. This regulation was promulgated to curb capital outflows and to defend the French franc. Similar exchange control measures have been imposed at times in other developed countries as well, including the United Kingdom (*dollar premium*), Belgium (*franc financier*), and the United States (*interest equalization tax*).

The U.S. Securities Act is typical of government regulations designed to ensure that its domestic investors are protected. The act requires that all public issues of securities be registered with the Securities and Exchange Commission (SEC). Any bond not registered with the SEC cannot be publicly offered to U.S. citizens at the time of issue. SEC registration is imposed to ensure that accurate information on bond issues is publicly available. Bonds issued in foreign markets and Eurobonds do not meet this requirement, but Yankee bonds do, because they undergo a simplified SEC registration. All other bonds cannot be purchased by U.S. citizens at the time of issue; they may be purchased only after they are seasoned (i.e., come to rest). Sometimes it is difficult to know when an issue is seasoned; usually three months, but sometimes a longer period, such as nine months, is necessary. U.S. banks can participate in Eurobond issuing syndicates only if they institute a procedure guaranteeing that U.S. investors cannot purchase the bonds. This can be difficult, because Eurobonds are issued in bearer form.

Fiscal Considerations

Fiscal considerations are important in international investment. Many countries impose withholding taxes on interest paid by their national borrowers. This means that a foreign investor is often taxed twice: once in the borrowing country (withholding tax) and again in the investor's home country through the usual income tax. Tax treaties help by allowing one to claim the foreign withholding tax as a tax credit at home; nontaxable investors can also reclaim all or part of a withholding tax, but this is a lengthy and costly process. Avoiding double taxation, in fact, was a major impetus behind the development of the Eurobond market. And that is why today the official borrower on the Eurobond market is usually a subsidiary incorporated in a country with no withholding tax (e.g., the Netherlands Antilles). Of course, the parent must fully guarantee the interest and principal payments on the bond. Nevertheless, the trend seems to be toward the elimination of withholding taxes for foreign investors. In 1984 the United States and Germany eliminated withholding taxes on foreign investment in their domestic markets. France also eliminated these taxes, but only on bonds issued after 1984. The United States allowed domestic corporations to borrow directly from foreigners on international markets without paying a 30% withholding tax. This removed the need to borrow through a subsidiary incorporated in the Netherlands Antilles or another tax-free base. Similar regulations already existed in other countries. For example, France grants an exemption from French withholding tax to French companies borrowing abroad (provided the bonds are not offered to French residents).

Exhibit 9.9 displays national withholding taxes as of 1994. Depending on the nationality of the investor, part or all of this tax may be reclaimed. The exhibit is arranged from the point of view of a taxable U.S. investor, but similar rates apply to residents of other countries. Again, there is no withholding tax on Eurobonds. International tax treaties allow for the reduction of the withholding tax rate or a

EXHIBIT 9.9

Summary of Withholding Tax Rates on Interest Payments in Selected Countries, 1994

Country	Tax Rate under U.S.-Country Tax Treaty (percent)
Australia	10
Canada	0–15
France	0–10
Germany	0
Netherlands	0
Sweden	0
Switzerland	0–35
United Kingdom	0–25

total or partial tax refund. Note that tax liability is sometimes more complex than is reflected in the exhibit. For example, all of the U.K. gilts except one (the war loan, which is taxed at 3.5%) are subject to a withholding tax that is frequently revised (the tax rate was 25% in 1994). Foreign investors can claim a full refund for any of the taxes paid under most double-taxation treaties. But more advantageous is the fact that foreigners can claim exemption on about half of the outstanding issues, known as the FOT, or free-of-tax stocks. This exemption is obtained by applying to the U.K. government at least six weeks before the coupon payment.

International tax treaties allow foreign tax withheld to be credited against domestic income tax payment. The same treaties apply to stock dividend withholding tax, as was discussed in Chapter 6. Tax-exempt investors face the risk of losing the tax withheld because they have no domestic tax to pay and therefore the foreign tax credit is lost. In many countries tax-exempt investors, such as pension funds, can obtain a total exemption from withholding taxes or a direct tax refund in the foreign country. A notable exception is Japan, where a minimum tax of 10% applies to all foreign investors. Foreign investors in Japan often resort to coupon hopping: They sell the Japanese bond just before the payment date and buy it back immediately thereafter. They incur no tax liability because the tax is levied only on the person receiving the coupon payment. Furthermore, there is a strong demand for coupons by Japanese institutions, so that a counterparty can easily be found, and transaction costs are minimal.

The repeal of withholding taxes promotes a greater integration of Eurobond and domestic markets, but not at the expense of the Euromarket. The Eurobond market continues to grow despite the removal of these taxes on major national markets.

Bond Indexes

Bond indexes are less commonly available than stock indexes, probably because of the close correlation between all bond price movements when the interest rate fluctuates on a single-currency market. However, total-return bond indexes serve many purposes and are increasingly used. A total-return index cumulates the price movement with accrued interest; it is a cumulative index of the total return on a bond portfolio.

These indexes are put to different uses: A bond index calculated daily for each bond market allows the quick assessment of the direction and magnitude of movements in the market. Using an index for assessment is much easier and more precise than looking at the price quotations of a list of bonds when many of the bonds are not even traded on that day. An index allows for quick comparisons between various markets in different segments or currencies. Total-return bond indexes also are required for measuring the performance of a bond portfolio in a domestic or multicurrency setting. This is usually done monthly or quarterly.

There are two approaches to the calculation of bond indexes. The first is to use a small but representative sample of actively traded bonds. Such an index provides good indications of short-term movements in the interest rate. The second is to build an exhaustive index covering all bonds in the market. Since many issues are not liquid and their prices may be old or out of line with the market, exhaustive market indexes tend to lag behind the interest rate movements, but they reflect the current valuation of a market portfolio. The first approach tends to be used to calculate daily indexes; the latter, monthly indexes. Given the high correlation between all bond prices on a given market, bond indexes tend to be highly correlated,[6] which is not the case for equity indexes. This is illustrated in Exh. 9.10, which compares the monthly value (income plus price appreciation) on two Japanese bond indexes: The first index is calculated monthly by Salomon Brothers in New York, and the second one is calculated daily by Lombard Odier and Cie in Geneva. Despite marked differences in index composition, the performance of the indexes is very close. This is not the case for equity indexes, as illustrated in Exh. 6.7.

EXHIBIT 9.10

Comparative Performance Indicated by Two Japanese Bond Indexes

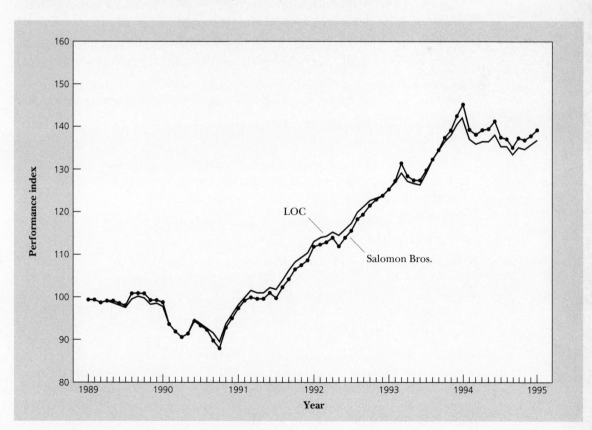

As for equity indexes, there are two major sources of bond indexes: domestic and international. In many countries domestic institutions calculate local bond indexes weekly, monthly, and sometimes daily. Examples of such institutions are the following:

United States	Lehman, Salomon Brothers, Merrill Lynch, J.P. Morgan
United Kingdom	Financial Times
France	Crédit Lyonnais, CDC-FININFO
Switzerland	Pictet, Vontobel, Lombard Odier

International investors find the indexes calculated by these institutions difficult to use because they must be obtained from numerous sources that are often difficult to access. Also, their construction and frequency of calculation make it difficult to compare them.

Several institutions have developed consistent bond indexes for the major domestic and Eurobond markets:

- Salomon Brothers has published monthly indexes for a long time on all major bond markets. They are now calculated daily. Their indexes are extensively used for performance measurement. Total-return indexes take into account both the price movement and the income earned.

- J.P. Morgan publishes indexes for all major bond markets, as well as regional indexes. These indexes are also widely used for performance measurement.

- Lombard Odier and Cie has published daily total-return as well as price-only indexes since 1982. They are published daily in the *Wall Street Journal* (*Europe*).

- *The Financial Times* publishes daily quotes on "benchmark" bonds representative of each market.

- Several banks have developed international bond indexes reported in their monthly publications (Merrill Lynch, First Boston Credit Suisse, Chase, Lehman Brothers).

- The ISMA publishes total-return and price-only indexes for the Eurobond market.

All these institutions and many others report average yields for various market segments.

The Eurobond Market

Of all the bond markets in the world, the Eurobond market is certainly the most attractive to the international investor. It avoids most national regulations and constraints. Because of its important role in international investment, we will examine in some detail how Eurobonds are issued and traded.

The Issuing Syndicate

Eurobonds are sold in a multistage process. The issue is organized by an international bank called the *lead manager*. This bank invites several *comanagers* to form the *management group* (from 5 to 30 banks, usually). For large issues there may be several lead managers. The managers prepare the issue, set the final conditions of the bond, and select the *underwriters* and *selling group*. One of the managers is appointed as the principal paying agent and fiscal agent. A large portion of the issue is directly subscribed by the management group.

The underwriters are invited to participate in the issue on the basis of their regional placement power. Their number varies from 30 to 300 and comprises international banks from all regions of the world. Together with the management group, they guarantee final placement of the bonds at a set price to the borrower.

The selling group is responsible for selling the bonds to the public and consists of managers, underwriters, and additional banks with a good selling base. Note that a participant may be, at the same time, manager, underwriter, and seller. Separate fees are paid to compensate for the various services. The total fee ranges from 1.25% to 2.5%. Unlike their U.S. counterparts, Eurobond underwriters are not obligated to maintain the bond's market price at or above the issue price until the syndicate is disbanded. This means that bonds are often placed at a price below the issue price. There is considerable price discrimination among clients, and selling members may pass along part of their fee to the final buyer of the bond.

The Timetable of a New Issue

Unlike national markets, the Eurobond market has neither registration formalities nor *waiting queues*. A new issue may be placed within three weeks. A typical timetable is depicted in Exh. 9.11.

EXHIBIT 9.11

Timetable of a New Issue

Discussion between borrower and lead manager, two weeks or more

One to two weeks of preplacement ("gray market")

Two-week public placement

| Decision to issue Eurobond | → | Announcement of Eurobond issue | → | Offering day with final terms | → | Closing day: Selling group pays for bonds | Total elapsed time: Five to six weeks |

First, the lead manager gets together with the borrower to discuss the terms of the bond (amount, maturity, fixed or floating rate, and coupon). The terms generally remain provisional until the official offering date. During this period, the lead manager arranges the management syndicate and prepares various documents, one of which is a preliminary prospectus called, at this stage, a *red herring*. On the *announcement day* the managers send telexes describing the proposed bond issue and inviting banks to join the underwriting and selling groups. Potential underwriters are sent the preliminary prospectus. A week or two later the final terms of the bond are set, and the syndicate commits itself to the borrower. A final prospectus is printed, and the bonds are publicly offered on the *offering day*. At the end of a public placement period of about two weeks, the subscription is closed on the *closing day*, and the bonds are delivered in exchange for cash paid to the borrower. A *tombstone* is later published in international newspapers to advertise the successful issue and to list the participating banks.

After the closing day, the bonds can be publicly traded. However, bond trading actually takes place well before the closing day. A *gray* market for the bonds starts before the final terms have been set on the offering day; trading is contingent on the final issue price. That is, bonds are traded in the gray market at a premium or discount relative to the future price. For example, a quote of *less* ¼ means that the bonds are exchanged at a price of 99¼% if the future issue price is set at 99½%. This is a form of forward market for bonds that are not yet in existence. The gray market is often used by members of the selling group to resell part of their bond allocation at a discount below the issue price but possibly at a net profit if their fee is large enough.

Dealing in Eurobonds

The Eurobond secondary market is truly international and comprises an informal network of market makers and dealers. A market maker quotes a net price to a financial institution in the form of a bid and ask price. No commissions are charged.

All market makers and dealers in Eurobonds are part of the ISMA based in Zurich and London. The ISMA bears some similarities to the U.S. National Association of Securities Dealers (NASD). But whereas NASD is under the supervision of the Securities and Exchange Commission, the ISMA is purely self-regulated and enjoys no government intervention.

Eurobond Clearing System

Let's assume that a Scottish investment manager wants to buy $100,000 worth of a specific Eurobond. The investment manager calls several market makers to get their best quotations and concludes the deal at the lowest price quoted. The trade is settled in seven calendar days,[7] and the transaction is cleared through one of the two major clearing systems, Euroclear or Cedel.

Both systems are owned by a group of financial institutions. Euroclear, which handles about two thirds of the total volume, was founded and is operated by J.P. Morgan from Brussels. Cedel is based in Luxembourg and was created by a group of Eurobond traders to compete with J.P. Morgan's Euroclear. Both systems operate in a similar fashion. Each member has both bond accounts and cash accounts in each of the currencies used to denominate Eurobonds. All transactions are entered in the books without any physical movement of the securities. Both systems cover around 10,000 different securities. German banks prefer to deposit their Deutsche mark Eurobonds in a domestic group of depositary banks, the Kassenverein, which have direct links with Euroclear and Cedel. Similarly, most Swiss franc bonds are deposited in Switzerland, usually with the local clearing system SEGA. The whole clearing system is highly efficient because there are electronic bridges between Euroclear and Cedel, as well as between the various domestic clearing systems (SICOVAM in France, NECIGEF in the Netherlands, CIK in Belgium, and others).

All transactions are performed on a net basis. In other words, the market maker quotes a bid-ask spread and charges no commission. The typical spread for a straight dollar bond is between 10 and 50 basis points (a basis point is one hundredth of a percentage point) for a normal ticket of 100 to 500 securities (a $100,000 to $500,000 transaction). This spread increases for Deutsche mark straight bonds and can reach 1% for some Swiss franc bonds and bonds denominated in other currencies. The spread for floating-rate notes is generally on the order of 0.25% and is larger than 1% for convertible bonds.

These spread figures are averages. The spread is larger for small transactions and may vary for each bond, depending on market conditions. The private investor is charged a commission by his or her bank on top of this spread.

Clearing and custody charges must also be paid. Euroclear and Cedel collect a transaction fee for each book entry, as well as a custody fee for holding the securities. The custody fees are a function of a client's transaction volume: If the member bank maintains a large bond turnover, the custodial fee is nil. Euroclear and Cedel also provide security lending facilities.

Emerging Markets and Brady Bonds

Investors wishing to buy bonds issued by emerging countries have several alternatives.

- They can access directly the *domestic* bond markets of some emerging countries. These emerging markets have been growing, and the capitalization of loans and bonds traded exceeds $200 billion. However, various restrictions and liquidity problems reduce the amount available to foreign investors. Latin America dominates the fixed-income market of emerging countries, but some

European and Asian markets are worth mentioning: Turkey, Hungary, Czech Republic, India, Indonesia, or the Philippines. Most of the bonds traded on emerging markets are *not* investment grade, i.e., rated Baa or above by Moody's or BBB or above by Standard & Poor's (see Chapter 10). This means that they are not eligible for many U.S. institutional investors. These instruments are generally denominated in the *local* currency and carry the *exchange risk* of that currency. On the other side, local governments are less likely to default on these bonds, because they can always print more national currency.

- They can buy *Eurobonds* issued by emerging countries. In the 1990s emerging countries have returned to the Eurobond market. In 1993 emerging countries issued over $50 billion of new Eurobonds. Latin American governments and firms represent the largest share of these new issues denominated in U.S. dollars and other major currencies. Major issuers come from Mexico, Argentina, Venezuela, and Brazil.

- They can buy *Brady bonds* on the international capital market. In 1990 the Brady plan allowed emerging countries to transform nonperforming debt into so-called Brady bonds, which are traded on the international bond market.

Brady Bonds: A Historical Perspective

In the 1980s many developing countries were hit hard by the drop in commodity prices and became unable or unwilling to service their loans from international banks. This led to an international debt crisis that threatened the international financial system. The emerging-country debt often took the form of bank loans, which are nontradable, as opposed to bonds. Although many emerging countries have not serviced their bank loans, leading to a negotiation to reschedule them, they have usually kept servicing their bond debt. The debtor banks formed the *Paris Club* to negotiate with emerging countries the rescheduling of their debts. A secondary market for nonperforming loans developed where these loans traded at a steep discount from their par value. The average discount reached two thirds of face value by 1989. Some debt-for-equity swaps were arranged by some countries, whereby loans could be exchanged for equity investment in the local economy. These measures were not sufficient for the debtor banks and did not allow the defaulting countries to obtain new international financing, for fear of repetition of debt servicing problems. The principles of Brady plans, named after the U.S. Secretary of the Treasury, were designed in 1989 and implemented from 1990 to provide a satisfactory solution to this debt crisis.

To negotiate its Brady plan, the emerging country must initiate a credible economic reform program that receives the agreement, and funding, from the World Bank, the IMF, and regional development banks, such as the Inter-American Development Bank, the African Development Bank, the Asian Development Bank, or the European Bank for Reconstruction and Development. Once the IMF and World Bank have agreed that the economic reform plan will reduce the risk of new insolvency problems, these organizations provide funding, which can be used partly to provide collateral and guarantees in the debt rescheduling. The debt transformation plan is usually coordinated by the Paris Club, which groups all major former creditors. One advantage for creditors is that they exchange commercial loans for tradable bonds. A Brady plan is basically a debt-reduction program whereby sovereign debt is repackaged into tradable Brady bonds, generally with collateral. In 1994 close to 20 countries had issued Brady bonds, including Argentina, Brazil, Bulgaria, Costa Rica, Nigeria, Poland, the Philippines, Uruguay, and Venezuela. These bonds are traded in the international capital market, with a total capitalization close to $100 billion.

International commercial banks, which were most active in lending to emerging countries, are the major market markers on the Brady bond market. An *Emerging Markets Traders Association* has been formed. The bid-ask spread on these bonds averages 25 basis points and is low relative to that of Eurobonds issued by emerging countries, because the issue size of Brady bonds can be very large and their market is quite active.

Characteristics of Brady Bonds

Brady bonds come with a large menu of options, which makes their analysis somewhat complicated. The basic idea is to replace existing government debt with Brady bonds, whose market value is *less* than the par value of the original debt but that are more attractive than the original debt because of the guarantees provided and their tradability on the international bond market.

Types of Guarantees   Three types of guarantees can be put in place. These guarantees are not available on all types of Brady bonds.

- *Principal collateral.* The U.S. Treasury issues long-term (e.g., 30-year) zero-coupon bonds to collaterallize the principal of the Brady bond. The collateral is paid for by a combination of the IMF, the World Bank, and the emerging country. The value of the collateral increases with time and reaches par at maturity of the Brady bond.

- *Rolling-interest guarantee.* The first semiannual coupons (generally three) are guaranteed by securities deposited in escrow with the New York Federal Reserve Bank, to protect the bondholder from interest suspension or default. If an interest payment is missed, the bondholder will receive interest payment from the escrow account. If the interest payment is made normally by the emerging country, the interest collateral will be rolled forward to the next interest payments.

- *Value recovery rights.* Some bonds issued by Mexico and Venezuela have attached warrants linked to the price of oil. Investors can get extra interest payments if the oil export receipts of these countries increase over time.

Types of Bonds   Two major types of Brady bonds have been issued: *par* bonds and *discount* bonds.

- *Par bonds.* These *PARs* can be exchanged dollar for dollar for existing debt. Typically these bonds have fixed coupons and a long-term maturity (30 years) and are repaid in full (*bullet* bonds) on the final maturity. In some cases the coupon is stepped up progressively over the life of the bond. The debt reduction is obtained by setting a coupon rate on the par value of the bond well below the current market interest rate. In other words, the market value of the bond is well below its face value, because of the low coupon. These bonds are sometimes known as interest-reduction bonds. The difference between the par value of the bond and its market value at issue time can be regarded as the amount of debt forgiveness. Generally, par bonds benefit from principal collateral and rolling-interest guarantee.

- *Discount bonds.* DISCs are exchanged at a discount to the par value of the existing debt but with a "market-rate" coupon. These bonds are sometimes known as principal-reduction bonds. Typically these bonds have floating-rate coupons (LIBOR plus a market-determined spread) and a long maturity (25 to 30 years) and are repaid in full on the final maturity. Generally, discount bonds benefit from principal collateral and rolling-interest guarantee.

Other types of Brady bonds can be negotiated.

- *Front-loaded interest-reduction bonds.* FLIRBs have fixed coupons that step up to higher levels for a number of years, after which they pay a floating rate. Typically FLIRBs have no principal collateral but a rolling-interest rate guarantee, only during the period of fixed coupons. To compensate for the absence of principal collateral, these bonds are amortized (reimbursed) progressively over their total life (usually around 20 years). Such bonds are not easy to value.

- *New-money bonds* (*NMBs*) *and debt-conversion bonds* (*DCBs*). These are generally issued together through the new-money option of the Brady plan. This option is designed to give debt holders incentives to invest additional capital (*new money*) in the emerging country. For every dollar of NMB subscribed, the investor can exchange existing debt for debt-conversion bonds in a ratio stated in the Brady plan (typically $5 of DCBs for each dollar of NMBs). The incentive is provided by making DCBs more attractive than the bonds available in other Brady options. These bonds tend to be floating-rate bonds amortized progressively over 20 or 25 years.

- *Past-due interest bonds.* PDIs are issued in exchange for unpaid past interest. In a way they pay interest on interest. Argentina issued some PDFIs simply named Floating Rate Bonds (*FRBs*). Brazil issued some PDIs named Interest Due and Unpaid (*IDUs*).

This list is not exhaustive, and the option menu of a Brady plan can be quite varied.

Summary

1. The international bond market is divided into three broad market groups: domestic bonds, foreign bonds, and Eurobonds. Whereas domestic and foreign bonds are issued and traded on a single national market, Eurobonds belong to an unregulated international market on which banks from all over the world participate.

2. The total world bond market capitalization has passed the $16 trillion mark. U.S dollar–denominated bonds account for about half of the world market; Japanese yen bonds for about 20%. Bonds denominated in European currencies account for more than one fourth of the world market.

3. The market for international bonds has been growing very rapidly. The U.S. dollar dominates as a denomination currency, but several other currencies are also used. The ECU, a composite basket of the European currencies, has been extensively used in the recent past. The Eurobond market is a free and innovative market. All types of instruments can be found with imaginative interest rates and multicurrency clauses.

4. Issuing and dealing practices differ among bond markets across the world. Yield calculation varies greatly between countries and markets. International investors must be aware of these practical differences.

5. Foreign withholding taxes on interest income are being progressively removed throughout the world. Where such taxes exist, international tax treaties allow them to be claimed as a tax credit against domestic income tax or to be used to get a tax refund from the withholding country. Eurobonds are exempt from any withholding tax.

6. The Eurobond market is an informal network of investment and commercial banks of all nationalities. New issues are made rapidly, since in the absence of supervising authorities, no special documents need to be prepared by the borrowing firm or underwriting syndicate. An international clearing system ensures efficient settling of all transactions.

7. The solvency problems encountered by many emerging countries in the 1980s led to their disappearance from international capital markets. The Brady plan prompted the development of an active market for emerging-country bonds in the 1990s. Numerous corporations from emerging countries have also issued bonds on the Eurobond market.

Questions and Problems

1. What is the difference between a foreign bond and a Eurobond?

2. Why did U.S. commercial banks have an interest in the development of the Eurobond market?

3. What is the attraction of an ECU bond for, respectively, the borrower and the investor?

4. An FRN (floating-rate note) is a bond that pays a quarterly or semiannual coupon indexed on a short-term interest rate such as the LIBOR. Why does it make sense to use a short-term interest rate as index? Why are banks heavy issuers of FRNs?

5*. Give at least two reasons why Eurobonds are issued in bearer form.

6*. To provide full protection against unexpected tax imposition, all Eurobond contracts have a convenant stating that the issuer will increase the interest payments to make up for any tax imposed. Assume that Paf Inc. has issued a Eurobond with a coupon of $10 per $100 bond. For some reason, Paf Inc. is forced by its government to transfer 15% of the coupon as withholding tax, so that the net coupon paid to the bondholder is only $8.50. What should Paf Inc. do according to the bond covenant?

7. Let's consider the NKK dual-currency bond shown in Exh. 9.5. It is a bond quoted in yen at 101%. What would happen to the market price if the following scenarios took place?

   ■ The market interest rate on (newly issued) yen bonds drops significantly.

   ■ The dollar drops in value relative to the yen.

   ■ The market interest rate on (newly issued) dollar bonds drops significantly.

   Would you give the same answers if the same bond were quoted in dollars?

8*. What are the potential biases of the simple interest rate calculation used in Japan? Take the example of two straight Eurobonds with the same maturity of five years. Bond A has a coupon of 12% and bond B, a coupon of 8%. The current market interest rate on yen bonds is 10%. These two bonds have the same yield-to-maturity of 10% and are correctly priced at 107.58% for bond A and 96.42% for bond B. What would be the yield-to-maturity indicated by the simple interest rate calculation?

9*. A zero-coupon bond with a five-year maturity is worth 68.06% of its final reimbursement value. Verify that its actuarial yield-to-maturity is equal to 8% by compounding 8% over five years. What is the simple yield of this bond, and why is it so different from the actuarial yield?

10. Two bond indexes of the same market tend to give the similar total return indications even if their composition is quite different. Why?

11. Assume that you are an international bank having lent money to some Latin American countries. Because of the nonpayment of interest due, you have already taken substantial reserves against these nonperforming loans. Why would you be willing to exchange these loans for Brady bonds?

12. Discuss the differences between a par and a discount Brady bond. Take successively the viewpoint of the emerging country and of the bondholder.

Notes

1. The Interest Equalization Tax was imposed on interest paid to U.S. bondholders by foreign borrowers. The supposed purpose was to equalize the after-tax interest rate paid by U.S. and foreign borrowers. This tax did not apply to some borrowers, such as those from Canada or less-developed countries or to such international organizations as the World Bank.

2. Remember that British traders use the word *stock* where U.S. traders use the word *bond*. Spanish bonds also trade on the basis of full or dirty price, not clean price.

3. On the other hand, the day count for U.S. Treasury bonds is based on the actual number of days in a year of 365 or 366 days.

4. Eurosterling FRNs are the sole exception, with the day-count following the rule of actual number of days in a year of 365 days.

5. The rationale for this method is that it is easy to calculate a yield for a bond issued at par with semiannual coupons. You just multiply the semiannual coupon by 2. However, the use of an annual actuarial yield (with compounding of semiannual yields) makes more sense and allows a direct comparison between instruments and markets. The actuarial (or compounding) method of calculating a yield-to-maturity is described in Chapter 10.

6. A good analysis of the correlation between major U.S. bond indexes is provided in F. Reilly, G.W. Kao, and D.J. Wright, "Alternative Bond Indexes," *Financial Analysts Journal*, May/June 1992.

7. The settlement period was shortened from five business days (seven calendar days) to three business days in 1995.

Bibliography

Bank for International Settlements, *Recent Innovations in International Banking*, April 1986.

————. *Annual Report*, various years.

Brown, P. *Formulae for Yield and Other Calculations*, London: International Securities Market Association, 1992.

Bruslerie, H. de la. *Gestion Obligataire Internationale*, Paris: Economica, 1990.

Doso, G. *The Eurobond Market*, Hermel Hempstead, UK: Woodhead-Faulkner, 1992.

Dufey, G., and Giddy, I. *The International Money Market*, Englewood Cliffs, NJ: Prentice Hall, 1978.

Euromoney, various publications on international bond markets, swaps, etc., London: Euromoney Publications.

Fabozzi, F.J., ed. *Handbook of Fixed Income Securities*, 3rd ed., Homewood, IL: Business One Irwin, 1991.

Kemp, L.J. *A Guide to World Money and Capital Markets*, New York: McGraw-Hill, 1982.

Kerr, I. *A History of the Eurobond Market: The First 21 Years,* London: Euromoney Publications, 1984.

OECD (Organization for Economic Co-operation and Development). *Financial Market Trends,* recent issues.

Park, Y.S., and Zwick, J. *International Banking in Theory and Practice,* Reading, MA: Addison-Wesley, 1985.

Reed, H.C. *The Pre-eminence of International Financial Centers,* Westport, CT: Praeger, 1981.

Reilly, F., Kao, G.W., and Wright, D.J. "Alternative Bond Indexes," *Financial Analysts Journal,* May/June 1992.

10

Bonds: Concepts and Techniques

I n Chapter 4 we established the case for diversification in international bond markets. We found that foreign bonds reduce the risk of a global portfolio. We also found that active international fixed-income management can achieve superior performance if a manager is skilled at forecasting interest rates and currency movements.

International fixed-income investment requires both a familiarity with the markets described in Chapter 9 and a thorough knowledge of the techniques required to manage bond portfolios. We begin this chapter by reviewing the main concepts and actuarial techniques used in fixed-income portfolio management. We also consider the dimension of multicurrency analysis. The rest of this chapter presents some of the more complex bonds issued worldwide and ideas about how they should be analyzed.

Straight Bond Prices and Yields

Bond portfolio management requires the use of mathematical techniques. International bond management adds a new dimension to these techniques, namely, a multicurrency strategy. It also implies the analysis of a large variety of unusual bonds, floating-rate notes, currency option bonds, and other instruments.

The following section could appear in any textbook that deals with domestic investment; as such, it is presented only briefly here. It is followed by a more detailed analysis of the techniques used in international portfolio management, especially the comparison of international yield curves, and an analysis of special bonds.

Bond Valuation Techniques: A Review

Yield-to-Maturity   The theoretical value of a bond is determined by computing the present value of all future cash flows generated by the bond discounted at an appropriate interest rate. Conversely, one may calculate the internal rate of return, or *yield-to-maturity* (YTM), of a bond on the basis of its current market price and its promised payments.

For example, a bond that promises a payment of $F_1 = \$110$ one year from now with a current market value of $P = \$100$ has a yield-to-maturity r given by

$$P = \frac{F_1}{1+r}$$
$$100 = \frac{110}{1+r}. \tag{10.1}$$

Hence

$$r = 0.10 = 10\%.$$

Similarly, one may use the following formula to compute the yield-to-maturity of zero-coupon bonds maturing in t years:

$$P = \frac{F_t}{\left(1+r\right)^t}, \tag{10.2}$$

where r is expressed as a yearly interest rate. The term $1/(1=r)^t$ is the discount factor for year t. The yield-to-maturity is defined as the interest rate at which P dollars should be invested today in order to realize F_t dollars t years from now:

$$P(1 + r)^t = F_t.$$

For example, a two-year zero-coupon bond paying $F_2 = \$100$ two years from now and currently selling at a price $P = \$81.16$ has a yield-to-maturity r given by

$$81.16 = \frac{100}{\left(1+r\right)^2}.$$

Hence

$$r = 0.11 = 11\%.$$

Yield Curves   The yields-to-maturity of two zero-coupon bonds in the same currency but with different maturities are usually different. However, bonds with similar characteristics (risks, coupons, and maturities) should provide the same return. Graphing the yields-to-maturity on bonds with different maturities allows us to draw a *yield curve*. The yield curve shows the yields-to-maturity computed on a given date as a function of the maturity of the bonds. It provides an estimate of the current *term structure* of interest rates. To be meaningful, a yield curve must be drawn from bonds with identical characteristics, except for their maturity.

A good example of a yield curve can be drawn for zero-coupon bonds with government guarantees and no call or *sinking-fund* clauses. This is a default-free yield curve. Two zero-coupon bonds are represented as two points on the hypothetical yield curve in Exh. 10.1. Other yield curves can be drawn for risky bonds, e.g., those with an AA quality rating or denominated in foreign currencies.

Forward Interest Rates   Yield-to-maturity is a sort of average rate of interest on a bond held to maturity. YTM assumes a constant rate of interest over the life of a bond, but as we have already seen, interest rates are contingent on the maturity of a bond. For example, the yields-to-maturity on one-year and two-year zero-coupon bonds, r_1 and r_2, are generally different.

Now we can introduce the notion of forward interest rates. Forward interest rates are future one-year interest rates implied by long-term interest rates.

The yield-to-maturity on a *t*-year bond, r_t, may be thought of as the rollover of one-year investments until the bond expires. Let's use R_1 to represent the interest rate on a one-year bond maturing in a year and R_2 to represent the forward interest rate on a one-year bond maturing in two years (i.e., issued one year from now). Similarly, R_3, R_4, etc., represent the forward interest rates on one-year bonds maturing three, four, or however many years from now. The values of the forward rates are determined by the following set of equations:

$$(1 + R_1)(1 + R_2) \ldots (1 + R_t) = (1 + r_t)^t. \tag{10.3}$$

EXHIBIT 10.1

Yield Curve for Zero-Coupon Bonds

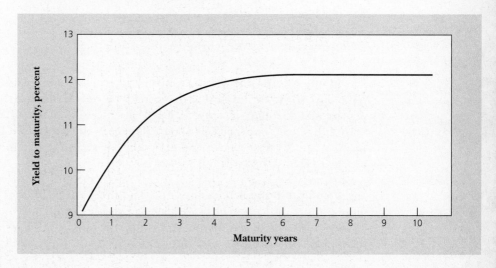

Note that R_1 must equal r_1. The next forward interest rate, R_2, is easily derived from the yield curve, knowing the yields-to-maturity on a one-year and a two-year bond.

$$(1 + r_1)(1 + R_2) = (1 + r_2)^2.$$

Hence

$$1 + R_2 = \frac{(1 + r_2)^2}{(1 + r_1)}$$

and so on for $R_3, R_4, \ldots, R_t$.

Going back to our original example, the forward interest rate one year from now is given by

$$1 + R_2 = \frac{(1.11)^2}{1.10} = 1.12009.$$

Hence

$$R_2 \approx 12\%$$

when

$$r_1 = 10\%$$

and

$$r_2 = 11\%.$$

In order to borrow at this forward rate, one can simply combine two transactions. At time zero, borrow for two years at $r_2 = 11\%$ and simultaneously lend for one year at $r_1 = 10\%$. Nothing happens during the first year, since the borrowing and lending are mutually offsetting. After one year, we are left in a borrowing position at a rate R_2 such that

$$1 + R_2 = \frac{(1 + r_2)^2}{1 + r_1}.$$

In other words, the one-year interest rate must move to 12% in the year 2001 for an investor to be indifferent to buying a two-year bond in 2000 or buying a one-year bond and rolling it over in 2001. Many investors believe that the implied forward rate reflects expectations about changes in the short-term interest rate.[1] The forward interest rate structure implied by the yield curve depicted in Exh. 10.1 may be easily computed and is shown in Exh. 10.2.

Valuing a Bond with Coupons   The theoretical value of a coupon-paying bond is more difficult to assess. It may be considered the present value of a stream of cash flows consisting of each coupon payment and the principal reimbursement. Since the cash flows occur at different times, they should be discounted at

EXHIBIT 10.2

Implied Forward Interest Rates

N Maturity (years)	1	2	3	4	5
N-years interest rate (percent)	10	11	11.5	11.75	11.9
Implied one-year forward interest rate (percent)	10	12	12.52	12.50	12.50

the interest rate corresponding to their date of disbursement. Accordingly, the coupon to be paid in one year should be discounted at the one-year interest rate on the yield curve

$$\left(\frac{1}{1+r_1}\right).$$

The coupon to be paid in two years should be discounted at the two-year rate:

$$\left(\frac{1}{1+r_2}\right)$$

and so forth. In essence, then, a coupon-paying bond is a combination of zero-coupon bonds with different maturities. For example, a 10-year $100 bond with an annual coupon of $10 is a combination of 10 bonds, each with a nominal value of $10 and a maturity of 1 to 10 years, and a bond with a nominal value of $100 and a 10-year maturity. As we will later see, the *duration* of this coupon bond is a weighted average of the maturities of this combination of bonds. It is a more accurate measure of a bond's economic life than final maturity.

One may still define the yield-to-maturity of a coupon bond as the internal rate of return, r, which equates the discounted stream of cash flows to the current bond market price. For an annual coupon bond, the equation is as follows:

$$P = \frac{C_1}{1+r} + \frac{C_2}{\left(1+r\right)^2} + \ldots + \frac{C_n}{\left(1+r\right)^n}, \tag{10.4}$$

where $C_1, C_2, \ldots, C_n$ are the cash flows 1, 2, $\ldots$, n years from now, including the final reimbursement. In practice, coupons may be paid semiannually or quarterly, and a valuation may be made at any time during the coupon period. This calls for the more general valuation formula to determine yield-to-maturity:

$$P = \frac{C_{t_1}}{\left(1+r\right)^{t_1}} + \frac{C_{t_2}}{\left(1+r\right)^{t_2}} + \ldots + \frac{C_{t_n}}{\left(1+r\right)^{t_n}}, \tag{10.5}$$

where r is the annualized yield-to-maturity, and $t_1, t_2 \ldots, t_n$ are the dates on which the cash flows occur, expressed in number of years from the current date. Hence these dates are usually fractional. For example, consider a bond with a semiannual coupon to be paid three months from now (one fourth of a year); the next cash flow dates are $t_1 = 0.25$, $t_2 = 0.75$, $t_3 = 1.25$, etc. The cash flows include coupons and principal redemption. It must be stressed that P represents the *total* value of the bond, quoted price plus accrued interest.

Equation (10.5) allows us to determine the annual yield-to-maturity on a bond if we know its cash flows and observe its market value. This is the standard compounding, or actuarial, method that can be used whatever the frequency and dates of coupons. This method is used worldwide except in the United States, where the tradition is to calculate a yield-to-maturity over a semester and multiply it by 2 to report an annualized yield. Hence the semiannual yield is a mixture of a compounding calculation to obtain the semester yield and of a simple yield calculation to transform it into an annualized yield. Bond traders often refer to the *European*, or *ISMA*, method when they use the standard method described in Eq. (10.5). They refer to the *semiannual* method when they use the U.S. convention.[2]

The appellation "semiannual yield" is somewhat confusing, since it refers to an annualized yield calculated with a semiannual method. To reduce confusion, we will use the term *semester yield* to refer to a yield over a six-month period and the term *semiannual yield* for its annualized equivalent using, the U.S. method.

This semiannual method to compute an annualized semiannual yield r' can be described by the formula

$$P = \frac{C_{t_1}}{\left(1 + r'/2\right)^{2t_1}} + \frac{C_{t_2}}{\left(1 + r'/2\right)^{2t_2}} + \ldots + \frac{C_{t_n}}{\left(1 + r'/2\right)^{2t_n}}, \tag{10.6}$$

where r' is the semiannual yield, and the cash flow dates are still expressed in number of years. The logic of Eq. (10.6) is to use the semester as the unit of time measurement. The reader can verify that one uses a semester yield $r'/2$ to discount the cash flows and that the exponents $(2t_1, 2t_2, \ldots, 2t_n)$ are the number of semesters from the valuation date. The difference between r' and r comes from the difference between compounding and linearizing semester yields to get annual yields. If a semester yield of 4% is found, the U.S. method will report a semiannual yield of $r' = 2 \times 4\% = 8\%$, whereas the European method will report an annual yield of $(1.04)(1.04)-1 = 8.16\%$.

One must not confuse the methodology used to calculate yields and the frequency of coupon payments on a specific bond. The semiannual (U.S.) method can be applied to bonds with annual coupon payments, and the annual (European) method can be applied to bonds with semiannual coupon payments.

The maturity of a bond is generally defined as the date on which the final payment is made on the bond, although its duration is less. This implies that the yield-to-maturity on a coupon bond can differ from that on a zero-coupon bond with the same maturity. In an upward-sloping yield curve, the YTM on a correctly priced coupon bond should be less than that of a zero-coupon bond because it has a shorter duration.[3] In a downward-sloping yield curve, the reverse is true.

EXHIBIT 10.3

Yield Differentials Between High- and Low-Coupon Government Bonds
Weekly data, June 1982 to June 1983

Country	Representative Bonds	Yield Differentials (basis points)		
		Average	Maximum	Minimum
Japan	8 '86 vs. 6.6 '87	–50	–23	–95
Switzerland	5¾ '93 vs. 3¾ '92	53	68	30
United Kingdom	15¼ '96 vs. 12 '98	34	92	23
United States	16⅛ '86 vs. 12¾ '87	12	54	–10
Canada	11¼ '89 vs. 10 '89	12	33	–29
West Germany	10¾ '91 vs. 8½ '92	6	16	–1

Source: J. Hanna and T.Q. Hung, "Coupon Based Trading Strategies," *Bond Market Research*, Salomon Brothers Inc., August 1983. Reprinted with permission.

But two other factors affecting yield-to-maturity should be taken into account. The first stems from the fact that coupons and capital gains usually have a different tax status. That is, investors must generally pay more taxes on income than on capital gains; therefore they prefer low-coupon bonds. Conversely, investors require a higher YTM from high-coupon bonds to compensate for this tax effect. It should be remembered, however, that this tax effect is not present to the same degree in all countries. Exhibit 10.3 shows the average yield differential for high- and low-coupon government bonds with comparable maturity in six different domestic markets. What we find is that YTM is an increasing function of the coupon rate in all countries except Japan.[4]

A second factor, particularly important in the Eurobond market, is the use of *call* provisions, as described later. Low-coupon bonds offer greater call protection than high-coupon bonds. This is because low-coupon bonds must sell at a higher market price than high-coupon bonds with a similar maturity in order to provide a comparable yield-to-maturity. Conversely, high-coupon bonds are more likely to be called (repaid at a set price) by the issuer, a risk that must be offset by a higher YTM for the investor.

Duration The cash flows on a coupon bond are periodically paid over the life of the bond in the form of coupons and, ultimately, a principal reimbursement. The duration of a bond is defined as its average maturity. It is a time-weighted average, with each date weighted by the present value of the cash flow paid by the bond on that date. On a coupon date the duration, *D*, is computed as follows:

$$D = \frac{1}{P}\left(1\frac{C_1}{1+r} + 2\frac{C_2}{(1+r)^2} + \ldots + t\frac{C_t}{(1+r)^t} + \ldots + n\frac{C_n}{(1+r)^n}\right)$$

or

$$D = \frac{\sum_{t=1}^{n} t \dfrac{C_t}{(1+r)^t}}{\sum_{t=1}^{n} \dfrac{C_t}{(1+r)^t}},$$

(10.7)

where the final cash flow, C_n, includes the coupon and the principal repayment. Duration is easily computed on dates other than coupon dates, using a compounding formula like Eq. (10.5).

Duration is a more precise definition of the average maturity of a coupon bond. It gained wide use when it was recognized that it also measures bond-price sensitivity to interest rate movements. The percentage change in price induced by a small change, dr, in interest rate (for example, a 10-basis point increase where $dr = 0.10\%$) is given by

$$\left(\frac{1}{P}\right)\left(\frac{dP}{dr}\right) = -\frac{1}{P}\sum_{t=1}^{n} t \frac{C_t}{(1+r)^{t+1}} = -D\frac{1}{1+r} = -D^*.$$

(10.8)

Interest rate sensitivity, or *modified duration*, is shown by

$$D^* = \frac{D}{1+r}.$$

The only difference between this and the former measure is the multiplicative constant

$$\frac{1}{1+r}.$$

For the remainder of the chapter, the latter definition of duration will be used: the measure of the sensitivity of the price of a bond to interest rate movements.[5]

A bond with a duration of 7.2 rises in price on the order of 0.72% when the interest rate drops by 10 basis points (0.10%):

Percent change in $P = -D^* \times$ Change in interest rate.

Let's consider two bonds, one with a duration of 7.2 and the other with a duration of 10. The second bond is more sensitive to interest rate movements, up and down, than the first one. Their relative sensitivity is the ratio of their duration:

$$\frac{10}{7.2}.$$

Note that mathematically, a coupon-bearing bond with duration of N years has the same sensitivity to changes in interest rates as an N-year zero-coupon bond. That is, a coupon bond with 10-year final maturity and a duration of 7.2 would react to changes in interest rates as a zero-coupon bond with 7.2 years remaining.

Two words of caution are in order here. First, the sensitivity of the bond as measured by its duration is an exact actuarial measure. Yet the price sensitivity of a bond price varies with the level of interest rates themselves. This means that for large changes in the market interest rate, $D^*(r)$ does not stay constant. Nonetheless, exact calculations of $D^*(r)$ can be performed. Second, the underlying assumption of Eq. (10.8) is that the whole term structure of interest rates moves by the same amount, dr. More complex multifactor duration models have been developed that assume different shifts for short- and long-term interest rates. But empirical evidence indicates that Eq. (10.8) performs just as well as the more complex models; see Nelson and Schaefer (1983).

The interest rate sensitivity or risk of a portfolio is the weighted average of the durations of individual bonds.

Sinking Fund   Many bonds are not repaid in fine, that is, in a lump at maturity (bullet bonds). Instead, they are progressively amortized over their maturity through a sinking-fund provision. Three methods are used by issuers for early bond redemption:

- *Lot drawing at par.* Following a grace period, part of the bond issue is repaid according to a fixed schedule. The bonds to be repaid are drawn at random and are reimbursed at par value.

- *Market repurchase.* Part of the bond issue is repaid according to a fixed schedule by which it is purchased by the issuer in the market at market prices.

- *Issuing of serial bonds.* Serial bonds each have a serial number, and each series has a different maturity and yield. Investors know at issue which bond will be reimbursed and when. This method is seldom used, because each series represents a different bond, which reduces the liquidity of the issue.

Sometimes a combination of methods is used. For example, the issuer may have the option of meeting the redemption schedule by either drawing bonds at par or repurchasing them in the market. This method greatly benefits the issuer, who can thus choose the cheapest redemption method possible at any given time. Conversely, it is a disadvantage to the investor.

For each bond purchased, an investor can compute the expected cash flows, taking into account the probability each year of being reimbursed. From these cash flows he or she can compute an internal rate of return. This is the yield obtained by an investor who, holding a large number of shares of a bond issue, knows exactly how many bonds will be drawn each year.

A bond with a mandatory redemption schedule has a smaller duration than a *bullet bond* with a similar maturity. The *average life* (AL) of a bond is usually defined as the average maturity of the whole issue. Average life takes into account the fact that some bonds are reimbursed early and others late, which makes it a weighted average of the maturities on each bond. Unlike duration, the calculation of the average life takes into account only the principal repayments, not the coupon. Also, it is only a linear average without discounting.

Worldwide, there is some confusion over the correct definition of yield-to-maturity for a bond with contractual amortization. Some institutions compute the YTM on Eurobonds as if there were no sinking fund. In actuality, this is a *yield-to-final-maturity* (YFM), and it is equal to YTM only for those bonds that are reimbursed on the final date. It does not measure the expected yield on either a typical bond or portfolios containing the bond. These same institutions often call *yield-to-average-life* (YTAL) what we would call YTM, i.e., the actuarial yield that takes the mandatory sinking fund into account. This computation is clearly a more exact measure of the expected rate of return on the bond. The YTM computed without reference to the mandatory redemption schedule is misleading. The difference between the two measures YFM and YTAL can be large for bonds selling at a price either far above or far below par value. Early redemption at par improves the true yield-to-maturity if a bond is selling under par in the market but reduces it if the bond is selling over par in the market. This feature does not apply if the bond is repurchased within the market (though there may be temporary upward pressure on its market price). An option to repurchase a bond in the market or drawing a bond at par always reduces the true yield-to-maturity.

To illustrate this, Exh. 10.4 shows the average life, duration, and yield-to-maturity for three hypothetical bonds *with a similar final maturity of ten years*. The three bonds are

1. A zero-coupon bond trading at 32.2.

2. A 10% coupon (annual) bond, repaid in full in 10 years. This bullet bond currently trades at 88.7.

3. A 10% coupon (annual) bond with sinking fund determined by lot drawing at par. The bond is redeemed in equal tranche amounting to one tenth of all bonds each year. This sinking fund bond currently trades at 92.7.

Note that all three bonds have the same final maturity. They were issued five years ago, and early redemption applies only to the third bond. The three bonds have the same yield-to-maturity of 12% once the coupons and redemption schedule are taken into account. The zero-coupon bond A has a (modified) duration

EXHIBIT 10.4

Characteristics of Three Bonds with Similar Final Maturity

Bond	Market Price (percent of par)	Final Maturity (years)	Average Life (years)	Yield-to-Final Maturity (percent)	Yield-to-Maturity (percent)	Interest-Rate Sensitivity (duration)
A. Zero-coupon	32.2	10	10	12	12	8.93
B. Coupon bond	88.7	10	10	12	12	5.85
C. Coupon bond with sinking fund	92.7	10	5.5	11.25	12	3.67

equal to 8.93 (10 years divided by $1 + r = 1.12$), which greatly exceeds that of the 10% coupon bond B with a maturity of 10 years and a duration of 5.85 years. Bond C has an average life of 5.5 years because of the sinking fund and a duration of only 3.67 years. This last bond is much less sensitive to changes in interest rates than the zero-coupon bond A with identical final maturity.

The true yield-to-maturity on each of these bonds is 12% when the sinking-fund schedule is taken into account. An institution calculating only the yield-to-final-maturity would find a yield of 11.25% for bond C, although its true YTM is 12% if one takes into account the fact that the bond is redeemed progressively.

Of course, there is no reason for these three bonds to have the same YTM, since they are so different in duration. The zero-coupon bond carries much more interest risk than the sinking-fund bond and should have a higher YTM in an upward-sloping yield curve.

Call Options Bonds are sometimes issued with a call or other options. This is very common in the Eurobond markets but less so in certain domestic markets, such as the British gilt market.

The most common call option is the right given to the issuer to call back the bond at a given date at a price set in the bond contract. This is profitable to the issuer if the market interest rate falls, because he or she can redeem high-coupon bonds and issue new bonds with a lower coupon.

Many other options are also found in the international market. For example, currency-option bonds give the investor an opportunity to benefit from currency movements. Bond options such as these are analyzed later.

Quality Spreads The interest rate required by a bondholder is a function of the default risk assumed: The greater the risk, the higher the yield that the borrower must pay. This implies that yields reflect a quality spread over the default-free rate.

In come countries credit-rating agencies asses the creditworthiness of borrowers with respect to specific obligations. The rating is based on both the likelihood of default and the nature, provisions, and protection afforded by specific obligations. Although such credit ratings are routinely provided on the U.S. bond market, they are rare on other national markets (with the exception of the United Kingdom and Japan). Standard & Poor's and Moody's now provide credit ratings on most international bonds (foreign bonds and Eurobonds). Exhibits 10.5 and 10.6 give the ratings scales used by these two agencies.

Governments are much heavier borrowers than corporations in the international market. To assess the creditworthiness of corporate borrowers, traditional analysis can be used, but for governments the task is trickier. That is why commercial banks and supranational lenders, such as the World Bank, have developed special techniques for forecasting sovereign default and assessing country risk. These techniques often rely on statistical methods. Two publications, *Euromoney* and *Institutional Investor,* regularly provide investors with country-risk rankings. *Euromoney* ranks countries according to the average spreads they pay on their

EXHIBIT 10.5

Moody's Long-Term Debt Ratings

Aaa

Bonds that are rated **Aaa** are judged to be of the best quality. They carry the smallest degree of investment risk and are generally referred to as *gilt edged*. Interest payments are protected by a large or by an exceptionally stable margin and principal is secure. While the various protective elements are likely to change, such changes as can be visualized are most unlikely to impair the fundamentally strong position of such issues.

Aa

Bonds that are rated **Aa** are judged to be of high quality by all standards. Together with the **Aaa** group they comprise what are generally known as high-grade bonds. They are rated lower than the best bonds because margins of protection may not be as large as in **Aaa** securities, fluctuation of protective elements may be of greater amplitude, or there may be other elements present that make the long-term risks appear somewhat larger than the **Aaa** securities.

A

Bonds that are rated **A** possess many favorable investment attributes and are to be considered upper-medium-grade obligations. Factors giving security to principal and interest are considered adequate, but elements may be present that suggest a susceptibility to impairment some time in the future.

Baa

Bonds that are rated **Baa** are considered as medium-grade obligations (i.e., they are neither highly protected nor poorly secured). Interest payments and principal security appear adequate for the present, but certain protective elements may be lacking or may be characteristically unreliable over any great length of time. Such bonds lack outstanding investment characteristics and in fact have speculative characteristics as well.

Ba

Bonds that are rated **Ba** are judged to have speculative elements; their future cannot be considered as well assured. Often the protection of interest and principal payments may be very moderate, and thereby not well safeguarded during both good and bad times over the future. Uncertainty of position characterizes bonds in this class.

B

Bonds that are rated **B** generally lack characteristics of the desirable investment. Assurance of interest and principal payments or of maintenance of other terms of the contract over any long period of time may be small.

Caa

Bonds that are rated **Caa** are of poor standing. Such issues may be in default or there may be present elements of danger with respect to principal or interest.

Ca

Bonds that are rated **Ca** represent obligations that are speculative to a high degree. Such issues are often in default or have other marked shortcomings.

C

Bonds that are rated **C** are the lowest-rated class of bonds, and issues so rated can be regarded as having extremely poor prospects of ever attaining any real investment standing.

Moody's applies numerical modifiers, **1**, **2**, and **3** in each generic rating classification from **Aa** through **B** in its corporate bond rating system. The modifier **1** indicates that the security ranks in the higher end of its generic rating category; the modifier **2** indicates a mid-range ranking; and the modifier **3** indicates that the issue ranks in the lower end of its generic rating category.

Source: Moody's Credit Ratings and Research, 1994.

EXHIBIT 10.6

Standard and Poor's Guide to International Ratings

Standard and Poor's debt rating is a current assessment of the creditworthiness of an obligor with respect to a specific obligation. This assessment may take into consideration obligors such as guarantors, insurers, or lessees.

The debt rating is not a recommendation to purchase, sell, or hold a security, inasmuch as it does not comment on market price or suitability for a particular investor.

The ratings are based on current information furnished by the issuer or obtained by S + P from other sources it considers reliable. S + P does not perform an audit in connection with any rating and may, on occasion, rely on unaudited financial information. The ratings may be changed, suspended, or withdrawn as a result of changes in, or unavailability of, such information, or for other circumstances.

The ratings are based, in varying degrees, on the following considerations:

1. Likelihood of default. Capacity and willingness of the obligor as to the timely payment of interest and repayment of principal in accordance with the terms of the obligation.
2. Nature and provisions of the obligation.
3. Protection afforded by, and relative position of, the obligation in the event of bankruptcy, reorganization, or other arrangement under the laws of bankruptcy and other laws affecting creditor's rights.

AAA

Debt rated **AAA** has the highest rating assigned by Standard & Poor's. Capacity to pay interest and repay principal is extremely strong.

AA

Debt rated **AA** has a very strong capacity to pay interest and repay principal and differs from the highest-rated issues only to a small degree.

A

Debt rated **A** has a strong capacity to pay interest and repay principal, although it is somewhat more susceptible to the adverse effects of changes in circumstances and economic conditions than debt in higher rated categories.

(continued on next page)

BBB

Debt rated **BBB** is regarded as having an adequate capacity to pay interest and repay principal. While it normally exhibits adequate protection parameters, adverse economic conditions or changing circumstances are more likely to lead to a weakened capacity to pay interest and repay principal for debt in this category than in higher rated categories.

BB, B, CCC, CC, and **C**

Debt rated **BB**, **B**, **CCC**, **CC**, and **C** is regarded, on balance, as predominantly speculative with respect to capacity to pay interest and repay principal in accordance with the terms of the obligation. **BB** indicates the lowest degree of speculation and **C** the highest degree of speculation. While such debt will likely have some quality and protective characteristics, these are outweighed by large uncertainties or major risk exposures to adverse conditions.

D

Debt rated **D** is in default, and payment of interest and/or repayment of principal is in arrears.

Plus (+) or minus (−)

The ratings from **AA** to **CCC** may be modified by the addition of a plus or minus sign to show relative standing within the major rating categories.

r

The letter **r** is attached to highlight derivative, hybrid, and certain other obligations that S + P believes may experience high volatility or high variability in expected returns due to non-credit risks.

N.R.

Indicates no rating has been requested, that there is insufficient information on which to base a rating, or that S + P does not rate a particular type of obligation as a matter of policy.

Debt obligations of issuers outside the United States and its territories are rated on the same basis as domestic corporate and municipal issues. The ratings measure the creditworthiness of the obligor to repay in the currency of denomination of the issue. However, S + P does not assess the foreign exchange risk that the investor may bear.

Source: Standard and Poor's Debt Rating Definitions, November 1994.

Euromarket borrowing. *Institutional Investor* surveys the lending officers of the largest banks in order to establish their country ranking. To be sure, no method is perfect. The spread over the London interbank offered rate (LIBOR) depends partly on market conditions at the time of borrowing. When markets are liquid, the spread is reduced for every borrower. Moreover, front-end and management fees should, to some extent, be taken into consideration. Also, the popularity-poll approach of the *Institutional Investor* survey introduces some bias into its ranking. As shown in Exh. 10.7, country-risk rankings sometimes differ according to the analysis techniques used. For example, the Swiss government is considered more risky than the Canadian government, according to the *Euromoney* ranking, but not according to the *Institutional Investor* ranking.

EXHIBIT 10.7

Risk Ranking for a Selected List of Localities as of March 1994

Locality	Institutional Investor Ranking	Euromoney Ranking
Switzerland	1	6
Japan	2	13
United States	3	1
Germany	4	9
Netherlands	5	5
France	6	7
United Kingdom	7	12
Austria	8	2
Luxembourg	9	3
Canada	10	4
Singapore	11	10
Spain	16	19
Hong Kong	26	24
Mexico	42	46

It should be clear that the currency borrowed can affect default risk. For example, there is little risk of the Mexican government defaulting on Mexican peso bonds, because it has the power to print its own money.

There is no consensus on the credit ratings of corporations and governments. The Swiss market, which is the second-largest international bond market, seems to favor private corporations over supranational entities and governments. Swiss, British, and U.S. assessments of creditworthiness for certain European borrowers can differ quite markedly at times. Several money-management institutions, in fact, have developed their own credit-rating methods. This implies that the link between a quality spread on a bond yield and its credit rating by an agency is not as close as it is in the United States.

Specific International Techniques

International bond investment demands special analysis techniques. Several of the more commonly used techniques are described here.

Bond issues in a specific currency are sometimes found in several markets. For example, U.S. dollar bonds are issued on both the domestic U.S. market and the Eurobond markets. There are several reasons for this. One is that foreign firms often prefer to raise money on the Eurobond market rather than the Yankee bond market, the U.S. market for foreign borrowers, simply to avoid U.S. regulations.

Differential tax treatment also encourages the development of parallel bond markets (see Chapter 9). By purchasing Eurobonds, foreign investors can avoid the withholding tax that is sometimes imposed on them in national markets. Confidentiality is another consideration, at least for those private investors who prefer to remain anonymous. This is possible on the Eurobond market but not on some domestic markets. These factors, in turn, influence the yield differential between various market segments in the same currency.

Another important aspect of the international bond market is its large number of nonstandard issues. A sizable portion of the U.S. dollar Eurobond market is made up of floating-rate notes commonly referred to as floaters, or FRNs. Technical analysis of FRNs is quite different from that of fixed-interest bonds. International bankers are extremely inventive in this area, and as a result there is a large number of bonds in all currencies with unusual clauses and options, including renewable bonds, currency options, and dual-currency bonds. New instruments appear almost daily; therefore investors must develop the ability to analyze innovative bonds quickly. The analysis of FRNs and *fancy* bonds is discussed later in this chapter.

The multicurrency dimension is the major complication of international bond investment. A strategic approach implies decisions about currencies and maturities and requires the use of analytical tools to merge interest and exchange rate analysis.

International Yield Curve Comparisons   A term structure of interest rates exists for each currency. Investors focus on the yield curve for government bonds. However, other yield curves may be drawn beside the default-free term structure, depending on the quality of the bond and the market sectors. Yields-to-maturity generally differ across currencies. As we discussed in Chapters 2 and 3, international interest rate differences are caused by a variety of factors, including differences in national monetary and fiscal policies and inflationary expectations. Furthermore, the interest rate differential for two currencies is not constant over the maturity spectrum.

Term structures for U.S. dollar and British pound bonds are given in Exh. 10.8. These are hypothetical yield curves for government securities and are meant to serve as an illustration. We see that the U.S. short-term interest rate is much lower than the British rate. The British yield curve peaks at around five years, and thereafter the difference in yield between the two curves goes from 300 basis points down to approximately 80 basis points for very long-term bonds. These two yield curves are not atypical: For some dates the yield curve may be upward sloping in one currency and downward sloping in others. Yield curves for various currencies are shown in Exh. 10.9.

Clearly the difference in yield curves between two currencies is caused by foreign exchange expectations. Otherwise, arbitrage would occur between bonds denominated in different currencies. This key relation between interest rate differences and exchange rate expectations for a given maturity is the subject of our next discussion.

EXHIBIT 10.8

Example of Yield Curves for U.S. Dollar and British Pound Bonds

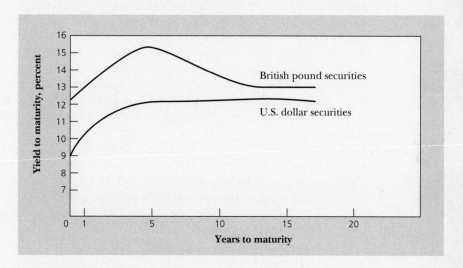

EXHIBIT 10.9

Yield Curves for Various Currencies Based on Eurobond Yields

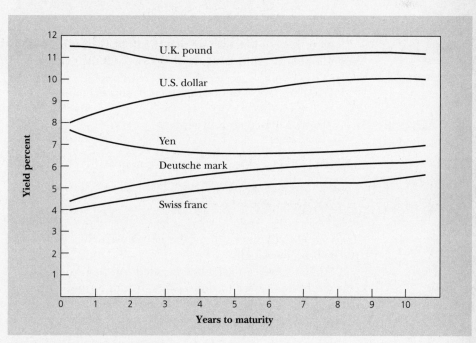

Source: James Capel and Co., November 1985.

Implied Forward Exchange Rates   The purpose of this section is to introduce the analytical tools that can help a manager to choose an optimal investment strategy given a particular exchange rate–interest rate scenario. Our main objective is to determine the implication for exchange rates of yield differentials on bonds denominated in different currencies but with similar maturities. In other words: How do we compare exchange rate movements and yield-to-maturity differentials?

A higher yield in one currency is often compensated, ex-post, by a depreciation in this currency and in turn an offsetting currency loss on the bond. It is important to know how much currency movement will exactly compensate the yield differential. This subject was already discussed for short-term instruments in Chapters 1 and 2.

Let's consider a one-year bond with an interest rate r_1 in domestic currency and $r_1{}^*$ in foreign currency. The current exchange rate is S, expressed as the domestic currency value of one unit of a foreign currency. One year from now the exchange rate must move to a level F_1 in order to make the two investments identical, i.e., have the same total return. In Chapter 1 we called the forward exchange rate F_1. It is expressed as follows:

$$1 + r_1 = \left(1 + r_1{}^*\right)\frac{F_1}{S}. \tag{10.9}$$

The implied offsetting currency depreciation is given by

$$\Delta S_1 = \frac{F_1 - S}{S} = \frac{\left(r_1 - r_1{}^*\right)}{1 + r_1{}^*}.$$

As an illustration, assume that the dollar one-year interest rate is $r_1 = 10\%$, the pound one-year interest rate is $r_1{}^* = 13\%$, and the current exchange rate is $S = 2.00$ dollars per pound.

From Eq. (10.9) we see that the forward exchange rate equals

$$F_1 = S\,\frac{1 + r_1}{1 + r_1{}^*} = 2.0\,\frac{1.10}{1.13} = 1.947.$$

The implied offsetting currency movement is therefore equal to

$$\Delta S_1 = \frac{\left(1.947 - 2.0\right)}{2.0} = -2.65\%.$$

Thus a 2.65% depreciation of the pound will exactly offset the yield advantage on the British investment.

Similarly, we can calculate implied forward exchange rates on two-year zero-coupon bonds, as well as on bonds of longer maturity. By comparing the yield curves in two currencies, we can derive the term structure of implied forward exchange rates and therefore of implied currency appreciation or depreciation.

The implied forward exchange rate for a *t*-year bond is given by Eq. 10.10):

$$\frac{F_t}{S} = \left(\frac{1+r_t}{1+r_t{}^*} \right)^t .$$

(10.10)

The implied currency appreciation or depreciation over the *t*-year period is equal to

$$\Delta S_t = \left(\frac{1+r_t}{1+r_t{}^*} \right)^t - 1 .$$

The calculations for the term structures shown in Exh. 10.8 are given in Exh. 10.10 and Exh. 10.11. We find that the implied pound/dollar exchange rate initially declines with time (pound depreciation). On a five-year investment, the break-even exchange rate is £1 = \$1.745, a 12.75% depreciation of the pound. In other words, an investor would get a similar five-year return on the British and U.S. bond investments if the pound were to depreciate 12.75% by the end of the period. Note that this result holds only for investments having this five-year maturity.

These simple calculations assume that we use yield curves for zero-coupon bonds. The formulas are slightly more complicated if we use the yield curves for coupon bonds, because we must assume that the coupons are reinvested each year or semester until final maturity. Computations for coupon bonds are given in the appendix to this chapter.

Applications   The implied forward exchange rate is not a forecast but rather a break-even point. It provides investors with a yardstick against which to measure their own foreign exchange forecasts. In our hypothetical example U.S. dollar bond investments are clearly not attractive if we expect a depreciation of the U.S. dollar relative to the British pound. By the same token, a 20% depreciation of the pound makes British bonds unattractive whatever their maturity.

In order to pick bond maturities, we examine the term structure of implied forward exchange rates shown in Exh. 10.11. If exchange rate trends are our major concern, a long-term investment (over seven years) in British pounds bonds is unattractive because the maximum implied depreciation obtains for less than seven years. It should be remembered, however, that this result is atypical. Most implied exchange rate curves are not bumped like that for British pounds; usually they just slope upward or downward.

Another illustration of the use of this concept is found in comparing the U.S. dollar and Swiss franc bond market in 1984. In August 1984 10-year bond yields for U.S. dollar and Swiss franc bonds of comparable quality were 12.25% and 5%, respectively. This disparity in yields suggests that the U.S. dollar would have to depreciate by 50% in order to make the Swiss investment attractive. In other words, the Swiss franc would have to move from roughly \$0.4 to \$0.8. Few investors at the time would have taken the risk of betting on so weak a dollar, but this dollar depreciation did take place.

EXHIBIT 10.10

Implied Forward Exchange Rates and Offsetting Currency Depreciation
(U.S. dollar per British sterling)

Maturity (years)	1	2	3	4	5	6	7
Sterling yield (percent)	13.00	13.75	14.25	14.75	15.00	14.80	14.20
Dollar yield (percent)	10.00	11.00	11.50	11.75	11.90	11.95	12.00
Forward exchange rate (dollar/pound)	1.947	1.904	1.859	1.799	1.745	1.720	1.754
Currency depreciation (percent)	2.65	4.78	7.05	10.06	12.75	14.00	12.73

A more precise scenario analysis can be performed for individual bonds. Consider an investor from the United Kingdom who wants to buy bonds denominated in a foreign currency, say Deutsche marks. Bonds are available on the market, with a variety of coupons and sinking-fund provisions. In order to evaluate them, our investor should posit several scenarios for the British pound/Deutsche mark exchange rate over time. Actuaries can compute the expected pound return for each bond, given these scenarios, by translating each bond payment at the expected exchange rate on the payment date. For example, a rapid Deutsche mark appreciation over the next two years followed by a period of stable exchange rate would make high-coupon short-term Euro-Deutsche mark bonds very attractive.

EXHIBIT 10.11

Implied Forward Exchange Rates and Offsetting Currency Depreciation

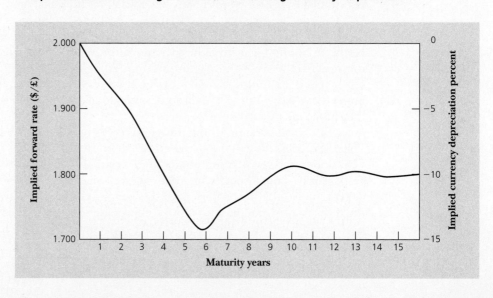

8	9	10	11	12	13	14	15
13.80	13.50	13.20	13.10	13.00	13.00	12.95	12.90
12.00	12.05	12.10	12.10	12.10	12.10	12.10	12.10
1.760	1.781	1.814	1.814	1.798	1.802	1.799	1.798
11.97	10.93	9.30	9.31	10.11	9.87	10.05	10.12

Banks are interested in bonds for both lending and borrowing, and several banks in Europe prepare tables simulating a variety of currency scenarios (i.e., one-time depreciation, trends, and combinations) and their influence on bond returns. A final step is to engage in active currency hedging on bonds, as explained in Chapter 14.

Floating-Rate Notes

Investment bankers on the international bond market are notoriously inventive when it comes to escaping domestic regulations. U.S. commercial bankers, on the other hand, are very active in floating new issues abroad. Investment bankers bring domestic expertise from around the world to bear on the international market, and that is why it boasts so many sophisticated techniques. This sophistication is evident in the incredible diversity of bonds issued, which in turn makes the analysis all the more difficult and technical.

Apart from the straight bonds discussed earlier, there are two other major categories of bonds: index-linked bonds and bonds with options.

Indexation

Several types of index-linked bonds are found on both domestic markets and international markets. In countries with high and volatile inflation, bonds indexed either to inflation or to the price of a specific commodity are common. In 1981, for instance, the U.K. government started issuing index-linked gilts. Both the coupon payments and the final payment at maturity of these bonds are adjusted in line with changes in the U.K. retail price index. The French and Danish governments have issued bonds indexed to the price of gold (*gold bonds*), and Mexican firms have issued bonds indexed to the price of oil (*petro bonds*). Other countries have issued inflation-indexed bonds, but these issues attract mainly local investors.

In the Eurobond market private corporations have occasionally indexed coupons to some quantity or price index. For example, Club Meditérranée issued a U.S. dollar bond with a coupon indexed to both the average price of a vacation in their U.S.-zone villages and their occupancy rate.

The most common index-linked bonds are floating-rate notes. The coupon paid on these bonds is indexed to some variable interest rate. Floating-rate notes do not exist on all national bond markets, but this is rapidly changing. France, where a large variety of FRNs has recently been issued, is a notable example. The clauses used in interest-rate indexation are also very diverse, as we see from the examples that follow:

- The coupon may be indexed to a short- or long-term interest rate.

- The reference interest rate may be a recent value or a yearly or quarterly average.

- The coupon may be pre- or postdetermined, i.e., either the coupon is known for the coupon period in reference to the interest rate valid at the start of the period, or the coupon is set on the payment date in reference to the current interest rate.

- The spread over the reference interest rate may be multiplicative or additive.

- Minimum and maximum values for the reference rate may be specified.

These diverse clauses make accurate valuation of an FRN a difficult but valuable exercise.

Floating-rate notes were first issued on the U.S. domestic market with a coupon set at a spread over the Treasury bill rate. Dollar-denominated FRNs are usually in great demand by U.S. thrift institutions because of the development of money-market deposit accounts and the rapid growth of the U.S. FRN market.

The largest FRN market is the U.S. dollar international market. Eurodollar FRNs represented 20% of all new U.S. dollar issues in the international bond market in 1993. There is also a market for floating-rate notes in other currencies. Euro-FRNs are generally indexed to the London InterBank Offered Rate[6] (LIBOR), which is the short-term deposit rate on Eurocurrencies. The coupon on Eurobond FRNs is generally reset every semester or every quarter. The maturity of the LIBOR chosen as index usually matches the coupon period; for example, FRNs with semi-annual coupons are indexed on the six-month LIBOR. The coupon to be paid is determined on the reset date, which usually coincides with the previous coupon date. On the reset date, the value of the index (say, the six-month LIBOR) is determined by looking at the quotations of major London banks. The coupon to be paid the next period is then set equal to the LIBOR plus a spread that has been fixed at the time of issue. In other words, the coupon, C_t, that will be paid at time t

is set at time $t-1$ (the previous coupon date) equal to the LIBOR rate, i_{t-1}, plus a fixed spread, m_0.

$$C_t = i_{t-1} + m_0 \qquad (10.11)$$

All rates are quoted in percent. The spread is fixed when the bond is issued and generally remains fixed for the maturity of the bond. Some FRNs are issued with various mismatches that deviate from the plain-vanilla FRN described earlier.

FRN prices behave quite differently from straight bond prices, which adjust to fluctuations in the market interest rate. The price of a straight bond must go down if the market interest rate goes up, in order to maintain a competitive yield-to-maturity. By contrast, floaters have coupons that adjust to interest rates, so the coupons react to interest rate movements rather than the bond price. This means that FRNs exhibit great price stability when compared to straight bonds. The difference in volatility is illustrated in Exh. 10.12, which shows the comparative performance (from December 1977 to mid-1983) of FRNs, U.S. government bonds, Euro-CDs, and three-month Treasury bills. All indexes assume that the income is reinvested. We see that the annualized standard deviation of returns on Euro-FRNs

EXHIBIT 10.12

Cumulative Total Return Indexes

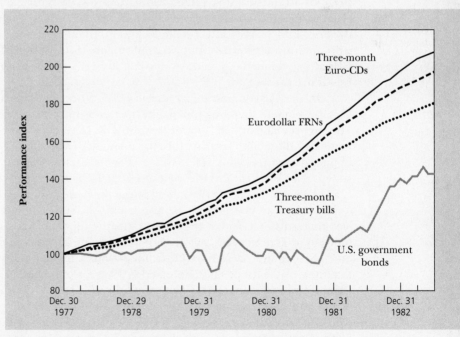

Source: J. Hanna and G. Pariente, *International Bond Market Analysis*, Salomon Brothers, July 1983. Reprinted with permission.

(1.5% per year) is historically much less than that on either U.S. government bonds (12.1% per year) or Eurodollar straight bonds (8.9% per year), although it is comparable to that of domestic- or Euro-CDs (1.5% per year).

From a theoretical point of view, we may ask why there is any price variability at all on floating-rate bonds. It turns out that there are several major reasons for this price variability, which we will illustrate by taking examples from the Eurodollar market.

Choice of Index

Borrowers must offer a spread, or margin, over the reference interest rate. This spread is determined by the credit quality of the borrower: The more risky the borrower, the higher the spread that must be paid. As with any other debt instrument, the price performance of FRNs depends on the market perception of the borrower's credit standing. Changes over time in a borrower's credit standing affect the price of outstanding bonds.

For top-quality issuers the spread is very small (⅛% or ¹⁄₁₆%), because some of them, like banks, can easily borrow in the Eurodollar short-term deposit market at LIBOR.[7] The minimum spread paid by these top-quality issuers changes only slightly over time in response to market conditions. This, in turn, affects the bond price of all outstanding FRNs. From 1981 to 1982, for example, institutional investors—pension funds, savings institutions, and insurance companies—entered the Euro-FRN market and accepted a lower minimum spread because the yield was still more attractive than that on money-market investment alternatives, such as CDs and commercial paper. All outstanding FRN prices benefited from this narrowed market spread.

On the U.S. domestic market, no corporation can borrow as cheaply as the U.S. Treasury, so that even top-quality borrowers must pay a sizable spread over the Treasury bill rate, which is lower than LIBOR. In recent years the yield differential between LIBOR and Treasury bills has fluctuated between one and five percentage points. The differential widens when there is a risk of disruption in the banking system. Not surprisingly, the yield on U.S. Treasury bills is very low (relative to LIBOR) when the U.S. government is the only safe borrower in U.S. dollars: The government can always print money to pay its debts. Unfortunately, FRN issuers lack that privilege, so that their credit quality is lower. That is why domestic FRNs indexed to Treasury bill rates are not an attractive investment during panicky periods. They are as risky as Euro-FRNs but provide a much lower yield, with the result that their prices drop. This happened in 1982 during the so-called flight to quality, when investors feared less-developed countries (LDC) bankruptcies and a collapse of the international banking system. For a time, the Treasury bill–versus–LIBOR yield differential reached 400 basis points, and the price of U.S. domestic FRNs dropped by 5%, yet Euro-FRNs remained stable. In fact, U.S. domestic FRNs indexed to Treasury bills always exhibit more price volatility than Euro-FRNs indexed to LIBOR, although domestic issues limit price variability by employing more frequent coupon revisions that have adjustable spreads and put clauses. This is shown in Exh. 10.13.

It pays to be careful in selecting the reference interest rate for an issue. In order to limit price variability, an index should behave like the short-term interest rate available on a typical top-quality borrower in the FRN market.

EXHIBIT 10.13

Price Volatility: Eurodollar versus Domestic FRNs
Semiannual, long maturity

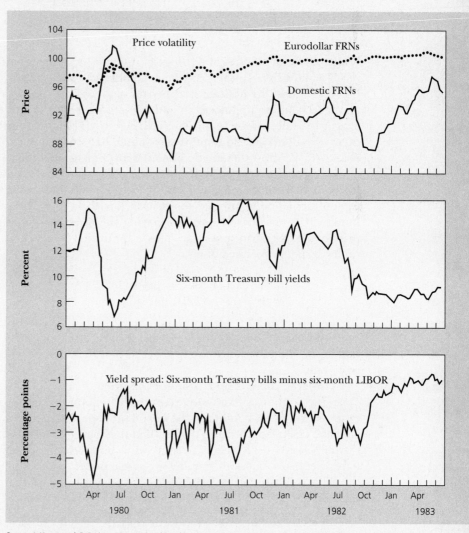

Source: J. Hanna and G. Pariente, *International Bond Market Analysis*, Salomon Brothers, July 1983. Reprinted with permission.

Reset Date

FRN coupons are periodically reset, or rolled over. The rollover may be annual, semiannual, or quarterly. This means that the coupon is fixed at the reset, or rollover, date for the coming period. The first question is to determine the theoretical price of the bond on reset date, when the previous coupon has just been paid and the new coupon has just been fixed for the coming period. To disentangle the effects, it is useful to start the analysis by assuming that the borrower has, and will have, no default risk and that the index has been chosen as the relevant short-term interest rate for that borrower. For example, assume that an FRN with annual reset is issued by a major bank, which has to pay exactly LIBOR without any spread, in the absence of default risk:

$$C_t = i_{t-1}. \tag{10.12}$$

Remember that all rates and prices are quoted in percent. Under this assumption of no default risk, we can show that the price of the bond should always be 100% on reset dates. To further simplify the analysis, assume that the coupons are annual. The reasoning needs to go *backward*. There is a future date when we know exactly the value of the bond: This is at maturity T. Right after the last coupon payment, the bond will be reimbursed at 100. Let's now move to the previous reset date $T-1$. We know that the bond contract stipulates that the coupon C_T will be set equal to the one-year LIBOR observed at time $T-1$. Of course, we do *not* know today (time 0) what this rate will be at $T-1$, but we know that it will be *exactly* equal, by contractual obligation, to the market rate for a one-year instrument. Hence a bond with a maturity of one year paying the one-year interest rate must have a price equal to its principal value. This is confirmed by discounting at time $T-1$, the future cash flow received at time T:

$$P_{T-1} = \frac{100\% + C_T}{1 + i_{T-1}} = \frac{1 + i_{T-1}}{1 + i_{T-1}} = 100\%. \tag{10.13}$$

We now know that the price one period before maturity must be equal to 100. We can apply the same reasoning to the price of the bond at time $T-2$, and so on, until time 0. We have therefore shown that the bond price must be equal to 100 at each reset date.

However, there is no reason for the price to stay constant *between* reset dates. Once the coupon is fixed on a reset date, the bond tends to behave like a short-term fixed-coupon bond until the next reset date. FRN prices are more volatile just after the reset date, because that is when they have the longest fixed-coupon maturity. FRNs with a semiannual reset tend to be more volatile than FRNs with quarterly reset dates, but both should have stable prices on reset dates.

This is illustrated in Exh. 10.14 for the price of a Midland Bank FRN with a semiannual reset. Note that in December 1980 the six-month Eurodollar rate climbed suddenly from 15% to over 20%, just after the coupon on the bond had

EXHIBIT 10.14

Eurodollar FRNs: The Stability of Rollover Date Prices
Midland Bank, May 1987

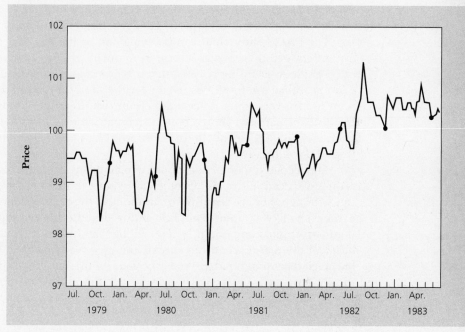

Source: J. Hanna and G. Pariente, *International Bond Market Analysis*, Salomon Brothers, July 1983. Reprinted with permission.

been reset. This induced a 2% drop in the bond price. By contrast, the prices on reset dates are very stable. Practitioners usually consider that the interest sensitivity to movements in the index interest rate is simply equal to the (modified) duration to the next reset date. Consider a bond with a new reset date in five months. Its sensitivity to a sudden change in LIBOR should be equal to:

$$D_i^* \approx \frac{5}{12} = 0.4 \text{ years}$$

or

$$\text{Percent change in } P = -D_i^* \times \text{Change in index rate.} \tag{10.14}$$

If the LIBOR rises by 10 basis points, the bond price should drop by 4 basis points.

In practice, issuers carry some default risk, and a spread over LIBOR is required by the market. This can explain why the prices on reset dates observed on Exh. 10.14 are not exactly equal to 100.

Spread, Maturity, and Price Volatility

Research shows that FRNs with long maturities tend to sell at a discount relative to those of short maturity. Long-term FRNs are also more volatile than short-term FRNs. Changes in the spread required by the marketplace explain these observations. The market-required spread changes with the perception of credit risk.

The first phenomenon can be explained by the fact that the default risk premium tends to increase with time to maturity. A 20-year loan to a corporation, rated single A, seems more risky than a 3-month loan to the same corporation. The coupon spread on an FRN is fixed over the life of the bond, whereas the market-required spread, which reflects the credit risk premium, tends to decrease as the bond nears maturity. Hence bond prices, at least on reset dates, should progressively increase. Of course, there is a survival bias, since defaulted bonds disappear from the comparison.

The second phenomenon can be explained by *unexpected* changes in the market-required spread. FRNs are "protected" against movements in the market interest rates, though they are sensitive to variations in the required spread, as we discussed earlier. The FRN coupon is not fully indexed to the market-required yield, because the interest rate component is indexed, but the spread is fixed over the life of the bond. If the market-required spread changes over time, the FRN behaves partly like a fixed-coupon bond, precisely because of this feature. And we know that technically, long-term bonds are more sensitive than short-term bonds to changes in market yield. By contrast, short-term bonds are repaid sooner, and this drives their price close to par.

This price volatility induced by the fixity of the spread is illustrated in Exh. 10.15 for the price of a Midland Bank perpetual FRN, with semiannual reset at LIBOR plus 0.25% (a spread of 25 basis points). The price remained relatively stable until 1987, when an international debt crisis threatened the international financial system. Investors became afraid that banks had too many bad loans, especially to many emerging countries, which stopped servicing their debts. They feared that the default of a few banks would lead to the collapse of the international banking system. Lenders shied away from the long-term debts of banks. The required risk premium for holding FRNs issued by banks increased by 100 basis points within a few weeks. This led to a huge drop in FRN prices, as can be seen in Exh. 10.15. In a way the sensitivity of an FRN bond price to a change in the market-required spread is like the sensitivity of a straight bond price to a change in the required yield. Some practitioners calculate a standard duration for the FRN, as shown in Eqs. (10.7) and (10.8), *assuming* that the index rate will stay *constant* over the life of the bond. They use this duration to evaluate the sensitivity of the FRN to changes in the required spread. This measure of duration is sometimes called the *spread duration* D_s^*. The volatility associated with a change in market-required spread is given by

$$\text{Percent change in } P = -D_s^* \times \text{Change in market-required spread.} \qquad (10.15)$$

EXHIBIT 10.15

Eurodollar FRNs: The Impact of a Change in Market-Required Spread
Perpetual Midland Bank FRN, LIBOR plus 0.25%

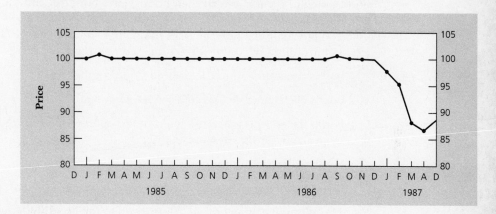

With a LIBOR around 7%, the perpetual FRN of Exh. 10.15 had a spread duration of 14, so an increase in the market-required spread of 100 basis points translated into a drop in bond price of 14%.

Other factors, such as minimum coupons, sinking-fund, and call provisions, may also affect FRN prices. Some exotic FRNs are discussed in the Questions and Problems section.

Bonds with Options

A variety of option clauses may now be found on all domestic bond markets but with varying frequency. A *call option* permits an issuer to redeem a bond early at a set price. It is the most common option clause in many markets but is still unusual in the French bond market and in many government bond markets, including those in Europe and Japan. A call option works to the advantage of the bond issuer whenever the market interest rate drops, because the issuer can call back the bond at a preset price and issue a new bond at a lower market rate. Conversely, this feature works to the disadvantage of the bondholder. In the absence of a call, the market price of a bond goes up when the market interest rate goes down. This is not so when a bond has a call because of the risk that the issuer will call the bond back. As such, the presence of a call deprives the investor of an opportunity for capital gain.

Some bonds are issued with a *put option*, which entitles the bondholder to redeem the bond at a preset price. It is to the bondholder's advantage to do so whenever interest rates go up and the bond price concomitantly drops. Some bonds, such as French and Belgian bonds, have both call and put options with different exercise prices.

The international bond market has seen a large number of innovative option clauses introduced in recent years. Other common options are as follows:

- bonds convertible into the common stock of the issuer

- bonds exchangeable for bonds with longer maturity

- bonds issued with warrants, i.e., with the option to buy more bonds with the same characteristics at a preset price

- bonds with warrants for common stock

- floating-rate bonds convertible into fixed interest rate bonds and vice versa.

The advantage of an option clause given to the bondholder is that the investor has the right to exercise it when it can yield the most benefit. It protects against risk without affecting the return on investment if the risk does not materialize. When an option has value to the holder, as with a put option, it can be issued at an interest rate lower than the market yield for straight bonds of comparable quality. The investor loses in terms of yield what is gained in terms of risk protection. A major challenge for the investor is determining the value of each option clause. Pricing of the bonds requires knowing how much interest rate reduction the market will accept as compensation for the option.

When an option is controlled by the bond issuer, e.g., a call provision, it is exercised only in the issuer's best interest, which means to the disadvantage of the bondholder. That is why a bond with a call option must offer a higher interest rate than a comparable straight bond.

Option Clause Valuation

A call provision is the easiest to value. Let's consider a perpetuity issued at par in the year 2000 with a coupon of 12%. The bond is callable in 2005 at a price of $100. Let's now assume that in 2004 interest rates have dropped. The very-long-term market rate is 10%, and the one-year interest rate is 9%. The term structure of interest rates is therefore upward sloping. Recalling Eq. (10.4), the market price of a perpetuity without a call option is easily computed[8] as follows:

$$P = \frac{C}{r},$$

where C is the coupon and r is the interest rate.

Here

$$P = \frac{12}{0.10} = 120.$$

There is a high probability that this bond will be called the following year at a price of \$100. If the bond is certain to be called, it should be valued in 2004 as a one-year bond yielding a one-year return of 9%. Its market price should be \$102.75 so that it provides a yield-to-next-call of 9%:

$$P = \frac{100 + 12}{1.09} = 102.75.$$

In practice we would expect the bond to be called while the market long-term interest rate stays below 12%. Given the 10% rate for the year ahead, it seems likely, but not certain, that the call will be exercised. The market price of this bond should be close to \$102.75.

Determining a precise theoretical market value requires an option valuation model similar to the Black-Scholes model presented in Chapter 13. Conceptually the call option price we derive from the option model should be subtracted from the straight bond price (\$120, in this example). Once the volatility of the bond's price has been estimated, the theoretical value of an option to repurchase the bond at a price P_E while it currently quotes P can be calculated. Let's call this value $P_0 (P)$. Then the theoretical value of the bond is equal to the value of the bond without the option clause (*naked bond*) minus the value of the option. The value of the naked bond is simply the present value of all coupon and principal payments discounted at the current market interest rate. In the example the value of the naked bond is $P_N = \$120$. In this simple approach the theoretical value of the callable bond is given by the following equation:

$$P = P_N - P_0(P_N). \tag{10.16}$$

As shown in Chapter 13, the option value can be broken down into two parts: the intrinsic value, which is the value of the option if it were exercised immediately, and the time value of the option. The intrinsic value is equal to 0 if the naked bond is worth less than the callable price P_E; it is equal to the difference between the bond price and the callable price (otherwise, $P_N - P_E$). Of course, the coupon should also be taken into account.

The formula becomes more complicated if the call option can be exercised at various dates in the future. Brennan and Schwartz (1977) have provided general valuation formulas for bonds with put and call options.

It should be stressed that the concept of a single yield-to-maturity on a callable bond becomes very fuzzy because of the uncertainty as to what the maturity will actually be. Practitioners often choose the minimum of the yield-to-next-call and the yield-to-maturity without the call. In other words, they assume that the most pessimistic scenario will take place. This convention tends to systematically under-estimate the true expected YTM, because interest rates can move widely before the call is exercisable. A year before the call date, exercise of the call may seem unlikely (high yield-to-next-call relative to YTM), but a year later interest rates could drop, so that it would be to the issuer's advantage to exercise the call. If that happened, the ex-post yield for the investor would turn out to be the higher, not the lower, of the two alternatives.

Currency Option Bonds

Because international investors invest in several currencies, some bond option clauses address currency risks. Bonds with these clauses are said to have a *currency option*. During the early 1970s, certain bonds were issued with a Deutsche mark/sterling currency option. This particular option gives the bondholder the right to receive principal and interest payments in either sterling or Deutsche marks, whichever is more advantageous to the investor. Both the coupon rate and the sterling/Deutsche mark exchange rate are fixed during the life of the bond. In June 1972 Rothmans International issued a 20-year sterling Deutsche mark bond of this type with a coupon rate of 6.25% and a fixed exchange rate of 7.80 Deutsche marks per sterling. The bond was issued in sterling so that each £1000 bond paid an annual coupon of either £62.50 or DM 487.5, whichever the bondholder preferred. The exchange rate of 7.80 Deutsche marks for a British pound was roughly the market exchange rate at the time of issue. Ten years later, in 1982, the sterling/Deutsche mark exchange rate had dropped by 50% to roughly 3.90 Deutsche marks per sterling. Naturally, investors preferred their interest payments in Deutsche marks at that time, since a coupon of DM 487.5 represented £125, or twice the amount the coupon paid in sterling. For all practical purposes, the Rothmans International bond had become a Deutsche mark bond with a coupon of 6.25%, because it is very unlikely that sterling will return to its 1972 exchange rate of 7.80 Deutsche marks. Moreover, as of 1982 the sterling coupon rate of this bond was a full 12.50%, since the bondholder could convert the coupon of DM 487.5 at the market exchange rate of 3.90 Deutsche marks per sterling and thereby receive 125 sterling for an initial investment of £1000.

A currency option bond benefits the investor, who can always select the stronger currency. On the other hand, the interest rate at issue is always lower than the interest rate paid on single-currency straight bonds denominated in either currency. A call redemption clause usually protects the issuer against a large movement in one of the currencies. Only a few currency option bonds have been issued lately, since they are considered too risky by issuers.

In 1972 Rothmans should have paid approximately 10% on a straight sterling bond and 8.75% on a straight Deutsche mark bond. It should be obvious that the currency option bond must be issued at a coupon below the lowest of the two interest rates if the option clause is to be of any value. In our case a Rothmans bond investor ended up with a Deutsche mark bond with a coupon of 6.25%, whereas he or she could have obtained 8.75% on a straight Deutsche mark bond. On the other hand, the investor is better off than if he or she had bought a 10% straight sterling bond.

The value of such a currency option bond can be broken down into two elements: the value of a straight 6.25% Deutsche mark bond and the value of an option to swap a 6.25% Deutsche mark bond for a 6.25% sterling bond at a fixed exchange rate of 7.8 DM/£. So the value of this bond is the sum of the value of a straight bond plus the value of an option on a currency swap contract. Basically the issuer is writing the currency swap option. Of course, the bond value could also be seen as the sum of a straight 6.25% sterling bond plus an option for a £/DM currency swap. The major difficulty in valuing such a bond is the theoretical valuation of the currency swap option.

Feiger and Jacquillat studied the application of option theory to currency option bonds.[9] As with any option model, they found that the value of a currency option bond depends mainly on two factors: the parameters set in the option clauses, such as the conversion rate and exercise date, and the volatility of the exchange rate. Various valuation exercises on currency-option bonds are proposed in the Questions and Problems section.

Dual-Currency Convertible Bonds

A more common currency option clause is found in bonds issued in one currency and convertible into common stocks (or bonds) quoted in another currency. Japanese issuers have frequently issued bonds in U.S. dollars (or sterling, Deutsche marks, Swiss francs, etc.) convertible into shares of the Japanese company. For example, Toshiba, a Japanese electronics firm, issued bonds denominated in Swiss francs and convertible into shares of Toshiba quoted in yen with a fixed rate of currency conversion. The bond issue is described in Exh. 10.16. The currency conversion rate is fixed at ¥ 103.44 = SF 1, and the stock-conversion price (¥ 449) determines exactly how many common stocks can be acquired if the SF 5000 bond is converted. At conversion, one common share of Toshiba is exchanged for 4.3407 Swiss francs worth of bonds (449/103.44). So for one bond of denomination SF 5000, the bondholder can get 5000/4.3407 = 1152 shares of Toshiba. Note that the U.S. dollar–based investor has three profit potentials:

1. The investor benefits if the Swiss interest rate drops and the Swiss franc rises relative to the investor's home currency (i.e., the dollar); this is true of any Swiss franc bond.

2. The investor benefits if Toshiba stock prices go up significantly. He or she will convert the bond and benefit from the difference between the conversion price and the share market price.

3. The investor benefits if the yen goes up significantly relative to the Swiss franc, because he or she can exchange the Swiss franc asset (the bond) for a yen asset (common stock).

These convertible bond issues also include a call provision, which makes the fair valuation of these bonds difficult.

EXHIBIT 10.16

Bond Description

INTERNATIONAL BONDS SERVICE
PART 2   **TOSHIBA**

ADDED TO SERVICE	UP-DATED TO 26 APR. 1984

2% CONV. 1984–92

TOSHIBA CORPN. (JAPAN)
2% CONVERTIBLE BONDS 1984-92.
Sw. Fr. 100m. issued at 100% in April 1984 for redemption 30 September 1992.

CONVERTIBLE INTO COMMON STOCK OF TOSHIBA CORPN.

BUSINESS   The Group is engaged primarily in the development, manufacture and sale of a wide variety of consumer electronic and electrical products, heavy apparatus and industrial electronic products and systems.

PRINCIPALS   Swiss Credit Bank; Swiss Bank Corpn.; Union Bank of Switzerland; Swiss Volksbank; Banque Leu S.A.; Groupement des Banquiers Privés Genevois; A. Sarasin & Cie.; Société Privée de Banque et de Gérance; Groupement de Banquiers Privés Zurichois; Union des Banques Cantonales Suisses; Nomura (Switzerland) Ltd.; Daiwa (Switzerland) S.A.; Mitsui Finanz (Schweiz) AG; Bank of Tokyo (Schweiz) AG; Deutsche Bank (Suisse) S.A.

CONVERSION & PAYING AGENTS   Swiss Credit Bank; Swiss Bank Corpn.; Union Bank of Switzerland; Swiss Volksbank; Banque Leu S.A.; Groupement des Banquiers Privés Genevois; A. Sarasin & Cie.; Société Privée de Banque et de Gérance; Groupement de Banquiers Privés Zurichois; Union des Banques Cantonales Suisses; Bank of Tokyo (Schweiz) AG; Deutsche Bank (Suisse) S.A.

INTEREST   Payable semi-annually on 31 March and 30 September without deduction of tax. The first interest payment will be made on 30 September 1984 in respect of the period from 8 May 1984 to 30 September 1984.

REDEMPTION   a)Mandatory.
Redeemable at par on 30 September 1992; no sinking fund.

b)Optional.

Upon 90 days' notice, as a whole only, on 30 September 1989 or any subsequent coupon date at the following redemption prices:

Coupon Date	%
30 Sept. 1989	102
31 Mar. 1990	101-1/2
30 Sept. 1990	101
31 Mar. 1991	100-1/2

and thereafter at par.
Co. may redeem all outstanding Bonds on or after 30 September 1988, if for at least 30 consecutive trading days, ending 15 days prior to redemption, the closing price of shares of Co.'s Common stock was at least 150% of effective Conversion Price. Such repayment will be made at the following redemption prices:

6-month Period Commencing	%	6-month Period Commencing	%
30 Sept. 1988	103	31 Mar. 1990	101-1/2
31 Mar. 1989	102–1/2	30 Sept. 1990	101
30 Sept. 1989	102	31 Mar. 1991	100-1/2

and thereafter at par.

CONVERSION   Convertible from 8 June 1984 to 21 September 1992 into shares of Common stock of Toshiba Corpn. at an initial price of ¥.449 per share (Y.103.44 = Sw.Fr.1). Fractions arising upon conversions will not be issued nor any cash adjustment be made.

DENOMINATIONS   Sw.Fr.5,000: Sw.Fr.100,000.

QUOTED   Zurich, Basle, Geneva, Lausanne and Berne.

DELIVERY   Europe.

BONDSPEC CODE   TSHE.

Source: Extel Statistical Service, April 1984. Reprinted with permission.

Special Issuing Techniques

New issuing techniques continue to appear (and disappear) on the international bond market as issuers adjust to changing markets. The most interesting are motivated by currency selection and speculation. These bonds focus on the currency element, but they have no optional clauses.

Dual-Currency Bonds

In 1983 and 1984 dual-currency bonds were popular. These bonds were issued mainly on the Swiss foreign bond market. A typical dual-currency bond is a straight foreign Swiss franc issue, with interest paid in Swiss francs and principal repaid in U.S. dollars. The amount of dollars repaid is determined at issue with reference to the current Swiss franc/U.S. dollar exchange rate. U.S. and Canadian corporations used this technique to tap the Swiss market, which was the second-largest bond market in the world after the U.S. dollar market. The issuer of a dual-currency bond can convert his or her Swiss francs into U.S. dollars on the spot foreign exchange market, hedge the stream of Swiss francs coupon payments on the forward exchange market (or through a bank), and thereby borrow U.S. dollars at a cheaper rate than is directly possible in the U.S. dollar market. Swiss-based investors were attracted to the issues by the opportunity for limited currency speculation (on only the principal) that they provided. Those who invested were betting on an appreciation of the dollar. Note that there is no option involved in dual-currency bonds, because all of their terms are fixed at issue.

Recently a large number of Japanese yen/U.S. dollar bonds have been issued. These bonds are issued and pay interest in yen but are reimbursed for a fixed dollar amount. The tombstone of a bond issued by NKK was reproduced in Chapter 9. Borrowers are not only Japanese corporations but also non-Japanese entities, such as the U.S. Federal National Mortgage Association (Fannie Mae). These bonds are attractive to Japanese investors because they are considered as yen bonds for regulatory purposes. The Ministry of Finance imposes limits on the amount of foreign currency bonds held by Japanese institutions. Dual-currency bonds allow investors to hold a dollar-linked asset, although it qualifies as a yen bond for regulatory purposes.

The value of a dual-currency bond can be broken down into two parts as follows:

- A stream of yearly coupon payments. The current value of this stream of cash flows is obtained by discounting at the yen interest rate.

- A dollar zero-coupon bond for the final dollar principal repayment. The current value of this single cash flow is obtained by discounting at the dollar interest rate.

Various evaluation exercises on dual-currency bonds are proposed in the Questions and Problems section.

Partly Paid Bonds

Partly paid bonds are issued in several currencies to attract foreign investors with expectations of downward currency and interest rate movements. This type of bond is partly paid by the investor at the time of issue and fully paid after a delay of several months. Of course, the terms of the issue are fixed on the issuing date.

Let's consider the example of a British investor who would like to lock in the high U.S. interest rate on currently issued bonds but fears a short-term drop in the value of the dollar. This investor may find a partly paid U.S. dollar bond issue attractive, locking in the high interest rate but fully subscribing the bond in only a few months, with the intention of using fewer pounds sterling to invest the same amount of U.S. dollars.

Partly paid bulldog sterling, as well as foreign Swiss franc issues, have also been offered.

The value of a partly paid bond can be broken down into two parts:

- The value of a straight bond for the part that is paid up immediately.

- A forward contract on a long-term bond for the part that is subscribed later. The maturity of the forward bond contract is the date of final liberation.

Because a forward contract requires no capital investment, it is not exposed to a down movement in the currency of denomination.

ECU and SDR Bonds

European Currency Unit (ECU) and Special Drawing Right (SDR) bonds are securities issued in a basket of currencies. The ECU is by far the most successful composite currency. In recent years, in fact, the ECU has surpassed the Dutch guilder and the Canadian dollar as a currency of denomination for new issues in the Eurobond market.

The ECU is the weighted average of the currencies of the European Monetary System (EMS). Its value relative to the U.S. dollar is computed daily. ECU bonds pay interest that is related to the weighted average of the interest rates of EMS members. A composite currency allows investors, especially European investors and borrowers, to limit currency risk. For a French investor, for example, the ECU is less volatile than any one of its currency components, such as the Deutsche mark or Dutch guilder. Moreover, whenever the French franc devalues with respect to other European currencies, the French franc value of the ECU correspondingly rises (even though this effect is dampened by the fact that the French franc is part of the basket). In short, the ECU is an attractive investment alternative to single foreign currencies because it is less sensitive to the volatility of a single currency and is revalued in the event of a depreciation of the investor's home currency. The

ECU market is also quite attractive, from a risk viewpoint, for European borrowers. Of course, an ECU bond should be valued as a portfolio of bonds in proportion to the ECU weights.

Portfolio Strategies

The diversification benefits brought by an international bond portfolio are stressed in Chapter 4. The approach to international bond diversification, presented here, may be passive or active.

Passive Management

Index Funds   In a passive approach the manager builds a world index fund. The ideal world bond index would consist of all securities contained in the markets, with each issue weighted by its market capitalization. An example of such an index for the U.S. domestic market is the Lehman Brothers Corporate/ Government Bond Index, which indicates the performance of the U.S. investment-grade institutional bond market. The task of constructing a portfolio tracking such a world bond index is formidable, since the index would contain more than 100,000 securities quoted over the world. It is not possible to hold a portfolio including all securities in their market value proportions. A practical alternative is to group bonds into homogeneous groups. A homogeneous group is defined as bonds with similar characteristics and holding-period returns. These portfolios can be formed by picking one or more liquid issues from each group. The weighting of the securities would be proportional to the weights of the groups they represent. For example, the Swiss franc market could be divided in five groups by category of issuers and then by maturity (short, medium, and long-term). The five categories of borrowers might be:

- foreign states and supranationals (EU, World, Bank)

- foreign corporations

- the Swiss Confederation and cantons

- Swiss banks and finance companies

- Swiss industrial and services

Note that the portfolio sampling concentrates on liquid issues, since some rebalancing is required to reflect changes in the market composition. Most of the issues are not actively traded, so rebalancing is limited as much as possible. Because interest rate movements are the major cause of all bond price variation (in any currency), the index is not too difficult to track. Furthermore, the stratified sampling accounts for changes in quality spread. Two major problems in the bond index fund approach are the large number of fancy bonds with callable clauses and the poor liquidity of the market for most issues. The technical aspects of bond indexation are discussed in Seix and Akhoury (1986) and Fabozzi (1991).

A third problem with this approach is the selection of bond indexes recognized worldwide. Some domestic bond markets publish daily, weekly, or monthly bond indexes, but they are not internationally comparable. As mentioned in Chapter 9, a few institutions now publish consistent bond indexes for domestic and international markets. Institutional investors tend to limit their international investments to top-quality risks, such as the best sovereign borrowers.

Despite all the technical problems, the great advantage of passive bond management is retaining the benefits of international diversification while reducing transaction costs.

Immunization   Immunization strategies are passive in the sense that they are a straightforward, disciplined application of simple and technical rules. Immunization is a strategy designed by pension funds or life insurance companies to construct and manage bond portfolios such that bond values are always in line with the value of their liabilities.

In *cash-flow matching*, the most direct method, a manager selects a portfolio of bonds such that the cash inflow (coupons plus repayments) exactly matches the expected cash outflow of the liabilities (pension plan or life insurance). Matching cash inflow and outflow precisely is difficult and often infeasible. The exact replication of cash flow is often impossible to find in the bond market; it might also lead to a dangerous concentration in a few bonds with little risk diversification.

A practical alternative to cash-flow matching is building a portfolio such that its value exactly matches that of the liabilities for any change in the interest rate. The institution could simply achieve this objective by selecting a portfolio of bonds with a duration and initial present value equal to the duration and present value of the scheduled liability cash flows. Note that a change in interest rate, as well as the investment time, will change the duration of both assets and liabilities, so that the portfolio of bonds must be continuously adjusted to maintain immunization.

As mentioned earlier, the single-duration measure is strictly valid only if there are parallel shifts in the term structure (i.e., if the yield-to-maturity on all bonds changes by the same amount when interest rates change). If these yields change by different amounts, the relative changes in bond values will not be exactly proportional to the duration, and the fund will not be perfectly immunized. Some equilibrium models[10] of the bond market have been developed assuming that interest rates follow a "multifactor" model allowing for twists in the term structure of interest rates. These models lead to multifactor measures of duration. However, all empirical tests indicate that the simple measure of interest rate sensitivity appears to be quite effective in immunizing portfolios and performs as well as the more sophisticated alternatives of the multifactor models.

The theory of immunization assumes that the only source of risk is interest rate risk. In practice, however, many managers attempt to improve their performance by investing in bonds with default risk (i.e., corporate bonds or municipals).

The process for default risk does not lend itself to the application of duration analysis. The application of immunization techniques to non-default-free bonds is expected to lead to imperfect results and should be used with caution. Similarly, the calculation of the duration for a bond with option clauses (e.g., early call option) is not simple; such calculations require an option valuation model for each optional clause. Again, the duration estimates for a bond with optional clauses should be used with caution, and it might be preferable to limit immunization strategies to straight, default-free bonds.

Financial futures are used to adjust the duration of a bond portfolio. The calculation of the duration of a Treasury bond futures contract is discussed in Chapter 12. Banks are extensive users of futures contracts to immunize the interest rate risk caused by a mismatch of duration between their assets and liabilities in many currencies.

A pure immunization strategy is passive in the sense that it is purely technical and does not involve any forecast about interest rates. Some active strategies might be designed to attempt to improve the performance of the fund. These strategies imply that the managers choose a portfolio duration different from the riskless duration and according to their forecasts about interest rates. For example, they will choose a lower duration if they expect a rise in interest rates compared to the market consensus implied in the term structure of interest rates. *Contingent immunization* strategies are designed to guarantee a predesignated minimum return and foster the likelihood of slightly higher returns.[11] Of course, the minimum return is less than that promised by a pure immunization strategy.

Immunization strategies are developed for a single currency. Multicurrency liabilities exist for pension plans of multinational firms or for life insurance companies operating in several countries; in this situation immunization strategies should be applied for each currency separately.

Active Management

An active management of international bond portfolios requires both a good technical knowledge of the various domestic and Eurobond markets and some ability to forecast interest rates and currencies. The neutral position, assuming no forecasting ability, should be market capitalization weights in the major currencies; deviations from these weights are induced by specific forecasts.

As for common stocks, the observation that all bonds issued in a given currency behave very similarly tends to justify a top-down currency approach. For an international investor, the major differences in performance are caused by the selection of currency markets. All fixed-interest bond prices are influenced by changes in interest rates in the respective currencies as well as the translation in the domestic currency. For example, the dollar performance of all British pound bonds is influenced primarily by two factors: movements in British interest rates and movements in the pound/dollar exchange rate. In comparison the difference in performance within a market segment is relatively small.

Typically an active management of multicurrency bond portfolios is broken into three stages:

- portfolio analysis

- strategic analysis

- bond selection and arbitrage techniques

Portfolio Analysis   The portfolio analysis stage provides the manager or trustee with a good synthesis of the current composition of the portfolio and its exposure (sensitivity) to the various risks involved. It is important to get the breakdown of the portfolio by currency, type of borrower, maturity, and so on. The information typically printed for each holding includes the following:

- issuer name

- coupon (annual or semester)

- maturity date

- call or sinking-fund provision (yes or no)

- credit rating

- market price

- yield-to-maturity

- yield-to-next-call

- duration

- average life

- capital invested (in local currency)

- accrued interest

- total value in base currency (capital plus accrued interest)

- percentage of portfolio value

Some summary information should be provided by currency. The duration provides an estimate of the portfolio's sensitivity to interest rate movements.

This portfolio analysis might be linked to a valuation system designed to compute the fair market value of bonds. Usually the valuation system works by isolating the important characteristics of bonds and then estimating market values for them, using sophisticated techniques involving option models. The analysis starts from an estimation of the term structure of default-free bonds and then takes into account the following:

- call or other interest rate–related options

- quality spreads

- default risks

- liquidity

- tax effects

Strategic Analysis   The investment strategy is based on forecasted scenarios for interest rates and currencies. Note that exchange rate movements are correlated, to some extent, with interest rate changes so that the two forecasts are not independent. Given the current portfolio, one can simulate the effect of a scenario on the value of the portfolio. This simulation also suggests which securities to sell and buy given the forecasted scenario. The three basic inputs are:

- changes in the term structure for each currency

- changes in quality or sector yield spreads (i.e., changes in the spread between the domestic and Euromarket segments)

- changes in exchange rates

This analysis suggests a revision in the multicurrency bond asset allocation. A comparison between the forward interest rates implied in the market yield curves and the manager forecasts of future interest rates indicates the preferred duration of the portfolio in each currency. This simulation model also allows for a sensitivity or risk analysis.

Bond Selection and Yield Enhancement   Numerous techniques are proposed to add value to the performance of the basic strategy. Some specialized trading techniques are used to provide incremental returns with very little risk (e.g., securities lending). These techniques evolved over time and are too specialized to be described here.

Valuation techniques are used to detect the cheapest bonds to buy (undervalued) when the portfolio has to be rebalanced. Spread analysis is often used to assess the relative value of two securities with fairly similar characteristics. This spread analysis can even lead to an arbitrage between two bonds. The idea is very simple. Two bonds with close characteristics trade at very similar prices and yield-to-maturity. Each day, a manager computes the spread between the two bond prices and plots them. Because of market inefficiencies, the spread is likely to be high above (or below) its average (normal) value at some point in time. This is the time to arbitrage one bond against the other. This spread analysis is conducted in terms of yield-to-maturity rather than in terms of prices.

Other bond portfolio management techniques are more complex and involve instruments such as futures or option contracts. For example, one might wish to invest in foreign bonds hedged against currency risks. All these hedging techniques involving other types of instruments allow for monitoring and adjusting the exposure of a bond portfolio to various sources of risk; they are presented in Chapter 14.

A typical way to enhance return on a bond portfolio is to add securities with higher promised yield because of the credit risk of the borrower. Some investors include bonds issued by high-credit-risk corporations. These bonds are issued by firms with a low credit rating and are often referred to as *junk* bonds. Investors can also obtain higher yields by investing in Brady bonds, where the risk of credit stems from the risk that a country will default on its debt servicing. One must be aware that the higher yield is a compensation for the risk of default. If this risk materializes, the realized yield on the bond investment can be very bad.

Other bonds have been designed as fairly complicated securities with uncertain cash flows. This is typically the case of mortgage-backed securities and corporates with option features. In mortgage-backed securities the borrower has the option of early prepayments, which is attractive if interest rates go down. Some models are used to estimate the normal spread over treasury rates justified by the bond's complicated structure.[12] Again, one should be careful that the yield enhancement provided by complicated bonds, with uncertain cash flows and option clauses, can lead to severe capital losses in periods of adverse market conditions. This was a painful experience for many investors in early 1994, when interest rates rebounded unexpectedly, and some complicated securities experienced very volatile price movements. Some of these complicated bonds, often called *structured notes*, are presented in Chapter 13.

Summary

1. We started with a review of the concepts and techniques used in analyzing straight bonds. Yield curves and duration are important concepts in bond management. A comparison of yield curves in different currencies allows one to assess the exchange rate movement implicit in bond yield differentials between two currencies. An investor should compare this implicit exchange rate with a personal forecast of the exchange rate fluctuations over the maturity of the bond.

2. Credit ratings of borrowers are available on the Eurobond market and on a few national markets. Governments, the largest borrowers, are rated by the research departments of banks, as well as by various agencies and publications. The assessment of sovereign risk often differs among the various rating organizations.

3. Floating-rate notes (FRNs) are bonds with a coupon indexed to some interest rate. Their price is much less volatile than that of a straight bond but still exhibits some volatility because of the indexation technique.

4. Many bonds are issued with various option clauses. The valuation of these option clauses is important, especially on the international market, where numerous currency option clauses can be found. In a currency option bond the bondholder can choose to receive coupon and principal payments in either of two currencies at a predetermined exchange rate. Two-currency convertible bonds are very common in the international market. These bonds are issued in one currency but are convertible into common stocks of a company from a country with a different currency. These bonds can be valued as the sum of a straight bond plus an option.

5. Special types of bonds and issuing techniques designed for the multicurrency investor are found in the Eurobond market. The major ones are dual-currency bonds, partly paid bonds, ECU, and SDR bonds.

6. International bond investment strategies are complex because of the large variety of available instruments. Active strategies start from forecasts on exchange rate movements and changes in the term structure of interest rates in each currency. Bond-selection techniques are then applied to each market segment.

Questions and Problems

1*. What are the yield-to-maturity and durations for the following bonds:
   - A zero-coupon bond reimbursed at $100 in 10 years and currently selling at $38
   - A straight bond reimbursed at $100 in 10 years, with an annual coupon of 10% and selling at $110
   - A perpetual bond with an annual coupon of $8 and currently selling at $110

2*. The market price of a two-year bond is 105% of its nominal value. The annual coupon to be paid in exactly one year is 7%. Its yield-to-maturity (European way) is 4.336%.
   - Calculate its modified duration.
   - Calculate its simple yield (Japanese way).
   - Calculate its semiannual yield (American way).

3. A French franc bond has been issued with an annual coupon rate of 10%. This bond has a sinking-fund provision: Half of the issue is reimbursed in two years and half in three years. You hold FF 10 million of nominal value of this bond.
   - Write the three future annual cash flows in francs, assuming that the previous coupon has just been paid.
   - The yield curve is currently flat at 9%. What is the value of the bond, its yield-to-maturity, its duration, and its modified duration?
   - How much do you stand to lose if the yield curve moves uniformly from 9% to 9.1% within one day?

4*. The yields are as follows:

Maturity	US$ %	DM %	FF %
1 month	2.10	8.00	7.00
6 months	2.50	7.75	7.15
1 year	3.00	7.00	7.30
2 years	3.50	6.90	7.50
5 years	4.00	6.80	7.60
10 years	4.25	6.75	7.70
Spot exchange rate (per US$)		1.80	5.50

Calculate the implied forward exchange rates, assuming that the interest rates are Eurocurrency rates for maturities of less than a year and yields on zero-coupon bonds for maturities of more than a year.

5. Some of the yields given in Exh. 10.9 are as follows:

Maturity	U.S. dollar	Deutsche mark	Japanese yen	Swiss franc	British pound
1 month	7.94	4.44	7.81	4.06	11.50
6 months	8.00	4.69	7.50	4.25	11.50
12 months	8.31	4.81	7.19	4.31	11.31
5 years	9.78	6.40	6.82	5.40	10.90
7 years	10.16	6.75	7.00	5.45	11.00
10 years	10.33	6.80	7.33	5.70	11.14
Spot exchange rate (per US$)		2.50	200.00	2.10	0.70

Calculate the implied forward exchange rates, assuming that the interest rates are Eurocurrency rates for maturities of less than a year and yields on zero-coupon bonds for maturities of more than a year.

6. Calculate the implied forward rates as done in Exh. 10.10, but assume that the yield curves are par yield curves, i.e., yield curves derived from coupon bonds selling at par rather than from zero-coupon bonds.

7*. A young investment banker considers issuing a DM/$ currency option bond for a AAA client and wonders about its pricing. Our banker knows that currency options are available on the market and that they could help set the conditions on the bond issue. As a first step, he decides to study a simple case: a one-year bond. The current market conditions are as follows:

- one-year dollar interest rate: 10%

- one-year Deutsche mark interest rate: 7%

- spot DM/$ exchange rate: $1 = DM2

Our banker could issue a bond in dollars at 10%, a bond in DM at 7%, or a currency option bond at an interest rate to be determined. One-year currency options are negotiated on the over-the-counter market. A one-year currency option to exchange one dollar for two Deutsche marks is quoted at 4%, i.e., four cents per dollar. This is a European option, which can be exercised only at maturity. The one-year forward exchange rate is:

$$F = 2\frac{1+7\%}{1+10\%}.$$

Given these data, what should the interest rate be on a one-year DM/$ bond? How would you determine how to set the interest rate on an n-year currency bond?

8*. The yield on zero-coupon bonds are as follows:

	US$ %	Yen %
1 year	3.00	5.00
2 years	3.50	6.00

A young investment banker considers issuing a $/yen dual-currency bond for ¥100 million. It is a bond with interest paid in yen and principal repaid in dollars. The current spot exchange rate is $1 = ¥100. The bond will be reimbursed for $1 million in two years. The interest is paid on year 1 and year 2. What should the interest paid in yen be?

9. A company hesitates to issue a one-year dual-currency bond or a one-year currency-option bond. The dual-currency bond would be issued in Deutsche mark (100 DM), with interest payable in DM and a principal repaid in U.S. dollars ($50). Denote x the interest at which this bond is issued. The currency-option bond is issued in DM (100 DM), and the interest and principal are repaid in DM or $ at the option of the bondholder. The principal repaid is either 100 DM or $50 and the interest rate is either y DM or ½ y dollars.

   As you guessed, the current spot exchange rate is 2 DM/$. The current one-year market interest rates are 6% in DM and 10% in $. One-year currency options are quoted in Chicago. A put DM is quoted at 1.2 US cents per DM; this option premium is for one DM, with a strike price of 50 US cents.

   ▪ What is the fair interest rate x on the dual-currency bond?

   ▪ What is the fair interest rate y on the currency option bond?

10. The yield curves in US dollars and Swiss francs are as follows:

	U.S dollar %	Swiss franc %
1 year	10	6
2 years	12	7

These are yields for zero-coupon bonds of one and two-year maturity. The spot exchange rate is SF/US$ = 1.5.

   ▪ What are the implied one-year and two-year forward exchange rates?

   ▪ You contemplate issuing a dual-currency bond. You could issue zero-coupon bonds in both currencies at the interest rates above. Instead, you wish to issue bonds of SF 150 with a coupon C in Swiss francs, paid each year for two years, and reimbursed for $100 at the end of two years. What is the interest rate c% ($c = C/150$) on the bond that would be consistent with the yield curves above?

   ▪ You contemplate issuing a two-year currency-option bond. The bond is issued for $100 and gives the option to receive the coupons and principal payment in either dollars or Swiss francs at a fixed exchange rate of SF/$ = 1.5. A bank gives us quotes on the premiums for calls SF with a strike price of $1/1.5 = 0.66666$ US$. The premium for a one-year call is 4 US cents (per Swiss franc) and for a two-year call is 7 US cents. What is the coupon rate that you should set on your currency-option bond?

11. Fuji Bank issued convertible Eurobonds in 1989. Convertible bonds were a popular way for Japanese banks to raise funds while the Tokyo stock market was booming in the 1980s. The lure of capital gains from converting the bonds to equity allowed the banks to issue the securities with a very low interest rate.

   Fuji Bank Eurobond was a 500-million Swiss franc zero-coupon bond, issued at par. A bond with a face value of 100 Swiss francs could be converted into two shares of Fuji Bank. At time of issue, Fuji's stock was worth 3590 yen, and a Swiss franc was worth 80 yen. The bond also had a put option that could be exercised at the start of 1991. Bondholders had the option of redeeming the bond at a premium of 2.625% over its face value. In other words, bondholders could obtain 102.625 francs for each bond. On January 14, 1991, the Tokyo stock market and the yen dropped. A stock of Fuji Bank was worth 2400 yen, and a Swiss franc was worth 95 yen. Most bonds were presented for early redemption.

   - Why was it interesting for a bondholder to exercise the put option?

   - What was the total yen loss for Fuji Bank?

12*. A company without default risk can issue a perpetual Eurodollar FRN at LIBOR. The coupon is paid and reset semiannually. It is certain that the issuer will never have default risk and will always be able to borrow at LIBOR. The FRN is issued on November 1, 2005, when the six-month LIBOR is at 4.5%. On May 1, 2006, the six-month LIBOR is at 5%.

   - What is the coupon paid on May 1, 2006, per $1000 bond?

   - What is the new value of the coupon set on the bond?

   - On May 2, 2006, the six-month LIBOR has dropped to 4.9%. What is the new value of the FRN?

13. A company without default risk can issue a 10-year Eurodollar FRN at LIBOR. The coupon is paid and reset semiannually. It is certain that the issuer will never have default risk and will always be able to borrow at LIBOR. The FRN is issued on November 1, 2005, when the six-month LIBOR is at 4.5%. Here are the Eurodollar yield curves on two different dates:

	May 1, 2006 %	August 1, 2006 %
1 month	5.00	4.00
3 months	5.00	4.50
6 months	5.00	5.25
12 months	5.00	6.00

What should the value of the FRN be on May 1 and August 1, 2006?

14*. A corporation rated AA issues a five-year FRN Eurobond in Deutsche mark on November 1, 2005. The coupon is paid quarterly and is equal to the DM LIBOR plus a spread of ½%. On November 1 the three-month DM LIBOR is at 4%. The issuer remains rated at AA during the life of the bond.

- Three months later, the three-month DM LIBOR has moved to 4.5%, and the market-required spread for AA borrowers has remained at ½%. What should the value of the bond on reset date be?

- Three months later (May 1, 2006), the three-month DM LIBOR is still at 4.5% but the market-required spread for AA borrowers has increased to ¾%. Give some estimation of the new value of the FRN on reset date.

15. A corporation rated A has issued a semiannual FRN in dollars. This is a perpetual bond, which will pay coupons indefinitely if the corporation does not default. The coupon is set at six-month LIBOR plus a spread of ¾%. The six-month dollar LIBOR is equal to 5%.

    Six months later the six-month dollar LIBOR has remained at 5%, but the market-required spread for A-rated corporations on long-term FRNs has moved to 1%. Give some estimation of the new value of the FRN on reset date.

16*. In March 1993 the Student Loan Marketing Association (Sallie Mae) issued five-year notes with a coupon set at 4.5% in the first year and reset quarterly subsequently. The floating quarterly coupon rate was set to be the higher of either 4.125% or 50% of the rate on 10-year Treasury notes plus 1.25%. At time of issue, the interest rates for all maturities were well below 4%, and investors were attracted by the high current yield (4.5%) compared to other straight bonds available.

    Assume that in March 1994 interest rates have risen dramatically and that the U.S. Treasury yield curve is now flat at 7% for all maturities.

- What is the new coupon rate set on the Sallie Mae bond?

- Try to explain why the Sallie Mae bond is now trading at a hefty discount.

17. The current dollar yield curve on the Eurobond market is flat at 7% for top-quality borrowers. A French company of good standing can issue plain-vanilla straight and floating-rate dollar Eurobonds at the following conditions:

- *Bond A: Straight bond.* Five-year straight dollar Eurobond with a coupon of 7.25%.

- *Bond B: FRN.* Five-year dollar FRN with a semiannual coupon set at LIBOR plus ¼% and a cap of 14%. The cap means that the coupon rate is limited at 14% even if the LIBOR passes 13.75%.

An investment banker proposes to the French company to issue Bull and/or Bear FRNs at the following conditions:

- *Bond C: Bull FRN.* Five-year FRN with a semiannual coupon set at: 13.75% − LIBOR

- *Bond D: Bear FRN.* Five-year FRN with a semiannual coupon set at 2 × LIBOR − 7%

The coupon on a Bull FRN will increase when LIBOR drops. This is sometimes known as a *reverse floater.* The coupon on the Bull FRN cannot be negative, so it has a floor of zero. The Bear FRN will benefit from a rise in interest rates. The coupon on the Bear FRN is set with a cap of 20.50%.

- Explain why a Bull FRN could be attractive to some investors.

- Explain why a Bear FRN could be attractive to some investors.

- Explain why it would be attractive to the French company to issue these FRNs compared to current market conditions for plain-vanilla straight Eurobonds and FRNs. The company assumes that LIBOR can never be below 3.5% or above 3.75%. This assumption is relaxed in Problem 17 of Chapter 13.

18. The French luxury-goods company LVMH, Louis Vuitton–Moët Hennesy, issued a series of perpetual floating-rate notes on the international capital market in the 1990s. These bonds have the advantage of being quasiequity, while benefiting from favorable tax treatment. Pioneered by state-owned French firms that cannot sell stock to the public, and subsequently used by a number of private European companies that were reluctant to dilute their stocks, the subordinated perpetual floating-rate note is an instrument that remains outstanding in name only. These securities are called instantly repackaged perpetuals, or *IRP*s.

   After a 5 billion francs issue in 1990, LVMH sold, in March 1992, 1.5 billion francs of IRPs. The company received 1.1 billion, the remaining 400 million being transferred to an offshore trust. The trust used the proceeds to buy 15-year zero-coupon bonds issued by banks underwriting the LVMH issue or by sovereign borrowers like Denmark and Austria. The 400 million investment in zero-coupon bonds will be redeemed for 1.5 billion in 15 years. The IRPs have the peculiarity that they pay interest only for the first 15 years; the interest becomes nil thereafter. After these 15 years, the trust is committed to repurchase the perpetuals at their face value of 1.5 billion francs. The trust, especially set up for this purpose, will then hold the IRPs forever, but their market value has become zero as they are perpetuals, which pay no interest. The semiannual coupon was set at six-month PIBOR (Paris InterBank Offer Rate) plus ½%.

   From an *accounting* viewpoint, these IRPs are treated as new equity of LVMH, because they are perpetual. From a *tax* viewpoint, the interest paid on the IRPs during 15 years can be deducted as interest expense (while dividend payments are not tax deductible).

   - Assume that you are an investment banker proposing such an IRP to another potential client. Explain in detail the advantage of such a package relative to a plain-vanilla 15-year FRN, or relative to a new stock issue.

   - In 1990 the French tax authorities decided to allow a writeoff of interest expense for only the net amount of capital the issuer actually takes on its books (1.1 billion for LVMH). Why does this decision reduce the attraction of issuing IRPs?

   - Following the 1992 LVMH issue, the tax authorities decide to introduce a new regulation for trusts, whereby capital gains would be taxed at the normal income tax rate. In effect, the trust would make a capital gain equal to the difference between the face value of the zero-coupon bonds and their issue price. This basically shut the market for IRPs. Why?

Notes

1. For a description of the various theories on forward interest rates, expectations, and risk premia, see W. Sharpe, *Investments*, Englewood Cliffs, NJ: Prentice Hall, 1991.

2. This method is also known as the *U.S. Street method*. There is a slight difference in the method traditionally used for discounting cash flows on the U.S. Treasury market. In the *U.S. Treasury method* partial periods are discounted, using simple rather than compound interest.

3. The yield-to-maturity should be equal on similar bonds with the same duration rather than same final maturity. For a more detailed explanation of this well-known result, see Sharpe, *op. cit.*

4. One explanation for this phenomenon is that insurance companies, which are large investors in Japan, prefer coupon income to capital gains for accounting and regulatory reasons.

5. For a detailed discussion of duration, see Bierwag, Kaufmann, and Toevs (1983), Fong and Fabozzi (1985), Fabozzi (1991), and Brown (1992). The modified duration gives the sensitivity of the bond price to small movements in the interest rate. Unfortunately this sensitivity estimate works well only for small changes in interest rates, because the relationship between bond prices and interest rates is curvilinear. The degree of curvature (or second derivative) is called the *convexity*, which varies from one bond to the next.

6. The London interbank offered rate is the rate at which banks offer to lend on Eurodeposits. Some FRNs are indexed to the London interbank bid rate (LIBID), the rate that a bank is willing to pay on Eurodeposits. Others are indexed to the LIMEAN, which is the mean of LIBID and LIBOR. (The spread between LIBID and LIBOR is generally approximately ⅛% or 1/16%)

7. Banks often issue FRNs for regulatory reasons. For example, FRNs are classified as capital in France and the United Kingdom and help banks meet their reserve and ratio requirements. Japanese banks are required to cover part of their short-term international lending with long-term financing.

8. Remember that the value of a perpetual bond with coupon C and market interest rate r is given by the formula:

$$P = \frac{C}{1+r} + \frac{C}{\left(1+r\right)^2} + \ldots = \frac{C}{r}.$$

9. See G. Feiger and B. Jacquillat, "Currency Option, Bonds Puts and Calls on Spot Exchange and the Hedging of Contingent Claims," *Journal of Finance*, December 1979. An analysis of currency option bonds on three currencies or with default risk is provided by R. Stulz, "Options on the Minimum or the Maximum of Two Risky Assets: Analysis and Applications," *Journal of Financial Economics*, July 1982.

10. See J. Cox, J. Ingersoll, and S. Ross, "Duration and Measurement of Basis Risk," *Journal of Business*, January 1979; M. Brennan and E. Schwartz, "Duration, Bond Pricing and Portfolio Management," in G.O. Bierwag, G. Kaufmann, and A. Toevs, eds., *Innovation in Bond Portfolio Management: Duration Analysis and Immunization*, Greenwich, CT: JAI Press, 1983; S. Schaeffer and J. Nelson, "Dynamics of the Term Structure and Alternative Portfolio Immunization Strategies," in Bierwag, Kaufmann, and Toevs, *op. cit.*

11. See M. Leibowitz and A. Weinberger, "Contingent Immunization," *Financial Analysts Journal*, November–December 1992, and January–February 1993.

12. See O. Cheyette, "OAS Analysis for CMOs," *Journal of Portfolio Management*, Summer 1994; and R.W. Kopprasch, "Option-Adjusted Spread Analysis: Going Down the Wrong Path?" *Financial Analysts Journal*, May–June 1994.

Bibliography

Bierwag, C., Kaufmann, G. and Toevs, A.L., "Duration: Its Development and Use in Bond Portfolio Management," *Financial Analysts Journal*, July/August 1983.

Bierwag, C., Kaufmann, G., and Toevs, A.L., eds. *Innovations in Bond Portfolio Management: Duration Analysis and Immunization*, Greenwich, CT: JAI Press, 1983.

Black, F., and Scholes, M. "The Pricing of Options and Corporate Liabilities," *Journal of Political Economy*, June 1973.

Brennan, M., and Schwartz, E. "Savings Bonds, Retractable Bonds and Callable Bonds," *Journal of Financial Economics*, January 1977.

Brown, P. *Formulae for Yield and other Calculations*, London: International Securities Market Association, 1992.

Fabozzi, F.J., ed. *Handbook of Fixed Income Securities*, 3rd ed., Homewood, IL: Business One Irwin, 1991.

_____. *Investing: The Collected Work of Martin Leibowitz*, Chicago, IL: Probus, 1992.

Feiger, G., and Jacquillat, B. "Currency Option Bonds Puts and Calls on Spot Exchange and the Hedging of Contingent Claims," *Journal of Finance*, December 1979.

Fong, H.G., and Fabozzi, F.J. *Fixed Income Portfolio Management*, Homewood, IL: Dow Jones–Irwin, 1985.

Ho, T.Y. *Strategic Fixed Income Investment*, Homewood, IL: Richard Irwin, 1990.

Journal of Fixed Income, various issues.

Nelson, J., and Schaefer, S. "The Dynamics of the Term Structure and Alternative Portfolio Immunization Strategies," in G. Bierwag, G. Kaufmann, and A.L. Toevs, eds. *Innovations in Bond Portfolio Management: Duration Analysis and Immunization*, Greenwich, CT: JAI Press, 1983.

Seix, C., and Akhoury, R. "Bond Indexation: The Optimal Quantitative Approach," *Journal of Portfolio Management*, Spring 1986.

Sharpe, W., *Investments*, Englewood Cliffs, NJ: Prentice Hall, 1991.

Stulz, R. "Options on the Minimum or the Maximum of Two Risky Assets: Analysis and Applications," *Journal of Financial Economics*, July 1982.

Chapter 10: Appendix
Advanced Section on Implied Forward Rates

Let's consider the yield curve for coupon bonds selling at their par value. Our aim is to calculate the terminal value of a bond investment, assuming that all coupons are reinvested in the same currency until maturity. Let's call V_t this final value for a domestic t year bond and V_t^* for a foreign t year bond. The implied forward exchange rate F_t for maturity t is given by

$$\frac{F_t}{S} = \frac{V_t}{V_t^*} \tag{10.A1}$$

Let's compute the value of V_t in one currency, assuming we know the par yield curve r_t. V_t is equal to the sum of the final repayment (and coupon) plus all reinvested coupons, so V_t can be decomposed into its components v_1 to v_t. For a unit investment (say, \$1) the final payment is equal to

$$v_t = 1 + r_t.$$

The annual coupon, which equals r_t, is paid every year. Now we must determine the interest rate at which this coupon is reinvested. We know that a coupon paid in year $t - 1$ is reinvested for one year, but we do not know at what rate it will be reinvested. The most natural assumption is that it will be reinvested at the forward interest rate derived from the term structure. As we have seen, the one-year forward interest rate from the period $t - 1$ to t is R_t. It is calculated using Eq.(10.A2):

$$\left(1 + R_t\right) = \frac{\left(1 + r_t\right)^t}{\left(1 + r_{t-1}\right)^{t-1}}, \tag{10.A2}$$

where we should recall that

$$1 + r_1 = 1 + R_1$$

and

$$(1 + r_t)^t = (1 + R_1(1 + R_2) \ldots (1 + R_t).$$

Therefore, the final value, in local currency, of the reinvested coupon from year $t-1$ is equal to

$$v_{t-1} = r_t\left(1 + R_t\right) = r_t \frac{\left(1 + r_t\right)^t}{\left(1 + r_{t-1}\right)^{t-1}}.$$

Similarly, the final value, in local currency, of the reinvested coupon from year $t-2$ is equal to

$$v_{t-2} = r_t\left(1 + R_t\right)\left(1 + R_{t-1}\right) = r_t \frac{\left(1 + r_t\right)^t}{\left(1 + r_{t-2}\right)^{t-2}},$$

and so on. For the first coupon paid at the end of the first year, we have

$$v_1 = r_t \frac{\left(1 + r_t\right)^t}{1 + r_1}.$$

This gives us the final value, in local currency, of our bond investment, V_t:

$$V_t = v_t + v_{t-1} + \ldots + v_1.$$

A similar computation can be performed for V_t^*, and Eq. (10.A1) gives the value of the implied exchange rate F_t.

11

Swaps

A bond is characterized by the stream of cash flows, or obligations, that it promises to pay. Bonds can be found with fixed or floating coupons and denominated in numerous currencies. The development of multicurrency financing and investment prompted the need for instruments that allow transforming a stream of obligations, or cash flows, into another stream of obligations denominated in another currency or with different characteristics. In other words, bridges across the various bond markets were needed. *Swaps* serve this purpose.[1] The market for swaps has become very active; the principal amount of outstanding swaps reaches several trillion U.S. dollars.

Description

The Historical Background

A swap is an exchange of periodic cash flows between two parties. The origin of swaps may be traced back to the *parallel*, or *back-to-back*, loans, which were popular in the 1970s. In a back-to-back loan two companies exchange loans in two different currencies.

A simple example might be useful in understanding the motivation and technical aspects of back-to-back loans and swaps. A French company would like to borrow $20 million to finance a foreign investment but is little known outside of France. At the time, French franc yields were higher than U.S. dollar yields. The French company would have to pay 9% on a five-year U.S. dollar loan and 10% on a five-year French franc loan. Similarly, a U.S. company needs 140 million French francs for its French subsidiary but has much easier access to the U.S. bond market. The U.S. company would have to pay 8% on a five-year U.S. dollar loan and 11% on a five-year French franc loan. The current spot exchange rate is FF/$=7.00. Each company has a comparative advantage to borrow on its home financial market. The U.S. company can borrow in dollars at 8%, compared to 9% for the French company. The French company can borrow in francs at 10%, compared to 11% for the U.S. company. At first this statement might seem paradoxical for the French company, which can borrow at 9% in dollars compared to 10% in francs. However, one must remember that U.S. interest rates are lower than French interest rates in this example, and the uncertainty about the franc/dollar exchange rate renders a direct comparison between the interest rates in the two currencies difficult.

The national comparative advantage can be captured by combining a borrowing on the home market with a back-to-back loan between the two companies. So the French company will borrow 140 million FF at 10%, whereas the U.S. company will borrow $20 million at 8%. In addition, they will enter into a back-to-back loan arrangement. The back-to-back loan will simply state that the French company lends French francs for five years to the U.S. company at a rate of 10%, whereas the U.S. company lends an equivalent amount of U.S. dollars to the French company at a rate of 8%, with the same schedule. The two companies have thereby exchanged both the principal and the interest payments. The French company has exchanged a stream of obligations in French francs for a stream of obligations in U.S. dollars.

The French company has entered into three financial operations:

- Borrowing on the French market in francs at 10%

- Lending francs to the U.S. company at 10% (back-to-back loan)

- Borrowing dollars from the U.S. company at 8% (back-to back loan)

If we combine the cash flows of the two operations, we see that the net result for the French company is to borrow dollars at 8%.

Two problems arise with back-to-back loans:

1. They appear on the balance sheet for accounting and regulatory purposes, although they effectively offset each other; debt ratios are increased.

2. Default by one party does not release the other party from its obligation to make its contractual payments.

In 1981 the first currency swap was designed, taking into account these two problems.[2] Soon interest rate swaps and mixed currency–interest rate swaps also developed. The market for swaps is now a multitrillion dollar market. All major commercial and investment banks participate in the swap market.

Description of Swaps

A swap is a contract whereby the two parties agree to a periodic exchange of cash flows. Only the *balance* of the two cash flows is exchanged on each payment date. A swap resembles a back-to-back loan arrangement but is packaged into a single contract, as opposed to two separate loans. On each swap payment date, the balance between the two cash flows exchanged is calculated, and a payment is made by the party owing money according to the calculation. In swap jargon each side of the swap is called a *leg*. It is important to remember that only the balance of the two legs will be exchanged at each payment date. A swap is simply a *contract* stating the formula to be used to compute the balance paid or received on each payment date. A swap must be studied independently of any initial borrowing or lending operation that motivates it.

Another important point to remember is that swaps appear off–balance sheet. They are simply commitments to perform future payments.

There are three major types of swaps.

Currency Swaps A *currency swap* is a contract to exchange streams of fixed cash flows denominated in two different currencies. A typical currency swap can be illustrated by using the previous example. Instead of concluding a back-to-back loan, an intermediary bank specialized in swaps may assist in getting the two parties together and arranging a U.S. dollar/French franc currency swap between them. This is a five-year swap for a principal of $20 million (or FF 140 million at the current spot exchange rate of FF/$=7.00), with fixed interest rates of 10% in francs and 8% in dollars. Under the swap agreement the French company contracts to pay the U.S. company annual interest and principal (in five years) in U.S. dollars and to receive annual interest and principal (in five years) in French francs. In this swap $20 million and FF 140 million are the principals, and the interest rates are 10% in French francs and 8% in U.S. dollars, with a maturity of five years. Each year, the U.S. company pays the French company the balance of FF 14 million (the annual interest of 10% on the French franc principal) minus $1.6 million (the annual interest of 8% on the U.S. dollar principal). When this balance is negative, the French company pays the balance to the U.S. company. After five years the principals of $20 million and FF 140 million will be swapped back: The French company will receive the balance of FF 140 million minus $20 million. This swap is diagramed in Exh. 11.1.[3]

Because the swap is designed to have the same principal value in francs and dollars at the time of contracting ($20 million equals FF 140 million at the spot exchange rate of FF/$=7), there is no initial payment between the two parties. Future swap payments depend on the evolution of the FF/$ exchange rate S_t. On each of the first four swap payment dates t, the French company will receive in million francs:

$$14 - S_t 1.6,$$

or in million dollars:

$$(14/S_t) - 1.6.$$

If this figure is positive, the French company will receive this amount from the U.S. company. If this figure is negative, the French company will have to pay the amount to the U.S. company. The cash flows are exactly the opposite for the U.S. company. If the dollar has risen to FF/$=7.50 in year 1, for example, the French franc value of the interest payment on the U.S. dollar leg of the swap is equal to

EXHIBIT 11.1

Currency Swap

Principal exchange (in million)

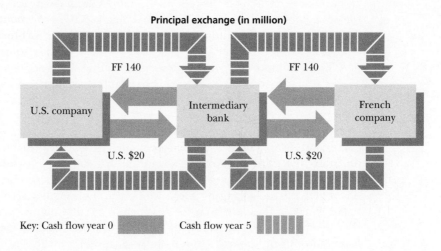

Key: Cash flow year 0 Cash flow year 5

Yearly interest exchange (in million)

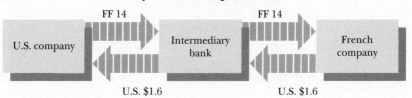

$1.6 million × 7.50, or FF 12 million when valued at the current spot exchange rate. This FF 12 million is to be compared with the FF 14 million interest payment on the French franc leg of the swap. The U.S. company simply remits to the French company the FF 2 million difference in cash flow. Equivalently this swap payment could be settled in dollars for $0.267 million, at the ongoing exchange rate of 7.5 FF/$.

On the last payment date, the French company will receive (or pay) in million francs the swap of the last interest payment plus principal:

$$154 - S_t \, 21.6.$$

Interest Rate Swaps An *interest rate swap* is a contract to exchange streams of cash flows in the same currency but based on two different interest rates. The most common interest rate swaps are U.S. dollar swaps involving a fixed interest rate and a floating rate. The floating rate index used is generally the six-month London interbank offer rate (LIBOR). As on a floating-rate note (see Chapter 10), the floating-rate leg is reset on a date that precedes the payment date, with a lead equal to the maturity of the floating interest rate. For example, the six-month LIBOR is preset six months before the next swap payment date.

A typical dollar interest rate swap could be concluded for a principal of $100 million, to exchange 8.5% fixed for six-month LIBOR. Payments are semiannual, and the fixed rate is a semiannual rate. Various other short-term rates (Treasury bill rate, commercial paper rate, prime rate, and so on) are sometimes used on the floating-rate leg.

Interest rate swaps do not involve exchange of principal, since the same amount and currency are involved on both legs of the swap. The uncertainty over the future swap payments on date t stems from the evolution of the floating rate reset on date $t-1$, i_{t-1}. On date t the floating-rate leg is set at $C_t = i_{t-1}$. In our example the swap party contracting to pay fixed and receive floating will receive a payment (in $ million) of:

$$C_t/2 - 4.25,$$

if this figure is positive. Otherwise it will have to pay the amount to the other party (contracting to pay floating and receive fixed). These interest rate swaps sometimes have an optionlike payoff. For example, there could be a cap on the floating rate, allowing for a maximum level of the floating interest rate. These options are described in Chapter 13.

Currency–Interest Rate Swaps   A *currency–interest rate swap* is a contract to exchange streams of cash flows in two different currencies, one with a fixed interest rate and the other with a floating interest rate. For example, a company could decide to swap a five-year French franc obligation with a fixed interest rate of 10% into a five-year dollar obligation at the six-month LIBOR plus 0.25%. Exhibit 11.2 describes such a currency–interest rate swap for $20 million U.S. (FF 140 million). The floating rate (LIBOR plus 0.25%) is applied to a principal of $20 million U.S.

Such a swap can be seen as a combination of a French franc/U.S. dollar currency swap as presented previously and a U.S. dollar–interest rate swap, exchanging a $20 million fixed interest rate liability for a floating rate (LIBOR plus 0.25%) liability. Future swap payments are uncertain because of the evolution of both the exchange rates and the floating interest rate.

Dollar–interest rate swaps developed after the currency swaps, but they now represent the largest share of the swap market. Interest rate swaps in French franc, Swedish krona, British sterling, Deutsche mark, Dutch guilder, Japanese yen, and many other currencies have also been arranged. It is estimated that a sizable portion of Eurobond issues are swapped.

Other Swaps   Swaps are often customized products. Banks quote swap rates for generic, or plain-vanilla, swaps, but customers often require some specific features on their swaps to match some specific characteristics of their existing liabilities or assets. Furthermore, exotic swaps are being marketed.[4] Swaps are often part of a more complex package of securities offered to a customer as a way to reduce its financing costs, speculate, or manage an interest rate or currency position. This

EXHIBIT 11.2

Currency–Interest Rate Swap

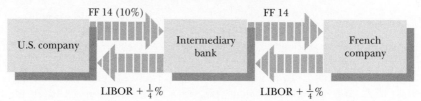

Principal exchange (in million)

FF 140   FF 140

U.S. company   Intermediary bank   French company

U.S. $20   U.S. $20

Key: Cash flow year 0   Cash flow year 5

Yearly interest exchange (in million)

FF 14 (10%)   FF 14

U.S. company   Intermediary bank   French company

LIBOR + $\frac{1}{4}$%   LIBOR + $\frac{1}{4}$%

package is tailor-made to take advantage of some specific aspect of the market environment, such as supply/demand imbalance and tax or regulation considerations.

Some interest rate swaps involve two floating rates; these are often referred to as *basis swaps*. A typical example is the exchange of a LIBOR-indexed obligation for a Treasury bill rate–indexed obligation. This basis swap is known as a *TED* (Treasury Eurodollar). Another example is the exchange of obligations indexed on the one-month and the six-month LIBOR.

A *differential swap*, or *switch LIBOR swap*, involves the LIBOR rates in two different currencies, but with both legs denominated in the same currency. For example, a Japanese insurance company engages in a differential swap, receiving the six-month Japanese yen LIBOR and paying the six-month U.S. dollar LIBOR plus 50 basic points (bp) but with both legs denominated in yen. No principal is exchanged at the end. The current LIBOR for the yen and the dollar are 6% and 4%, respectively, and the principal is 100 million yen. Hence the first swap payment will be based on a differential of 1.5% in yen [6% − (4% + 0.5%)]. The current yield pick-up is 150 bp. There is no currency risk on this swap. Such a swap, which was commonly arranged in the early 1990s, is explained by the different slopes on the yen and dollar yield curves. The dollar yield curve was very steep (long-term rates are much higher than short-term rates), whereas the yen yield curve was almost flat. The steep dollar yield curve reflects expectations that dollar short-term interest rates will rise in the future, offsetting the current yield differential. The motivation of the Japanese institution is to increase its current income; hence the swap permits such an increase.

A *forward swap* begins at some specified future date but with the binding terms set in advance. A *zero swap* is an interest rate swap in a single currency but such that no payments are exchange until maturity. A zero swap is equivalent to swapping a zero-coupon bond with a floating-rate bond whereby the floating-rate payments are capitalized until maturity. An *amortizing swap* has coupon payments on one or both legs, and those coupon payments are stepped up in a prespecified way. The stepping up could be conditional on some interest rate movements. A *commodity swap* is an exchange of fixed monetary payments against a spot commodity price.

Swaps may also come with numerous options. A *callable swap* gives the fixed-rate payer the option of canceling the swap before maturity, against up-front payment of a premium. A *putable swap* gives the fixed-rate receiver the option of canceling the swap before maturity, against up-front payment of a premium. A *swaption* is an option on a swap. Swaptions come in many formats; the most simple one is the option to enter a swap at a specified future date, against up-front payment of a premium.

Organization of the Swap Market

For illustration purposes, the example of a currency swap presented earlier suggested that a bank put in contact two customers, the French and U.S. companies. In practice, however, this seldom happens, and the customer deals directly with a bank. Typically a customer wishing to arrange a swap will call one or several banks specialized as swap dealers and providing swap rate quotes. Real-time quotes for generic, or plain-vanilla, swaps from various banks are also available on the major news services (Reuters, Bloomberg, Telerate, and so on).

The Primary Market The *primary* swap market is an over-the-counter market with the participation of all major commercial and investment banks of the world. Of course, banks tend to specialize in swaps involving their home currency; for example, French banks tend to specialize in swaps involving the French franc. So a corporate customer or a smaller bank tends to always have another major bank as counterparty in a swap deal. In turn, the major bank manages its swap book and tries to hedge any deal with an opposite swap with another customer or with specific risk-hedging techniques. Major market participants belong to the *International Swap and Derivatives Association,* or *ISDA.* The ISDA has prepared a master swap agreement contract, which serves as the basic model for most swap contracts. However, various modifications to the master contract are often enacted to suit national regulations and traditions or specific customers' requests.

Swaps are an attractive source of off–balance sheet earnings for commercial banks and investments banks alike. They also facilitate other types of businesses, such as Eurobond underwriting. Commercial banks tend to consider swaps an extension of their traditional credit activities as an intermediary. They stress their expertise in assessing credit risk and their ability to carry long-term market and credit risks. They also rely on their large customer base to find swap counterparts. In contrast, investment banks consider swaps negotiable securities. They attempt to reduce the default risk from a swap and to standardize the contract as much as possible. They stress their trading and hedging expertise.

It should be stressed that the credit risk of a swap is rather small. It does not apply to the principal but only to the differential in interest payments and, in the case of currency swaps, to the differential of principal repayments due to currency movements. Clearly the risk of a currency swap is higher than that of an interest rate swap. Because of their large capital base, commercial banks are more willing to assume long-term credit risk than are investments banks, which frequently request collateral. Corporate customers engaging in a swap with a bank are also worried about the credit standing of the bank offering the swap. Many major investment banks have a single-A credit rating, which most customers deem insufficient. To be a major swap dealer, a bank must have a rating equal to at least double-A.

To circumvent this problem, investment banks have often created specific subsidiaries to deal in swaps and derivative products. These units are set up to receive a double-A or triple-A credit rating from Moody's and Standard and Poor's. In 1991 Merrill Lynch set up a subsidiary, Merrill Lynch Derivative Products, which gained a triple-A rating. To win this rating, Merrill Lynch capitalized its subsidiary, agreed to deal only with customers that had ratings of double-A or better, and limited the type of derivatives that it could deal. In early 1993 Salomon Brothers, rated single-A at the time, formed Swapco, which also received a triple-A rating. The concept of Swapco was quite innovative. Salomon put an initial capital of $175 million, but the capital is continuously adjusted to reflect growth in swap activity and marked-to-market dynamically to reflect potential losses on the swap portfolio of Swapco. Finally, some adverse events can trigger the automatic termination of Swapco and the cash settlement of all derivative contracts written by Swapco. This automatic termination clause ensures that the capital will always be sufficient to cover the daily losses of Swapco and avoid its bankruptcy. On the other hand, this termination clause could be unattractive to some potential clients wishing to be sure to hold the swap until its maturity.

Goldman Sachs followed another route to create a triple-A subsidiary. Goldman Sachs Mitsui Marine Derivative Products L.P. (GSMMDP) is a joint venture with Mitsui Marine, Japan's third-largest nonlife insurer. Mitsui Marine and Goldman Sachs are jointly obligated to maintain GSMMDP's net worth at $10 million and to provide the capital and liquidity on a timely basis if needed. Hence this subsidiary benefits from the triple-A rating of Mitsui Marine. In turn, Goldman Sachs brings its expertise in derivative products to the joint venture. Other investment banks have followed either the Salomon route, with subsidiaries structured with marked-to-market capital and termination clauses (e.g., Paribas Dérivés

Garantis), or the Goldman Sachs route by enlisting a top-quality partner (e.g., Baring Brothers using the triple-A rating of Abbey National).

The Secondary Market   The *secondary* market for swaps has evolved unevenly because many swap contracts are highly customized. Furthermore, the other party must agree to the sale of the swap and often objects because of the change in credit risk. Three other possibilities are open to a party wanting to get out of a swap contract:

- *Agree on a voluntary termination with the original counterparty.* This popular agreement is simple and implies only a lump-sum payment to reflect the changes in market conditions. Once this cash payment is settled, the counterparty can always look for another swap at current market conditions if it wants to maintain the same economic position. This cash termination is negotiated between the two parties.

- *Write a mirror swap with the original counterparty.* A swap is reversed by writing an opposite swap contract with the same maturity and amount but at current market conditions. For example, company A enters into a seven-year swap agreement with bank B. Company A receives LIBOR and pays 10.5% fixed. A year later the two parties could write a six-year mirror swap whereby company A receives 9.5% and pays LIBOR to company B (the current swap conditions). The difference from a termination is that the settlement is paid over the remaining six years (1% per year), and some credit risk remains on the differential interest rate payment.

- *Write a reverse swap in the market with another counterparty.* This is the easiest deal to arrange but has two drawbacks. First, it is unlikely and expensive to find a swap that exactly offsets the previous one in terms of payment frequencies, price reset, and floating-rate base. Second, engaging in another swap doubles credit risk.

Investment banks encourage the development of the secondary market by standardizing swaps and trying to minimize credit risk. After all, swaps are long-term futures contracts and could be traded as futures on an organized exchange. Credit risk would be eliminated by a margin system with a marking-to-market procedure, as described in Chapter 12. Investment banks also attempt to eliminate credit risk by collateralization. They incorporate collateral revisions in the swap contract, giving the intermediary the right to call for an amount of collateral equal to the credit exposure on the contract.

At present, corporations and banks use swaps primarily to manage the currency and interest rate exposure of their assets and liabilities. The minimum size of the contracts (a few million dollars and usually much more), as well as the lack of a developed secondary market, do not make them attractive to the small investor. The standardization of swap contracts could change that situation. Numerous corporations and some institutional investors use swaps as an investment vehicle to take bets on interest rates and currency movements.

Swap Quotations

Banks quote swap rates for generic swaps in the major currencies. The quotations are given for a top-quality customer (rated double-A or above). The rates on a customized swap are derived from these quotations.

Interest Rate Swap Rates   For the U.S. dollar, interest rate swaps are usually quoted with the floating leg set as the six-month LIBOR. The fixed leg is usually quoted as the Treasury yield plus a spread. Examples of quotations are given in Exh. 11.3

The fixed rates are equal to the rates on the Treasury yield curve for the corresponding maturity plus a spread expressed in basis points. The spread is given as a bid/ask quote. For example, assume that the yield on five-year Treasury bonds is 8%. The swap dealer is willing to write a five-year swap whereby it receives LIBOR and pays 8.83% fixed (UST plus 83 bp) or to write a swap whereby it pays LIBOR and receives 8.88% fixed (UST plus 88 bp). So the *bid* refers to the fixed rate that the quoting swap dealer is willing to pay to receive LIBOR; the *ask* refers to the fixed rate that the swap dealer is asking to receive to pay LIBOR. The reason for quoting the floating leg at LIBOR *flat* is that it is the floating rate at which the bank (swap dealer) can access the floating-rate market. The reason for quoting the fixed leg at a Treasury yield plus a spread is to provide a fairly stable quote; the spread usually stays the same during the day, whereas the Treasury yield moves continuously over time, following changes in market bond prices. An alternative would be to quote directly a fixed rate against LIBOR, e.g., 8.83–8.88%, but this quotation would have to be continuously adjusted to reflect price movements in the bond market. Interest rate swaps in other currencies are quoted against the LIBOR in that currency. The fixed leg is expressed with reference to the government yield curve or, most frequently, as a fixed rate. For example, a five-year DM swap could be quoted at 8.23–8.30 against the six-month Euro-DM LIBOR.

EXHIBIT 11.3

US $ Interest Swap Quotes against Six-Month LIBOR	
Years	Fixed (s.a.)
2	UST+82–86 bp
3	UST+83–87 bp
4	UST+83–87 bp
5	UST+83–88 bp
7	UST+84–89 bp
10	UST+85–90 bp

Currency–Interest Rate Swaps In a currency–interest rate swap, the floating rate is generally in U.S. dollars, whereas the fixed rate is generally in a foreign currency. The swap quotations are usually given as a fixed foreign currency rate against six-month US $ LIBOR. A quotation example for a yen fixed/US $ LIBOR swap is given in Exh. 11.4. For example, the swap dealer is willing to write a five-year swap whereby it receives the US $ LIBOR and pays 5.05% fixed in yen or to write a swap whereby it pays LIBOR and thereby receives 5.13% fixed in yen.

Currency Swaps The quotations for currency swaps (fixed against fixed) can easily be reconstructed from the quotes on the two previous types of swaps. For example, the swap dealer would be willing to pay 8.83% fixed US $ and to receive 5.13% fixed yen (or receive 8.88% in US $ and pay 5.05% in yen). The swap dealer will probably make a direct quote for a yen/dollar currency swap within those spreads. The quote can also be set directly as a foreign currency fixed rate against the U.S. Treasury yield for the maturity. For example, a five-year US $/yen currency swap with annual swap payment could be quoted at 4.25–4.33% fixed yen against UST.

Some Further Precision It is important to specify how the fixed rate is calculated. In U.S. dollar interest swaps, the fixed rate is usually a semiannual rate (see Chapter 10), to reflect the conventions used in the United States. Following the national bond market conventions, most nondollar swaps are quoted using annual yield on the fixed leg. We must be very careful in distinguishing between the frequency of swap payments and the convention used to report a fixed rate.[5] Various types of mismatches can also be introduced in swaps. For example, the floating rate could be a three-month rate and the swap payments semiannual. This would require compounding the three-month rates over two successive quarters. Each kind of mismatch requires some technical adaptation to the formula for generic swaps discussed previously. These technical adjustments are discussed in Kopprasch, Macfarlane, Ross, and Showers (1987), Sundaresan (1991), or Saber (1994).

EXHIBIT 11.4

Fixed Yen Swap Quotes against Six-Month US $ LIBOR

Years	Fixed (annual)
2	5.00–5.07
3	5.03–5.10
4	5.04–5.12
5	5.05–5.13
7	5.06–5.13
10	5.06–5.13

Motivations for Swaps

As usual in finance, the major motivations for using swaps are *return* and *risk*. Companies use swaps to reduce their cost of financing (return motivation). They also use swaps to manage their long-term exposure to currency and interest rate risks, especially when they are faced with risks to existing assets and liabilities. For example, if a U.S. corporation borrowed in Swiss francs two years ago and is concerned about an anticipated strong appreciation of the Swiss franc, a U.S. dollar/Swiss franc swap can be used to transform the Swiss franc liability into a U.S. dollar liability.

Cost Benefits of Swaps

The usual argument for the use of swaps in new borrowing is cost saving. The main motivation in the early stage of the market was to take advantage of borrowing cost differentials between two markets to raise funds cheaply. The swap by itself does not provide a cost benefit, but it does provide a bridge across several financing markets. Given competition, swaps are priced at fair value, but they allow the transfer of some cost advantage obtained by borrowing in one market to another market.

Simple Cost-Financing Advantage   The motivation for a classic currency swap operates as follows. A supranational borrower (say, the World Bank) can tap the U.S. dollar market on favorable terms but would prefer to borrow Swiss francs because of the low interest rate in that market and because it needs to diversify its financing currencies. Supranational borrowers, such as the World Bank, the EU, or the European Investment Bank, are not favorites of Swiss investors, who prefer nonstate borrowers. Alternatively, a large U.S. corporation can borrow on very attractive terms in the foreign Swiss franc market but needs dollars. Each party is better off by borrowing in the market where it holds a comparative advantage and entering separately a swap with a bank to obtain the desired structure of cash flows. For example, the supranational borrower issues a bond in the U.S. dollar market and swaps the proceeds for the low–interest rate Swiss francs. Conversely, the U.S. corporation issues a Swiss franc bond and swaps the francs for dollars. Each party is bound to benefit from this swap by obtaining funds more cheaply than if it had directly accessed its desired-currency market.

The cost benefits of swaps are illustrated in the example provided at the start of this chapter. For the French company, the net result of borrowing in French francs combined with the franc/dollar swap is to borrow in dollars at 8%. This is 100 basis points below the rate of 9% that it should have paid, had the company borrowed directly in dollars. The cost reduction obtained by the U.S. company is also equal to an annual 1% on its franc borrowing.

It was not uncommon to achieve a 100 basis-point reduction in interest costs thanks to a combined swap/borrowing arrangement. The idea is to use financing on a specific market where a borrower has a *comparative advantage* and to transfer that advantage to another market or currency by a swap made at prevailing market conditions. The swap helps only as a bridge across markets. However, these cost savings based on the comparative advantage of some companies in some market segments are a form of market inefficiency. Financial arbitrage, such as a swap, exploits these market inefficiencies. As the volume of swaps increases, these simple inefficiencies are bound to disappear; they are arbitraged away.

As a swap trader observed about U.S. dollar interest rate swaps:

> . . . at the outset of the market, a "AAA" issuer could reasonably expect to achieve 75–100 basis points below LIBOR on a bond/swap; under current conditions, this same issuer might expect only 25–30 basis points below. . . . Many issuers now find it more cost-effective to approach the floating rate note market than the bond/swap market.[6]

More Complex Engineering   Many swap dealers believe that the growth of the market depends on the ability to identify and exploit new arbitrage opportunities as they develop in world markets. Some of these temporary or persistent arbitrage opportunities are caused by the regulatory and fiscal environment. For example, some domestic firms have access to subsidized lending (some government agency subsidizes part of the interest cost) at home but wish to borrow foreign currencies to finance their foreign operations. An interesting example can be found in the yen market, in which Japanese regulatory pressure is strongly felt.

Until recently, three Japanese regulatory and fiscal situations could have led to an interesting packaging of securities:

1. The Ministry of Finance limited the amount of nonyen bonds held by Japanese institutions, such as pension funds and insurance companies.

2. A dual-currency bond issued in yen, with interest payments in yen but principal repayment in a foreign currency, qualified as a yen bond for purpose of the yen limit imposed by the Ministry of Finance. This was attractive to Japanese institutions as a legal way to invest in foreign currency assets.

3. Zero-coupon bonds were taxed as non-income-generating assets. At maturity the difference between the face value and purchase price of the bond was taxed as capital gain, at a lower tax rate than income. Zero-coupon bonds were attractive to taxable Japanese investors.

In response to this regulatory and fiscal environment, a corporation wanting to borrow U.S. dollars could instead have engaged in the following operations:

- Issued a five-year dual-currency bond with an 8% interest coupon in yen and principal repayment in dollars. The face value would be $50 million U.S., and the issue amount would be 10 billion yen. The spot exchange rate is 200 yen/dollar.

- Issued a five-year zero-coupon yen bond with the same maturity as the dual-currency bond and a face value of 10 billion yen. There would be no interest payment, simply a principal repayment of 10 billion yen in five years.

- Entered into an agreement to swap a five-year yen fixed-rate obligation of 10 billion yen for a U.S. dollar liability (yen/dollar currency swap).[7]

Let's look at the economic position taken. The combination of the zero-coupon and dual-currency loan is equivalent to a straight yen bond, with a principal of 10 billion yen and annual coupons of 0.8 billion yen, plus a U.S. dollar zero-coupon bond with a face value of $50 million. The reasoning is simple if one looks at the cash flows by currency, as shown in Exh. 11.5. To get back to purely dollar borrowing, the corporation would swap the yen obligation of 10 billion yen into a U.S. dollar obligation (as indicated in the third operation of Exh. 11.5). The issue of the two bonds would capitalize on a regulatory and a fiscal attraction to Japanese investors, but the final product for the corporation would be a U.S. dollar loan, preferably at a cheaper cost than a straight U.S. dollar loan.

Asset Swaps   So far we have discussed situations in which swaps permitted the transfer of a cost-financing advantage from one market to another. These are sometimes called *liability swaps*. Swaps are also used to transform the cash flows on

---

EXHIBIT 11.5

Example of a Complex Package

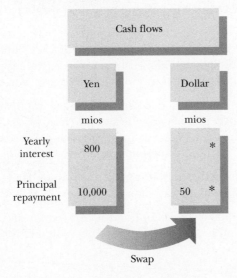

an asset into another stream of cash flows. These swaps are sometimes called *asset swaps*. Bond markets tend to be quite illiquid for most issues. Some bonds trade temporarily in one market at a "low" price because investors in that market cannot absorb the large amount offered by this type of issuer. An international investor could buy those bonds at a discount and then engage in a swap to transfer the cash flows into the desired interest/currency structure. Hence asset swaps are a play on liquidity and credit risk perception in one market. For example, some Euroyen bonds issued by Nordic governments could be selling at a discount because of liquidity conditions in that market. An investor could buy those bonds and swap yen for dollars. Japanese ex-warrant bonds are another example of the motivation for swaps on assets. In the late 1980s and early 1990s, Japanese companies issued bonds in dollars or Swiss francs with an equity warrant (long-term option on the shares of the Japanese company) attached. After issue, these bonds were stripped from their warrant and carried very low coupons. These bonds traded at a discount from their "fair" value because institutional investors preferred high-yield bonds. An asset swap could repackage these bonds into high-yielding LIBOR, taking advantage of the abnormally low price of the bond. Another motivation of asset swaps is to "unbundle" some complex bonds, called structured notes (see Chapter 13).

Swaps also contribute to the integration of financial markets by creating contracts that do not currently exist in the marketplace. They make the market more complete. Currency swaps are a typical example of long-term forward contracts that did not exist previously.

Risk Management

Interest rate swaps can be used to alter the exposure of a portfolio of assets or liabilities to interest rate movements. Swaps are all the more useful when assets or liabilities cannot be traded, as is the case for bank loans.

Take the example of a French company that borrowed $100 million U.S. at 9.5% a year ago. The long-term U.S. dollar interest rate has started to drop, and the French company believes that it will continue to fall. To take advantage of this drop in interest rates, the company decides to enter an interest rate swap in U.S. dollars. It swaps $100 million U.S. at a fixed interest rate of 9% for a floating rate equal to the six-month LIBOR. In effect the French company is now protected against a downward movement in interest rates. Conversely, a reverse swap is arranged if one believes that a rise in interest rates is due.[8] Futures contracts on bonds can also be used to hedge interest rate exposure, but they need to be rolled over frequently and require administrative attention because of the marking-to-market procedure described in Chapter 12.

Currency swaps are used to hedge the currency exposure of assets and liabilities. For example, a French bank can have made numerous loans in dollars to French corporations with subsidiaries abroad. If the bank fears a depreciation of the dollar relative to the franc, it could enter franc/dollar swaps. The bank would agree to receive francs and to pay dollars for a principal equal to the amount of the loans outstanding.

Liabilities or assets need not take the form of loans. For example, Gaz de France (GDF) is the French utility company selling natural gas to French homes and corporations. It has long-term gas purchase contracts with numerous countries, with a price denominated in dollars. To hedge the dollar risk on its forward commitment to buy gas, GDF has entered franc/dollar swaps. In these swaps GDG receives dollars and pays francs.

Risk management using swaps requires several steps:

1. Identify the source of uncertainty that could induce losses.

2. Measure the amount of exposure to this risk.

3. Identify the type of swaps that could best be used to hedge the risk.

4. Decide on the amount of hedging that should be undertaken. It is useful to start from the risk-minimizing hedge and to deviate from this position as a function of expectations and risk aversion.

For example, let's consider a small British bank that provided a loan in Deutsche mark to a top-quality customer that had to finance some acquisition in Germany. The amount of the loan is 50 million DM, with a fixed annual coupon of 7% and three years remaining. The British bank finances this DM loan by rolling over short-term borrowing on the Eurocurrency market. This bank is mostly domestic, and this loan and its associated DM floating-rate borrowing are the only asset and liability in DM appearing on the bank's balance sheet. The current six-month rate on Euro-DM is 6%, and the bank fears a rise in DM interest rates that would affect short- and long-term rates in a similar fashion. This interest rate increase is specific to the German economy, and no particular movements in the exchange rates are predicted. The following analysis of this simple example could be performed:

1. The source of risk is a movement in the general level of German interest rates. This can be seen in two ways. In terms of annual *cash flows*, the rise in interest rates will increase the financing costs (floating) of the bank without a corresponding increase in its interest income (fixed). However, the overall impact on the bank is best measured by looking at the change in *market value* of its assets and liabilities. A rise in German interest rates should not affect the value of the floating-rate borrowing; however, the value of the fixed-rate loan would drop as market yields increase. A rise in DM interest rates would hurt the bank; a drop in DM interest rates would benefit the bank.

2. The exposed amount is DM 50 million.

3. A DM interest rate swap is a good hedge against this risk. The bank should enter in a swap to pay fixed and to receive floating.

4. The risk-minimizing strategy would be to swap DM 50 million. If the bank is very sure of its rate prediction, it could enter a swap for a larger amount. This would be equivalent to "speculating" on this prediction.

For the same reasons that swaps can be used to hedge risks on existing positions, they can also be used to take speculative bets on interest and exchange rates. Corporations have often used swaps as investment vehicles. They regard swaps as highly levered long-term contracts that help them capitalize on predictions about exchange rate or interest rate movements. Because swaps are off–balance sheet contracts that are sometimes not fully understood by the top management of the firm, they can lead to large and unpredicted losses (or gains). Huge losses were incurred by Procter & Gamble, for example, during the U.S. interest rate upturn of 1994; these publicized losses have increased the awareness of the risks involved with derivative contracts.

In summary, the market for swaps developed both to exploit international financial arbitrage opportunities and to offer unique tools for currency and interest rate management.

Valuation of Swaps

We now turn to the important question of the value of a swap contract. At the time of contracting, the two parties agree on the terms of the swap, and no money is exchanged. It is a pure commitment that is acceptable to the two parties, which require no side-payment to enter the swap. Hence the value of the swap at the time of contracting is zero. However, as market conditions change over time, so does the value of the swap.

The financial profession uses standard methods to value a swap; a discussion follows. We will first assume that there is no default risk on either party of the swap. Later we will introduce credit risk.

Valuation in the Absence of Default Risk

Currency Swap   Let's take the example of the franc/dollar swap introduced at the start of this chapter. Twenty million U.S. dollars are swapped against 140 million French francs. The spot exchange rate is FF/$ = 7.00; the interest rates on dollars and francs are 8% and 10%, respectively. The maturity of the contract is five years, and interest coupons are swapped once a year.

At the time of issue, interest rates in the two currencies are set at prevailing market conditions, so that there is no actual exchange of money. In our example, $20 million is worth FF 140 million at the current exchange rate, and no money needs be exchanged to enter into this swap agreement. The market value of this currency swap is zero on the contracting day. However, the market value of this swap will change because of movements in interest rates and in the spot exchange rate. The question is: How should we value a swap in the secondary market? For example, assume that a corporation entered this swap contract to pay dollars and receive French francs and wants to sell it a year later. How should we price this swap?

Two approaches can be used:

- Value a currency swap as a package of long-term forward currency contracts

- Value a swap as a portfolio of two bonds

A currency swap can be broken down into a series of forward currency contracts for each cash flow. In our example the swap can be treated as a package of five forward contracts with maturity from one to five years, as depicted in Exh. 11.6. We can price the swap as a sum of forward currency prices.[9] In other words, we can unbundle the package of forward currency contracts.

There are two problems with this approach, however. First, it is not obvious that a fixed bundle of contracts would be priced exactly as the sum of its components, because markets are incomplete, and the unbundling of a package of contracts is difficult. Second, forward contracts are not frequently traded for long-term maturities, so forward currency rates have to be inferred from interest rate yield curves, as discussed previously. As a matter of fact, it is more common to derive forward currency prices from swap prices rather than the reverse.

Swaps can be treated as a portfolio of two bonds, short in one currency and long in the other. Basically the swap is treated as a back-to-back loan, and each leg of the swap is valued separately. The value of this hedged portfolio changes if interest rates in either of the two currencies move or if the spot exchange rate moves.

Let's denote $P_1(r_\$)$ and $P_2(r_{FF})$ the respective values of the dollar and French franc bonds, given the current market interest rates, $r_\$$ and r_{FF}, on bonds in the

EXHIBIT 11.6

Currency Swap as a Package of Forward Currency Contracts (in millions)

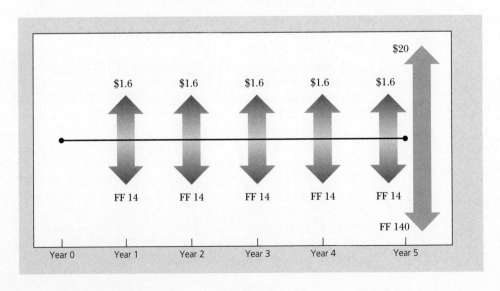

two currencies. Then the franc value of the swap, given the spot exchange rate, S, expressed as French francs per dollar, is:

$$\text{Swap value} = P_2(r_{FF}) - S P_1(r_\$). \tag{11.1}$$

This is the value of a swap to pay dollars and receive francs. The dollar value of the swap is simply deducted from the franc value of the swap by dividing by the spot exchange rate, S. The value of the swap for the other party, which agreed to pay francs and to receive dollars, is exactly the opposite of that computed in Eq. (11.1).

An application of the previous example will illustrate this formula. At the time of issue, the two interest rates were equal to the market yield-to-maturity on five-year default-free bonds in dollars (8%) and francs (10%). Assume that *a year later*, the yield curves in dollars and francs are flat and that interest rates have dropped to 7% on U.S. dollar default-free bonds and 8% on French franc default-free bonds. The spot exchange rate has dropped to FF/$=6.8. A swap payment of FF 3.12 million has just been made $[14 - 6.8 \times 1.6]$. We now wish to value the swap for the party that agreed to receive francs and pay dollars.

We value separately the two bonds implied in the swap. The dollar bond was worth $20 million (its par value) when the swap was contracted with a dollar interest rate of 8% $[P_1(8\%) = 20 \text{ million}]$. A year later the bond is worth $20.677 million at the current market yield of 7%. This is the present value of a stream of yearly coupons of $1.6 million and a principal of $20 million repaid in four years, discounted at 7%.

$$P_1 = \frac{1.6}{(1.07)} + \frac{1.6}{(1.07)^2} + \frac{1.6}{(1.07)^3} + \frac{21.6}{(1.07)^4} = 20.677. \tag{11.2}$$

Similarly, the French franc bond was worth FF 140 million (its par value) when the swap was contracted with a franc interest rate of 10% $[P_2(10\%) = 140 \text{ million}]$. A year later the bond is worth FF 149.274 million at the current market yield of 8%. This is the present value of yearly coupons of FF 14 million and a principal of FF 140 million repaid in four years, discounted at 8%.

$$P_2 = \frac{14}{(1.08)} + \frac{14}{(1.08)^2} + \frac{14}{(1.08)^3} + \frac{154}{(1.08)^4} = 149.274. \tag{11.3}$$

The franc value of the swap (to pay dollars and receive francs) is equal to:

$$\text{Swap value (in francs)} = 149.274 \text{ million} - (6.8 \times 20.677 \text{ million})$$
$$= \text{FF } 8.670 \text{ million}.$$

In dollars the swap is worth $1.275 million. For the other party the swap now has a negative value of –1.275 million.

The only practical problem in this approach is determining the relevant market interest rates used on both legs of the swap. For each cash flow on the fixed-rate leg, one should use a zero-coupon term structure. The practice in the finance profession—see Litzenberger (1992)—is to derive a zero-coupon structure from the current swap rates quotations and to use it to price outstanding swaps. This term structure is usually called *zero swap rates*.

Interest Rate Swaps   Interest rate swaps can be valued likewise using a portfolio of a fixed-rate bond and a floating-rate bond. The floating-rate leg is assumed to have a market value that remains set at par on reset date (see Chapter 10). The fixed-rate leg is valued as described earlier, using the current zero swap rates. The same applies to a mixed currency–interest rate swap.

For example, consider a dollar interest rate swap written with an 8% annual coupon against LIBOR. The remaining life of the swap is four years. For simplicity assume that the payments are annual with a principal of 20 million. The current zero swap rates are now at 7% for all maturities. The fixed-rate leg is now worth 20.677 million, and the floating-rate leg is still worth 20 million. The current market value of the swap for the party receiving fixed and paying floating is now 0.677 million [20.677–20].

Valuation in the Presence of Credit Risk

The swap quotations should differ for a party with credit risk. For example, a triple-A bank quoting swap rates to a single-A client is likely to increase the bid-ask spread on the swap rates. Typically the credit quality spread for a single-A party would be from one to five basis points on either side. For example, the five-year dollar interest rate swap rates for a top-quality client was given in Exh. 11.3 as UST + 83–88 bp. For a single-A client, the swap rates quoted could be UST + 80–90 bp.

A quality spread of a few basis points may seem very low to compensate for the risk of default on a swap. However, one must understand that the potential losses on swaps, especially interest rate swaps, are much smaller than for a loan. The default risk does not apply to the principal and interest payments but only to the *differential* in interest payments in the case of an interest rate swap. The default risk also applies to the differential in principal repayment in the case of a currency swap, so the quality spread should be somewhat higher. Further note that the default of a risky client will affect the bank (swap dealer) only if the interest rate and currency movements were such that the client is in a position to owe money to the bank. This can be seen by looking at the previous dollar interest rate swap example. Assume that the defaulting party had contracted to receive fixed and pay floating. The swap has a net market value of $0.677 million for the client. The bank was already in an unfavorable position on this swap (liability due to the negative value of its swap), and the default of the client does not worsen the bank's position.

Swap contracts specify how the swap will be terminated in case of bankruptcy of one of the parties. These termination clauses can vary across swaps and market participants. The most common clause is the "full two-way payments" option proposed in the ISDA master agreement. Under this clause, a party is deemed to default on the swap if it becomes insolvent on its debt. All outstanding swaps are "netted," and the settlement is based on the replacement values of the outstanding swaps. In other words, one computes the net market value of the swap position between the two parties, using standard methods and quotes from major swap dealers. Any accrued but unpaid swap and interest payments are taken into account to determine the amount owed. To simplify the analysis, let's call "bank" the nondefaulting party and "client" the defaulting party. If the net market value is negative for the bank (positive for the defaulting client), it is to be paid by the bank.[10] If the net market value is positive for the bank (negative for the defaulting client), it is to be paid by the defaulting client.

Because a swap comes very late in the seniority order of debt, it is unlikely that the solvent party will recover all or much of this value. A total loss is probably a reasonable assumption. Due to this asymmetry, swaps take an optionlike characteristic.[11] In case of default of the client, the bank will pay the maximum of the swap market value (if the swap value is positive for the client) and zero (if the swap market value is positive for the bank).

Summary

1. Swaps have rapidly developed since 1981. Currency swaps involve the exchange of obligations in two currencies. Interest rate swaps involve the exchange of two obligations in the same currency: one with a fixed interest rate, the other with a floating rate (usually LIBOR). Currency–interest rate swaps involve the exchange of a fixed interest rate in one currency for a floating interest rate in another currency.

2. Major commercial and investment banks are swap dealers. Investment banks that suffer from a low credit rating had to set up a specific subsidiary for dealing in swaps and other derivatives. The secondary market has evolved unevenly because swaps are customized contracts.

3. Interest rate swaps are quoted as a fixed rate against the reference floating rate *flat*. In U.S. dollar–interest rate swaps, the fixed rate is usually quoted as the U.S. Treasury bond yield for that maturity plus a spread. Hence this spread is really what is quoted and evolves over time. Currency–interest rate swaps are quoted as a fixed rate in one currency against the LIBOR flat in the other currency. Currency swaps are quoted as two fixed rates in each currency, or as a fixed rate in one currency against the U.S. Treasury bond yield *flat* when the dollar is one of the two currencies.

4. Swaps are used to reduce financing costs by transferring a comparative advantage enjoyed in one market to another market. Swaps are also used to manage the long-term exposure of a company to currency and interest rate risk.

5. Swaps are generally valued as a portfolio of two bonds.

6. Default risk on a swap involves smaller potential losses than on a loan. This explains why the quality spread (the difference between the swap rate for a default-risky and for a default-free party) amounts to only a few basis points.

Questions and Problems

1*. A swap with a maturity of five years was contracted by Papaf Inc. three years ago. Papaf swapped $100 million for DM 250 million. The swap payments were annual, based on market interest rates of 8% in dollars and 4% in DM. In other words, Papaf Inc. contracted to pay dollars and receive DM. The current spot exchange rate is 2 DM/$, and the current interest rates are 6% in DM and 10% in $ (the term structures are flat).

   ▪ What is the swap payment at the end of year 3? Does Papaf pay or receive?

   On the final date of the swap, the spot exchange rate is 1.5 DM/$.

   ▪ What is the final swap payment at the end of year 5?

2*. A corporation enters into a two-year DM interest rate swap on April 1, 2000. The swap is based on a principal of DM 100 million, and the corporation will receive 7% fixed and pay six-month Euro-DM LIBOR. Swap payments are semiannual. The 7% fixed rate is quoted as an *annual* rate using the European method, so the implied semiannual coupon is 3.44% [since $(1.0344)^2 = 1.07$]. Two years later the swap is finally settled, and the following Euro-DM rates have been observed:

Apr. 1, 2000	Oct.1, 2000	Apr. 1, 2001	Oct. 1, 2001	Apr.1, 2002
6.5%	7.5%	8%	7.5%	6%

   What have the swap payments or receipts for the corporation been on each swap payment date?

3. The same German corporation also entered another two-year DM interest rate swap on April 1, 2000. The swap is based on a principal of DM 100 million, and the corporation contracted to receive 7% fixed and pay six-month Euro-DM LIBOR. On this swap the payments are annual. Hence the two successive six-month LIBOR are compounded. Assuming that the Euro-DM rates given in the previous problem have been observed, what have the two annual swap payments been?

4*. A swap dealer provides the following quotations for a DM/$ currency swap. The quotes are for a DM fixed rate against the U.S. Treasury yields flat, with annual payments.

Years	Fixed (ann.)
2	6.00–6.08
3	6.12–6.21
4	6.14–6.23
5	6.15–6.24
7	6.18–6.28

   A client wishes to enter a five-year swap, paying DM and receiving US $. The current yield on five-year U.S. Treasury bonds is 7.20%, using the semiannual method, which amounts to 7.33%, using the annual European method.

   What will the exact terms of the swap be if the client accepts these quotations?

5. A French corporation plans to invest in Thailand to develop a local subsidiary to promote its French products. The creation of this subsidiary should help boost its exports from France. The Thai bath is pegged to a basket of currencies dominated by the U.S.

dollar, so borrowing in U.S. dollars would reduce the currency risk on this investment. The corporation needs to borrow $20 million for five years. A bank has proposed a five-year dollar loan at 7.75%. The French government wishes to support this type of foreign investments helping French exports. A French government agency can subsidize a 1.50% improvement in French franc interest costs. In other words, the corporation can get a five-year, FF 100 million loan at 7.5% instead of the current market conditions of 9%. The current spot exchange rate is 5.00 FF/$. A bank offers to write a currency swap for a principal of $20 million, whereby the corporation would pay dollars at 7.75% and receive francs at 9%.

What could the corporation do to get an obligation in dollars, its desired currency position, while capturing the French interest rate subsidy?

6*. Pouf is a rapidly growing and pleasant country in the Austral hemisphere. Its inhabitants are called Poufans, and its currency is the pof. The bond market is fairly active with many issues by Poufan companies, but there are no foreign investors or issuers. The current yield on Pof bonds is 10%. Poufan investors have to pay a 15% tax on interest income received. The newly elected Poufan government wishes to internationalize its bond market and attract foreign issuers. To do so, it decides to remove any taxation of income on bonds issued by foreign corporations in Pouf. Several changes take place after the enactment of this tax provision:

- Several well-known foreign corporations issue Pof-denominated bonds in the Poufan bond market.
- Several well-known Poufan corporations issue Eurobonds denominated in U.S. dollars.
- Several dollar/pof swaps are arranged.

Could you provide a sensible explanation for this phenomenon?

7*. A Dutch institutional investor has decided to bet on a drop in U.S. dollar bond yields. It engages in a leveraged strategy, borrowing $100 million at LIBOR plus 0.25% and investing the proceeds into attractive newly issued, long-term dollar Eurobonds. Suddenly the investor becomes worried that bond yields have hit bottom and will rise because of inflationary pressures. The investor wishes to keep the specific Eurobonds that have been selected, partly because of their attractiveness and partly because of their lack of market liquidity. What kind of swap could be arranged to hedge this U.S. dollar bond yield risk?

8*. A German bank has the following portfolio of loans in US dollars:

Assets	Liabilities
$50 million of a five-year loan at LIBOR plus 0.5%	$10 million of a five-year loan at a fixed rate of 9%

The German bank fears a long-term depreciation of the U.S. dollar relative to the Deutsche mark and believes in stable U.S. interest rates. What type of swap arrangements should it contract? What should the principal of the swaps be?

9. Take the swap of Papaf Inc. described in problem 1. Immediately after the third payment, what is the market value of the swap for Papaf?

10*. A five-year currency swap involves two triple-A borrowers and has been set at current market interest rates. The swap is for $100 million against DM 200 million at the current spot exchange rate of DM/$ = 2.00. The interest rates are 10% in dollars and 7% in Deutsche mark, or annual swaps of $10 million for DM 14 million. A year later the interest rates have dropped to 8% in U.S. dollars and 6% in Deutsche mark, and the exchange rate is now DM/$ = 1.9.

- What should the market value of the swap be in the secondary market?

Assume now that the swap is instead a currency–interest rate swap whereby the dollar interest is set at LIBOR.

- What would the market value of the currency–interest rate swap be if these conditions prevailed a year later?

11. A five-year currency swap involves two triple-A borrowers and has been set at current market interest rates. The swap is for $100 million against DM 200 million at the current spot exchange rate of DM/$ = 2.00. The interest rates are 4% in dollars and 7% in Deutsche mark, or annual swaps of $4 million for DM 14 million. A year later the interest rates have dropped to 3% in U.S. dollars and 6% in Deutsche marks, and the exchange rate is now DM/$ = 1.9.

- What should the market value of the swap be in the secondary market?

Assume now that the swap is instead a currency–interest rate swap whereby the dollar interest is set at LIBOR.

- What would the market value of the currency–interest rate swap be if these conditions prevailed a year later?

12. Four years ago, a Swiss firm contracted a currency swap of $100 million U.S. for 250 million Swiss francs, with a maturity of seven years. The swap fixed rates are 8% in dollars and 4% in francs, and swap payments are annual. The Swiss firm contracted to pay dollars and receive francs. The market conditions are now (exactly four years later) as follows:

Spot exchange rate: 2.00 Swiss franc/U.S. dollars

Term structure of zero swap rates:

Maturity years	U.S. dollar % (ann.)	Swiss franc % (ann.)
1	9	5
2	9.5	5.75
3	10	6
4	10.25	6.25
5	10.75	6.5
6	11	7
7	11.5	7.5

- What should the swap payment (receipt) be at the end of the fourth year, i.e., today?
- Right after this payment, what is the swap market value for the Swiss firm?

13*. A small French bank has the following balance sheet, based on historical (nominal) values.

Assets

Loan of 100 million:
   3 years, @ 3-month PIBOR + ½

Liabilities

Debt of 50 million:
   5 years, @ 10%

Net worth: 50 million

    All assets and liabilities are denominated in French francs. PIBOR is the Paris Interbank Offer Rate; this is the interbank short-term interest rate in francs. The net worth is calculated as the difference between the value of assets and liabilities. The current franc interest-rate term structure is flat at 8%. The risk premium over PIBOR required on the loan to a client remains at 50 basis points.

- Value the balance sheet based on *market* value.

The bank fears a sharp drop in French interest rates.

- Would this drop be good for the bank?

    The current market conditions for interest rate swaps with a maturity of three or five years are 8% against PIBOR.

- Assume that the bank simply wishes to immunize its market value against *any* movements in interest rates (drop or rise). What swap would you do to hedge this interest rate risk?

- Assume that the bank is quite confident in its interest rate prediction (a drop). What would you suggest?

    The next day, all interest rates move down to 7%.

- Value again the balance sheet, assuming that the floating rate debt remains at 100% and that the bank has undertaken the swap that you recommended.

14. A small Dutch bank has the following balance sheet, based on historical or nominal values.

Assets

Loan of 200 million:
   3 years, @ 7%

Liabilities

Euroguilder borrowing of 150 million:
   @ 3-month LIBOR

Net worth: 50 million

    All assets and liabilities are denominated in Dutch guilders. The bank borrows short-term on the Euro-DG market. The bank and its client are triple-A quality. The net worth is calculated as the difference between the value of assets and liabilities. The current guilder term structure for triple-A borrowers is flat at 6.5%.

- Value the balance sheet based on *market* value. Compute the interest-rate sensitivity (modified duration) of the asset. Infer some estimate of the interest rate sensitivity of the net worth of the bank. For example, how much would stockholders lose if Dutch interest rates moved up by 0.10%?

- The bank fears a rise in Dutch guilder interest rates. The current market conditions for interest rate swaps with a maturity of three years are 6.5% against Dutch guilder LIBOR. What would you do to hedge this interest rate risk?

- The next day all interest rates move down to 6%. Value again the balance sheet, assuming that the floating-rate debt remains at 100% and that the bank has undertaken the swap that you recommended. Is the hedge perfect? Why?

15. A *differential swap*, or *switch LIBOR swap*, involves the LIBOR rates in two different currencies but with both legs denominated in the same currency. Let's take the example provided in the text. A Japanese insurance company engages in a differential swap whereby it receives the six-month Japanese yen LIBOR and pays the six-month U.S. dollar LIBOR plus 50 bp but with both legs denominated in yen. No principal is exchanged at the end. The current LIBOR for the yen and the dollar are 6% and 4%, respectively, and the principal is 100 million yen. Hence the first swap payment will be based on a differential of 1.5% in yen [6% − (4% + 0.5%)]. The current yield pick-up is 150 bp. There is no currency risk on this swap.

    Provide some intuitive explanation for the pricing of such a swap, knowing that at the time, the dollar yield curve was very steep (long-term rates are much higher than short-term rates) and the yen yield curve was almost flat.

16*. Assume that a triple-A customer pays 8% on a five-year loan and can contract a five-year interest rate swap (paying fixed) at 8% against LIBOR. Assume that a triple-B customer pays $(8 + m)\%$ on a five-year loan and can contract a five-year interest rate swap (paying fixed) at $(8 + \mu)\%$ against LIBOR. Should a customer pay the same credit-quality spread (m and μ) on a loan and on a swap?

17. The current market conditions for a triple-A client are 8% on a one-year dollar loan, and 8% fixed U.S. dollar for 9% fixed British pound on a one-year dollar/pound currency swap. Let's consider a triple-B client borrowing at $(8 + m)\%$ on a one-year dollar loan. The same client can enter a dollar/pound currency swap, paying $(8 + \mu)\%$ fixed dollar and receiving 9% fixed pound. Assume that the customer has a probability of $p\%$ to default within a year. In case of default the bank knows that it will recover nothing on either transaction. The probability of default p (e.g., 5%) is known and independent of movements in interest and exchange rates. The spot exchange rate is $S_0 = 1\ \$/\pounds$.

    Assuming that you can observe the prices of $\$/\pounds$ currency options, can you suggest some approach to determine the fair values of m and μ? (Assume that the bank has a large number of clients whose probabilities of default are independent; therefore the bank can diversify away the uncertainty of default on this specific client.)

Notes

1. Swaps are derivative products and could also have been included in Part Five. They are closely linked to the international bond market and therefore provide a transition between fixed-income instruments and derivative products.

2. The World Bank and IBM are believed to have initiated the first currency swap.

3. A currency swap can also be seen as a package of forward currency contracts (see Chapters 1 and 2). For example, the swap cited with annual interest payments is a package of five forward currency contracts. The year 1 forward commitment is for $1.6 million; the implicit forward exchange rate is equal to the ratio of the sums

exchanged, or FF/$ = 8.75 (FF 14/$1.6). The year 5 forward commitment is for $21.6 million (principal plus last interest payment); the implicit forward exchange rate is equal to the ratio of the sums exchanged, or FF/$ = 7.13 (FF 154/$21.6).

4. Exotic swaps are periodically discussed in various issues of *Euromoney* and *Risk* magazine. See also Brady (1992).

5. For example, a yield of 8%, using the U.S. semiannual yield convention, implies a six-month coupon of 4%. A yield of 8%, using the European annual yield convention, implies a six-month coupon of 3.923%, since $(1 + 3.293\%)^2 = 1 + 8\%$. This is discussed in Chapter 10.

6. Bankers Trust Company, "The International Swap Market," Supplement to *Euromoney*, September 1985.

7. Such an example has also been presented by Smith, Smithson, and Wakeman (1986).

8. As mentioned in Chapter 10, a drop in interest rates increases the present value of a fixed-rate debt obligation, whereas a rise in interest rates reduces the present value.

9. See Smith, Smithson, and Wakeman (1986) and Smith, Smithson, and Wilson (1990).

10. Alternatively, the ISDA master agreement suggests a "one-way payment" option whereby the nondefaulting party is not obligated to settle the swap market value if it owes money to the defaulting party. It is doubtful that such a one-sided clause would withstand the test of courts.

11. A simple analysis of the optionlike feature of swaps in the presence of default risk is provided by Solnik (1990). See also Bollier and Sorensen (1994), Cooper and Mello (1991), Sun, Sundaresan, and Wang (1993), and Brown and Smith (1993).

Bibliography

Beidelman, C.R. (ed.). *Cross-Currency Swaps*, Homewood, IL: Business-One Irwin, 1992.

Bollier, T.F., and Sorensen, E.H. "Pricing Swap Default Risk," *Financial Analysts Journal*, May–June 1994.

Brady, S. "Derivatives Sprout Bells and Whistles," *Euromoney*, August 1992.

Brown, K.C., Harlow, W.V., and Smith, D.J. "An Empirical Analysis of Interest Rate Swap Spreads," *Journal of Fixed Income*, March 1994.

Brown, K.C., and Smith, D.J. "Default Risk and Innovations in Design of Interest Rate Swaps," *Financial Management*, Summer 1993.

Cooper, I., and Mello, A.S. "The Default Risk of Swaps," *Journal of Finance*, June 1991.

Kopprasch, R., Macfarlane, J., Ross, D.R., and Showers, J. "The Interest Rate Swap Market: Terminology and Conventions," Salomon Brothers, 1987.

Litzenberger, R.H. "Swaps: Plain and Fanciful," *Journal of Finance*, July 1992.

Saber, N. *Interest Rate Swaps: Valuation, Trading and Processing*, Homewood, IL: Business-One Irwin, 1994.

Smith, C., Smithson, C.W., and Wakeman, L.M. "The Evolving Market for Swaps," *Midland Corporate Finance Journal*, Spring 1986.

Smith, C., Smithson, C.W., and Wilson, D.S. *Managing Financial Risks*, New York: Harper and Row, 1990.

Solnik, B., "Swap Pricing and Default Risk: A Note," *Journal of International Financial Management and Accounting*, Spring 1990.

Sun, T.S., Sundaresan, S., and Wang, C. "Interest Rate Swaps: An Empirical Investigation," *Journal of Financial Economics*, 34, 1993.

Sundaresan, S. "Valuation of Swaps," in S.J. Khoury, (ed.), *Recent Developments in International Banking and Finance*, Vol 5, New York: Elsevier, 1991.

P A R T   F I V E

Futures, Options, and Others

12

Futures

S peculative investments offer financial leverage. The capital invested is less than the price of the underlying asset, allowing one to multiply the rate of return on the underlying asset. Because of this leverage, speculative investments may be used either to take better advantage of a specific profit opportunity or to hedge a portfolio against a specific risk.

Investments used in these ways are usually traded on futures and options markets, which allow an investor to speculate, or hedge risk, without much capital investment. Other types of leveraged investments exist in the form of private contracts between two parties, such as swaps. Once signed, these contracts are not easily traded. The scope of this book is limited to financial markets; therefore we consider only publicly available investments.

This chapter describes futures; options are covered in the next chapter. Strategies using futures and options to cash in on specific forecasts or to hedge specific risks are considered in Chapters 14 and 15.

Markets and Instruments

The Principle of a Futures Contract

In a *futures contract*, all terms of a goods exchange are arranged on one day, but the physical delivery takes place at a later date. More precisely, a futures contract is a commitment to purchase or deliver a specified quantity of goods on a designated date in the future for a price determined competitively when the contract is transacted.

Let's consider the gold futures traded on the commodity exchange in New York. Contracts on the exchange specify delivery of 100 troy ounces; all futures prices are quoted per unit, here per ounce of gold. On December 1, 1993, one could have bought a futures contract for delivery in April 1994 at a price of $420 per ounce. This means that the buyer of the futures contract was obliged to buy 100 ounces of gold in April from the seller of the contract, who likewise was obliged to sell to the buyer. The seller may pick the actual date of delivery during the month of April. The amount of money transacted was $42,000. Exchanges offer contracts with different delivery months: On the commodity exchange in New York (COMEX), gold futures are traded with delivery months in February, April, June, August, October, and December over a two-year period.

A futures contract is simply a commitment to buy or sell. There is no money exchanged when the contract is signed. In order to ensure that each party fulfills its commitment, therefore, some form of deposit is required. This is called the margin. The exchanges set a minimum margin for each contract, but brokers often require larger margins from clients. In fact, two types of margins are required: When the client first enters a contract, an initial margin must be posted. The amount, which depends on the volatility of the contract price and hence on the risk being taken, typically varies from 1% to 10%, depending on the commodity. The initial margin on our gold contract was $1500 for a 100-ounce contract. The maintenance margin is the minimum level below which the margin is not allowed to fall once losses on the contract value have been taken into account. The maintenance margin is usually 70% to 80% of the initial margin but is often equal to the initial margin on non-U.S. futures exchanges. Margins are usually deposited in the form of cash, and the broker pays no interest. But brokers often allow large customers to use interest-bearing securities, such as Treasury bills, as deposits. In that case, there is no opportunity cost associated with a futures contract investment, since the margin position continues earning interest.

Futures prices fluctuate every day and even every instant. Therefore all contract positions are marked to market at the end of every day. If net price movements induce a gain on the position, the customer immediately receives cash in the amount of this gain. Conversely, if there is a loss, the customer must cover the loss. As soon as a customer's account falls below the maintenance margin, the customer receives a margin call to reconstitute the margin. If this is not done immediately, the broker will close the position on the market. The following example illustrates how this works.

Assume that a customer buys an April contract in gold at $420 per ounce on December 1 and puts up an initial cash margin of $1500. The maintenance margin is $1200. The next day the futures price moves down to $415, and the position is marked to market. The customer loses $5 per ounce, or $500 per contract. This amount is debited from the customer's cash position, which is reduced to $1000. The customer receives a margin call for $500 to reconstitute the initial margin to $1500. The next day the futures price moves up to $425 per ounce, and the customer's cash account is credited $1000 [(425 − 415)100 ounces]. The cash account now has a balance of $2200, and the customer may draw up to $700 from the account.

The procedure of marking to market implies that all potential profits and losses are immediately realized. This is a major difference between futures and forward contracts. Practically every day futures contracts are canceled and replaced by new contracts with a delivery price equal to the new futures price, that is, the settlement price at the end of the day. In our gold example, the contract was replaced at the end of the second day by a new April contract with a delivery price of $415 instead of $420.

The internationalization of futures markets started in 1984. Some exchanges have linked their operations on identical contracts. For example, the Chicago Mercantile Exchange (CME) and the Singapore International Monetary Exchange (SIMEX) created a mutual offset system for their currency and Eurodollar contracts in September 1984. This interexchange trading system allows a market participant to open a position on one exchange and to liquidate that position on another exchange during two different trading sessions. These links provide additional trading hours for investors around the globe. In 1989 the CME announced its intention to develop GLOBEX, a computerized trading system that would allow international, round-the-clock trading. MATIF, the largest futures exchange in Europe, has decided to join GLOBEX. However, the development of these global links has been slow and disappointing.

Futures Versus Forward Contracts

Like futures contracts, *forward contracts* are made in advance of delivery. But a forward contract is a private agreement between two parties. A forward contract cannot be resold, since there is no secondary market for it. For the same reason, forward contracts cannot be marked to market, and the customer has to wait for the delivery date to realize the profit or loss on the position. The margin is set initially and never revised. This could lead to fairly large initial margins, in order to cover default risk over the life of the contract.

Futures contracts have succeeded because they are standardized. A clearinghouse handles the two sides of a transaction. For any transaction two contracts are written: one between the buyer and the clearinghouse and one between the clearinghouse and the seller. Through this procedure all contracts are standardized in terms of name of the other party, as well as size and delivery date. To cancel a position the customer simply has to reverse the trades by selling contracts previously bought or buy back contracts previously sold. This creates a highly liquid market in standardized contracts. Forward contracts do not offer the same liquidity, because all contracts are different in terms of size, delivery date, and name of the other contracting party. Even if a reverse trade was possible in the forward market (and it would require an identical amount and delivery date), the customer has to carry both contracts until the delivery date, since both are private commitments with two different parties. The reverse trade locks in the profit (or loss) on the initial contract, but this profit (or loss) will be realized only on the delivery date. Exhibit 12.1 summarizes the major differences between the two types of markets.

It should be stressed that futures contracts are seldom used for physical delivery. These contracts are used to hedge, or take advantage of, price movements rather than to delay the sale or the purchase of goods. Most customers reverse their position in the futures market before expiration of the contract.

EXHIBIT 12.1

Major Differences Between Forward and Futures Contracts

Forward Contracts	Futures Contracts
1. Customized contracts in terms of size and delivery dates.	1. Standardized contracts in terms of size and delivery dates.
2. Private contract between two parties.	2. Standardized contract between a customer and a clearinghouse.
3. Impossible to reverse a contract.	3. Contract may be freely traded on the market.
4. Profit or loss on a position is realized only on the delivery date.	4. All contracts are marked to market; profits and losses are realized immediately.
5. Margins are set once, on the day of the initial transaction.	5. Margins must be maintained to reflect price movements.

Commodities

There has always been a need for future markets in commodities with volatile spot prices. Farmers and harvest buyers have long used futures markets to hedge price risks arising from climatic conditions. A large variety of commodities are now traded on futures markets throughout the world, including perishable goods, such as soybeans or live cattle; metals, such as copper or silver; energy sources, such as oil; and a variety of financial contracts. For each commodity the quality and quantity of the product traded are precisely specified, as are the locations and conditions of delivery.

The same commodity is often traded on several futures markets, although the quality of the commodity may vary slightly from one market to the next. With gold, for instance, gold bullion is traded on several futures and forward markets throughout the world. Futures contracts in gold bullion of 100 troy ounces are traded on the following major markets:

- New York Commodity Exchange (COMEX)
- International Monetary Market of the Chicago Mercantile Exchange (IMM)
- Chicago Board of Trade (CBT)
- Mid-America Commodity Exchange
- London International Financial Futures Exchange (LIFFE)
- Hong Kong
- Singapore International Monetary Exchange (SIMEX)

Forward transactions can also be arranged on the major spot gold markets, i.e., London and Zurich.

Currencies

The *interbank foreign exchange market* is usually considered the largest market for forward or futures transactions in currencies, although there are no statistics available on its trading volume. As seen in Chapter 1, this forward market is closely linked to that of Eurocurrency deposits because of the technical relationship between forward exchange rates and interest rate differentials between two currencies. It is also very large and efficient and boasts minimal transaction costs for normal transactions (several millions). Moreover, the market is open around the clock with participants throughout the world.

As mentioned, forward contracts are not standardized, and there is no organized secondary market. Forward contracts are usually negotiated with maturities of one month, two months, three months, six months, or twelve months, but contracts with other maturities can also be arranged. Because the length of the contracts rather than the delivery date is fixed, each day a new contract is traded on the market. For example, someone buying a one-month contract on June 2 with maturity July 1 cannot resell it on June 6, since one-month contracts traded on this day expire on July 5.

Furthermore, these contracts involve two private parties, and a reverse transaction to cover the position is not possible, so that the contract has to be held until delivery. Of course, it is possible to cover economic positions by making an offsetting transaction on a contract with the same delivery date, but these contracts are usually not traded on the interbank market. To assist a customer, a bank may propose a forward contract tailored to the customer's needs and charge a large commission for this service. Thus a bank could propose on June 6 a forward contract with a maturity of 25 days expiring on July 1. The currency swaps described in Chapter 11 are a form of forward exchange rate contract. They involve swapping at a fixed exchange rate a series of cash flows denominated in one currency for a series of cash flows denominated in another currency. This swap may be regarded as a package, or strip, of forward currency contracts on each of the coupon and principal payment dates. This currency swap market allows for long-term currency hedging. The forward and futures markets cover contracts ranging from one month to two years, whereas swaps extend this range to ten years.

Futures markets in currencies follow the same rules as commodity futures. The Chicago Mercantile Exchange trades in futures contracts for French francs, Canadian dollars, Dutch guilders, Mexican pesos, British pounds, Japanese yen, Deutsche marks, and Swiss francs.[1] Active trading takes place in the last four currencies. As shown in Exh. 12.2, all prices are expressed in U.S. dollars per unit of foreign currency. One could have bought one Deutsche mark contract with a December delivery wherein one would have agreed to buy 125,000 Deutsche marks in December for a price of 0.4654 dollars per Deutsche mark. If the Deutsche mark appreciated and went above 0.4654 dollars by December, the buyer would have made a profit; if not, the buyer would have taken a loss.

The currency futures quotations shown in Exh. 12.2 illustrate the type of information available in the international financial press.[2] For example, note the futures

EXHIBIT 12.2

Quotations for Currency Futures

CURRENCY FUTURES

	Open	High	Low	Settle	Change	Lifetime High	Low	Open Interest
BRITISH POUND (IMM)—25,000 pounds; $ per pound								
Sept	1.4735	1.4820	1.4675	1.4765	— .0125	1.5435	1.3240	28,123
Dec	1.4630	1.4695	1.4560	1.4560	— .0125	1.5360	1.3250	881
Est vol 8,877; vol Fri 16,430; open int 29,024, +329.								
CANADIAN DOLLAR (IMM)—100,000 dlrs.; $ per Can $								
Sept	.7244	.7247	.7239	.7246	+ .0011	.7305	.6809	8,529
Dec	.7210	.7215	.7205	.7212	+ .0011	.7285	.6790	1,675
Mar87	.7175	.7182	.7175	.7178	+ .0011	.7256	.6770	393
Est vol 763; vol Fri 1,004; open int 10,670, −41.								
JAPANESE YEN (IMM) 12.5 million yen; $ per yen (.00)								
Sept	.6238	.6288	.6230	.6282	+ .0072	.6317	.4690	44,512
Dec	.6270	.6321	.6264	.6314	+ .0072	.6348	.4720	1,511
Mar87	...	...	.6350	+ .0072		.6354	.5850	295
Est vol 16,968; vol Fri 21,955; open int 46,318, −2,247.								
SWISS FRANC (IMM)—125,000 francs-$ per franc								
Sept	.5601	.5663	.5593	.5657	+ .0084	.5717	.4790	29,502
Dec	.5631	.5688	.5612	.5680	+ .0083	.5743	.4878	2,124
Est vol 18,735; vol Fri 26,630; open int 31,660, −1,690.								
W. GERMAN MARK (IMM)—125,000 marks; $ per mark								
Sept	.4587	.4632	.4577	.4631	+ .0063	.4675	.3762	42,469
Dec	.4610	.4652	.4601	.4654	+ .0063	.4703	.4090	1,107
Est vol 19,655; vol Fri 29,266; open int 43,670, −835.								

Source: Reprinted by permission of *The Wall Street Journal (Europe)*, July 16, 1986, © 1986, Dow Jones & Co., Inc. All rights reserved worldwide.

prices for the Deutsche mark contracts. All contract prices are given per unit of goods traded, i.e., one Deutsche mark. The December contract opened at 0.4610 dollars per Deutsche mark and closed, or *settled*, at 0.4654. The high and low prices of the day were 0.4652 and 0.4601 dollars. The *change* gives the price change from the settlement price on the previous day. The settlement price is also the price used for the marking-to-market procedure. The buyer of one December Deutsche mark contract would have gained $787.50 from the previous day of quotation (DM 125,000 × 0.0063 $/DM). The *open interest* is the amount of contracts outstanding.

The advantage of currency futures is that the investor may transact in small amounts for reasonable transaction costs. Moreover, the market is very liquid. An investor may engage in active currency exposure management, since clearing procedures permit covering positions at any time by reverse transactions in the futures contracts. In addition, the margins are less than on the interbank market, and the procedure of marking to market allows an investor to realize a profit or a loss immediately rather than having to wait until delivery. As with commodity futures, few contracts result in actual delivery, because reverse trades are usually made to cancel the position before the delivery date.

Some currency futures contracts are traded in several markets throughout the world (e.g., London, Singapore, Chicago Mercantile Exchange). Trading links between the markets sometimes allow positions that are opened in one market to be liquidated in another.

Futures contracts usually express the exchange rate of the U.S. dollar relative to another currency. A Swiss investor wanting to hedge the currency risk of British assets has to take two positions: one in British pounds (relative to U.S. dollars) and the other in Swiss francs (relative to U.S. dollars). For example, to hedge British assets against the risk of a pound depreciation relative to the Swiss franc, an investor would sell British pound futures and buy Swiss franc futures.

In general, investors use forward and futures currency contracts to manage their exposure to currency risk. Their purposes range from hedging exchange risk on the foreign part of their portfolio to pure speculation on currencies.

Interest Rate Futures

The most actively traded futures contracts in the world are interest rate futures, such as Eurodollar or U.S. Treasury bonds contracts. Commercial banks and money managers use these futures to hedge their interest rate exposure, i.e., to protect their portfolios of loans, investments, or borrowing against adverse movements in interest rates. They are also used by speculators as leveraged investments, based on their forecasts of movements in interest rates.

Organized markets for interest rate futures exist for instruments in several currencies. Following the United States and the United Kingdom, most countries with a major bond market have either already developed, or are in the process of developing, a futures market for long-term bonds and sometimes short-term paper.

Active U.S. dollar markets exist in three-month U.S. Treasury bills and Eurodollar deposits for short-term interest rates and in 20-year 8% Treasury bonds for long-term rates. Other futures contracts have been introduced for certificates of deposit (CDs), commercial paper, 5- and 10-year Treasury bonds, and the mortgage bonds known as Ginnie Maes, or GNMA. Similarly, the London International Financial Futures Exchange offers a 3-month sterling deposit contract, a 3- to 4½-year 12% U.K. gilt contract, and a 20-year 12% U.K. gilt contract. The Paris Bourse (MATIF) proposes a 15-year 10% government bond contract and 3-month Treasury bill and PIBOR contracts. The Tokyo Stock Exchange offers contracts on 10-year bonds with a 6% yield. The Sydney Futures Exchange proposes contracts for 3-month Australian bills and 10-year Australian bonds. Eurodollar contracts are traded on several exchanges in the United States, Canada, London, and Singapore. These interest rate futures markets are growing rapidly throughout the world, and new contracts are continually created to fit the needs of banks and investors. Major bond contracts are given in Exh. 12.3

The quotation method used for these contracts is difficult to understand but tends to be similar among countries. Quotations for U.S. interest rate futures are given in Exh. 12.4. Contracts on short-term instruments are quoted at a discount from 100. At delivery, the contract price equals 100 minus the interest rate of the underlying instrument. For example, three-month Eurodollar contracts are denominated in units of $1 million; the price is quoted in points of 100%. For this reason the September contract in Exh. 12.4 is quoted at 93.61% on the CME. The

EXHIBIT 12.3

Major Bond Contracts Worldwide, 1994

Exchange,[a] Contract	Contract Size
CBOT, US 15-year T-bond	$100,000
CBOT, US 10-year T-note	$100,000
CBOT, US 5-year T-note	$100,000
CBOT, US 2-year T-note	$200,000
BM, Government of Canada 6½–10-year bond	Canadian $100,000
SFE, 10-year Commonwealth treasury bond	Australian $100,000
SFE, 3-year Commonwealth treasury bond	Australian $100,000
TSE, 10-year Japanese government bond	JPY 100m
LIFFE, Japanese government bond future	JPY 100m
LIFFE, UK government long gilt	£ 50,000
MATIF, 7–10 year French government bond	FF 500,000
MATIF, 6–10 year notional ECU bond	ECU 100,000
BELFOX, Belgian government bond	BF 2.5m
FUTOP (CSE), Danish government bond	DKK 1m
DTB, 8½–10-year German government bond	DM 250,000
LIFFE, 8½–10-year German government bond	DM 250,000
LIFFE, Italian government bond	ITL 200m
MEFF, 10-year Spanish government bond	Pta 10m
SOFFEX, Swiss government bond	SF 100,000

[a]CBOT: Chicago Board of Trade; MACE: Mid-America Commodity Exchange; BM: Bourse de Montréal; SFE: Sydney Futures Exchange; TSE: Tokyo Stock Exchange; LIFFE: London International Financial Futures and Options Exchange; MATIF: Marché à Terme International de France; BELFOX: Belgian Futures and Options Exchange; CSE: Copenhagen Stock Exchange; DTB: Deutsche Terminbörse; MEFF: Mercado de Opciones Y Futuros Renta Fija; SOFFEX: Swiss Options and Financial Futures Exchange.

price of 93.61% is linked to an interest rate on three-month Eurodollar deposits of 6.39% (100 minus 93.61). If the three-month interest rate at delivery is less than 6.39%, the buyer of the contract at 93.61% will make a profit.

This quotation method is drawn from the Treasury bill market. However, further calculations are required to derive the profit or loss on such a futures position, since the interest rates for three-month instruments are quoted on an annual basis. The true interest paid on a three-month instrument is equal to the annual yield divided by four. Therefore the profit or loss on one unit of a Eurodollar contract (or any other three-month financial contract) equals the futures price variation divided by four. The total gain or loss on one contract is therefore equal to

$$\text{Gain (loss)} = \left(\frac{\text{Futures price variation}}{4} \right) \text{Size of contract.}$$

EXHIBIT 12.4

Quotations for Interest Rate Futures

EURODOLLAR (IMM)
$1 million; pts of 100%

	Open	High	Low	Settle	Chg	Yield Settle	Yield Chg	Open Interest
Sept	93.56	93.63	93.54	93.61	+ .04	6.39	– .04	76,011
Dec	93.46	93.55	93.43	93.53	+ .06	6.47	– .06	38,366
Mr87	93.26	93.35	93.25	93.34	+ .07	6.66	– .07	19,393
June	93.00	93.08	92.98	93.08	+ .07	6.92	– .07	10,705
Sept	92.71	92.80	92.70	92.79	+ .07	7.21	– .07	6,757
Dec	92.42	92.51	92.42	92.51	+ .07	7.49	– .07	5,110
Mr88	92.15	92.23	92.14	92.24	+ .08	7.76	– .08	4,970
June	91.89	91.96	91.88	91.98	+ .08	8.02	– .08	1,632

Est vol 31,938; vol Fri 40,189; open int 162,944, +422.

TREASURY BONDS (CBT)
$100,000; pts. 32nds of 100%

	Open	High	Low	Settle	Chg	Yield Settle	Yield Chg	Open Interest
Sept	99–16	100–17	98–31	100–14	+ 34	7.956	– .107	164,959
Dec	98–23	99–23	98–05	99–20	+ 34	8.038	– .109	23,623
Mr87	97–28	98–28	97–14	98–26	+ 34	8.121	– .110	5,197
June	97–15	98–02	97–15	98–01	+ 34	8.202	– .111	3,372
Sept	96–14	97–11	96–14	97–09	+ 34	8.280	– .113	2,517
Dec	96–13	96–23	96–08	96–20	+ 34	8.350	– .114	1,288
Mr88	95–28	96–03	95–21	96–01	+ 34	8.413	– .116	1,266
June	...	...	...	95–16	+ 34	8.471	– .116	759
Sept	94–24	95–03	94–24	95–01	+ 34	8.522	– .117	304
Dec	...	...	...	94–19	+ 33	8.570	– .114	112

Est vol 200,000; vol Fri 222,906; open int 203,397, +6,152.

Source: Reprinted by permission of *The Wall Street Journal* (*Europe*), July 16, 1986, © 1986, Dow Jones & Co., Inc. All rights reserved worldwide.

Assume that in September the Eurodollar interest rate drops to 6% on the delivery date. The futures price will be 94% on that date. The profit to the buyer of one contract is

$$\text{Gain} = \left(\frac{94\% - 93.61\%}{4} \right) \$1 \text{ million} = \$975.$$

The same quotation technique is used for Treasury bills and other short-term interest rate contracts.

The quotation method for contracts on long-term instruments is quite different. The contract is usually defined in reference to a theoretical bond of well-defined characteristics, usually called a *notional bond*. For example, the U.S. Treasury bond contracts traded on the Chicago Board of Trade and on the LIFFE are defined in reference to a notional Treasury bond with an 8% yield and a 20-year maturity. The contract is to buy or deliver 100,000 U.S. dollars of par value of any U.S. Treasury bond that has a minimum life of 15 years and is noncallable over that period. However, the futures price quoted applies strictly to the notional 20-year 8% coupon bond. If the seller of a contract wants to physically deliver a bond, the seller can do so with any U.S. Treasury bond that has a maturity of more than 15 years and is noncallable for 15 years. The price received for a specific bond is equal to the settlement price of the notional bond adjusted by a conversion factor that takes into account the different characteristics in terms of coupon and maturity of the bond delivered.

For example, a high-coupon security is worth more than a comparable low-coupon bond. The conversion factor equals the present value of the bond discounted at 8%. Thus bonds with coupons in excess of 8% have conversion factors greater than one. Bonds with coupons below 8% have conversion factors less than one. The invoice price of a delivery is therefore equal to the futures settlement price times the contract size times the conversion factor:

Principal invoice = Futures settlement × Contract size × Conversion factor.

The delivery invoice paid by the futures buyer is adjusted for accrued interest on the delivered bond. At each point in time some bonds will be cheaper to deliver than others; their market price is low compared to the invoice price received on delivery. Futures prices tend to correlate most closely with the price of the cheapest-to-deliver security.

As shown in Exh. 12.4, the quotations are expressed in points and thirty-seconds of 100%. The quotation is in percentage of the par value of the bond. For example, the December 1986 contract of Treasury bonds settled at $99^{20}\!/_{32}$ on July 14. The change from the previous day's settlement price was $^{34}\!/_{32}$, or more than one percentage point (100 basis points). This exhibit also gives the calculated yield to maturity and its change from the previous day. With a price of $99^{20}\!/_{32}$, the notional bond has a yield to maturity of 8.038%. Because of the inverse relationship between the long-term interest rate and the market price of a bond (see Chapter 10), the buyer of a bond contract gains if the interest rate drops (the bond price rises) and loses if the interest rate rises. The gain or loss is simply equal to the futures price variation, in percent, times the size of the contract. In our illustration the gain made on one U.S. Treasury bond contract from the previous trading day is equal to:

$$\text{Gain} = \frac{34}{32}\% \times \$100,000 = \$1062.50.$$

The mechanics of other national bond futures markets are very similar to that of the United States. In each market the conversion factor for a deliverable bond is equal to the present value of the bond on delivery date, discounted at the yield of the notional bond (10% in France, 12% in the United Kingdom). An exception is China, where futures contracts for individual government bonds are traded.

The degree of international interest in financial futures is illustrated by the fact that the most active futures contract in terms of dollar value of the underlying security is the Eurodollar contract. As shown in Exh. 12.4, the total dollar value of Eurodollars exchanged in July 1986 was 31,938 × $1 million = $31.9 billion, as opposed to $20 billion for U.S. Treasury bonds. In 1995 a typical daily transaction volume on the Eurodollar futures was 500,000 contracts, or $500 billion of underlying value. A typical daily volume on the U.S. Treasury bond futures was also 500,000 contracts, or $50 billion of underlying value. Interest rate contracts in other currencies are also extremely active. This is typically the case of the Japanese, French, and British bond futures.

Some interest rate contracts are negotiated outside organized exchanges. Future rate agreements (FRA) are private contracts usually written by banks, which guarantee a client the borrowing or lending interest rate at a future time. On the expiration date of the FRA, the bank pays or receives the interest rate difference between the agreed rate and the interest rate prevailing in the marketplace at the time. It should be stressed that the FRA is disconnected from the actual lending or borrowing. The bank simply pays or receives the interest rate difference at maturity but does not lend to or borrow from the client. FRAs allow a client to lock in a future interest rate, so that they can be used in the same way as interest rate futures. However, FRAs are customized contracts that cannot be traded until maturity. Their advantage is that they can be tailored to the client's needs in terms of both exact expiration date and type of interest rate desired (e.g., six-month Eurodollar or twelve-month CD). In turn, the bank attempts to hedge its position, using other FRAs or interest rate futures.

Interest rate swaps described in Chapter 11 are also akin to forward contracts. As mentioned, they may be considered long-term packages of forward contracts.

Stock Index Futures

Stock index contracts are linked to a published stock index. The contract size is a multiple of the index. For example, the dollar size of the Standard and Poor's 500 contracts traded on the Chicago Mercantile Exchange is 500 times the S & P 500 index. As with all futures contracts, the futures price depends on the expected final settlement price, since the futures price converges at expiration toward the spot price of a good or financial instrument. A unique characteristic of stock index futures is that the underlying good, the stock index, does not exist physically as a financial asset. As a result, all final settlements take place in cash rather than by delivery of a good or security. On the delivery date, the buyer of a stock index contract receives the difference between the value of the index and the previous futures price. The procedure works as if the contract were marked to market on the last day, with the final futures price replaced by the stock index value. The cash delivery procedure avoids most of the transaction costs involved in buying and selling a large number of stocks. That is why cash settlement is sometimes used for other financial futures contracts. Eurodollar futures contracts have a cash settlement, and many new contracts are being created with cash settlement rather than physical delivery.

Numerous stock index contracts are available in the United States and all major countries. Futures or forward markets for individual stocks also exist in some stock markets, such as Rio de Janeiro and Paris. The most active contracts are described in Exh. 12.5. These indexes are usually broadly based to allow for broad

EXHIBIT 12.5

Major Stock Index Contracts Worldwide, 1994

Exchange,[a] Contract	Index Specifications	Futures Value Multiplier
CME, S&P 500	Weighted index of top 500 industrial stocks on NYSE	$500 × index
CBOT, Major Market Index	Weighted index of top 20 stocks on NYSE	$500 × index
NYFE, NYSE Composite Index	Comprised of 1500 shares on NYSE	$500 × index
TFE, TSE 35	Weighted index of top 35 Canadian stocks on Toronto Stock Exchange	Canadian $500 × index
SFE, All Ordinary	Weighted index of top 250 Australian stocks	Australian $100 × index
HKFE, Hang Seng	Weighted index of top 33 shares on Hong Kong Stock Exchange	Hong Kong $50 × index
CME, Nikkei 225	Unweighted index of top 225 shares on Tokyo Stock Exchange	$5 × index
OSE, Nikkei 225	Unweighted index of top 225 shares on Tokyo Stock Exchange	JPY 1000 × index
SIMEX, Nikkei 225	Unweighted index of top 225 shares on Tokyo Stock Exchange	JPY 500 × index
TSE, Topix	Weighted index of Japanese shares on TSE	JPY 10,000 × index
LIFFE, FT-SE 100	Weighted index of top 100 British stocks on LSE	£25 × index
MATIF, CAC 40	Weighted index of top 40 French stocks	FF 200 × index
DTB, DAX	Weighted index of 30 shares on Frankfurt Stock Exchange	DM 100 × index
FFMA, EOE Stock Index	Weighted index of 25 leading Dutch stocks quoted on Amsterdam Stock Exchange	FL 200 × index

[a]CME: Chicago Mercantile Exchange; CBOT: Chicago Board of Trade; NYFE: New York Futures Exchange; TFE: Toronto Futures Exchange; SFE: Sydney Futures Exchange; HKFE: Hong Kong Futures Exchange; OSE: Osaka Securities Exchange; SIMEX: Singapore International Monetary Exchange; TSE: Tokyo Stock Exchange; LIFFE: London International Financial Futures Exchange; MATIF: Marché à Terme International de France; DTB: Deutsche Terminbörse; FFMA: Financial Futures Market Amsterdam; CSE: Copenhagen Stock Exchange; MEFF: Mercado de Futuros Financieros; OM: Stockholm Options Exchange; OTOB: Osterreichische Terminbörse; SOFFEX: Swiss Options and Financial Futures Exchange.

Exchange,[a] Contract	Index Specifications	Futures Value Multiplier
FUTOP (CSE), KFX Stock Index	Pure price index composed of 20 equities with the highest market capitalization among the 40 most liquid share listed on Copenhagen Stock Exchange	DKK 1000 × index
MEFF, IBEX 35	Comprised of the most important Spanish shares	Pta 100 × index
OM, OMX Stock Index	Weighted index of the 30 most heavily traded stocks on Stockholm Stock Exchange	SEK 100 × index
OTOB, ATX Index	Comprised of the largest Austrian stocks	ASch 100 × index
SOFFEX, Swiss Market Index (SMI)	Comprised of 25 shares of the most important Swiss companies	SF 50 × index

participation in the market. One exception is the Chicago Maxi Market index, which consists of only 20 stocks. It is favored because it closely tracks the Dow Jones index and is easier to arbitrage, given the small number of stocks involved.

All stock index futures prices are expressed as the value of the underlying index. As an illustration, let's assume that the December contract of the Sydney All Ordinary index contract is 1150. The next day this contract quotes at 1170. The gain in Australian dollars for the holder of one contract is equal to:

$$\text{Gain} = (1170 - 1150)\ A\$100 = A\$2000.$$

In general,

$$\text{Gain (loss)} = \text{Futures price variation} \times \text{Contract value multiplier.}$$

One may wonder why stock index futures have become so popular. The reason is that, like any other futures contracts, stock index futures offer an investor leverage. One can speculate on or hedge stocks with only a small cash investment equal to the margin. The specific advantage of a stock index contract is that an investor can directly invest in the stock market in a broad sense, without having to bear the specific risk of individual securities. Let's consider an investor who is bullish on an economy but has no knowledge or expectations about individual firms in that economy. What the investor wants is a diversified portfolio that will appreciate with the market rather than a few individual issues, which are vulnerable to specific factors. The investor has two alternatives: to buy an index fund with the associated costs or to buy stock index futures. Stock index futures are a convenient, highly liquid, and relatively inexpensive way to get a position similar to that of a well-diversified portfolio. They can even be used to short the market.

There are numerous situations in which stock index futures are useful:

- Because of their leverage and liquidity, they allow for active up-and-down speculation.

- Large institutional investors may hedge their portfolios by selling stock index contracts when they anticipate a decline in the market. Hedging avoids the large transaction costs involved in rapidly liquidating a large portfolio. Moreover, the hedge can be undone instantly should expectations be revised.

- An investor may be very bullish on specific companies and expect their stock price performance to outperform the market. However, the market as a whole may decline, pushing all stock prices down. The investor can hedge the associated market risk of the selected securities by taking a short position in stock index futures contracts.

- Institutions that move large sums of money in the stock market use these contracts to immediately take a position in the market, while slowly lining up sellers of shares at the best price. Even if the stock market goes up before the purchase program is completed, the institution benefits from the rise thanks to its *long position* in stock index futures. An alternative strategy is to ask brokers and dealers for a firm price immediately; because brokers require a certain amount of time to line up sellers, they charge a marked-up asking price. This compensates them for the risk of the market's going up while they are lining up sellers. With stock index futures, the need for this procedure, and the risk premium required, is eliminated. The same applies to institutions wanting to sell large portfolios.

- Foreign investors are interested in stock index futures to reduce cash movements between countries and manage their currency risk exposure better. This is illustrated in Chapter 14.

Futures Valuation

Payoff Structure

A whole-term structure of futures prices is quoted for every asset. For example, a term structure of gold futures prices for December 1, 1993, is given in Exh. 12.6. In the spot (cash) market an ounce of gold traded for $400. The futures price quoted for delivery April 1994 was $420, with a margin of $15 per ounce. Since gold is traded in contracts of 100 ounces, the total margin for one contract was

EXHIBIT 12.6

Gold Contract of 100 Troy Ounces; Futures Price per Ounce on December 1, 1993

Delivery Date	Futures Price (dollars)
December 1993	403
February 1994	413
April 1994	420
June 1994	428
August 1994	435
October 1994	444
December 1994	452
February 1995	457
April 1995	467
June 1995	475
August 1995	485
October 1995	493

$1500. It is clear that the financial leverage is on the order of 28, i.e., 420 over the margin deposit of 15. In other words, a 10% gold price appreciation would have been transformed into a 280% profit on the capital invested (less commissions and taxes). In a sense, the gold beta of this speculative position (i.e., the rate of return sensitivity to a gold price movement) is equal to 28, the financial leverage:

$$\frac{\mathrm{d}M}{M} = \beta \frac{\mathrm{d}G}{G},$$

where

ß   is equal to G/M, or the financial leverage
M is the amount of margin, and
G is the price of gold.

Potential gains or losses on the position may be represented either in dollars per ounce or in rate of return as a function of the price of gold at maturity (see Exh. 12.7). It is clear that the loss may exceed 100% (the original margin).

The Basis

A futures price approaches the spot price at delivery, though not during the life of the contract. The difference between the two prices is called the *basis*:

Basis = Futures price − Spot price.

EXHIBIT 12.7

Potential Gain-Loss Structure as a Function of Gold Price

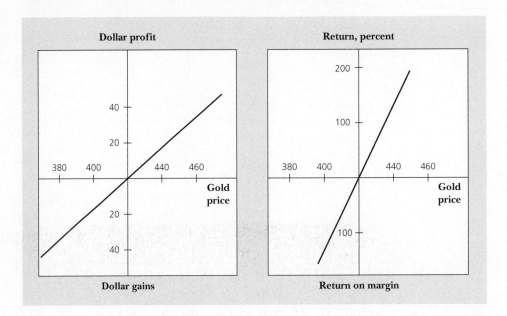

Futures valuation models determine a theoretical value for the basis. The basis for perishable goods depends on complex factors that are often difficult to forecast, including harvesting cycles and expected crop sizes. But the bases for financial contracts, such as currencies, interest rates, stock indexes, or gold, depend on much simpler factors.

The theoretical value of the basis is constrained by the existence of profitable riskless arbitrage between the futures and the spot markets for the good. This arbitrage is often referred to as a *cash and carry*. Taxes and transaction costs can make futures prices deviate from their arbitrage values.

Gold Futures   If the futures price gets to be too high relative to the price of gold in the spot market, operators start an arbitrage involving spot and futures positions. They buy cash gold and sell gold futures contracts. As an illustration, assume that the February futures 1994 price given in Exh. 12.6 was $430 instead of $413. Furthermore, assume that the annual interest rate on three-month borrowing was 12% (or 3% for three months) and that gold storage costs were equal to $0.40 per ounce per month. An arbitrager could have bought spot gold at $400 per ounce, financed the purchase at a 12% interest rate, and stored gold until the end of February. A February futures contract would have been sold at the same time the spot was purchased, for a futures price of $430. At the end of February the spot gold would have been used for delivery of the futures contract. The final result would have looked as follows:

Spot purchase
Cash	$400.00
Financing cost (3%)	12.00
Storage cost (0.40 × 3 months)	1.20
	$413.20
Futures sale	$430.00
Net profit	$16.80

Arbitrage takes place to eliminate this profit opportunity. Prices adjust until the futures price is such that the basis is inferior or equal to the *carrying costs*, which are the costs of storage, insurance, and financing the spot purchase. Financing and storage costs are, in turn, linked to the quantity of goods and the length of time they are stored. Storage costs may be either fixed or a function of the value insured (the spot price). As a matter of fact, the basis generally approximates carrying costs. If it were significantly less, sophisticated investors would sell gold from their hoardings and replace it with gold futures contracts. Therefore arbitrage implies that the basis should be close to carrying costs. We assume that the margin is interest bearing, so that there is no financing opportunity cost associated with depositing it.

If we denote F the futures price for delivery at time t and S the current spot price, a simple theoretical value of the basis is given by

$$\text{Futures price} = F = S(1 + r) + k\,(t, S), \tag{12.1}$$

or

$$\text{Basis} = F - S = Sr + k\,(t, S),$$

where

r is interest rate over the period t, and
k is the cost of storage, which is a function of t and S.

As an illustration, assume that the three-month interest rate is 3% (12% annual) and that the cost of storage is $0.40 per ounce per month. Then the basis should be equal to $13.2:

$$F - S = (400 \times 3\%) + (0.40 \times 3) = 13.2.$$

To simplify the mathematical formula, we refer in this chapter to interest rates over the time period considered. If annual rates are used instead, they have to be adjusted by multiplying by the number of days in the period and dividing by 360. For example, the 12% annual rate translates into

$$r = 12\% \frac{90}{360} = 3\%.$$

Commissions should not be neglected in this arbitrage. They are often quite large and affect the theoretical valuation model given here. Moreover, contract prices for different delivery dates may be negotiated at different times of the day, which means that they may be based on different spot prices. Combined with the cost of arbitrage, this introduces apparent discrepancies into the term structure of the futures prices we see published in newspapers. This problem arises more frequently in markets that either are illiquid or have little trading activity on certain delivery dates.

Note that the basis increases with the maturity of the contract, as illustrated in Exh. 12.6. Similar arbitrage valuation models hold for other financial futures.

Currency Futures   A futures pricing argument was already developed in Chapter 1. It has been shown that the currency futures exchange rate cannot differ from the spot exchange rate adjusted by the interest rate differential in the two currencies.

Let's suppose that the spot exchange rate S is FF/\$ = 8.00, that the U.S. dollar one-year interest rate is $r_\$ = 10\%$, and that the French franc one-year interest rate is $r_{FF} = 14\%$. Then the one-year futures rate, F, has to be equal to 8.2909. To illustrate again how the arbitrage works, let's suppose for a moment that the futures rate is only FF/\$ = 8.10. Then the following (riskless) arbitrage would be profitable for a French investor:

Borrow \$1 and transfer it into
French francs on the spot market: FF 8.00

Invest the francs for a year
at 14% with an income of   1.12
                                         ─────────
                                         FF 9.12

Sell a futures contract to repatriate
enough of these francs to cover the
dollars borrowed plus the financing
cost, i.e., \$1.10. At delivery, \$1.10
will be obtained for FF 8.10 × 1.10   FF 8.91

The FF net profit is   FF 0.21

Arbitrage will take place until the futures rate is such that

$$F = S\frac{1 + r_{FF}}{1 + r_\$},$$ (12.2)

or

$$\text{Basis} = F - S = S\frac{r_{FF} - r_\$}{1 + r_\$}.$$

In the example the futures rate must be equal to FF/\$ = 8.2909.

Interest Rate Futures: Bonds   A similar arbitrage reasoning holds for bond futures. Let's consider the example in which a British investor can buy either a bond futures with delivery in three months at 99.8 or a long-term bond selling at 100% in the cash market with a coupon equal to the current long-term yield of 12%. The three-month short-term interest rate is equal to 8%. If the futures price is too high, e.g., with futures price of 99.8, the investor should work the following arbitrage:

Buy the bond in the cash market	−100
Incur three months financing costs (at 8%)	−2
Receive three months of bond accrued interest (at 12%)	+3
	−99
Sell bond futures (at 99.8) and take delivery in three months	99.8
Net profit	0.8

Clearly the basis has to be equal to the difference between the short- and long-term interest rates (−1% in this example) to rule out any obvious arbitrage opportunities. The bond futures price will be below spot prices if the yield curve is upward sloping (long-term interest rates above short-term rates).

The previous example is, however, somewhat misleading. First, several bonds can be used for delivery, so the basis must be calculated for each of these bonds; these bases are usually referred to as the *cost of carry*. In each cost-of-carry calculation, the futures price should be adjusted by the conversion factor. Second, whereas the seller of a futures contract may deliver any of the acceptable bonds, the buyer of a futures contract must accept the bonds chosen by the contract's seller. The seller will generally choose the bond cheapest to deliver, which means that the futures prices are generally influenced by the cost of carry of the bond cheapest to deliver. The option to choose the cheapest bond to deliver is a definite advantage to the contract's seller (or short). The relative value of deliverable bonds changes when the interest rate changes. The option to choose the bond to be delivered is impounded in futures prices bidding them down.[3] This may make the futures look inexpensive compared to the cash value of bonds. Conversely, the futures yield may appear high compared to the average bond yield as found on the cash market.

Interest Rate Futures: Short-Term Deposits   These futures create a deposit commencing several months hence. Their valuation is somewhat difficult, because the futures are written on a security that has not been issued and therefore has no spot price. For example, the September Eurodollar indicated in the July 14 quotations in Exh. 12.4 relates to a three-month deposit that will start in September. Even if three-month bills are traded in July, they are not the ones that will be issued in September. This is a marked difference from other financial contracts, for which the underlying security is simultaneously traded in the cash market. (Stock index futures have no underlying securities, but the spot value of the index can easily be calculated at any moment in time.) The short-term interest rate futures are often referred to as *forward/forward rates*; the valuation of such a contract is usually obtained by observing two interest rates currently quoted in the market.

Assume that we want to determine the futures interest rate on the September Eurodollar contract. As of July 14 the contract is deliverable in about two months; since the contract is written on a three-month deposit, the final maturity takes place in five months (two plus three). Buying the futures contract in July is equivalent to a contract to lend Eurodollars for three months in September (two months from now) at the futures interest rate. This is similar to lending in July for five months and simultaneously borrowing for two months. Therefore the futures interest rate, r_F, is given by the formula

$$1 + r_F = \frac{1 + r_m}{1 + r_d}, \tag{12.3}$$

where

r_F is the futures interest rate,

r_m is the current interest rate to maturity (five months, in the example), and

r_d is the current interest rate to delivery (two months, in the example).

Since interest rates are usually quoted on an annual basis, they should be multiplied by the time to maturity: r is equal to the annual interest rate multiplied by (period = days/360). Annual interest rates are calculated over 365 days, rather than 360, in a few countries, e.g., the United Kingdom. It might be useful to work this formula through an example.

Let's assume that the five-month annual interest rate is equal to 6.3% and that the two-month annual interest rate is equal to 6.068%. The interest rate over the periods are

$$r_m = 6.3\% \frac{5}{12} = 2.6250\% \text{ and}$$

$$r_d = 6.068\% \frac{2}{12} = 1.0113\%.$$

So, by Eq. (12.3) we find that

$$1 + r_F = \frac{1.026250}{1.010113} = 1.015975.$$

Hence $r_F = 1.5975\%$, and the annual interest rate is

$$1.5975 \frac{12}{3} = 6.39\%.$$

Therefore the futures price should be equal to 100% minus the interest rate of 6.39%, which is 93.61.

Stock Index Futures   Again, the basis for stock index futures is determined by an arbitrage argument. The basis should be equal to the opportunity cost of directly buying the stocks in the cash market; the cost of financing the stocks is linked to the short-term interest rate, and the arbitrager receives the dividend yield, which is not paid on the futures contract. The theoretical value is given by

$$F = S(1 + r_S - r_D),\tag{12.4}$$

where

r_D is the dividend yield,
r_S is the financing cost (short-term interest),
S is the spot value of the stock index, and
F is the futures value of the stock index.

If the futures price were much larger than this theoretical value (the futures quotes at a large premium), an arbitrager could buy the index and sell the futures. At expiration, he or she would receive the value of the futures, F, plus the dividend yield on the index, Sr_D, while he or she would have spent the value of the spot index plus the financing of the spot position $(S + Sr_S)$. Arbitrage takes place until the receipt and expenses are equal, as in Eq. (12.4).

Transaction costs to build the arbitrage make all these valuation models somewhat approximate. This is more vividly the case for stock index futures where a large number of different securities have to be transacted to build an arbitrage. Buying and selling programs take place anyway and may affect the stock prices on the delivery date.

Futures and Forward

The pricing relations just described ought to be better verified for forward than for futures contracts. This is because forward contracts have a fixed margin that is not revised over the life of the contract. So far, we have assumed that the initial margin was deposited in the form of interest-bearing securities, so that there was no financing cost for this margin. However, futures contracts are marked to market, so that any loss on the futures position must be paid for and financed. This financing cost is uncertain because it depends on the future price variation. Also, the interest rate used to finance this margin may vary over time. It has been shown that futures and forward prices should be equal if the interest rates are constant over the life of the contract. If interest rates are uncertain, the correlation of interest rate and asset price movements has been shown to be an important variable in the relationship between forward and futures prices.[4]

Other futures contract quirks affect futures pricing. For example, many contracts traded in the United States can be delivered at any time during the delivery month, so that the exact maturity of the contract is uncertain.

Bond contracts traded on the Chicago Board of Trade have an *implied put option*, or *wild card play*. The seller may choose to deliver securities on any day during the delivery month. The invoice price is based on the futures settlement price at the close of trading (around 2:00 P.M.). But the seller has until 8:00 P.M. the same day to decide whether to deliver, during which time the bonds continue to be traded in the cash market. If bond prices drop sharply between 2 and 8 P.M., the seller may buy cheap bonds in the cash market, bonds that can be used to deliver at the settlement price fixed at 2:00 P.M. Of course, this option affects futures pricing[5] and lowers the value of the futures contract.

Hedging with Futures

Leveraged securities allow hedging of specific risks with minimal capital investment. Hedging the risk of an individual asset is easy if futures contracts on that specific asset exist. A U.S. investor holding 1000 ounces of gold bullion may sell ten 100-ounce gold futures contracts when the outlook for gold becomes poor. This action will basically remove the uncertainty linked to gold price fluctuations. However, futures contracts do not exist for every asset, so that somewhat imperfect hedging strategies have to be designed. The major question is: Which futures contracts should be used and in what amount? This problem is all the more important in portfolios with an international asset allocation and numerous sources of risk.

As an illustration, let's consider a Swiss manager worried about the British bond part of his portfolio. The manager might fear an increase in British interest rates, while forecasting a strong British pound relative to the Swiss franc. This would lead the manager to selectively hedge against the British interest rate risk, while retaining the British pound currency exposure. Similarly, the manager might be bullish on a few U.S. companies, while fearing an adverse movement in both the general level of U.S. stock prices and the value of the U.S. dollar. Multicurrency risk management is addressed in Chapter 14; here we focus on the hedging approach to a single national market (commodity, equity, or fixed income).

A hedge can generally be classified as a *cash hedge* or an *anticipatory hedge*. A cash hedge is the hedging of an existing position in the spot (cash) market. An anticipatory hedge involves hedging a cash position that has not yet been taken but is expected to be taken in the near future. A cash hedge generally involves selling futures contracts to cover a cash position and is usually referred to as a *short hedge*. In contrast, an anticipatory hedge generally involves buying futures contracts in anticipation of a cash purchase. This is usually referred to as a *long hedge*, since the investor is long in futures contracts.

Examples in fixed-income management may illustrate these two types of hedges. Financial futures are often used by bond portfolio managers following an active strategy when they fear a sudden, adverse move in interest rates. Futures contracts allow them to adjust a position quickly, without incurring the high transaction costs involved in rapidly rebalancing a portfolio. Two examples illustrate how this works:

Short hedge. An investor has a portfolio of Treasury bonds with a face value of $1 million worth $769,000 in the market. She is worried that the weekly money supply figure, announced on Thursday, will push long-term interest rates up. Rather than sell the bond portfolio, she can temporarily hedge the portfolio against interest rate movements by selling ten Treasury bond contracts on the CBT (one contract for each $100,000 in face value). The futures price for a December contract is $76^{16}\!/_{32}$%, which is the price of a theoretical 8% coupon Treasury bond. The investor's portfolio of Treasury bonds may be used as collateral. If long-term interest rates go up, the futures price will drop, and the investor will show a profit because her contracts will be marked to market.

One week later the futures price drops to 76, and the market value of her Treasury bond portfolio falls to $764,000. The profit on the ten futures contracts is

$$\left(76^{16}\!/_{32}\% - 76\%\right) \times \$100,000 \times 10 = \$5000.$$

This realized profit offsets the loss of value on the bond portfolio, as illustrated in Exh. 12.8.

EXHIBIT 12.8

Short Hedge	
Cash Market	**Futures Market**
September 1: Holds $1 million of a bond at 76.9% ($769,000)	Sells $1 million of Treasury bond futures at 76.5% ($765,000)
September 8: Holds $1 million of a bond at 76.4% ($764,000)	Buys $1 million of Treasury bond futures at 76% ($760,000)
Gain: –$5000	+$5000

Long hedge. A Swiss portfolio manager has just learned that a client will add $1 million to his account in a week. This cash flow will be invested in short-term Eurodollar deposits. The current short-term interest rates on the Eurodollar market are at 10%, but the manager is afraid that interest rates will drop before the cash flow is received and invested. In order to lock in the 10% interest rate, the manger buys one Eurodollar futures contract on the London International Financial Futures Exchange (LIFFE). Recall that short-term futures contracts are quoted as 100 minus the annual interest rate, even for three-month deposits. The futures price on the LIFFE is 90.

One week later the three-month interest rate drops to 9%, and the Eurodollar futures price is 91. The cash flow has arrived and is invested at the current 9% interest rate. The futures contract may then be resold at a profit. The profit per unit is equal to the futures price variation (91 – 90) divided by 4, because the annual yield must be converted to a quarterly rate for a three-month instrument. The total realized profit on one contract is therefore

¼(91% −90%) $1,000,000 = $2500.

Meanwhile, the cash flow is invested at 9%, with a return after three months of

$1,000,000 × 9% × ¼ = $22,500.

Compared to the 10% interest rate initially contemplated (an interest income of $25,000), there is an opportunity loss of $2500, but the realized profit on the futures contract exactly offsets this opportunity cost. In other words, the manager has locked in the initial high interest rate of 10%. This strategy works perfectly only if the maturity of the deposit or loan is three months and if the starting date corresponds exactly to the delivery date. Unfortunately this is seldom the case for real transactions. Short-term interest rate futures can be used to hedge despite the mismatched dates and maturities. However, cross-hedge risk is introduced.

It should be stressed that hedging with futures allows the reduction, or even the elimination, of the price uncertainty. However, it works both ways: It also reduces the chance of a gain in case of a favorable move in the price of the cash position. In the short-hedge example, the manager will not benefit from a drop in interest rates, because a loss on the futures position will offset a gain on the cash position.

Unfortunately perfect hedges as shown in these two examples are usually difficult to build. In a hedge risk is eliminated to the extent that the gain (loss) on the futures position exactly offsets the loss (gain) on the cash position. A perfect hedge is generally impossible to construct, because futures prices are not perfectly correlated to their spot prices, and futures contracts do not exist for all assets to be hedged.

Problems

Basis Risks   In a few cases one can find futures contracts written on the asset that needs to be hedged, as is the case for gold bullion. Even then, a perfect hedge will work only if the futures and spot prices of the asset vary exactly in parallel. Unfortunately the basis, i.e., the difference between the futures and the spot prices, tends to vary in an unpredictable manner. The basis is linked to the cost of carrying a futures versus a spot arbitrage position and can be positive or negative. As has been shown, the basis should, in theory, be equal to the difference between the income from the deliverable asset and the cost of borrowing this asset (short-term interest rate plus storage costs, for commodities).

Fluctuations in interest rates lead to variations in the basis. In the case of gold futures, the basis increases if short-term interest rates rise. The basis for most financial instruments involves a spread between two rates. For example, the basis for stock index futures is linked to the spread between the short-term interest rate and the dividend yield on the stock index. The basis for bond futures is linked to the spread between the short-term and long-term interest rates. Fluctuations in the spread induce variations in the basis. Therefore, a futures price will not exactly track the spot price of the underlying asset. Also, the basis, as calculated in the valuation formulas given, is only an arbitrage condition that holds within transaction costs. Even if interest rates do not move, the basis can fluctuate within the transaction cost band before arbitrage occurs. For example, buy (or sell) stock market arbitrage programs are automatically triggered if the basis (premium or discount) in stock index futures reaches the transaction cost band. The uncertainty about the variation in the basis creates basic risk, which precludes the possibility of establishing a perfect hedge. Strictly speaking, only unexpected variations in the basis create a risk; the basis is expected to converge to zero at delivery. The basis risk is a function of the time to expiration of the futures contract: The longer the maturity of the contract, the larger the basis. This is a major reason why investors tend to hedge with near-term contracts despite the commissions involved in rolling over the hedge, if desired, at the expiration of the futures contract.

The perception of basis risk depends on the investment horizon set by the investor. One usually attempts to preserve capital on a daily basis and to reduce the daily volatility of a portfolio. In a few cases investors care only about the value of the portfolio at specific dates, say, end of quarter. One would then try to hedge with futures contracts expiring on the date nearest to the investment horizon in order to minimize basis risk. Note that basis risk disappears totally if one shorts futures contracts whose delivery dates coincide exactly with the investment horizon. This happens because, on that delivery date, the futures price is equal to the spot price, and all uncertainty in the basis is resolved.

The existence of basis risk is illustrated in Exh. 12.9. A gold bullion position is hedged by selling futures contracts of equal amounts of ounces. The spot gold price is $400 per ounce, and the futures price is $413. Many things can happen in a week, and gold prices may go up or down. Gold price risk will be fully hedged, because the futures contract is precisely written on gold bullion, the asset being hedged. However, the basis may fluctuate. Several scenarios are presented in Exh. 12.9, which indicates the net gain or losses per ounce on the fully hedged position. We use the February futures given in Exh. 12.6.

If the basis remains unchanged, the return on the position is always zero,[6] and all gold price risk is eliminated. The only uncertainty borne is that of a change in the basis. As shown in Exh. 12.9, the net gain is equal to the change in basis whatever the movement in the price of gold. The asset price risk is fully eliminated, because the futures contract is precisely written in the asset to be hedged, and the only risk borne on this position is basis risk. A short hedger will gain if the basis decreases (a negative basis gets smaller in absolute value or even becomes positive) and will lose if the basis increases. The reverse holds true for a long hedger.

EXHIBIT 12.9

Hedge and Basis Risk *(Profit and loss per ounce under various scenarios of a short hedge)*					
Scenario:	**Cash (Spot) Market**		**Futures Market**		**Basis**
Drop in gold price					
December 1	Buy	400	Sell	413	13
December 8	Sell	380	Buy	393	13
		−20		+20	Change = 0
	Net = 0				*No change in basis*
December 1	Buy	400	Sell	413	13
December 8	Sell	380	Buy	396	16
		−20		+17	Change = +3
	Net = −3				*Basis increases*
December 1	Buy	400	Sell	413	13
December 8	Sell	380	Buy	391	11
		−20		+22	Change = −2
	Net = +2				*Basis decreases*
Increase in gold price					
December 1	Buy	400	Sell	413	13
December 8	Sell	420	Buy	433	13
		+20		−20	Change = 0
	Net = 0				*No change in basis*
December 1	Buy	400	Sell	413	13
December 8	Sell	420	Buy	436	16
		+20		−23	Change = +3
	Net = −3				*Basis increases*
December 1	Buy	400	Sell	413	13
December 8	Sell	420	Buy	431	11
		+20		−18	Change = −2
	Net = +2				*Basis decreases*

Cross Hedging　Unfortunately futures contracts exist for only a few assets; the chance of matching a futures contract to a specific portfolio of bonds or stocks is slim. A *cross hedge* has to be constructed in order to hedge the volatility of a specific security in a portfolio. A cross hedge means that the futures contract used is different from the initial asset to be hedged. For example, a U.K. gilt (long-term government bond) contract can be used to hedge a specific British corporate bond. Clearly the cross hedge will be established so that the price of the selected futures contract most closely correlates with the price of the initial asset. The following are a few examples of cross hedges on individual assets:

- Use Eurodollar contracts to hedge Euro-CDs.

- Use gold bullion contracts to hedge gold price uncertainty in a Canadian gold mining stock.

- Use Deutsche mark futures contracts to hedge Dutch guilders.

- Use U.K. stock index contracts to hedge a specific British stock portfolio.

The prices of the two instruments involved in the cross hedge do not correlate perfectly, so that cross-hedge risk is introduced. For example, the spread between Euro-CDs and Eurodollar rates may increase, or the specific U.K. stock portfolio may have a worse performance than the general market index.

Cross-hedge risk can seldom be avoided on portfolios of securities. The only exceptions are portfolios that are specifically designed to track a given market index (e.g., the Standard and Poor's 500) for which futures contracts are available. Hedging each individual security in the portfolio would be a costly and unfeasible task, since few futures contracts exist for individual assets. Instead, the strategy is to hedge homogeneous groups of securities (e.g., U.K. stocks or U.S. bonds) with global futures contracts, such as stock index contracts or government bond contracts.

The combination of basis and cross-hedge risk means that a perfect hedge can seldom be established, which means that an optimal hedging strategy has to be designed to get the best possible hedge.

Hedge Ratio

The result of a hedging strategy depends on finding the proper *hedge ratio*, because price movements of the asset and of the futures are often of different magnitudes. The hedge ratio is usually defined as the ratio of the principal (face value) of the futures contracts used to hedge relative to the principal (face value) of the cash asset position.

The multiplicity of asset types and contracts makes it difficult to give an encompassing definition of the hedge ratio; the one used here fits interest rate futures. In the two examples illustrating short and long hedges, the investors had to hedge a position with a face value of $1 million. In both cases they hedged using futures with a $1 million face value, so that the hedge ratio was equal to one. The application of this definition to other types of assets is somewhat difficult, especially when cross hedges are involved.

A practical and general extension of the hedge ratio definition is as follows;

$$\text{Hedge ratio} = \frac{\text{Number of contracts} \times \text{Size of contract} \times \text{Spot price}}{\text{Market value of asset position}}$$

$$= \frac{N \times Size \times S}{V}, \tag{12.5}$$

where

N is the number of futures contracts used to hedge;

Size of contract is the quantity of assets (e.g., 100 ounces of gold or 125,000 Deutsche marks), or the face value of securities (e.g., $100,000 worth of treasury bonds or $1,000,000 worth of Eurodollars), or the stock index multiplier (e.g., $500 times the S & P 500);

S is the spot price of the asset; and

V is the market value of the cash asset position.

It is easy to check that this definition of a hedge ratio is consistent with the previous one for fixed-income securities where $V/_S$ is the face value of the cash assets, and $N \times Size$ is the face value of the futures contracts. This definition applies equally to gold and other commodities. If an investor holds 1000 ounces of gold (spot price $400 per ounce) and decides to short ten contracts of 100 ounces (futures price $413 per ounce), the hedge ratio is equal to 1, since

$$\text{Hedge ratio} = h = \frac{N \times Size \times S}{V} = \frac{10 \times 100 \times 400}{400,000} = 1.$$

The hedge ratio for a stock portfolio can be calculated in a similar fashion. Note, however, that for stock portfolios the notion of physical quantities (as with a single commodity) or face value (as with bond portfolios) becomes very fuzzy. In this definition S represents the spot price of the index. Let's consider a portfolio of U.S. stocks with a market value of $1.5 million, hedged with 20 Standard and Poor's 500 futures contracts. The spot value of the S & P 500 is 150, and the futures price is 155. The hedge ratio is then equal to 1:

$$\text{Hedge ratio} = h = \frac{N \times Size \times S}{V} = \frac{20 \times 500 \times 150}{1,500,000} = 1.$$

The determination of an optimal hedge ratio is a controversial issue. The method used depends both on what the investor wants to optimize and on the stochastic behavior of asset prices. The methods currently used are listed here. The appendix to this chapter focuses on determining the optimal hedge ratio for a bond portfolio, which is somewhat more technical than determining one for commodities and stocks. Examples of hedging a gold and a stock investment will be used in the following discussion.

The Naive Approach: Equal Position   In the naive approach the principal value of a futures contract is chosen to be equal to the principal value of the asset position. The hedge ratio is therefore one. This is the traditional approach in commodities, in which hedging is based on the exact quantity of goods held. Brochures prepared by futures exchanges often suggest this hedging strategy. It makes sense for commodities in which futures are traded on an identical commodity. However, if the quality of the commodity differs among the cash futures or if cross hedges are required, this hedging strategy may not be optimal. For example, we may be hedging a small-company stock portfolio with S & P 500 futures. A higher hedge ratio would be required because small-company stocks are more volatile than the S & P 500 index.

The Naive Approach: Dollar Matching   A variant of the naive approach is to build a futures position so that its dollar market value will be equal to that of the asset position. Instead of matching quantities in position, we match dollar market values. The two hedge ratios differ because the futures price is different from the spot price.

Using gold as an example, our investor would sell $400,000 worth of gold futures, or approximately 9.69 contracts (for the purpose of this illustration, we assume that futures contracts can be fractionated), since each futures contract has a market value of 413×100 ounces = $41,300. Therefore 9.69 contracts will match the cash position of 1000 ounces at $400. The resulting hedge ratio is

$$\text{Hedge ratio} = \frac{9.69 \times 100 \times 400}{400,000} = 0.969.$$

Similarly, the small-companies investor would sell $1.5 million worth of S & P futures contracts. At market value this would amount to 19.355 contracts, since each contract has a market value of $500 \times 155 = \$77,500$. The resulting hedge ratio is

$$\text{Hedge ratio} = \frac{19.355 \times 500 \times 150}{1,500,000} = 0.968.$$

This dollar-matching strategy assumes that the percentage price movements of spot and futures prices are identical. The equal-position and dollar-matching strategies differ because of the difference between futures and spot prices. The equal-position approach makes more sense. We know that a futures price may be broken down into two parts: the spot price and the basis. The basis is moved by factors that may be quite independent from movements in the spot price, so that the basis component does not provide a hedge against uncertainty in the spot price. Hedges should be constructed to have equal spot value, as in the equal-position approach.

This naive approach may be acceptable for direct hedges when futures exist for the asset to be hedged. However, better strategies have to be used for cross hedges or even when basis risk is significant.

Minimum Variance Approach   Because of cross-hedge and basis risks, it is usually impossible to build a perfect hedge. One objective is to search for minimum variability in the value of the hedged portfolio. Investors usually care about the rate of return on their investment and the variance thereof. So if they decide to hedge, investors would like to minimize the variance of the return on the hedged portfolio. It is shown in the appendix that the optimal hedge ratio is equal to the covariance of the asset, or portfolio, return to be hedged with the return on the futures, divided by the variance of the return on the futures:

$$\text{Hedge ratio} = h = \frac{\sigma_{PF}}{\sigma_F^2}. \tag{12.6}$$

This optimal hedge ratio can be estimated as the slope coefficient of the regression of the asset, or portfolio, return on the futures return:

$$R_p = a + hR_F,$$

where R_p is the return on the asset or portfolio, R_F is the return on the futures, and a is a constant term. The futures return is defined as the futures price change divided by the spot price. (See discussion in the appendix.)

The minimum-variance hedge ratio for gold is likely to be close to one: Gold spot and futures prices are strongly correlated, with a regression slope of one. This is not the case for many cross hedges. Take the example of our small-companies portfolio. The optimal hedge is derived by regressing the portfolio return on the stock index return. This hedge ratio is the traditional beta used in modern portfolio theory. A slight difference is that we use the index futures return instead of the index return. This introduces a very small difference.

Let's consider a portfolio of small stocks that is more volatile than the market. It tends to amplify the movement in the market index by 50%. In other words, its ß relative to the market is equal to 1.5, the slope of the regression of the portfolio return on the market index return. The minimum-variance optimal hedge ratio is equal to 1.5. Whenever the market drops by $X\%$, the portfolio tends to drop by $1.5X\%$.

Utility-Based Approach   The objective set thus far has been to minimize the volatility of the hedge position. But this may be achieved at the expense of sacrificing expected return. More general theories of hedging attempt to maximize expected utility rather than simply minimize risk.[7] The optimal hedging strategy depends on the investor's utility function, so that no general practical results can be found. In the traditional mean-variance approach, an investor would attempt to minimize risk and maximize expected return simultaneously.

Hedging Market Risk   Financial futures are often used to hedge against market risk. The hedge allows the elimination of market risk while retaining specific risk. This is a typical portfolio approach with stocks and bonds. A few examples may illustrate this point.

1. An investor, thinking that a couple of companies are undervalued, will then buy the stocks of these companies and simultaneously sell stock index futures to avoid the risk of a slide in the stock market. When the mispricing of these companies is corrected, our investor will profit regardless of the movement in the market level. If she invests $1 million in these stocks, she should follow these two steps:

   a. Calculate the regression slope, ß, of her portfolio return with the stock index return. Since the ß of a portfolio is the weighted average of the ßs of the individual companies, the portfolio ß can easily be calculated from the company ß values published by many brokers and research services. Assume that the ß of the portfolio is equal to 1.5 in this case.

   b. Sell Standard and Poor's 500 futures. The hedge ratio should be 1.5. Each contract has a multiplier of $500, and the spot value of the index is 150. The number of contracts required is given by Eq. (12.5), assuming that the hedge ratio is 1.5.

$$1.5 = \frac{N \times 500 \times 150}{1,000,000},$$

   where N is the number of contracts. Hence our investor should sell 20 contracts.
   If the coefficient ß stays constant over time, the portfolio will be well hedged against stock market risk.

2. To illustrate the working of such a hedge, let's consider an American who wants to purchase shares of Australian natural resources companies, e.g., mines. He believes that this portfolio of stocks will strongly outperform the Australian stock market. The beta of this portfolio is estimated at 1.15. He wants to acquire protection against adverse movements in the Australian stock market and sells futures contracts on the All Ordinary Stock Index. The current level of the stock index is 1140, and the December futures are quoted at 1150. He decides to buy a natural resources stock portfolio of A$1 million and to sell ten contracts. The number of contracts is again derived from Eq. (12.5). Since All Ordinary Stock Index contracts have a multiplier of A$100 and the beta is equal to 1.15, the number of hedging contracts is given by

$$1.15 = \frac{N \times 100 \times 1140}{1,000,000}.$$

Hence $N = 10.09$, or approximately ten contracts.
   The portfolio is now protected against a down movement in the market. A month later the market drops by 10%, but the portfolio loses only 6.9%. A market drop of 6% is implicit in the loss of 6.9% incurred on a portfolio with a beta of 1.15, since $6.9\% = 1.15 \times 6\%$. The outcome of the operation is as follows:

	Futures Market	**Stock Market**
September 1	Sell 10 December All Ordinary futures at 1150	Buy natural resource stock ($ß = 1.15$), cost = A $1,000,000
October 1	Market declines 10%, but natural resources decline 6.9%	
	Buy 10 December All Ordinary futures at 1036	Sell natural resource stocks, proceeds = A $931,000
	Profit on futures = A $114,000	Loss on stocks = A $69,000
	Net profit on trade = A $45,000	

Despite the fact that the value of the stocks fell, because the market as a whole fell further, the short futures created a greater profit than the loss incurred on the stocks. A profit would also show if the stock market rose (instead of falling) and the natural resource stocks appreciated more than the market, adjusted for beta. For example, assume that the market rose 10% but natural resource stocks rose by 16.1%. A market rise of 14% is implicit in the gain of 16.1% incurred on a portfolio with a beta of 1.15, since $16.1\% = 1.15 \times 14\%$.

	Futures Market	**Stock Market**
October 1:	Buy 10 December All Ordinary Futures at 1264	Sell natural resource stocks, proceeds = A $1,161,000
	Loss on futures = A $114,000	Profit on stocks = A $161,000
	Net profit on trade = A $47,000	

Note that the hedge allows the investor to benefit not from the market appreciation but from the differential performance of the natural resource stocks. Because of the basis, the percentage movement in futures prices is somewhat different from that of the spot stock index.

3. An investor expects the spread between Eurobond yields and U.S. Treasury bond yields to narrow; that is, she expects the price of Eurobonds to rise relative to that of Treasury bonds. However, she is uncertain about the prospects of general interest rate levels. She should therefore buy Eurobonds and sell Treasury bond futures. The hedge ratio can be determined as shown in the appendix.

4. A gold bug believes that some Canadian gold mines and French gold-linked bonds are undervalued. He should buy a portfolio of these assets, calculate their ß relative to gold price movements, and use this ß as the hedge ratio. The sale of gold futures will protect the portfolio against adverse movements in the gold price, while allowing the investor to cash in on the correction of the securities mispricing.

Summary

1. Futures and forward contracts offer high financial leverage and liquidity.

2. Futures contracts are standardized in terms of size and delivery dates. They may be freely traded on the market. They are marked to market every day so that profits and losses are immediately realized.

3. Forward contracts are private contracts between two parties. They are customized in terms of size and delivery date and have to be held until delivery. The margin is set once and never revised.

4. There is a very large interbank forward exchange market as well as a significant currency futures market for the major currencies. Other commodities and financial instruments tend to be traded in futures rather than forward contracts.

5. Futures and forward contracts have a symmetrical payoff structure.

6. Futures and forward prices are usually broken down into the spot, or cash, price of the asset plus a basis. The basis is referred to as a discount, or premium, for currency or stock index contracts.

7. The major question in futures valuation is how to determine the theoretical value of the basis. This is usually done using an arbitrage argument taking offsetting positions in the spot and futures or forward markets. The cost of carrying this arbitrage puts limits on the basis. In all cases the basis tends to reflect the financing cost of holding a cash position minus the income lost, if any, in holding a futures position. Various technical aspects render the valuation of bond futures more difficult.

8. Futures and forward contracts are used to hedge assets or portfolios of assets against price risk. Several types of hedges can be designed. Two major decisions are the contracts to be used and the amount of hedging. Since few futures contracts exist, investors must often engage in cross hedging by using contracts that are close, but not identical, to the assets to be hedged. The aim is to use contracts whose futures price most closely correlates with that of the assets to be hedged.

9. Perfect hedges can seldom be created, because of basis risk (unexpected fluctuations in the basis) and cross-hedge risk (imperfect correlation between the asset and the contract). Various strategies for optimal hedging in a single-currency context have been proposed. These strategies range from a naive approach to a minimum-variance optimization approach.

Questions and Problems

1. A German corporation finalized a sale to an Italian client on April 15. The German corporation will deliver some gardening equipment on May 31 and will be paid 345 million lira on June 30. The current spot exchange rate is 1040 lira/DM. The German corporation is very worried about a depreciation of the lira in the coming two months and wishes to sell those lira forward against DM. Give some reasons why the German corporation should use forward rather than futures currency contracts. Exactly what contract should the German corporation arrange with its bank?

2. A Swiss portfolio manager has a significant portion of the portfolio invested in dollar-denominated assets. The money manager is worried about the political situation surrounding the next presidential election and fears a potential drop of the dollar. The manager decides to sell forward the dollars against Swiss francs. Why would the Swiss money manager use futures rather than forward currency contracts?

3. It is often said that futures contracts are less subject to default risk than futures contracts. Why is that?

4. In Chicago the size of a yen futures contract is 12.5 million yen. The initial margin is $2025, and the maintenance margin is $1500. You decide to buy ten contracts, with maturity in June, at the current market futures price of 0.01056 $/¥. The contract expires on the second to last business day before the third Wednesday of the delivery month (expiration date: June 17). We are on April 1, and the spot exchange rate is 0.01041 $/¥. Indicate the cash flows that affect your position if the following prices are subsequently observed. (Assume that spot and futures prices stay equal to the previous quotes on the dates that are not indicated below.)

	April 1	April 2	April 3	April 4	June 16	June 17
Spot $/¥	0.01041	0.01039	0.01000	0.01150	0.01150	0.01100
Futures $/¥	0.01056	0.01054	0.01013	0.01160	0.01151	0.01100

5*. In Hong Kong the size of a futures contract on the Hang Seng stock index in HK $50 times the index. The margin (initial and maintenance) is set at HK $32,500. You believe in a drop of the Hong Kong stock market following some economic problems in China and decide to sell one June futures contract on April 1. The current futures price is 7200. The contract expires on the second to last business day of the delivery month (expiration date: June 27). We are on April 1, and the current spot value of the stock market index is 7140.

- Guess why the spot value of the index is lower than the futures value of the index.

- Indicate the cash flows that affect your position if the following prices are subsequently observed:

	April 1	April 2	April 3	April 4
H.S. Futures	7200	7300	7250	6900

6*. Eurodollar futures contracts are traded on the Chicago Mercantile Exchange with a size of US $1 million. The initial margin is $540, and the maintenance margin is $400. You are the treasurer of a corporation, and you know on April 1 that you will have to pay cash for some goods worth $10 million and delivered on June 10. In turn you will sell those goods with a profit, but the payment will be received only on September 10.

Hence you know that on June 10, you will have to borrow $10 million for three months. We are on April 1, and the current LIBOR is 6.25%. On the Chicago Mercantile Exchange the Eurodollar futures contract with June delivery is quoted at 93.280%. The contract expires on the second business day before the third Wednesday of the delivery month (expiration date: June 17).

- What is the forward interest rate implicit in the Eurodollar futures quotation (93.280%) on April 1? Any guess why it is higher than the current three-month Eurodollar rate (6.25%)?

- What position would you take in futures contracts to freeze a three-month borrowing rate for June 10?

- On June 10 the Eurodollar futures contract quotes 90.97% while the current Eurodollar rate in London is 9%. You unwind your position on that date. Describe the cash flows involved.

7*. Derive a theoretical price for each of the following futures contracts and indicate why and how the market price should deviate from this theoretical value. In each case consider one unit of underlying asset. The contract expires in exactly three months, and the annual interest rate on three-month bills is 12%. All interest rates quoted are *annualized*.

Gold futures:	Spot gold price = $400 per ounce;
	cost of storage = $0.50 per ounce per month
Currency futures:	$/DM spot exchange rate = 50 cents per DM;
	3-month Deutsche mark interest rate = 4%
Eurodollar futures:	6-month Eurodollar interest rate = 10%
Stock index futures:	Current value of stock index = 240;
	annual dividend yield = 4%

8*. You wish to establish the theoretical futures price on a Euro-DM contract quoted on the LIFFE in London. The futures contract is for a 90-day Euro-DM rate at expiration of the futures contract. You look at the current term structure of Euro-DM interest rates. Following the standard conventions for short-term rates, all interest rates are quoted as annualized linear rates. In other words, the interest paid for a maturity of T days is equal to the annualized rate quoted, divided by 360 and multiplied by T. The observed rates are as follows:

	60-day	**90-day**	**150-day**	**180-day**
Euro-DM rate	4.125%	4.250%	4.500%	4.550%

- What should be the Euro-DM futures price quoted today with an expiration date in exactly 90 days?

- What should be the Euro-DM futures price quoted today with an expiration date in exactly 60 days?

9*. You are specialized in arbitrage between the futures and the cash market on the Paris Bourse. The CAC stock index is made up of 40 leading stocks. The futures price of the CAC contract with delivery in a month is 2120. The size of the contract is FF 200 times the index. The spot value of the index is given as 2000. Actually, there are transaction costs in the cash market; the bid-ask spread is around 40 points. You can buy a basket of stocks representing the index for 2020 and sell the same basket for 1980.

Transaction costs on the futures contracts are assumed to be negligible. During the next month, the stocks in the index will pay dividends amounting to 5 per index. These dividends have already been announced, so there is no uncertainty about this cash flow. The current one-month interest rate in francs is 6¼–⅜%.

- Do you detect any arbitrage opportunity?
- What profit could you make per contract?
- What is the theoretical value of the futures price?

10. The MATIF has a very active market for the French government bond contract. The underlying asset is a notional long-term government bond with a yield of 10%. The size of the contract is FF 500,000 of nominal value. Futures prices are quoted in percentage of the nominal value. On April 1 the French term structure of interest rate is flat. The bond futures price for delivery in June is equal to 106.21%. The three French government bonds that can be used for delivery have the following characteristics:

	Market price	Modified duration	Conversion factor
Bond A	107.46%	7.00	101.1771%
Bond B	105.57%	7.90	98.1441%
Bond C	106.32%	8.80	99.3104%

- Is the futures price consistent with the spot bond prices? (Find the bond cheapest to deliver.)
- Give an estimate of the interest rate sensitivity (modified duration) of the futures price.

    You are an American investor with a portfolio of French government bonds. The portfolio has a nominal value of FF 100 million and a market value of FF 110 million. Its average modified duration is 3.5. You are suddenly worried that social unrest in France could lead to an increase in French interest rates. Rather than selling the bonds, you wish to temporarily hedge the French interest rate risk.

- How many futures contracts would you sell and why?

11. An investor wants to invest in a diversified portfolio of Japanese stocks but can invest only a rather small sum. Our investor also worries about fiscal and transaction-cost considerations. Why would futures contracts on the Nikkei/Dow Jones index be an attractive alternative?

12*. A money manager holds $50 million worth of top-quality Eurobonds denominated in dollars. Their face value is $40 million, and most issues are highly illiquid. She fears a rise in U.S. interest rates and decides to hedge, using U.S. Treasury bonds futures. Why would it be difficult to achieve a perfect hedge (list the various reasons)?

13*. In problem 12 the average modified duration of the Eurobond portfolio is four years. The manager shares the market view that Eurobond yields for top-quality issues will closely track the yield on U.S. Treasury bonds. The current futures price is 80, and the modified duration of the notional bond is 9. What hedge ratio would you recommend? What about using a combination of different futures contracts?

14*. A manager holds a diversified portfolio of British stocks worth £5 million. He has short-term fears about the market but feels that it is a sound long-term investment. He is a firm believer in betas, and his portfolio's beta is equal to 0.8. What are the alternatives open to temporarily reduce the risk on his British portfolio?

15. You are an American pension fund holding a portfolio of French stocks. The market value of the portfolio is FF 20 million, with a beta of 1.2 relative to the CAC index. Here are some quotes on November:

- Spot value of CAC index: 2000
- Spot value of the franc: 5 FF/$

The dividend yield and FF and US $ interest rates are all equal to 4% (flat yield curves).

- What should be the futures price of the CAC?

- You fear a drop in the French stock market (but not the FF). The size of CAC index contracts is 200 times the CAC index. How many contract should you buy or sell to hedge the French stock market risk?

- You like the French stock market (different scenario from above) but fear a depreciation of the French franc. How many FF should you sell forward?

Notes

1. The contract sizes are 250,000 French francs, 100,000 Canadian dollars, 125,000 Dutch guilders, 1 million Mexican pesos, 25,000 British pounds, 12.5 million Japanese yen, 125,000 Deutsche marks, and 125,000 Swiss francs.

2. Exhibit 1.3 gave similar quotations for forward exchange rates.

3. See Garbade and Silber (1983); Gay and Manaster (1986) and (1991); and Benninga and Smirlock (1985).

4. See Black (1976); Jarrow and Oldfield (1981); Cox, Ingersoll, and Ross (1981); Richard and Sundaresan (1981); and Modest and Sundaresan (1983). Cornell and Reiganum (1981) studied the relation between futures and forward exchange rates; they found no significant differences. Most authors conclude that forward and futures prices should be empirically very close.

5. See Kane and Marcus (1986); and Fleming and Whaley (1994).

6. The expected return on the position is really the risk-free interest rate. The basis should progressively converge toward zero on the delivery date. If interest rates do not move, it can be shown that the expected daily change on this fully hedged position is the daily interest rate. This can be deducted by looking at the pricing equation (Eq. 12.1). The daily posting of marked-to-market margins renders the theoretical analysis more complicated for futures than for forward contracts.

7. See Anderson and Danthine (1981); and Benninga, Eldor, and Zilcha (1984).

Bibliography

Anderson, R.W., and Danthine, J.P. "Cross-Hedging," *Journal of Political Economy*, December 1981.

Benninga, S., and Smirlock, M. "An Empirical Analysis of the Delivery Option, Marking to Market and the Pricing of Treasury Bond Futures," *Journal of Futures Markets*, Fall 1985.

Benninga, S., Eldor, R., and Zilcha, I. "The Optimal Hedge Ratio in Unbiased Futures Markets," *Journal of Futures Markets*, Spring 1984.

Black, F. "The Pricing of Commodity Contracts," *Journal of Financial Economics*, March 1976.

Chicago Board of Trade. *Interest Rate Futures for Institutional Investors*, various issues.

Cornell, B., and French, K. "The Pricing of Stock Index Futures," *Journal of Futures Market*, Spring 1983.

Cornell, B., and French, K. "Taxes and the Pricing of Stock Index Futures," *Journal of Finance*, June 1985.

Cornell, B., and Reiganum, M. "Forward and Futures Prices: Evidence from the Foreign Exchange Market," *Journal of Finance*, December 1981.

Cox, J., Ingersoll, J., and Ross, S. "The Relation Between Forward and Futures Prices," *Journal of Financial Economics*, December 1981.

Duffie, D. *Futures Markets*, Englewood Cliffs, NJ: Prentice Hall, 1989.

Fleming, J., and Whaley, R.E. "The Value of the Wildcard Option," *Journal of Finance*, March 1994.

Garbade, K., and Silber, W.L. "Futures Contracts in Commodities with Multiple Varieties: An Analysis of Premiums and Discounts," *Journal of Business*, July 1983.

Gay, G.D., and Manaster, S. "Implicit Delivery Options and Optimal Delivery Strategies for Financial Futures Contracts," *Journal of Financial Economics*, May 1986.

————. "Equilibrium Treasury Bond Pricing in the Presence of Implicit Delivery Options," *Journal of Futures Markets*, Fall 1991.

Hill, J., and Schneeweiss, T. "A Note on Hedging Effectiveness of Foreign Currency Futures," *Journal of Futures Markets*, Spring 1986.

Ho, T., *Strategic Fixed Income Investment*, Homewood, IL: Dow–Jones Irwin, 1990.

Hull, J.C., *Options, Futures and other Derivatives*, Englewood Cliffs, NJ: Prentice Hall, 1993.

Jarrow, R.A., and Oldfield, G.S. "Forward Contracts and Futures Contracts," *Journal of Financial Economics*, December 1981.

Kane, A., and Marcus, A.J. "Valuation and Optimal Exercise of the Wild Card Option in the Treasury Bill Futures Market," *Journal of Finance*, March 1986.

Kolb, R.W. *Understanding Financial Futures*, Miami, FL: Kolb, 1991.

Modest D., and Sundaresan, M. "The Relationship Between Spot and Futures Prices in Stock Index Markets," *Journal of Futures Market*, Spring 1983.

Richard, S., and Sundaresan, M. "A Continuous Time Equilibrium Model of Forward Prices and Futures Prices in a Multigood Economy," *Journal of Financial Economics*, 9, December 1981.

Schwarz, E., Hill, J., and Schneeweis, T. *Financial Futures: Fundamentals, Strategies and Applications*, Homewood, IL: Irwin, 1986.

Siegel, D.R., and Siegel, D.F. *Futures Markets: Arbitrage, Risk Management and Portfolio Strategies*, Chicago, IL: Dryden Press, 1990.

Stoll, H.R., and Whaley, R.E. *Futures and Options*, Southwestern Publishing, 1993.

Toevs, A.L., and Jacob, D. "Futures and Alternative Hedge Ratio Methodologies," *Journal of Portfolio Management*, Spring 1986.

Chapter 12: Appendix
Advanced Section on Hedging

Derivation of the Minimum-Variance Hedge Ratio

Let's consider a portfolio of assets with market value V. This portfolio is hedged selling N futures contracts of a specific size. The spot and futures prices are S and F.

From period 0 to period t, the profit (or loss) on the hedged position is given by

$$\text{Profit} = (V_t - V_0) - [N \times Size \times (F_t - F_0)]. \tag{12.A1}$$

Introducing the hedge ratio h

$$h = \frac{N \times Size \times S_0}{V_0},$$

we have

$$\text{Profit} = \left(V_t - V_0\right) - \left[\frac{N \times Size \times S_0}{V_0}\left(V_0 \frac{F_t - F_0}{S_0}\right)\right]. \tag{12.A2}$$

The rate of return on the hedged position, R_H, is equal to

$$\text{Rate of return hedged} = R_H = \frac{V_t - V_0}{V_0} - \left[\left(\frac{N \times Size \times S_0}{V_0}\right)\left(\frac{F_t - F_0}{S_0}\right)\right], \tag{12.A3}$$

where

R_H is the rate of return on hedged portfolio,
R_P is the rate of return on asset portfolio,

R_F is the rate of return on futures $\dfrac{F_t - F_0}{S_0}$, and

h is the hedge ratio.

Eq. (12.A3) is equivalent to

$$R_H = R_P - hR_F.$$

The variance of return is equal to

$$\sigma_H^2 = \sigma_P^2 + h^2\sigma_F^2 - 2h\sigma_{PF}, \tag{12.A4}$$

where σ_H^2, σ_P^2, and σ_F^2 are the variances of R_H, R_P and R_F, respectively; and σ_{PF} is the covariance of R_P and R_F. Setting the derivative of σ_H^2 to zero, one can see that the variance of the hedged position is minimized for a hedge ratio given by

$$2h\sigma_F^2 = 2\sigma_{PF}, \text{ so}$$

$$h = \frac{\sigma_{PF}}{\sigma_F^2}. \tag{12.A5}$$

Note that this optimal hedge ratio is also the slope of the regression:

$$R_P = a + hR_F. \tag{12.A6}$$

The minimum-variance strategy is sometimes applied to price changes or price levels rather than rates of return, depending on the investor's risk-minimization objective. Rates of return are used in portfolio theory, since one generally cares about returns per dollar (or other unit of currency) invested. Even if some investors cared only about absolute dollar losses, they would still be better off estimating the optimal hedge ratio by running a regression such as in Eq. (12.A6). As pointed out by Hill and Schneeweis (1981) and Benninga, Eldor, and Zilcha (1984), the econometric properties of price levels or price changes require the estimation of h using a regression on percentage price changes, i.e., rates of return.[1]

Estimation Problems The optimal hedge ratio is usually estimated on past data. Besides the econometric problems mentioned, the procedure is helpful only to the extent that the past provides useful information on the future. A few months of daily or weekly data are required to estimate the regression slope. If the composition of the asset portfolio is frequently rebalanced, a past estimation of the optimal hedge ratio may be useless for the current portfolio. Therefore the method used to estimate h should be forward looking rather than backward looking. Even if the composition of the asset portfolio stays constant, the regression slope can be unstable with a low R^2. This is typically the case for the ßs of stocks. This means that the hedge will be imperfect ex-post and that great care should be devoted to estimating the optimal hedge ratio.

Multicontract Hedging Investors may want to hedge simultaneously several types of risk. For example, the value of a gold-linked bond is influenced both by movements in long-term yields and by gold prices (see Chapter 15). The holder of such a bond might sell Treasury bond futures and gold futures. The minimum-variance hedge ratios are obtained by running a multiple regression:

$$R_P = a + h_1R_{F1} + h_2R_{F2}, \tag{12.A7}$$

where h_1 and h_2 are the hedge ratios on each of the two futures contracts, and a is a constant term. A joint estimation of the two hedge ratios is required, since the two futures prices tend to be correlated. In our example gold prices are negatively correlated with movements in interest rates.

Hedging Strategies with Bonds

Despite a large variety of bonds, only a few bond futures contracts exist. Therefore hedging a bond portfolio is a difficult task. In this section we recall the various methods used to determine optimal hedge ratios, while focusing on those methods that are specific to bond management.

The Naive Approach   The simplest approach to hedging bond portfolios is to sell futures contracts with a face value equal to that of the bond portfolio, thereby attaining a hedge ratio of one. A simple example based on a single bond can illustrate the differences in hedging strategies according to the approach followed. In practice managers care about diversified portfolios of bonds rather than single issues. Let's consider a Treasury bond with a 12% coupon maturing in 2010. On June 1, this bond is priced at 90 percent of par value. The September Treasury bond futures trade at 70 percent of par value. Assume that the investor holds $1 million of face value of the bond. By definition of the hedge ratio, the equal-position hedge requires the investor to sell a number of contracts, N, such that the hedge ratio is equal to one in Eq. (12.5):

$$\frac{N \times 100,000 \times 90\%}{900,000} = 1.$$

Hence $N = 10$ contracts. This hedge would work well if the cash and futures positions experience the same price change.

Another alternative would be to match the dollar values of the cash and futures positions. This hedge would work well if the two positions experienced the same percentage return (rather than the same price change). Here the hedge ratio is equal to

$$h = \frac{90}{70} = 1.286.$$

The hedger should sell 12.86 contracts for each $1 million of bond face value.

Since the 12% Treasury bond maturing in 2010 is deliverable for the futures contract, a minor variation in the dollar-matching approach is to use the conversion factor. This bond has a conversion factor of 1.30, which means that it will be worth 1.3 times the futures price at delivery. This method is applicable only if the bond is deliverable. Furthermore, the hedge works well only if this bond is the cheapest to deliver, since futures prices tend to track more closely the price of the cheapest-to-deliver security. The conversion factor method cannot be applied to general bond portfolios.

Although these methods are very convenient, they seldom provide efficient hedging.

Minimum-Variance Approach   To apply the minimum-variance approach to hedging a bond portfolio, one would collect a few months of daily data on the portfolio values and futures prices. A regression of the portfolio's return, R_P, on the futures return, R_F, is run over the data set

$$R_P = a + hR_F.$$

For example, the slope of the regression in our illustration is equal to 1.15. Note that this hedge ratio is quite different from the dollar-matching value of 1.286. The number of contracts to be sold is equal to N such that

$$\frac{N \times 100,000 \times 90\%}{900,000} = 1.15.$$

Hence $N = 11.5$ contracts.

However, this method suffers from several problems. First, the slope estimate is likely to be unstable and reflect past relations. A change in the bond portfolio composition would affect the future slope coefficient. Second, the relationship between the two regression variables R_P and R_F is not expected to be linear. Remember that a bond price is a complex function of the interest rate. Interest rate changes will affect R_P and R_F differently. Indeed the coefficient h is likely to be a complex function of the interest rate and move over time.

This regression method is theoretically questionable and impractical, since it necessitates the collection of a large number of daily observations on each portfolio. A specific method has been developed to assess the optimal hedge ratio for bond portfolios. It is usually referred to as the instantaneous price sensitivity approach or duration approach.[2]

Instantaneous Price Sensitivity   The objective of a good minimum-variance hedge strategy is to offset any unexpected price change in the bond portfolio with price changes in the futures position. Actuarially, we know how a bond price reacts to a change in interest rates. The instantaneous price sensitivity, D^*, has been described in Chapter 10. The absolute value, D^*, is equal to the standard duration divided by one plus the yield-to-maturity on the bond. The sensitivity D^* is often referred to as modified duration:

$$\frac{dV}{V} = -D^* \, dr,$$

where dr is the instantaneous change in interest rate and dV the change in value of a bond or portfolio of bonds. Since a similar duration, D_F^*, exists for the notional bond futures, an optimal hedge can be constructed as the ratio of the price sensitivity of the bond portfolio to the price sensitivity of the futures contract. Then the optimal hedge ratio is equal to

$$h = \frac{SD_P^*}{FD_F^*} \qquad\qquad\qquad (12.A8)$$

where D_P^* and D_F^* are the modified durations for the portfolio and futures, and S is the average price of the bond portfolio. The modified duration of the bond cheapest-to-deliver is used for D_F^*.

In the example the modified duration of the 12% Treasury bond maturing in 2010 is equal to 6.5 years, while the notional bond in the futures contract has a modified duration of 7.1 years. Hence the optimal hedge ratio is equal to

$$h = \frac{90 \times 6.5}{70 \times 7.1} = 1.177.$$

Note that this instantaneous price sensitivity approach gives results equal to those of the dollar-matching approach when the duration of the portfolio is equal to that of the notional bond.

The advantage of this approach is that it is forward looking. It can easily be applied to a portfolio by calculating the weighted average duration of the portfolio. This is easy, since duration figures are routinely available from commercial services and brokers; no historical data are required. On the other hand, the hedge is supposed to work instantaneously only for small movements in interest rates. As the durations vary, the hedge ratio should be readjusted periodically.

Note that the instantaneous price sensitivity approach assumes that the interest rate is the only source of uncertainty and that there are parallel shifts in the term structure of interest rates. Indeed, the concept of duration relies on the assumption of parallel shifts in the term structure. An example of a situation in which this method is not expected to provide a perfect hedge is the hedging of a corporate bond portfolio of three-years' duration using 20-year Treasury bond futures; changes in the corporate-government interest rate spread, plus twists in the term structure, would lead to unexpected returns on the hedged position.

Appendix Notes

1. Running a regression on price levels results in significant autocorrelation of residuals. Running a regression on price changes results in heteroskedasticity of residuals.

2. The advantages of this approach are discussed in Toevs and Jacob (1986).

13

Options

O ption contracts, like futures contracts, are leveraged investments. They offer an attractive risk structure and are used for hedging and speculation. But their main advantage is that, because of their risk-return characteristics, they can be used to insure an existing portfolio.

Bonds and many other financial contracts include one or several optional clauses, so that the valuation of options is a very important task in finance. In this chapter we first describe the options market and its instruments. We then discuss the risk-return characteristics of options and their valuation. Finally, we discuss the use of options in portfolio management.

The Markets and Instruments

The Principle of an Option

Definition   In general, an option gives to the buyer the *right*, but not the *obligation*, to buy or sell a good, whereas the option seller must respond accordingly. Many different types of option contracts exist in the financial world. The two major types of contracts traded on organized options exchanges are calls and puts.

A call gives to the buyer of the option contract the right to buy a specified number of units of an underlying asset, at a specified price called the exercise, or strike price, on or before a specified date, called the expiration date, or strike date. A put gives to its buyer the right to sell a specified number of units of an underlying asset at a specified price on or before a specified date. In all cases the seller of the option contract, the writer, is subordinate to the decision of the buyer, and the buyer exercises the option only if it is profitable to him or her. The buyer of a call benefits if the price of the asset is above the exercise price at expiration. The buyer of a put benefits if the asset price is below the exercise price at expiration.

The complete definition of an option must clearly specify how the option can be exercised. A European-type option can be exercised only on a specified date, usually the expiration date. An American-type option can be exercised by the buyer at any time until the expiration date. American options are used on most of the organized options exchanges in the world. Both types of options can be freely traded at any time until expiration.

Organization of the Market   Before 1973 and the creation of the Chicago Board of Options Exchange (CBOE), options contracts were private contracts between two parties. The contracts were generally not standardized, and there was little or no secondary market activity. It was simply too difficult or costly to find someone to take over the obligation of a specific option contract. The procedure introduced by the CBOE revolutionized options trading and stimulated tremendous development of the market worldwide.

The organization of the market for listed, or traded, options is somewhat similar to that of the futures market. An options clearing corporation plays a central role. All option contracts are represented by bookkeeping entries on the computers of clearing corporations. As soon as a buyer and a seller of a particular contract decide to trade, a clearing corporation steps in and breaks down the deal into two option contracts: one between the buyer and the clearing corporation acting as seller, and the other between the seller and the clearing corporation acting as buyer. This procedure completely standardizes the contracts. It allows one to close a position by simply selling out the options held, while a seller may buy into a previous position. If a buyer decides to exercise an option, the clearing corporation randomly selects a seller of the option and issues an exercise notice. Specific selection rules are set by each exchange.

In most cases investors offset their position by making a reverse trade before the expiration date. Option buyers usually find it more profitable to resell an option on the market than to exercise it. But there are times when exercising an option is more profitable, such as when a large dividend is about to be paid on the underlying stock.

Some of the old options markets still offer only private nontraded options, but these markets are steadily disappearing. For example, dealers in the American over-the-counter market received authorization from the Securities and Exchange Commission to organize a Chicago-type options market for over-the-counter stocks. The Paris Bourse has also transformed its traditional options market into a Chicago-type market. Notable exceptions to this trend are the markets for currency options. Banks have begun writing European-type currency options tailored to the specific needs of commercial customers. This interbank market has successfully developed despite competition from the listed currency options market, which got its start on the Philadelphia Stock Exchange, and is now found on markets in London, Chicago, Amsterdam, Singapore, Sydney, Montreal, and other places.

Listed options markets can be found all over the world and are growing quickly. Options markets are opening in most countries, including emerging countries. International links between options exchanges have also slowly developed.

Trading in Listed Options   The option to buy an asset has a price that must be paid at the time of contracting. The price of an option, usually called the premium, fluctuates over time, depending on the value of the underlying asset and other parameters. Option quotations are given in the press as illustrated in Exh. 13.1, 13.2, and 13.3. An option is usually defined by the underlying asset, the exercise price, and the expiration month. Several options are usually traded on the same asset. Looking at London-traded options on BP in Exh. 13.1, one finds that nine calls and nine puts were traded for three exercise prices (500, 550, and 600 pence) and three expiration months (July, October, and January). The premium for the January 550 call option was 55; that for the October 600 put was 50. At the time of the transaction, buyers of the January call paid 55 pence per share. The standard size of an option contract is usually 100 shares, so buyers of one January 550 BP call contract paid $100 \times 55 = 5500$ pence, or 55 pounds. At expiration the buyer would have exercised the call option only if the BP share price had been higher than the exercise price of 550. In Exh. 13.1 the closing price of a BP share is given in the first column below the name of the underlying asset. The option buyer would have profited if the difference between the share price and the exercise price had been larger than the initial investment, namely, the premium of 55 pence. The investor could also have resold the option at any time after the initial purchase. Whether this investment resulted in a profit or a loss depended on the evolution of the option premium.

One must be careful when directly comparing published option prices, since they may be based on transactions taking place at different times of the day. The underlying asset price can change over the course of a day, thereby changing the option price.

The various quotations from Chicago, London, and Amsterdam are published in slightly different formats, as shown in Exhs. 13.1 to 13.3, but they all include the same information. In the United States and the United Kingdom the first three option prices listed are for calls, and the latter three, for puts. On the European Options Exchanges in Amsterdam (Exh. 13.2) the three prices in each row apply either to a call, if the underlying asset name is followed by a *C*, or to a put, if it is followed by a *P*. The current price of the underlying asset is given in all tables. It appears under the asset name in U.S. and British quotations and in the last column on the EOE. The information on the EOE is slightly more complete: The publication indicates the number of contracts traded each day. Note that some options were not traded on July 14. A nontraded option is indicated by a dash (—) on European exchanges. In the United States, however, a nontraded option is often indicated by the letter *r*, if the option was not traded during the day, or an *s*, if the option does not exist but is included to complete the matrix format of the publication. Each exchange has a fixed cycle of expiration months. Because active trading takes place in the last month of an option, some exchanges have introduced options expiring at the end of the current month.

Option Combinations   Investors can assemble various types of options into combinations that have such colorful names as *straddles*, *strips*, and *straps*.

EXHIBIT 13.1

Options Quotation in London

LONDON TRADED OPTIONS						
		·······Calls·······			·······Puts·······	
Option		Jul	Oct	Jan	Jul	Oct	Jan
■ **Allied Lyons**	300	32	45	55	1	7	8
(*333)	330	8	25	38	8	18	25
	360	2	12	20	33	38	40
■ **B.P.**	500	65	75	90	1	6	10
(*563)	550	20	40	55	4	19	27
	600	1½	17	30	40	50	57
■ **Cons. Gold**	420	24	47	57	3	22	30
(*434)	460	3	28	38	34	47	55
	500	1	11	23	70	77	84
■ **Courtaulds**	260	26	36	45	1	5	9
(*286)	280	8	25	31	4	10	15
	300	2	14	22	18	22	27
	330	1	6	14	48	49	50
■ **Com. Union**	280	33	38	—	1	3	—
(*312)	300	13	27	37	4	12	14
	330	2	14	24	20	26	28
■ **Cable & Wire**	600	90	120	140	1	10	13
(*685)	650	40	77	900	3	22	32
	700	10	35	60	20	45	55
	750	1	20	38	65	70	80
■ **Distillers**	600	145	160	—	1	4	—
(*740)	650	95	115	—	2	10	—
	700	45	70	—	4	25	—
■ **G.E.C.**	180	14	28	36	1	5	8
(*192)	200	3	16	22	10	15	18
	220	1	8	13	30	32	34
■ **Grand Met.**	360	—	—	55	—	—	13
(*383)	382	9	27	—	9	23	—
	390	—	—	38	—	—	30
	420	1	12	25	43	48	50
■ **I.C.I.**	850	147	160	182	2	4	7
(*994)	900	97	112	140	2	9	15
	950	47	78	105	4	24	30
	1000	13	50	72	17	42	52
■ **Land Sec.**	300	39	52	60	1	3	5
(*339)	330	10	30	39	3	10	15
	360	1½	13	21	24	26	29
■ **Marks & Spen.**	180	19	28	35	1	4	7
(*197)	200	3	16	23	5	12	16
	220	0½	7	14	24	26	27
■ **Shell Trans.**	700	78	100	117	1½	7	14
(*778)	750	30	60	82	5	18	27
	800	7	30	52	27	47	52
■ **Trafalgar House**	280	8	22	30	7	16	19
(*281)	300	2	10	18	22	28	30
	330	1	4	10	52	52	53

Option		Jul	Aug	Sept	Oct	Jul	Aug	Sept	Oct
■ **FT-SE**	1550	58	75	—	—	5	11	—	—
Index	1575	38	55	73	—	8	22	27	—
(*1599)	1600	20	38	53	82	17	33	38	52
	1625	90	27	42	65	33	45	55	70
	1650	3	20	35	52	57	62	70	84
	1675	2	15	23	38	80	83	87	100
	1700	1	—	—	—	105	—	—	—
	1750	1	—	—	—	155	—	—	—

Source: Financial Times, July 15, 1986. Reprinted with permission.

EXHIBIT 13.2

Options Quotations on European Options Exchange

EUROPEAN OPTIONS EXCHANGE								
		Aug.		Nov.		Feb.		
Series		Vol.	Last	Vol.	Last	Vol.	Last	Stock
GOLD C	$370	15	1	21	4.80	—	—	$346
GOLD P	$320	4	0.50	—	—	20	4.50	"
GOLD P	$330	—	—	20	3.50	—	—	"
		Sept.		Dec.		March		
SILV C	$550	8	19	5	19A	—	—	$505
SILV P	$550	—	—	20	35	—	—	"
£/FL C	Fl.355	25	10.50	—	—	—	—	Fl.366.25
£/FL C	Fl.365	1	5.50	5	7.50	—	—	"
£/FL C	Fl.385	—	—	10	2	—	—	"
£/FL P	Fl.350	8	1.30	—	—	—	—	"
£/FL P	Fl.355	25	2.50	—	—	—	—	"
£/FL P	Fl.360	13	4.30	—	—	—	—	"
£/FL P	Fl.370	15	10.50	—	—	—	—	"
£/FL P	Fl.380	8	18	—	—	—	—	"
$/FL C	Fl.240	150	10	—	—	—	—	Fl.246.55
$/FL C	Fl.245	12	6.50	—	—	—	—	"
$/FL C	Fl.250	111	4.200	1	7.20	—	—	"
$/FL C	Fl.255	5	2.90	—	—	—	—	"
$/FL C	Fl.260	44	1.70	1	3.80	—	—	"
$/FL C	Fl.265	—	—	7	2.50	—	—	"
$/FL C	Fl.270	8	0.50	—	—	—	—	"
$/FL P	Fl.235	4	1.70	—	—	—	—	"
$/FL P	Fl.240	11	3.40	5	6.80A	—	—	"
$/FL P	Fl.245	44	5.30	—	—	—	—	"
$/FL P	Fl.250	2	7.50	—	—	—	—	"
$/DM C	Dm.225	20	3	—	—	—	—	DM.218.75
		July		Oct.		Jan.		
ABN C	Fl.600	278	8	136	27	41	41A	Fl.606
ABN P	Fl.600	25	1.80	108	17	44	20	"
AEGN C	Fl.110	207	0.20	21	4.50	20	7.50A	Fl.106.20
AEGN P	Fl.115	208	8.50	10	9.50	—	—	"

TOTAL VOLUME IN CONTRACTS: 31,767
A = Ask　　B = Bid　　C = Call　　P = Put

Source: Financial Times, July 15, 1986. Reprinted with permission.

A straddle is the combination of one put and one call on the same asset with the same exercise price and the same expiration date. A strip is the combination of one call and two puts with similar exercise prices and expiration dates. A strap is the combination of two calls and one put with similar characteristics. More complex combinations involve calls and puts with different exercise prices or expiration dates.

Options on Futures versus Options on Spot　So far we have discussed only options that require the physical delivery of an asset when they are exercised. Options on futures contracts have also been introduced. The buyer of a futures

EXHIBIT 13.3

Currency Options Quotations

Currency Options

PHILADELPHIA EXCHANGE

Option & Underlying Price	Strike Price	Calls—Last			Puts—Last		
		Jul	Aug	Sep	Jul	Aug	Sep

12,500 British Pounds-cents per unit.

		Jul	Aug	Sep	Jul	Aug	Sep
BPound	135	r	s	r	r	s	0.30
148.57	.140	r	s	8.70	r	s	0.90
148.57	.145	r	r	5.35	r	1.30	2.70
148.57	.150	r	1.75	2.60	r	3.80	5.20
148.57	.155	r	0.50	1.05	r	r	r
148.57	.160	r	0.15	r	r	r	r

50,000 Canadian Dollars-cents per unit.

		Jul	Aug	Sep	Jul	Aug	Sep
CDollr	...74	r	r	0.19	r	r	r

62,500 West German Marks-cents per unit.

		Jul	Aug	Sep	Jul	Aug	Sep
DMark	..43	r	r	2.95	r	r	0.21
46.06	...44	r	2.25	r	r	r	0.26
46.06	...45	r	1.42	1.78	r	0.30	0.61
46.06	...46	r	0.86	1.23	r	0.78	r
46.06	...47	r	0.41	0.77	r	r	r
46.06	...48	r	0.19	0.42	r	r	r
46.06	...49	r	r	0.26	r	s	r

6,250,000 Japanese Yen-100ths of a cent per unit.

		Jul	Aug	Sep	Jul	Aug	Sep
JYen	...54	r	s	r	r	s	0.04
62.57	...56	r	r	6.50	r	r	r
62.57	...57	r	r	r	r	r	0.16
62.57	...58	r	r	4.68	r	r	0.19
62.57	...59	r	r	r	r	0.14	r
62.57	...60	r	r	3.16	r	0.21	r
62.57	...61	r	r	2.46	r	0.43	0.74
62.57	...62	r	1.15	1.77	r	0.70	1.21
62.57	...63	r	0.87	1.32	r	1.16	r
62.57	...64	r	r	0.90	r	r	r
62.57	...65	r	0.35	r	r	r	r

62,500 Swiss francs-cents per unit.

		Jul	Aug	Sep	Jul	Aug	Sep
SFranc	...53	r	r	r	r	r	0.32
56.39	...54	r	r	r	r	0.22	r
56.39	...55	r	r	r	r	0.42	0.88
56.39	...56	r	r	r	r	1.00	r
56.39	...57	r	0.74	1.10	r	r	r
56.39	...58	r	0.41	0.65	r	r	r
56.39	...60	r	0.14	0.38	r	r	r

Total call vol.	9,885		**Call open int.**	325,104
Total put vol.	9,966		**Put open int.**	282,224

r — Not traded. s — No option offered.
Last is premium (purchase price).

CHICAGO BOARD OPTIONS EXCHANGE

Option & Underlying Price	Strike Price	Calls—Last			Puts—Last		
		Jul	Aug	Sep	Jul	Aug	Sep

25,000 British Pounds-cents per unit.

		Jul	Aug	Sep	Jul	Aug	Sep
BPound	140	r	r	r	r	r	0.95
148.63	.146	r	r	r	r	1.55	2.35
148.63	.150	r	1.60	2.35	r	r	r

125,000 West German Marks-cents per unit.

		Jul	Aug	Sep	Jul	Aug	Sep
DMark	..45	r	1.16	1.73	r	r	r
46.07	..47	r	0.59	r	r	r	r

12,500,000 Japanese Yen-100ths of a cent per unit.

		Jul	Aug	Sep	Jul	Aug	Sep
JYen	...60	r	r	3.17	r	0.32	r
62.58	...62	r	1.37	1.82	r	r	r
62.58	...63	r	0.88	1.26	r	r	r
62.58	...64	r	r	r	r	2.13	r
62.58	...65	r	0.28	r	r	r	r

125,000 Swiss Francs-cents per unit.

		Jul	Aug	Sep	Jul	Aug	Sep
SFranc	...54	r	r	r	r	0.18	r
56.38	...55	r	r	r	r	0.37	0.68
56.38	...56	r	1.10	r	r	0.80	r
56.38	...58	r	0.38	r	r	r	r

Total call volume 2,279		**Total call open int.**		17,250
Total put volume 804		**Total put open int.**		12,837

r—not traded. s—No option offered.
Last is premium (purchase price).

Currency Futures Options

EURODOLLAR (CME) $ million; pts. of 100%

Strike Price	Calls—Settle			Puts—Settle		
	Sep-c	Dec-c	Mar-c	Sep-p	Dec-p	Mar-p
9300	0.63	0.64	0.64	0.03	0.13	0.32
9325	0.41	0.48	0.50	0.06	0.22	0.42
9350	0.23	0.33	0.37	0.12	0.30	...
9375	0.12	0.22	0.27	0.26	0.42	...
9400	0.06	0.13	0.19	0.44	...	0.82
9425	0.02	0.08	0.13	0.65	...	...

Est. vol. 3,327, Fri.; vol. 3,913 calls, 10,563 puts
Open interest Fri.; 53,723 calls, 41,282 puts

BRITISH POUND (CME) 25,000 pounds; cents per pound

Strike Price	Calls—Settle			Puts—Settle		
	Sep-c	Dec-c	Mar-c	Sep-p	Dec-p	Mar-p
1425	6.40	7.35	...	1.30	3.50	5.20
1450	4.75	6.00	...	2.10	4.60	6.40
1475	3.35	4.80	5.50	3.20	5.80	7.70
1500	2.25	3.80	4.55	4.60	7.25	9.10
1525	1.50	2.95	...	6.30	8.00	10.70
1550	0.95	2.25	3.05	8.20	10.55	...

Est. vol. 2,078, Fri.; vol. 1,073 calls, 338 puts
Open interest Fri.; 23,645 calls, 11,949 puts

W. GERMAN MARK (CME) 125,000 marks, cents per mark

Strike Price	Calls—Settle			Puts—Settle		
	Sep-c	Dec-c	Mar-c	Sep-p	Dec-p	Mar-p
44	2.54	3.14	...	0.25	0.67	0.94
45	1.79	2.48	2.96	0.49	0.98	1.26
46	1.16	1.91	2.39	0.85	1.37	1.66
47	0.71	1.44	1.95	1.40	1.88	2.16
48	0.41	1.06	1.55	2.09	2.48	...
49	0.25	0.81	...	2.91	...	...

Est vol. 4,329, Fri.; vol. 4,152 calls, 2,193 puts
Open interest Fri.; 49,122 calls, 38,721 puts

SWISS FRANC (CME) 125,000 francs; cents per franc

Strike Price	Calls—Settle			Puts—Settle		
	Sep-c	Dec-c	Mar-c	Sep-p	Dec-p	Mar-p
55	2.18	3.02	...	0.61	1.26	...
56	1.55	2.46	3.06	0.98	1.66	...
57	1.06	1.95	2.57	1.47	2.13	2.49
58	0.70	1.54	2.14	2.13	2.70	...
59	0.45	1.21	...	2.86	3.28	...
60	...	...	...	...	...	...

Est. vol. 2,419, Fri.; vol. 1,087 calls, 886 puts
Open interest Fri.; 17,936 calls, 17,574 puts

JAPANESE YEN (CME) 12,500,000 yen, cents per 100 yen

Strike Price	Calls—Settle			Puts—Settle		
	Sep-c	Dec-c	Mar-c	Sep-p	Dec-p	Mar-p
61	2.45	3.36	...	0.65	1.26	1.68
62	1.82	2.76	...	1.01	1.65	...
63	1.29	2.24	2.99	1.47	2.10	...
64	0.90	1.80	2.54	2.06	...	...
65	0.61	1.43	...	2.76	...	...
66	...	...	...	...	...	...

Est. vol. 3,797, Fri.; vol. 2,614 calls, 1,221 puts
Open interest Fri.; 25,142 calls, 16,569 puts

STERLING (LIFFE) — b-£25,000; cents per pound

Strike Price	Calls—Settle			Puts—Settle		
	Sep-c	Dec-c	Mar-c	Sep-p	Dec-p	Mar-p
140	8.38	9.06	9.67	0.93	2.81	4.47
145	4.87	6.11	6.98	2.42	4.86	6.78
150	2.43	3.88	4.85	4.98	7.63	9.65
155	1.03	2.32	3.26	8.58	11.07	13.06
160	0.37	1.30	2.11	12.92	15.06	16.91
165	0.11	0.69	...	17.66	19.44	...

Actual Vol. Monday, 798 Calls, 238 Puts.
Open Interest Friday; 3,147 Calls, 4,309 Puts.
b-Option on physical sterling.

option has the right to buy (call) or sell (put) a specified futures contract. When the option is exercised, the writer, or seller, of the option pays the buyer the difference between the current price of the futures contract and the exercise price of the option. This cash settlement must be paid, because futures contracts are marked to market every day.

For some financial instruments one can find both options on an asset and options on futures contracts in that asset at the same time, as is the case for interest rate, currency, and stock index options. Futures options are usually listed on futures exchanges.

The Different Instruments

Commodity Options   Options are also traded on certain commodities; the most active trading takes place in gold and silver options, which many money managers use for their gold-linked assets. In the past, private commodity options have been successfully offered, especially by Credit Suisse First Boston. But they have been steadily replaced by listed options traded on many exchanges, including the European Options Exchange, the New York Commodity Exchanges, Amex Commodity Corporation, Chicago Board of Trade, and the exchanges in London, Montreal, Vancouver, and Hong Kong.

It should be stressed that some of the exchanges trade in bullion options, which require physical delivery of the metal, whereas others trade in gold futures contracts.

Stock Options   Trading in listed options started with options on individual common stocks. Markets have developed throughout the world to the point where options on most active stocks are now traded. Options have also been introduced for stocks of smaller companies that have attractive characteristics, such as high growth or membership in a specialized industry. In the United States the volume of shares traded through options is sometimes larger than the volume of the actual stocks traded on the New York Stock Exchange.

Stock options are usually protected against capital adjustments, such as splits, but not against dividend payments, which is why it can be more profitable to exercise a stock option just before a dividend is paid than to keep it and lose the dividend.

Stock Index Options   Options on stock indexes have developed in several countries in the Americas, Europe, and the Far East. Exhibit 13.1 shows quotations for the UK *Financial Times* index. Stock index options are options on the level of the index. The contract size is equal to the index times a *multiplier* set by the exchange. For example, the Standard and Poor's 500 options traded on the Chicago Mercantile Exchange have a contract multiplier of 500. In other words, the investment required to purchase one contract is equal to the premium multiplied by $500. All settlement procedures require cash rather than physical delivery of an index.

Some options (e.g., options traded on the CBOE, the American Exchange, and the New York Stock Exchange) are directly linked to an index value, whereas most active contracts are options on futures contracts of stock indexes. Options listed on futures exchanges are usually futures options, whereas options listed on stock exchanges are usually spot options. Major stock index options traded worldwide are described in Exh. 13.4.

EXHIBIT 13.4

Major Stock Index Options Worldwide, 1994

Exchange, Contract[a]	Index Specifications	Contract Size	Exercise Style
CBOE, Standard and Poor's 100	Weighted index of top 100 industrial stocks on NYSE	$100 × index	American
CBOE, Standard and Poor's 500	Weighted index of top 500 industrial stocks on NYSE	$100 × index	European
AMEX, Major Market Index	Weighted index of top 20 stocks on NYSE	$100 × index	European
CME, Standard and Poor's 500 Index Futures	Weighted index of top 500 stocks on NYSE	$500 × index	American
NYFE, NYSE Composite Index Futures	Comprised of 1,500 shares on NYSE	$500 × index	American
TFE, TSE 35	Weighted index of top 35 Canadian stocks on Toronto Stock Exchange	Canadian $100 × index	European
SFE, All Ordinary Index Future	Weighted index of top 250 Australian stocks	Australian $100 × index	American
OSE, Nikkei 225	Unweighted index of top 225 shares on Tokyo Stock Exchange	JPY 1,000 × index	European
CME, Nikkei 225 Index Future	Unweighted index of top 225 shares on Tokyo Stock Exchange	$5 × index	American
SIMEX, Nikkei 225 Index Futures	Unweighted index of top 225 shares on Tokyo Stock Exchange	JPY 500	American
LIFFE, FT-SE 100	Weighted index of top 100 British stocks on LSE	£10 × index	European
LIFFE, FT-SE 100	Weighted index of top 100 British stocks on LSE	£10 × index	American
MONEP, CAC 40	Weighted index of top 40 French stocks	FF 200 × index	American
DTB, DAX	Weighted index of 30 shares on Frankfurt Stock Exchange	DM 10 × index	European

Exchange, Contract[a]	Index Specifications	Contract Size	Exercise Style
DTB, DAX Index Futures	Weighted index of 30 shares on Frankfurt Stock Exchange	DM 100 × index	American
EOE, EOE Stock Index	Weighted index of 25 leading Dutch stocks	FL 100 × index	European
FUTOP (CSE), KFX Stock Index	Pure price index composed of 20 leading Danish stocks	DKK 1,000 × index	European
FOM, FOX Index Futures	Weighted index of top 25 Finnish stocks	FIM 100 × index	European
MEFF, IBEX 35	Weighted index of the 35 largest Spanish shares	Pta 100 × index	European
OM, OMX	Weighted index of the 30 most heavily traded Swedish stocks	SEK 100 × index	European
OSSE, OBX	Weighted index of the 25 largest Norwegian stocks	NOK 100 × index	European
OTOB, ATX	Comprised of the largest Austrian shares	Asch 100 × index	European
SOFFEX, Swiss Market Index	Comprised of 24 shares of the most important Swiss companies	SF 5 × index	European

[a]CBOE: Chicago Board Options Exchange; AMEX: American Stock Exchange; PHLX: Philadelphia Stock Exchange; CME: Chicago Mercantile Exchange; NYFE: New York Futures Exchange; TFE: Toronto Futures Exchange; SFE: Sydney Futures Exchange; HKFE: Hong Kong Stock Exchange; OSE: Osaka Stock Exchange; SIMEX: Singapore International Monetary Exchange; LIFFE: London International Financial Futures Exchange, MONEP: Marché des Options Négociables de Paris; DTB: Deutsche Terminbörse; EOE: European Options Exchange; CSE: Copenhagen Stock Exchange; FOM: Finnish Options Market; MEFF: Mercado de Opciones y Futuros Financieros; OM: Stockholm Options Exchange; OSSE: Oslo Stock Exchange; OTOB: Osterreichische Terminbörse; SOFFEX: Swiss Options and Financial Futures Exchange.

Currency Options   Markets in currency options have become essential for coping with the volatility of the U.S. dollar. As shown in Exh. 13.3, currency options are now traded on markets throughout the world, including markets in the United States, London, Amsterdam, Hong Kong, Singapore, Sydney, Vancouver, and Montreal. In all of these markets three types of contracts are negotiated:

1. Over-the-counter currency options are not tradeable and can be exercised only at maturity; that is, they are European-type options. Commercial customers often turn to a bank when they need a large number of options of this type for a specific date. For example, a German car exporter may expect a payment of $10 million three months from now on September 7. Listed options do not offer this specific expiration date, and the amount involved (500 contracts) may be too large for the volume of transactions on the exchange. Moreover, a commercial exporter would not be interested in the

possibility of early exercise or sale of the options, anyway. Once the bank has written the option, it uses forward contracts or listed currency options to hedge actively the position it has created. Options are also written for longer terms (over two years) than the maturity available on the exchange-listed options.

2. In the early 1980s the Philadelphia Stock Exchange introduced option contracts on currencies. When a currency option is exercised, foreign currency must be delivered to a bank account, usually in the country in whose currency the delivery is made.

3. Other listed currency options are options on currency futures contracts. For example, the Chicago Mercantile Exchange trades options on its own currency futures.

The price of an option on spot and futures exchange rates may differ slightly. Technical differences are also important. For example, spot currency options on the Philadelphia Stock Exchange expire on the Saturday before the third Wednesday of the month (i.e., around the middle of the month). But futures currency options on the Chicago Mercantile Exchange stop trading two Fridays before the third Wednesday of the month (i.e., at the start of the month).

Currency options are quoted in several ways. In the United States options are quoted in terms of U.S. dollars per unit of foreign currency. For example, in Exh. 13.3 the call Deutsche mark August 45 quoted in Philadelphia is an option contract giving to the investor the right to buy 62,500 Deutsche marks at an exercise price of 45 cents per Deutsche mark on or before mid-August. At the time, the spot exchange rate was 46.06 cents per Deutsche mark, and the premium was 1.42 cents per Deutsche mark. If the Deutsche mark had gone up, the price of the option would have increased, and the holder of the call would have profited. One could also have bought a Deutsche mark put, which would have given to the investor the right to sell 62,500 Deutsche marks at a fixed exercise price. For example, the put Deutsche mark August 45 was worth 0.30 cent per Deutsche mark. If the Deutsche mark had depreciated (i.e., if its value had gone down in terms of U.S. dollars), the holder of the put would have profited. Remember that currency options traded in the United States are options written on a foreign currency, so that the prices of the currency and of the option are expressed in U.S. dollars and cents just like a U.S. stock option. There are different conventions in different countries. Exhibit 13.5 indicates the major currency options traded worldwide.

Interest Rate Options: Listed Options Options were traded on U.S. debt instruments, such as specific Treasury bonds, Treasury bills, and certificates of deposit. But a more active market has developed for options on futures contracts in bonds and short-term deposits. Futures contracts allow a more liquid, less costly exercise procedure. Options exist worldwide for most major interest rate futures contracts.

EXHIBIT 13.5

Major Currency Options Worldwide, 1994		
Exchange,[a] Contract	**Contract Size**	**Exercise Style**
PHLX, GDP/USD	£31,250	American and European
PHLX, DEM/USD	DM 62,500	American and European
PHLX, FF/USD	FF 250,000	American and European
PHLX, JPY/USD	JPY 6.25m	American and European
PHLX, CHF/USD	SF 62,500	American and European
PHLX, CAD/USD	Canadian $50,000	American and European
PHLX, DEM/JPY	DM 62,500	European
PHLX, GDP/DEM	£31,250	European
CME, GDP/USD Futures	one £62,500 futures contract	American
CME, DEM/USD Futures	one DM 125,00 futures contract	American
CME, JPY/USD Futures	one JPY 12.5m futures contract	American
CME, CHF/USD Futures	one SF 125,000 futures contract	American
CME, CAD/USD Futures	one Canadian $100,000 futures contract	American
MATIF, USD/FF	$100,000	European
MATIF, USD/DEM	$100,000	European
EOE, USD/FL	$10,000	American
EOE, USD/FL	$100,000	European
EOE, GDP/FL	£10,000	American

[a]PHLX: Philadelphia Stock Exchange; CME: Chicago Mercantile Exchange; MATIF: Marché à Terme International de France; EOE: European Option Exchange.

Options on bond futures contracts are listed in Exh. 13.6. In each country the underlying asset is generally the notional bond futures contract, using the conventions described in Chapter 12. For example, a call on the long-term U.K. gilt with a strike of 101% and an exercise month June is quoted on April 1 at 0.70%. The underlying asset is a gilt futures contract with a nominal value of £50,000 and delivery in June. Hence the premium on one option contract is 0.70% of £50,000, or £350. This gives the right to get one gilt futures contract in June at a price of 101%. If the gilt futures quotes 102% on expiration, the call option contract will be worth 1% times £50,000, or £500.

EXHIBIT 13.6

Major Bond Options Worldwide, 1994

Exchange,[a] Contract	Contract Size Nominal value	Exercise Style
CBOT, 15-year US T-bond futures	$100,000	American
CBOT, 10-year US T-bond futures	$100,000	American
CBOT, 5-year US T-note futures	$100,000	American
TSE, 10-year JGB futures	¥ 100 million	American
SFE, 10-year Commonwealth Treasury bond futures	A$100,000	American
SFE, 3-year Commonwealth Treasury bond futures	A$100,000	American
LIFFE, UK long gilt futures	£ 50,000	American
MATIF, French government Treasury bond 7–10-year futures	FF 500,000	American
MATIF, 6–10-year notional ECU bond futures	ECU 100,000	American
LIFFE, Italian government bond futures	Lit 200 million	American
LIFFE, German government bond futures	DM 250,000	American
DTB, futures on the 3- to 5-year bond futures	DM 250,000	American
EOE, Dutch government bonds	FL 10,000	American
EOE, guilder bond futures	FL 250,000	American
MEFF, 10-year Spanish government bond futures	Pta 10 million	American

[a]CBOT: Chicago Board of Trade; TSE: Tokyo Stock Exchange; SFE: Sydney Futures Exchange; LIFFE: London International Financial Futures and Options Exchange; MATIF: Marché à Terme International de France; DTB: Deutsche Terminbörse; EOE: European Option Exchange; MEFF: Mercado de Opciones y Futuros Financieros Renta Fija.

Options on short-term interest rates are generally options on a short-term interest rate futures. Active contracts exist only in a few currencies that have an active Eurocurrency market (e.g., U.S. dollar, Deutsche mark, U.K. pound, French franc). Options use the same convention as futures. For example, a put on PIBOR with a strike of 94% and an exercise month June is quoted on April 1 at 1.2%. The underlying asset is a French three-month PIBOR futures contract with a nominal value of FF 5 million and delivery in June. Following the futures convention, the premium on one option contract is 1.2% of FF 5 million, *divided by four*, or FF 15,000. This gives the right to sell one PIBOR futures contract in June at a price of 94%. If the PIBOR futures quotes 93% on expiration, the put option contract will be worth 1% times FF 5 million, divided by four, or FF 12,500.

Interest Rate Options: Over-the-Counter   Besides these exchange-traded options, some interest rate options are negotiated over the counter. These tend to be longer-term options on short-term interest rates. They often take the form of *caps* and *floors*. The basic contract in an interest rate cap option is an agreement between the buyer and the seller of the option stating that if a chosen index, such as the three-month London interbank offer rate (LIBOR), is above the agreed exercise price at prespecified dates in the future, the seller will reimburse the buyer for the additional interest cost until the next specified date. (LIBOR is the short-term Eurodollar interest rate most commonly used in floating-rate notes and loans.) A floor option has the reverse characteristics. A five-year cap on the three-month LIBOR can be broken down into a series of 19 European options with quarterly strike dates. The option premium may be paid in the form of a single front-end price (e.g., 2% of the amount specified in the option) or a yearly cost paid up regularly (e.g., 0.5% per year).

As an illustration, consider a five-year 10% cap on the three-month LIBOR for $1 million. The current LIBOR is 8%, and the yearly cap premium is 0.5%. If the LIBOR stays below 10% over the next five years, the cap option will be useless. Conversely if the LIBOR rises above 10% at some of the specified exercise dates, the seller will pay the difference in interest costs. For example, if the LIBOR rises to 12%, the cap buyer receives a payment in the amount of the difference between the market LIBOR (12%) and the exercise price (10%). In this case the quarterly payment is

$$\$1,000,000\left(\frac{12\% - 10\%}{4}\right) = \$5000.$$

The motivation for engaging in these caps and floors contracts is financial costs insurance. The contracts are most often used by companies as an insurance against a rise in interest costs on existing floating-rate borrowings. The options are usually written by banks with extensive international underwriting activities. These banks often hedge their option writing by borrowing funds at a variable rate with an interest cap. For example, a bank may engage in the following operations:

- Lend money to company A at the LIBOR + ⅛%

- Borrow money from investors at the LIBOR + ⅜% with a cap at 10%

- Sell a cap option at 10% to company B for ½% per year

As seen in Exh. 13.7, a bank has hedged its cap writing and ends up with a margin of 1%. An alternative for the bank might simply have been to lend to company A at the LIBOR plus $\frac{7}{8}$% and borrow from investors at the LIBOR plus $\frac{1}{8}$% without any cap. In effect, the margin would have been equal to $\frac{3}{4}$% ($\frac{7}{8}$% − $\frac{1}{8}$%). The cap packaging allows the bank to increase its profit margin without taking additional risks.

Collars, which offer both a floor and a cap on interest rates, have also been introduced on the international market. They are another attractive instrument for management of long-term interest rate risk.

As seen with swaps, these complex packagings are quite common in international finance. Their use requires expertise on the part of bankers and a good understanding of the pricing of these multiple options.

Over-the-counter dollar options are available against most bases, such as the LIBOR, CDs, Treasury bills, commercial paper, and prime rates. However, the most active contracts are those for the three- and six-month LIBOR. Dealers writing options on bases other than the LIBOR tend to hedge their position using the three-month LIBOR. They tend to charge fairly high costs to buyers because they assume the mismatch risk. Nondollar caps and floors are also available in Deutsche marks, yen, and sterling.

The great advantage of these nontraded options is their maturity, which extends from a year to ten years or more. However, they tend to involve large sums of money and are designed for corporations rather than small private investors.

Other Instruments with Options   Many securities have option features. Among the most common securities with options are the following.

EXHIBIT 13.7

Hedging the Sale of a Cap

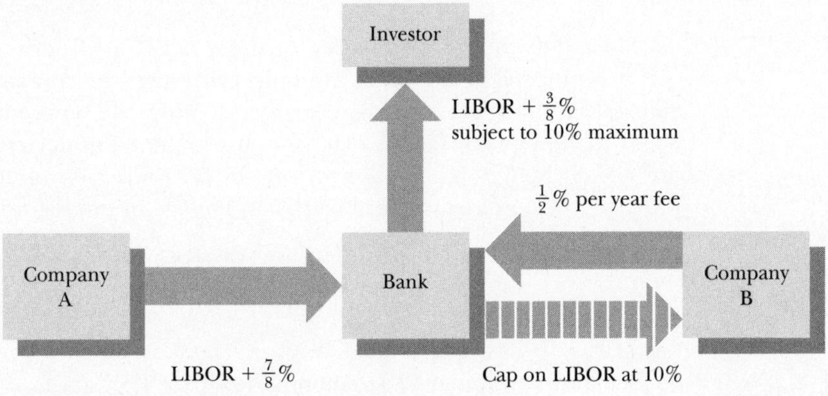

- *Warrants* are like long-term call options. They are traded securities issued by a firm whose stock serves as the underlying asset of the option. Although stock warrants are more common, bond warrants are also found, especially on the Eurobond market and in France. A bond warrant is a security giving to the holder the right to buy a given bond at a specified exercise price over the life of the warrant. The terms stipulated in the warrant are sometimes complex. For example, the exercise price can vary over time.

- *Convertible bonds* are bonds convertible into another security at the option of the bondholder. The most common convertibles are bonds that are convertible into common stock of the firm that issued them. These securities trade on most national capital markets and on the Eurobond market.

- *Bonds with optional clauses* are very common on all markets. Many bonds are issued with a call provision, which gives the issuer the right to call back, or reimburse, the bondholder at a specified price. Bonds with put options give to the bondholder the right to force the issuer to reimburse the bondholder at a specified price. Specific bonds, called *structured notes*, to fit the needs and market forecasts of various investors, are discussed in the last section.

Option Valuation

Profit and Loss at Expiration

The profit and loss structure of an option that is held until expiration is shown in Exh. 13.8. The exercise price is assumed to equal the current spot price of gold, which is $400. The premium is $10, and commissions are ignored. All profits and losses are expressed in dollars per ounce of gold. The example of a gold option is taken because it is the simplest option to analyze. Interest rate options, currency options, or stock index options introduce further complexities.

Exhibits 13.8(a) and (b) show the profit structures for long and short positions on an underlying asset. We see from the diagram that the profit structures on these two positions exactly mirror each other. This stems from the fact that for any dollar gain in the price of gold, the buyer of gold earns a dollar profit, and the seller loses a dollar.

The profit structures for options must take premiums into account. The buyer and the writer of a call option have opposite profit opportunities at expiration. The maximum loss for an option buyer is limited to the premium, although the profit may be quite large. The reverse holds true for the option writer, which is why Exhs. 13.8(c) and (d) also are mirror images of each other.

Another way of saying this is that the risk structure of options is asymmetric when compared to a direct investment in the spot or futures market. That is, though the option buyer risks losing the premium, the seller of that same option bears the risk of an almost unlimited loss.

EXHIBIT 13.8

EXHIBIT 13.8

Profits and Losses from Various Positions

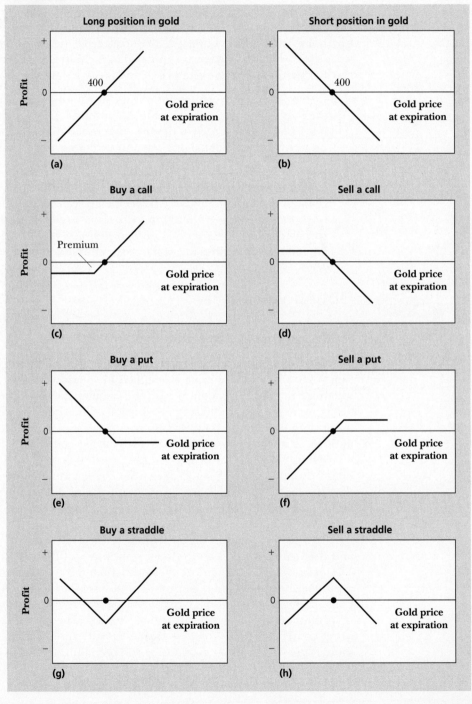

The six basic positions of buying or selling an asset, a call, or a put may be combined in complex investment strategies. For example, buying a call and a put with the same exercise price is called a *straddle*. Its profit structure is shown in Exh. 13.8(g). The attraction of this strategy is that a substantial gold price movement in either direction will generate a profit. Another strategy for achieving the same thing is to buy two calls and sell short the underlying asset (in this case, gold). This does not mean that all securities or combinations of securities with similar profit structures have exactly the same price. They may differ in exercise price and amount of capital invested, but their risk-return structures are similar, and their market values are linked.

To be sure, Exh. 13.8 depicts only examples of securities that are held until expiration. However, option buyers usually resell contracts before maturity, and sellers, likewise, repurchase them. The rate of return on a call option is depicted in Exh. 13.9.

Valuation Models

Option premiums fluctuate so rapidly as a function of price movements in underlying assets that computerized models are necessary to properly value them. These models are so extensively used by traders and money managers that simple versions of them can be found even on programmable hand-held calculators.

In order to understand how options are valued, recall both the parameters that determine option premiums and the famous valuation formula proposed by Black and Scholes (1973).

Most options traded in the world are American options in the sense that they can be exercised any time before expiration, which means that premiums must at least equal the profit one could obtain by immediately exercising the option.

EXHIBIT 13.9

Potential Return on a Call Option

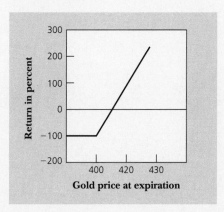

Intrinsic value is the value of an option that is immediately exercised. A rational option buyer would never exercise a call when the underlying asset price is below the exercise price, because he or she would lose money. An option exercised under such circumstances is said to be *out of the money*, and the intrinsic value of the option is zero. When an asset price is above the exercise price, the call is said to be *in the money*, and its intrinsic value is the difference between the asset price and the exercise price. The intrinsic value of a call as a function of asset price is shown in Exh. 13.10.

An option will generally sell above its intrinsic value. For example, a gold option with a strike, or exercise, price of $400 is worth $10 when the spot price of gold, the underlying asset, is $402. The difference between the option premium and its intrinsic value is usually referred to as the time value of the option. Here the intrinsic value is $2 ($402 – $400), and the *time value* is $8 ($10 – $2). The major valuation problem is to determine the time value of an option.

On all markets option premiums vary with the underlying asset prices along a curve similar to that shown in Exh. 13.11. For very low values of the asset price relative to the exercise price, the intrinsic value is zero, and the time value of the option is close to zero, since the probability that the option will ever be exercised is almost zero. For very high asset prices relative to the exercise price, the option premium is almost equal to the option's intrinsic value. The option is almost sure to be exercised at expiration, since it is unlikely that the asset price will ever drop below the exercise price; therefore the time value of the option is close to zero, and the premium approaches the intrinsic value. When the asset price is in the neighborhood of the exercise price, the time value of the option may be large, and the premium is well above its intrinsic value. In our example the time value is $8.

EXHIBIT 13.10

Option Intrinsic Value

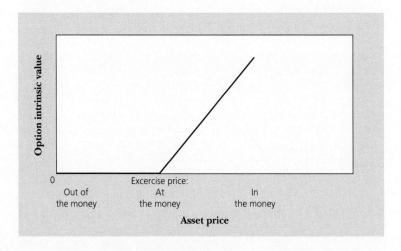

EXHIBIT 13.11

Option Value as a Function of Asset Price

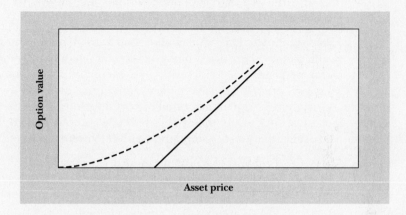

If the gold price goes up, say, to $450, the option holder will benefit from the price appreciation; on the other hand, the investor will be protected from a fall in gold prices because his or her maximum loss is limited to the option premium: If gold drops to $300, the investor will lose only $10. This attractive asymmetric risk structure calls for a positive time value.

Note that the slope of a tangent to the curve shown in Exh. 13.11 gives the instantaneous reaction of the option premium to a change in the asset price. This slope is usually called delta (δ).

On all markets, option premiums vary with asset prices along a curve similar to that shown in Exh. 13.11. Investigators have found that option values depend on just four variables. The influence of each of these variables on a call option can be described as follows:

Exercise price. We have seen that the value of an option depends critically on its exercise price, E, relative to its current asset (e.g., gold) price, G. The higher the exercise price, the lower the premium for options on the same asset that have an identical expiration date.

Interest rate. The value of a call option is an increasing function of the interest rate. Buying a call enables an investor to lay claim to an asset, although making a much smaller capital investment. Options reduce the opportunity or financing cost for claiming an asset. Naturally, as interest rates rise, this characteristic of options becomes more valuable, thereby raising the price of the option; in a sense the present value of the asset to be purchased at expiration is reduced.

Volatility. The value of an option increases with the volatility of the underlying asset because options are perfectly protected against downside risk. The buyer can never lose more than the premium paid. Yet simultaneously, the buyer may potentially realize big gains on the upside. The more volatile the asset, the larger the expected gain on the option and, hence, the larger its premium.

Time to expiration. The value of an option is an increasing function of the time to expiration. There are two reasons for this. First, the leveraging advantage mentioned earlier increases with time. Second, the opportunity for the underlying asset price to far exceed the exercise price increases over time. Of course, there is also an increased opportunity for the asset price to drop by more, but once again, the call holder's loss is always limited to the premium paid. Time, therefore, compounds both the interest rate and volatility effects.

All the determinants of option premiums, except underlying asset volatility, can be measured precisely. Underlying asset volatility is represented by the standard deviation of returns (or its squared value, the variance) and must be estimated.

From these four parameters, a simple valuation model for call options can be constructed. The most famous valuation model was developed by Black and Scholes and is currently used on option markets worldwide. It is available on a variety of computer time-sharing systems, financial packages, and even hand-held calculators. The reason valuation models are so necessary is that a small change in the underlying asset price can cause an immediate, large percentage change in the option premium. The Black-Scholes formula is based on an arbitrage model for a European-type call option. It assumes that no commissions, taxes, or dividends are paid; that the interest rate is constant and risk-free; and that the return on the asset follows a normal distribution with a constant variance, σ^2. Under these assumptions, a call premium may be valued by the following, relatively simple, formula:

$$P_0 = GN\left(d\right) - Ee^{-rt}N\left(d - \sigma\sqrt{t}\right), \tag{13.1}$$

where

$$d = \frac{\ln\left(G/E\right) + \left(r + 0.5\sigma^2\right)t}{\sigma\sqrt{t}}$$

and where

G is the price of the asset (e.g., gold),

E is the exercise price,

r is the risk-free interest rate expressed on a continuous compounding basis,

σ is the standard deviation of the asset's annual rate of return,

t is the time to expiration (in years),

e is 2.71828,

$\ln$ is the natural logarithm, and

$N(d)$ is the probability that a deviation less than d will occur in a normal distribution with a mean of zero and a standard deviation of one.

A polynomial approximation of $N(d)$ is often used on computers in the following form:

$$N(d) = 1 - [0.5(1 + 0.04986734d + 0.0211410061d^2 + 0.0032776263d^3$$
$$+0.000380036d^4 + 0.0000488906d^5 + 0.0000005383d^6)^{-16}].$$

The derivation of this formula is generally based on an arbitrage construction using options and their underlying asset. The hedge is constructed by looking at the derivative of the option premium with respect to the underlying asset's price. In Exh. 13.11 this derivative would be δ, the slope of the tangent to the option value at any given point. The inverse of this slope is usually called the *hedge ratio, h.* A good hedge can be formed by buying one unit of the underlying asset and selling h units of the option. Alternatively, one could buy one unit of the option and sell δ units of the underlying asset. By construction, this hedge portfolio should not be sensitive to small changes in the asset's price. The hedge ratio continually changes with the asset's price, so that the composition of the hedge portfolio should be continually rebalanced. The expected return on this riskless portfolio should be equal to the risk-free interest rate. This reasoning leads to a differential equation whose solution has been given. Other authors have derived the theoretical value of an option using a binomial process.[1]

Applying the Black-Scholes formula is straightforward once the variance of the asset over the life of the option, σ^2, has been estimated. It can be estimated either from past data or through other prospective methods. Though it is the only estimated variable in the formula, it is an important one.

In some cases particular characteristics of the underlying asset require revision of the formula. Buying options on bonds, for example, does not allow one to claim the accrued interest, whereas buying a bond does. Some options are not written on assets but on indexes or prices, such as futures prices or exchange rates. To accommodate these differences, slight changes are required in the arbitrage model used to derive the valuation formula. The changes made in the model to accommodate currency options are discussed in the appendix.

These valuation formulas provide useful approximations. With the help of computers, they can be used to continually adjust premium estimates, thereby reflecting changes in underlying asset prices and allowing for rapid management of a position. Unfortunately several of the assumptions required by the Black-Scholes model are not actually valid in the real world: Interest rates and variances are not constant, and stocks pay dividends that are not precisely known ahead of time. It is therefore sometimes profitable to exercise an option before its expiration date. For example, it is occasionally profitable to exercise a stock option before a dividend payment or a currency option that is deep in the money.

Since the Black-Scholes formula assumes no early exercise, its theoretical value is clearly incorrect. The problem is even more pronounced for put options.[2] Transaction costs and taxes also undermine the Black-Scholes model. Some of these imperfections are taken into account in more sophisticated formulas, but an exact analytical model for option premiums will never exist. However, it appears that Black-Scholes-type formulas provide a good practical approximation of option pricing.[3] Computer valuation programs can simulate various scenarios for the underlying asset's price and thereby indicate the best investment alternative given the manager's expectations. Such models assist in the day-to-day management of a complex position, so that a manager can understand how sensitive his or her total position is to changes in key parameters over time.

Insuring with Options

Options provide a unique tool with which to insure portfolios. Insurance means that a portfolio is protected against a negative performance while it retains its positive performance potential. By contrast, hedging removes both negative and positive performance potentials. An example will illustrate this concept.

An investor holds 1000 ounces of gold. On December 1 the spot price is equal to $400 per ounce, and the premiums of put gold options are as reproduced in Exh. 13.12. Our investor decides to buy ten put options February 400. The premium is equal to $8 per ounce, so that the total cost is equal to

10 options × 100 ounces × $8 = $8000.

If the price of gold goes up by the end of February, the options will be worthless. It is useless to have the right to sell at $400 gold that is worth more on the spot market. However, if the price of gold drops, the investor will use the option to sell her gold holdings at $400 per ounce. The net value of the insured portfolio as a function of the future price of gold is given in Exh. 13.13. The value of the portfolio is always greater than $400,000 minus the premium cost of $8000. This premium is the insurance cost.

EXHIBIT 13.12

Premiums of Put Options on Gold
Contracts of 100 ounces, premium per ounce

Strike Price	Expiration Month		
	February	May	August
390	2.00	5.00	7.00
400	8.00	10.00	12.00
410	13.00	14.00	15.00

EXHIBIT 13.13

Value of the Insured Portfolio for Various Scenarios of the Price of Gold

Price of Gold (Dollars per Ounce)	Value of the Portfolio (Dollars)
380	392,000
390	392,000
400	392,000
410	402,000
420	412,000
450	442,000

Several different options could be chosen. An out-of-the-money option, such as the put February 390, is less costly but protects the portfolio for gold prices only below \$390 per ounce. In-the-money options provide better protection at a higher cost, as seen in Exh. 13.14. An insurance could be sought for a longer time horizon, but naturally the premium is higher given the larger time value of the option.

Selling a call would not provide a good protection, since the option to exercise lies with the buyer of the call. However, dynamic strategies for changing the options position when the spot price of gold moves may be implemented. Also investors may replicate a put position even if such a contract is not traded. These synthetic securities may be created by combining several other securities or adopting dynamic buy and sell strategies.[4]

This example assumes that the option is held until expiration. In many cases the option will be sold in the market before expiration; the total insurance cost is simply the difference in the time values of the option. In some cases options, instead of futures, are used to hedge portfolios. Hedging is designed to eliminate the uncertainty of a future outcome, whereas insurance is designed to eliminate only the negative outcomes. Of course, there is a cost to the attractive risk-return characteristic of insurance. The use of options for hedging and insurance is discussed further in Chapter 14.

The example of insuring a stock portfolio with stock index options is also illustrated in some problem sets provided later. Institutional investors periodically wish to reduce the downside risk on an existing stock portfolio. In the mid-1980s institutions relied on *portfolio insurance*, a strategy that attempted to recreate an optionlike hedge by dynamic trading of actual blocks of stocks in the portfolio. The failure of portfolio insurance strategies during the crash of 1987 led to a renewed interest for put options on stock indexes. The premium of a put is known ahead of time, and there is little risk that the option will not perform as expected, given the design of the option market with the guarantee of a clearing corporation.

EXHIBIT 13.14

Value of Insured Portfolios with Different Options

Price of Gold (Dollars per Ounce)	Value of the Portfolio (Dollars) Insured with		
	Feb. 390	Feb. 400	Feb. 410
380	388,000	392,000	397,000
390	388,000	392,000	397,000
400	398,000	392,000	397,000
410	408,000	402,000	397,000
420	418,000	412,000	407,000
450	448,000	442,000	437,000

Other Uses of Options

Listed options are also used in investment strategies with different motivations. Furthermore exotic options and special bonds with various options (structured notes) have also been designed by banks to meet the desires of particular investors.

Investing with Downside Protection

Buying a call allows one to participate in the price appreciation of the underlying asset with a good downside protection in case of a drop in the asset price. For example, call options on stock indexes permit the management of market risk with a fairly low transaction cost. Trading in stock index options is very active. In a typical day some 100,000 option contracts on the Standard & Poor's 500 are traded. The underlying asset volume is sometimes higher than that of stocks traded on the NYSE. The same observation applies to some non-American stock index options. This was illustrated in a recent article:

> Giant American pension funds and mutual funds are eager to exploit any tools that increase their flexibility. They've found index options useful not only in hedging their portfolios against adverse market swings, but also in boosting their returns. . . . The boom in index options largely reflects a more-active stance among institutional investors toward adjusting asset mix when market conditions change.[5]

Global investment strategies have prompted the use of options as an alternative to buying the individual stocks. For example, buying a call on the CAC index allows foreign investors to take a diversified position on the French stock market, with low transaction costs and downside risk protection. Furthermore options permit one to reduce the exchange risk borne, as stressed in Chapter 14. Options are often preferred to futures by institutional investors for a couple of reasons. One obvious reason is the different risk structure of an option. Another reason is that buying an option requires an immediate cash-outlay but no further investment or administrative burden. Futures are subject to constant marking-to-market, and the risk is not limited to the initial margin deposited. Furthermore many institutional investors are not legally allowed to deal in futures contracts.

Another strategy is a *zero-cost collar* to reduce the cost of insurance linked to the purchase of options. In this strategy the portfolio manager sells call options and uses the proceeds to buy put options. The put protects the portfolio from a down movement in the market, and this protection is obtained at zero monetary cost. The drawback is obvious. If the market rises strongly, the investor will not need the downside protection and will be hurt by the sale of the call.

Other investors are stock pickers and wish to buy selected stocks without incurring market risk. In other words, they believe that the selected stocks will outperform the market index but fear that a fall of the whole market will lead to a negative return on their portfolio. Of course, they could hedge market risk by selling stock index futures. Alternatively, they could buy stock index puts. This strategy offers downside protection if the market drops but carries an insurance cost, the put premium. The advantage of using options rather than futures is that this strategy still allows one to participate in a global market appreciation if it materializes. Some institutional investors go beyond simply insuring an existing portfolio; they buy stock index puts on national markets that they believe overvalued.

Yield Enhancement

Some institutional investors are looking for additional cash income, without having to trade securities in their portfolio. Writing (selling) an option can provide such yield enhancement. Assume that an institution writes an out-of-the-money call option on part of its portfolio. If the stock market drops or remains stable, the call will not be exercised, and the institutional investor will pocket the premium in cash. If the market rises the call will be exercised by the buyer, and the option writer will have to sell part of the portfolio. Although this sale can be performed at a price higher than what it was when the option was written, the fact that the sale is done below the current market price still is a serious opportunity cost.[6] This risk can be reduced in various more complex option strategies.

Banks have offered investment products or structured notes that offer the potential of yield enhancement with limited risk. These bonds basically are option plays linked to a plain-vanilla bond. They may involve some exotic options, which will be reviewed before a discussion of some of these structured notes.

Exotic Options

Many types of exotic options have been offered in the over-the-counter market. The underlying asset is often a currency, an interest rate, or a stock index. Some of these options are briefly described below to give a flavor of these new products.

Zero-cost collars are a package of options (buying some and selling others) so that the net investment is nil. These packages carry flowery names, such as *tunnel, cylinder, hybrids, range forward*, etc.

Barrier options are activated if the underlying asset price reaches some predetermined barrier during the life of the option. A *knock-in* option is activated if the price crosses the barrier, whereas a *knock-out* option is deactivated if the price reaches the barrier.

Asian (or average) options are written on the average price of the underlying asset during the life of the option. The price of the asset is averaged over the entire life of the option. At expiration, the value of an Asian call is equal to the difference between this average price and the exercise price (if positive). For example, assume an Asian call on the CAC index with an exercise price of 2000. The CAC index starts with a value of 1900, goes up to 2250, and is worth 2000 at expiration; the average value of the index over the life of the option is 2100. The Asian call will be worth 100 (or 2100 minus 2000) at expiration.

Ladder (or ratchet) options specify some lock-in levels. If the underlying asset price reaches the lock-in level, this minimum level of the asset price will be guaranteed at time of exercise, even if the asset price later reverts to lower levels. For example, assume a ladder call on the CAC index with an exercise price of 2000 and a 2200 lock-in level. Under the scenario just described, where the CAC index starts at 1900, goes up to 2250, and is worth 2000 at expiration, the lock-in will be activated when the CAC index reaches 2200. The final value of the ladder option will be 200.

Digital (or binary) options can have only two payoffs at maturity. If the strike condition set in the option is met, the buyer will receive the full prespecified payoff. If not, the buyer receives no payoff. This is different from a traditional option where there exists an infinite number of payoffs. For example, we could have a digital option on the CAC index, stating that the option buyer will get 200 if the CAC index is above 2000 at expiration and zero otherwise. On this digital option, the buyer will get exactly 200 as soon as the CAC index is above the 2000 level at expiration, whether it be 2001, 2100, or 3000.

Look-back options have a variable exercise price. On a look-back call, the strike price is set as the minimum value of the asset price during the life of the option (or some specified time interval). On a look-back put, the strike price is set as the maximum value of the asset price during the life of the option.

Rainbow options are options on two or more assets.

Quanto (or differential) options are options on a foreign asset price but with a fixed exchange rate. For example, an American investor could get a call on the French CAC stock index but where the index level is written in dollars, not francs. This reduces exchange risk on a foreign investment. An example of such an option is given in Exh. 13.15. It is a quanto call warrant issued in February 1994 by Paribas Capital Markets.

EXHIBIT 13.15

Quanto Call Warrant

ṅ Paribas
CAPITAL MARKETS

QUANTO CALL WARRANT ON THE DAX INDEX

Strike Price: USD 2179.67
Maturity: 31st January 1995

TERMS AND CONDITIONS OF THE WARRANT

Market	: USD
Issuer	: Paribas Capital Markets Group Ltd.
Instrument	: QUANTO CALL warrants on DAX Index
Warrant type	: American Quanto Call Warrants (continuous exercise)
Number of Warrants	: 700,000
	10 warrants represent 1 call on 1 unit of the Index
Minimum trading size	: Multiples of 100 warrants
Minimum exercise size	: 1,000 warrants
Maximum exercise size	: No more than 10% of the issue in a single day.
Launch date	: 31st January 1994
Strike price	: USD 2179.67
Issue price	: USD 21.8
Maturity	: 31st January 1995
Exercise period	: Any Business Day from the next Business Day after Payment Date to Expiration Date inclusive. A Business Day is a day on which banks are open for business in London and on which Euroclear or Cedel is open for business.
Settlement	: Cash settlement in USD (value 5 business days)
Currency	: US Dollar
Clearing	: EUROCLEAR, and CEDEL
Listing	: London Stock Exchange

Paribas will make a market in this issue. Paribas' quote can be found on REUTERS page PCMM. Under normal market conditions the bid/offer spread will not exceed 5% of the warrant price quoted and prices will be good for at least 10,000 warrants.

EUROCLEAR and CEDEL common code: 4887166

Source: Paribas Capital Markets (PCM), the Capital Market Division of Banque PARIBAS. Reprinted with permission.

There exist many variations on these definitions. The valuation of these options is usually a difficult exercise, unless they can be replicated by a package of simple options. A detailed description of the use and valuation of these exotic options is beyond the scope of this book.

Structured Notes

A *structured note* is a bond (note) issued with some unusual optionlike clause. These notes are bonds issued by a name of good credit standing and can therefore be purchased as investment-grade bonds by most institutional investors, even those that are prevented by regulation from dealing in options or futures. Another attraction for investors is that these structured notes offer some long-term options that are not publicly traded. We will present a couple of examples of structured notes offered to the international investors and will avoid some technical domestic products, e.g., CMO (Collateralized Mortgage Obligations).

Structured notes are designed for some specific investors wishing to take a bet on some forecasts. If their forecasts are correct, the yield on the note will be enhanced. In turn, the issuer is basically taking the opposite bet. However, the bank structuring the note proposes to the issuer some hedging structure that will eliminate this risk. The idea is that the issuer should end up with a plain-vanilla bond (with fixed or floating-rate coupons) but at a total cost that is less than the prevailing market conditions for those bonds. To determine the "fair" price of the bond, the investment bank constructs a replication portfolio using elementary securities (like plain-vanilla FRNs, straight bonds, and options). The structured note can be issued at better conditions for the issuer, because it satisfies the needs of some investors.

Structured notes are often classified by generations. Some structured notes are only *interest rate* plays. They are called below first- and second-generation notes. Other structured notes offer a play on some other variables, such as *equity* or *commodity* prices. They are called third-generation notes.

First-Generation Notes
First-generation notes offer some interest rate play, or potential yield enhancement, based on a simple formula, usually involving some optionlike clause.

Bull FRNs are notes that benefit *investors* if interest rates drop. A typical example is a reverse floater, where the coupon is set at a fixed rate minus LIBOR. An example is a five-year dollar FRN with a semiannual coupon set at 13.75% minus LIBOR. We know that the market price of a fixed-coupon bond will go up if interest rates drop. In a bull FRN, the coupon will increase if LIBOR drops; hence its market price will rise *more sharply* than for a fixed-coupon bond. A coupon cannot become negative, even if LIBOR goes above 13.75%. In effect the bull FRN includes a coupon of 13.75% minus LIBOR, as well as a 13.75% cap option on LIBOR (see description of caps above). If LIBOR goes above 13.75%, this cap is activated and offsets the potentially negative coupon. In summary, the bull FRN could be seen by investors as the sum of:

- Two straight bonds with a 6.875% coupon

- A short position in a plain-vanilla FRN at LIBOR flat

- A 13.75% cap option on LIBOR

In turn the issuer can hedge and transform this bull note into a straight fixed-coupon bond by buying a 13.75% cap option on LIBOR and swapping the short position in the FRN into a short position in a fixed-coupon obligation (see problem 17).

FRNs with a cap on the coupon also offer a *bull* play on the interest rate. For example a triple-A name could issue a plain-vanilla ten-year FRN at LIBOR flat; current LIBOR is 6%. Instead, it issues a ten-year FRN at LIBOR plus 60 basis points, with a cap of 7.6%. This structured note is attractive to investors who believe in stable or dropping interest rates. If LIBOR does not move over 7% during the life of the bond, they will get 60 basis points of yield enhancement. However, if LIBOR moves above 7%, they will receive only 7.6%. In summary, this capped FRN can be seen by investors as the sum of:

- A plain-vanilla FRN at LIBOR plus 0.6%

- Selling a 7% cap option on LIBOR

In turn the issuer can hedge and transform this capped note into a plain-vanilla FRN by selling to a bank a ten-year interest rate option. This is a 7% cap on LIBOR with an annual premium turning out to be 70 basis points. The net result for the company is to issue a plain-vanilla FRN at LIBOR minus 10 basis points.

Bear FRNs are notes that benefit investors if interest rates rise. An example of a bear FRN is a note with a coupon set at twice LIBOR minus 7%. The coupon will increase rapidly with a rise in LIBOR. Such a bond could be valued by the investor as a portfolio long in two plain-vanilla FRNs and short in one straight bond with a coupon of 7%. Because the value of the plain-vanilla FRNs should stay at par on reset dates, even if LIBOR moves, the net result is that the portfolio should appreciate if market interest rates rise. However, the coupon on the note cannot become negative, which is attractive to the investor in case of a drop in LIBOR below 3.5%. In summary, this bear note could be seen by investors as the sum of:

- Two plain-vanilla FRNs at LIBOR flat

- A short position in a straight bond (with a coupon of 7%)

- A 3.5% floor option on LIBOR

In turn the issuer can hedge and transform this bear FRN into a plain-vanilla FRN by issuing simultaneously a straight fixed-coupon bond and buying a 3.5% floor option from the bank.

Another example of a structured note is provided by the $200 million, ten-year note issued by J.P. Morgan in August 1992. At the time, six-month LIBOR was at 3⅜%, and the bank would have to pay some 25 basis points above LIBOR on a plain-vanilla FRN. Investors were unhappy with the low rates paid at the time and were looking for yield enhancement. J.P. Morgan offered notes with an interest-rate collar: The coupon is capped at 10% but floored at 5%. The floor rate is an attractive element for investors, as it means that they are assured of a coupon of at least 5%, well above the current LIBOR. Because of this attractive clause, J.P. Morgan could issue the structured note at LIBOR *minus ⅛%*. It appears that these notes were sold to private European investors. The unusual feature of this note is that the collar is already in-the-money (the floor is operative). In summary, this note could be seen by investors as the sum of:

- A plain-vanilla FRN
- Selling a 10% cap option
- Buying a 5% floor option

In turn the issuer is able to hedge out the collar in the interbank market. Effectively J.P. Morgan sold the 10% cap and bought the 5% floor at a net annual cost of ⅛%. Hence the actual borrowing cost is around LIBOR flat instead of LIBOR plus 25 basis points. As is often the case with notes structured for a specific investors' need, the deal was quickly imitated, and the demand for such structured notes dried up within a week.

Second-Generation Notes   Second-generation notes involve the more exotic options reviewed. *Digital structured notes*, much in favor in the mid-1990s, are created by embedding a series of digital interest-rate options throughout the life of the note. These notes take the form of a Eurobond issued by a good-quality issuer, with a maturity of one to a few years. Redemption of the capital is guaranteed, but the coupon can be enhanced by the addition of a digital cap or a digital floor. In a *digital-capped note* the enhanced coupon will be paid as long as the reference interest rate (say, LIBOR) remains below a preset cap selected by the investor. Hence a digital-capped note is a bull play on the interest rate; the investor forecasts a stable or dropping rate. A *digital-floored note* will pay an enhanced coupon as long as the reference interest rate remains above a preset floor. Hence a digital-floored note is a bear play on the interest rate. Société Générale has structured numerous digital notes whose principles are described in Exh. 13.16.

The difference between a note with a traditional cap and a note with a digital cap can be illustrated on a simple example. A plain-vanilla FRN could have been placed by a top-quality issuer at one-month LIBOR flat. Let's now consider a floating-rate note by the same issuer with a coupon indexed on one-month LIBOR plus 0.30% and capped monthly at 9.3%. The traditional cap means that the coupon paid each month will be either LIBOR plus 0.3% or 9.3%, whichever is smaller. The capped FRN can be regarded by investors as the sum of a plain-vanilla floater plus a 9% cap option on one-month LIBOR *sold* by the investor. Hence the yield enhancement of 30 basis points can be viewed as the annualized price of the cap option sold by investors. A FRN with a *digital cap* at 9% could be placed by the same issuer at LIBOR plus 1%. Each month when LIBOR is below 9%, the investor

EXHIBIT 13.16
Digital Structured Notes: Société Générale

SOCIÉTÉ GÉNÉRALE–STRUCTURED PRODUCTS

BOND INVESTOR DIGITAL STRATEGIES

Definition of Digital Note

Digital Notes can be created by embedding a series of Digital Options throughout the life of the note. For example, a 1 year Digital Note would pay an investor 1% each month where the underlying interest fulfills the strike conditions. This note would have 12 embedded options, each with the same payoff and strike. The note may be structured with options with varying strike levels to more closely match the investor's forecasts of the underlying rate.

Digital Note Strategies

The Digital Note comes in many forms, such as the Digital Capped and Floored FRN's, Digital Range Notes, and Resettable Range Notes. The exact nature of a Digital Option allows investors to create notes which specifically meet their interest rate forecasts on a daily, monthly, or yearly basis.

All Digital Note strategies are issued on the following Euro-Medium Term Note or Euro-Bond structure:	
Issuer:	A to AAA
Type:	EMTN or Eurobond
Maturity:	6 months to 3 years
Currency:	All Major Markets
Index:	OAT, US T-Note, BUND, PIBOR, LIBOR USD / DEM / ITL/JPY
Digital Strikes	Defined by investor
Amount:	Minimum Issue $10 Million
Coupon:	Enhanced Coupon × (% of time index meets digital conditions), fixed or floating
Redemption:	100% Guaranteed

Digital Capped and Floored FRN's

A Capped FRN pays an enhanced spread over LIBOR when the indexed LIBOR rate is below the Digital Cap level. For example, the coupon would equal (FRF PIBOR + 60) × (% of time the PIBOR is less than 9.50%). Due to the all or nothing pay-off of the digital option, the strike of a Digital Cap may be set much higher than the strike level of a regular cap which pays the same enhanced return. A Digital Floored FRN pays an enhanced coupon when the underlying rate stays above the strike level.

Digital Range Notes

The Range Note allows the investors to receive an enhanced return on days when the rate is within a range (combination of a digital cap and a digital floor) by taking the risk of earning no coupon on days the rate is outside of the range. The narrower the range and the further the range differs from the implied forward rates, the greater the potential return enhancement. The 1 year Range Note we issued at the start of this year is shown below with the historic PIBOR rates. The note has already accrued a coupon of 8% × (200/365), and SG economists are forecasting a 3 month PIBOR rate within the notes range through maturity.

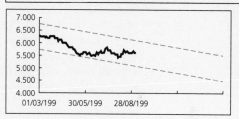

8% DIGITAL 6.INDEXED ON 3-MONTH PIBOR
1 March 1994

Resettable Range Note

The Resettable Range Note gives the investor the ability to reposition a constant-width range periodically (every 3 months for example) throughout the life of the note. At issue date, the investor defines a constant width range in which the underlying rate is expected to trade and the frequency in which this range may be reset. At each reset date, the investor may reposition the constant width range anywhere in relation to the underlying spot rate. For example, a floating rate note in USD would give a return of (LIBOR + 60) × (% of time) with a resettable range of 100 basis points.

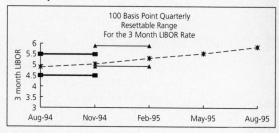

100 Basis Point Quarterly Resettable Range For the 3 Month LIBOR Rate

Source: Société Générale. Reprinted with permission.

receives LIBOR plus 1%. Each month when LIBOR is at 9% or above, the investor receives no coupon payment. The digital-capped FRN can be regarded by investors as the sum of a plain-vanilla floater plus the sale of a periodic 9% digital cap option, with a digital payoff equal to LIBOR. Hence the yield enhancement of 100 basis points can be viewed as the annualized price of the digital cap option sold by investors.

Third-Generation Notes

Third-generation notes involve a play on some equity or commodity index. Typical examples are *guaranteed notes with equity participation* and *bull and bear equity-linked notes*.

Guaranteed notes with equity participation are bonds having guaranteed redemption of capital and a minimum coupon; in addition, some participation in the price movement of a selected index is offered if this price movement is positive. For example, let's consider a two-year note that guarantees the initial capital (redemption at 100%) plus an annual coupon of 3% and that offers a 50% *participation rate* in the percentage price appreciation in the Japanese Nikkei index over the two years. At time of issue, the yield curve was flat at 8%. The 50% participation rate works as follows: If the stock index goes up by x%, the investor will get 50% of x. For example, if the Nikkei stock index goes up by 30% from the time of issue to the time of redemption, the option will yield a profit of 15% = ½.30%, and the bond will be redeemed for 115. The participation rate is in effect the percentage of a call option on the index obtained by the investor. In summary, the structured note can be viewed by investors as the sum of:

- A straight bond with a coupon of 3%

- Plus 50% of a call option on the Nikkei

The present value of the straight bond is:

$$P = \frac{3}{\left(1.08\right)} + \frac{103}{\left(1.08\right)^2} = 91.08\%.$$

As the bond is issued at 100, the implicit value of 50% of a call option on the Nikkei is therefore equal to

$$100 - 91.08 = 7.92\%,$$

and the full value of one call option on the Nikkei index is equal to:

$$2 \times (100 - 91.08) = 17.84\%.$$

There is clearly a negative relation between the amount of the *guaranteed coupon* and the *participation rate* that can be offered in the option. For example, a structured note with a zero coupon will leave more money to invest in the call option:

$$P = \frac{0}{\left(1.08\right)} + \frac{100}{\left(1.08\right)^2} = 85.73\%.$$

The difference between the redemption value and the current market value of the zero-coupon bond (14.27=100 − 85.73) can be invested by the issuer in call options. The remaining question is to determine the number of call options that can be purchased with this amount of 14.27. The number of call options that can be purchased is equal to the participation rate that is set in the structured note. In the example, one call option on the Nikkei index is worth 17.84, and 14.27 is available to invest in options. Hence this allows a participation rate of:

$$14.27/17.84 = 80\%,$$

instead of 50% as above.

Bull and bear equity-linked notes are often issued together but offered to two different kinds of investors. On September 30, 1986, the Kingdom of Denmark issued FF 800 million of bull and bear notes linked to the French CAC stock index and maturing on October 1, 1991. At time of issue, the French stock index stood at 405.97. Each note was issued at par with a face value of FF 10,000 and with an annual coupon of 4.5%, or FF 450 per five-year bond.[7] In addition, they were structured to offer an optionlike play on the stock index as follows:

- The bear equity-linked note is redeemed for a value equal to FF 23,200 minus 25.88 times the stock index on October 1, 1991, with a floor of zero. It should be noted that 23,200 is equal to 25.88 times 896.45. If I_t is the level of the stock index at maturity, the redemption value can be written as:

  $$25.88 \, [\text{Max} \, (0, 896.45 - I_t)].$$

- The bull equity-linked note is redeemed for a value equal to 25.88 times the stock market index on October 1, 1991, with a maximum of 896.45 per index (or 23,200 per the note). Hence the maximum redemption value is FF 23,200. The redemption value can be written as a function of the stock index at maturity I_t:

  $$25.88 \, [896.45 - \text{Max}(0, 896.45 - I_t)].$$

The bear note is structured as a put on the index with an exercise price of 896.45; the bull note is structured as a fixed amount of 896.45 per index minus a put on the index. This can be seen on Exh. 13.17, which describes the redemption values of the two notes as a function of the stock index level at maturity. The theoretical valuation of each structured note could be derived from:

- The value of a five-year annuity of FF 450

- The value of a five-year, European-type put option on the French stock index with a strike price of 896.45.

Bull notes and bear notes attract two different types of investors wishing to bet on the French stock market. These notes are quite risky, as they offer no guaranteed redemption value. In 1986 futures or options markets on the French stock index had not yet been approved, so these notes provided an attractive alternative.

EXHIBIT 13.17

Bull and Bear Notes: Redemption Value

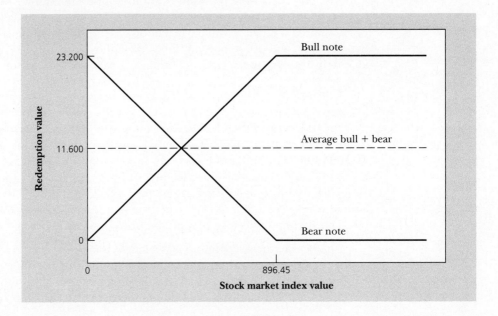

From the issuer's viewpoint, the risk analysis is quite different. The redemption value of the *sum* of the bear note and of the bull note is effectively set at FF 23,200 for the two notes, or an average FF 11,600 per note. There is effectively no equity risk for the issuer, as long as the same amounts of the two notes are issued. The yield to maturity on these bonds issued at FF 10,000 with a coupon of FF 450 and reimbursed at FF 11,600 is 7.27%, well below the rate paid by the French government on five-year straight bonds (around 8%). Hence the Kingdom of Denmark could issue debt at a fairly low cost because it catered to the needs of investors who had little alternatives to find similar plays on the stock market.

Summary

1. Options, like futures, are leveraged instruments but have an attractive asymmetric risk-return characteristic. Calls and puts are the major types of options traded on organized exchanges. Combinations of options and other securities allow the creation of numerous positions designed to capitalize on specific expectations about return and risk. Customized options can be arranged,

especially for currencies and interest rates, with long-term horizons extending up to 10 or 15 years. These customized products are written by banks for large amounts.

2. Exchange-traded options are written on all types of financial instruments, including commodities, currencies, individual stocks, stock indexes, fixed-income instruments, and interest rates. Options exist on spot asset prices as well as on futures contracts.

3. The valuation of options is somewhat complex and depends on the underlying asset. Analytical valuation models have been derived for European-type options, which cannot be exercised until expiration. They offer an operational approximation for American-type options, which can be exercised at any time, as is the case for a majority of options traded in the world.

4. Options can be used to invest in a specific security or market, while limiting the downside risk potential. They are also used to "insure" an existing portfolio. For example, buying a put on an asset (or portfolio) allows the reduction, or elimination, of loss in case of a drop in value of the asset. In-the-money options offer better protection than out-ot-the-money options but at a higher cost.

5. Numerous investment products, called *structured notes*, have recently been offered to investors. These are bonds structured with some optionlike clauses that allow specific plays on movements in interest rates or stock markets. These structured notes sometimes involve exotic options.

Questions and Problems

1*. An American investor believes in the depreciation of the dollar and buys one call option on the Deutsche mark at an exercise price of 45 cents per DM. The option premium is 1 cent per DM, or $625 per contract of 62,500 DM (Philadelphia):

- For what range of exchange rates should the investor exercise the call option at expiration?
- For what range of exchange rates will the investor realize a net profit, taking the original cost into account?
- If the investor had purchased a put with the same exercise price and premium, instead of a call, how would you answer the previous two questions?

2*. If the average premium on gold call options declines, does it mean that they are becoming undervalued and therefore should be bought? Using valuation models, give at least two possible causes for this decline.

3. The average premium on currency calls has decreased, whereas the premium on currency puts has increased. What explanations can you provide?

4*. You will receive $10 million at the end of June and will invest it for three months on the Eurodollar market. The current three-month Eurodollar rate is 6%, and you are worried that the rate will drop by the end of June. Here are some market quotes:

Eurodollar LIBOR futures, June delivery: Price 94%

Call Eurodollar, June expiration, strike price 94%:   Premium 0.4%

Put Eurodollar, June expiration, strike price 94%:   Premium 0.4%

The contract sizes are $1 million.

- Should you buy or sell futures to hedge your interest rate risk?
- Should you buy (or sell) calls (or puts) to insure a minimum rate when you will invest your money? What is this rate?
- In June the Eurodollar rate has moved to 4%. What is the result of both strategies? What if the rate is equal to 8% in June?

5. The French futures market, MATIF, trades PIBOR contracts. The PIBOR is the three-month interbank interest rate (the equivalent in francs of the LIBOR). The contract size is FF 5 million, and the margin is FF 15,000. On January 10 March futures trade at 90.74%. Options on the PIBOR futures contract are also listed. The premiums (in %) on March options are as follows:

Strike price	Call	Put
90.40	0.30	0.06
90.80	0.17	0.18
91.00	0.09	0.34

A few days later (January 14) the futures price moves to 89.50.

- What is the gain or loss, in francs, for someone who had sold a futures contract on January 10? What is the return, as a percentage of the initial investment (margin)?
- Are all option premiums quoted on January 10 reasonable?
- You know that you will have to borrow FF 50 million in March and fear a rise in interest rates. What are the maximum borrowing rates that you can insure using the various options?

   To cap your borrowing rate, you decide to use options with a strike price of 90.80.

- How many calls (or puts) should you buy (or sell)?

On January 14 the premium on the call March 90.80 moves to 0.02, and the premium on the put March 90.80 moves to 1.33.

- What is the FF profit (or loss) on your option position? What is the rate of return on your option position?

6*. You are currently borrowing $10 million at six-month LIBOR + 0.5%. The LIBOR is at 4%. You expect to borrow this amount for five years but are worried that LIBOR will increase in the future. You can buy a 6% cap on six-month LIBOR over the next five years with an annual cost of 0.5%. Describe the evolution of your borrowing costs under various interest rate scenarios.

7. A French importer will be paid $1 million in three months (March). He hesitates to sell $1 million forward or to buy currency options for that amount. What are the differences between the two strategies?

The current market prices are as follows:

Exchange rates: Spot $/FF = 0.20
                        3-month forward: $/FF = 0.19

Call FF March 0.20:   0.010 $ per FF

Put FF March 0.20:   0.012 $ per FF

8. What are the major determinants of the value of a currency option (call and put)? Briefly justify each determinant and its direction.

   What is the relation between a currency put and a currency call (put-call parity)? Suggest the circumstances in which an American-type option should be exercised before expiration.

9. You would like to protect your portfolio of British equity against a down movement of the British stock market. What are the relative advantages of stock index futures and options? Should you prefer in-the-money or out-of-the-money options?

10*. You hold a diversified portfolio of German stocks with a value of DM 50 million. You are getting worried by the outcome of the next elections and wish to hedge your German stock market risk. However, you like the companies that you hold and believe that the German stock market will do well in the long run. Transactions costs are too high to sell the stocks now and buy them back in a few weeks. Instead, you decide to use DAX futures or options to temporarily protect the value of your portfolio. Current market quotations are given below:

    DAX index value: Spot, 2000
                    June Futures, 2000

    DAX Call June 2000:   62

    DAX Put June 2000:   60

    DAX Put June 1950:   30

    DAX Put June 1900:   10

    The standard contract size for futures and options is DM 100 times the index.

    ▪ Why are the spot and futures values of the DAX index equal?

    ▪ What would you do to hedge your portfolio with futures?

    ▪ What would you do to insure your portfolio with options?

    ▪ Simulate the results of the four protection strategies: selling June futures, buying puts June 2000, buying puts June 1950, and buying puts June 1900. Look at the value of your portfolio, assuming that it follows exactly the movements in the market. Assume successively that the DAX index in June is equal to 1800, 1900, 2000, 2100, 2200.

11. You are American and hold a portfolio of French stocks. The market value of the portfolio is FF 20 million, with a beta of 1.2 relative to the CAC index. In November the spot value of the CAC index is 2000. The dividend yield, FF, and US$ interest rates are all equal to 4% (flat yield curves).

    ▪ You fear a drop in the French stock market (but not the FF). The size of CAC index contracts is 200 times the CAC index. There are futures contracts quoted with

December delivery. How many contracts should you buy or sell to hedge the French stock market risk? Calculate the futures price of the index.

- Puts on the CAC index with December expiration and a strike price of 2000 quote 50. How many puts should you buy or sell to insure your portfolio? Compare the results of this insurance with the hedge suggested above.

- You now fear a depreciation of the French franc relative to the U.S. dollar. Will the strategies above protect you against this depreciation?

12. Bank PAPOUF decides to issue two bonds and wonders what the fair interest rate on these bonds should be:

- *A one-year currency option bond*. The bond is issued in dollars with a face value of $100. The bondholder can choose to have the coupon and principal paid in dollars or in DM, at a specified exchange rate of DM/$ = 2, i.e., receive either $100 or DM 200 as principal repayment, and receive either $ C or DM 2C as interest if C is the coupon set in dollars.

- *A two-year currency option bond*. The bond is issued in dollars, with a face value of $100 and pays an annual coupon C'. The bondholder can choose to have the coupons and principal paid in dollars or in DM, at a specified exchange rate of DM/$ = 2, i.e., receive either $100 or DM 200 as principal repayment, and receive either $ C' or DM 2C' as interest if C' is the coupon set in dollars.

Compute the two interest rates C and C' that would be consistent with market conditions at time of issue:

Interest rates (zero-coupon rates):	1-year	2-year
US$	8%	8%
DM	4%	4%

Spot exchange rate: DM/$ =2

Currency options:

DM call, strike price 50 US cents, Expiration 1-year: 2 US cents

DM call, strike price 50 US cents, Expiration 2-year: 5 US cents

DM call, strike price 50 US cents, Expiration 1-year: 1 US cents

DM call, strike price 50 US cents, Expiration 1-year: 3 US cents

13*. Titi, a Japanese company, issued a six-year Eurobond in dollars convertible into shares of the Japanese company. At time of issue, the long-term bond yield on straight dollar bonds was 10% for such an issuer. Instead, Titi issued bonds at 8%. Each $1000 par bond is convertible into 100 shares of Titi. At time of issue, the stock price of Titi is 1600 yen, and the exchange rate is 100 yen = 0.5 dollar($/¥=0.005).

- Why can the bond be issued with a yield of only 8%?

- What would happen if:

The stock price of Titi increases?

The yen appreciates?

The market interest rate of dollar bonds drops?

A year later the new market conditions are as follows:

The yield on straight dollar bonds of similar quality has risen from 10% to 11%.

Titi stock price has moved up to ¥ 2000.

The exchange rate is $/¥=0.006.

- What would be a minimum price for the Titi convertible bond?
- Could you try to assess the theoretical value of this convertible bond as a package of other securities, such as straight bonds issued by Titi, options or warrants on the yen value of Titi stock, and futures and options on the dollar/yen exchange rate?

14. Strumpf Ltd. decides to issue a convertible bond with a maturity of two years. Each bond is issued with a nominal value of £100 and an annual coupon C; of course, C has to be determined. Each bond can be redeemed for £100 or converted into one share of Strumpf at the option of the bondholder.

The current stock price of Strumpf is £90. The yield curve for an issuer like Strumpf is flat at 6%. Barings is ready to issue long-term options on Strumpf shares. The premiums on calls with one- and two-year expirations are given below:

Strike price	European-type: 1-year	2-year	American-type: 1-year	2-year
90	11	16	12	17
100	6	8	6.5	9

- American-type calls are more expensive than European-type calls. Is it reasonable?
- Assume that the bond can be converted only at maturity, after payment of the second coupon. What should be the fair coupon rate C, consistent with the market conditions above?
- Assume that the bond is issued with the coupon rate determined above. The yield curve suddenly moves from 6% to 6.1%, and the option premiums stay the same. What should the new market price of the convertible bond be?
- Assume now that the bond can be converted on two dates (rather than one) These dates are the first year (right after the first coupon payment) and the second year as above. It is not possible to convert the two-year bond at any other date. Is it possible to construct an arbitrage portfolio allowing to price the fair coupon C with the data above? Be precise in your explanation, and state what type of options you would need to price the bond.

15*. The French bank BNP issues *exchangeable bonds.* These are bonds issued for FF 100 on April 1, 1990, with an annual coupon of FF 5, plus an exchange right. The bonds can be redeemed for FF 100 on April 1, 1996. The right can be exchanged on April 1, 1991, with payment of an additional FF 100, for another bond identical to the old bond (annual coupon of FF 5 and redeemed for FF 100 on April 1, 1996). If you exercise your right, you will have paid an additional FF 100 on April 1, 1991, but you will then hold two BNP bonds with maturity 1996.

- Under what scenario would you exercise the exchange right (exchange the right plus FF 100 for an additional bond) on April 1, 1991? Hence what is the attraction of such an exchangeable bond for investors?
- On April 1, 1990, the yield curve is flat at 6%. You can buy a call on a five-year bond with a coupon of 5%. The call has a strike price of 100% and expires on April 1, 1991. Its premium is 2%. Construct a replication portfolio to determine at what price the exchangeable bond can be issued by BNP.

16. Draw the profit and loss curve at expiration (as in Exh. 13.8), as a function of the CAC index for those two options:

- *Traditional call on the CAC index:* Exercise price: 2000, premium: 40
- *Digital call on the CAC index:* Exercise price: 2000, payoff if exercised: 200, premium 40.

What are the relative advantages of the two options? Should the premium on the digital call be an increasing or decreasing function of the payoff? Assume that the volatility of the French stock market increases suddenly. Should the premium on the digital call increase more (or less) than the premium on the traditional call?

17. The current dollar yield curve on the dollar Eurobond market is flat at 7% for top-quality borrowers. A company of good standing can issue plain-vanilla straight and floating-rate dollar Eurobonds at the following conditions:

- *Bond A: Straight bond.* Five-year straight dollar Eurobond with a coupon of 7.25%.
- *Bond B: FRN.* Five-year dollar FRN with a semiannual coupon set at LIBOR plus ¼% and a cap of 14%. The cap means that the coupon rate is limited at 14% even if the LIBOR passes 13.75%.

An investment banker proposes to the French company to issue bull and/or bear FRNs at the following conditions:

- *Bond C: Bull FRN.* Five-year FRN with a semiannual coupon set at: 13.75% − LIBOR
- *Bond D: Bear FRN.* Five-year FRN with a semiannual coupon set at: $2 \times$ LIBOR − 7% and a cap of 20.5%

The floor on all coupons is zero. The investment bank also proposes a five-year floor option at 3.5%. This floor will pay to the French company the difference between 3.5% and LIBOR, if it is positive, or zero if LIBOR is above 3.5%. The cost of this floor is spread over the payment dates and set at an annual 0.1%. The company can also enter in a five-year interest-rate swap 7% fixed against LIBOR.

- Explain why it would be attractive to the French company to issue these FRNs compared to current market conditions for plain-vanilla straight Eurobonds and FRNs.
- Find out the borrowing cost reduction that can be achieved by issuing those bear and bull notes compared to a fixed-coupon rate of 7.25% or to an FRN at LIBOR plus ¼%.

18*. You are a young investment banker considering the issuance of a guaranteed note with stock index participation for a client. The current yield curve is flat at 8% for all maturities. Long-term at-the-money options on the stock market index are traded by banks. Two-year at-the-money calls trade at 17.84% of the index value; three-year at-the-money calls trade at 20% of the index value.

You hesitate about the terms to set in the structured note. You know that if you guarantee a higher coupon rate, the level of participation in the stock appreciation will be less. Your boss asks you to compute the "fair" participation rate that would be feasible for various guaranteed coupon rates and maturities. In other words, you will take the current market conditions (as described above) to estimate the participation rates that are feasible with a maturity of two or three years, and a coupon rate of: 0, 1, 2, 3, 5, and 7%.

Notes

1. See Cox and Rubinstein (1985).

2. A review of some of the problems can be found in Cox and Rubinstein (1985) and Hull (1993).

3. This is shown in the foreign-currency options markets by Shastri and Tandon (1986) and Bodhurta and Courtadon (1986).

4. See Cox and Rubinstein (1985) and Rubinstein and Leland (1981).

5. "Stock Index Options are Gaining More Popularity with Institutions," *Wall Street Journal* (*Europe*), November 11–12, 1994.

6. Such strategies are often used for cost-accounting motivations. For example, assume that an asset had been purchased at 110, while the current market price is 107. Selling a call with an exercise price of 110 and a premium of 3 will allow insuring a revenue of 113, above historical cost, in case of exercise and an income of 3 otherwise.

7. This example is analyzed in Jacque (1993).

Bibliography

Black, F. "The Pricing of Commodity Contracts," *Journal of Financial Economics*, March 1976.

Black, F., and Scholes, M. "The Pricing of Options and Corporate Liabilities," *Journal of Political Economy*, May/June 1973.

Bodhurta, J., and Courtadon, G.R. "Efficiency Tests of the Foreign Currency Options Market," *Journal of Finance*, March 1986.

Brenan, M., and Schwartz, E. "The Valuation of American Put Options," *Journal of Finance*, May 1977.

Cox, J., Ross, S., and Rubinstein, M. "Option Pricing: A Simplified Approach," *Journal of Financial Economics*, September 1979.

Cox, J., and Rubinstein, M. *Options Markets*, Englewood Cliffs, NJ: Prentice Hall, 1985.

Garman M., and Kohlagen, S. "Foreign Currency Option Values," *Journal of International Money and Finance*, December 1983.

Geske, R., and Johnson, H. "The American Put Valued Analytically," *Journal of Finance*, December 1984.

Gibson, R. *Option Valuation*, New York: McGraw-Hill, 1991.

Grabbe, J.O. "The Pricing of Call and Put Options on Foreign Exchange," *Journal of International Money and Finance*, December 1983.

Hull, J.C. *Options, Futures and other Derivative Securities*, Englewood Cliffs, NJ: Prentice Hall, 1993.

Jacque, L. "Myths and Realities of the Global Capital Market: Lessons for Financial Markets," *Continental Bank Journal of Applied Corporate Finance*, Fall 1993.

Jarrow, R., and Rudd, A. *Option Pricing*, Englewood Cliffs, NJ: Prentice Hall, 1993.

Merton, R.C. "A Rational Theory of Option Pricing," *Bell Journal of Economics and Management Science*, Spring 1973.

"Options: Origins of the Species," *Risk Magazine*, October 1991.

Roll, R. "An Analytical Formula for Unprotected American Call Options with Known Dividends," *Journal of Financial Economics*, November 1977.

Rubinstein, M., and Leland, H. "Replicating Options with Positions in Stock and Cash," *Financial Analysts Journal*, July/August 1981.

Shastri, K., and Tandon, K. "On the Use of European Models to Price an Option on Foreign Currencies," *Journal of Futures Markets*, Spring 1986.

Stoll, H.R., and Whaley, R.E. *Futures and Options*, Southwestern, 1993.

Chapter 13: Appendix
Valuing Currency Options

Traditional option valuation models can be readily adapted to currency options.[1] The main revision stems from the fact that the opportunity cost to invest in a foreign currency is not the domestic risk-free rate, as for an ordinary asset, but rather the interest rate differential (domestic minus foreign). The intuitive explanation for this is that the direct investment in a foreign currency costs the domestic interest rate (to finance the purchase of currency) but earns the foreign interest rate. This leads to a simple revision of the Black-Scholes formula, Eq. (13.A1). For a European-type call option the revised formula is

$$P_0 = e^{-r^*t}\left[SN(d) - e^{-rt}EN\left(d - \sigma\sqrt{t}\right)\right]$$

(13.A1)

where

S is the exchange rate (the domestic currency price of one unit of foreign currency),

E is the exercise price,

r and r^* are the domestic and foreign interest rates expressed on a continuous compounding basis,

$N(X)$ is the probability that a deviation of less than X will occur in a unit normal distribution,

d is $\dfrac{\ln\left(S/E\right) + \left(r - r^* + 0.5\sigma^2\right)t}{\sigma\sqrt{t}}$,

t is the time to expiration, and

σ is the standard deviation of percentage exchange rate changes.

This formula can also be written as a function of the forward, or futures, exchange rate, rather than the spot exchange rate. With continuous compounding, the interest rate parity relation between the forward rate, the spot rate, and the interest rate differential is written as

$$F = Se^{(r-r^*)t}. \tag{13.A2}$$

This implies that the valuation of the option premium may be written as

$$P_0 = e^{-rt}\left[FN\left(d\right) - EN\left(d - \sigma\sqrt{t}\right)\right], \tag{13.A3}$$

where

$$d = \frac{\ln\left(F/E\right) + 0.5\sigma^2 t}{\sigma\sqrt{t}}.$$

Note that this formula equals the Black-Scholes formula for options on currency futures.[2] Therefore a European-type option on spot exchange rate or on futures exchange rate should have the same value. This is not the case for an American-type option, which can be exercised any time before expiration. Although the spot and futures exchange rates converge at expiration, they are not equal during the life of the option. Depending on the value of the basis (futures discount or premium), an American-type option on spot exchange rates (as traded in Philadelphia) may be worth more or less than an American-type option on futures exchange rates (as traded in Chicago).

In the valuation formula for European-type currency options, the coefficient δ is equal to

$$\delta = e^{-rt}N(d).$$

Valuing a currency put is identical to valuing a currency call because of the inverse relationship between exchange rates. A put on the pound/dollar rate is identical to a call on a dollar/pound rate.

The formula above was derived by Black and Scholes for European-type options, which cannot be exercised before expiration. In reality, however, listed currency options can usually be exercised at any time before expiration. And unlike many other call options, it is sometimes more profitable to do so. This is true, for example, for deep-in-the-money calls (or put options) when the foreign interest rate is much higher (or lower) than the domestic interest rate. In general, in fact, the probability of early exercise increases with the interest rate differential, especially for in-the-money options. The intuitive explanation for this is that it is better to exercise a call immediately and invest at a high foreign interest rate than wait until expiration and, in the meantime, earn a low domestic interest rate on the cash to be converted. When the probability of early exercise increases, the premium becomes driven by the conversion value of the option, so that the Black-Scholes formula systematically underestimates it. Under those circumstances, we must use more complicated models involving numerical estimation techniques.

Other things being equal, the value of an option decreases over time. Intuitively, this relationship between time and the value of an option makes sense for two reasons. First, the cash investment in the option is less than the amount required to buy the security, which means that money is left over to invest elsewhere. The longer the time to expiration, the more valuable this financing advantage is. Second, the longer the time to expiration, the more likely it is that there will be a large positive move in the price of the underlying security. Of course, large adverse moves are just as likely to occur, but this does not affect the option buyer, because his or her loss is limited to the premium. For currency options, the time premium component is usually less than it is for stock options because the financing opportunity cost for currency options is only the interest rate differential, not the domestic risk-free rate. But the second component, i.e., security price volatility of the time premium, is still present, and that is why the premium tends to decline over time.

The premium of a currency option is affected by the interest rate differential and, more important, by the estimated volatility of the exchange rate. Exchange rate markets go through periods of calm and periods of turbulence, depending on the international environment. Options can be considered as undervalued by an investor if his or her volatility assessment is more than that of the market. Option valuation models can be used to estimate the market assessment of the exchange rate volatility implied in current option premiums. Basically, one would use models such as Eq. (13.A1) and solve for σ given the premium P_0. This is routinely done by most option dealers. Exhibit 13.18 shows the evolution of the volatility of the $/DM exchange rate changes as calculated by Salomon Brothers from January 1993 to June 1994. The solid line is the estimated annualized volatility implied in at-the-money currency options. The dashed line is an estimate of the volatility based on historical data. This estimate, called GIFT, uses a GARCH model of past data (see Appendix to Chapter 3) to get an estimate of current volatility. The volatility moves between 8% and 15% per year. Some investors and traders use these charts to determine when options look under- or overvalued.

EXHIBIT 13.18

Volatility Profile of DM/US$ Exchange Rate

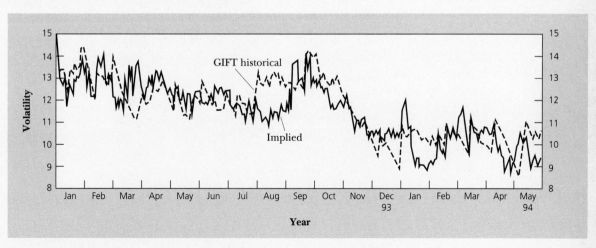

Source: Salomon Brothers Inc.

Appendix Notes

1. For a straightforward derivation of the Black-Scholes valuation formula for options, see Garman and Kohlagen (1983) and Grabbe (1983).

2. The formula for European-type options on futures contracts has been derived by Black (1976).

14

Currency Risk Management

The traditional and most consistent international investment strategy is first to decide on an international asset allocation. An allocation breaks down a portfolio by both asset class (short-term deposit, bond, equity, commodity) and country or currency of investment (U.S. dollar, British pound, French franc). The resulting allocation can be used to form a matrix of currencies and asset classes. Ten percent of a typical portfolio's value may be allocated to Japanese stocks, 5% to Deutsche mark bonds, and so forth. Specific bonds and stocks are selected using the various techniques discussed in previous chapters. Once a portfolio is structured, it must be managed according to changes in expectations. For example, periodical revisions of the forecasted earnings of specific companies can lead to equity arbitrage within a portfolio. More common revisions in expectations, however, are the result of macroeconomic variables. News of economic growth or changes in money supply may cause a manager to alter his or her asset allocation, at least temporarily. But frequent reallocation can lead to heavy transaction costs, especially on bonds and some illiquid foreign stocks.

Leveraged instruments, such as options and futures, are used domestically to hedge risks that arise suddenly. They protect a manager from being forced to arbitrage or liquidate a large part of his or her portfolio. For example, interest rate futures or options may be used to hedge a long-term bond portfolio if fears about a rise in interest rates materialize. Similarly a domestic manager who is heavily invested in bonds but suddenly becomes bullish on the stock market can immediately act on his or her expectation by buying stock index futures or options and thereafter slowly switching his or her portfolio from bonds to stocks. This technique reduces transactions costs, gives the manager time to select the best stocks, and locks in potential profits on the anticipated rise in the stock market. Moreover, if after a few days the manager changes his or her mind about how well the stock market will perform, the manager need only close his or her futures and options position and stick with the initial portfolio allocation. These and other short-term risk management techniques are extensively used in the

United States and other countries where speculative instruments on stocks and bonds exist (see Chapters 12 and 13). The use of financial futures and options in controlling portfolio risk is described in textbooks that deal with domestic investment. The most important area of risk management in international investment is currency risk.

This chapter is devoted to the art of fine-tuning an international portfolio, so that it will benefit from both sudden changes in expectations and market uncertainties. Its focus is currency risk management.

Most portfolio managers are often confronted with practical problems such as the following:

- An investor is bullish about his portfolio of French stocks but is concerned that the franc may drop sharply in the wake of local elections. On the other hand, the franc may also appreciate strongly if the election goes the other way.

- An investor holds British gilts. She expects the long-term UK interest rate to drop, which in turn would cause a depreciation of the pound.

- An investor would like to buy KLM stock because he is very bullish about the Dutch airline, but he is concerned that the Dutch guilder may depreciate.

- A British investor specializes in forecasting monetary variables, such as interest and exchange rates. Which strategies should she choose to capitalize on her forecasts?

This chapter is intended to assist the reader in better handling these kinds of situations. The issue of whether to systematically hedge currency risk is addressed in Chapters 5 and 17.

Hedging with Futures or Forward Currency Contracts

Either futures or forward currency contracts may be used to hedge a portfolio. They differ in several ways, which are outlined in Chapter 12, but more important, both types of contracts allow a manager to take the same economic position. Therefore in this chapter futures will denote both futures and forward contracts.

The Basic Approach: Hedging the Principal

Hedging with futures or forward contracts is very simple. One takes a position with a foreign exchange contract that is the reverse of the principal being hedged. In other words, a citizen of country A who wants to hedge a portfolio of assets denominated in currency B would sell a futures contract to exchange currency B for currency A. The size of the contract would equal the market value of the assets hedged. For example, a U.S. investor with £1 million invested in British gilts (Treasury bonds) would sell futures for £1 million worth of dollars. The direction of a foreign exchange rate contract is often confusing because it involves the exchange rates of two currencies.

On the International Monetary Market at the Chicago Board of Trade one can buy and sell contracts of £25,000 where the futures price is expressed in dollars per pound. The same-size contract is also found on the London International Financial Futures Exchange (LIFFE). Let us assume that on September 12 our U.S. investor buys futures with delivery in December for 1.95 dollars per pound; the spot exchange rate is 2.00 dollars per pound. In order to hedge his £1 million principal, the investor must sell a total of 40 contracts. Now let us assume that a few weeks later, the futures and spot exchange rates drop to $1.85 and $1.90, respectively, whereas the pound value of the British asset rises to 1,010,000. To help the U.S. investor assess the value of his portfolio, we introduce the following notation:

V_t is the value of the portfolio of foreign assets to hedge, measured in foreign currency at time t (e.g., £1 million),

V_t^* is the value of the portfolio of foreign assets measured in domestic currency (e.g., $2 million),

S_t is the spot exchange rate: domestic currency value of one unit of foreign currency quoted at time t (e.g., 2.00 $/£), and

F_t is the futures exchange rate: domestic currency value of one unit of foreign currency quoted at time t.

Exhibit 14.1 shows that as the pound value of the British assets appreciates by 1%, the sterling exchange rate drops by 5%, causing a loss in dollar value on the portfolio of 4.05%. In dollar terms this loss in portfolio value is $81,000:

$$V_t^* - V_0^* = V_t S_t - V_0 S_0 \tag{14.1}$$

Hence

$$\$1,919,000 - \$2,000,000 = (£1,010,000 \times \$/£1.90)$$

$$- (£1,000,000 \times \$/£2.00)$$

$$= -\$81,000.$$

EXHIBIT 14.1

Relationships Between Portfolio Value and Rate of Return

	Period 0	Period t	Rate of Return (percent)
Portfolio value (in pounds), V	1,000,000	1,010,000	1
Portfolio value (in dollars), V^*	2,000,000	1,919,000	−4.05
Exchange rate ($/pounds), S	2.00	1.90	−5
Futures rate ($/pounds), F	1.95	1.85	—

On the other hand, the realized gain on the futures contract sale is $100,000, as follows:

$$V_0 \left(-F_t + F_0\right) = \text{Realized gain.} \tag{14.2}$$

Hence

$$£1,000,000 \times \$/£(1.95 - 1.85) = \$100,000.$$

Therefore the net profit on the hedged position is $19,000:

$$\text{Profit} = V_t S_t - V_0 S_0 + V_0 \left(F_0 - F_t\right). \tag{14.3}$$

Hence

$$\text{Profit} = \$100,000 - \$81,000 = \$19,000.$$

The rate of return in dollars on the hedged position is

$$\text{Return} = \frac{19,000}{2,000,000} = 0.95\%.$$

This position is almost perfectly hedged, since the 1% return on the British asset is transformed into a 0.95% return in U.S. dollars, despite the drop in value of the British pound. The slight difference between the two numbers is explained by the fact that the investor hedged only the principal (£1 million), not the price appreciation or the return on the British investment (equal here to 1%). The 5% drop in sterling value applied to this 1% return exactly equals $1\% \times 5\% = 0.05\%$.

The efficiency of a hedge depends on the return on the hedged assets. The larger the return, the less efficient the hedge. This is seen by examining the rate of return on the hedged position. It is necessary to introduce some further notations to better understand the technical effects of exchange rate movements. Let us call R, R^*, and s the rates of return on V, V^*, and S, and let's call R_F the variation on the futures exchange rate as a proportion of the spot exchange rate, that is, $R_F = (F_t - F_0)/S_0$. The relationship between dollar and pound returns on the foreign portfolio is as follows:

$$R^* = R + s(1 + R). \tag{14.4}$$

Hence

$$-4.05\% = 1\% - 5(1.01)\%.$$

The cross-product term $sR = 0.05\%$ explains the difference between the return on the portfolio and the return on the futures position. The currency contribution, $R^* - R$, is equal to exchange rate variation *plus* the cross-product sR. When the value of the portfolio in local currency fluctuates widely, the difference is significant. So the question is what the exact amount hedged should be to reduce or fully eliminate the influence of the currency movement.

Optimal Hedge Ratio

The objective of a currency hedge (see the appendix) is to minimize the uncertainty of the influence of an exchange rate depreciation. This is usually taken to mean the following: A currency hedge should achieve on a foreign asset the same rate of return in domestic currency as can be achieved on the local market in foreign currency terms. For example, a U.S. investor would try to achieve a dollar rate of return on a British gilts portfolio equal to what he or she could have achieved in terms of sterling. Creating a perfect currency hedge is equivalent to nullifying a currency movement and translating a foreign rate of return directly into a similar domestic rate of return.

As shown in Chapter 12, the rate of return on a hedged position is equal to

$$R_H = R^* - hR_F, \tag{14.5}$$

where R_H is the rate of return on a portfolio hedged against currency risk, and h is the hedge ratio as defined in Chapter 12.

The optimal amount to hedge is determined by finding the value of h such that the hedged return in domestic currency terms, R_H, equals the return in foreign currency terms, R. Substituting the value of R^* given in Eq. (14.4) into Eq. (14.5), we find

$$R_H = R + s(1 + R) - hR_F.$$

Therefore the objective of a hedging policy is to minimize the variance of the return differential $R_H - R$, where

$$R_H - R = s(1 + R) - hR_F. \tag{14.6}$$

We will now study the operational implications of this currency hedging strategy, starting with a simple case and moving on to a more general case.

No Basis Risk   Let's first assume that the basis (see Chapter 12) remains constant. Then the rate of return on a futures contract, $R_F = (F_t - F_0)/S_0$, is equal to the spot exchange rate movement, $s = (S_t - S_0)/S_0$. Equation (14.6) can now be written as follows:

$$R_H - R = s(1 + R - h). \tag{14.7}$$

The optimal hedge ratio h is most easily determined for assets that have nonstochastic returns, such as interest-bearing securities with fixed prices (e.g., short-term deposits). To eliminate the influence of currency translation, one must hedge both the principal and the expected return on the principal $(1 + R)$. In the previous example the investor should ideally have hedged £1,010,000 had he been able to anticipate that the return would be 1% on his British gilts. When the return on foreign assets is uncertain, however, an investor should take into account the covariance between exchange rates and asset returns.

We saw in Chapter 4 that because in practice stock prices have little correlation with exchange rates, the last covariance term may be dropped. The optimal hedge for stocks, therefore, includes both the principal and any expected dividend payment or price appreciation. Where there are unexpected price movements, an investor's holding of futures contracts should be adjusted to reflect the change in market value of the foreign stock portfolio.

Bond portfolios are generally more sensitive to exchange rate movements because of the link between exchange rates and interest rates. In the introduction we described a U.S. investor who was expecting a decline in British interest rates (rise in bond prices) leading to a depreciation of the pound. This scenario implies that there is a negative covariance between R and s. The hedging implications of this covariance are studied in the appendix.

Basis Risk   Forward and futures exchange rates are directly determined by two factors: the spot exchange rate and the interest rate differential between two currencies. (This was discussed in Chapters 1 and 2). The forward discount, or the premium, which is the percentage difference between the forward and the spot exchange rates, equals the interest rate differential for the same maturity as the forward contract. In futures jargon we say that the basis equals the interest rate differential. If we express the exchange rate in sterling as the dollar value of one pound (e.g., $\$/\pounds = 2.00$) and call $r_\$$ and $r_\pounds$ the interest rates in dollars and pounds, respectively, with the same maturity as the futures contract, the relation known as interest rate parity is

$$\frac{F}{S} = \frac{1+r_\$}{1+r_\pounds} \quad \text{and}$$

$$\frac{F-S}{S} = \frac{r_\$ - r_\pounds}{1+r_\pounds}. \tag{14.8}$$

Because this relation is the result of arbitrage on very liquid markets, it technically holds at every instant. On the interbank Eurocurrency market, banks trade only in short-term interest rates. There forward prices are simply quoted to clients by applying the interest rate parity formula. When a forward contract is written for a client, the bank simply takes an offsetting position in the Eurocurrency market. Arbitrage between futures and forward prices ensures that interest rate parity applies to futures contracts as well. Note that such an exact valuation of the basis does not work for futures or forward contracts on other commodities and instruments: Arbitrage transaction costs are much higher in other markets, and optional clauses exist in many other futures contracts. As discussed in Chapter 12, bond futures are an extreme case where basis valuation is a rather difficult exercise. Forward and futures currency contracts are an interesting exception, since the basis is precisely defined as the interest rate differential, and changes in the interest rate differential have a strong influence on currency movements.

Minimum-Variance Hedge   The optimal hedge ratio is equal to the covariance of the currency contribution $(R^* - R)$, with the futures return R_F divided by the variance of the futures return (see Eq. 12.6 and the Chapter 14 appendix). A correlation between currency movements and changes in the interest rate differential will lead to an optimal hedge ratio different from one. This is because a component of the futures return is the change in interest rate differential or basis. Accordingly the hedge ratio should compensate for this correlation.

The correlation between futures and spot exchange rates is a function of the futures contract term. Futures prices for contracts near maturity closely follow spot exchange rates because at this time the interest rate differential is a small component of the futures price. To illustrate, let us consider the futures price of British pound contracts with one, three, and twelve months left until delivery. The spot exchange rate is currently $2.00 per pound, and the interest rates and the calculated values for the futures are as given in Exh. 14.2. The one-month futures price should equal $2.00 plus the one-month interest rate differential applied to the spot rate. The interest rate differential for one month equals the annualized rate differential of –4% divided by 12:

$$F = S + S\frac{r_\$ - r_£}{1 + r_£} = 2.00 - 2.00\frac{\frac{4}{12}\%}{1 + \frac{14}{12}\%}.$$

Hence

$$F = 1.993.$$

We see, then, that even though the interest rate differential is very large, its effect on the one-month futures price is minimal because the spot exchange rate is the driving force behind short-term forward exchange rate movements. This is less

EXHIBIT 14.2

Importance of Interest Rate Differentials to Futures Prices

	Maturity		
	One month	**Three months**	**Twelve months**
Pound interest rate (percent)	14	13.5	13
Dollar interest rate (percent)	10	10	10
Futures price (dollars)	1.993	1.983	1.947
Interest rate component (dollars)	–0.007	–0.017	–0.053

Spot rate: £1 = $2.00.

true for longer-term contracts. More specifically, a reduction of 1% (100 basis points) in the interest rate differential causes a futures price movement of approximately 0.25% (³⁄₁₂) for the three-month contracts and 1% (¹²⁄₁₂) for the one-year contract, as compared to 0.08% (¹⁄₁₂%) for the one-month contract.

Hedging Strategies

A major decision in selecting a futures or forward currency hedge is the choice of contract terms. Short-term contracts track the behavior of the spot exchange rates better, have greater trading volume, and offer more liquidity than long-term contracts. On the other hand, short-term contracts must be rolled over if a hedge is to be maintained for a period longer than the initial contract.

For longer-term hedges, a manager can choose from three basic contract terms:

1. Short-term contracts, already mentioned, which must be rolled over at maturity

2. Contracts with a matching maturity, that is, one that matches the expected period for which the hedge is to be maintained

3. Longer-term contracts with a maturity extending beyond the hedging period

Futures contracts for any of the three terms may be closed by taking an offsetting position on the delivery date. This avoids actual physical delivery of a currency. Exhibit 14.3 depicts three such hedging strategies for an expected hedge period of six months. The choice of strategy depends on the evolution of interest rates. Long-term contracts are more attractive if the interest rate differential (domestic minus foreign) falls in absolute value. *Ceteris paribus*, a drop in the interest rate differential means lower futures prices (relative to spot prices), which is beneficial to the seller of a futures contract.

EXHIBIT 14.3

Three Hedging Strategies for an Expected Hedge Period of Six Months

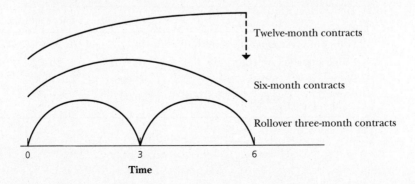

Twelve-month contracts

Six-month contracts

Rollover three-month contracts

Time

Another consideration in picking a hedging strategy is transaction costs. Rolling over short-term contracts generates more commissions because of the larger number of transactions involved. Also, the number of futures contracts used in order to reflect changes in the market value of the hedge portfolio should be frequently adjusted to reflect changes in the asset value.

Longer hedges can be built using currency swaps, which can be arranged with horizons up to a dozen years long. However, currency swaps are used primarily by corporations in the currency management of their assets and liabilities. Portfolio managers usually take a shorter horizon.

Portfolio of Currencies

Cross hedges are sometimes used for closely linked currencies. For example, a U.S. investor could use Deutsche mark futures to hedge a currency risk on Dutch stocks, since the Dutch guilder and the Deutsche mark are strongly correlated. Futures and forward currency contracts are actively traded only for the major currencies. International portfolios are often invested in assets in Spain, Italy, Norway, Sweden, Singapore, and other countries where futures contracts are not actively traded in the domestic currency. In these cases one must try to find contracts on other currencies that are closely correlated with the investment currencies.

Investment managers sometimes fear the depreciation of only one or two currencies in their portfolio and therefore hedge currency risk selectively. Other managers fear that their domestic currency will appreciate relative to all foreign currencies. For example, the strong U.S. dollar appreciation from January 1983 to March 1985 was realized against all currencies. This domestic currency appreciation induced a negative currency contribution on all foreign portfolios. Foreign stock investments had outstanding performances, but an overall currency hedge on their foreign investments would have drastically improved their performance by nullifying the negative currency contribution to the total dollar performance of non-U.S. portfolios.

Systematic currency hedging also reduces the total volatility of the portfolio, as seen in Chapter 4. A complete foreign currency hedge can be achieved by hedging the investments in each foreign currency. But this is unfeasible for many currencies and very cumbersome administratively. Also, it is not necessary to hedge all of each currency component in a multicurrency portfolio. In a portfolio with assets in many currencies, the residual risk of each currency gets partly diversified away. Optimization techniques can be used to construct a hedge with futures contracts in only a few currencies (e.g., the yen, Deutsche mark, and sterling). Although the residual risk of individual currencies is not fully hedged, the portfolio is well protected against a general appreciation of the home currency.[1] Another alternative is to use futures on a basket of currencies, such as the European currency unit.

The stability of the estimated hedge ratios is of crucial importance in establishing effective hedge strategies especially when cross hedging is involved. Empirical studies indicate that hedges using futures contracts in the same currency as the asset to be hedged are very effective but that the optimal hedge ratios in cross hedges that involve different currencies are quite unstable over time.[2]

Insuring and Hedging with Options

Two approaches are used for reducing currency risk exposure with options. The traditional method exploits the asymmetric risk-return characteristic of an option, so that it is used as an insurance vehicle. The second, and more dynamic, approach takes into account the relationship between the option premium and the underlying exchange rate. This second approach is closer to a hedging strategy.

Insuring with Options

Many investors continue to focus on the characteristics of options at expiration. Currency options are purchased in amounts equal to the principal to be hedged. As with currency futures, it is not easy to determine which options to use, because they involve the rate of exchange between two currencies. Our previous example described a U.S. investor with £1 million of British assets. Let us assume that on the Philadelphia Stock Exchange he buys British pound puts for December at 200. A British pound put gives him the right, but not the obligation, to sell British pounds at a fixed exercise price with payment in dollars. Similarly a British pound call gives him the right to buy British pounds with U.S. dollars. We should note that a call to buy British pounds with U.S. dollars is equivalent to a put to sell U.S. dollars for British pounds. Options markets in some countries sometimes offer reverse contracts, so that investors must be sure that they understand the position they are taking. In all cases, however, a good hedge implies buying options (puts or calls), not selling or writing them.

Returning to our example, the spot exchange rate is $2.00 per pound. The exercise price for the December put is 200 cents per pound (or 2 dollars per pound), and the premium is 6 cents per pound. On the Philadelphia Stock Exchange one contract covers £12,500, so that the investor must buy 80 contracts to hedge £1 million. In this traditional approach puts are treated as insurance devices. If the pound drops below $2.00 at expiration, a profit will be made on the put that exactly offsets the currency loss on the portfolio. If the pound drops to $1.90, the gain on the put at expiration is

$$80 \times 12,500 \times (2.00 - 1.90) = \$100,000.$$

The advantage of buying options rather than futures is that options simply expire if the pound appreciates rather than depreciates. For example, if the British pound moves up to $2.20, the futures contract will generate a loss of $200,000, nullifying the currency gain on the portfolio of assets. This does not happen with options that simply expire. Of course, one must pay a price for this asymmetric risk structure, namely, the premium, which is the cost of having this hedging insurance.

Note that the premium keeps an investor from having a perfect hedge. In the previous example the net profit on the put purchase equals the gain at expiration minus the premium. If we call V_0 the number of pound puts, P_0 the premium per £, and E the exercise price, the net dollar profit on the put at the time of exercise t is

Net dollar profit $= V_0\,(E - S_t) - V_0 P_0$, that is,

Net dollar profit = £ quantity (Exercise price – Spot price)
$\qquad\qquad\qquad$ – £ quantity (Premium).

Hence

$£1,000,000 \times \$/£(2.00 - 1.90) - £1,000,000 \times \$/£0.06 = \$40,000.$

This profit does not cover the currency loss on the portfolio (equal to roughly $100,000), because the option premium cost $60,000. It would have been even less profitable if the pound had dropped to only $1.95. An alternative solution is to buy out-of-the-money puts with a lower exercise price and a lower premium. But with those, exchange rates would have to move that much more before a profit could be made on the options. In short, what is gained in terms of a lower premium is lost in terms of a higher exercise price.

In fact the traditional approach does not allow for a good currency hedge except when variations in the spot exchange rate swamp the cost of the premium. Instead this approach uses options as insurance contracts, and the premium is regarded as a sunk cost. Note, however, that options are usually resold on the market rather than left to expire; when the option is resold, part of the initial insurance premium is recovered. On the other hand, the approach still exploits the greatest advantage of options, namely, that an option can be allowed to expire if the currency moves in a favorable direction. Options protect a portfolio in case of adverse currency movements, as do currency futures, and maintain its performance potential in case of favorable currency movements, whereas futures hedge in both directions. The price of this asymmetric advantage is the insurance cost implicit in the time value of option.

Dynamic Hedging with Options

Listed options are continually traded, and positions are usually closed by reselling the put in the market instead of exercising it. The profit on a position is the difference between the two market premiums and, therefore, completely dependent on market valuation. The modern approach to currency option hedging recognizes this fact and is based on the relationship between changes in option premiums and changes in exchange rates.

The definition of a perfect currency option hedge is simple and similar to the one given previously. A perfect hedge is a position where every dollar loss from currency movement on a portfolio of foreign assets is covered by a dollar gain in the value of the options position.

We know that an option premium is related only indirectly to the underlying exchange rate. Exhibit 14.4 shows the relationship we usually observe. Beginning with a specific exchange rate, say, $/£ = 2.00, a put premium can go up or down in response to changes in the exchange rates. The slope of the curve at point A denotes the elasticity of the premium to any movements in the dollar exchange rate. In Exh. 14.4 the premium is equal to 6 cents when the exchange rate is 200 U.S. cents per pound, and the tangent at point A equals –0.5. This slope is usually called delta, as described in Chapter 13.

In this example a good hedge would be achieved by buying two pound puts for every sterling of British assets. One pound put is defined here as a put option on one unit of British currency. One contract includes several pound puts, depending on the contract size. If the pound depreciated by 1 U.S. cent, each put would go up by approximately 0.5 cent, offsetting the currency loss on the portfolio. In general, if n pound options are purchased, the gain on the options position is

$$\text{Gain} = n(P_t - P_0),$$

where P_t is the put value at time t, and P_0 is the put value at time zero. For small movements in the exchange rate,

$$P_t - P_0 = \delta(S_t - S_0).$$

EXHIBIT 14.4

Value of a Pound Puts in Relation to the Exchange Rate

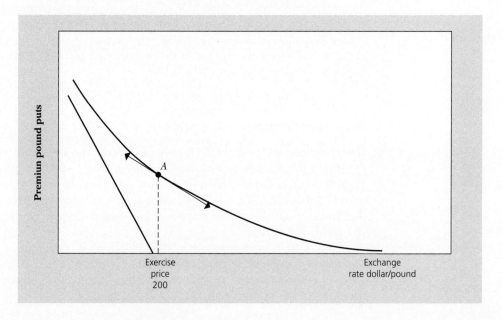

Hence a good currency hedge is obtained by holding $n = -V_0/\delta$ options. The hedge ratio is equal to $-1/\delta$. The profit on the options position is then equal to $-V_0(S_t - S_0)$, which offsets the currency loss on the portfolio. In the first approximation the pound value of the portfolio is assumed not to move.

We must emphasize that δ and the hedge ratio vary with the exchange rate, so that the number of options held must be adjusted continually. Transaction costs make this both impractical and expensive. In reality a good hedge can be achieved only with periodical revisions in the options position, i.e., when there is a significant movement in the exchange rate. Between revisions, options offer their usual asymmetric insurance within the general hedging strategy. This strategy may be regarded as a mixed hedging-insurance strategy.

Implementing such a strategy requires a good understanding of option valuation and the precise estimation of the hedge ratio. As with futures, the strategy should take into account the expected return on the foreign portfolio, as well as its correlation with exchange rate movements.

Hedging Strategies

Hedging strategies with options can be more sophisticated than those with futures, for two reasons: The hedge ratio of options fluctuates but is constant for futures; and an investor can play with several maturities and exercise prices with options only.

The following example illustrates a dynamic strategy. At time zero, an investor buys n currency puts to hedge a portfolio of British assets. If the pound depreciates, options protect the portfolio but its δ changes. For example, the slope δ could move to -0.8 if the pound drops to $1.95. Then the hedge ratio should be equal to $\frac{1}{0.8} = 1.25$. To avoid overhedging, the investor must either sell some puts or switch to options with a lower exercise price (and lower delta); in both cases a profit will be realized. A typical strategy is to keep a fixed number of options but to replace in-the-money options with cheap out-of-the-money options to maintain the same hedge ratio. If the pound later reverses its down trend, the puts will become worthless; however, most of the profit will have been previously realized and saved.

A hedging strategy can combine futures and options.[3] Futures markets are very liquid and charge low transaction costs. Options offer the advantage of an asymmetric risk structure but have higher costs, in terms of both the fair price for this insurance risk structure and their transaction costs.

If a hedging decision is necessary because an investor faces an increasing volatility in exchange rates and doesn't have a clear view of the direction of change, currency options are a natural strategy. In the scenario described in the introduction, French elections created uncertainties about the future of the franc. In that case options would have allowed the investor to hedge a drop in the franc while maintaining the opportunity to profit in case it rose.

Where the direction of a currency movement is clearly forecasted, currency futures provide a cheaper hedge. In setting the hedge, however, one should take into account the expected return on the portfolio and its correlation with currency movements.

Other Methods for Managing Currency Exposure

Many methods are used to reduce currency exposure and to take positions in foreign markets without incurring excessive exchange risk. First, an investor can rearrange a portfolio so as to increase its risk level in a foreign market without increasing its currency exposure. For stocks this means buying equities with higher betas (relative to the market index) and selling those with lower betas. This makes the portfolio more sensitive to local market movements without increasing its sensitivity to currency fluctuations. For bonds this means adjusting the duration of the foreign portfolio to play on foreign interest rates without increasing its currency exposure.

An international portfolio manager who wants to invest in countries where the currency is expected to weaken has a couple of choices. He or she can buy common stock outright and hedge the exchange risk with currency futures or options, or the manager can take another alternative and buy options on the stock. For example, a U.S. investor may want to buy call options on the British firm ABC rather than ABC shares. The reason is simple: If ABC stock goes up by the same percentage as the British pound drops, the dollar value of a direct investment in ABC stock will remain unchanged. On the other hand, options on ABC will yield both a pound profit and a dollar profit. Currency fluctuations affect only the translation of the profit into dollars, not the principal. The price quotations given in Exh. 14.5 illustrate how this strategy works.

EXHIBIT 14.5

Price Quotations on ABC Shares

	Prices		Price Variation (percent)
	December 1	January 15	
Dollars per pound	1.50	1.25	
Pounds per dollar	0.667	0.800	+20
ABC stock (in pounds)	200	240	+20
ABC stock (in dollars)	300	300	0
ABC February 200 options (in pounds)	11	42	
ABC February 200 options (in dollars)	16.5	52.5	

The dollar profit of buying one share of ABC is zero because the currency loss on the principal offsets the capital gain in pounds. If the investor had instead purchased an option, the profit per share would have been $36 despite the currency loss. Also, note that the initial investment in options is only $16.50 compared to $300 for shares. The difference could have been invested in U.S. cash instruments. Since the initial foreign currency investment in an option is very small, the currency impact is always limited to the direct investment in the asset.

A similar approach can be used to invest in an entire foreign market rather than just specific securities. This is done by buying stock index futures or options. Like regular stock futures, stock index futures limit an investor's foreign currency exposure to the margin. Any realized profit can be immediately repatriated in the domestic currency. For example, a Swiss investor who is bullish on the U.S. stock market but not on the U.S. dollar can buy Standard and Poor's 500 index futures. In addition, hedging the margin deposited in dollars against currency risk would provide the Swiss with complete currency protection. Stock index options can likewise be used. A similar strategy applies to bond investments. For example, a U.S. investor who is bullish on interest rates in the United Kingdom can buy gilt futures on the LIFFE rather than bonds and thereby simultaneously hedge against exchange risk. Other alternatives include buying bond warrants or partly liberated bonds.

Futures and options on foreign assets reduce currency exposure as long as an investor does not already own the assets in question. In addition, costs involved in taking such positions are less than those for actually buying foreign assets and hedging them with currency futures or options. On the other hand, if the assets are already part of a portfolio, more conventional methods of currency hedging are probably better, especially for assets that will remain in the portfolio for a long time.

In the same spirit, one should be aware of the currency impact on an investment strategy involving different types of instruments whose currency exposures are not identical. As an illustration, let's consider one of the strategies introduced in Chapter 12. An American investor buys Australian natural resource companies and sells stock index futures to hedge the Australian stock market risk. The motivation for this strategy is the belief that natural resource stocks are undervalued relative to the Australian market. Such a position, which is long in stocks and short in futures, requires an Australian dollar net investment and is therefore exposed to the risk of the Australian dollar. A 10% depreciation would induce a currency loss in the stock position that would not be offset by a currency gain on the stock index futures. As a matter of fact, there will even be a small currency loss in the initial margin deposited for the futures contracts. (This aspect is neglected in the example.) This can be illustrated using the first scenario presented in Chapter 12 with the additional assumption that the Australian dollar drops from one U.S. dollar on September 1 to 0.90 U.S. dollar on October 1. Our investor would have made a gain of 45,000 U.S. dollars if the US$/A$ exchange rate had remained stable at one. Instead, the 10% depreciation of the Australian dollar induced a loss of 59,500 U.S. dollars, as shown in the following table.

	Futures Market	Stock Market
September 1 (US$/A$ = 1)	Sell 10 December All Ordinary futures at 1150	Buy natural resource stocks; cost = A $1,000,000, US $1,000,000
October 1 (US$/A$ = 0.9)	*Market declines 10%, but natural resource stocks decline 6.9%*	
	Buy 10 December All Ordinary futures at 1036	Sell natural resource stocks; proceeds = A $931,000, US $837,900
	Profit on futures = A $114,000, US$102,600	Loss on stocks = US $162,100
	Net loss on trade = US $59,500	

It would be wise to hedge the stock portfolio against currency risk if our investor fears a depreciation of the Australian dollar. Note that the stock beta is irrelevant to our currency hedge, where the hedge ratio should be close to one.

Several investment vehicles and strategies may be used either to take advantage of or to hedge against monetary factors. Many of these strategies have been discussed before, so that we already know that they usually involve a combination of investments in money, capital, and speculative markets. For example, a British investor expecting a weak U.S. dollar and falling U.S. interest rates could buy long-term U.S. bonds, or zero-coupons, to maximize the sensitivity of his or her portfolio to U.S. interest rate movements and at the same time to hedge against exchange risk with currency futures or options. A matrix of alternative investments in the U.S. dollar fixed-income markets is given in Exh. 14.6. Each quadrant represents a specific scenario concerning U.S. interest rates and the U.S. dollar. Group I, for example, represents a set of strategies designed to capitalize on a strong U.S. dollar and falling dollar interest rates.

The purpose in outlining strategies is to help an investor to take advantage of his or her specific forecasts with respect to interest rates and currencies. Of course, the actual performance of these strategies depends on the accuracy of the investor's forecasts. A similar strategy matrix can be designed for nondollar investments, even though the absence of speculative markets in some currencies sometimes limits the range of strategies an investor can choose.

Summary

1. Currency futures, forward, and option contracts are used primarily to protect a portfolio against currency risks. Managers adapt their hedging strategies to their expectations of an asset's performance in local currency and of exchange rate movements.

2. The basic approach to the use of currency futures contracts is to hedge the foreign currency value of the foreign asset. One would sell short currencies in the amount of an asset's value. Ideally one should hedge the future value of

EXHIBIT 14.6

A Strategy Matrix of Alternative Investments in the U.S. Dollar Fixed-Income Markets

Securities/strategies are generally listed with the more traditional, or less risky, at the top of each group; the more highly leveraged, or risky, are toward the bottom of the list. In some instances the same instruments/strategies appear in more than one quadrant. In such cases they appear only with a code letter in that quadrant where they are especially appropriate. They appear without a code letter in the other quadrants.

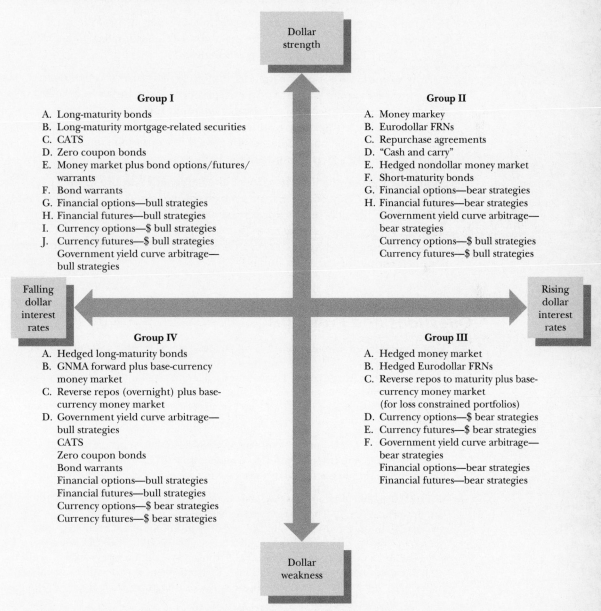

Dollar strength

Group I
A. Long-maturity bonds
B. Long-maturity mortgage-related securities
C. CATS
D. Zero coupon bonds
E. Money market plus bond options/futures/ warrants
F. Bond warrants
G. Financial options—bull strategies
H. Financial futures—bull strategies
I. Currency options—$ bull strategies
J. Currency futures—$ bull strategies
   Government yield curve arbitrage— bull strategies

Group II
A. Money markey
B. Eurodollar FRNs
C. Repurchase agreements
D. "Cash and carry"
E. Hedged nondollar money market
F. Short-maturity bonds
G. Financial options—bear strategies
H. Financial futures—bear strategies
   Government yield curve arbitrage— bear strategies
   Currency options—$ bull strategies
   Currency futures—$ bull strategies

Falling dollar interest rates

Rising dollar interest rates

Group IV
A. Hedged long-maturity bonds
B. GNMA forward plus base-currency money market
C. Reverse repos (overnight) plus base- currency money market
D. Government yield curve arbitrage— bull strategies
   CATS
   Zero coupon bonds
   Bond warrants
   Financial options—bull strategies
   Financial futures—bull strategies
   Currency options—$ bear strategies
   Currency futures—$ bear strategies

Group III
A. Hedged money market
B. Hedged Eurodollar FRNs
C. Reverse repos to maturity plus base- currency money market (for loss constrained portfolios)
D. Currency options—$ bear strategies
E. Currency futures—$ bear strategies
F. Government yield curve arbitrage— bear strategies
   Financial options—bear strategies
   Financial futures—bear strategies

Dollar weakness

Source: J. Hanna and P. Niculescu, "The Currency and Interest Rate Strategy Matrix: An Investment Tool for Multicurrency Investors," Bond Market Research, Salomon Brothers Inc., September 1982. Reprinted with permission.

an investment, taking into account the expected price change and income. The covariance between the asset return and the currency movements should be considered. The interest rate differential is the forward basis, the percentage difference between the futures and the spot exchange rates. The correlation between changes in interest rate differentials and currency movements should also be taken into account in determining the optimal hedge ratio.

3. Hedging strategies for multicurrency portfolios usually involve the use of futures in the major currencies. The instability of the estimated hedge ratios reduces the effectiveness of hedging strategies.

4. Currency options are used for their asymmetric risk-return characteristic. They provide insurance against adverse currency movements while retaining the profit potential in case of a favorable currency movement. There is a cost associated with this attractive insurance characteristic. More dynamic hedging strategies also can be implemented using currency options. They require option valuation models to estimate the hedge ratio.

5. Other methods can be used to manage the currency exposure of international portfolios. Leveraged instruments on foreign assets, such as futures and options, have little currency exposure, since the capital invested in foreign currency is very small compared to the value of the underlying asset. The impact of a currency movement on a combined position of several assets and contracts should be carefully studied.

Questions and Problems

1*. An American investor holds a portfolio of Japanese stocks worth ¥ 160 million. The spot exchange rate is ¥/$ = 158, and the three-month forward exchange rate is ¥/$ = 160. Our investor fears that the Japanese yen will depreciate in the next month but wants to keep the Japanese stocks. What position can the investor take based on three-month forward exchange rate contracts? List all the factors that will make the hedge imperfect.

2*. A Dutch investor holds a portfolio of Japanese stocks similar to that of our U.S. investor. The current three-month Dutch guilder forward exchange rate is DG/$ = 2.5. What position should the Dutch investor take to hedge the yen/guilder exchange risk?

3*. You are a U.S. dollar–based investor. You currently have a portfolio worth DM 100 million in German bonds. The current spot exchange rate is 2 DM/$. The current one-year market interest rates are 6% in DM and 10% in $. One-year currency options are quoted in Chicago with a strike price of 50 U.S. cents per DM; a call DM is quoted at 1 U.S. cent and a put DM is quoted at 1.2 U.S. cents; these option prices are for one DM.

You are worried that the integration of East and West Germany will cause inflation in Germany and a drop in the DM. So you consider using forward contracts or options to hedge the currency risk.

- What is the one-year forward exchange rate DM/$?

- Simulate the dollar value of your portfolio assuming that its DM value stays at DM 100 million; use spot exchange rates equal in one year to (DM/$): 1.6, 1.8, 2, 2.2, 2.4. First consider a currency-forward hedge, then a currency-option insurance.
- What could make your forward hedge imperfect?

4*. You advise a wealthy old Swiss lady who has $10 million in short-term dollar deposits. You are going away for a one-month vacation in the jungle, and she is worried that the dollar will drop relative to the Swiss franc in your absence. She cares only about the Swiss franc value of her assets. She has heard that currency options exist that would guarantee that her $10 million would be worth a minimum amount on your return in March, if the dollar dropped, but would benefit from a dollar appreciation if her fears became unfounded. You are on the telephone with her, facing your screen. You see that the March forward exchange rate is 0.7389 $/SF (or 1.3534 SF/$). The quotes for Swiss franc currency options in Chicago are:

March SF options (all prices are in US cents per SF)

Strike	Call SF	Put SF
73	2.43	1.54

- What minimum amount of SF can you *guarantee* for March, using these options? Make the simplifying assumption that all interest rates are equal to zero and that you can buy exactly the desired number of SF options. You must use some of the $10 million to get the options. Be quick; she is waiting on the phone.
- What would be the difference if you used forward contracts?

5*. You are American and hold a portfolio of French stocks. The market value of the portfolio is FF 20 million, with a beta of 1.2 relative to the CAC index. Here are some quotes in November:

Spot value of CAC index: 2000

Spot value of FF: 5 FF/$

The dividend yield, FF and US$ interest rates, are all equal to 4% (flat yield curves).

- You fear a drop in the French stock market (but not the FF). The size of CAC index contracts is 200 times the CAC index. How many contracts should you buy or sell to hedge the French stock market risk? Calculate the futures price of the index.
- You like the French stock market (different scenario from above) but fear a depreciation of the French franc. How many FF should you sell forward?

You have the following quotes in Chicago on French franc options, maturity March.

March FF options (all prices are in US cents per FF)

Strike	Call FF	Put FF
20	1.1	1

- Should you buy or sell calls or puts to insure against currency risk?
- Simulate the result of your strategies (unhedged, hedge with March forward, insured with March options), assuming that your French stock portfolio is still worth FF 20 million in March. Simulate for different values the spot FF in March, namely, 1FF = 0.10$, 0.20$, 0.30$.

6. The spot exchange rate is FF/$=5. We are on November 4. The three-month interest rates are 12% in FF and 8% in US$. A French franc call traded in Chicago with a strike price of 20 U.S. cents per FF has a premium of 1 U.S. cent (the FF call gives the right to buy one FF for a strike price of 20 cents). A French franc put traded in Chicago with a strike price of 20 U.S. cents per FF has a premium of 1.2 U.S. cents. The size of the option contract is FF 100,000. Both calls and puts can be exercised on February 4 (in three months).

   ▪ What is the three-month forward exchange rate FF/$?

   ▪ You are French and will receive $1 million U.S. on February 4. Should you buy or sell forward francs to hedge your future U.S.$ cash flow? How many francs will you get on February 4 if you hedge?

   ▪ Should you buy or sell FF calls or puts to insure your cash flow? Assuming that you have some cash available to buy the options, how many option contracts should you buy? Simulate the resulting FF cash flow on February 4 for spot exchange rates of 4, 4.5, 5, 5.5, and 6 FF/$.

7. A U.S. investor is attracted by the high yield on British bonds but is worried about a British pound depreciation. The currency market data are as follows;

	United States	United Kingdom
Bond yield (%)	7	12
Three-month interest rate (%)	6	8
Spot exchange rate, $/£ = 2		

A bond dealer has repeatedly suggested that the investor purchase hedged foreign bonds. This strategy can be described as the purchase of foreign currency bonds (here, British pound bonds) with simultaneous hedging in the short-term forward or futures currency market. The currency hedge is rolled over when the forward or futures contract expires.

   ▪ What is the current three-month forward exchange rate ($/£)?

   ▪ Assuming a £1 million investment in British bonds, how would you determine the exact hedge ratio necessary to minimize the currency influence?

   ▪ When will this strategy be successful (compared to a direct investment in U.S. bonds)?

8*. Futures and forward currency contracts are not readily available for most currencies. However, many currencies are closely linked. For example, the European Monetary System (EMS) described in Chapter 1 implies a close link among several European currencies.

   An American investor has a portfolio of Belgian stocks that she wishes to hedge against currency risks. No futures contracts are traded on the Belgian franc, so she decides to use Deutsche mark futures contracts traded in Chicago, since both currencies belong to the EMS. Here are some quotes:

Value of the portfolio	BF 100 million
Spot exchange rates	BF/$ = 50
	DM/$ = 2.5
Futures price (contract of DM 125,000)	$/DM = 0.41

- How many Deutsche mark contracts should our U.S. investor trade?

9. Let's go back to our first problem; our U.S. investor owns a portfolio of Japanese securities worth ¥160 million. He considers buying currency puts on yen instead of selling futures contracts. In Philadelphia a yen put with a strike price of 62 U.S. cents per 100 yen and three-month maturity is worth 0.70 U.S. cents per 100 yen (0.007 cents per yen).

    Assume that three months later, the portfolio is still worth ¥ 160 million; simulate various values of the spot yen/dollar exchange rate. Compare the results of the following two currency hedging strategies for your different values of the exchange rate three months later. In the first strategy the investor sells ¥160 million forward; in the second strategy he buys yen puts for ¥ 160 million (25.6 contracts on the Philadelphia Stock Exchange).

10*. On October 1 a German investor decides to hedge a U.S. portfolio worth $10 million against exchange risk using Deutsche mark call options. The spot exchange rate is DM/$ = 2.5, or $/DM = 0.40. The German investor can buy November Deutsche marks with a strike price of $0.40 U.S. per Deutsche mark at a premium of 1 cent per Deutsche mark. The size of one contract is DM 62,500. The delta of the option is estimated at 0.5.

    - Reflecting this delta, how many Deutsche mark calls should our investor buy to *hedge* (not *insure*) the U.S. portfolio against the DM/$ currency risk (*dynamic* or *delta* hedge)?

        A few days later the U.S. dollar has dropped to DM/$2.439, or $/DM = 0.41, and the dollar value of the portfolio has remained unchanged at $10 million. The November 40 Deutsche mark call is now worth 1.6 cents per Deutsche mark and has a delta estimated at 0.7.

    - What is the result of the hedge?
    - How should the hedge be adjusted?

11. You are a French investor holding a portfolio of U.S. stocks worth $10 million. You wish to engage in a dynamic hedge of the $/FF exchange risk by buying FF calls. On April 1 a June 20 FF call quotes 1 U.S. cent per franc. This gives you the right to buy one franc for 20 cents in June. The delta of this call is equal to 0.5. The spot exchange rate is 5 FF/$. The size of an option contract is FF100,000.

    - How many FF calls should you buy to get a good dynamic hedge?

        A few days later your portfolio is still worth $10 million. But the dollar, however, has dropped to 4.5 FF/$. The call is now worth 2.5 U.S. cents, and its delta is equal to 0.9.

- What is the global result, in FF, of your strategy? Has the hedge been satisfactory and why?

- What should you do to rebalance your hedge?

12. Why is a purchase of a futures contract or an option on a foreign asset not exposed to much currency risk?

Take the following example for a U.S. investor:

	November	December
Financial Times Stock Exchange (FTSE) Index	1600	1700
December futures on FTSE	1615	1700
December 1650 FTSE Call	20	50
Dollar/Pound spot rate	2.00	1.80

As mentioned in Chapter 12, one FTSE futures contract has a multiplier of 25 pounds. The margin deposit is £1500 per contract. FTSE options have a contract size of £25 times the index. What is the amount of currency loss per index unit if the U.S. investor had bought:

- The index in the form of stocks (e.g., £1600 worth of an FTSE index fund)

- A December futures on FTSE

- A December 1650 FTSE call

13. The current yield curve is much lower in the United States than in Great Britain. You read in the newspaper that it is unattractive to hedge currency risk on British assets for an American investor. The same journal states that British investors should hedge the currency risk on their U.S. investments. What do you think?

14. Salomon Brothers proposes to investors a contract called "Range Forward Contract." Here is an example of such a U.S. dollar/British pound contract:

- The contract has a size of £100,000 and a maturity of three months. At maturity the investor will purchase the pounds at a price that is a function of the spot exchange rate.

- If the spot exchange rate at maturity is less than 1.352 $/£, the investor will pay 1.352 dollars to get one pound.

- If the spot exchange rate at maturity is between 1.352 $/£ and 1.470 $/£, the investor will pay the current spot exchange rate to get one pound.

- If the spot exchange rate at maturity is more than 1.470 $/£, the investor will pay 1.470 dollars to get one pound.

Assume that you are a British exporter who will receive $10 million in three months that will have to be transferred into British pounds at the time. Currently the spot and forward exchange rates are 1.4200 $/£ and 1.4085 $/£, respectively.

- Explain why such a Range Forward Contract could be attractive if you fear a depreciation of the dollar during the three months.

- Explain why Salomon Brothers can sell such a contract at a very low price.

15*. An American investor holds a British bond portfolio worth £100 million. The portfolio has a modified duration of seven. She temporarily fears a depreciation of the pound but wishes to retain the bonds. To cover this risk, she decides to sell pounds forward. Our investor observed that the British government tends to adopt a "leaning-against-the-wind" policy. When the pound depreciates, British interest rates tend to rise to defend the currency. A regression of "variations in long-term British yields" on "percentage $/£ exchange rate movements" has a slope coefficient of 0.1. In other words, British yields tend to go up by 10 basis points (0.1%) when the pound depreciates by 1% relative to the dollar.

- What should be the optimal hedge ratio used by our investor if she wishes to reduce the uncertainty caused by exchange risk? [The investor uses only forward currency contracts to hedge this risk, not bond futures contracts.]

- Detail the many factors that could make this hedge imperfect if the depreciation of the pound materializes.

16. *Project*: Collect some monthly data over five years for the following prices: French, German, and British stock and bond indexes; the dollar exchange rates of their respective currencies.

- Using a regression between asset returns and percentage currency movements, calculate for each asset class the minimum-risk currency hedge ratio for an American investor.

- Same question assuming that you are a German investor. Are the conclusions different?

  Now collect some data on Argentinean and Brazilian stock indexes and their respective currencies.

- Using a regression, calculate for each asset class the minimum-risk currency hedge ratio assuming that you are an American investor.

- Are your conclusions similar to those obtained for developed markets? Why?

Notes

1. For an empirical examination of the multicurrency betas of international portfolios, see Adler and Simon (1986).

2. See Eaker and Grant (1987); Dale (1981); and Grammatikos and Saunders (1983). The importance of basis risk (movements in interest rate differential) for determining the risk-minimizing hedge ratio has been illustrated by Briys and Solnik (1992). Kroner and Sultan (1993) derive risk-minimizing dynamic hedging strategies if the distribution of returns change over time and follow some GARCH process.

3. For a detailed description of currency options strategies, see "Currency Options Strategy Manual" by the Chicago Mercantile Exchange, as well as various brochures prepared by the Philadelphia Stock Exchange, the London International Financial Futures Exchange, the European Options Exchange, and so forth.

Bibliography

Adler, M., and Dumas, B. "International Portfolio Choices and Corporate Finance: A Synthesis," *Journal of Finance*, June 1983.

Adler, M., and Simon, D. "Exchange Rate Surprises in International Portfolios," *Journal of Portfolio Management*, Winter 1986.

Bodurtha, J., and Courtadon, G. "Efficiency Tests of the Foreign Currency Option Market," *Journal of Finance*, March 1986.

Briys, E., and Solnik, B. "Optimal Currency Hedge Ratios and Interest Rate Risk," *Journal of International Money and Finance*, December 1992.

Dale, C. "The Hedging Effectiveness of Currency Futures Markets," *Journal of Futures Markets*, Spring 1981.

Eaker, M., and Grant, D. "Cross-Hedging Foreign Currency Risks," *Journal of International Money and Finance*, March 1987.

Grammatikos, T., and Saunders, A. "Stability and the Hedging Performance of Foreign Currency Futures," *Journal of Futures Markets*, Fall 1983.

Hanna, J., and Niculescu, P. "The Currency and Interest Rate Strategy Matrix: An Investment Tool for Multicurrency Investors," Bond Market Research, Salomon Brothers, September 1982.

Kroner, K.F., and Sultan, J. "Time-Varying Distributions and Dynamic Hedging with Foreign Currency Futures," *Journal of Financial and Quantitative Analysis*, December 1993.

Madura, J., and Reiff, W. "A Hedge Strategy for International Portfolio," *Journal of Portfolio Management*, Fall 1985.

Stultz, R. "Optimal Hedging Policy," *Journal of Financial and Quantitative Analysis*, June 1984.

Chapter 14: Appendix
Advanced Section on Optimal Currency Hedging

In theory the optimal hedging policy for an individual investor is the one that max-imizes his or her expected utility. Policies would be individual-specific and a func-tion of the parameters of the individual's utility function. But it is unclear why an investor should isolate exchange rate risk as a specific source of risk to be hedged. The mere definition of exchange risk in a general equilibrium framework is con-troversial, as discussed in Chapter 5 and by Adler and Dumas (1983). Market imperfections and segmentation render the theoretical analysis an impossible task. A remark often made is that common economic factors may affect both return on the asset and the exchange rate. So why should an investor single out the currency translation risk and hedge it independently?

In practice, stock returns and currency movements are quite independent; an investor will want to specifically hedge currency translation risks when he or she fears a depreciation of the foreign currency. If a foreign asset is uncorrelated with short-term currency movements, a hedge ratio of one is a reasonable strategy. The foreign asset represents a given quantity of foreign currency, and the same amount of currency is sold short. This is a rather simple strategy based on the quantity of currency to be hedged. No cross hedging is involved. The analysis can be refined by calculating the minimum-variance hedge given by the minimization of the vari-ance of

$$R_H - R = s(1 + R) - hR_F, \qquad (14.A1)$$

where all variables have been defined in the text of Chapter 14. The first-order optimization condition can be written as in the appendix for Chapter 12. It implies that the optimal hedge ratio is equal to

$$h = \frac{\text{cov}\left[s\left(1 + R\right), R_F\right]}{\sigma_F^2}, \qquad (14.A2)$$

where σ_F^2 is the variance of R_F. This hedge ratio is also equal to the regression slope of the currency contribution, $R^* - R = s(1 + R)$, on the futures return, R_F.

At this point it is useful to detail the components of R_F:

$$R_F = \frac{\left(F_t - F_0\right)}{S_0}.$$

We can write $F_t - F_0$ as

$$F_t - F_0 = F_t - S_t - (F_0 - S_0) + S_t - S_0.$$

Hence

$$R_0 = \frac{S_t}{S_0} \frac{F_t - S_t}{S_t} - \frac{F_0 - S_0}{S_0} + \frac{S_t - S_0}{S_0} \text{ and}$$

$$R_F = \left(1 + s\right)B_t - B_0 + s,$$

where B_0 and B_t are the bases (interest rate differential) at times zero and t. This might be written as

$$R_F = s + B_t - B_0 + sB_t. \tag{14.A3}$$

$$\begin{array}{ccc} & \text{Currency} & \text{Change in} \\ \text{Futures return} = & \text{movement} + & \text{interest rate} + \text{Cross product.} \\ & \text{in percent} & \text{differential} \end{array}$$

Basically, the futures return is equal to the spot exchange rate variation plus the change in interest rate differential plus a smaller cross-product term. Clearly the covariance of the currency movement with the change in interest rate differential will affect the optimal hedge ratio in Eq. (14.A2). A rise in the U.S. interest rate that is unmatched by the British rate tends to strengthen the dollar relative to sterling. Given our notation, this leads to a negative covariance and a smaller hedge ratio.

Another objective of a currency hedging policy is to remove totally the direct and indirect influences of a currency movement on the portfolio return. As mentioned in Chapter 2, a depreciation of sterling may lead to a rise in British interest rates in defense of the currency. In turn this rise in local interest rates induces a drop in bond prices. In the end both the sterling return and a currency translation yield a loss for the U.S. investor. The optimal hedge ratio is obtained by running a regression of the portfolio dollar return, R^*, on the futures return R_F:

$$R^* = a + hR_F, \tag{14.A4}$$

where a is a constant term, and all other variables have been defined above. One can verify that this optimal hedge ratio will differ from the previous one if the foreign currency return, R, is correlated with the futures return, R_F.

A diversified international portfolio can be hedged using only the futures contracts available in a few currencies, as discussed previously. The currency influence on the portfolio can be reduced by following the following procedure:

- Select the major most independent currencies with futures contracts available. For an American investor these may be the yen, Deutsche mark, and sterling. For a Swiss-based investor, these may be the yen, sterling, and the U.S. dollar.

- Calculate the hedge ratios jointly by running a multiple regression between the domestic currency returns on the portfolio (U.S. dollar return for a U.S. investor) and the futures returns in the three selected currencies.

$$R^* = a + h_1 R_{F1} + h_2 R_{F2} + h_3 R_{F3} \, .$$

- Use the regression coefficients h_1, h_2, and h_3 as the hedge ratios in each currency. Because the spot currency movement is the major component of futures volatility, the hedge ratios obtained would be fairly close if we used currency movements in the regression instead of futures return.

Of course, this procedure requires historical data on the portfolio and will work well only if the estimated regression coefficients are stable over time. Eaker and Grant (1987) provide some evidence on the instability of these coefficients.

15

*Commodities, Real Estate,
and Alternative Investments*

A lternative investments can be considered to complement stocks, bonds, and other financial instruments traded on international financial markets. *Private* investors have always been attracted by alternative investments, but *institutional* investors have also started to be interested, as shown by Healey and Hardy (1994). There is a large variety of alternative investments, and the list evolves over time. In some cases investors wish to own directly real assets as opposed to financial paper; this is a clear motivation for buying precious metals or real estate. In other cases investors seek specialized investment vehicles that are based on an investment strategy taking bets on specific concepts. We will now review successively commodities, real estate, and other alternative investments, including hedge funds.

Commodities

Commodities are not extensively used by money managers. Actually the physical purchase of most commodities can hardly be considered as a reasonable investment by the average investor. Commodities require special storage facilities. For example, it is not easy to buy one ton of frozen orange juice and hold it physically for one year. Costs would just be too high for most investors. The idea is to purchase indirectly those real assets that should provide a good hedge against inflation risk. There exist at least three more or less direct ways to invest in commodities:

- Futures contracts

- Bonds indexed on some commodity price

- Stocks of companies producing the commodity

515

Investing in commodity futures is the most common strategy. We will start by a general discussion of commodity investment and detail the example of gold investment, because of its historical importance in international investment.

Commodity Futures

Futures contracts are the easiest and cheapest way to invest in commodities. Commodities can be grouped into three major categories:

- Agricultural products, including fibers (wool, cotton), grains (wheat, corn, soybean), food (coffee, cocoa, orange juice), and livestock (cattle, hogs, pork bellies). These are often called soft commodities by professionals.

- Energy, including crude oil, heating oil, and natural gas.

- Metals, such as copper, aluminum, gold, silver, and platinum.

The major commodity futures markets are located in the United States, but some limited commodity trading exists elsewhere, especially in London.

Numerous commodity indexes have been developed. Some traditional indexes are broadly based with a global economic perspective; they aim to track the evolution in input prices. This is the case of *The Economist* Commodity Price Index and of the *Knight-Ridder Commodity Research Bureau Index*, or *CRB*. Dow Jones, Moody's, Reuters, and other information services also provide commodity futures price indexes.

Other indexes have been developed to be *investable* indexes. They are based on the most liquid commodity futures contracts, so they can be easily replicated by taking positions in individual commodities.

- The *Goldman Sachs Commodity Index* (*GSCI*) was launched in 1991 and comprises some 20 individual commodities. Each commodity is weighted according to an assessment of its importance in the world economic production. It does not include less active futures contracts, such as lumber and coal, which are included in the CRB. In 1992 the Chicago Mercantile Exchange introduced futures and options contracts on the GSCI.

- The *J.P. Morgan Commodity Index*, or *JPMCI*, was launched in 1994 and includes base metals, precious metals, and energy-related commodities; it excludes all soft commodities (agricultural products).

- *Merrill Lynch Enmet Index* includes only six energy and metal ("Enmet") commodities: crude oil, natural gas, aluminum, copper, gold, and silver.

- *Bankers Trust Commodity Index* (*BTCI*) includes only five commodities: crude oil, heating oil, aluminum, gold, and silver.

The composition of these indexes differs widely, and so does their performance. The GSCI includes soft commodities; the other three are much less diversified. In 1995 gold accounted for less than 3% of the GSCI but for some 20% of each of the other three indexes.

Motivations and Investment Vehicles

Commodities are sometimes treated as an asset class because they represent a direct participation in the real economy. The motivations for investing in commodities range from the diversification benefits achievable by a *passive* investor to the speculative profits sought by an *active* investor. The design of the investment vehicle used will reflect these different motivations.

Passive Investment A *passive* investor would buy commodities for their risk diversification benefits. When inflation accelerates, commodity prices go up, whereas bond and stock prices tend to go down. A passive investor would typically invest through a collateralized position in futures contract. Many banks and money managers offer collateralized futures funds based on one of the investable commodity indexes. For example, a GSCI collateralized fund consists of an unleveraged long position in the GSCI futures contract, fully collateralized by U.S. Treasury bills. An example will help understand the procedure.

Assume that the futures price is currently 100. If 100 million is added to the fund, the manager will take a long position in the futures contract for 100 million of underlying value and simultaneously buy 100 million worth of U.S. Treasury bills (part of this will be deposited as margin). If the futures price drops to 95 the next day, the futures position will be marked-to-market, and the manager will have to sell 5 million of Treasury bills to cover the loss. Conversely, if the futures price had risen to 105, the manager would have received a marked-to-market profit of 5 million, which would be invested in additional Treasury bills.

The return on the collaterlized futures position comes from the change in futures price and the interest income on the Treasury bills. The position earns a *total return* equal to the risk-free interest rate plus an *excess return* equal to the price movement in the futures price. The various investable indexes are published both in excess-return and in total-return form. The long-term performance of the JPMCI and of the GSCI are presented in Exhs. 15.1 and 15.2. The indexes reported assume that the total return on the index is continuously reinvested. So the performance corresponds to that of collateralized futures indexes. It appears that both commodity indexes had a higher return than U.S. or international equity investments. The volatility of commodity futures is higher than that of domestic or international equity, but commodities have a negative correlation with stock and bond returns and a desired positive correlation with U.S. inflation.

The excellent long-term performance of the two commodity indexes requires a word of caution. The GSCI and JPMCI have been back-calculated from the 1970s

EXHIBIT 15.1

Return and Risk of GSCI, 1970–1992

Investment	Mean Return (% per year)	Standard Deviation (% per year)	Correlation with GSCI
GSCI	14.8	18.3	1
EAFE	13.1	7.6	–0.27
S&P 500	11.5	16.2	–0.42
Treasury bond	9.0	11.3	–0.32
Treasury bill	7.5	0.8	–0.20
Inflation	6.0	1.2	0.26

Source: S.L. Lummer and L.B. Siegel, "GSCI Collateralized Futures: A Hedging and Diversification Tool for Institutional Portfolios," *Journal of Investing*, Summer 1993.

to 1990. These indexes have been constructed in the 1990s, and the commodities and weights selected to enter the index reflect a selection bias. Commodities that have become less important in modern economic development, and whose prices have therefore dropped during the 1970–1990 period, have not been selected. This biases the back-calculated performance.

Active Investment   Besides inflation bets, another motivation for investing in commodities is that they provide good performance in periods of economic growth. This is not an inflation story, as for the risk-diversification benefits, but a growth story. In periods of rapid economic growth, commodities are in strong demand to satisfy production needs, and their prices go up. Because of productivity gains, the prices of finished goods are unlikely to rise as fast as those of raw materials. This leads to active management whereby specific commodities are bought and sold at various times. Actively managed commodity funds are proposed by a large number of institutions. These funds managed by *Commodity Trading Advisers (CTA)* are sometimes called *Managed Futures* funds. Although the performance of some of these funds can be impressive, their volatility in return is also quite high.

The Example of Gold

Gold has always played a special role in investments. It is a commodity traded worldwide, but more important, it was regarded by many Europeans and Asians as the ultimate store of value. It is considered an international monetary asset that offers protection in case of a major disruption. Ibboston, Siegel, and Love (1985) found that gold bullion represents some 5% of total investable world wealth. Furthermore gold is regarded by central banks and most non-U.S. investors as a monetary asset because it has been the core of domestic and international monetary systems for many centuries. This section focuses on gold investment because

EXHIBIT 15.2

Relative Performance of JPMCI Commodity Index, U.S. Bonds, U.S. Stocks, and EAFE Stocks

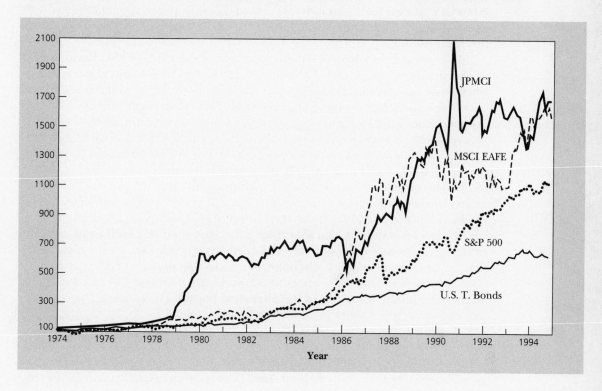

of the traditional and quasimystical importance of gold in investment strategies and also as an example of a real asset investment. Of course, precious stones, stamps, or paintings could also be profitable long-term investments. But they usually require high transaction costs, and moreover, each stone or painting is in a sense unique, which reduces its marketability. Gold offers a wide variety of investment vehicles that can be used in passive or active strategies. Gold-linked investments include gold bullion, coins, bonds, mining equity, futures, and options on gold and on mining equity or bonds.

The Motivation for Investing in Gold   The traditional role of gold as the ultimate hedge and store of value is well known. For centuries Europeans and Asians alike have regarded gold as the best possible protection against inflation and social, political, or economic crises because it can easily be traded worldwide at any time, and its real value increases during crises. Europeans and others who have suffered revolutions, invasions, and periods of hyperinflation need no correlation coefficients to be convinced of this attractive portfolio hedge characteristic. For example, gold kept its real value during the U.S. stock market crash from 1929 to

1932 and the London Stock Exchange collapse in equity and bonds from 1973 to 1975. Furthermore the central role gold has played in domestic and international monetary systems for thousands of years makes it in part a monetary asset with exceptional liquidity. Other real assets, such as diamonds or stamps, do not have this characteristic.

In general, gold allows one to diversify against the kinds of risks that affect all stock markets simultaneously. For example, in 1973 and 1974 bullion price tripled when stock markets worldwide dropped dramatically during the oil crisis; the New York Stock Exchange dropped approximately 50%. Conversely, the price of gold dropped from 1982 to 1983, when most stock markets rose during the economic recovery. Several studies have shown the existence of a small, and often negative, correlation between gold and stock prices. As shown in Exh. 15.3, gold had a negative correlation of –0.4 with the U.S. stock market for more than 25 years (1948 to 1975). The conclusion can be drawn from this exhibit that the price of gold tends to go up when inflation accelerates and stock prices drop. The same conclusion can be reached if one looks at the correlation of gold with non-U.S. stock markets. This weak correlation is also found for other commodities used in investment strategies. To illustrate the diversification benefits of gold, Exh. 15.4 compares the risk and performance of a portfolio invested solely in stocks (the Morgan Stanley Capital International world index) with a portfolio of 90% stocks and 10% gold. The risk (standard deviation) of the diversified portfolio is reduced. The comparison with a purely U.S. stock portfolio is even more telling.[1]

A theoretical comment is in order here. In modern portfolio theory, a small or negative beta implies that the expected return on gold should be small. For example, a negative beta caused by a negative correlation between gold and the market portfolio implies that in the Capital Asset Pricing Model (CAPM) framework, the expected return on gold should be less than the risk-free interest rate. Indeed, it can be claimed that we should expect, and certainly hope for, a modest long-term performance in gold and a greater return on the other assets in the portfolio; however, gold assets will reduce the risk of the portfolio in case of adverse economic

EXHIBIT 15.3

Correlation of Annual Rates of Inflation and U.S. Stock Returns with Gold Price Movements, 1948 to 1975

	Correlation Coefficient	Arithmetic Mean of Yearly Return (percent)	Yearly Standard Deviation (percent)
Gold	1.0	8.8	20.8
Inflation	0.6	3.8	4.2
S & P 500 Stocks	–0.4	12.8	18.3

Source: J.G. McDonald and B. Solnik, "Valuation and Strategy for Gold Stocks," *Journal of Portfolio Management*, Spring 1977. Reprinted with permission.

EXHIBIT 15.4

Risk and Performance of Simulated Portfolios (monthly U.S. dollar returns, 1971 to 1993)

	Risk (% per year)	Return (% per year)
100% gold bullion	24.2	10.7
100% U.S. stocks	15.5	11.0
100% World stocks	14.6	12.2
90% U.S. stocks and 10% gold	14.0	11.0
90% World stocks and 10% gold	13.6	12.1

conditions. The question for a prudent portfolio manager, then, is whether these hedge benefits are worth the implicit premium he or she must pay in the form of a modest, expected long-term performance of a small part of the portfolio.

Gold Price Determinants   The purpose of this book is not to provide the reader with recipes in financial analysis. The following material is intended only to indicate the kind of information and methods utilized by analysts and investment managers to analyse real-asset investments. Commodities other than gold could serve as an example.

Gold is a tangible international asset in limited supply. Gold can be extracted at a cost but cannot be produced artificially. The current estimate of the total past worldwide mining extraction is over 100,000 metric tonnes. Although gold is immune to the effects of weather, water, and oxygen, it suffers from human habits. The tradition of hiding gold treasures in the ground is consistent with the observation that gold is the ultimate physical store of value during major disruptions, such as civil unrest, coup d'état, and war. During World War II, most Europeans dug a hole in their gardens or cellars to hide their gold holdings. Part of this hidden gold is never recovered if the owner dies. Most of the gold used in dentistry also disappears with the owner. Despite these losses, the stock of gold keeps slowly increasing with the amount extracted.

In a sense the price of gold should be easy to forecast: The product is well defined. The supply sources are well identified, and reserves can be reasonably estimated. The major demands are clearly identified: carat jewelry, industrial needs, coins, and investment. Historical supply and demand for gold is shown in Exh. 15.5. This analysis is limited to supply and demand for gold in the Western world, since we have no indications for the former Communist bloc. The variations in the official reserves of governments and of the International Monetary Fund have been included in the supply: The bottom half of the table is simply the private demand. It appears that Western gold production has been quite steady.

EXHIBIT 15.5

Western World Gold Supply and Demand (metric tonnes)

	1984	1985	1986	1987	1988	1989	1990	1991	1992	1993
Supply										
Mine production	1167	1236	1296	1383	1551	1682	1750	1782	1861	1891
Net communist sales	205	210	402	303	263	266	388	230	65	175
Net official sales	85	—	—	—	—	366	9	28	626	475
Old gold scrap	306	334	506	448	369	374	509	449	445	516
Gold loans	3	38	17	55	164	78	5	—	—	—
Forward sales	35	18	20	72	126	116	224	96	165	198
Option hedging	—	6	8	22	63	—	7	15	103	2
Implied disinvestment	61	167	—	—	163	—	—	263	—	—
Total supply	**1861**	**2009**	**2249**	**2284**	**2699**	**2882**	**2892**	**2862**	**3265**	**3257**
Demand										
Fabrication										
Jewelry	1113	1212	1192	1238	1557	1924	2063	2143	2474	2302
Electronics	132	116	124	126	135	139	149	153	143	156
Other	284	243	470	325	261	273	260	288	260	289
Total fabrication	1529	1571	1786	1688	1953	2336	2471	2584	2877	2748
Net official purchases	—	132	145	72	285	—	—	—	—	—
Bar hoarding	332	306	214	259	461	514	203	233	234	97
Gold loans	—	—	—	—	—	—	—	45	85	65
Option hedging	—	—	—	—	—	15	—	—	—	—
Implied investment	—	—	104	264	—	18	218	—	69	348
Total demand	**1861**	**2009**	**2249**	**2284**	**2699**	**2882**	**2892**	**2862**	**3265**	**3257**

Source: Gold 1994, Gold Fields Mineral Services Ltd.

Production slowly rose through the 1980s. The dramatic increase in gold price from 1971 has allowed the exploitation of higher-cost mines. The South African production has remained remarkably stable, but other countries have emerged as major gold producers. Today South Africa produces roughly a third of the gold produced in the non-Communist world. But various countries, including Canada, the United States, Brazil, Colombia, the Philippines, Australia, and Papua New Guinea, are also major producers; they have been the source of growth in production in the recent years.

Jewelry is the major source of gold demand. It seems quite sensitive to movements in gold prices. The dramatic gold price increases in 1974 and 1980 temporarily reduced the carat jewelry demand; for example, in 1980 it was eight times below that of the period from 1977 to 1978. However, jewelry demand has slowly increased, except for occasional dramatic moves in reaction to gold prices. The demand for industrial needs is stable.

Supply and demand clearly determine the price of gold. It is therefore necessary to study the various components of supply and demand to forecast the price of gold. A different model may be required for each component. For example, Western mine production is affected by technological considerations, South African extraction policy, and political situations in sensitive countries. Russian gold sales depend on their need for hard currencies. Official sales may also be induced by monetary and balance-of-payments problems. The industrial demand depends on technological innovation and the discovery of cheaper substitutes. Jewelry demand is sensitive to short-term gold price movements as well as fashion; the investment motivation is often present in jewelry purchases. Investment demand for bullion and coins is a component of the total demand affecting gold price but is also determined by expectations of future price movements.

As we can see, gold is a single, well-identified, extensively researched product, but its analysis and valuation are not a simple exercise. This difficulty may add another dimension to its mystical attraction.

Commodity-Linked Securities

Holding commodities provides no income, so the sole return to the owner is through price increase. Investors can also select securities that are linked to some commodity prices and also provide some income. This can be an attractive alternative for investors who wish, or are constrained, to hold financial investments rather than real assets. The two major types of commodity-linked securities are bonds and equity. The indexation clause is explicit for commodity-linked bonds but implicit for equity. Again we will focus on the example of gold.

Commodity-Linked Bonds   There are many examples of commodity-linked bonds in the world capital markets.[2] Governments faced with large interest rate risk because of high inflation have often been forced to offer loans with coupons or principal indexed to either the price of a specific good or a global inflation index. Inflation-indexed gilts became popular in the United Kingdom during the 1980s. The capital and coupons of these bonds are indexed to British retail prices. High-inflation countries, such as Brazil and Israel, have also issued inflation-indexed bonds, and corporations and governments have issued bonds indexed to a variety of specific prices. The Mexican Petrobonos indexed on Mexican gas prices is one such bond.

Gold bonds have been an attractive alternative to holding gold ingots. Among the few private issuers of gold bonds are Refinement International and Lac Mineral, Ltd. Refinement International, a U.S. corporation, issued 3.5% gold-indexed bonds. Each bond is worth 10 ounces of gold, and the coupon is worth 0.35 ounce of gold. Lac Minerals Ltd., a Canadian corporation, issued 8% debentures with warrants. Each warrant entitles the holder to buy 0.5 troy ounce of gold from Lac Minerals Ltd., at a price of $230. More important are the public issues of gold bonds, and among them two famous French state loans. One is a bond with a 4.5% coupon rate usually referred to as the Pinay, after the French finance minister responsible for its issue. The other is a bond with a 7% coupon rate usually referred to as the Giscard. The principal, but not the coupon, of the Pinay was indexed to the Napoleon, the French gold coin, in a complex manner. The Giscard had a straightforward indexation clause on the price of gold ingots in Paris. The Giscard may be thought of as a bond that is reimbursed in full at maturity in the form of 95.3 grams of gold (or rather, its value at the time) and pays a coupon worth 6.67 grams of gold every year. Although payment is made in French francs, the amount is determined solely by the gold price during the month of payment. If the bond sold at (gold) par, it would amount to a bond yielding exactly 7% in real gold terms. These bonds are famous because they were issued at a time of monetary crisis in France, when the gold indexation became one of the only ways to attract the confidence of private investors.

Commodity-Linked Equity   The value of some companies is directly affected by commodity prices. This is clearly the case of the so-called *energy companies*. For example, companies in the oil and gas industry are affected by the evolution of oil prices. The link between commodity prices and stock prices is more evident for small, undiversified companies that specialize in one type of activity, e.g., oil and gas exploration and production. However, large oil companies tend to be quite diversified across activities. For example, the revenue from gas stations comes from selling not only gas but also groceries and various other products.

Gold mining companies are another example of commodity-linked equity. The relationship between gold mining share prices and the price of gold is shown in Exh. 15.6. This exhibit presents the price evolution of gold bullion (in dollars per ounce) and of the MSCI Gold Mine index from 1971 to the end of 1993. The correlation between the two curves is readily apparent, although the gold mine stock index amplifies movements in gold price. The yield on gold shares was very high (10% to 20%) over the period, given the mines' payout policy, but is not taken into account in the graph. Therefore the total performance of a gold mine portfolio would be much higher than shown on the graph. Note that the correlation between gold mine share prices and the price of gold is far from perfect. Gold mine values are influenced by factors other than gold prices: For example, social and political factors have strongly affected South African share prices.

Gold mining shares differ from commodity-linked bonds in that the indexation clause is not fixed by contract but depends on mining economics. In fact, the mining industry is probably the simplest activity to describe in a valuation model. The economics of mining can be described by a simple discounted-profit model. The principal relationship in the model is the cost structure of the mine as measured by the ratio of costs to revenues. The cost to remove an ounce or a gram of gold from so-called storage and refine it depends on several factors: technology, wage rates, power rates, and the grade and depth of the mine.

EXHIBIT 15.6

Comparative Performance of Gold Bullion and MSCI Gold Mines

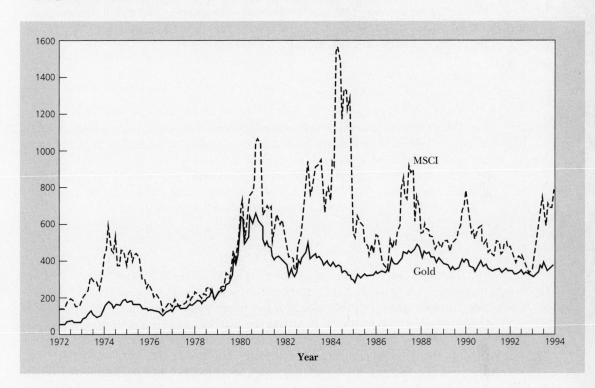

Revenues depend on the world price of gold, adjusted for any government subsidies or withholdings. And mine earnings, E, depend on the quantity of gold sold, Q, the gold price received, G, and the total cost per unit, C.

$$E = Q\,(G - C).\tag{15.1}$$

To value the mine, we assume for the time being a dividend policy with a fixed percentage of distributed earnings, d. That gives us a value P for the mine of

$$P = d\frac{Q_1\big(G_1 - C_1\big)}{1+r} + d\frac{Q_2\big(G_2 - C_2\big)}{\big(1+r\big)^2} + \ldots + d\frac{Q_n\big(G_n - C_n\big)}{\big(1+r\big)^n} + \ldots$$

$$P = d\sum \frac{Q_t\big(G_t - C_t\big)}{\big(1+r\big)^t},\tag{15.2}$$

where r is the discount rate required by investors, and the earnings, $E_t = Q_t(G_t - C_t)$, vary over time.

Our next question is how the mine stock price reacts to a change in gold bullion price. In other words: What is its gold beta? A statistical answer to this question may be found by using past market data on price elasticity, ß, as an estimate of the future elasticity. A gold beta may then be obtained by regressing stock returns on percentage changes in gold prices over a recent period:

$$R = \alpha + \beta \frac{dG}{G}. \tag{15.3}$$

Gold betas find their origin directly in the technical aspects of mining activities. Different betas are the result of the differences in cost structure found among mines because of their differential influence on mine earnings. Let us assume that production plans at a given mine have been made, wages negotiated, and the quantities to be produced specified for the coming quarter. The percentage change in earnings (dE/E) depends on the percentage change in the gold price (dG/G) and a multiplier, b, that we define for each mine as

$$\frac{dE}{E} = b \frac{dG}{G}.$$

The multiplier b is calculated using Eq. (15.1). This is done as follows: Assume that quantities, Q, and costs, C, are held constant over the period. That makes the percentage change in profit equal to the percentage change in gold price times the multiplier b. One can think of b as the elasticity of profit with respect to gold price.[3] In the mining profession, the factor b is called the *operating leverage*, the reciprocal of the mining company's profit margin, $1/(1 - C/G)$.

To illustrate how this affects earnings, we should compare the multiplier in a high-cost mine with that of a low-cost mine. A high-cost mine may have a ratio to total cost to gold price (C/G) of 0.8 per ounce; in other words, a profit margin of 20%. Here the multiplier b equals 5 (that is, 1 divided by 0.2). The multiplier measures the operating leverage of this company. In this case a short-term 10% rise in the price of gold would boost earnings by 50% as long as both the quantity produced and costs remain constant over the period in question. By contrast, a low-cost mine may have a C/G ratio of only 0.2; that is, a profit margin of 80%, which translates to a multiplier of 1.25 (1 divided by 0.8). The lower multiplier would boost earning by only 12.5% for a 10% rise in the price of gold.

In reality, both gold production and mining costs rise over time in response to gold price increases. Mines adjust production plans, unions respond to higher gold price with higher wage demands, and utility companies raise the energy prices mines must pay. This process of rolling adjustment can only be approximated with a static model.

Stock brokers use such discounted cash flow analysis to value mining stocks, but uncertainty and extraction policy reaction to changes in gold price are poorly taken into account. Brennan and Schwartz (1985), Miller and Upton (1985) and

Sundaresan (1984) have proposed valuation models consistent with modern finance theory. These models are presented in the appendix.

McDonald and Solnik (1977) have shown that for all gold mines, a strong relationship exists between the operating leverage multiplier, *b*, the gold beta estimated over a given time period, and the elasticity of stock returns to gold returns over the subsequent time period. The high correlation they found between greater common stock elasticity and higher cost-revenue ratios is consistent with the old-fashioned notion that the cost structure and average ore grade of a mine are the key determinants of market response to a change in gold price.

Real Estate

Real estate (private housing or commercial or agricultural properties) is also an important category of investment. In many countries domestic real estate is a common investment vehicle for pension funds and life insurance companies. Dutch pension funds are one of the few institutional investors that invest in *foreign* real estate. Their holding of foreign properties (mostly in the United States) is quite large. Japanese institutions seem to be moving in the same direction. But as a rule, foreign real estate is seldom considered by institutional investors. The reasons are obvious: First, it is difficult to monitor properties located abroad. Second, taxes, paperwork, and unforeseen risks make foreign real estate investment impractical on a large scale. To be sure, private deals can be arranged for special projects, but these are well beyond the scope of this book. For the same reason, we do not address other forms of international private money management. However, one should mention that there is a definite trend toward the development of negotiable forms for real property interest. In many countries pooled funds have been created with the specific purpose of real estate investment. Mortgage-backed Eurobonds are rapidly growing in popularity. The time may not be too far off when real estate will be a normal component of international investment strategies.

As mentioned repeatedly, real estate assets are quite different from securities traded on a financial market:

> Because the real estate market is not an auction market offering divisible shares in every property, and information flows in the market are complex, these features place a premium on investment judgment. Managers who want to own some of IBM simply buy some shares. Managers who want to participate in the returns on, say, a $300 million office building must take a significant position in the property.[4]

Some major differences of the real estate market with securities markets are:

- Properties are basically indivisible and unique.

- There is no national, or international, auction market for properties. Hence the "market" value of a given property is difficult to assess.

- Transaction costs and management fees are high.

- Information is not freely available and there is no, or little, public protection from insider trading.

Some real estate indexes have been developed to attempt to measure the average return on investment. Good-quality indexes with a long-term historical record exist in the United States and United Kingdom, but they are more recent or even nonexistent in other countries.

Real estate returns consist of income and capital gain or loss. The income on a property can usually be measured in a straightforward fashion. The value appreciation is more difficult to assess. The most common method is to use changes in *appraised* value. Appraisal of each property is conducted by specialists fairly infrequently (typically once a year). Appraisals are generally based on two approaches: discounted cash flows and transaction prices of comparable properties. In practice, appraisal prices exhibit remarkable inertia. The value of a real estate portfolio is further smoothed because properties are appraised infrequently (typically once a year), so their prices remain constant between appraisals. The major U.S. real estate indexes based on appraisal values are:

- The *Frank Russell Company (FRC)* and the *National Council of Real Estate Investments Fiduciaries* indexes. These are quarterly indexes starting in 1978 and broken down by regions and property types.

- The *Commingled Real Estate Equity Fund (CREF)* index published by Evaluation Associates. This is a quarterly index starting in 1969 of major tax-exempt funds.

Another method of measuring price appreciation is to use a reference to some real estate commingled funds that are traded on the stock market. In the United States Real Estate Investment Trusts (REIT) are traded on the stock market. REITs are investment trusts owning and managing properties. The total return on a REIT is made up of the income paid to shareholders as well as of the stock market appreciation of the REIT share price. Various REIT indexes are used to proxy the average total return on real estate investments. They are easier to construct, as they are simply some weighted average of market traded shares. The major REIT indexes are:

- The *National Association of Real Estate Investment Trusts (NAREIT)*, a monthly equal-weighted index of some 100 REITs starting in 1972

- REITs indexes published by various institutions, e.g., Wilshire or Goldman Sachs

The two types of indexes provide very different performance and risk characteristics, which have been studied by Firstenberg, Ross, and Zisler (1988), Goetzman and Ibbotson (1990), and Gyourko and Keim (1993). REIT indexes outperformed appraisal-based indexes by a considerable amount over the past 15 years. Appraisal-based indexes are much less volatile than REIT indexes. For example, Goetzman and Ibbotson found that a REIT index had an annual standard deviation of 15.4%, comparable to that of the Standard and Poor's 500 index, but six times larger than that of the CREF index, of 2.6%. Furthermore appraisal-based indexes and REIT indexes have very little correlation. Appraisal-based indexes exhibit a large persistence in returns (returns are correlated over time), showing the inertia in appraisals. REIT indexes are strongly correlated with the rest of the stock market.

The wide differences in the risk and return characteristics of real estate indexes confirm that it is difficult to assess the value and performance of real estate investments. It is probably difficult to integrate real estate, like most of the alternative investments outlined below, into the global quantitative framework that is used throughout this book. An asset allocation optimization of the portfolio should reserve a special, more qualitative, treatment for real estate investments.

Alternative Investments

It is difficult to give a broad characterization of alternative investments. But they are usually equity investment in some nonpublicly traded asset. These investments are sought because of their potential for superior return as well as their diversification benefits. Healey and Hardy (1994) surveyed alternative investments undertaken by U.S. endowment, foundation, and pension funds. They found that endowments and foundations committed some 10% of their assets to alternative investments, compared to 5% for corporate pension funds and only 3% for public pension funds. Investors are generally using limited partnerships to enter alternative investment (80% of the deals). Direct investment or the use of specialized funds is much less common. In a limited partnership a specialist of the type of investment considered acts as general partner, and the investors (institutional or private) act as limited partners. Each limited partnership operates one or several investment projects. According to this survey, the most popular alternative investments were in that order:

- *Leveraged buyouts.* Leveraged buyouts (LBOs) are significant equity investments in publicly held or privately held companies. The deals often have a large size and result in a significant equity control in the company.

- *Venture capital.* Venture capital refers to equity investment in companies with excellent growth potential. As opposed to buyouts, venture capital deals are of a smaller size and generally involve only a noncontrolling minority interest in the company. The return on the successful ventures should be very high to compensate the losses on a probable large number of failures. Although venture capital started in the United States, it has now spread to Europe and Asia. Institutional investors have been actively seeking foreign venture capital investments. Venture capital and leverage buyouts represent by far the largest share of alternative investments by institutional investors.

- *Mezzanine financing.* This refers to investment in privately held companies in the form of subordinated debt with various optional clauses that allow equity participation. This is a form of less-direct equity investment.

- *Distressed-company investing.* This refers to the purchase of debt of companies that are in financial distress, in bankruptcy, or in a reorganization process. This implies buying debt at a discount in the hope that the company will recover. Again international investment has grown rapidly in this area.

- *Special economic programs.* These programs refer to investment projects in specific economic areas, such as oil and gas exploration, mining, timberland, or farmland.

- *Economically targeted investments.* Economically targeted investments (ETI) refer to investments that are made in the joint interests of society and of investors. This is sometimes described as *social investing.* The idea is to direct pension funds to socially desirable projects lacking capital. Public pension funds are often under pressure of local authorities, worldwide, to undertake such ETI, and a vocal controversy on the opportunity of such investments is ongoing in many countries. The opposite is sometimes called *ethical investing* and refers to the principle that some types of investments should be prohibited for social or ethical reasons, e.g., investing in South African interest at the time of apartheid or in tobacco companies.

- *Others.* A variety of other real investments have been considered by investors, depending on fashion and national tastes. For example, Japanese investors have taken interest in French vineyards or works of art.

Hedge Funds

The early 1990s saw the explosive development of *hedge funds.* The attraction for these funds was tempered by many huge losses suffered in 1994.

Definition

It is difficult to provide a general definition of hedge funds, which numbered several thousands by the mid-1990s. The original concept of a hedge fund was to offer plays *against* the markets, using short-selling, futures, and other derivative products. Today funds using the "hedge fund" appellation follow all kinds of different strategies and cannot be considered as a homogeneous asset class. Some funds are highly leveraged; others are not. Some engage in hedging activities, and others do not. Some focus on making macroeconomic bets on commodities, currencies, interest rates, and so on. Some are mostly "technical" funds trying to take advantage of the mispricing of some securities within their market. Futures funds belong to the world of hedge funds. In fact, the most common denominator of hedge funds is not their investment strategy but the *search for absolute returns.*

Money management has progressively moved toward a focus on performance *relative to preassigned benchmarks.* The performance of an institutional money manager is generally evaluated relative to some market index that is assigned as a mandate. In turn these benchmarks guide (some would say "unduly constrain") the investment policy of the money manager. The risk of deviating from the performance of the benchmark has become huge, given all the publicity surrounding relative performance in a very competitive money management industry. The development of hedge funds can be seen as a reaction against this trend with the search for absolute return in all directions. Hedge funds managers seek freedom to achieve high absolute returns and wish to be rewarded for their performance. These objectives are apparent in the legal organization and the fee structure of hedge funds. These two aspects are probably the only uniform characteristics of hedge funds.

The fund is set up as a *partnership* or as an *offshore corporation*, and the manager is compensated through a fee based on the value of assets under management (typically 1% to 3% of the asset base) *plus* an incentive fee proportional to the realized profits (typically 15% to 30% of total profits). This legal structure allows the fund manager to take short and long positions in any asset, to use all kinds of derivatives, and to leverage the fund without restrictions.

Hedge funds started in the United States in the form of *private investment partnerships*, which are limited to 99 partners, who must be "accredited investors" (with a net worth of at least $1 million), and are prohibited from advertising. Given the small number of partners a minimum investment is typically $1 million. Institutional investors can become partners. *Offshore funds* have also proved to be an attractive legal structure. These are incorporated in countries like the British Virgin Islands, Bermuda, or other locations attractive from a fiscal and legal viewpoint.

Hedge funds have become very global. This shows in the wide international array of investments used by these hedge funds. It also shows in the international diversity of their client base.

Classification

Some classification of hedge funds by investment strategy is provided in the media. These classifications are somewhat arbitrary and exhibit a large degree of overlap. A possible classification is given below.

- *Short funds* are the traditional type of hedge funds, taking short and long bets in common stocks. They vary their short and long exposure according to forecasts, use leverage, and now play on numerous markets in the world.

- *Global/macro funds* take bets on the direction of a market, a currency, an interest rate, a commodity, or any macroeconomic variable. These funds tend to be highly leveraged and make extensive use of derivatives.

- *Event arbitrage funds* take bets on some event specific to a company or a security. These include arbitrage in case of mergers and acquisitions (for example, buying the acquired company and selling the acquiring company), restructurings, bankruptcies, rights offerings, and so on.

- *Market-neutral funds* take bets on valuation differences within some market segment. This could involve simultaneous long and short positions in closely related securities. For example, one could buy some bond deemed to be underpriced with a simultaneous short position in bond futures or other fixed-income derivatives. This type of fund is sometimes called *risk-arbitrage fund*. Among the various techniques used by market-neutral funds, we can mention:

  - Fixed-income hedging

  - Pairs trading

  - Warrant arbitrage

  - Convertible bond arbitrage

  - Statistical arbitrage

  It must be understood that these funds are not riskless, as they can never be perfectly hedged, although they are often highly leveraged. For example, David Askin's Granite Fund, specialized in arbitrage on mortgage-backed securities, lost its total $600 million value in a couple of weeks.

- *Funds of funds* have been created to allow easier access to small investors. The participation in a hedge fund requires a large initial investment. A "fund of funds" is open to small investors and, in turn, invests in a selection of hedge funds. If a "fund of funds" has a large client base, it can invest large sums of money in each hedge fund. A "fund of funds" provides the small investor with two benefits:

  - It allows diversifying the risk of a single hedge fund.

  - The manager of the "fund of funds" is supposed to have expertise in finding reliable and good-quality hedge funds, in a world where information on the investment strategies of hedge funds is difficult to obtain.

  However, there are a couple of drawbacks with a "fund of funds":

  - The fee charged by its manager comes on top of that already charged by each hedged fund. The total fee can be quite hefty.

  - Individual hedge funds are mostly selected by the "fund of funds" on the basis of past performance. This gives little indication of future performance.

Performance and Risk

Because of their heterogeneity, it is not possible to talk about the performance of hedge funds as an asset class. Some indexes of hedge fund performance are available from consultants, such as Managed Account Report (MAR) or E. Lee Hennessee Group. A great statistical caution should be exercised when looking at the historical track record of hedge funds. Survivorship bias is a serious problem in the world of these nonpublic hedge funds. Although several thousand hedge funds were in operation in the mid-1990s, another large number of them had disappeared because their losses made them lose their client base. Only successful ones publish a track record. However, good past performance brings no certainty for future performance. This was illustrated by the highly publicized performance of George Soros's Quantum funds in 1993, which was followed by similarly highly publicized losses in 1994. Any investor should realize that hedge funds are high-risk investments, with high-potential profits or losses.

Summary

1. Commodity investments provide some diversification benefits, as well as an opportunity to speculate.

2. Gold is a major example of commodity investment. It has always played a special role in international investment. It is regarded both as an international monetary asset and as the ultimate store of value. Gold keeps its real value in times of severe hardship, such as wars, revolution, and extreme monetary crises (stock market crashes and hyperinflation). In the past, gold has provided good long-term protection against inflation and currency devaluation. In general, gold allows diversification against risks that affect all stock and bond markets simultaneously.

3. Commodity-linked investments exist in various forms: futures, options, bonds, and stocks. The valuation of commodity-linked securities is a typical example of relative pricing.

4. Real estate investments are regarded by some investors as a bona fide asset class. However, the investment characteristics of real estate are quite different from those of a financial security traded on a capital market.

5. Various alternative investments are also considered by some investors. They usually amount to an equity participation in some nonpublicly traded assets. Major alternative investments are leverage buyouts, venture capital, mezzanine financing, special economic programs, or economically targeted investments.

6. Hedge funds have become quite fashionable in the 1990s. They are not an asset class per se, but rather a form of investing that searches for large

absolute returns with few investment constraints. The risk of such investments is commensurate with the potential profits that could be realized.

Questions and Problems

1. Explain why the figures shown in Exh. 15.1 suggest that commodities are an attractive investment.

2*. Let's assume that you believe in the Capital Asset Pricing Model (CAPM). The beta of gold relative to the market portfolio is –0.3. The risk-free rate is 7%, and the market risk premium is 4%. Therefore your current expectation of the market return is 11%.

   ■ What is the expected return on gold?

   ■ Give an intuitive explanation for such a low expected return.

3. Bel Or Mine issues a five-year Eurobond with the following characteristics:

   ■ Par value 100 gold ounces. Each bond is issued and repaid in dollars at the market value of 100 ounces of gold.

   ■ Annual coupon payment of the dollar market value of three ounces of gold.

   ■ Maturity of five years with no early redemption.

   A few days after issue, the yield on straight dollar-Eurobonds, for issuers of the quality of Bel Or Mine, is 10%. The price of gold is $400 per ounce. The gold-linked bond sells for $35,000. What can you say about the market expectations of gold prices?

4*. Let's assume that you are a U.S. investor who wants to invest $10,000 in gold. The current price of gold is $400, and you expect it to go up by 10% in the very short term. You consider buying shares of gold mines; you hesitate between Bel Or and Schoen Gold. Your broker gives you the following information:

	Bel Or	Schoen Gold
Cost per Ounce	147	340
Gold Beta	1.6	6

   The gold beta is obtained by running a regression of the gold mine stock price changes on the gold bullion price changes. It indicates the stock market price sensitivity to gold.

   ■ Which mine would you buy and why?

   ■ What is your expected return, given your scenario?

5. To capitalize on your expectation of a 10% gold price appreciation, you consider buying futures or option contracts. Near-delivery futures contracts are quoted at $410 per ounce with a margin of $1000 per contract of 100 ounces. Call options on gold are quoted with the same delivery date. A call with an exercise price of $400 costs $20 per ounce.

   ■ What is your expected return at maturity of both contracts (assuming a 10% rise in gold price)?

- Simulate the return of the two investments for various movements in the price of gold.

- Would you prefer in-, at-, or out-of-the money options?

6. G.O. Bug wants to invest $12,000 in gold. In December the spot price of gold is $400 per ounce. G.O. Bug is very confident that gold will appreciate by at least 10% before the end of January and is willing to assume fairly risky positions to maximize the return on this forecast. G.O. Bug is considering several alternatives:

- *Gold bullion.* G.O. could buy 30 ounces, or roughly one kilogram.

- *Gold futures.* G.O. Bug could buy February futures. These contracts trade at $413 per ounce, with an initial margin of $1500 per contract of 100 ounces. Therefore G.O. could buy eight contracts (12,000/1500).

- *Gold options.* G.O. Bug considers two February call options with different strike prices. Each option contract covers 100 ounces. The February 410 call quotes at $8 per ounce; the February 430 call quotes at $4 per ounce. Therefore G.O. could buy 15 contracts of the first option or 30 contracts of the second option.

- *Two gold mines.* Mines A and B have the same stock price: $10 per share. A British broker has estimated the gold beta of both mines using a discounted cash flow model as well as historical regression analysis. Mine A is a rich mine with a gold beta equal to two; mine B has much higher production costs with a gold beta equal to five. G.O. could buy 1200 shares of one of the gold mines.

G.O. Bug quickly rules out investing directly in bullion, which does not offer enough leverage.

- Assuming that G.O.'s expectations are realized by the end of February, compute the realized returns on the various alternative strategies considered. Simulate various values of the spot price of gold in February (320, 360, 380, 400, 420, and 480).

- Which investment strategy would you suggest to G.O. Bug?

7. Let's consider an industrial firm using some raw material and energy to produce some inexpensive consumer goods. Here is what happened over the past ten years:

- The price of raw material went up much more quickly than the price of goods produced.

- The share price of the company went up much more quickly than the price of goods produced.

Financial analysts claim that this was easy to predict.

- Is this statement logical?

8*. The issue of *survivorship bias* is a serious potential problem when one draws conclusions from historical track records. Try to show why the following statements can be misleading:

- "There are today 100 Type-A hedge funds in operation. Their average return over the past two years is 20%. Hence they have outperformed the stock market (return of 15%)" [actually some 50 funds disappeared during these two years].

- "The Poupou commodity index has been back-calculated from 1970 to 1990 using the leading commodity futures contracts; by leading we mean those that have been most active. The Poupou commodity index had a remarkable performance from 1970 to 1995" [actually several commodity futures contracts have been removed from the commodity exchange or have experienced a drop in trading activity].

9*. Let's consider the four major commodities traded on Poupou Commodity Futures exchange in 2009. The following table lists the average annualized price movements from 2000 to 2009, as well as the production volumes, expressed in the local currency unit, today (2009) and ten years ago (2000):

Commodity	Average return	Annual production	
		2000	2009
Plastik	20%	10	50
Lumin	20%	5	20
Woodo	–10%	50	10
Ironi	0%	35	20

The futures exchange decides in 2009 to create a commodity index based on the four commodities, with weights equal to their current relative importance in economic production. These indexes are back-calculated from 2000 but using today's weights.

- Would such an index give unbiased indications over the past ten years?
- Do you have any suggestions regarding weights that can be used to back-calculate the indexes?

10. The SOL group specializes in hedge funds invested on the Paf stock market. Over the year 1999, the Paf stock market index went up by 20%. The SOL group had three hedge funds with very different investment strategies. As expected, the 1999 returns on the three funds were quite different. Here are the performance of the three funds before and after management fees set at 20% of gross profits:

Fund	Gross return	Net return
SOL A	50%	40%
SOL B	20%	16%
SOL C	–10%	–10%

One can observe that the average gross performance of the three funds is exactly equal to the performance on the PAF stock index. At year end, most clients had left the third fund, and SOL C was closed. At the start of 2000, the SOL group launched an aggressive publicity campaign among portfolio managers, stressing the remarkable return on SOL A. If potential clients asked whether the SOL group had other hedge funds invested in Paf, SOL group mentioned the only other fund, SOL B, and claimed that their average gross performance during 1999 was 35%.

- What do you think of this publicity campaign?

11. Real estate appraisal values are very smooth, whereas transaction costs for properties are very high compared to other financial assets.

- Would you suggest using real estate appraisal–based indexes in a global portfolio optimization?

12. The correlation of two real estate indexes (FRC and NAREIT) and of the Wilshire 5000 U.S. stock index for the period 1984–1989, as computed by Ennis and Burik (1991), is given as:

	Wilshire	NAREIT	FRC
Wilshire 5000	1.00	0.79	0.18
NAREIT	0.79	1.00	0.02
FRC	0.18	0.02	1.00

- Are the two real estate indexes comparable?

13*. The investment fund of the Lemon County of Kalifornia is investing $1 billion in a leveraged-bond hedge fund. This hedge fund has the following structure:

- $4 billion invested in a reverse-floater (also called Bull FRN). This is a five-year bond with a coupon set at 8% minus LIBOR
- $3 billion borrowed at LIBOR

The current yield curve is flat at 4%. The reverse-floater is currently priced at 100%.

- Estimate the yield enhancement over LIBOR that the hedge fund would provide if the yield curve drops uniformly by ten basis points (0.1%).

Actually, the whole yield curve moved up to 7% within a couple of weeks.

- What would be the new income (coupon rate) on this $1 billion investment made by Lemon County?
- Can you provide some rough estimate of the new market value of this $1 billion investment? (Assume that a 100 investment in the reverse floater can be priced as the sum of a 200 long position in a straight five-year bond with a fixed coupon of 4% *plus* a 100 short position in a plain-vanilla FRN with a coupon set at LIBOR.)

Notes

1. Further evidence may be found in Renshaw and Renshaw (1982), Sherman (1982 and 1984), Carter, Afflecte-Graves, and Money (1982), and Jaffe (1989).

2. Jacquillat and Roll (1979) provide an empirical analysis of the benefits of commodity-linked bonds. Schwartz (1982) provides a theoretical model for an index-linked bond with an option to repay the bond at face value or at an index-linked price. Such a model was tested on a silver-linked bond issued by Sunshine Mining in Brauer and Ravichandran (1986). An interesting analysis of oil-linked securities is provided by Gibson and Schwartz (1990).

3. The value of b is obtained by taking, in Eq. (15.1), the derivative of E relative to G: $dE/dG = Q$.
   That means

$$\frac{dE}{E} = \frac{dG}{G}\frac{G}{G-C};$$

   hence the value of b.

4. P.M. Firstenberg, S.A. Ross, and R.C. Zisler, "Real Estate: The Whole Story," *Journal of Portfolio Management*, Spring 1988.

Bibliography

AIMR, *Real Estate Investing in the 1990s: ICFA Continuing Education*, Charlottesville, VA, AIMR, 1995.

Ankrim, E.M., and Hensel, C.R. "Commodities in Asset Allocation: A Real-Asset Alternative to Real Estate?" *Financial Analysts Journal*, May-June 1994.

Brauer, G.A., and Ravichandran, R. "How Sweet Is Silver?" *Journal of Portfolio Management*, Summer 1986.

Brennan, M., and Schwartz, E. "Evaluating Natural Resource Investments," *Journal of Business*, March 1985.

Brown, S.J., Goetzman, W., Ibbotson, R.G., and Ross, S.A. "Survivorship Bias in Performance Studies," *Review of Financial Studies*, 5 (4), 1992.

Carter, K., Afflecte-Graves, J., and Money, A. "Are Gold Shares Better Than Gold for Diversification?" *Journal of Portfolio Management*, Fall 1982.

Ennis, R.M., and Burik, P. "Pension Fund Real Estate Investment under a Simple Equilibrium Pricing Model," *Financial Analysts Journal*, May-June 1991.

Firstenberg, P.M., Ross, S.A., and Zisler, R.C. "Real Estate: The Whole Story," *Journal of Portfolio Management*, Spring 1988.

Gibson, R., and Schwartz, E. "Stochastic Convenience Yield and the Pricing of Oil Contingent Claims," *Journal of Finance*, July 1990.

Goetzmann, W.M., and Ibbotson, R.G. "The Performance of Real Estate as an Asset Class," *Journal of Applied Corporate Finance*, Fall 1990.

Green, T., *The World of Gold*, London: Rosendale Press, 1993.

Gyourko, J., and Keim, D.B. "Risk and Return in Real Estate: Evidence from a Real Estate Index," *Financial Analysts Journal*, September-October, 1993.

Healey, T.J., and Hardy, D.J. "Alternative Investments Grow Rapidly at Tax-Exempt Funds," *Journal of Investing*, Spring 1994.

Ibbotson, R.G., and Brinson, G.P. *Global Investing*, New York: McGraw-Hill, 1993.

Ibbotson, R.G., Siegel, L., and Love, K. "World Wealth: Market Value and Returns," *Journal of Portfolio Management*, Fall 1985.

Jacquillat, B., and Roll, R. "French Index-Linked Bonds for U.S. Investors?" *Journal of Portfolio Management*, Spring 1979.

Jaffe, J. "Gold and Gold Stocks as Investments for Institutional Portfolios," *Financial Analysts Journal*, March/April 1989.

Lummer, S.L., and Siegel, L.B. "GSCI Collateralized Futures: A Hedging and Diversification Tool for Institutional Investors, *Journal of Investing*, Summer 1993.

McDonald, J.G., and Solnik, B. "Valuation and Strategy for Gold Stocks," *Journal of Portfolio Management*, Spring 1977.

Miller, M.H., and Upton, C.W. "A Test of the Hotelling Valuation Principle," *Journal of Political Economy*, February 1985.

Pindyck, R. "Uncertainty and Exhaustible Resource Markets," *Journal of Political Economy*, December 1980.

Renshaw, A., and Renshaw, E. "Does Gold Have a Role in Investment Portfolios?" *Journal of Portfolio Management*, Spring 1982.

Schwartz, E. "The Pricing of Commodity-Linked Bonds," *Journal of Finance*, May 1982.

Sherman, E.J. "Gold: A Conservative, Prudent Diversified," *Journal of Portfolio Management*, Spring 1982.

Sherman, E. "Performance of Gold Versus Stocks, Bonds and Money Markets in Six Countries: 1968–1983," *International Gold Corporation*, March 1984.

Sundaresan, M. "Equilibrium Valuation of Natural Resources," *Journal of Business*, 1984.

Chapter 15: Appendix
Advanced Section on Evaluating Natural Resource Investments

The general valuation formula for a natural resource investment, such as a mine or an oil field, is given by Eq. (15.2), *assuming* all earnings paid as dividend:

$$P = \sum \frac{Q_t(G_t - C_t)}{(1+r)^t}.$$

In this appendix we make the common assumption that all profits are distributed to the owner.

One major problem is that future extraction costs are likely to be a function of the current extraction, Q_t, as well as the past extraction policy. The current costs will be higher if the mine already produced a lot and is left with low-grade ore than if it produced at a slower pace without exhausting its rich ore. Of course, past and present extraction policies are a function of the output price, G, of gold, in our case. Microeconomics analysis can help us simplify Eq. (15.2) if we assume that producers attempt to maximize profits at each point in time. Miller and Upton (1985) provided such an analysis in a simple discrete-time certainty framework. They assumed a finite horizon date, N, beyond which production could safely be presumed to have ceased, and known total reserves, R_0. They first considered the case where costs were only a function of current production, $C_t(Q_t)$. The first-order condition for profit maximization in every period is

$$\frac{(G_t - c_t)}{(1+r)^t} = \lambda, \text{ for } t = 0, \ldots, N,$$

where c_t is the marginal cost of producing Q_t. Since the same condition applies at time 0, we have

$$(G_0 - c_0) = \lambda.$$

Hence

$$G_t - C_t = (G_0 - c_0)(1 + r)^t.$$

Miller and Upton make the further simplifying assumption that the marginal costs of production are constant; then the valuation equation of the mine reduces to

$$P = \left(G_0 - c_0\right) \sum_{t=0}^{N} Q_t = \left(G_0 - c_0\right) R_0.$$

The value of the mine is equal to current earnings times the total reserves. In this case the gold beta of the mine is exactly equal to its current operating leverage. They also worked out the more complex formula for situations in which costs are an increasing function of current production and cumulative past production.

One problem with this traditional microeconomics analysis is the existence of uncertainty. Pindyck (1980) considered the case of uncertainty assuming risk neutrality; Sundaresan (1984) also considered constant risk aversion. However, they did not consider the possibility of closing a mine and reopening it at a later time in response to current market conditions. Indeed, some gold mines were closed in the late 1960s, when the low price of gold, around $40 an ounce, made it very costly to continue their operation. Many of these mines reopened in the mid-1970s, when the gold price surged to $200 an ounce. Brennan and Schwartz (1985) took a different approach to tackling this problem. They resorted to an arbitrage approach similar in spirit to the one developed for option pricing. This is based on constructing arbitrage portfolios on the mine equity and futures contracts on the underlying commodity, gold. Using stochastic optimal control theory, they derive a set of differential equations that could be solved numerically. Although the mathematics are tough, the implications and potential uses of the model are attractive.

P A R T S I X

Strategy, Organization, and Control

16

International Performance Analysis

*T*he management of a global portfolio is a complex task with numerous parameters to take into account. The portfolio's performance and risk can be attributed to many management decisions, including the choice of instruments, markets, currencies, and individual securities. This book has shown the wide diversity of institutional features, investment techniques, and concepts that a capable international money manager must master. Given this complexity, a detailed and frequent analysis of the performance and risk of international portfolios is required, for both internal and external purposes. A money management firm typically has several portfolio managers with responsibility for a large number of accounts under very diverse mandates. It is of the utmost importance for the firm to perform an in-house assessment of the performance of each account and manager, of the risks and bets taken, and of the areas where expertise, or lack of expertise, has been demonstrated. From an external viewpoint, clients wish to compare the performance of competing money managers; this requires that performance on managed accounts be analyzed in a comparable fashion. This chapter deals with the principles, mathematics, and implementation of performance analysis in an international context.

The Basics

Principles and Objectives

The first thing to remember is that accounting valuation should not be confused with performance measurement. *Multicurrency accounting* systems keep track on a daily basis of transactions, including forward commitments, and provide a valuation of the account based on current market prices from around the world and computed in one *base currency* (also called reference currency). The base currency is the currency chosen by the investor to value the portfolio; for example, an American pension fund would use the U.S. dollar as base currency. Every item, including stocks, bonds, and, of course, cash, is included in an accounting valuation.

International performance analysis (IPA) systems measure the return on a portfolio and various portfolio segments, usually on a monthly or quarterly basis. A huge amount of valuation and transaction information is synthesized into a few performance figures. IPA systems are developed in-house or applied by outside services:

- *In-house IPA* systems are driven by the firm's daily accounting system and allow quick monitoring of the performance and risks of all major accounts. They are used for presentation of performance analysis to clients, as well as for internal control of the investment process.

- *Outside IPA* services analyze the performance of a universe of managers, based on information provided monthly or quarterly by those money managers. They allow an objective measure of performance by a client and a comparison across competing managers. Outside IPA services act mostly on behalf of trustees whose funds are under management. The oldest established IPA services are provided by InterSec, Frank Russell International, and WM (World Markets).

The objective of an IPA is to be able to answer the following types of questions about a portfolio, and in so doing assess the effectiveness of its manager:

- What is the total return on the portfolio over a specific period?

- What is the breakdown of the return in terms of capital gains, currency fluctuations, and income?

- To what extent is the performance explained by asset allocation, market timing, currency selection, or individual stock selection?

- How does the overall return compare to that of certain benchmarks? For example, does it outperform the EAFE index in terms of return, given its level of risk? How closely does the portfolio track the benchmark (tracking error)?

- How does the overall return compare to that of a universe of competing money managers with similar mandates?

- Is there evidence of unusual expertise in a particular market (e.g., Japanese stocks or British bonds)?

- Has the risk diversification objective been achieved?

- How aggressive is the manager's strategy?

Total rates of return are usually computed on a quarterly or monthly basis and compared to one or more benchmarks. The benchmark can be either a passive index, such as the Morgan Stanley Capital International World or EAFE index, or the mean return of a universe of managed funds. Calculating total return is easy once the manager provides the advisor with a total valuation for the start and the end of a period and the major cash flows that occurred during the period. In fact, it is just like calculating the return on a purely domestic fund. The interesting part lies in:

- Breaking the performance down into its various components, such as yield, capital gain in local currency, and currency contribution.

- Analyzing the impact on performance of various management decisions, such as asset allocation, currency management, and security selection.

The performance of a manager in each market is estimated by calculating the rate of return for every segment of the portfolio that is associated with a national stock or bond market (e.g., Japanese stocks) and comparing it to the return on the corresponding national index. Any disparity between the two reflects the manager's stock-selection ability. If the performance is measured relative to an internationally weighted index, this disparity can be further broken down into the following: (1) the portion resulting from a difference in market weighting between the portfolio and the international index, and (2) the portion resulting from the manager's security selection and timing ability in each market. To perform this analysis, IPA services obtain the periodic valuations for each portfolio segment, as well as the cash flows affecting each segment.

Unfortunately, technical and conceptual problems arise, in part due to the quality of the data used as inputs to the analysis. These problems are present, to some extent, in a domestic performance analysis, but they are magnified in an international setting.

Calculating a Rate of Return

The first, and somewhat unexpected, problem encountered in performance analysis is the basic method to be used in calculating a basic rate of return on a portfolio or on a portfolio segment (a segment is defined as some homogeneous class of assets, e.g., French stocks).

The rate of return over a period on a portfolio segment or on a total portfolio is easy to calculate *if there are no cash inflows or outflows*. Then the rate of return r is simply equal to the change in value over the period $(V_1 - V_0)$ divided by the initial value V_0:

$$r = \frac{V_1 - V_0}{V_0} \text{ or}$$

$$1 + r = \frac{V_1}{V_0}.$$

However, let's now assume that a cash withdrawal, C_t took place on day t during the period. Then the calculation of the rate of return is less obvious. There are several methods of calculating the rate of return on a portfolio affected by cash movements.[1] The most common are the money-weighted rate of return (MWR), the internal rate of return (IRR), and the time-weighted rate of returns (TWR).

It is useful to consider the following simple example:

- Value at start of the year is $V_0 = 100$

- Cash withdrawal on day t is $C_t = 50$, $t = 30$ days

- Value on day t, before the cash flow, is $V_t = 95$

- Final value at year end is $V_1 = 60$

We use the usual convention that a *positive* cash flow for the client is a *withdrawal* from the portfolio (a reduction in invested capital) and that a *negative* cash flow is an *addition* to the portfolio. The change in value over the year is unquestionably equal to $V_1 + C_t - V_0 = 10$. However, methods differ on how to calculate the rate of return. Dividing the change in value by the initial capital value, V_0, would be a mistake, since a much smaller capital was invested during most of the year.

Money-Weighted Rate (MWR)   This is the return on the average invested capital and is obtained by dividing the change in value of the portfolio by the average capital invested during the period. A problem in this "accounting" ratio is the measure of average invested capital. The most simple method is to measure the net cash flow during the period and assume arbitrarily that it takes place at the middle of the period. Then the *average* invested capital is simply equal to the starting capital minus 50% of the net cash flow. The resulting rate of return is equal to:

$$MWR_1 = \frac{V_1 + C_t - V_0}{V_0 - \frac{1}{2} C_t} = \frac{60 + 50 - 100}{100 - 25} = \frac{10}{75} = 13.33\%.$$

This approach does not take into account the exact timing of cash flows; it assumes that they take place in the middle of the period so that the average contribution is half their value. A more accurate method is to divide not by $V_0 - \frac{1}{2}C_t$, but by a term that takes into account the length of time the funds have been invested. In our example, we have:

$$MWR_2 = \frac{V_1 + C_t - V_0}{V_0 - \dfrac{365 - t}{365} C_t} = \frac{10}{100 - \dfrac{335}{365} 50} = 18.48\%.$$

If several cash flows take place, each is weighted according to the portion of the period for which the funds have been left in the portfolio. This requires keeping track of the date of each cash flow. This can be a cumbersome task if we calculate the performance of each portfolio segment as all transactions (sales and purchase of securities, income receipts, etc.) must basically be accounted for.

Internal Rate of Return   This linear method of calculating a money-weighted rate of return is questionable. Financiers are used to calculating the rate of return on an investment with multiple cash flows using discounting. The *Internal Rate of*

Return (*IRR*) is a money-weighted rate computed by taking into account the time-value of money. The IRR is the discount rate that equals the start-of-period value to the sum of the discounted cash flows, including the end-of-period value.

In our example the internal rate of return is the value of r in the following equation:

$$V_0 = \sum_t \frac{C_t}{\left(1+r\right)^{t/365}} + \frac{V_1}{\left(1+r\right)}.$$

In our example the internal rate of return is equal to:

$$r = MWR_3 = 18.90\%.$$

However, the calculation of an IRR is a cumbersome task; the simpler MWR are generally accepted as a measure of the rate of return on a portfolio. A problem with the IRR is that it must be computed using some algorithm that may yield several solutions, especially if there is an alternance of positive and negative cash flows. Also the calculation is very sensitive to measurement errors and the exact dating of cash flows.

Time-Weighted Return   By contrast with the MWR methods, the *time-weighted rate* of return (*TWR*) is the performance *per dollar invested* (or per unit of base currency) and is calculated independently of the cash flows to or from the portfolio segment.

In other words, the TWR measures the performance that could have been realized had the same capital been under management over the whole period. This method is necessary for comparing performance among managers or to a passive benchmark. The TWR is obtained by calculating the rate of return between each cash flow and chain linking those rates over the total period under study. As mentioned above, the rate of return over a period without cash flows suffers no controversy, and the TWR simply compounds the rates or return per unit of base currency. The calculation of a TWR requires the valuation of a portfolio segment each time a cash flow takes place.

The calculation requires knowledge of the value of the portfolio segment, V_t, just before a cash flow takes place. In our example the rate of return for the first subperiod is given by:

$$1 + r_t = \frac{V_t}{V_0}.$$

The rate of return for the second subperiod is given by r_{t+1}.

$$1 + r_{t+1} = \frac{V_1}{V_t - C_t}$$

The total time-weighted rate of return, r, is given by

$$\left(1+r\right)=\left(1+r_t\right)\left(1+r_{t+1}\right)=\left(\frac{V_t}{V_0}\right)\left(\frac{V_1}{V_t-C_t}\right).$$

In the example the portfolio was worth 95 at the time cash was withdrawn, so the TWR is equal to 26.66%, as shown below:

$$1+r_t=\frac{95}{100}=0.95 \qquad\qquad r_t=-5.00\%,$$

$$1+r_{t+1}=\frac{60}{45}=1.33 \qquad\qquad r_{t+1}=33.33\%,$$

$$1+r=\left(0.95\right)\left(1.33\right)=1.27 \qquad r=26.66\%.$$

Clearly the various methods of calculating a rate of return yield very different results: from 13.33% to 26.66%. The MWR is useful to measure the return of invested capital; however, everyone agrees that the TWR is the method to use to measure and compare the performance of money managers. The comparison should be independent of the cash movements imposed by the clients.

Implementation   In the international context the problems associated with using quarterly MWR figures are compounded by the multicurrency and multimarket nature of performance measurement. Many IPA services base their analyses on monthly or quarterly money-weighted rates of return for both the entire portfolio and each national segment. Monthly or quarterly MWR are then chain-linked into TWR for longer periods. This crude substitute for a genuine quarterly TWR is a necessary evil in the absence of precise daily transaction data. Unfortunately, the approximation introduces some potential biases, especially if one is interested in the performance of the manager in specific markets. A short hypothetical example should illustrate this point.

Let us consider a small $10 million fund that is restricted to a 10% investment limitation in Japan. ¥100 million ($1 million) are invested in the Japanese stock market and managed by a local money manager. The fund's trustee wants to evaluate the security-selection skill of the manager in this market. Assuming no currency problem (i.e., assuming a fixed 100¥/$ rate), we will consider the following scenario.

The Japanese manager invests ¥100 million in the Japanese stock index, via an index fund, *thereby exactly tracking the index*. After two weeks, the index rises from 100 to 130, and the fund's trustee decides to transfer ¥30 million to a falling market (such as the U.K. market) to keep within the 10% limitation on Japanese investment. Over the next two weeks, the Japanese index loses 30% of its value (falling to 91), so that by the end of the month the Japanese portfolio is down to ¥70 million. The calculation for the MWR and the TWR of the portfolio follow and are indicated in Exh. 16.1.

EXHIBIT 16.1

TWR and MWR of a Hypothetical Japanese Portfolio				
	Day:			
	1	**15**	**30**	**TWR %**	**MWR %**
Index	100	130	91	−9	−9
Portfolio	100	130			
(¥ mios)		100	70	−9	0

$$1 + TWR = \frac{130}{100} \times \frac{70}{100} = 0.91 \qquad TWR = -9\%$$

$$MWR = \frac{70 + 30 - 100}{100 - \frac{1}{2}(30)} = 0.$$

The TWR on that Japanese portfolio is −9%; that is the performance of the Japanese index, which was perfectly tracked and fell from 100 to 91. The money-weighted rate of return computed by the IPA service will be 0% (a net profit equal to 0), wrongly implying that the manager outperformed the Japanese market and has great skills in Japanese stock selection. In fact, he precisely tracked the Japanese market and no more.

Although the MWR is useful for measuring a fund's total return, it does not accurately measure its performance relative to a preselected index. In the domestic context serious distortions can be avoided by valuing a portfolio in total every time a large cash flow occurs. In a detailed international analysis of the performance of each national segment, shifting funds between markets creates the same cash flow problem. Since these internal cash flows are frequent, the total portfolio should be valued frequently. The larger the flow relative to the average investment in a given market, the larger the potential bias. Thus statistical errors can obscure real overperformance or underperformance in a national market, especially in small markets. Since international funds are often diversified over ten or more different bond and stock markets, this statistical error will affect the performance measurement of any reasonably active manager. Moreover, there is no reason to believe that these measurement errors will average out over several months, especially in recently created funds that are still receiving injections of cash (as are many international pension funds). The only way to remedy this bias is to use precise daily data to compute the TWR. But accounting for portfolio transactions on a daily basis is no easy task when there are so many currencies, types of investments (stocks, bonds, cash, precious metals, forward and future contracts, options, etc.), and difference in national trading procedures to reconcile.

Using quarterly returns to compute operational *risk* measures is not realistic, either. At least four years of quarterly data are required to obtain statistically significant estimates of a fund's volatility, and this assumes stationary currency and market returns over that period, as well as a constant risk objective on the part of the manager. These assumptions are risky (especially for currencies) in light of the marked instability that many financial markets have displayed over time. Furthermore, risk averages over four years do not help the manager to evaluate and monitor his or her current risk exposure. Monthly returns, at least, should be used.

The importance of exact computations cannot be overstressed even to non-mathematicians. Astute stock selection is supposed to be a significant contribution made by a manager. This is computed as a residual, subtracting the currency and market effect from the overall performance of the portfolio's segments. Unfortunately this residual is also the repository for a variety of errors arising from poor data, incorrect calculations and approximations, and transaction and management fees.

Designing an IPA System

A portfolio is broken down into various segments according to type of asset (e.g., stocks, bonds, cash, convertible bonds, gold) and currency. Each homogeneous segment (say, Japanese stocks) is valued separately in its local currency as well as in the base currency of the portfolio. Thus Japanese stocks are valued in yen and German bonds in Deutsche marks.

The Mathematics of Multicurrency Return

The basic unit of measurement is the rate of return on each segment before any cash movement between segments. The adjustment for cash flows affecting the segment have been discussed above and will not be repeated here.

Return in Local Currency   If we call V_j the value of one segment j, in local currency, the rate of return in local currency for period t is given by

$$r_j = \frac{V_j^t - V_j^{t-1} + D_j^t}{V_j^{t-1}} = \frac{V_j^t - V_j^{t-1}}{V_j^{t-1}} + \frac{D_j^t}{V_j^{t-1}} = p_j + d_j, \qquad (16.1)$$

where

D_j is the amount of dividends or coupons *paid* during the period,

p_j is the capital gain (price appreciation) in percent, and

d_j is the yield.

Further precision is needed for fixed-income segments. In most countries, as well as on the Eurobond market, accrued interest, A, is computed and quoted separately from the price of a bond, P. An investor must pay both the price and accrued interest to the seller. Therefore the total *value* of the bond is $V = P + A$. The rate of return on the bond segment is given by

$$r_j = \frac{V_j^t - V_j^{t-1} + D_j^t}{V_j^{t-1}} = \frac{P_j^t - P_j^{t-1}}{P_j^{t-1} + A_j^{t-1}} + \frac{A_j^t - A_j^{t-1} + D_j^t}{P_j^{t-1} + A_j^{t-1}} = p_j + d_j. \tag{16.2}$$

Note that accrued interest should be taken into account for nonnegotiable interest-bearing instruments (e.g., Eurodollar deposits) but not for securities that are negotiated on a flat or discounted basis (e.g., some British bonds, Treasury bills, common stocks, etc.).

Over a longer period, these unit rates of return can be chain-linked to get a time-weighted rate of return for each segment. An example of calculations for the equity and gold segments of a portfolio is shown in Exh. 16.2.[2]

Return in Base Currency The base-currency rate of return is easily derived by translating all prices[3] into the base currency 0 at exchange rate S_j:

$$r_{j0} = \frac{V_j^t S_j^t + D_j^t S_j^t - V_j^{t-1} S_j^{t-1}}{V_j^{t-1} S_j^{t-1}}. \tag{16.3}$$

EXHIBIT 16.2

Geographical Breakdown and Return Statistics on Equity and Gold Investments (the base currency is the Swiss franc)

Portfolio   Composition (in %)

July 8	Average over period	Sept. 30	Market	Total return in local currency	Total return on equity index
11.53	8.62	5.62	West Germany	6.37	5.58
1.36	1.38	1.50	Canada	13.53	17.39
20.85	19.87	16.73	United States	18.00	11.32
1.37	1.01	0.90	United Kingdom	2.07	11.05
3.40	3.49	3.52	Japan	13.44	0.72
2.75	2.73	2.76	Netherlands	9.52	1.27
7.52	3.98	7.16	Other countries	—	—
51.22	58.92	61.81	Gold related	26.05	23.61

After some algebraic reshuffling, this may be written as

$$r_{j0} = p_j + d_j + s_j (1 + p_j + d_j), \text{ or} \tag{16.4}$$

$$r_{j0} = p_j + d_j + c_j$$

Total return in base currency	=	Capital gain component	+	Yield component	+	Currency component

where s_j denotes the percentage exchange rate movement and c_j denotes the influence of the exchange rate movement on the estimated return in the base currency. Note that the currency component, c_j, is equal to zero if the exchange rate, S_j, does not move, but differs slightly from s_j because of the cross-product terms.

The compounding of currency and market movements on a foreign security is illustrated in Exh. 16.3. The value of a foreign investment is represented as a rectangle, where the vertical axis represents the exchange rate, and the horizontal axis represents the value of the investment in local currency. As an illustration, consider a U.S. investor holding £10,000 of British assets with an exchange rate of $/£ = 2. The dollar value of the assets is represented by area A, or $20,000. Later the British assets have gone up by 10% to £11,000, and the pound has appreciated by 5% to $/£ = 2.10. The total dollar value is now £23,100, or a gain of 15.5%. The dollar gain, if the currency had not moved, is represented by the area B (10% of initial value). Because of the currency movement, this gain is transformed to a

EXHIBIT 16.3

Market and Currency Gains

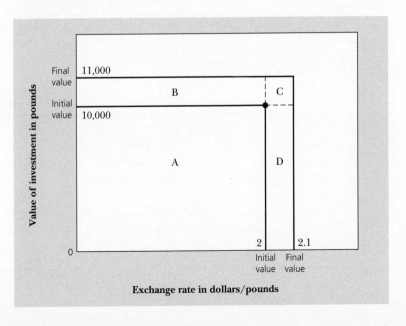

total gain of 15.5%, equal to the sum of areas B, C, and D. Area C plus D is the exchange rate component to the total return. Note that it can be seen as a pure exchange rate movement (area D) and a cross-currency-market term (area C).

Total-Return Decomposition

The first objective of IPA is to decompose the portfolio's total return, measured in base currency, into the three main sources of return:

- Capital gain (in local currency)
- Yield
- Currency

The total return is simply the weighted average of the returns on all segments. Over period t, the total portfolio's return r is computed in the base currency as follows:

$$r = \sum_j w_j r_{j0} = \sum_j w_j \left(p_j + d_j + c_j \right),$$

(16.5)

where w_j represents the percentage of segment j in the total portfolio at the start of the period. The various sources of return may be regrouped into three components:

$$r = \sum w_j p_j + \sum w_j d_j + \sum w_j c_j$$

Capital gain component + Yield component + Currency component

(16.6)

As an illustration, the last column of Exh. 16.4 breaks down the total return of an account (which is 12.95% in Swiss francs) into capital gains in the local currency (11.33%), yield (0.67%), and exchange rate gains (0.95%). The middle column breaks these numbers down further into the contribution of fixed and non-fixed income securities.

Performance Attribution

The relative performance of a manager may be measured by making several comparisons. The basic idea is to provide a comparison with some passive benchmarks. Active management decisions will induce deviations from the benchmarks' return. Some of the many management decisions that are commonly analyzed are discussed below.

Security Selection   A manager's security selection ability is determined by isolating the local market return of the various segments. Let's call I_j the return, in local currency, of the market index corresponding to segment j (e.g., the Tokyo Stock Exchange index). The rate of return on segment j (Japanese stocks) may be broken down into the following components:

$$r_{j0} = I_j + (p_j - I_j) + d_j + c_j.$$

(16.7)

EXHIBIT 16.4

Performance Analysis

	Returns (percent)	
Total return		**12.95**
Capital gains (losses)		11.33
Fixed income	0.84	
Equity and gold	10.49	
Market return	*9.24*	
Security selection	*1.25*	
Currency movements		0.95
Fixed income	0.23	
Equity and gold	0.72	
Yield		0.67
Fixed income	0.41	
Equity and gold	0.27	

The total portfolio return may be written as

$$r = \sum w_j I_j + \sum w_j \left(p_j - I_j \right) + \sum w_j d_j + \sum w_j c_j$$

(16.8)

$$\underset{\substack{\text{Market} \\ \text{return} \\ \text{component}}}{} + \underset{\substack{\text{Security} \\ \text{selection} \\ \text{contribution}}}{} + \underset{\substack{\text{Yield} \\ \text{component}}}{} + \underset{\substack{\text{Currency} \\ \text{component}}}{}$$

The first term on the right-hand side measures the performance that would have been achieved had the manager invested in a local market index instead of individual securities. This contribution is calculated net of currency movements, which are picked up by the last term in the formula. The second term measures the contribution made by the manager's individual security selection. To illustrate this type of analysis, Exh. 16.4 shows a breakdown of the performance of an equity investment. The 10.49% capital gain in equity breaks down into a 9.24% market index return and a 1.25% individual stock selection contribution. For this particular portfolio, the impact of exchange rates on total return (which was 12.95% for the quarter) was quite weak (only 0.95%). Most of the return, in fact, is explained by capital gains in the local markets (11.33%). In terms of security selection, the manager did well overall, since the portfolio outperformed some markets substantially (1.25% on average). (More detailed results for each market are shown in Exh. 16.2.)

Asset Allocation   Another step is to study the performance of the total portfolio relative to that of a global benchmark. This comparison is usually made with respect to the return I^* on an international index, such as the Morgan Stanley Capital International EAFE or World index. The objective is to assess the portfolio manager's ability as measured by the difference in return, $r - I^*$.

To do this, additional notations are required. Let's call I_{j0} the return on market index j, translated into base currency 0. We have

$$I_{j0} = I_j + C_j,$$

where C_j is the currency component of the index return in base currency, i.e., $C_j = s_j(1+I_j)$. Let's call w_j^* the weight of market j in the international benchmark chosen as a standard. In base currency, the return on this international index equals

$$I^* = \sum w_j^* I_{j0}.$$

Equation (16.8) may be rewritten and transformed into Eq. (16.9) by simultaneously adding and subtracting $\sum w_j^* I_{j0}$:

$$r = \sum w_j^* I_{j0} + \sum \left(w_j - w_j^* \right) I_j + \sum \left(w_j c_j - w_j^* C_j \right) + \sum w_j d_j + \sum w_j \left(p_j - I_j \right) \qquad \text{(16.9)}$$

International benchmark return I^*	Market allocation contribution	Currency allocation contribution	Yield component	Security selection contribution

This breakdown allows us to estimate the contribution to total performance of any deviation from the standard asset allocation $w_j - w_j^*$.

The word *contribution* in this context indicates performance relative to a selected benchmark; the word *component* refers to a breakdown of the portfolio's total return. Equation (16.9) states that the relative performance of a manager, $r - I^*$, is the result of the two factors (after allowing for the yield on the portfolio) described below.

1. *An asset allocation different from that of the index.* This factor is a source of positive performance for the manager who overweighs ($w_j > w_j^*$) the best-performing markets and underweighs the poorest-performing markets. This factor can be further broken down into market and currency contributions.[4] So it is possible for a manager to have chosen his or her markets very effectively (resulting in a positive market allocation contribution) but be penalized by adverse currency movements (resulting in a negative currency allocation contribution).

2. *Superior security selection.*

This breakdown of relative performance is the simplest of many possibilities. IPA services use a variety of similar approaches and employ graphics in presenting their results.

Market Timing   Asset allocation varies over time, so that over a given performance period, there is a contribution made by *market timing*, due to the time-variation in weights w_j. Moreover, the contribution made by market timing can be further broken down and measured for each market (e.g., Japanese equity) by simply adjusting the risk level (beta) of each segment.

Factors and Styles   The performance within a segment can further be attributed to the choice of an investment style (see Sharpe (1992)). We discussed the factor/attribute approach in Chapter 7. Once a manager takes bets on various factors within a national market segment, an IPA system can analyze how much of the performance relative to the national market index can be attributed to each factor bet. For example, BARRA proposes a within-market performance attribution linked to the factors described in Chapter 7. If the manager of a Japanese stock segment overweighs some industry relative to the industry weight of the Japanese stock index, a deviation in performance will generally be attributable to this industry bet.

An Example of Output

Graphic displays of performance attribution are proposed by most IPA services. As mentioned, these services collect information on a large number of portfolios with comparable investment mandates. Exhibit 16.5 presents the comparison of the performance of a specific portfolio with that of a universe of managers with a similar mandate (non–North American equity). The performance attribution is presented here for one year. The left part of the exhibit gives the total return on the fund, the MSCI EAFE index, and a universe of 117 portfolios. The return of the studied portfolio is represented by a dot; that of the EAFE index is represented by a square. The distribution of the same statistics for the universe of managed funds surrounds the dot. For example, the return on the portfolio is 17.3% over the year, whereas the EAFE index went up by only 10.0%. The median of the universe had a return of about 13.1% (full line). The first quartile of the distribution (top 25% of the universe) is around 16.8% (dashed line), whereas the third quartile (bottom 25% of the universe) is around 10.8% (other dashed line). The best manager had a return of 21.6%, the worst one had a return of 6.3%. The portfolio ranked quite high in the universe; on a percentile scale of 0 to 100, its rank is 19. The performance relative to the EAFE index is attributed in the right part of Exh. 16.5. The relative performance of the portfolio is 7.3% (a return of 17.3% minus the return on the EAFE index of 10.0%). This can be decomposed into a market allocation contribution of 7.7%, a currency allocation contribution of –2.0%, and a stock selection contribution of 1.6%. The manager ranked high in the universe on asset allocation and stock selection but poorly on currency allocation.

More on Currency Management

Part of the total portfolio could be hedged against currency risk. This is usually done by *selling forward* foreign currencies against the base currency. As mentioned in Chapters 1 and 2, a forward currency *purchase* is equivalent to being long in

EXHIBIT 16.5

Analysis of Performance: Non-North American Equity Return in U.S. Dollars
(*One year ending September 1994*)

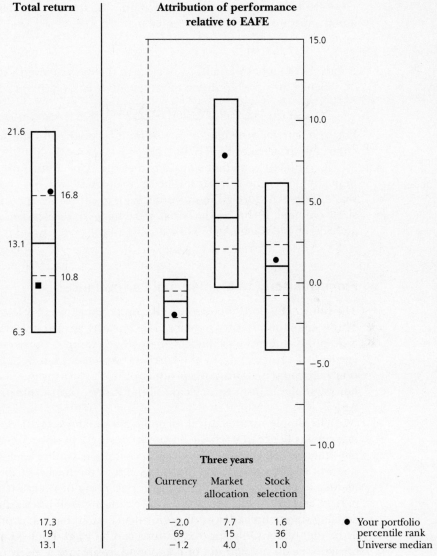

	Currency	Market allocation	Stock selection	
17.3	−2.0	7.7	1.6	Your portfolio
19	69	15	36	percentile rank
13.1	−1.2	4.0	1.0	Universe median

Source: InterSec Research Corp., Stamford, CT. Reprinted with permission.

foreign cash and short in the domestic (base-currency) cash. Assume that a portfolio is hedged for a proportion of w^f_j in currency j. This means that the forward *sale* of currency j represents $w^f_j\%$ of the total value of the portfolio, where w^f_j is a *negative* number (a sale). Then the equations above could be used assuming that $-w^f_j$ is invested in the base-currency short-term interest rate R_0 and that w^f_j is invested in the short-term interest rate of R_j of currency j. For example, if the portfolio is worth \$100 million and \$10 million worth of yen are sold forward, we have $w^f_j = -10\%$. Using a linear approximation,[5] the forward purchase of currency j has a pure-currency component c^f_j equal to:

$$c^f_j = s_j + R_j - R_0.$$

Remember that both c^f_j and c_j are close to the movement in exchange rate s_j.

Hence the decomposition of return given in Eq. (16.5) can be rewritten as:

$$r = \sum w_j p_j + \sum w_j d_j + \sum w_j c_j + \sum w^f_j c^f_j. \tag{16.10}$$

Likewise, currency hedging can also be incorporated in the "currency allocation contribution" term of Eq. (16.9).

A comment sometimes made is that the "fair" return on a currency component should not be zero, as implicitly assumed above, but should be the interest rate differential (foreign minus domestic), as this is the return that would be passively obtained if the currency risk were hedged; see Ankrim and Hensel (1994) and Singer and Karnosky (1995).

From Quarterly to Multiannual Performance

The return of a portfolio has been decomposed above in a *linearly additive* fashion. This is common industry practice. The linearity has been achieved by affecting all cross-product terms to a specific effect.[6] For example, the product of the percentage capital appreciation by the currency movement has been affected to the currency component. This cross-product of two returns is generally a smaller term. For example, if both returns are equal to 1%, their cross-product will be only 0.01%.

The simple mathematical formulas shown above break down when there are movements between portfolio segments during a period. Adjusting for these cash movements (i.e., changes in w_j over time) is not easy. The linearity of the decomposition of total time-weighted return, as well as the linear attribution of the performance, are not preserved in the compounding of successive periods. A multi-period extension of Eq. (16.9) with changing weights would prevent us from deriving simple breakdowns of performance such that each component could easily be identified. Only approximations can be used. Four quarterly performance breakdowns do not add up, or compound, easily into a yearly performance breakdown, even when time-weighted returns are used.

To summarize, we can get good indications on the attribution of performance, but one must realize that the numbers obtained are not, and can never be, more than good indicators.

Risk and Performance

Risk

The final step in performance analysis is to analyze the risk borne by the manager. The total risk of a portfolio is usually measured by the standard deviation of its rate of return. As we mentioned previously, return should be measured frequently (at least monthly) to get a reliable estimate of the standard deviation. Quarterly valuation does not give an up-to-date risk estimate in a rapidly changing environment, since at least four years of data (sixteen quarters) are required for a decent estimation of risk. Over several years, the risk estimate is likely to be very unstable.

Exhibit 16.6 compares risk and return on the portfolio in our previous example with that of several preselected indexes, where risk estimates (standard deviations) are computed from daily returns. To allow for meaningful risk and return comparisons, all estimates are presented on a monthly basis. The mandate of the manager was quite broad: The portfolio is to be global, and the base currency is the Swiss franc. We see that this portfolio had a higher return than the EAFE index (4.46% per month versus 1.05%) but had more risk (4.50% per month versus 3.02%). It also outperformed the U.S. Standard and Poor's and the Swiss SBC stock indexes. The risk of the portfolio measured assuming that all exchange rates stay fixed was 4.08%. This is called "risk in local currency."

The total risk of a portfolio is not the only relevant measure of risk. Investors who are interested primarily in diversification typically spread their assets among several funds. Pension funds, for example, invest abroad partly to diversify their domestic holdings. Calculating the correlation of a portfolio to other preselected

---

EXHIBIT 16.6

Risk Analysis
Risk-return statistics in Swiss francs: July 8–September 30

	Total Return (percent per month)	Risk (percent per month)	Correlation with Portfolio
Portfolio	4.46	4.50[a]	1
S & P 500 Index	4.24	6.50	0.43
EAFE Index	1.05	3.02	0.68
SBC Swiss Index	0.48	5.61	0.36

[a]Risk in local currency: 4.08

indexes reveals whether the benefits of diversification have been achieved. A low correlation means that there are great diversification benefits relative to the index; a correlation close to one indicates that the portfolio closely followed the performance of the index, even over the short run. Some services compute betas rather than correlation coefficients to derive the same type of information. (A beta coefficient is equal to the correlation coefficient times the ratio of the standard deviation of the portfolio over that of the market index.)

Risk estimates are often highly unstable over time because they are derived from a mixture of many types of assets and sources of uncertainty. Currency markets are particularly prone to periods of calm followed by periods of extreme volatility. Portfolios that are low risk during one period can experience a larger standard deviation, or beta, the next period. That is why an analysis of both past and present risk exposures is necessary.

Risk-Adjusted Performance

In a domestic setting performance measurement services often attempt to rank managers on their risk-adjusted performance. It seems attractive to derive a single number taking into account both performance and risk. This is often done by calculating a *reward* (mean excess return over the risk-free rate) *to variability* (standard deviation of return). This measure, introduced by Sharpe, is both simple and intuitive. However, it can be used only for the investor's global portfolio. A portfolio whose objective is to be invested in foreign assets to diversify risk of the domestic assets cannot be evaluated separately from the total portfolio. The standard deviation of the foreign portfolio will get partly diversified away in the global portfolio. The pertinent measure of risk of a portfolio devoted to foreign assets should be its *contribution* to the risk of the global portfolio of the client (see Jorion and Kirsten, 1991). Other methods take the ratio of mean excess return to the market risk (ß). These are often called the Treynor, or Jensen, measures. Unfortunately, the application of these methods poses some problems, as outlined by Roll (1978), in a domestic context. The problems are even worse in an international context, where we lack an asset pricing theory that precisely defines what is meant by market risk.

If risk is a complex, multidimensional notion, no single reward-to-risk ratio can be used, and we are left with a more qualitative discussion of the risk-return trade-off. IPA services display risk-return performance comparisons for the universe of managers they evaluate. An example for World equity portfolios is reproduced in Exh. 16.7. Each point in the exhibit is one managed portfolio from a universe of 45 portfolios with a global equity mandate. The annualized rate of return over four years is given on the *Y*-axis. The annualized standard deviation is given on the *X*-axis. The large dot represents the MSCI World index, which is a natural benchmark. The median return (about 12%) and risk (about 9.75%) of the universe are represented by a straight line. The best portfolios should lie in the upper-left quadrant of this graph (more return and less risk).

EXHIBIT 16.7

Risk-Return Performance Comparisons: World Equity Portfolios (US $)
(Four years ending 31 December 1994)

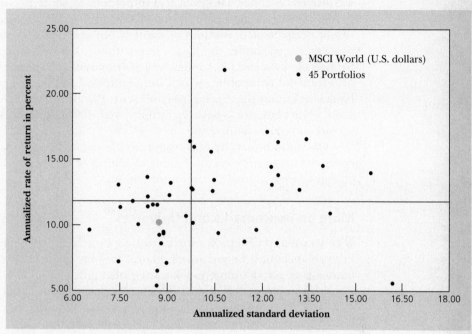

Source: Frank Russell Company. Reprinted with permission

Implementation

In-house performance measurement is useful in determining the strengths and weaknesses of an organization. This is even more important in an international than in a domestic setting because of the number of factors influencing return and risk. The development of an IPA system requires some sophisticated computer software, given the enormous mass of data that must be summarized into a few performance figures. The diversity of instruments, quotation and trading techniques, as well as information sources, renders the analysis susceptible to errors. However, a good investment organization should be able to master this issue. Ready-made performance software that can be linked to the money manager's accounting system has been developed by numerous companies. The difficult task is to bridge the performance software with the manager's database.

An IPA system can also be used by a client to select managers on the basis of their historical track records. This requires that the performance be measured by an independent service that computes performance on a universe of managers in a consistent manner. However, it is difficult to separate performance due to luck from that due to expertise. Past performance is often not a good indicator of future performance, whereas switching from one manager to the next is a costly process. For example, the Japanese portfolios of most foreign managers outperformed the Japanese stock index by a wide margin in the early 1980s. They focused on industrial companies, which outperformed the overall index, and held few bank stocks. But these same portfolios drastically underperformed the index in 1984, when bank stocks went up by more than 100% while stock prices in industrial sectors had only a modest rise.

One must be careful with respect to the statistical significance of performance comparisons to prevent inefficient churning of the portfolio and management changes based on insignificant information.

More on Benchmarks and Universes

A conceptual problem lies in choosing a benchmark for performance analysis. Performance must be measured relative to some norm. If the objective set by the trustee is to surpass some well-known global indexes, such as the Morgan Stanley Capital International World or EAFE stock index, or to invest solely in Japan, the standard for comparison is obvious. But what if the objectives are several or the fund comprises a variety of instruments, including bonds, time deposits, and gold? There is no such thing as a truly global index; nor is it clear what the proper weightings would be for such an index. Moreover, what if the objective is to create a portfolio having a minimum (or even a negative) correlation to U.S. assets or inflation? This objective might be chosen in order to maximize the diversification benefits of a foreign portfolio to the total fund. To what standard should we measure a fund's performance in that instance? The answer, once again, is unclear.

Standard global indexes are weighted by market capitalization. Some clients prefer indexes whose national allocation is based on different sets of weights—for example, relative national Gross Domestic Products (GDP). This gives to each country a weight proportional to its economic importance in world production. The problem with global indexes based on GDP weights is that they are difficult and costly to track in the managed portfolio. GDP figures stay constant for a few months and then are adjusted, whereas stock market prices move continuously; hence the portfolio must be continuously rebalanced to adjust to GDP weights. No passive investment strategy can replicate a GDP-weighted benchmark. Other clients wish to follow a global strategy with partial or total currency hedging. A specific currency-hedged benchmark must be designed to reflect this currency-hedging objective.

The manager's performance can be compared to that of a large universe of funds with similar objectives. Building a representative universe is not an easy task, because the guidelines imposed on international managers are very diverse. The universe is likely to include portfolios with fairly different mandates. Portfolio performance should therefore be measured both relative to the median return on the universe of similar funds and relative to the complete return distribution of those similar funds. But existing or prospective clients must be careful in assessing the dispersion in performance induced by the difference in investment guidelines of each fund.

AIMR and Other Performance Presentation Standards

Some countries have adopted performance presentation standards that apply to international portfolios. In the United States various regulations apply to different types of portfolios. Mutual funds have to follow rules edicted by the *Securities and Exchange Commission (SEC)*. Corporate pension funds apply the *Employee Retirement Income Security Act (ERISA)*. Public pension funds follow regulations edicted by the federal or local governments. These performance presentation regulations are not very restrictive and provide little guidance for internationally diversified portfolios.

The *Association for Investment Management and Research (AIMR)* implemented performance presentation standards in 1993. AIMR comprises the Financial Analysts Federation and the Institute of Chartered Financial Analysts (ICFA). The *AIMR Performance Presentation Standards*[7] are a set of detailed guiding ethical principles intended to promote full disclosure and fair representation by investment managers in reporting their investment results to existing and prospective clients. A secondary objective is to ensure uniformity in reporting so that results are directly comparable among investment managers. To this end some performance presentation aspects are mandatory, whereas others are only recommended. AIMR standards detail carefully the calculation and presentation of historical records of performance by base currency.

All AIMR members, CFAs, and candidates for the CFA designation are required to inform their employers about the existence and content of the standards and to encourage their employers to use the standards. An investment management firm must clearly state whether its performance presentation complies with AIMR standards.

The concept of *composites* is central to AIMR standards. All portfolios invested solely in U.S. or Canadian securities managed for U.S. or Canada-based clients must be presented in composites that adhere to AIMR standards. The idea is that an investment firm cannot present to existing or prospective clients a track record that is based only on a few selected accounts. The notion of composite is therefore central to the AIMR presentation standards and ensures that prospective clients have a fair and complete representation of a manager's past performance record. Each composite must comprise portfolios or asset classes representing a similar strategy or investment objective. Compliance must be met on a firmwide basis so that it applies to all portfolios. The definition of a firm entity has to be clarified for investment firms managing international assets and based in several countries. Investment managers have the option of defining firm entity as all assets managed to one or more base currencies. For example, two separate firm entities can be defined for assets managed with a U.S. dollar–base currency and for assets managed with a British pound–base currency. An investment firm has the option of complying with the standards for one base currency and not for the other.

Given the growing number of CFAs worldwide and the quality of the AIMR Performance Presentation Standards, their detailed reading is strongly recommended. However, the AIMR recognizes that performance presentation practices vary across the world and that it may not be practical for AIMR members residing outside the U.S. and Canada to meet compliance requirements. For example, British actuaries have edicted rules for U.K. pension funds. The *National Association of Pension Funds* (*NAPF*) has established British standards that *require* that performance be calculated by an outside service. This British industry practice of relying on outside services to calculate and present historical performance makes the aggregation into a composite more difficult if different outside services are used for different portfolios. The diversity of outside services is the rule for large investment firms, with many clients requesting that performance be calculated by their preferred actuarial service. In general, British standards are of good quality for international portfolios.

Industry practices in Continental Europe are lagging Anglo-American standards. The focus on performance is only recent among Europeans, partly because of the extensive reliance by institutional investors on in-house portfolio management. But performance presentation standards are likely to be formulated in the near future, given the development of pension funds and the internationalization of competition among investment managers.

Japan still relies extensively on book-value accounting of performance. In other words, unrealized profits or losses are not included in the calculation of the total rate of return. Deregulation and competition are progressively pushing Japan toward the Anglo-American approach to performance measurement.

Summary

1. The rate of return on a portfolio or on one of its segments can be measured using various methods to account for cash flows. The money-weighted rates measure the return on the average invested capital, whereas the time-weighted rate measures the return per unit of invested currency. The time-weighted rate should be used for performance analysis.

2. International performance analysis is important to understanding how performance has been achieved. A good performance analysis relies on the availability of data, and the problems are magnified in the international context. A major problem is that cash flows among the various portfolio segments are frequent, and calculation of the performance of each segment (e.g., Japanese equity) requires the valuation of segments on each cash flow date. Ideally, an international performance measurement system should be linked to the daily accounting system.

3. In active management superior performance can result from any of the major investment decisions: asset allocation (market and currency choices), market timing, and security selection on each market. The total performance should therefore be broken down and attributed to the various management decisions.

4. Risk reduction is an important motivation for international diversification, and the realized performance should be evaluated in light of the risk assumed. In terms of risk, the contribution of the foreign portfolio to the total risk of the global portfolio should be considered. In the absence of a clear model of international risk pricing, no simple measure of risk-adjusted performance can be used.

Questions and Problems

1*. An American pension fund wants to invest $1 million in foreign equity. Its board of trustees hesitates between investing in a commingled index fund tracking the EAFE index or giving the money to an active manager. The board learns that this active manager turns the portfolios over about twice a year. Given the small size of the account, the transaction costs are likely to be an average of 1.5% of each transaction's value. The active manager charges 0.75% in annual management fee, and the indexer charges 0.25%. By how much should the active manager outperform the index to cover the extra costs in the form of fees and transaction costs on the annual turnover?

2*. A U.S. pension fund has a domestic portfolio with a return of 10% and a standard deviation of 12%. It also invests in a foreign equity fund that has a dollar return of 11% and a dollar standard deviation of 20%. The correlation of the foreign and U.S. portfolio is 0.2. The current dollar interest rate is 8%. Would you say that the foreign equity portfolio is attractive from a risk/return viewpoint?

3. Is the total risk (standard deviation) of a foreign portfolio the relevant measure of risk? As an illustration, consider a U.S. pension fund with the following performance:

	Percentage Total Portfolio (percent)	Total Dollar Return (percent)	Standard Deviation of Return (percent)	Correlation with U.S. Stock Index
U.S. Equity	90	10	15	0.99
Foreign Equity	10	11	20	−0.10

- Is the risk-return performance of the foreign portfolio attractive?

4*. You are managing a portfolio worth 200 at the start of the period. After one month, the value of the portfolio is up to 220, and the client, who needs cash, withdraws 40. Two months later, the portfolio is still worth 180.

- Give various measures of the return on the portfolio over the three-month period.

5. A client has given you $100 million to invest abroad in an equity GDP-indexed fund. There are only two foreign countries, A and B, and their GDPs are currently equal to

$100 billion each. Their respective stock market capitalizations are $150 and $100 billion. The performance of the fund is compared monthly to the GDP-weighted index. Assume that exchange rates remain fixed and that there are no new listings on the stock markets, so that national market capitalizations go up and down in line with movements in the national stock indexes. Here are the stock market indexes and the published GDPs for the next six months:

Month	GDP_A	GDP_B	$Index_A$	$Index_B$
0	100	100	100	100
1	100	100	95	110
2	100	100	100	100
3	102	101	100	120
4	102	101	105	125
5	102	101	110	135

- Calculate the values at the end of each month of the two international indexes: GDP-weighted index and market-capitalization-weighted index. In both cases use the international weights (GDP and market capitalization) valid at the start of the month. Explain the difference.

- Assume that you build a portfolio using two national index funds. What operation should you do each month to track the GDP-weighted index?

6*. You own a portfolio of French and American stocks. There have been no movements during the year (cash flows, sales or purchase, dividend paid). Valuation and performance analysis is done in French francs. Here are the valuations at the start and the end of the year:

	January 1	December 31
French stocks	600,000 FF	660,000 FF
U.S. stocks	600,000 FF	702,000 FF
Total	*1,200,000 FF*	*1,362,000 FF*
Exchange rate	6 FF/$	5.4 FF/$
CAC Index	100	120
S&P Index	100	125

- What is the total return on the portfolio?
- Decompose this return into capital gain, yield, and currency contribution.
- What is the contribution of security selection?

7*. You own a portfolio of British assets worth £100,000 on January 1. The portfolio is worth £90,000 on January 10, and you withdraw £20,000. On January 20 the value of your portfolio has gone up to £90,000, and you add £50,000. On January 31 your portfolio is worth £145,000.

- Compute the rate of return in January, using the methods proposed in the text.

8. Investors are competing against one another. Professional investors now dominate the market. What should the average performance of all investors be compared to market indexes? If international investment managers, as a group, beat some national market index, what does it tell us about the performance of local investment managers?

Would you reach the opposite conclusion if international managers underperform, as a group, some local market index?

9. Take, successively, the viewpoint of a Japanese, European, and American investor. Can their foreign portfolio outperform their domestic portfolio simultaneously? Does it mean that international diversification cannot be beneficial to all of them from a risk-adjusted viewpoint?

10. Case Study

Mr. Smith is an investor of foreign nationality who has an account with a small Luxembourg bank. He does not pay taxes on his account. He gave a complete management mandate to the bank and wants to judge the performance of the manager. He is using the U.S. dollar as his base currency.

1. He is looking at the two most recent valuation monthly reports, which are given in Exh. 16.8, and wonders how to compute the performance. He reads in the financial press that the Morgan Stanley Capital International world index has risen by 2% this month (in U.S. dollars). Basically, he would like to answer the following questions:

▪ What is the total return on his portfolio?

▪ What are the sources of this return, i.e., how much is caused by capital appreciation, yield, and currency movements?

▪ How good is the manager in selecting securities on the various markets?

You must give him precise, quantified information that will help him to answer these questions. (First, compute the return for each segment of the portfolio and its components, i.e., price, yield, currency; then combine these returns to answer the last two queries.)

2. Mr. Smith is aware that cash flows, as well as movements among the various segments of his portfolio, may obscure his analysis. He tries to compute the performance during the next month where the manager has been more active.

He wants to make sure he understands how a valuation report is constructed before doing his analysis (he does not trust his banker). He gets the following information to prepare his own version of the valuation report:

Cash flow. Mr. Smith added $10,000 to his account.

Transactions. The manager sold the 500 Exxon. The total proceeds of the sale, net of commissions, were $20,000. He bought 400 Pernod-Ricard on the Paris bourse for a total cost of $30,860.

Income received. A semiannual coupon was paid on the EIB bond for a total receipt of $575. AMAX dividends were $357.

Market prices on February 28.

AMAX	24	Dollar/yen	0.0047
Hitachi	880	Dollar/French franc	0.105
TDK	6000	U.S. stock index	103
Club Méditerranée	850	Japan stock index	97
Pernon-Ricard	720	France stock index	110
Government 6% 92	92	Yen bond index	101
(accrued interest, 1.55%)		World index	104
EIB 8.5% 93	98		
(accrued interest, 0.62%)			

Mr. Smith has no indication of the exact day of the transactions, and it would be too complicated to break down the month into subperiods, anyway. He therefore decides to make the assumption that every transaction or cash flow occurred just before the end of the month and at month-end exchange rate. To help him, you should

- Establish a new valuation report (see Exh. 16.8)
- Discuss the methodology for adjusting for cash movements
- Analyze the performance of the manager

EXHIBIT 16.8

Account Valuation Reports (explanation)

The valuation report is set up following a standard method:

- Column 1 describes the security and its quotation currency.

- Column 2 gives either the number of securities for common stocks or the nominal invested for fixed income.

- Column 3 gives the market price in local currency. For bonds, this is given in percentage of the nominal (par) value.

- The accrued interest is given in column 4 as the percentage of the nominal (par) value. Usually a yen bond with a coupon of, say, 8% will bear an interest of 8/365% per day. This is cumulated in the accrued-interest column until the coupon is paid (semiannual, here).

- Column 5 gives the capital amount in base currency (here, U.S. dollars). It is the market price (column 3) multiplied by the column 2 values multiplied by the exchange rate.

- Column 6 gives the amount of accrued interest in base currency. It is the accrued interest in percentage (column 4) multiplied by the column 2 values multiplied by the exchange rates.

- Columns 7 and 8 give subtotals in capital and percentage.

(continued on next page)

EXHIBIT 16.8 (CONTINUED)

Account valuation for Mr. Smith, December 31, 1990

Description of Security (1)	Number of Securities or Nominal (2)	Market Price (local cur.) (3)	Accrued Interest (%) (4)	Capital Amount (US$) (5)	Accrued Interest (US$) (6)	Sub- total (US$) (7)	Sub- total (%) (8)
Equity							
United States (in $)							
AMAX	1,000	24.50		24,500			
Exxon	500	37.25		18,256		43,125	29.8
Japan (in Yen)							
Hitachi	10,000	800		34,320			
TDK	1,000	6,500		27,885		62,205	43.0
France (in FF)							
Club Med	200	770		18,326		18,326	12.7
Bonds							
Yen							
Govt 6% 92	2,000,000	91.0%	0.52%	7,807	45		
EIB 8.5% 93	3,000,000	98.5%	3.47%	12,677	447	20,976	14.5
Cash							
US dollars	0			0	0	0	0
Total				**144,140**	**492**	**144,632**	**100**

Exchange rates:
Yen = 0.00429 dollar
FF = 0.119 dollar

Market indexes (price only):
U.S. stocks = 100   Yen bonds = 100
Japan stocks = 100   World index = 100
France stocks = 100

(continued on next page)

EXHIBIT 16.8 (CONTINUED)

Account valuation for Mr. Smith, January 30, 1991

Description of Security (1)	Number of Securities or Nominal (2)	Market Price (local cur.) (3)	Accrued Interest (%) (4)	Capital Amount (US$) (5)	Accrued Interest (US$) (6)	Sub-total (US$) (7)	Sub-total (%) (8)
Equity							
United States (in $)							
AMAX	1,000	23.50		23,500			
Exxon	500	38.00		19,000		42,500	28.8
Japan (in Yen)							
Hitachi	10,000	820		36,900			
TDK	1,000	6,100		27,450		64,350	43.5
France (in FF)							
Club Med	200	870		19,140		19,140	12.9
Bonds							
Yen							
Govt 6% 92	2,000,000	90.0%	1.04	8,100	94		
EIB 8.5% 93	3,000,000	96.9%	4.16	13,081	562	21,837	14.8
Cash							
US dollars	0			0	0	0	0
Total				**147,171**	**656**	**147,827**	**100**

Exchange rates:
  Yen = 0.0045 dollar
  FF = 0.1100 dollar

Market indexes (price only):
  U.S. stocks = 102.5   Yen bonds = 99
  Japan stocks = 98   World index = 102
  France stocks = 108

Notes

1. See Bank Administration Institute (1968), Tapley (1986), or AIMR (1993).

2. The author is grateful to Lombard Odier for providing this example. The example is further detailed in T. Lombard and B. Solnik, "International Performance Measurement," Lombard Odier & Cie, June 1983.

3. For simplicity, assume that the dividend is paid at the exchange rate prevailing at the end of the period.

4. Remember that c_j and C_j are close to s_j, the exchange rate movement, so that the currency allocation contribution is close to $\Sigma(w_j - w_j^*)s_j$.

5. The exact movement in the forward exchange rate can be deducted from equations provided in Chapters 1 and 2.

6. This is sometimes justified by saying that the linear decomposition of returns would be exact (i.e., not imply any cross-product terms) if continuously compounded returns were used. This statement is incorrect, as all students of continuous-time finance and of Ito's lemma learn.

7. The following analysis is derived from AIMR, *Performance Presentation Standards 1993*, Charlottesville, VA: AIMR, 1993.

Bibliography

AIMR. *Performance Presentation Standards 1993*, Charlottesville, VA: AIMR, 1993.

Ankrim, E.M., and Hensel, C.R. "Multicurrency Performance Attribution," *Financial Analysts Journal*, March-April 1994.

Bank Administration Institute. *Measuring the Investment Performance of Pension Funds*, Parkridge, IL: 1968.

Brinson, G.P., and Fachler, N. "Measuring non-US Equity Portfolio Performance," *Journal of Portfolio Management*, Spring 1985.

Brinson, G.P., Singer, B.D., and Beebower, G.L. "Determinants of Portfolio Performance II: An Update," *Financial Analysts Journal*, May-June 1991.

Gillies, J. "Performance Measurement. The Practical Aspects," *Benefits International*, November 1982.

Jorion, P., and Kirsten, G. "The Right Way to Measure International Performance," *Journal of Investing*, Spring 1991.

Karnosky, D.S., and Singer, B.D. *Global Asset Management and Performance Attribution*, Charlottesville, VA: The Research Foundation of the IFCA, 1994.

Lombard, T., and Solnik, B. "Computing Complexities of Foreign Investment," *Pensions and Investment Age*, October 29, 1984.

————. "International Performance Measurement," Lombard Odier & Cie, June 1983.

Nowakowski, C. "International Performance Measurement: Problems and Solutions," *Columbia Journal of World Business*, May 1982.

Roll, R. "Ambiguity When Performance Is Measured by the Securities Market Line," *Journal of Finance*, September 1978.

Sharpe, W.F., "Asset Allocation: Management Style and Performance Measurement," *Journal of Portfolio Management*, Winter 1992.

Singer, B.D., and Karnosky, D.S. "The General Framework for Global Investment Management and Performance Attribution," *Journal of Portfolio Management*, Winter 1995.

Tapley, M. "Accounting and Performance Measurement," in *International Portfolio Management*, Euromoney Publications, 1986.

17

Structuring the International Investment Process

A n organization that is planning to invest internationally first needs the information on institutions and techniques provided in the beginning of this book. Then the organization needs to properly structure its entire international investment decision process, from research to management and control. Among the many international investment organizations in the world today, there are a great variety of approaches to structuring the international investment process. Different approaches reflect different investment philosophies and strategies.

This chapter starts with a review of the major choices facing an international investment organization. We then discuss some important issues in terms of international asset allocation. This chapter concludes with an example of an integrated approach to international money management.

Investment Philosophy

International investment has been growing rapidly among institutional investors of all nationalities. This is shown in Exh. 17.1, which indicates the growth in institutional assets and in the proportion invested abroad. Investment managers worldwide can no longer treat foreign investments as an exotic, minor decision, and they must now have a clear view of how they approach global investing. An organization must make certain major choices in structuring its international decision process, based on several factors:

- Its view of the world regarding price behavior

- Its strengths, in terms of research and management

- The available data, communication, and computer technology

- Its marketing strategy

EXHIBIT 17.1

Pension Funds: Growth in Total and Foreign Assets (in billions of dollars)

Country	Pension Fund Assets			% Invested Abroad		
	1988	1993	1998 est.	1988	1993	1998 est.
United States	2,085	3,650	5,470	3.0	7.2	11.5
Japan	522	1,022	1,600	6.3	9.0	12.0
Britain	456	814	1,050	18.7	28.0	28.0
Canada	145	250	350	6.1	10.3	16.0
Netherlands	178	245	340	9.5	15.2	21.1
Switzerland	129	201	310	4.0	8.6	11.6
Germany	75	118	165	3.5	4.5	5.1
Australia	44	80	145	9.8	15.4	19.4
Sweden	54	78	120	0	1.1	6.0
Denmark	28	52	85	0.4	5.7	8.7
France	16	44	60	1.0	3.5	6.0
Hong Kong	7	23	67	62.1	56.5	61.1
Ireland	8	15	23	23.0	30.0	35.0
Rest of the world	129	256	311	5.3	8.2	12.2

Source: InterSec Research Corporation

These important choices are discussed below in terms of investment philosophy and strategy.

Active or Passive

The Passive Approach   A fund managed according to a passive approach simply reproduces a market index of all securities. This type of fund is often called an *index fund.* The sole purpose of an index fund is to exactly track the return on a selected market index, to capitalize on its long-term performance while keeping all costs at a minimum. The passive approach is an international extension of modern portfolio theory, which claims that the market portfolio should be efficient. In the United States the domestic index fund approach is supported by extensive empirical evidence of the efficiency of the stock market. A similar domestic index fund approach has developed in the United Kingdom and, more recently, in Japan and in other European countries. Large pension funds have extensively moved to indexing their *domestic* assets. In the early 1990s U.S. public pension funds had indexed over 40% of their domestic equity investments. U.S. corporate pension funds and U.K. pension funds had indexed over 25% of their domestic equity investments.

The trend toward *international* indexing is strongly felt among institutional investors. A large number of pension funds worldwide have moved to passive international investment strategies. The basic argument supporting the passive index approach is that the alternative, an active strategy, requires above-average ability at forecasting markets or currencies or both. Forecasting is never easy and, moreover, entails higher commissions and costs. With a passive strategy, the fund can achieve the full benefits of international risk diversification without incurring these high costs.

Various indexing methods can be used:

- *Full replication.* All securities in the index are bought, with proper weighting. This method is impossible internationally, given the huge number of securities involved.

- *Stratified sampling.* This approach tracks the index by holding a representative sample of securities. The securities are grouped according to various criteria (country, firm's size, industry, yield), and the index fund sample attempts to replicate the characteristics of the index along the various criteria.

- *Optimization sampling.* This is a sampling method using factor models (see Chapter 7) to minimize the tracking error of the index. It is a sophisticated statistical method based on a large number of factors, or firm's attributes, and using optimization techniques based on historical relationships.

- *Synthetic replication.* A stock index can be replicated by using a futures contract on the index plus a cash position. The fair pricing of the futures ensures a good tracking of the index, and transaction costs are low. For many investors legal aspects constrain the use of this approach on a global scale. For example, only a few foreign futures contracts have been approved by the U.S. CFTC (Commodity Futures Trading Commission).

One should be aware that indexing reduces costs but that perfect tracking of an international index is not feasible. For example, whenever a dividend is paid in one currency—say, the Italian lira—it should be simultaneously reinvested in all international securities with proper weights, an impossible task. Indexing requires superior computer, administrative, and trading technology and exhibits large economies of scale. As the quality of the indexor shows up quickly, and objectively, in the form of a low tracking error, only the best indexors are likely to capture a large market share of this management style.

The remaining issue that is discussed later is the choice of the international benchmark to be passively tracked.

The Active Approach   In an active strategy, investors place bets on the various factors that affect securities behavior. Of course, the strategy itself depends on the investor's view of the world. Active decisions of a manager show up at various levels:

- *Asset allocation.* This is the choice of national markets and currencies. The manager can select long-term weights that differ from those of market indexes, such as the EAFE index. This long-term allocation is often called *strategic* allocation. Periodic revisions in the weights can be justified by changes in market expectations or risk estimates. This is often called *tactical* asset allocation. These decisions are further discussed later in the chapter.

- *Security selection.* To achieve a given asset allocation, the manager can engage in an active selection of securities within each market, to beat that market.

- *Market timing.* The manager can resort to market timing to temporarily increase or reduce the exposure in one or more markets or currencies. This is a short-term trading tactic (as opposed to long-run strategies for allocating assets) that often involves the use of derivatives.

A manager can be active in some dimension and not in others. For example, an active asset allocation management can be achieved using national index funds for each market. Conversely a manager could stick to a fixed asset allocation, using active security selection within each market.

The risk diversification argument is usually at the heart of the marketing pitch made by both active and passive international money managers. In the quickly changing international environment, active money managers have a special need to evaluate and to control the risk of their portfolios as rapidly as possible. Taking active bets on markets, currencies, or securities could result in portfolios that turn out to be quite risky and do not provide the international risk diversification benefits so widely claimed.

The Empirical Evidence The case for indexing a large *domestic* portfolio is clear. Since most securities follow the domestic market behavior to a large degree, any well-diversified domestic portfolio tends to track the domestic market index. Indexing allows the manager to capture this domestic market performance while minimizing management and transaction costs. However, foreign markets tend to be very independent of one another. This independence, when combined with substantial currency movements, means that different international asset allocations will yield very different returns.

Academic research has demonstrated the efficiency of individual national stock markets (see Chapter 5 references) and has shown that passive national indexes were not easy to beat systematically. However, no study has yet established that the world market portfolio is indeed optimal and that active international asset allocation strategies cannot consistently outperform the passive approach. An examination of the performance of international investment managers shows that different active strategies can lead to very different returns and that the passive approach is not consistently the best strategy. The wide dispersion of performance among international portfolios is illustrated in Exhs. 17.2 and 17.3. Exhibit 17.2 shows the distribution of the non-U.S. equity returns of a large number of U.S. pension fund portfolios, as tracked by InterSec for each year from 1986 to 1994. As in Exh. 16.5, InterSec gives the median, first, and third quartiles of the distribution of all portfolios, as well as the return on the EAFE index. As a group, the universe

EXHIBIT 17.2

Annual Return on Non-U.S. Equity Universe of Managers
(in U.S. dollars, based on 85 to 117 portfolios)

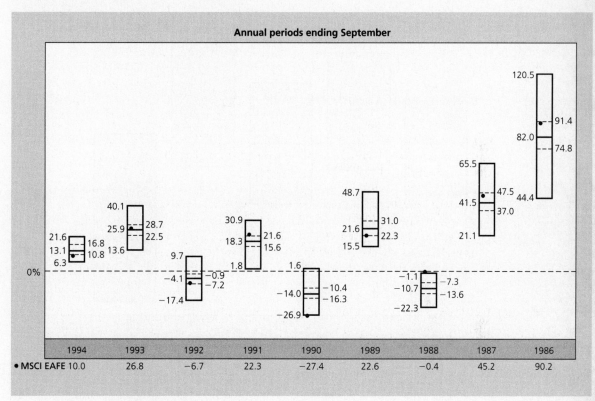

Annual periods ending September

	1994	1993	1992	1991	1990	1989	1988	1987	1986
● MSCI EAFE	10.0	26.8	−6.7	22.3	−27.4	22.6	−0.4	45.2	90.2

Source: InterSec Research Corp., Stamford, CT. Reprinted with permission.

of managers has systematically underperformed the EAFE benchmark in 1988 and outperformed it in 1990. This can be explained by the fact that international managers tend to allocate to Japan a smaller share than its market-capitalization weight used in the EAFE index. When the Tokyo stock market booms, international managers will tend to underperform the EAFE index, and vice versa. Over the ten years ending in December 1994, the median return of the InterSec universe is exactly equal to that of the EAFE index (an annualized 18.6% in dollar terms). Exhibit 17.3 provides return information on a universe of World equity portfolios, as tracked by Frank Russell Company. Over the five-year period ending December 1994, the median manager has beaten the World index by an annualized 3.3%. Risk-adjusted comparisons over the same universe have been provided in Exh. 16.7.

EXHIBIT 17.3

Return on World Equity Universe of Managers
(annualized rates in U.S. dollars, based on 45 to 50 portfolios)

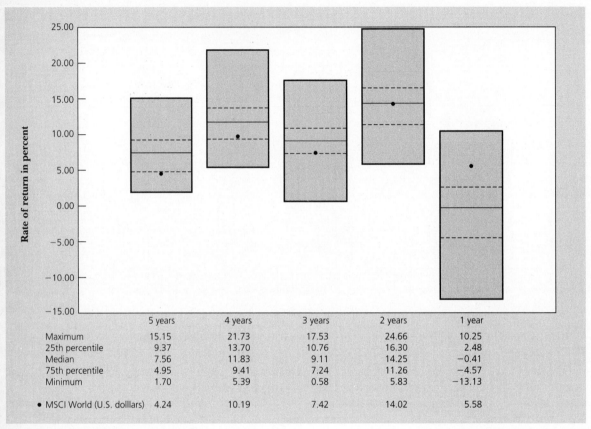

	5 years	4 years	3 years	2 years	1 year
Maximum	15.15	21.73	17.53	24.66	10.25
25th percentile	9.37	13.70	10.76	16.30	2.48
Median	7.56	11.83	9.11	14.25	−0.41
75th percentile	4.95	9.41	7.24	11.26	−4.57
Minimum	1.70	5.39	0.58	5.83	−13.13
● MSCI World (U.S. dolllars)	4.24	10.19	7.42	14.02	5.58

Source: Frank Russell Company. Reprinted with permission.

Top-Down or Bottom-Up

Domestically, portfolio managers use either a top-down or a bottom-up approach to the investment process. The same is true internationally.

Top-Down Approach   The manager using a top-down approach first allocates his or her assets and then selects individual securities to satisfy that allocation. The most important decision in this approach is the choice of markets and currencies. In other words, the global money manager must choose from among several markets (stocks, bonds, or cash) as well as a variety of currencies. Once these choices have been made, the manager selects the best securities available in each market.

Bottom-Up Approach   The bottom-up approach is most often used in international equity portfolios. The manager using this approach studies the fundamentals of many individual stocks, from which he or she selects the best securities (irrespective of their national origin or currency denomination) to build a portfolio. For example, a manager may be bullish on car manufacturers and buy shares in all of them (GM, Toyota, Volkswagen, Peugeot, etc.); or the manager may buy shares in only the best electronics firm in the world, regardless of its national origin. The product of this approach is a portfolio with a market and currency allocation that is more or less the random result of the securities selected. Implicit in this approach is the manager's greater concern with risk exposure in various sectors than with either market or currency risk exposure.

Conclusion   Many organizations claim to combine a top-down with a bottom-up approach. But this is not easy to achieve: To be consistent, the entire investment decision process should be structured along a single approach. For example, a research department using the top-down approach focuses on country and currency analysis. Typically, financial analysts in the department are specialized by country. On the other hand, financial analysts using the bottom-up approach are specialized by worldwide industry. Accommodating these contrasting professional requirements is not easy.

The empirical evidence presented in previous chapters showed that all securities within a single market tend to move together, but national markets and currencies do not. This underscores the fact that the major factor contributing to portfolio performance is the choice of markets and currencies, not individual securities. Indeed, a variety of international performance measurement services have shown that the performance of international money managers is attributable mainly to asset allocation, not to superior security selection. This, in turn, suggests that an international investment organization should be organized along primarily top-down lines, and its analysts should be specialized by country, and possibly by a few international sectors, such as energy companies or automobile manufacturers. The dominance of a top-down approach with a priority on country analysis is evidenced in Exh. 17.4. Frank Russell found that the average international manager puts 50% of his or her resources into country analysis, only about 15% into industry analysis, and 35% into company analysis (see Botkin, 1986).

Global or Specialized

European managers have traditionally been global money managers. Typically, a Swiss bank will manage all the assets of a customer and determine both the asset allocation and the selection of each security for the portfolio. By contrast, American managers often tend to specialize in particular investment areas, such as Japanese stocks, Eurobonds, or energy stocks. These specialized managers often handle specific funds that a customer can buy into, to diversity away his or her portfolio risk. The allocation decision is then made by the customer based on advice he or she gets from one or several managers. Thus it is not unusual to find

EXHIBIT 17.4

Investment Philosophy: Relative Emphasis Universe of 30 International Investment Firms

	Low	Medium	High
Country analysis	7	9	14

	Low	Medium	High
Industry analysis	15	9	6

	Low	Medium	High
Company analysis	5	16	9

Source: Frank Russell Company. Reprinted with permission.

investors with the bulk of their international portfolio in a passive, well-diversified fund and the remainder invested in a few active funds in specialized areas.

The trend toward specialized international management is derived from the fact that no manager is a superior expert on all markets, though some are superior on one or a few markets. Because asset allocation is potentially the most profitable decision, a combination of global and specialized management is required. Global management is the only reasonable solution for the small investor, whereas large investors may afford both global and specialized management.

Currency

Some managers treat currencies only as residual variables; their currency breakdown is determined by the countries, industries, and securities they select for the portfolio. They generally consider currency risk a necessary evil and argue that currency movements are impossible to predict and wash out in the long run, anyway, since it is the real economic variables that ultimately determine a portfolio's performance.

Other managers fully hedge their foreign portfolios or decide on a permanent hedge ratio based on a historical estimate. This strategy is based on some of the theories outlined in Chapter 5 or on the belief that foreign currency risk premia are small or unpredictable and hence that one is not compensated for carrying foreign exchange risk.

Still other managers take a proactive approach to currency forecasting. They try to minimize the contribution currency makes to total risk and cash in on opportunities created by currency movements. These managers prefer the currency-asset allocation method.

At the extreme end of the spectrum, we find a new brand of international money managers. These *currency-overlay* managers actively manage the currency exposure of a portfolio and often resort to currency options and forward or futures contracts for selective hedging and speculation.

Naturally, the approach an investment manager takes toward currencies leads to very different portfolio strategies.

Quantitative or Subjective

Quantification of the investment process is very helpful in international investment management because of the large number of parameters and decision variables it involves. Quantification can be applied to various models or aids used in the investment process, including:

- Econometric or technical forecasting models of markets and currencies

- International asset allocation optimizers

- Dividend-discount models, factor models, duration models, or option valuation models (for quantitative assessment of individual securities)

- Risk management models

- Performance and risk analysis

Other managers rely primarily on subjective judgment. In either case a great deal of information is required before decisions can be made. The difference between the two approaches is that managers who favor the subjective approach argue that the international environment is too complex to permit formal quantification. They say that models based on past data are not helpful, because constant changes in the international environment distort them.

A breakdown of international institutional managers according to investment philosophy and strategy is shown in Exh. 17.5. A vast majority of investment managers claim some degree of active management (82%). Although the top-down approach dominates the bottom-up approach, a majority of managers claim to do both.

From Strategic to Tactical

The most important international investment decision is the selection of an asset allocation. The first step for an international investor is to decide on a *strategic asset allocation,* or the structure of the portfolio for the long term. The asset allocation is periodically adapted to reflect changes in the market environment; this is referred to as *tactical asset allocation.*

EXHIBIT 17.5

Investment Philosophies of 112 International Money Managers of U.S. Pension Funds

Investment Philosophy	Managers Claiming the Philosophy (%)
Active	82
Passive	18
Top-down	34
Top-down and bottom-up	53
Bottom-up	13
Active asset allocation process	39
Currency emphasis	32
Quantitative overlay	39
Value orientation	26
Contrarian	4

Source: InterSec Research Corporation, Stamford, CT. Reprinted with permission.

Strategic Asset Allocation

In *institutional* money management the strategic asset allocation often takes the form of an investable benchmark that is assigned as an objective by the fund trustee to the manager. As the performance of the portfolio is measured against this benchmark, it provides a strong guide to the manager's investment policy.

The question that remains is the choice of the proper international benchmark. Three important issues are:

- The scope of the benchmark

- The set of weights chosen

- The attitude toward currency risk

Scope of International Benchmark   A truly global investor should include all asset classes, domestic and foreign, in the global benchmark. This global benchmark could then be broken down into various subbenchmarks that can be assigned to different investment managers. In practice many investors treat domestic and foreign investments as different asset classes. For example, a Dutch pension fund could decide to invest 25% of its assets out of the Netherlands, with half invested in foreign stocks and half invested in foreign bonds. Then the Dutch pension fund could assign the MSCI or FT-Actuaries World index to the foreign equity manager and the Salomon Brothers or J.P. Morgan World bond index to the foreign bond manager. These international indexes could be calculated by excluding the Netherlands from the indexes. Note that the global asset allocation will be strongly biased toward Dutch assets, so that the natural benchmark for the total assets of the pension fund will not be some market-capitalization weighted World index. Even within equity, the distinction is often made between investments in developed and emerging markets, which are usually treated as different asset classes.

Weights in the International Benchmark   A whole range of approaches is used to determine the benchmark weights. The simplest, most commonly used approach is to use some *published international market index*. The weights are proportional to the relative market capitalizations. A market-capitalization-weighted index is a natural implication of the theory. It can be easily replicated in a passive strategy as the weights change in line with price movements in the portfolio. This type of international index is widely published and used commonly by institutional investors throughout the world. Hence the performance can easily be compared across funds and managers.

However, market-capitalization-weighted indexes suffer form some problems. In Chapter 6 we indicted that extensive cross-holding of shares by Japanese companies significantly inflates the reported market capitalization for Japan. When two companies hold shares in the other one, one cannot simply add their stock market capitalization; their share cross-holding has to be removed from the addition. This phenomenon also affects other markets, such as Germany and some other European countries. Some managers have suggested using *GDP country weights* instead of market capitalization country weights. The idea is interesting, since it gives each country a weight proportional to its economic strength. But implementing it is not easy and is fairly costly in a passive portfolio that needs to be rebalanced each time a new GDP figure is published or revised in any country. The same problem shows up when a given stock market goes up or down, while the GDP weights stay constant.

The inclusion of bonds and cash investments in a variety of currencies makes the concept of a world market portfolio very difficult to measure and implement. As mentioned in Chapter 5, the World market portfolio would not be optimal, even in efficient markets, because of differences in currency, consumption preferences, transaction costs, or differential tax treatments. A large institutional investor will therefore treat each asset class separately. For example, it could assign three separate benchmarks for developed stock markets, emerging stock markets, and foreign bonds. This leaves open the question of the strategic global asset allocation across all asset classes. Different investor groups should follow different core strategies that reflect their situation and comparative advantage in terms of costs, taxes, and risks. This has led numerous institutional investors to select a *customized international benchmark*. The strategic allocation is often determined by conducting optimization studies based on long-term historical results for the various asset classes. Long-term usually means the past 25 or 100 years. Although historical returns and risk figures provide useful insights, one cannot claim that they will exactly repeat in the future. Hence various visions of the world for the next decade will lead to various strategic allocations of funds. The problem with these customized benchmarks is the lack of comparability across managers and portfolios.

Currency   Should foreign investments be systematically hedged against currency risks? This question has led to an extensive controversy already addressed in Chapters 4 and 5.

In theory the optimal asset allocation should be the world market portfolio, *partly* hedged against currency risk (Solnik, 1974; and Adler and Dumas, 1983). From an operational viewpoint, the optimal hedge ratios cannot be determined, as they are functions of unobservable parameters, such as the distribution of investors' risk aversion and relative wealth. Under very special assumptions, Black (1990) has suggested that the currency hedge ratios should be constant and the same for all investors.[1] This is a result of market equilibrium in a theoretical world where, among other assumptions, each investor holds the market portfolio and exhibits the same risk aversion and where there is no net foreign investment (the wealth of each country is exactly equal to its assets value). Clearly this approach is not satisfactory. In reality the composition of all portfolios exhibits a strong domestic bias.

An extreme version of this approach is the full-hedging recommendation of Perold and Schulman (1988).[2] Their argument is that holding foreign currencies provides no systematic return compensation in the form of a risk premium (expected return in excess of the risk-free rate) but forces one to bear additional risk, in the form of exchange risk. Hence the only preoccupation in the strategic currency allocation should be risk-minimization, leading to full hedging. This point is stressed by looking at the volatility of various foreign asset classes with and without currency hedging. Unhedged investments are systematically more volatile than currency-hedged investments. This simple approach has been severely attacked from many angles:

- First, theory tells us that currency risk premia should exist if some countries are net foreign investors (say, Japan) or exhibit more risk aversion than others.

- Second, numerous empirical studies have claimed the existence of currency risk premia, although of a time-varying nature (see Chapter 3).

- Third, the relevant measure of risk should not be the volatility of the foreign assets taken in isolation but their contribution to the total risk of the global portfolio (domestic and foreign). Indeed, currencies provide an element of monetary risk diversification to the domestic portfolio. As long as the proportion of foreign assets in the total portfolio is small (say, less than 10%), the contribution of currency risk is minimal and not worth the trouble and costs of engaging in systematic currency hedging (see Nesbitt, 1991; and Jorion, 1989).

Even the underlying side of this full-hedging approach, namely, that currency hedging reduces the volatility of return on foreign assets, has been contradicted. The question is the investor's time horizon. A pension fund has a long-term objective and should not care about short-horizon risk, such as monthly or quarterly volatility. Given the structure of its liabilities, a pension fund should rather focus on the risk that a sufficient return will not be realized over a long horizon, e.g., five or ten years. Froot (1993) shows, theoretically and empirically, that the risk-minimizing currency hedge is a function of the investment horizon. With a horizon of five years foreign stocks display a greater return volatility when hedged than unhedged. The reason for this finding is the mean-reversion in exchange rates. Over the short run, currency returns are explained mostly by changes in the real exchange rate. In the long run the purchasing powers of two currencies tend toward parity, and exchange rate trends are explained mostly by the inflation differential between the two currencies. Whether a fund trustee or an investment manager, whose jobs are at stake in the short run, will feel easy with measuring performance and risk solely on such a long horizon is another question.

To summarize, the extent of strategic currency hedging remains an open theoretical and empirical question. In the absence of a natural benchmark dictated by theory or systematic empirical observation, investors have taken different routes. Some are using different currency-hedging strategies for different asset classes. They keep their foreign-stock benchmark unhedged while fully hedging their foreign-bond benchmark, because currency risk is relatively more important for bonds than for stocks (see Chapter 4). Currency-hedged international indexes are now available for both stocks and bonds from the major index providers.

Tactical Asset Allocation

Active managers adjust their asset allocation periodically, typically monthly but sometimes more often, to reflect changes in the market environment. This is called dynamic, or *tactical asset allocation* (*TAA*). This revision is *conditional* on some new information. There is now extensive evidence that the direction of stock and bond prices can be predicted to some extent by using a set of information variables. As mentioned in Chapter 5, this does not necessarily imply that markets are inefficient; this predictability could also be explained by a time variation in risk premia justified by a change in the socioeconomic environment. In statistical jargon the strategic asset allocation could be based on long-term, unconditional risk premia; the tactical asset allocation, on conditional risk premia.

Predictability of International Asset Returns   Several variables have been shown to help predict the direction of stock and bond prices worldwide.[3] We are talking here about national market movements, not individual securities. The forecasting models are called *conditional risk-premium models* because they provide an estimate of the expected asset return in excess of the risk-free rate, conditional on a set of information variables. Most of the studies use publicly observable financial variables (such as various measures of interest rates or dividend yield), some average national valuation variables (such as the ratios of "price to book value" or "price to earnings"), and some technical characteristics of asset returns (such as serial correlation and January seasonality). Emanuelli and Pearson (1994) further suggest that "revisions in analysts' earning estimates for the companies in a country can be used to select countries that will provide above-average returns." They use the I/E/B/E/S International database. Arnott and Henriksson (1989), Ferson and Harvey (1994) and Dumas (1994) used some macroeconomic indicators to forecast subsequent national stock price movements. Of course, the economic indicators must be publicly available before the forecast is formulated. The poor quality of economic data make them more difficult to use than financial data that do not suffer from measurement error.

To illustrate these findings, Exh. 17.6 indicates the forecasting power reported by Solnik (1993*b*) for the eight major stock and bond markets in the world over the period 1971–1991. These are the adjusted R-square of a regression of various financial variables observed at time t, on the excess return of the various indices at time $t + 1$. A similar forecasting model is estimated for the seven exchange rates of the foreign currencies relative to the U.S. dollar. The frequency of observation is monthly; the forecasting variables used are:

EXHIBIT 17.6

Explanatory Power for Various Markets
(percentage of variance explained (adjusted R-square))

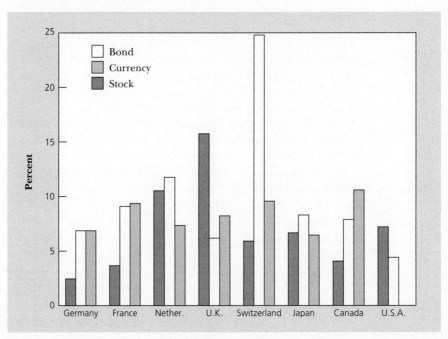

Source: B. Solnik, *Predictable Time-Varying Components of International Asset Returns*, Charlottesville, VA: The Research Foundation of the Institute of Chartered Financial Analysts, 1993.

- The national one-month interest rate

- The national term spread (long- minus short-term interest rate)

- The national dividend yield

- The interest rate differential (national minus U.S. short-term rate)

- The lagged asset return (serial correlation)

- A January seasonal

The explanatory power ranges from 2% to 25%. The conditional risk–premium models are statistically significant at the 5% level. The predictability of the Swiss bond market is somewhat artificial, as it is caused partly by the high serial autocorrelation induced by the illiquidity of the market; many bond prices adjust slowly to a market movement. The major question in investment management is not the "statistical" significance of a forecasting model but rather its "financial" significance. So we will now review the performance of tactical allocations using those models.

Performance of TAA   The financial relevance of the forecasting model can be evaluated by simulating TAA strategies based on the model. Solnik (1993*b*) assumed that informed investors revise their beliefs according to risk-premium models. They adapt their asset allocation accordingly. At the start of each month, the informed investor sequentially:

- Reestimates the risk-premium model in the light of last month's data

- Forecasts excess returns using the currently observed values of the conditioning information variables

- Decides on an optimal conditional mean-variance asset allocation

At the end of the month, the investor can observe the realized excess return; thus a time series of asset allocations and realized returns is obtained. The average realized return is compared to that of passive benchmarks. The tests are conducted *out-of-sample* in the sense that the model is estimated on a data sample that is different from the data used to test its performance.

Solnik looked at international asset allocation with the same volatility as the corresponding U.S. index. There are no transaction costs, and short-selling is not allowed. Results are reported in Exh. 17.7. TAA is conducted separately among the universe of eight stock markets and among the universe of eight bond markets. Three types of strategies are considered:

- *Full hedge*: Only fully hedged investments are allowed.

- *No hedge*: No currency hedging is allowed.

- *Partial hedge*: The amount of currency hedging is decided each month and for each currency based on the risk-premium models.

EXHIBIT 17.7

Performance of TAA with Different Currency-Hedging Policies
(in U.S. dollars, January 1971–December 1991)

| | | Mean Monthly Excess Return (%) | | | |
Asset	Volatility (in % per month)	U.S. market	Full hedge	No hedge	Partial hedge
Stocks only	4.67	0.247	0.694	0.962	1.149
Bonds only	2.56	–0.017	0.395	0.508	0.663

Source: B. Solnik (1993*b*)

The results for stock-only allocations are striking. The U.S. stock market had an excess return of 0.247% per month over the 21-year period, with a monthly standard deviation of 4.67%. Over the same period, the MSCI World index had an excess return of 0.35%, with a standard deviation of only 4.2%. The fully hedged TAA, with the same risk level as the U.S. stock index, had a monthly excess return of 0.694%. This is an annualized difference of more than 5%. The result for a TAA fully exposed to currency risk is even better (0.962%), but it is dominated by the results of a TAA with active currency hedging (1.149%). The importance of selective currency hedging has been confirmed by Glen and Jorion (1993), Levich and Thomas (1993), and Arnott and Pham (1993).

Harvey (1994) looks at the predictability of time-varying risk premia for emerging markets. He reports impressive out-of-sample performance for TAA.

Three strong words of caution are in order. Transaction costs have not been included. If futures contracts on currencies, stock indexes, and government bonds are used in TAA, transaction costs will be small compared to the returns presented above. As shown in Solnik (1993*a*), these performance results look impressive, but their statistical significance is not very high. In other words, one needs to wait several years to be reasonably assured that a TAA will outperform a passive benchmark. This could turn out to be too long for an investment manager who could lose impatient clients. Another problem is that, although the tests have been performed out-of-sample, they are to some extent guilty of data snooping, as described in Chapter 3 (see also MacBeth and Emanuel, 1993).

Structuring and Quantifying the Global Asset Allocation Process: An Illustration

The process described, with its separation between strategic and tactical asset allocation, is very common among *institutional* investors, such as pension funds. *Private* investors make a lesser use of benchmarks and tend to state their investment objectives in a less formal manner. They seem to care more about absolute returns than about deviations from a prespecified benchmark. This does not mean that the investment process should not be structured. We now introduce an example of an international investment structure designed for an organization with a large number of accounts stating a global investment objective and making extensive use of information technology.

Apart from the obvious technical and practical problems inherent in investing abroad, the key issue in international investing is how to structure the *asset allocation* process. Essential to this decision process are a variety of uncertain forecasts concerning exchange rates, interest rates, and stock market patterns. The task is further complicated by the fact that many of these variables are, to varying degrees, interdependent in the international context. For example, all the major stock markets are linked, but some are more closely linked than others, depending on the integration of the underlying economies. Similarly, a change in the interest rate of one currency will affect the exchange rates and interest rate of other currencies, but not to the same degree. Domestic asset allocation is simplified by the fact that an investor chooses from only a limited variety of assets, namely, cash, bonds, common stocks, and possibly commodities. In the international context, however, these choices are multiplied by the number of countries and currencies available, which themselves can present certain practical problems. For example, an investor may be bullish on the Japanese stock market but not on the yen. The complexity of the international scene, which involves so many interactions, makes quantification all the more useful and calls for computer technology. Ideally, an asset allocation system should enable a portfolio manager to react quickly and efficiently to any change in the international environment.

This section describes a quantified system for portfolio management based on a top-down approach that is currently used by several international money management firms.[4] Because it is internally consistent, it avoids the pitfalls often found in the bottom-up approach. The purpose of this system is to ensure the most efficient use of existing expertise within an organization. It relies on the multicountry view of the world described in Chapter 7. The system must therefore be structured along the lines of the major common factors (here, national market influences) affecting a security's price behavior. A different model of the world capital market would lead to a different system.

Our portfolio management system has four major stages: market analysis, asset allocation optimization, portfolio construction, and performance and risk control. The attraction of the system lies not in its components but rather in the way it integrates the four stages, with the aid of computers, to benefit money managers. The idea is not to generate more reliable forecasts but to use currently available forecasts better, which requires capitalizing most efficiently on the existing expertise within an organization. A diagram of this system is shown in Exh. 17.8.

Research and Market Analysis

To cope with the complexity and rapid changes of the international environment, a manager must use an interactive computer system. Ideally, everyone involved in

EXHIBIT 17.8

An Integrated Investment Process

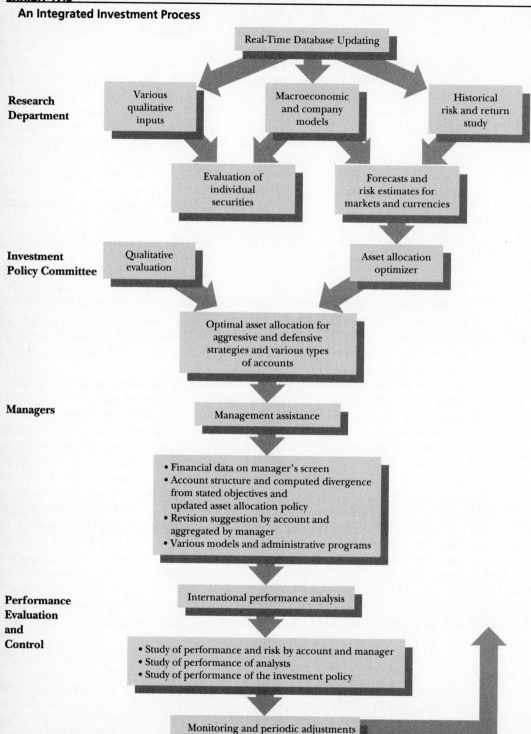

the investment decision process, i.e., analysts, investment committee members, and managers, should have interconnected computers.

To monitor markets, a large international database with on-line connections to major outside data bank services is necessary. The database should contain both price histories and information on economic statistics, markets, and individual securities. Ideally, the data should cover several previous years and be updated frequently, preferably daily. Only by having access to the most current data can managers update their correlation matrix properly, giving greater weight to more recent observations. A properly updated correlation matrix, in turn, helps managers to sort the interdependencies among the various markets (stocks, interest rates, exchange rates, etc.) that affect the portfolios under management.

A major responsibility of the research department in an investment organization is to provide forecasts on currencies, interest rates, commodity prices, and national stock indexes. The forecasts should then be translated by a computer into estimates of total return in particular base currencies.

Asset Allocation Optimization

Asset allocation has a major influence on fund performance. Of course, astute security selection on a given market can enhance the return on that segment of the account but not as much as astute currency or market allocation can.

The objective of any investment policy is to achieve a superior performance for a given risk. This may be achieved through subjective discussion among the members of an investment policy committee or by using formal optimization models. An investment policy should aim to achieve an efficient asset allocation matrix by country (or currency) and type of investment (stocks, bonds, money markets). Toward this end, a mean-variance quadratic program is often used to merge the forecasts and risk estimates generated by an investment organization. Such an optimization model is described in the appendix. Providing it is optimal; the resulting asset allocation will outperform a passive strategy only to the extent that the organization's forecasts reflect superior expertise in one or more markets, such as stocks, bonds, or foreign exchange. Another thing to remember is that the allocation must conform to the objectives and constraints of the various accounts managed by an organization. Some accounts permit only equity investment, others impose restrictions on selling short, and still others do not permit investment in specific asset classes. Plainly, constraints such as these will affect the potential return on an account, just as the choice of risk level or any other limitation will affect it.

Optimal asset allocations will differ according to the base currency of the client. In theory, one should care about real returns, not nominal returns. In other words, one should consider the returns calculated in the currency of the investor and adjusted by the appropriate inflation rate. Because the volatility of inflation rates is very small compared to that of most asset returns or currency movements, the use of real or nominal returns would not make much difference in the results of the optimization procedure. The optimization can be conducted on absolute returns, as done above. It can also be conducted relative to a prespecified bench-mark, with return and risk being measured in deviation from the benchmark.

The computer programs should be interactive so that an investment commit-tee can simulate several scenarios and thereby determine the most profitable investment policy. They should also enable the investment committee to check the sensitivity of the optimal asset allocation against a variety of other projected scenar-ios. Once the committee has chosen a policy, the resulting investment policy matri-ces should appear on each manager's terminal. The money managers can also use this optimization package to introduce their own scenarios. A sample output from an interactive program is shown in Exh. 17.9.

The institution whose asset allocation matrix is depicted in Exh. 17.9 consid-ers 10 countries and 3 asset types. Basically, the asset allocation matrix is made up of 30 cells to be determined. Maximum constraints have been put on some asset types (10% for cash, 20% for bonds), and no short-selling is allowed. The optimiza-tion model as described in the appendix allows the derivation of the optimal asset allocation for each risk level, given the forecasted returns, the correlation matrix, and the investment constraints.

The optimal allocation given in Exh. 17.9 is derived for a risk level deemed average and valid for a typical client; this is called a *balanced strategy*. Calculating the entire efficient frontier allows the portfolio manager to estimate expected return on the optimal international asset allocation for all risk levels (see Exh. 17.10). The composition of the portfolio on the efficient frontier is quite sensitive to small changes in forecasted returns.[5] The inclusion of transaction costs and various sta-tistical techniques can alleviate this problem.

EXHIBIT 17.9

Asset Allocation Matrix
(balanced strategy in U.S. dollars)

	Total	Cash	Bonds	Equities
United States	0.0	0.0	0.0	2.5
Switzerland	9.2	0.0	0.0	9.2
West Germany	18.5	0.0	6.5	12.0
Netherlands	12.1	2.1	5.0	5.0
United Kingdom	11.5	2.9	8.5	0.0
Japan	36.2	5.0	0.0	31.2
France	0.0	0.0	0.0	0.0
Australia	7.3	0.0	0.0	7.3
Hong Kong	0.0	0.0	0.0	0.0
Singapore	2.8	0.0	0.0	2.8
Total	**100.0**	**10.0**	**20.0**	**70.0**

Expected return = 29.0%; risk estimate = 12.9%.

Ultimately the quality of inputs is what counts. Bad forecasts will not generate superior performance, no matter what optimization method is used. However, any forecasting ability will best be exploited through such an approach.

Portfolio Construction

Active stock and bond selection in each market is a natural complement to active market selection. With the aid of computers, a research department should maintain an *active list* of individual securities in each market. This regularly updated list should provide a manager with an analyst's recommendation, possibly in the form of an expected return in local currency, as well as major risk characteristics of the security, including sensitivities to various factors, and, for bonds, actuarial yields and a measure for duration. The manager can then use this active securities list to construct the portfolio according to the asset allocation policy right on his or her terminal.

Managers of a large number of medium-sized accounts find that rebalancing those accounts to reflect even modest alterations in the organization's (or their own) investment policy is extremely time consuming and unduly repetitive. Reacting to a drastic policy change takes that much longer. To cope with this problem, a manager should first value each portfolio in the asset allocation matrix format. Next, each manager should modify the new investment policy matrix so that it reflects client guidelines for his or her major classes of accounts. The extent of this modification will depend on the type of client, base currency, and size of the

EXHIBIT 17.10
Efficient Frontier

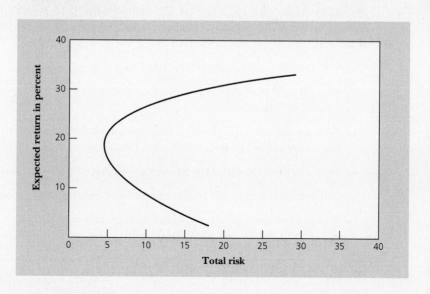

account. Any deviations of the current asset allocation from the new policy matrix will show up on the manager's screen in a format similar to that of Exh. 17.9. Drawing on the active securities list, the computer will make sell and buy recommendations for stocks and bonds that would enable the account to satisfy the new asset allocation guideline. The manager can either validate the proposed transactions on the screen or make his or her own. The market orders and attendant paperwork required for implementing the validated transactions are generated by the computer automatically.

More quantitatively oriented managers would probably make extensive use of the several models described in Chapters 7 and 10. One could adjust the sensitivity of the portfolio to specific market factors in each cell of the asset allocation matrix: For example, a manager very bullish on interest rates in Germany could select Deutsche mark bonds with a long duration to increase the sensitivity to a drop in Deutsche mark bond yields.

At this level, fine-tuning of the risk management strategy should also come into play. Futures and options can be used to react to sudden threats of a large market movement in some currency or asset classes.

Performance and Risk Control

The final step in the investment process is to monitor the performance and risk of individual portfolios. A common problem is that many money managers are concerned with international risk diversification but do little in their allocation process to achieve it. This problem is all the more serious for managers with active strategies, which tend to concentrate on a few currencies and markets and are therefore vulnerable to the high risk associated with those currencies and markets.

Performance control should be driven by an organization's daily accounting system. As mentioned in Chapter 16, the objective is to be able to answer the following questions about a portfolio and in so doing assess the effectiveness of its manager:

- What is the total return on the fund over a specific period?

- What is the breakdown of the return in terms of capital gains, currency fluctuations, and income?

- To what extent is the performance explained by asset allocation, market timing, currency selection, or individual stock selection?

- How does the overall return compare to that of certain standards?

- Is there evidence of particular expertise in various asset classes and markets?

- Has the risk diversification objective been achieved?

- How aggressive is the manager's strategy?

The characteristics and use of an account review of an international performance analysis (IPA) system have been discussed in Chapter 16. It should be stressed that the performance of a research department should also be studied to pinpoint the areas of expertise. This can be done by constructing paper portfolios based on analyst recommendations for each country and comparing the subsequent returns to those on the corresponding national indexes.

Some Practical Considerations

Databases   An international money manager must have access to financial information from all over the world. Fortunately foreign brokers now provide up-to-date financial analysis on most foreign stocks traded globally. American, Japanese, and some European brokers even provide forecasted earnings and investment advice directly to customers on computer time-sharing systems. To be sure, language differences are still a problem, even though many investment research houses publish reports in English, as well as in their native languages.

Market prices are also available worldwide on computerized information systems. Three types of international information systems are available:

- Real-time news systems, such as Telerate, Bloomberg, and Reuters, provide real-time news and prices on selected markets and securities.

- Price systems, such as Exshare and Telekurs, provide exhaustive price coverage of all capital and money markets in the world. These services focus on prices rather than analysis, although some (like Quotron) provide both services. They also provide information on capital adjustments, dividends, and ex dates.

- Portfolio management packages provide both price quotations and databases to assist financial research. These services, such as Datastream, feature easy-to-use software that can be run on desk-top computers.

Basically, a money manager can get real-time information from anywhere in the world as long as he or she can bear the heavy cost of subscribing to one or more of these international databases.

Accounting   An international portfolio accounting system is by definition complex. To begin with, it must incorporate a multicurrency system that both adjusts for the differences among national markets and allows any currency to serve as a reference. Transactions should be accounted for on the trade date, not on the settlement date. In addition, adjustments should be made for the trading procedures of different countries—for example, the "account period" on the U.K. stock market or the "reglement mensuel" on the French stock market (see Chapter 6). The system should also be able to accurately account for accrued interest on bonds. As shown in Chapter 9, countries have different methods for calculating interest. Another problem is foreign withholding tax, which should be reclaimed either in full or in part by the investor.

Custody   Several banks provide global securities custody.[6] The Securities and Exchange Commission and ERISA closely regulate custodians used by U.S. investors. A truly international custodial service requires subcustodians in each home market, as well as Euroclear or Cedel for the Eurobond market. Several countries have already developed central clearing and deposit systems for their domestic stocks and bonds, and these should be used whenever possible. In spite of the services and systems that are currently available, numerous practical problems arise in international custody. Accurate information from across the world should be gathered rapidly. Automated trade notification is necessary. Computer-to-computer links with the subcustodians, clearing services, and the manager should be set up. Income collection should be swift and correctly reported. Tax recovery should be automated and carefully checked with each government. Finally, a cash management system in many currencies should be implemented.

Summary

1. Major choices in terms of investment philosophy and strategy have to be made by an organization structuring its international investment process. These choices are based on a view of the world and, more important, the behavior of security prices. A major question is how active an international strategy should be. In an active strategy a manager can decide on (1) international asset allocation by type of asset and currency, (2) security selection, and (3) market timing. An active manager can also selectively hedge certain types of risks, such as currency risk. Another important question is whether the major emphasis should be on market analysis (top-down approach) or on security analysis (bottom-up approach). These and other choices dictate how the organization should be structured.

2. The most important decision in international investing is the selection of an asset allocation. The first step for an international investor is to decide on a *strategic asset allocation*. This is the structure of the portfolio for the long term. The asset allocation is periodically adapted to reflect changes in the market environment; this is referred to as *tactical asset allocation*.

3. The strategic asset allocation is formalized in the form of one or several benchmarks set as guidelines to investment managers. A passive manager will simply attempt to track the benchmark. The choice of a benchmark is a difficult decision, with no obvious answer.

4. Tactical asset allocation has shown some promise in international investing.

5. Structuring and quantifying the investment process is a difficult task because of the large number of parameters involved. A disciplined and efficient

approach calls for a quantified integrated system. The objective is to make optimal use of all expertise and control risk.

Notes

1. For a criticism of this model, see Adler and Solnik (1990), Adler and Prasad (1992), Solnik (1993), or Jorion (1994). We must clearly differentiate between the *strategic* currency decision, which sets the long-term policy regarding currency hedging, and *tactical* currency decision, which suggests temporary deviation from this long-term policy based on changes in expectations and risks. We talk here about the strategic allocation.

2. The idea is that a foreign exchange transaction is *symmetric* and that the gain for one party is offset by a loss for the other party. Because forward currency contracts are in zero net supply, currencies should offer no risk premium: Why would an investor engage in a forward currency transaction if he or she knows that it has to pay a risk premium to the other party? As Jorion (1994) and others have stressed, this reasoning is faulty. All futures contracts are in zero-net supply, but they can still provide long-term excess returns in the form of risk premia. For example, the buyer of a futures contract on a stock index does expect to earn money, on the average, but has no problem in finding a willing seller.

3. See, for example, Arnott and Henriksson (1989), Harvey (1991), Bekaert and Hodrick (1992), Solnik (1993*a* and 1993*b*), Harvey (1994), Ferson and Harvey (1994), and Emanuelli and Pearson (1994).

4. See Lombard and Solnik (1984) and the July 1985 issue of *Institutional Investor.*

5. See Michaud (1989).

6. A description of international custody problems is given in Grimsley (1986).

Bibliography

Adler, M., and Dumas, B. "International Portfolio Choice and Corporation Finance: A Synthesis," *Journal of Finance,* June 1983.

Adler, M., and Prasad, B. "On Universal Currency Hedges," *Journal of Financial and Quantitative Analysis,* February 1992.

Adler, M., and Solnik, B. Letter to the Editor, "The Individuality of 'Universal' Hedging," *Financial Analysts Journal,* May/June 1990.

Arnott, R.D., and Henricksson, R.D. "A Disciplined Approach to Global Asset Allocation," *Financial Analysts Journal,* March-April 1989.

Arnott, R.D., and Pham, T.K. "Tactical Currency Asset Allocation," *Financial Analysts Journal,* September-October 1993.

Bank Administration Institute. *Measuring the Investment Performance of Pension Funds,* Parkridge, IL, 1968.

Bekaert, G., and Hodrick, R.J. "Characterizing Predictable Components in Excess Returns on Equity and Foreign Exchange Markets," *Journal of Finance*, June 1992.

Black, F. "Equilibrium Exchange Rate Hedging," *Journal of Finance*, July 1990.

Botkin, D. "Strategy Setting and Expectations," in M. Tapley, ed. *International Portfolio Management*, Euromoney Publications, 1986.

Dumas, B. "A Test of the International CAPM Using Business Cycle Indicators as Instrumental Variables," *The Internationalization of Equity Markets*, Chicago, IL: NBER–The University of Chicago Press, 1994.

Emanuelli, J.F., and Pearson, R.G. "Using Earnings Estimates for Global Asset Allocation," *Financial Analysts Journal*, March-April 1994.

Ferson, W.E., and Harvey, C.R. "Sources of Risk and Expected Returns in Global Equity Markets," *Journal of Banking and Finance*, September 1994.

Ferson, W.E., and Harvey, C.R. "An Exploratory Investigation of the Fundamental Determinants of National Equity Returns," in J.A. Frankel, ed. *The Internationalization of Equity Markets*, Chicago, IL: NBER–The University of Chicago Press, 1994.

Froot, K.A. "Currency Hedging over Long Horizons," NBER Working Paper #4355, May 1993.

Glen, J., and Jorion, P. "Currency Hedging for International Portfolios," *Journal of Finance*, December 1993.

Grimsley, G.C. "Global Custody," in M. Tapley, ed. *International Portfolio Management*, Euromoney Publications, 1986.

Harvey, C.R. "The World Price of Covariance Risk," *Journal of Finance*, March 1991.

_____. "Conditional Asset Allocation in Emerging Markets," Working Paper, Fuqua School of Business, Duke University, January 1994.

Jorion, P. "International Portfolio Diversification with Estimation Risk," *Journal of Business*, July 1985.

_____. "Asset Allocation with Hedged and Unhedged Foreign Stocks and Bonds," *Journal of Portfolio Management*, Summer 1989.

_____. "Mean/Variance Analysis of Currency Overlays," *Financial Analysts Journal*, May-June, 1994.

Levich, R.M., and Thomas, L.R. "The Merits of Active Currency Risk Managment: Evidence from International Bond Portfolios," *Financial Analysts Journal*, September-October 1993.

Lombard, T., and Solnik, B. "Computing Complexities of Foreign Investment," *Pensions and Investment Age*, October 29, 1984.

Lombard, T., and Solnik, B. "International Performance Measurement," Lombard Odier & Cie, June 1983.

McBeth, J.D., and Emmanuel, D.C. "Tactical Asset Allocation: Pros and Cons," *Financial Analysts Journal*, November-December 1993.

Michaud, R.O. "The Markowitz Optimization Enigma: Is "Optimized" Optimal?" *Financial Analysts Journal*, January-February 1989.

Nesbitt, S.L. "Currency Hedging Rules for Plan Sponsors," *Financial Analysts Journal*, March-April 1991.

Perold, A., and Schulman, E. "The Free Lunch in Currency Hedging: Implications for Investment Policies and Performance Standards," *Financial Analysts Journal*, May/June 1988.

Roll, R. "Ambiguity When Performance Is Measured by the Securities Market Line," *Journal of Finance*, September 1978.

Solnik, B. "An Equilibrium Model of the International Capital Market," *Journal of Economic Theory*, July/August 1974.

_____. "Currency Hedging and Siegel's Paradox: On Black's Universal Hedging Rule," *Review of International Economics*, June 1993.

_____. "The Performance of International Asset Allocation Using Conditioning Information," *Journal of Empirical Finance*, March 1993a.

_____. *Predictable Time-Varying Components of International Asset Returns*, Charloitesville, VA: The Research Foundation of Chartered Financial Analysts, 1993b.

Tapley, M. "Accounting and Performance Measurement," in *International Portfolio Management*, London: Euromoney Publications, 1986.

Chapter 17: Appendix
Advanced Section on Optimal Asset Allocation

In this appendix we describe the asset allocation optimizer that is derived from mean-variance optimization theory.

Notations

The asset allocation is presented in a matrix by country (i.e., currency) and asset type, as shown in Exh. 17.9, where the base currency is the U.S. dollar. One cell of this matrix is referred to as an *asset class*, or a *segment*. The proportion of the account invested in the asset type j of currency i is denoted X_{ij}. For example, $X_{ij} = 10\%$ could be invested in Japanese (i) stocks (j). With these notations, we have a matrix where the rows are the currencies (or countries) i, and the columns are the asset types j. An asset class (e.g., Japanese stocks) is the combination of an asset type j and a currency i. For example, $i=6$ and $j=3$ for Japanese stocks in Exh. 17.9. The various proportions, X_{ij}s add up to 100%. Some institutions may use an asset allocation matrix in which small markets are grouped by region. A typical country breakdown could be: Domestic, North America, Japan, other Far East, U.K., Continental Europe, Emerging markets.

Futures contracts are implicitly allowed in this matrix. As mentioned in Chapter 1, a currency futures contract is equivalent to a short-term borrowing-lending swap in two currencies. For example, an American investor wanting to sell yen forward can simply borrow yen short term, transfer it into U.S. dollars, and invest it in dollar short-term deposits. Accordingly, selling a currency forward shows up as a negative proportion X_{ij} for the foreign currency cash investment and an offsetting positive proportion for the domestic cash investment. For example, an American investor hedging 10% of the total portfolio against yen/dollar risk would be described by:

$$X_{11} = +10\% \text{ and } X_{61} = -10\%.$$

A similar reasoning applies to other futures contracts on stock indexes or bonds.

The base currency used for the account has been chosen and all rates of returns are calculated in this base currency, denoted o.

The forecasted rate of return on an asset class is denoted E_{ij}. This is obtained by compounding the forecasted return in local currency by the expected currency movement. For example, if the Japanese stock market is forecasted to provide a return of 10% in yen (capital gain plus yield) and if the yen is expected to appreciate by 5% relative to the base currency, the U.S. dollar, the total forecasted return for a U.S. investor is:

$$E_{ij} = (1 + 10\%)(1 + 5\%) - 1 = 15.5\%.$$

The return on a bond asset class can be derived by multiplying the forecasted change in yield by the average duration of the market. The expected return on the total account is simply written as E.

The covariance between returns on two asset classes is denoted $\sigma_{ij,kl}$. The covariance between two assets is equal to the correlation of returns multiplied by the standard deviations of the two assets. The variance of the total account is simply written as σ^2.

Optimization

The objective of an optimal asset allocation is to maximize the expected return, E, while minimizing the risk level, σ^2. Operationally, this can be achieved by minimizing the risk level for a given level of expected return.

However, investment constraints are often imposed on the asset allocation. These take numerous forms but are usually expressed as linear combinations of the investment proportions X_{ij}. The most typical constraints are

- No short sales are allowed on some or all assets ($X_{ij} \geq 0$).

- A maximum limit is put on asset class, currency, or asset type. A typical constraint on a currency i would be written as $\sum_j X_{ij} \leq \max_i$. For example, we could set a maximum of 10% on French franc assets ($\max_7 = 10\%$ on the sum of the seventh row of Exh. 17.9). A typical constraint on an asset type j would be written as $\sum_i X_{ij} \leq \max_j$. For example, we could set a maximum of 10% on all cash assets.

- Currency short selling cannot exceed the amount of currency-exposed assets held in the portfolio.

Mathematically the optimization problem can be written as

$$\min_X \sum_{ijkl} X_{ij} X_{kl} \sigma_{ij,kl}$$

subject to

$$\sum_{ij} X_{ij} E_{ij} = E$$

and linear constraints on X_{ij}.

The optimal asset allocation can be obtained using standard quadratic programming packages. The estimation of the covariance matrix is an important prerequisite. The covariance estimates are somewhat unstable over time, so the statistical procedure used to estimate the covariance matrix makes a difference (see Jorion, 1985). Transaction costs and some nonlinear constraints can also be incorporated into the optimization.

Glossary

Accrued interest Interest earned but not yet due and payable. This is equal to the next coupon to be paid on a bond multiplied by the time elapsed since the last payment date and divided by the total coupon period. Exact conventions differ across bond markets.

Actuarial yield The total yield on a bond obtained by equaling the bond's current market value to the discounted cash flows promised by the bond. Also called Yield to maturity.

AIMR The U.S. AIMR (Association for Investment Management Research) delivers the CFA certification and edicts professional standards that must be applied by its members worldwide.

American depositary receipts (ADR) A certificate of ownership issued by a U.S. bank to promote local trading in a foreign stock. The U.S. bank holds the foreign shares and issues ADRs against them.

American-type option An option that can be exercised at any time before expiration.

Arbitrage approach A common approach used to value derivative securities, based on an arbitrage strategy involving primitive securities.

Arbitrage The simultaneous purchase and sales of different securities in order to obtain a riskless profit on the price differential. Taking advantage of a market inefficiency in a risk-free manner.

Ask price The price at which a market maker is willing to sell a security (also called Offer price)

At-the-money option An option for which the strike (or exercise) price is close to the current market price of the underlying asset.

Balance of payments A record of all financial flows crossing the borders of a country during a given time period (a quarter or a year).

Basis The difference between the futures (or forward) price of an asset and its spot (or cash) price. The basis can be expressed as a value or as a percentage of the spot price.

Basis point One hundredth of 1% (0.01%).

Bearer security A negotiable security. All cash flows paid on the security are remitted to its bearer. No register of ownership is kept by the issuing company.

Benchmark A standard of measurement used to evaluate the performance of a portfolio. The benchmark can be some passive index or the aggregate performance on a universe of comparable portfolios (see Composite).

Benchmark bond A bond representative of current market conditions and used for performance comparison.

Beta A statistical measure of market risk on a portfolio. Traditionally used to estimate the elasticity of a stock portfolio's return relative to that of the market index.

Bid price The price at which a market maker is willing to buy a security.

Black-Scholes formula Derived by F. Black and M. Scholes, an option pricing formula that is universally used by the industry to price options.

Bond A long-term debt security with contractual obligations regarding interest payments and redemption. A bond is called stock in Britain.

Book value The accounting value of a firm.

Bourse A term of French origin often used to refer to stock markets.

Brady bonds Bonds issued by emerging countries under a debt-reduction plan named after Mr. Brady, a former U.S. Secretary of the Treasury.

Break-even exchange rate The future exchange rate such that the return in two bonds markets would be even for a given maturity. Also called Implied forward exchange rate.

Call option A contract giving the right to buy an asset at a specific price on or before a specified date.

Cap A contract on an interest rate, whereby the writer of the cap pays at periodic payment dates the difference between the market interest rate and a specified cap rate if, and only if, this difference is positive. This is equivalent to a stream of call options on the interest rate.

Capital account A component of the balance of payments covering all short-term and long-term capital transactions.

Capital asset pricing model (CAPM) An equilibrium theory that relates the expected return of an asset to its market risk (See Beta).

Cash-and-carry arbitrage An arbitrage strategy with a simultaneous spot purchase and forward sale of an asset. The reverse transaction (borrowing the asset, selling it spot, and buying it forward) is known as a reverse cash-and-carry, or as a carry-and-cash arbitrage. These arbitrages lead to a relation between spot and forward, or futures, prices of the same asset.

Clean price The price of a bond obtained by taking the total price of the bond minus accrued interest. Most bonds are traded on the basis of their clean price.

Clearinghouse An organization that settles and guarantees trades in some financial markets.

Closed-end fund A fund with a fixed number of shares. New shares cannot be issued and old shares cannot be redeemed. Shares are traded in the marketplace, and their value may differ from the underlying net asset value of the fund.

Composite A universe of portfolios with similar investment objectives.

Conditional expected value Expected value of a variable conditional on some available information set. The expected value changes over time with a change in the information set.

Conditional variance Variance of a variable conditional on some available information set.

Convexity A measure of the change in duration with respect to changes in interest rates.

Cost of carry The cost associated with holding some asset, including financing, storage, and insurance costs. Any yield paid on the asset comes as a negative carrying cost.

Currency swap A contract to exchange streams of fixed cash flows denominated in two different currencies.

Current account A component of the balance of payments covering the country's payments for goods, services, income, and foreign aid.

Default risk The risk that an issuer will be unable to timely meet interest and principal payments.

Delta (option) Ratio of change of the option price to a small change in the price of the underlying asset. Also equal to the derivative of the option price with respect to the asset price.

Delta hedge A dynamic hedging strategy using options with continuous adjustment of the number of options used, as a function of the delta of the option.

Derivatives Securities bearing a contractual relation to some underlying asset or rate. Options, swaps, and many forms of bonds are derivative securities.

Dirty price Total price of a bond, including accrued interest.

Dual-currency bond A bond with coupons fixed in one currency and principal repayment fixed in another currency.

Duration A measure of a bond's average maturity. Specifically, the weighted average maturity of all future cash flows paid by a security, where the weights are the discounted present value of these cash flows. More important, a measure of a bond's price sensitivity to interest rate movements (see Modified duration).

Efficient frontier The set of all efficient portfolios for various levels of risk.

Efficient market A market in which any available information is immediately impounded in asset prices.

Efficient portfolio A portfolio that provides the best expected return for a given level of risk.

Eurocurrency market Interbank market for short-term borrowing and lending in a currency outside of its home country. For example, borrowing and lending of U.S. dollars outside the United States. Thus it is an offshore market escaping national regulations. This is the largest money market for the few major currencies.

Eurodollar market The U.S. dollar segment of the Eurocurrency market.

Eurobond A bond underwritten by a multinational syndicate of banks and placed outside of the countries of the issuer and of the currency of denomination. The issue thus escapes national restrictions.

European currency unit (ECU) A theoretical currency basket constructed as a weighted average of several European currencies.

European Monetary System A formal arrangement linking some, but not all, of the currencies of the EU.

European Union (EU) A formal association of European countries founded by the Treaty of Rome in 1957. Formerly known as the EEC, the EU had 15 members in the mid-1990s.

European-type option An option that can be exercised only at expiration.

Exercise price See Strike price.

Face value The amount paid on a bond at redemption and traditionally printed on the bond certificate. This face value excludes the final coupon payment.

Fair value The theoretical value of a security based on current market conditions. The fair value is such that no arbitrage opportunities exist.

Floating-rate note (FRN) Bond issued with variable quarterly or semiannual interest rate payments, generally linked to LIBOR.

Floor A contract on an interest rate, whereby the writer of the floor pays at periodic payment dates the difference between a specified floor rate and the market interest rate if, and only if, this difference is positive. This is equivalent to a stream of put options on the interest rate.

Foreign bond A bond issued by a foreign company on the local market and in the local currency (e.g., Yankee bonds in the United States, Bulldog bonds in the United Kingdom, or Samurai bonds in Japan).

Foreign exchange controls Various forms of controls imposed by a government on the purchase (sale) of foreign currencies by residents or on the purchase (sale) of local currency by nonresidents.

Forward contract A customized contract to buy (sell) an asset at a specified date and a specified price (forward price). No payment takes place until maturity.

Forward discount or premium Refers to the percentage difference between the forward exchange rate and the spot exchange rate (premium if positive, discount if negative).

Frankfurt Interbank Offer Rate (FIBOR) The equivalent of the LIBOR for Deutsche marks borrowed on Frankfurt interbank market.

Futures contract A standardized contract to buy (sell) an asset at a specified date and a specified price (futures price). The contract is traded on an organized exchange, and the potential gain/loss is realized each day (Marking to market).

Generic See Plain-vanilla.

Gilt (or Gild-edged) A U.K. government bond.

Gray market A forward market for newly issued bonds before the final terms on the bond are set. Bonds are traded at a discount or premium to the (unknown) issue price.

Group of Seven (G-7) The seven leading countries (Canada, France, Germany, Italy, Japan, United Kingdom, and the United States) meeting periodically to enhance cooperative action on international economic matters. The G-5 is made up of France, Germany, Japan, United Kingdom, and the United States and assumes a similar role.

Hedging The process of reducing the uncertainty on the future value of a portfolio by taking positions in various derivatives (e.g., forward and futures contracts).

Implied forward exchange rate See Break-even exchange rate.

Implied volatility The volatility of an asset that is implicit in the current market price of an option (using a standard Black-Scholes formula).

In-the-money option An option that has a positive value if exercised immediately. For example, a call when the strike price is below the current price of the underlying asset, or a put when the strike price is above the current price of the underlying asset.

Index-linked bond A bond whose interest rate payments and/or redemption value are linked in a contractual way to some specified index (e.g., a commodity price).

Insuring The process of setting a minimum level for the future and uncertain value of a portfolio by taking positions in various derivatives (e.g., options).

Interest rate parity An arbitrage process that ensures that the forward discount or premium equals the interest rate differential between the two currencies.

Interest rate swap A contract to exchange streams of fixed-interest rate for floating-interest rate cash flows denominated in the same currency.

Internal rate of return (IRR) The discount rate that equates the present value of a future stream of cash flows to the initial investment.

International CAPM An equilibrium theory that relates the expected return of an asset to its world market and foreign exchange risks.

International Monetary Fund (IMF) An organization set up in 1944 to promote exchange rate stability and to assist member countries in economic difficulties.

International Securities Market Association (ISMA) An association formed in 1969 to establish uniform trading procedures in the international bond markets. Formerly named AIBD.

International Swap and Derivatives Association (ISDA) An association of swap dealers formed in 1985 to promote uniform practices in the writing, trading, and settlement procedures of swaps and other derivatives.

Intrinsic value The value obtained on an option if it were to be exercised immediately.

Lead manager The bank in charge of organizing a syndicated bank credit or a bond issue.

Limit order An order to buy or sell a security at a specific price or better (lower for a buy and higher for a sell).

London Interbank Offer Rate (LIBOR) The rate at which international banks lend on the Eurocurrency market. This is the rate for a top-quality borrower. The most common maturities are one-month, three-month, and six-month. There is a LIBOR for the U.S. dollar and a few other major currencies. See also Frankfurt Interbank Offer Rate (FIBOR) and Paris.

Margin deposit The amount of cash or securities that must be deposited as guarantee on a futures position.

Market maker An institution or individual quoting firm bid and ask prices for a security and standing ready to buy or sell the security at those quoted prices. Also called Dealer.

Market order An order to buy and sell immediately at the best obtainable price.

Marking to market Procedure whereby potential profits and losses on a futures position are realized daily. The daily futures price variation is debited (credited) in cash to the loser (winner) at the end of the day.

Modified duration Measure of a bond's price sensitivity to interest rate movements. Equal to the duration of a bond divided by one plus its yield to maturity.

Officer price The price at which a market maker is willing to sell a security (also called Ask price).

Official reserves The amount of reserves owned by the central bank of a government in the form of gold, Special Drawing Rights, and foreign cash or marketable securities.

Option premium An often-used term for the price of an option.

Out-of-the-money option An option that has no value if exercised immediately. For example, a call when the strike price is above the current price of the underlying asset, or a put when the strike price is below the current price of the underlying asset.

Par value The principal amount repaid at maturity of a bond. Also called Face value.

Par yield curve The yield curve drawn for straight bonds of different maturities that are priced at par.

Paris Interbank Offer Rate (PIBOR) The equivalent of LIBOR for French francs borrowed on the Paris interbank market.

Perpetual bond A bond with no stated maturity.

Plain-vanilla Refers to a security, especially a bond or a swap, issued with standard features. Sometimes called Generic.

Present value The current worth of a future cash flow. Obtained by discounting the future cash flow at the market-required interest rate.

Purchasing power parity A theory that states that the exchange rate between two currencies will exactly reflect the purchasing power of the two currencies.

Put option A contract giving the right to sell an asset at a specified price, on or before a specified date.

Random-walk theory A theory that states that all current information is reflected in current security prices and that future price movements are random because they are caused by unexpected news.

Rating Evaluation by a credit rating agency, such as Moody's or Standard and Poor's, of an issue's investment quality.

Real exchange rates The exchange rate adjusted by the inflation differential between the two countries.

Real interest rate The interest rate adjusted by the inflation rate of the country.

Risk aversion Describes the fact that investors tend to be reluctant to take risk, for the same level of expected return. To take more risk, they require being compensated by a risk premium.

Risk premium The difference between the expected return on an asset and the risk-free interest rate.

Sovereign risk The risk that a government may default on its debt.

Special Drawing Right (SDR) An artificial official reserve asset held on the books of the IMF.

Spot price Current market price of an asset. Also called Cash price.

Spread Difference between the ask and the bid quotations. Also refers to a mark-up paid by a given borrower over the market interest rate paid by a top-quality borrower.

Straight bond Refers to a plain-vanilla bond with fixed coupon payments and without any optional clauses.

Strike price Price at which an option can be exercised (same as Exercise price).

Swap A contract whereby the two parties agree to a periodic exchange of cash flows. Only the balance of the two cash flows is exchanged on each payment date.

Tap Procedure by which a borrower can keep issuing additional amounts of an old bond at its current market value. This procedure is used for bond issues, notably by the British and French governments, as well as for some short-term debt instruments.

Technical analysis A forecasting method for asset prices based solely on information about past prices.

Term structure See Yield curve.

Tombstone Advertisement that states the borrower's name, the conditions of an issue, and lists the various banks taking part in the issue. The tombstone is published in the press after the issue for advertising purposes.

Trade balance The balance of a country's exports and imports.

Tranche Refers to a portion of an issue that is designed for a specific category of investors. A French word for "slice."

Volatility A measure of the uncertainty about the future price of an asset. Typically measured by the standard deviation of returns on the asset.

Withholding tax A tax levied by the country of source on income paid.

World Bank A supranational organization grouping several institutions designed to assist developing countries. The International Bank for Reconstruction and Development (IBRD) and the International Finance Corporation (IFC) are the more important members of the World Bank group.

Writing of an option A term used for the person who sells an option and therefore grants the right to exercise it to the buyer of the option.

Yield curve A curve showing the relationship between yield (interest rate) and maturity for a set of similar securities. For example, the yield curve can be drawn for U.S. Treasuries. Typically different yield curves are drawn for zero-coupon bonds (zero-coupon yield curve) and for coupon bonds quoted at par (par yield curve).

Yield to maturity The total yield on a bond obtained by equaling the bond's current market value to the discounted cash flows promised by the bond. Also called Actuarial yield.

Zero-coupon bond A bond paying no coupons until final redemption. Such bonds trade at a discount to their face value so that the price differential (face value minus market price) ultimately provides a return to the investor commensurate with current interest rates.

Answers to Selected Problems

Chapter 1

3. The French franc depreciated by 16.67% against the dollar.

4. These quotes are unreasonable. One can buy Bank A's dollars for 1562 lira per dollar, sell those dollars to Bank B for 1563 lira per dollar, and thereby make a pure arbitrage profit of one lira per dollar traded.

6. The implicit FF/DM quotation is 3.2978–3.3050.

8. The one-year FF/$ forward rate is 8.2552. The one-month FF/$ forward rate is 7.9894.

10. The quotes for the DM/$ one-month forward exchange rate are 2.4085–2.4130. The quotes for the DM/$ one-year forward exchange rate are 2.3987–2.4140.

Chapter 2

1. The expected value for the exchange rate (SF/$), a year from now, is 1.9429.

4. The Japanese consumer price index inflation is equal to 6.67%. The exchange rate is constant. Since the Japanese inflation rate is 6.67% and the American inflation rate is 0%, PPP is not verified. Indeed, PPP should not be verified in this case, the consumption baskets that we used to calculate inflation being different in Japan and in the United States. Production gains can explain the real appreciation of the yen.

6. The nominal interest rate can be defined as the compounding of the real interest rate and the expected inflation rate over the term of the interest rate. National rates can vary because of different real rates and/or expected inflation.

8. The appropriate answers (linear approximation) are a U.S. inflation rate of 5%, a spot exchange rate of 5.94 FF/$, and a one-year forward exchange rate of 6.00 FF/$.

10. I can sell FF forward against DM. I can also borrow FF, transfer them into DM, and lend those DM. If the DM appreciates in a few weeks, I will make a profit on both operations.

12. Due to political uncertainties, investors are more likely to fear devaluations in France than in Germany. A a result, they will rather invest their capital in Germany than in France. This supply of DM should lower German interest rates relative to FF interest rates. The real interest rates in France would be higher than in Germany to reflect devaluation risk.

Chapter 3

2. Paf's balance of payments for the quarter, in million pifs:

Current account	**3.51**
Exports	10
Imports	–6.3
Trade balance	*3.7*
Balance of services	0.45
Net income	–0.91
Unrequited transfers	0.27
Capital account	**–2.7**
Official reserve account	**–0.81**

The increase in official reserves (a negative account) results from a positive trade balance that more than compensates the portfolio investment deficit.

3. The permanent reduction of the monthly current account of Japan is bad news for the home currency, everything else being equal. This drop in monthly current account leads to a reduction in the country's reserves and, ultimately, to a depreciation of the Japanese yen. Of course, this reduction in the current account surplus could also be matched by a reduction in the capital account deficit.

5. Exports of goods and services exceed imports by $28.2 billion. This positive figure is partly offset by negative net income received and unrequited transfers, leading to an $11.9 billion positive current account. Direct investment is $0.4 billion. Portfolio investment is $3.3 billion. Other capital flows, which include short-term deposits made by foreigners in France and by residents abroad, is negative at –$12.3 billion. Adjusted for net errors and omissions, the capital account remains negative at –$4.5 billion. The balance of the current account and the capital account causes an increase in official reserves by $7.4 billion, which shows as a negative official reserve account.

8. A traditional Fisherian approach would suggest that the home currency should depreciate because of increased inflation. An increase in domestic consumption could also lead to increased imports and a deficit in the balance of trade. This deficit should lead to a weakening of the home currency in the short run.

   The asset-market approach claims that this scenario is good for the home currency. Foreign capital investment is attracted by the high return caused by economic growth and high interest rates. This capital inflow leads to an appreciation of the home currency.

10. The forecast is the implicit forward exchange rate: 1.1886 SF/DM.

11. The current forward exchange rate is 1.9439 DM/$. To capitalize on my forecast for the exchange rate at the end of the year (DM/$ = 2.06), I can buy forward dollar contracts for delivery in one year (DM/$ = 1.9439). If every market participant were using my model, everyone would simultaneously conduct my type of forward transaction. Hence the current forward exchange rate would instantaneously become equal to 2.06. The spot exchange rate and the interest rates would have to move to be consistent with this forward exchange rate value.

14. ■ Assume that you speculate on $1000. To take advantage of a pif's eventual devaluation, you could borrow 900 pif for a month at $\frac{18}{12}$%, buy $1000, and lend $1000 for a month at $\frac{6}{12}$%.

   ■ Your total loss will be equal to 9 pifs, or 1.0% of the capital speculated.
   ■ Your total gain will be equal to 91.5 pifs, or 10.17% of the capital speculated.

Chapter 4

1. The variance of the portfolio is 14.15%.

2.

Proportion Invested in Asset 1	Proportion Invested in Asset 2	Portfolio Expected Return	Portfolio Risk
100	0	10.00	10.00
80	20	10.80	9.19
60	40	11.60	9.61
50	50	12.00	10.25
40	60	12.40	11.11
20	80	13.20	13.34
0	100	14.00	16.00

4. Return: 12.8%   Volatility: 14.46%
   Return: 12.8%   Volatility: 15.08%

7. Canada (0.71) is obviously highly dependent on the U.S. economy. Switzerland (0.59) and the Netherlands (0.58) are small economic powers with very active multinational groups on the U.S. market. Although the U.K. (0.56) is less dependent, it has a great number of banks, insurance companies, and other financial institutions investing on the U.S. market, which explains the high correlation. Italy (0.24) and Spain (0.30) have southern European–oriented economies with lesser relation to the U.S. economy.

8. Foreign bonds have a higher return (6.80% versus 5.70%) and a lower volatility (6.88% versus 7.16%) than U.S. bonds. Besides, we can assume that there is no perfect correlation between U.S. bonds and foreign bonds (i.e., correlation factor < 1). Foreign bonds are therefore a good vehicle of diversification and allow one to reduce significantly the volatility of the portfolio. This makes foreign bonds attractive for a U.S. investor despite an additional foreign exchange risk.

13. The dollar volatility of the German market would simply be equal to 21.63%. Since the real figure is only 21.2%, we conclude that the correlation between stock market returns and exchange rate movements is slightly negative.

Chapter 5

1. Buy when a stock just went up. Sell if it just went down.

3. Broad-based indexes include many smaller stocks that trade infrequently. They have higher autocorrelation than narrow-based indexes. It is difficult to hedge or arbitrage a futures in a broad-based index, because it requires taking a spot position in a large number of illiquid stocks. The illiquidity leads to high transaction costs and risk of stale prices unrepresentative of current market conditions.

5. All trades are settled only at the end of the month. Hence a buyer benefits from free financing until the end of the month. All quoted prices are therefore forward prices. There is no marking-to-market.

   Let's denote:

   F the observed quoted price,

   S the underlying spot price (unobserved),

   r the daily interest rate assumed constant during the month,

   t the number of days till the end of month.

   If no dividends are paid during the month, we should have:

   $$F = \frac{S}{(1+r)^t}.$$

   The daily return on F is the return on S minus one day of interest. However, the first day of a new month is a special case. The forward price should suddenly jump by an amount equal to one month of interest. The reader could verify this by assuming that the spot rate is constant and looking at the value of F given by the equation over time. Hence the daily return (day close to day close) observed on F should be identically distributed except on the first day of the month, when the return should be much higher (by one month of interest). An empirical examination is provided in Solnik, "The Distribution of Daily Stock Returns and Settlement Procedures: The Paris Bourse," *Journal of Finance*, December 1990.

7. Foreign nationals can diversify the high volatility of Pafpaf in their global portfolio. Hence they should require a lower risk premium and be willing to buy the shares at a higher price than Paf nationals. The share price should be bid up by foreigners when the restriction is lifted.

13. You would choose Australia I.

15. No. A rapid depreciation of a currency is generally caused by rampant inflation. Stocks are claims on real assets, and their prices tend to go up with inflation. The question is whether they go up faster or slower than the inflation rate. During 1993, the Polish inflation rate was around 40%, which explained the zolty's depreciation. The Polish stock market appreciation was extremely high. The privatization program drew enormous interest in 1992 and 1993. The rise in stock prices was either based on expecta-

tions of very high future economic growth or was somewhat irrational. The 1994 performance of the stock market was very bad.

16. The local currency price of foreign bonds tends to go up when the dollar depreciates relative to the local currency. Hence foreign bonds would be good for American investors if a depreciation of the dollar took place. The dollar value of the foreign bonds would rise both because the foreign currency appreciates relative to the dollar and because the foreign bond prices rises.

Chapter 6

4. Due to the depreciation of the U.S. dollar, other markets' capitalization (measured in dollars) increased. Besides, the depreciating dollar made investments in the U.S. market less attractive as long as investors thought that the dollar would further depreciate. Hence turnover on the New York Stock Exchange decreased from $1,374 billion to $1,072 billion (1986–1990). As a result, the U.S. market capitalization fell from 54% in 1984 to 29% in 1988.

6. The dollar cost for 1000 shares will be (1000 × 45 ¼ × 1.002 = $45,340.5. Given the 5.31 FF/$ ask rate, I will have to pay 45,340.5 × 5.31 = FF240,758.05

7.

	French Francs	U.S. Dollars
Final value	95,200	14,000
Initial investment	84,000	12,000
Capital gain	**11,200**	**2,000**
Gross dividend	2,840	400
Withholding tax	426	60
Dividend received	**2,414**	**340**
Income tax	1,420	
Capital gain tax	1,680	
Gross return	16.714%	20%
Net return	13,024%	

The gross return in French francs is less than in U.S. dollars because of the dollar depreciation by year's end. The net return is calculated assuming that the U.S. withholding tax is used as a credit against French income tax.

11. Cheapest cost per share: $86.1040 (in London, versus $86.7925 in Paris). The shares should be bought in London at a total cost of $861,040. These will be an arbitrage opportunity if I can sell a stock that I bought in London at a profit in Paris. The proceeds from a sale in Paris will be $84.75. There is no arbitrage opportunity.

16. There is some truth to it. The lack of turnover means that a new order arriving on the system can be executed at a fairly bad price immediately or remain posted for a long time, exposing the client to the risk of some adverse news while the order remains posted. The Japanese trading halt allows one to avoid the automatic execution of a new market order, giving time for traders to provide competitive quotes or for other matching orders to reach the floor.

17. In a price-driven system, the bid-ask quotes of a market maker are publicly exposed. The market maker runs the risk of being picked off by an informed trader. This risk is compounded by liquidity problems. For example, a market-maker will have a difficult time reselling illiquid shares that he or she just bought. One protection is to quote huge bid-ask spreads. However, very few people will then be willing to trade at those prices. The net result is that no market maker will find it economically feasible to maintain a continuous market in less traded issues. On an order-driven system, some dealers could easily specialize in specific illiquid issues. If an order is posted by some clients, the dealer can decide to submit a matching order. The dealer is less exposed to liquidity risk, as he or she can decide when to match a posted order.

Chapter 7

3. ■ Constitution of "hidden reserves."
■ Inventories are carried at historical cost.
■ Reported earnings are tax earnings, which are subject to many actions taken to reduce taxation.
■ Publication of nonconsolidated statements.
■ Accelerated depreciation is often used for tax purposes, even if the actual life of the asset is longer than its tax-accepted life.

6. The consolidated accounts under the various methods are given below:

	Papa SA Nonconsolidated	Fille SA	Papa Full consolidation	Papa Proportional consolidation	Papa Equity method
Balance Sheets, end-1997					
Fixed assets	400	80	480	440	400
Investment in subsidiary	50				60
Current assets	50	40	90	70	50
Total assets	**500**	**120**	**570**	**510**	**510**
Share capital	440	100	440	440	440
Net income 1997	60	20	70	70	70
Stockholders equity	*500*	*120*	*510*	*510*	*510*
Minority interests					
Total Liabilities	**500**	**120**	**570**	**510**	**510**
Income statement 1997					
Revenues	300	80	380	340	300
Expenses	240	60	300	270	240
	60	**20**	**80**	**70**	**60**
Income from subsidiary					10
Minority interests(−)			(10)		
−Net income	**60**	**20**	**70**	**70**	**70**

■ The lowest earnings for Papa SA are obtained on nonconsolidated statements. The three methods of consolidation give the same consolidated earnings in this case.
■ The book PE ratio is equal to stockholders equity divided by earnings. The highest accounting PE ratio obtains for nonconsolidated statements. The three methods of consolidation give the same accounting PE ratio in this case.

7. Consolidated earnings are 13 million for A and 32 million for B.
   The PEs are:

	Company A	Company B
Nonconsolidated	200/10 = 20	450/30 = 15
Consolidated	200/13 = 15.4	450/32 = 14.1

9. In an efficient market, all available information is already discounted in current stock prices. The fact that economic growth is currently higher in country A than country B implies that current stock prices are already "higher" in A than in B. Only unanticipated news about future growth rates should affect future stock prices. Current growth rates can explain past performance of stock prices, but only differences in future growth rates from their current anticipated levels should guide your country selection. Hence you should decide whether your own economic growth forecasts differ from that implicit in current stock prices.

11. If British Telecom followed the British stock market, it should have moved up by 2% in London and about 3% in New York (given the pound appreciation). However, there is extensive American ownership in British Telecom, which is among the top 10 most-heavily traded shares on the NYSE. A down movement in the NYSE could push down the value of British Telecom ADR and hence its share price in London.

13.

	Portfolio
Confidence	0.4
Time horizon	0.7
Inflation	−0.3
Business cycle	3.0
Market-timing	0.85

   You should overweight stock A because of its large exposure to the business cycle and its low exposure to inflation.

14. Let's note β_{1i}, the exposure of stock i to the interest rate factor, and β_{2i}, the exposure of stock i to the popularity factor. We could use some factor analysis to estimate the exposures. A casual look at the data suggests that the second factor has no (or little) influence on stock returns ($\beta_{2i} \cong 0$). The intercept and exposure to the first factor are estimated approximately at $a = 2\%$, $\beta_{1A} = -4$, $\beta_{1B} = -3$, $\beta_{1C} = -2$, $\beta_{1D} = -1$, $\beta_{1E} = 0$, and $\beta_{1F} = +1$.

15. In both periods small firms outperform big firms. In both periods value stock (low P/BV ratio) outperform growth stocks (high P/BV ratio). Size and P/BV ratio seem to be significant attribute factors.

Chapter 8

3.

Portfolio A		**Portfolio B**	
Return:	17.7%	Return:	21.1%
Volatility:	14.5%	Volatility:	15.4%
Portfolio C		**Portfolio D**	
Return:	19.3%	Return:	21.6%
Volatility:	16.9%	Volatility:	23.9%

4. ▪

	Portfolio A		Portfolio B		Portfolio C
Return:	11.0%	Return:	11.4%	Return:	11.8%
Volatility:	14.3%	Volatility:	13.5%	Volatility:	13.2%

▪

Mean Return	Volatility	% U.S.	% EAFE	% Composite
11.76	13.24	42	38	20
11.80	13.24	41	38	21
12.00	13.29	36	41	24
12.40	13.59	24	46	30
12.80	14.16	13	51	35
13.00	14.53	08	54	38
13.40	15.46	00	53	47
13.80	17.05	00	40	60
14.00	18.10	00	34	66
14.40	20.57	00	20	80
14.80	13.40	00	07	93
15.00	25.00	00	00	100

Note: Portfolio weights have been rounded to the nearest percentage point in this table. The return and volatility of the efficient portfolios are based on the exact weights.

6. No. A rapid depreciation of a currency is generally caused by rampant inflation. Stocks are claims on real assets, and their prices tend to go up with inflation. The question is whether they go up faster or slower than the inflation rate. During 1993, the Polish inflation rate was around 40%, which explained the zolty's depreciation. The Polish stock market appreciation was extremely high. The privatization program drew enormous interest in 1992 and 1993. The rise in stock prices was either based on expectations of very high future economic growth or was somewhat irrational. The 1994 performance of the stock market was very bad.

7.

	Dollar Return
A	300%
B	44%
C	–40%
D	–100%

The return on an equal-weighted portfolio is 51%.

8. ▪ There is no alternative to investing in the closed-end fund for foreign investors. Foreigners find Paf shares attractive from a risk/return viewpoint. They are willing to compete and bid up the price to get them.
    ▪ The scenario is reasonable. The rate of return for the foreign investor is –7.7%.

Chapter 9

5. ▪ Registration by the issuing company of all international bondholders across the world would be a daunting and costly task.
    ▪ The work of clearinghouses, such as Euroclear or Cedel, is greatly simplified (and cheaper) because the bonds are in bearer form and therefore totally fungible.

- Registration of bondholders in a centralized location would increase the risk of sudden (and retroactive) tax imposition or regulation by the country of the registrar.
- International bondholders seek anonymity, possibly for tax-evasion reasons.

6. The coupon must be increased so that the net receipt by the bondholder is still $10 per $100 bond. Hence the new coupon rate is 11.7647%.

8. Yield for bond A: 9.745%. Yield for bond B: 10.296%

9. $68.06 \times (1.08)^5 = 100$ (1)
   The simple yield r' is 9.386%   (2)

    A zero-coupon bond always quotes well below par, so the simple yield systematically overstates the actuarial yield-to-maturity. The intuitive reason is that the simple yield computes an annual linear depreciation of the future capital gain (100–68.06) instead of compounding it as in Eq. (1).

Chapter 10

1. | **Zero-Coupon Bond** | **Straight Bond** | **Perpetual Bond** |
   |---|---|---|
   | Yield-to-maturity: 10.16% | Yield-to-maturity: 8.48% | Yield-to-maturity: 7.27% |
   | Modified duration: 9.08 years | Modified duration: 6.38 years | Modified duration: 14.76 years |
   | Standard duration: 10 years | Standard duration: 6.92 years | Standard duration: 14.76 years |

2. Standard duration: 1.936 years
   Modified duration: 1.86 years
   Simple yield: 4.286%
   Semiannual yield: 4.290%

4. The forward rates are as follows:

Maturity	DM/$	FF/$
1 month	1.8088	5.5224
6 months	1.8467	5.6263
1 year	1.8699	5.7296
2 years	1.9202	5.9333
5 years	2.0557	6.5201
10 years	2.2813	7.6166

7. Interest rate: 5.36%.

8. Interest rate: 3.61%

12.
   - The coupon paid on May 1, 2006, is a $22.5 coupon per $1000 bond.
   - The new coupon to be paid on November 1, 2006, is set at $25.
   - The new value of the FRN is $1000.49, or 10.049%.

14.
   - 100%.
   - The modified duration is 16 quarters, or 4 years. A 6.25 bp increase in the quarterly spread (equal to 25 bp on an annualized spread) causes a 1% drop (16 times 0.0625%, or 4 times) in the market value of the bond.

16. ▪ The new coupon is set to 4.75%
    ▪ The coupon of the Sallie Mae bond is well below that of U.S. Treasuries with similar maturity (4.75% compared to 7%). The only advantage of the Sallie Mae FRN is to provide a minimum coupon of 4.125% if yields drop in the future. Given the current level of interest rates for top-quality notes, the value of this protective option must be very small. This Sallie Mae bond did trade at a large discount in March 1994.

Chapter 11

1. ▪ Papaf has to *pay* DM 6 million (or $3 million).
   ▪ Papaf *receives* DM 98 million (or $65.33 million).

2. The swap receipts by the corporation (based on the DM LIBOR observed at the start of the six-month period) are as follows:

Date	Net receipt in DM million (payment if negative)
October 1, 2000	100 (3.44 – 3.25)% = 0.19
April 1, 2001	100 (3.44 – 3.75)% = –0.31
October 1, 2001	100 (3.44 – 4.00)% = –0.56
April 1, 2002	100 (3.44 – 3.75)% = –0.31

4. As stated in the table, the swap quotes use the European, or annual yield, method. A client entering a five-year swap to pay DM and receive $ will pay an annual yield of 6.24% in DM and receive an annual yield of 7.33% in $, with both yields using the annual European method.

6. Foreign corporations can issue bonds in pof at a lower yield than Poufan corporations because of the tax advantage (income is tax-free for Poufan investors). This tax advantage (15% of the yield) is shared between Poufan and foreign corporations through the pof/dollar swap.

7. The Dutch investor should swap fixed for floating in dollars. The investor should contract to pay fixed and receive floating (LIBOR).

8. The net exposure to the $ exchange rate is a net asset position of $40 million. The bank should enter in a swap to pay $ and receive DM. The swap amount that minimizes the currency exposure is $40 million.

10. ▪ The swap to receive DM and pay dollars is worth DM 4.34 million, or $2.28 million.
    ▪ This second swap is now worth DM 16.93 million, or $8.911 million.

13. ▪ The market value of the assets, *A*, is FF 100 million.
    ▪ The market value of the liability, *L*, is FF 53.99 million.
    ▪ The net worth, *V*, of the bank is now FF 46.01 million.
    ▪ This drop in interest rates is bad for the bank, as the market value of its liability will rise, while the market value of its assets would remain unchanged.
    ▪ The bank would enter into a five-year swap to receive fixed and pay floating. A swap of FF 50 million would transform the cash flow on the debt from a fixed 10% to a floating PIBOR + 2% (since the swap is 8% fixed for PIBOR). If the bank focuses on market values, it would be a better idea to contract for a swap amount of FF 53.99 million, the current market value of the debt.

- If the bank is quite confident of a drop in interest rates, it will swap more than that amount to speculate.
- A = FF 100 million
  L = FF 56.15 million
  V_1 = FF 45.90 million (if a FF 50 million swap was done)
  V_2 = FF 46.06 million (if a FF 53.99 million swap was done)

16. No. On the loan, the bank stands to lose all interest payments $(8 + m)\%$ *plus* the principal of 100%. On the swap, the bank stands to lose only an interest rate differential (fixed minus floating) and no principal. Furthermore if the floating rate rose above the fixed rate, the bank would have to pay the difference anyway, so the default of the other party does not worsen the situation. The credit-quality markup on the swap μ should be much smaller than on the loan m.

Chapter 12

5. - The futures price is higher than the spot price probably because the short-term interest rate is higher than the dividend yield (positive basis).
   -

	April 1	April 2	April 3	April 4
Gain/loss	0	−5,000	2,500	17,500
Margin before cash flow	0	27,500	35,000	50,000
Cash flow	−32,500	−5,000	2,500	17,500
Margin after cash flow	32,500	32,500	32,500	32,500

6. - The implicit interst rate is 6.72%.
   - You should *sell* 10 Eurodollar contracts.
   - There must have been various marking-to-market gains and losses from April 1 to June 10. The net result, neglecting financing costs (or profits) on the margin, is a gain of:
     $$10 \times 1 \text{ million} \times (93.28\% - 90.97\%)/4 = \$57,750.$$

7. Gold futures: $413.5
   Currency futures: 0.5099 $/DM
   Eurodollars futures: 92.2330
   Stock index: 244.8

8. - The annualized forward interest rate is 4.80%. F = 95.20%.
   - The annualized forward interest rate is 4.72%. F = 95.28%.

9. - The basis is equal to 120 per index, or 6% of the spot value. This seems very large. An arbitrage would be to sell futures, buy spot, and carry the position until expiration of the futures contract. At expiration, both positions would be liquidated.
   - Profit = 73.85.
   - F_{ask} = 2046.15.
   - F_{bid} = 1965.72.

12. Among the factors that could make the hedge imperfect:
    - The maturity (and duration) of the portfolio of bonds is different from that of the notional bond.

- Movements in the Treasury bond rates are not perfectly correlated with those on Eurobonds, which are mainly corporate bonds.
- Basis risk.

13. Hedge ratio: 0.694.

One might also consider using a combination of Eurodollar futures and U.S. Treasury bond futures.

14. One alternative is to sell the British shares and buy them back when his fears disappear. At least he could buy and sell shares to reduce the beta of his portfolio. This is a costly solution in terms of transaction costs. Another alternative is to sell *Financial Times* stock index futures contracts to hedge the British market risks and remove the hedge when the fears disappear. Given the beta of his portfolio, the investor should sell for $0.8 \times 5 = $ £4 million. Another alternative would be to buy put options on individual shares in the portfolio or on the stock index (see Chapter 13).

Chapter 13

1.
- The $/DM spot exchange rate must be above $0.45 at expiration.
- The $/DM spot exchange rate must be above $0.46. This does not take into account the financing cost of the purchase of the call.
- The investor would exercise the put if the $/DM spot exchange rate were below $0.45 on the last day of the option and would make a net profit if the $/DM rate moved below $0.44.

2. No. The premium on a gold call could decline because:
- The price of gold declines.
- The short-term interest rate drops.
- The perceived volatility of the price of gold declines.
- The time to expiration declines.

4.
- You should buy Eurodollar futures and thereby freeze a 6% investment rate.
- You should buy Eurodollar calls and thereby insure a minimum investment rate of 5.6%.
- If the Eurodollar rate moves to 4%, you invest at 6% in the first strategy or 5.6% in the second strategy. If the Eurodollar rate moves to 8%, you invest at 6% in the first strategy or 7.6% in the second strategy.

6. The annualized borrowing rate will be:

LIBOR + 1%   if LIBOR < 6%

6% + 1% = 7%   if LIBOR > 6%

This borrowing cost can change on each semester payment date.

10. n The basis is zero. This could be justified by the fact that the DM interest rate is equal to the German dividend yield.
- I would sell:

$$\frac{50,000,000}{2000 \times 100} = 250 \text{ DAX futures contracts.}$$

- I would buy 250 DAX put contracts. The cost for June 2000 puts is:

DM $250 \times 100 \times 60 = $ DM 1.5 million.

4. Simulation of the portfolio value at maturity (in DM million) is as follows:

DAX Index	Unhedged	Hedged with Futures	Insured with Puts June 2000	Insured with Puts June 1950	Insured with Puts June 1900
1800	45.00	50.00	48.50	48.00	47.25
1900	47.50	50.00	48.50	48.00	47.25
2000	50.00	50.00	48.50	49.25	49.75
2100	52.50	50.00	51.00	51.75	52.25
2200	55.00	50.00	53.50	54.25	54.75

13. ▪ This low yield is compensated by the conversion option clause.
    ▪ If the stock price of Titi in yen appreciates, so does the dollar price of the convertible bond.
    ▪ If the yen appreciates, so does the dollar price of the convertible bond.
    ▪ If the market interest rate of dollar bonds drops, the dollar price of the convertible bond goes up.
    ▪ The bond should sell at least for its conversion value: $100 \times 2000 \times 0.006 = \$1200$.
    ▪ This is a very difficult exercise. In theory it would require use of the valuation of options on options. The problem comes from the fact that the conversion value of the bond is uncertain; therefore it is not possible to use conventional currency futures or currency options to hedge the currency risk. The amount to hedge is variable.

15. ▪ The option is exercised on April 1, 1991, if the current market price of the BNP bond is more than FF 100. Thus using such an option is interesting in the case of a sharp fall in interest rates. This bond allows the investor to speculate on a drop in interest rates with only limited risk.
    ▪ The replication portfolio includes a six-year 5%-coupon bond and a one-year call option on this bond (strike = 100). The value of this portfolio is:

$$P = \frac{5}{1.06} + \ldots + \frac{5}{1.06^5} + \frac{105}{1.06^6} + 2 = 97.082.$$

18. The following table gives the fair participation rates for various coupon rates:

Coupon Rate	p (2-year bond)	p (3-year bond)
0%	80%	103%
1%	70%	90%
2%	60%	77%
3%	50%	64%
5%	30%	39%
7%	10%	13%

Chapter 14

1. The investor could sell ¥160 million forward at a forward exchange rate of ¥/$ = 160. The hedge will be imperfect if the price of the Japanese stocks moves. The investor should continually adjust the amount hedged. Another reason for an imperfect hedge is a change in the forward basis caused by a change in interest rate differential.

2. The investor should sell ¥160 million forward against Dutch guilders.

3. ▪ The one-year forward exchange rate is 1.9273 DM/$.
   ▪ The following table shows the simulation of the portfolio value (in $ million).

Exchange Rate	Unhedged	Hedged	Insured
1.6	62.50	51.89	61.30
1.8	55.56	51.89	54.36
2.0	50.00	51.89	48.80
2.2	45.45	51.89	48.80
2.4	41.67	51.89	48.80

   ▪ Basis risk and cross-hedge risk.

4. ▪ You should buy calls SF to insure the SF value of the portfolio. The amount of SF calls purchased is 13.2573 million. The premium paid is $322,153.
   ▪ The portfolio will have a fixed value of SF 13,533,631 (versus SF 13,257.324). The disadvantage is that the hedged value will remain fixed even if the dollar appreciates against the SF.

5. ▪ The futures price is 2000. You should sell 60 contracts.
   ▪ You should sell FF 20 million forward. The forward rate is 5 FF/$. If you worry about a FF depreciation, you should buy FF puts for FF 20 million. The cost is $200,000. The following table shows the simulation of the portfolio value (in $ million).

Exchange rate $/FF	Unhedged	Hedged	Insured
0.10	2.0	4.0	3.8
0.20	4.0	4.0	3.8
0.30	6.0	4.0	5.8

8. She would use DM futures as a proxy for Belgian franc futures, since the two exchange rates, DM/$ and BF/$, tend to move together. At the current spot exchange rate, the Belgian stock portfolio is worth:

$$BF\ 100\ \text{million} * \frac{2.5\ DM/\$}{50\ BF/\$} = DM\ 5\ \text{million}.$$

Therefore our American investor should sell for DM 5 million of futures contracts against dollars, or 40 contracts. In practice the proposed strategy uses a hedge ratio of 1. This would be optimal if there were no correlation between interest rate and exchange rate movements.

10. The delta hedge of the option should be taken into account for a dynamic hedge.
    ▪ 800 contracts [i.e., 25 million/(62,500 × 0.5)]. This requires payment of a premium of $500,000, or DM 1,250,000.
    ▪ The net gain is equal to DM 91,200. The portfolio has been overhedged, because the delta of the option has increased with the appreciation of the DM. In a dynamic strategy the German investor could sell part of his option contracts to adjust to the new delta. The investor now needs only 557 contracts. The new DM value of the portfolio: DM 24.39 million. The contracts needed for a delta-hedge: 557.5 [i.e., DM 24.39 million/(62,500 × 0.7)].

15. The optimal hedge ratio that would allow one to reduce the influence of exchange rate movements is 1.7.

Chapter 15

2. ■ The expected return on gold is 5.8%.
   ■ Gold is a good hedge. We hope (expect) that the global market will show a good performance and expect a modest performance from gold. However, gold is still an attractive diversification vehicle: If our expectations on the market are not realized and the market drops badly, gold will tend to show a superb performance and offset part of the loss on the rest of the portfolio.

4. We can compute the operating leverage of the two mines, $G/(G-C)$:

	Bel Or	**Schoen Gold**
Operating leverage	1.58	6.67
Gold beta	1.60	6.00

Schoen Gold is much more sensitive to gold price movements than Bel Or. This can be explained primarily by its cost structure. Given my expectation of a 10% gold price increase, I should buy Schoen Gold and expect to make 60% on my investment.

8. ■ The bad performance of the 50 funds that have disappeared is not included in the average performance of 20%, but it should be.
   ■ There is a selection bias based on past historical performance. Back in 1970, it was not possible to guess with certainty which commodities would experience a drop in activity. This is a serious problem because there is a correlation between the activity in a commodity futures contract and its price movement. All contracts, even those that later disappeared, should be included in a back-calculation of an index.

9. ■ Yes. It overweighs those commodities that have become important over the period and simultaneously went up in price.
   ■ For each year, use as weights their current relative economic importance (i.e., use 2000 weights for the index calculated in 2000, and so on).

13. ■ The yield enhancement is 0.70%.
   ■ The new annual coupon rate on the $1 billion investment is –17%. This is an annual loss of $170 million.
   ■ Price (hedged): 1.6% of initial investment. The total investment is almost wiped out.

Chapter 16

1. The active manager must outperform the indexer by at least 6.50%.

2. Yes. Here are some return and risk characteristics for global portfolios with increasing proportions of foreign assets:

% U.S.	% Foreign	Return (%)	Volatility (%)
100	0	10.00	12.00
90	10	10.10	11.37
80	20	10.20	11.11
70	30	10.30	11.26
60	40	10.40	11.78
50	50	10.50	12.65

4. $MWR_1 = 11.11\%$
   $MWR_2 = 11.54\%$
   $MWR_3 = 11.51\%$
   TWR $= 10\%$

6. ▪ The total return on the portfolio, measured in French francs, is 13.5%.
   ▪ Capital gain amounts to 20%. Currency contribution is equal to –6.5%.
   ▪ Security selection contributed negatively for –2.5%

7. $MWR_1 = 13.04\%$
   $MWR_2 = 14.52\%$
   $MWR_3 = 14.58\%$
   TWR $= 19.85\%$

Index